ASCENT®

CENTER FOR TECHNICAL KNOWLEDGE

AutoCAD® Electrical 2025 Fundamentals with NFPA Standards

Learning Guide

Edition 1.0

ASCENT - Center for Technical Knowledge®
AutoCAD® Electrical 2025
Fundamentals with NFPA Standards
Edition 1.0

Prepared and produced by:

ASCENT Center for Technical Knowledge
630 Peter Jefferson Parkway, Suite 175
Charlottesville, VA 22911

866-527-2368
www.ASCENTed.com

Lead Contributor: Renu Muthoo

ASCENT - Center for Technical Knowledge (a division of Rand Worldwide Inc.) is a leading developer of professional learning materials and knowledge products for engineering software applications. ASCENT specializes in designing targeted content that facilitates application-based learning with hands-on software experience. For over 25 years, ASCENT has helped users become more productive through tailored custom learning solutions.

We welcome any comments you may have regarding this guide, or any of our products. To contact us please email: feedback@ASCENTed.com.

AS-AEL2501-FND1NF-SG // IS-AEL2501-FND1NF-SG

Contents

Preface

The *AutoCAD® Electrical 2025: Fundamentals with NFPA Standards* guide is designed for those using AutoCAD® Electrical 2025 with a Windows operating system. This guide is not designed for the AutoCAD for Mac software.

The *AutoCAD Electrical 2025: Fundamentals with NFPA Standards* guide covers the indispensable core topics for working with the AutoCAD Electrical software. In this guide, you will learn how to use many of the powerful electrical drawing creation tools in the AutoCAD Electrical software. You will create schematic drawings (ladder logic and point to point), panel drawings, and PLC-I/O circuits using automated commands for symbol insertion, component tagging, wire numbering, and drawing modification. In addition, you are introduced to methods of customizing AutoCAD Electrical symbols, circuits, and databases. Other topics covered include titleblock linking, reporting tools, templates, and project files.

Topics Covered

- Understanding project files
- Creating and editing schematic and panel drawings
- Working with PLC symbols
- Creating custom symbols
- Generating reports

Prerequisites

Access to the 2025.0 version of the software, to ensure compatibility with this guide. Future software updates that are released by Autodesk may include changes that are not reflected in this guide. The practices and files included with this guide might not be compatible with prior versions (e.g., 2024).

Note on Software Setup

This guide assumes a standard installation of the Windows version of the AutoCAD Electrical 2025 software using the **NFPA (Inches) Symbol Libraries** and **all** the Manufacturers for the Content Libraries. Lectures and practices use the standard software templates.

Note on Learning Guide Content

ASCENT's learning guides are intended to teach the technical aspects of using the software and do not focus on professional design principles and standards. The practices aim to demonstrate the capabilities and flexibility of the software rather than following specific design codes or standards.

Lead Contributor: Renu Muthoo

Renu is a learning content developer for Autodesk products at ASCENT. She has over 25 years of experience working with Autodesk products and specializes in AutoCAD and design visualization software.

Holding a bachelor's degree in Computer Engineering, Renu began her career as an Instructional Designer, co-authoring 3ds Max and AutoCAD books. At ASCENT, she continues her passion for instructional design by developing off the shelf and custom courseware for AutoCAD, AutoCAD Toolsets (Electrical, Mechanical, and Plant 3D), Autodesk 3ds Max, and other software products. An Autodesk Certified Professional in AutoCAD, Renu also enjoys educating users by sharing her knowledge through webcasts and blogs.

Renu Muthoo has been the Lead Contributor for *AutoCAD® Electrical: Fundamentals* since 2013.

In This Guide

The following highlights the key features of this guide.

Feature	Description
Practice Files	The Practice Files page includes a link to the practice files and instructions on how to download and install them. The practice files are required to complete the practices in this guide.
Chapters	A chapter consists of the following: Learning Objectives, Instructional Content, Practices, Chapter Review Questions, and Command Summary. • **Learning Objectives** define the skills you can acquire by learning the content provided in the chapter. • **Instructional Content**, which begins right after Learning Objectives, refers to the descriptive and procedural information related to various topics. Each main topic introduces a product feature, discusses various aspects of that feature, and provides step-by-step procedures on how to use that feature. Where relevant, examples, figures, helpful hints, and notes are provided. • **Practice** for a topic follows the instructional content. Practices enable you to use the software to perform a hands-on review of a topic. It is required that you download the practice files (using the link found on the Practice Files page) prior to starting the first practice. • **Chapter Review Questions**, located close to the end of a chapter, enable you to test your knowledge of the key concepts discussed in the chapter. • **Command Summary** concludes a chapter. It contains a list of the software commands that are used throughout the chapter and provides information on where the command can be found in the software.
Appendices	Appendices provide additional information to the main course content. It could be in the form of instructional content, practices, tables, projects, or skills assessment.

Practice Files

To download the practice files for this guide, use the following steps:

1. Type the URL *exactly as shown below* into the address bar of your Internet browser to access the Course File Download page.

   Note: If you are using the ebook, you do not have to type the URL. Instead, you can access the page by clicking the URL below.

   https://www.ascented.com/getfile/id/neogynaPF

2. On the Course File Download page, click the **DOWNLOAD NOW** button, as shown below, to download the .ZIP file that contains the practice files.

3. Once the download is complete, unzip the file and extract its contents.

   The recommended practice files folder location is:
   C:\AutoCAD Electrical 2025 Fundamentals Practice Files

   Note: It is recommended that you do not change the location of the practice files folder. Doing so may cause errors when completing the practices.

Chapter 1

Introduction to AutoCAD Electrical

Understanding the various types of electrical symbols, files, and components used in the AutoCAD® Electrical software is fundamental in the creation of electrical designs. In addition, learning the basic layout of the interface and how to use the working environment increases your designing efficiency.

Learning Objectives

- Identify and navigate the AutoCAD Electrical interface.
- Identify the different types of electrical drawings.
- Identify the various symbols that are used in the AutoCAD Electrical software.
- Recognize the typically used design methodology workflows.

1.1 What is AutoCAD Electrical?

The AutoCAD Electrical software is a purpose built controls design tool that is used to automate the creation of electrical schematic and panel drawings. It also tracks component information between drawings and can create reports containing this information.

- Electrical symbols carry the intelligence of AutoCAD Electrical drawings and are the foundation of the functionality in AutoCAD Electrical software.
- Symbols are simply AutoCAD® blocks with attributes. Several standard symbol libraries can be installed with the AutoCAD Electrical software, including NFPA, IEC, IEEE, JIC, JIS, and GB.
- The AutoCAD Electrical software contains all of the standard AutoCAD commands and many automated commands for controls design. Use the AutoCAD Electrical commands when possible rather than the AutoCAD commands. Typically, AutoCAD Electrical commands have additional functionality that helps when designing. For example, the AutoCAD **Erase** command versus the AutoCAD Electrical **Delete Component** command.
    - The **Erase** command erases the component.
    - The **Delete Component** command erases the component, attempts to heal the wires, and updates any references.

Interface

The AutoCAD Electrical interface, shown in Figure 1–1, contains three main areas in which to access the AutoCAD Electrical specific commands. The color theme for the interface components has been changed to **Light** and the Drawing Window background color has been changed to white for printing clarity.

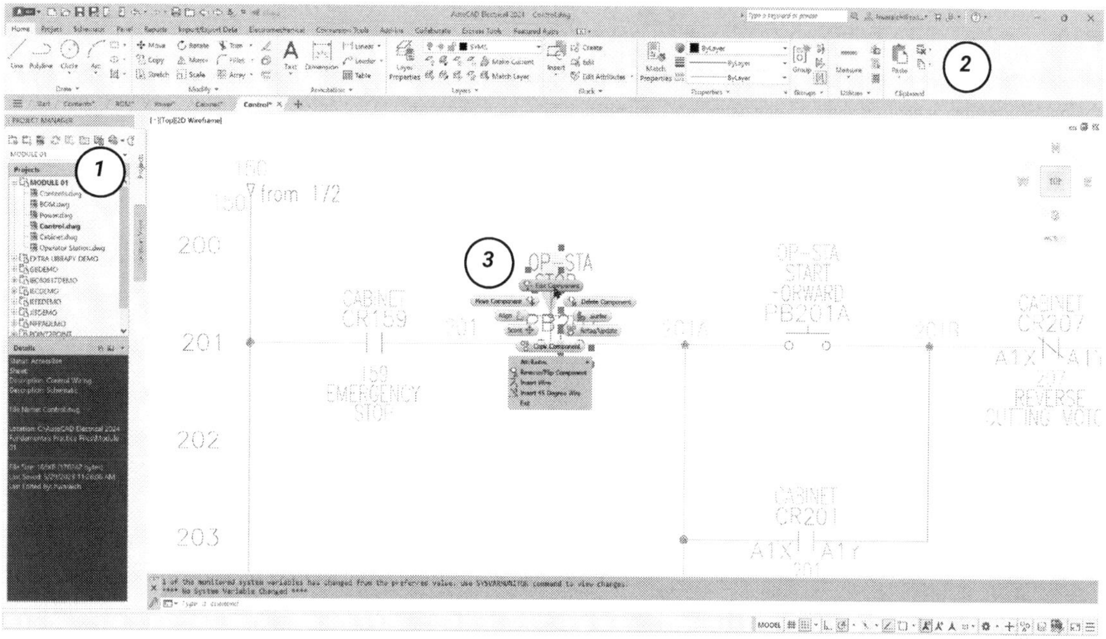

Figure 1–1

1. Project Manager Palette

The Project Manager enables you to access project files, drawing files, and the settings for the active project. It enables you to open, close, activate, and edit project files, as well as update and print drawing files.

2. Ribbon

In the AutoCAD Electrical software, you use the ribbon to access the commands. The ribbon consists of a series of tabs and panels that contain a variety of tools grouped by function.

3. Right-click Marking Menus

The AutoCAD Electrical interface contains context sensitive right-click marking menus. When you right-click on different objects, the menus that open contain commands specific to the selected object. These menus are very effective when editing or adding the electrical drawings.

Hint: Interface Color Theme

You can set the color theme for your interface components to be **Light** or **Dark** (default) in the *Options* dialog box, as shown in Figure 1–2.

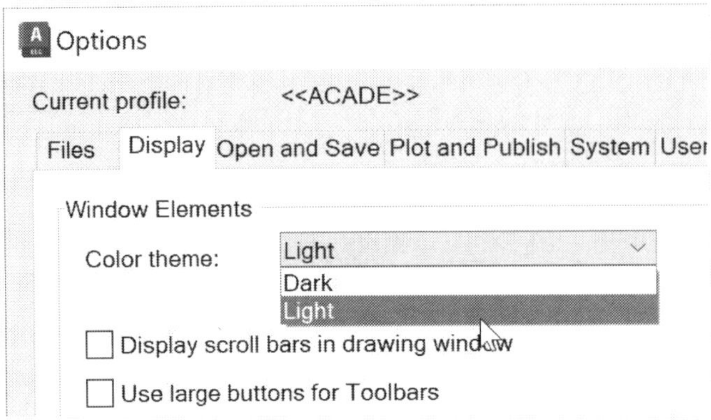

Figure 1–2

Start Tab

When you launch the software or if you click in the *Start* tab while working in an active drawing, the initial Start window displays, as shown in Figure 1–3.

- By default, the *Start* tab is always available in the *File Tabs* bar.
- You can click it to display the initial Start window anytime.
- You can switch between multiple open drawings and the *Start* tab by selecting the required tab.
- You can use <Ctrl> +<Home> to jump from an active drawing to the *Start* tab.
- The Start window contains the following options, as shown in Figure 1–3:
  - The **Open** and **New** options enable you to open and create drawings.
  - The **Recent** option enables you to access recently used files.
  - **Autodesk Projects** enables you to connect to Autodesk Desktop Connector to see your Autodesk projects.
  - **Learning** enables you to access online training resources, videos, and tips to help you learn the software.

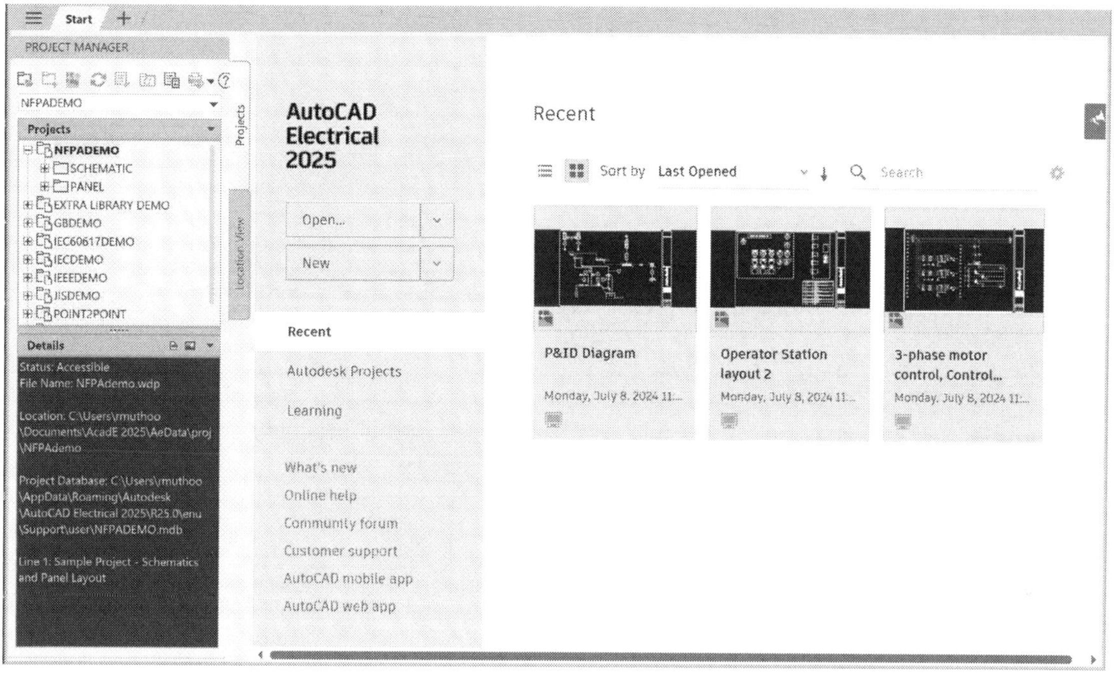

Figure 1–3

Electrical Help

AutoCAD Electrical Help files can be accessed by expanding  (Help) in the Infocenter Bar, as shown in Figure 1–4.

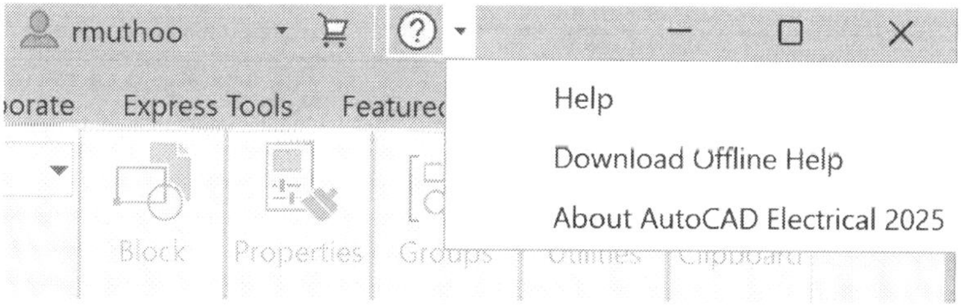

Figure 1–4

- You can also press <F1> to open the AutoCAD Electrical Help system.
- When hovering over a tool (tooltip displayed) or when a command is active, pressing <F1> opens the Help that is specific for that command.

1.2 Drawing Files

The AutoCAD Electrical software uses DWG files. They can be opened and modified in the different software, such as:

- AutoCAD software
- AutoCAD® WS software
- AutoCAD LT® software
- DWG TrueView™ and Design Review software
- Any software that supports DWG files

The AutoCAD Electrical software contains different types of drawing files. These include schematic drawings, panel drawings, and reference drawings.

Schematic Drawings

Schematic drawings (as shown in Figure 1–5) contain ladder logic documentation. This includes schematic symbols, wires, reports, and any other documentation that is required for the design.

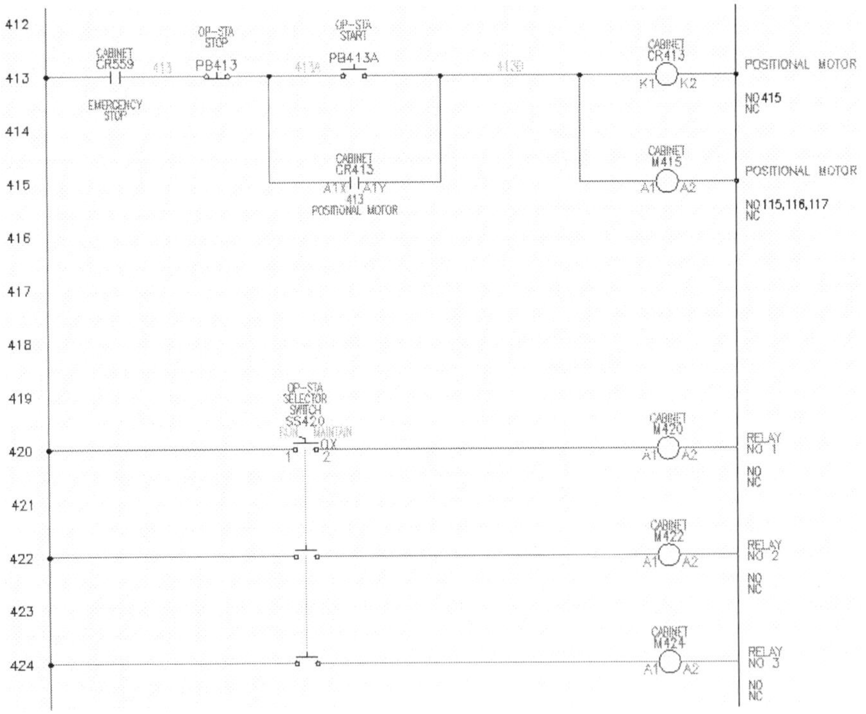

Figure 1–5

Panel Drawings

Panel drawings (as shown in Figure 1–6) are used to document the physical location of components in the panel. They can contain footprints for components, nameplates, balloons, and reports.

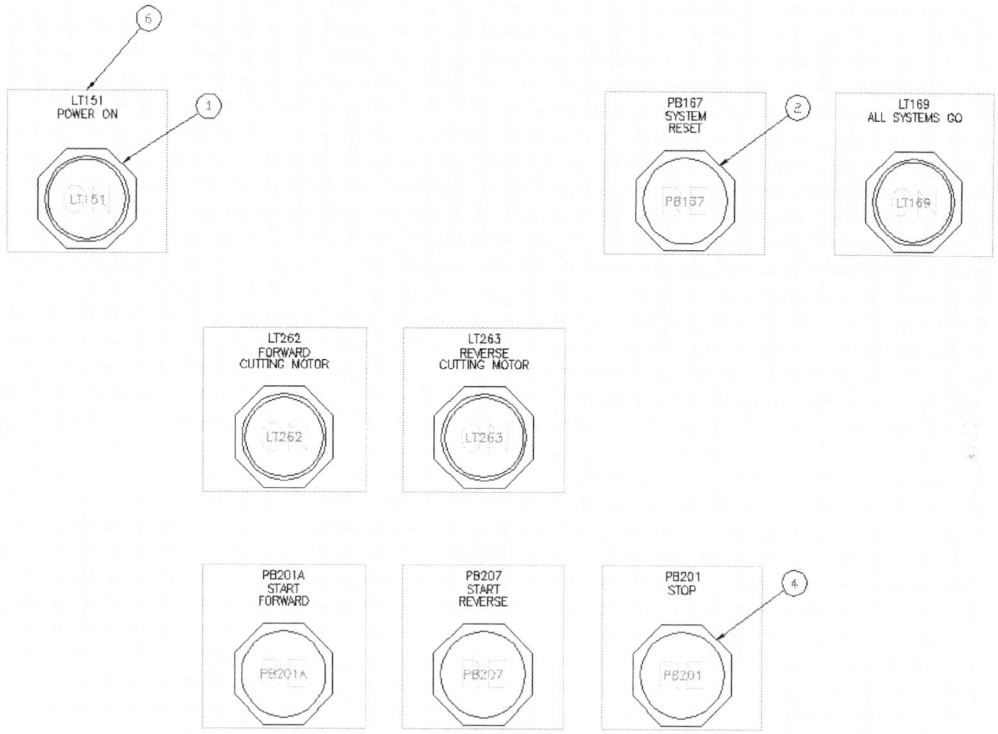

Figure 1–6

Reference Drawings

Reference drawings (as shown in Figure 1–7) are drawings used to document designs, including table of contents or customer drawings. Reference drawings are included in the project but not in the tagging, cross-referencing, or reporting processes.

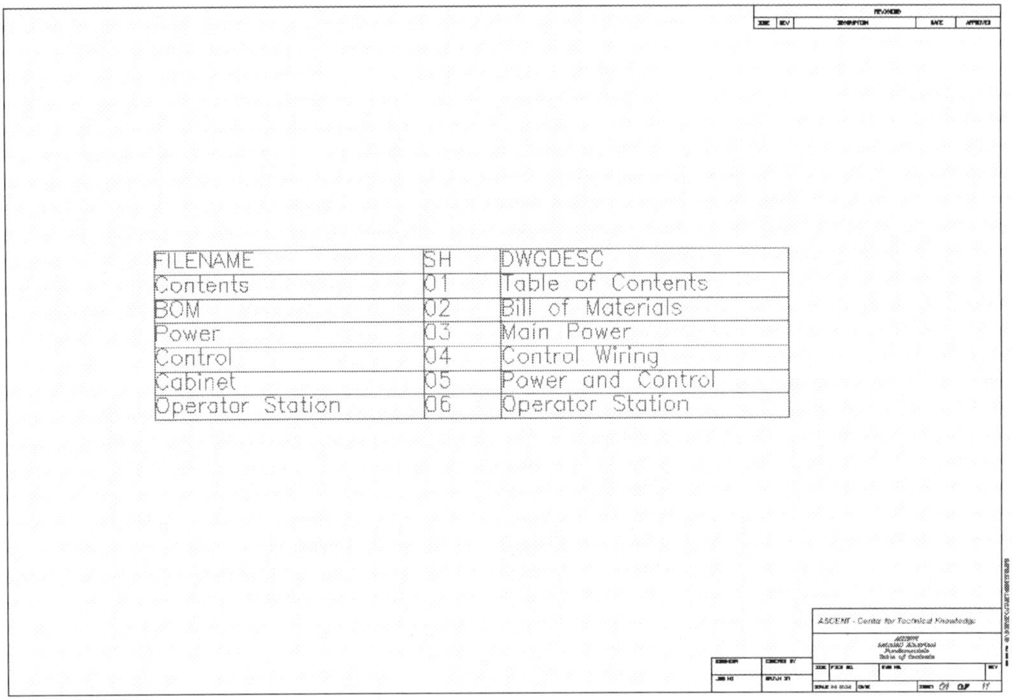

Figure 1–7

1.3 Electrical Components and Wires

The AutoCAD Electrical software uses symbols to represent components and lines to represent wires. It contains several commands for inserting and maintaining them.

Schematic Symbols

Schematic symbols, including push buttons, relays, and switches (as shown in Figure 1–8) are used to represent components in the electrical logic drawings of the system.

- Schematic symbols are AutoCAD blocks with attributes.
- The AutoCAD Electrical software contains several different libraries of symbols that support different standards, including NFPA, IEC, IEEE, JIC, JIS, and GB, among others.

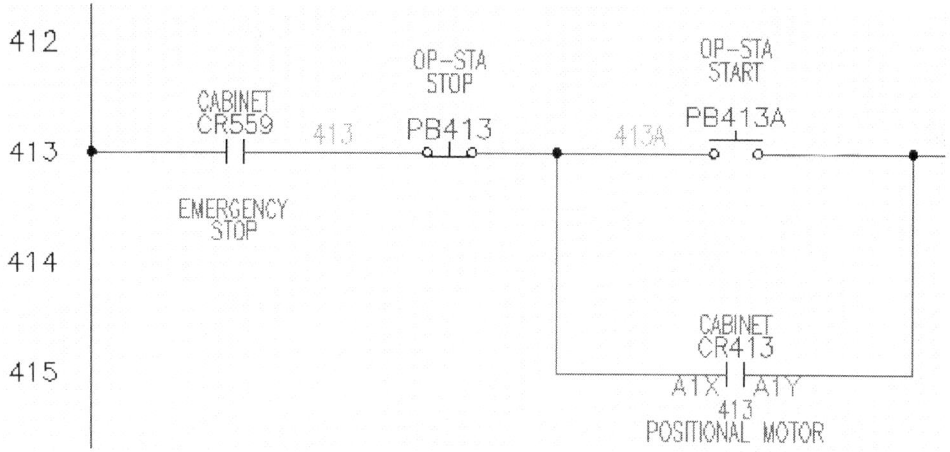

Figure 1–8

- The **Symbol Builder** utility can be used to create custom symbols.

PLC Modules

The AutoCAD Electrical software contains a library of PLC modules from different manufacturers, and display in a schematic drawing, as shown in Figure 1–9.

- The PLC library can be customized to add manufacturers or modules.
- The modules are AutoCAD blocks with attributes.
- The software contains automated commands for inserting the modules into a drawing.

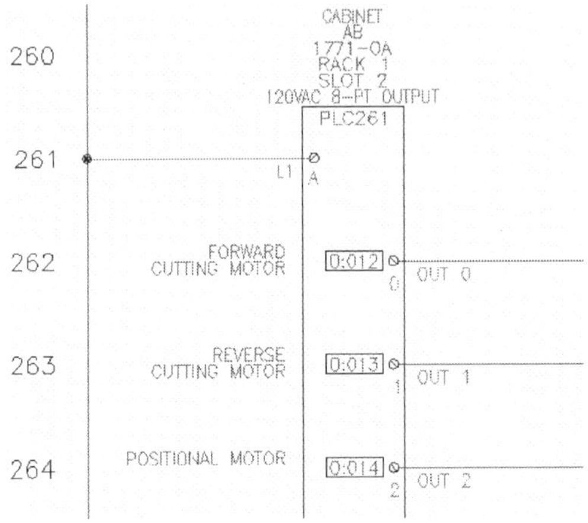

Figure 1–9

Panel Footprints

Panel footprints are used to represent components in the design, and schematic symbols are used to document the electrical logic of the system. The AutoCAD Electrical software contains a library of panel footprints based on manufacturer information, and display in a panel drawing, as shown in Figure 1–10. The library is customizable to enable you to add new footprints.

Figure 1–10

Wires

Wires are an integral part of any electrical design, as shown in Figure 1–11. The AutoCAD Electrical software contains automated commands for inserting, trimming, and numbering wires, which are AutoCAD line objects on special layers.

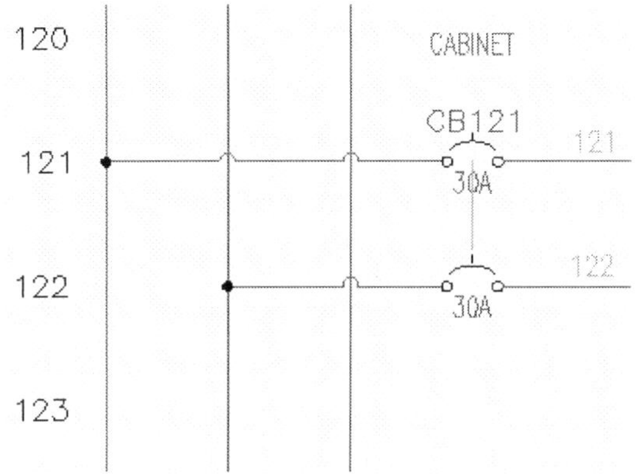

Figure 1–11

Cable Markers

Wires can be linked to create cables using cable marker symbols, as shown in Figure 1–12. Cable markers carry information about the cable manufacturer, color, and other attributes. The AutoCAD Electrical software contains commands for inserting, deleting, and modifying cable markers, and for creating reports containing information about the cables.

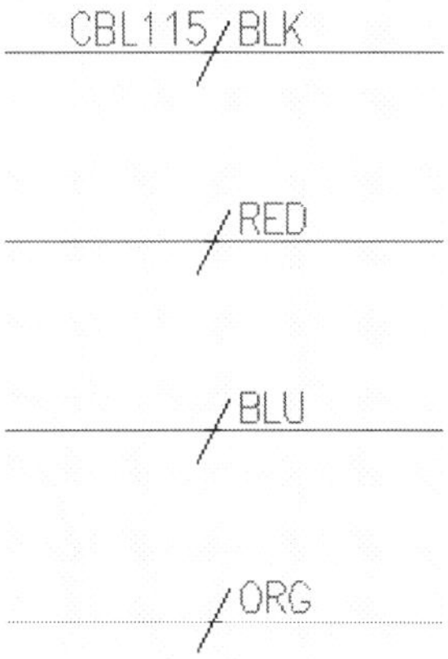

Figure 1–12

1.4 Design Methodologies

The AutoCAD Electrical software is a flexible and customizable system. A typical workflow includes:

1. Creating a new project file or copying an existing project file.
2. Configuring the settings for the project.
3. Building the schematic drawings.
4. Building panel drawings based on components in the schematic drawings.
5. Creating reports from the panel or schematic drawings.

The AutoCAD Electrical software enables you to have variations of the workflow. You can create panel drawings first, and then create schematic drawings based on components in the panel. Both workflows can be used: schematic to panel or panel to schematic.

Practice 1a
Introduction Overview

Practice Objective

- Open electrical drawings and investigate the information for the symbols.

In this practice, you will open a schematic drawing (as shown in Figure 1–13) and use the right-click marking menus to see the information attached to the symbols. You will then open a panel drawing and edit a panel footprint to see its attached information.

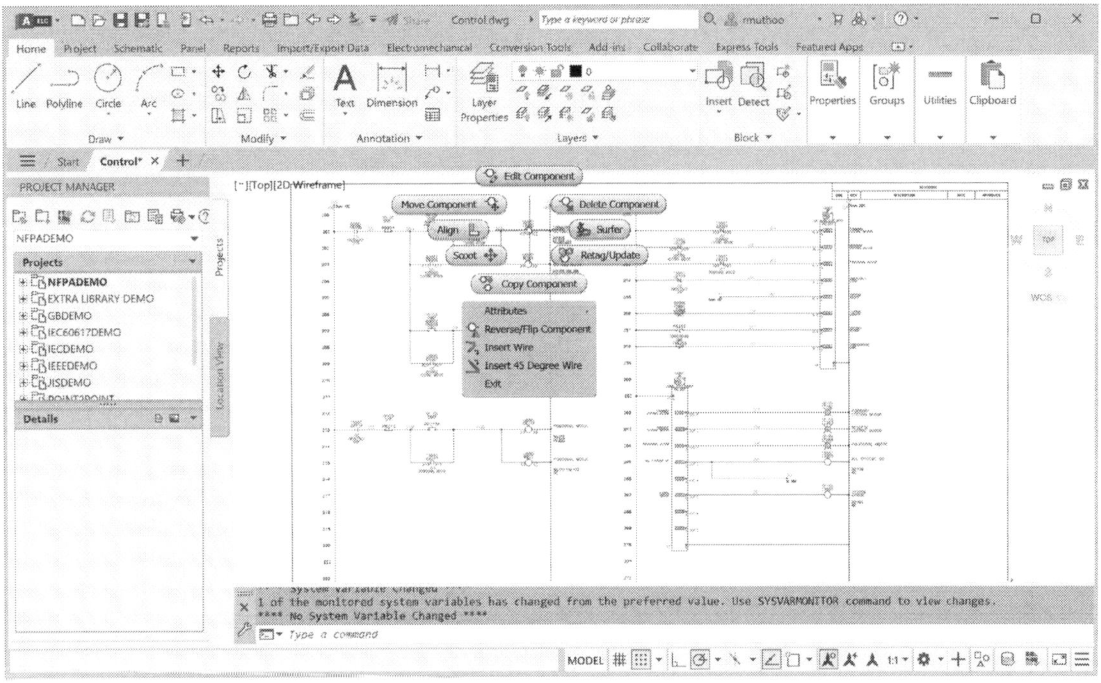

Figure 1–13

1. In your practice files folder, in the *Module 01* folder, open **Control.dwg**. (Use the AutoCAD **Open** command.)
2. Zoom to different areas of the drawing to investigate the different symbols. This is a schematic drawing containing two motor control circuits and two PLCs.
3. Zoom to the top half of the ladder on the right side of the drawing. This is the input PLC for this design.
4. Zoom to the lower half of the ladder on the right side of the drawing. This is the output PLC for this design.
5. Zoom to the top portion of the ladder on the left side of the drawing.

6. Right-click on the relay coil symbol labeled **CR201** to display the Marking Menu. Select **Edit Component**, as shown in Figure 1–14. The *Insert / Edit Component* dialog box opens, as shown in Figure 1–15. The data attached to the symbol includes its component tag, manufacturer, descriptions, and pin numbers.

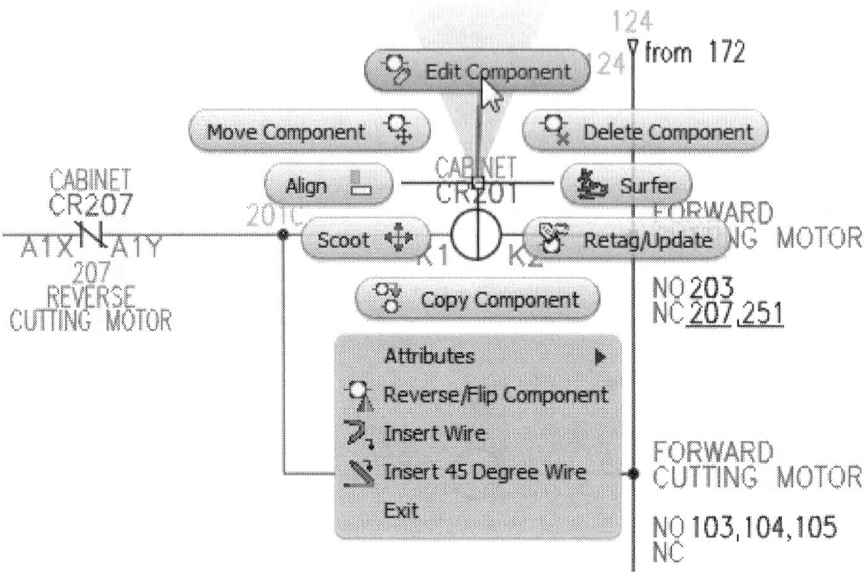

Figure 1–14

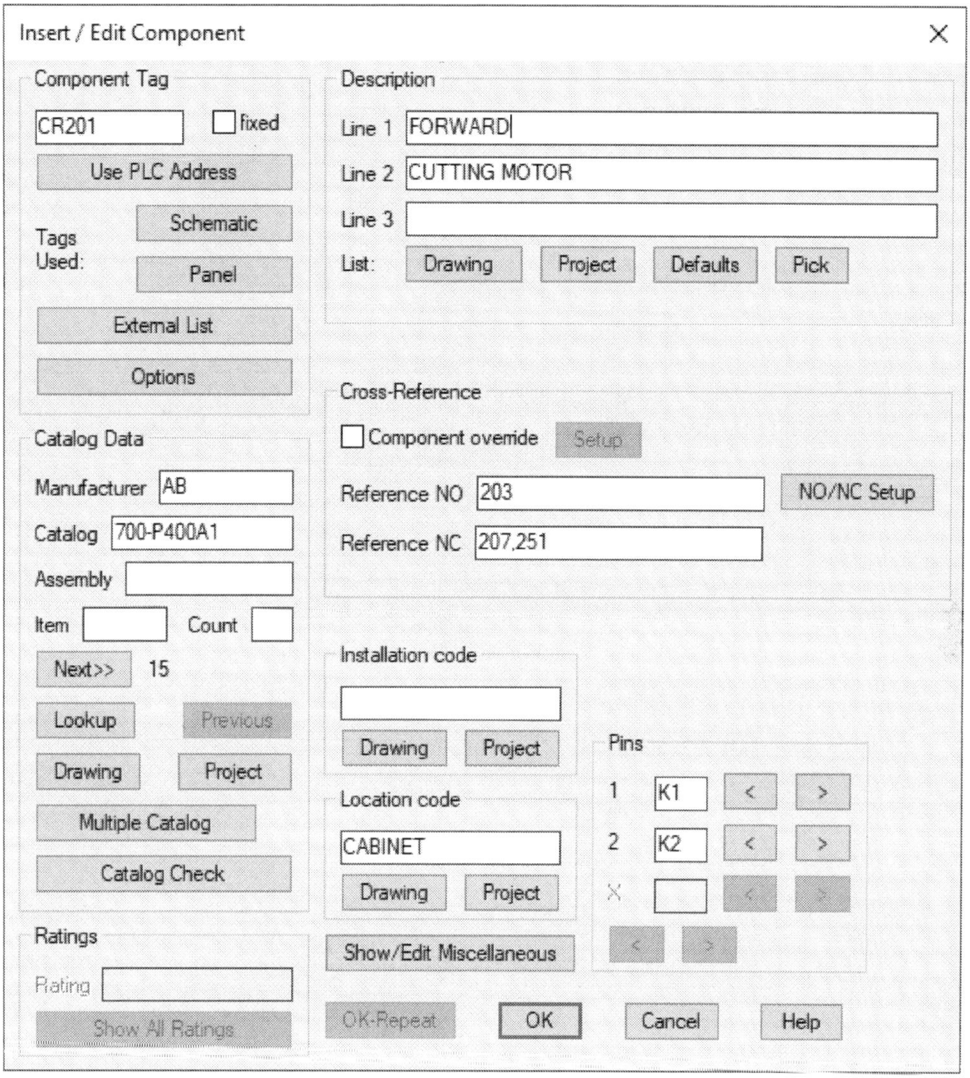

Figure 1–15

7. Click **Cancel** to close the dialog box.

8. Right-click on the push button symbol labeled **PB201A** and select **Edit Component** from its Marking Menu, as shown in Figure 1–16. The *Insert / Edit Component* dialog box opens, as shown in Figure 1–17. The same data fields are available, but they contain values pertaining to the push button.

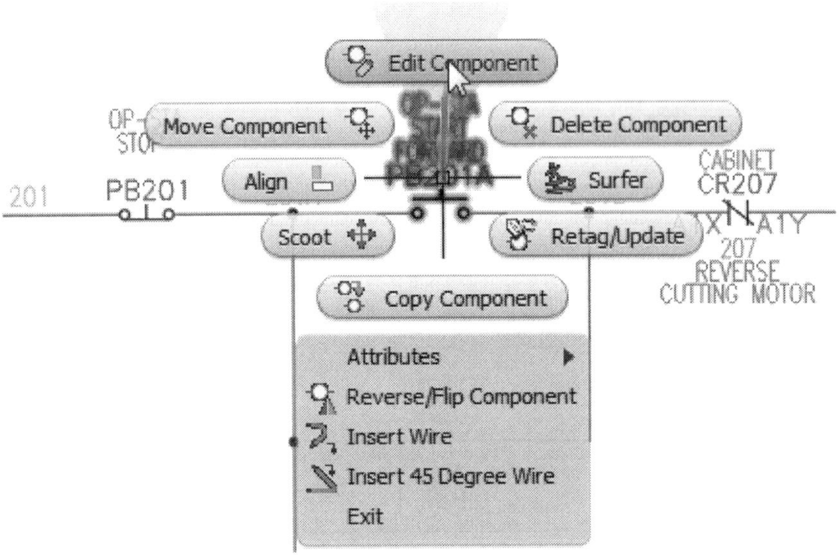

Figure 1–16

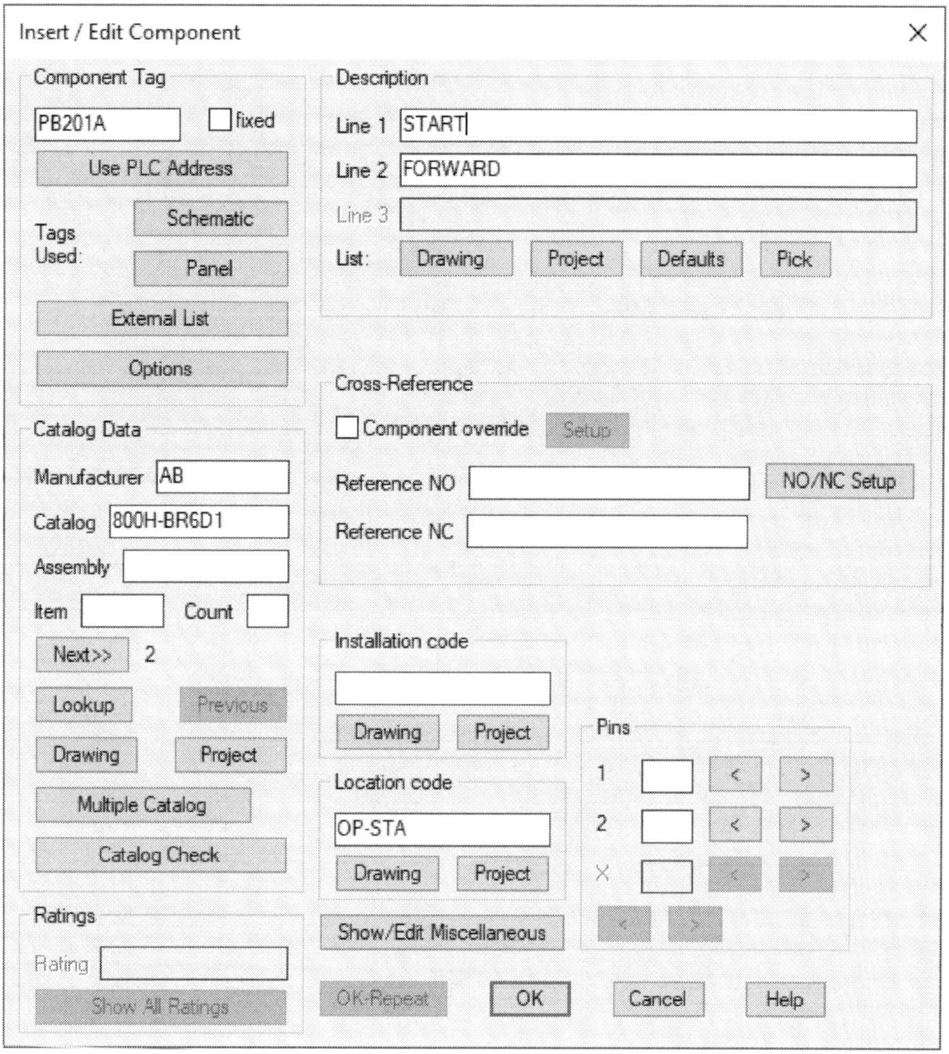

Figure 1–17

9. Click **Cancel** to close the dialog box.
10. Close **Control.dwg**. When prompted to save changes, click **No**.
11. In your practice files folder, in the *Module 01* folder, open **Operator Station.dwg**. The drawing represents the operator panel drawing and a bill of materials for the panel drawings.

12. Zoom in to the three push buttons near the middle of the panel, as shown in Figure 1–18. They are labeled **PB201A**, **PB207**, and **PB201**.

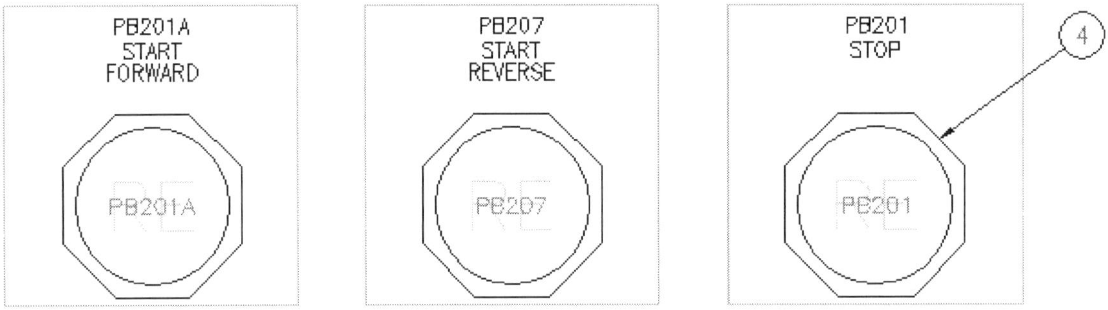

Figure 1–18

13. Right-click on the push button on the left, labeled **PB201A** and select **Edit Footprint**, as shown in Figure 1–19. (Right-click on the black geometry and not on the outside green square.)

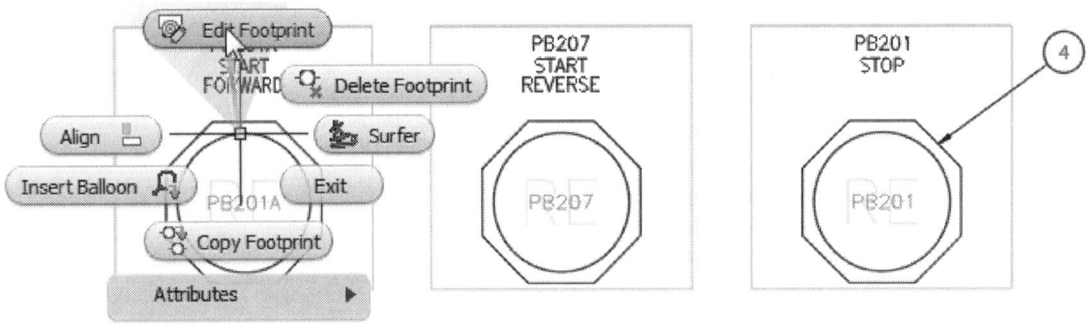

Figure 1–19

14. The *Panel Layout – Component Insert/Edit* dialog box opens, as shown in Figure 1–20. The panel footprint symbol represents the push button that was edited in the schematic drawing.

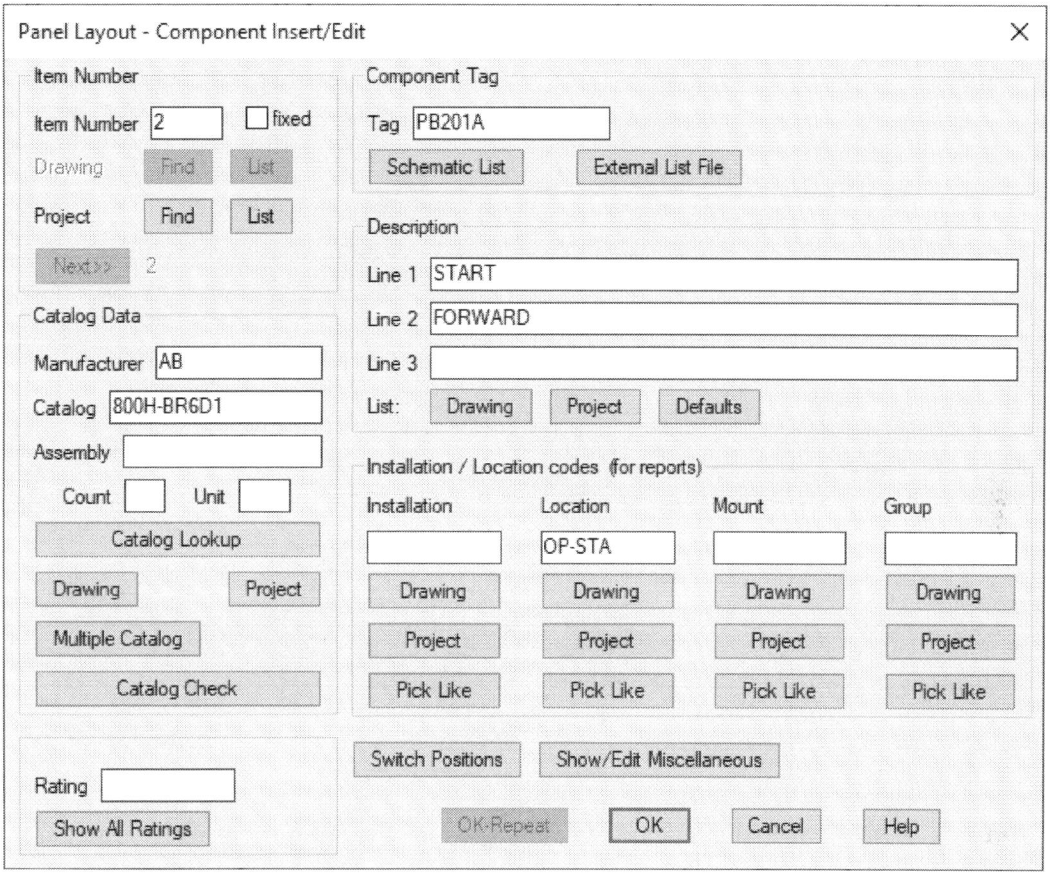

Figure 1–20

15. Click **Cancel** to close the dialog box.

16. Close **Operator Station.dwg**. When prompted to save changes, click **No**.

17. If time permits, open and investigate the other drawings in the *Module 01* folder, in your practice files folder. **Contents.dwg** contains a list of the drawings that are part of the project. **BOM.dwg** contains the bill of materials report for the project. **Power.dwg** contains the schematic symbols for the power circuit for the project. **Cabinet.dwg** contains the panel footprints for the cabinet components in the project.

End of practice

Chapter Review Questions

1. How do you access the AutoCAD Electrical commands? (Select all that apply.)
   a. Project Manager Palette
   b. Ribbon
   c. Status Bar
   d. Right-click Marking Menu

2. How do you access the AutoCAD Electrical Help system?
   a. Application Menu>Help
   b. Help>Electrical Help Topics in the Infocenter Bar
   c. Status Bar>Help
   d. Press <F2>

3. The AutoCAD Electrical symbols are composed of what object type(s)?
   a. Blocks and fields
   b. Lines and fields
   c. Blocks with attributes
   d. Lines and attributes

4. There are automated commands for creating and managing wires made of line objects.
   a. True
   b. False

Chapter 2

Project Files

The AutoCAD® Electrical software supports the use of multiple drawings using project files, which are managed through the *Project Manager* palette. Understanding the *Project Manager* palette enables you to efficiently navigate, work, and manage multiple drawings in projects to successfully create electrical designs.

Learning Objectives

- Recognize the importance of project files and the type of information they contain.
- Navigate through the *Project Manager* palette interface.
- Create, open, activate, and close project files and drawing files.
- Create new drawing files and add existing ones to an active project.
- Open a drawing file using the *Project Manager*.
- Manage the drawings and subfolders in the active project.
- Automatically save and close the open drawing.
- Customize the drawing list display in a project.

2.1 Project Manager Interface

Project Files

Typically, an electrical design requires many drawings. The AutoCAD Electrical software supports the use of multiple drawings using project files.

- A project file is a text file that contains a list of drawings that are part of a particular design. Project files contain settings for the project and are created and maintained using the *Project Manager* palette, as shown in Figure 2–1.

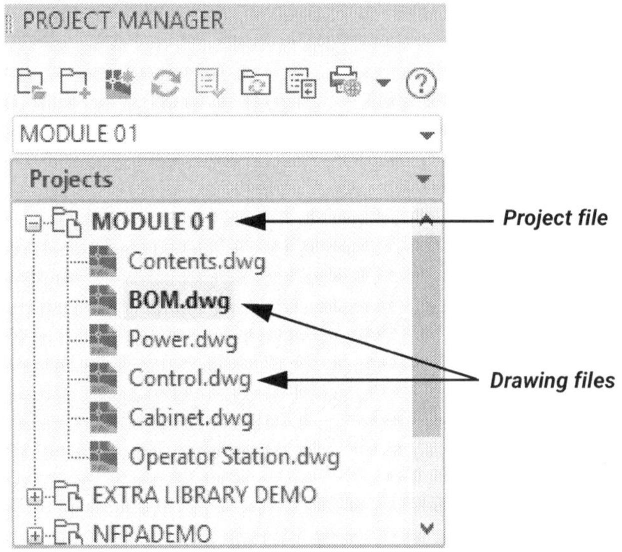

Figure 2–1

- There is no limit to the number of drawings that a project file can contain.
- Project files have a .WDP file extension.
- You can have multiple projects open, but only one is active at a time. The active project is the set of drawings that are processed using AutoCAD Electrical commands.

Project Manager

The *Project Manager* is a palette interface used to create and manage AutoCAD Electrical project files. It has the same functionality as any other AutoCAD® Tool Palette and contains options for docking, anchoring, and auto-hiding.

The *Project Manager* palette contains the *Projects* tab and the *Location View* tab along the right side of the palette, as shown in Figure 2–2. The display of the *Project Manager* interface depends on the tab you have selected.

Projects Tab

When the *Projects* tab is selected, the interface of the *Project Manager* displays as shown in Figure 2–2.

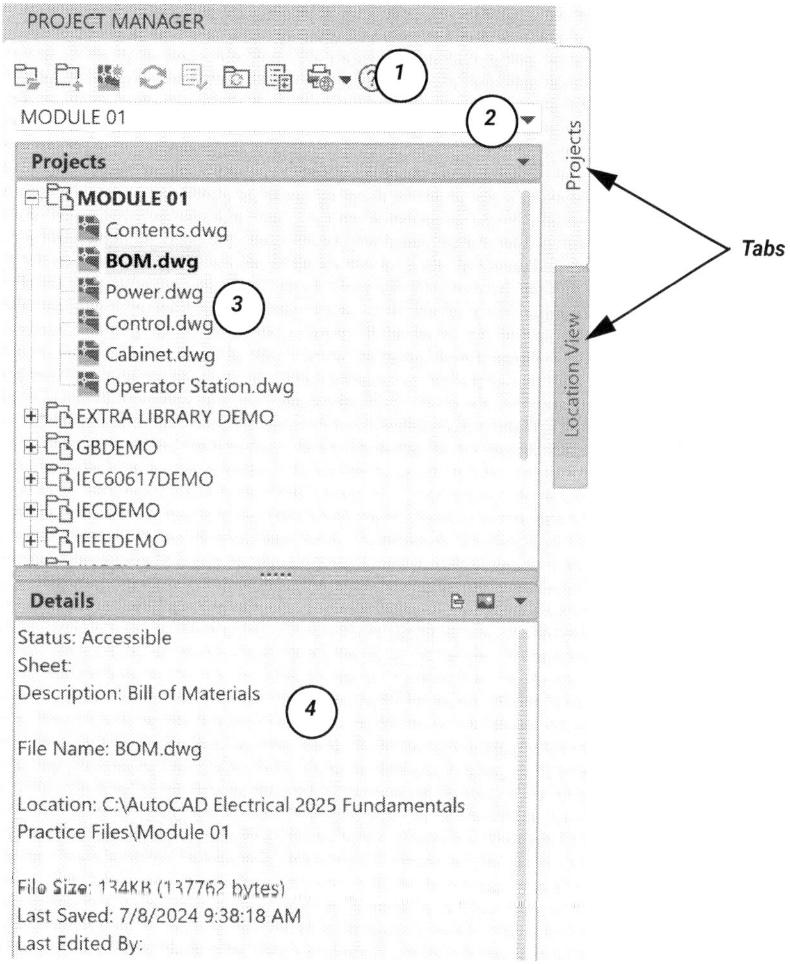

Figure 2–2

1. Toolbar

The *Project Manager* contains a toolbar across the top, as shown in Figure 2–3. It enables you to open an existing project, create a new project or drawing, make project-wide updates, access the print commands, access the AutoCAD Electrical Help system, etc.

Figure 2–3

2. Drop-down List

A drop-down list is available just below the toolbar, as shown in Figure 2–4. You can use it to activate a project, open an existing project, or create a new project.

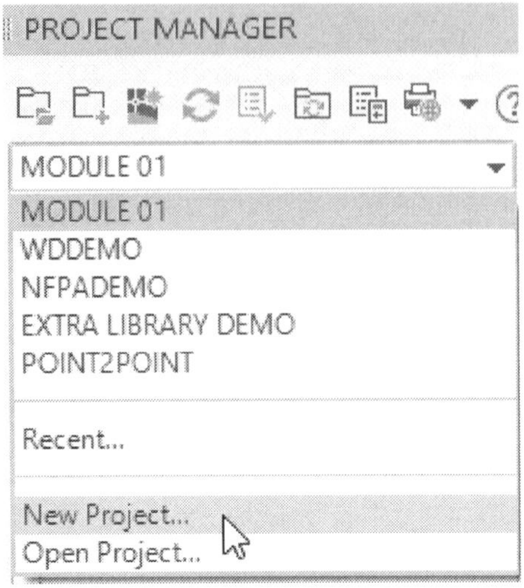

Figure 2–4

3. Projects Area

The *Projects* area lists open projects. When expanded, it displays the drawings and subfolders that are part of each project in a tree structure, as shown in Figure 2–5. Shortcut menu options are available by right-clicking on project files and drawing files in the *Projects* area.

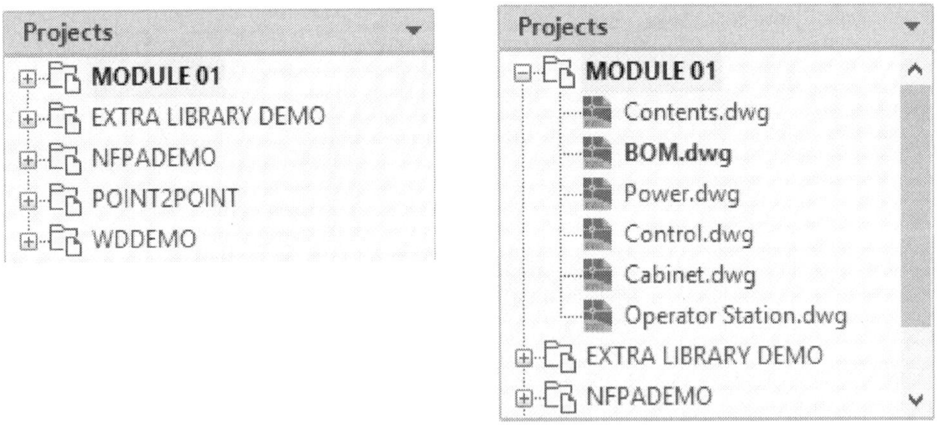

Figure 2–5

- A project can be organized into subfolders that group related drawings, as shown in Figure 2–6.

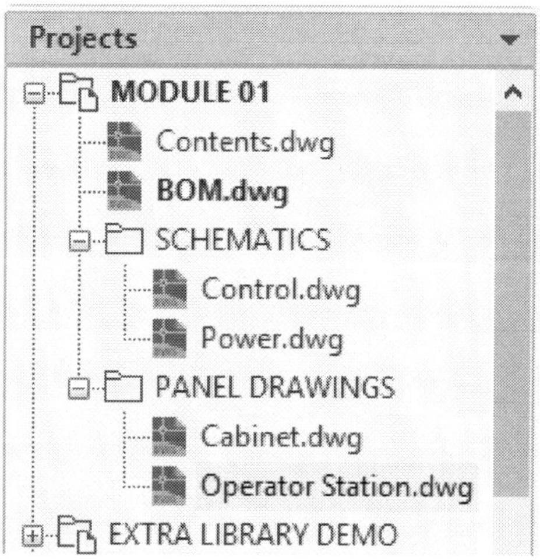

Figure 2–6

- The *Projects* area contains specific shortcut menus for DWG files, project files, and subfolders.
- The *Projects* area can be customized to display a combination of a DWG filename and its AutoCAD Electrical specific properties, as shown in Figure 2–7.

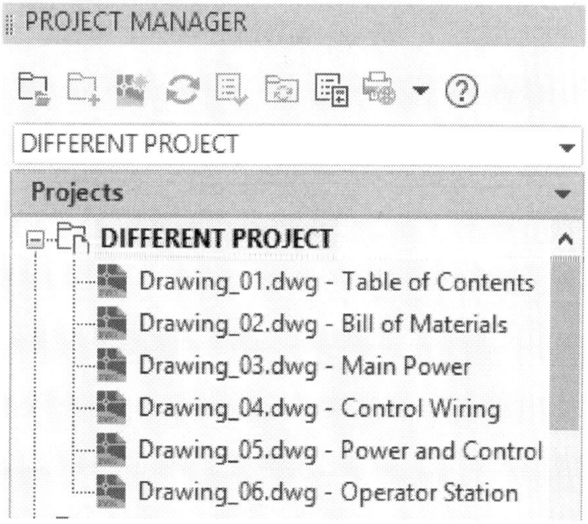

Figure 2–7

4. Details/Preview Area

The *Details/Preview* area (shown in Figure 2–8) can be found below the *Projects* area. The area displays information about the selected project file or drawing, including its name, location, and AutoCAD Electrical properties. Click (Preview) in the upper right corner to display a preview of a drawing file. Click (Details) to return to the *Details* area.

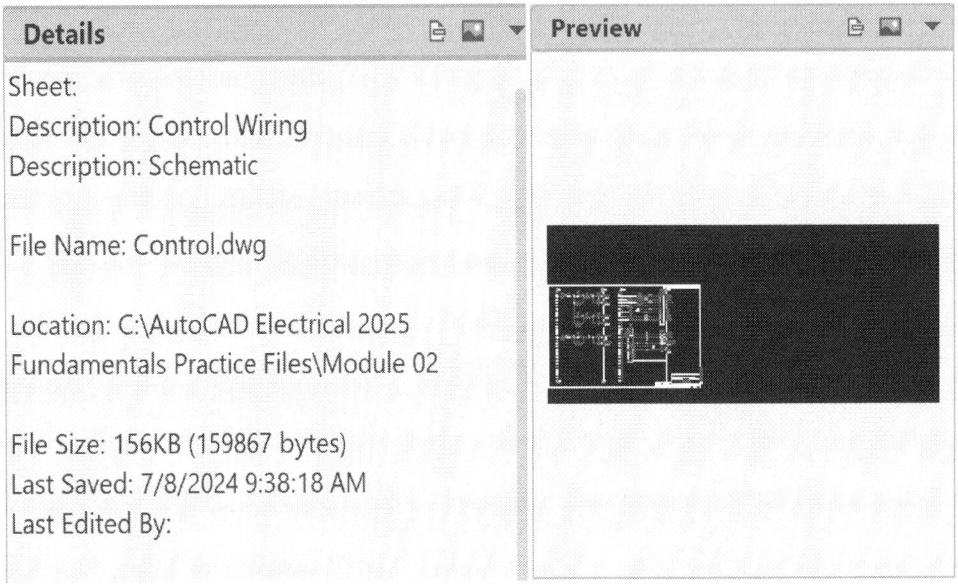

Figure 2–8

Location View Tab

When the *Location View* tab is selected, the interface of the *Project Manager* palette displays as shown in Figure 2–9.

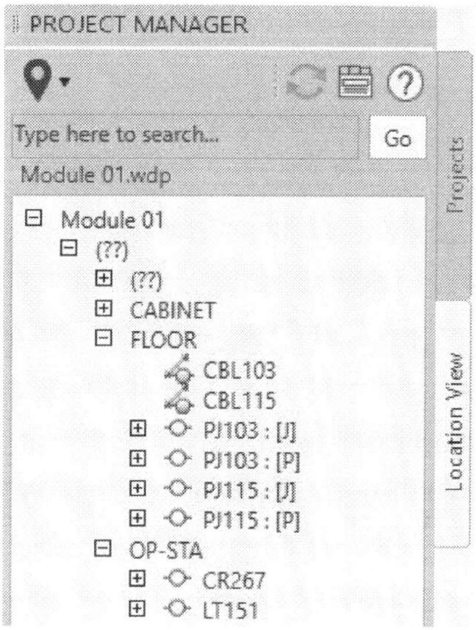

Figure 2–9

- The *Project Manager* palette (*Location View* tab) displays information about the connections and components in the projects. All the devices that are present in the project are listed along with their location in a tree structure.
- Hover the cursor over a component in the list to display its information, as shown in Figure 2–10.

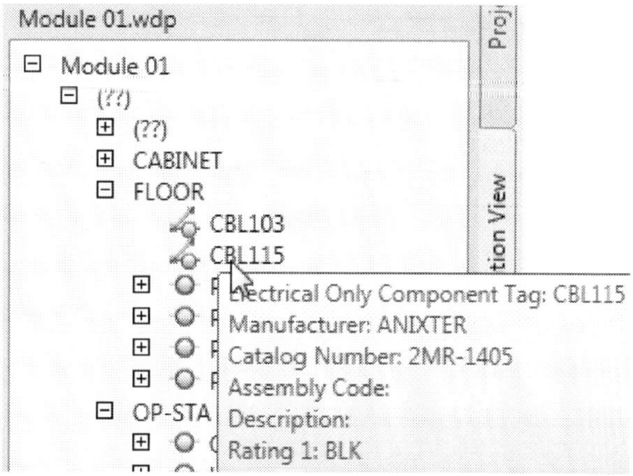

Figure 2–10

- Right-click on a component and select **Surf**. This opens a dialog box displaying the component references and location, as shown in Figure 2–11.

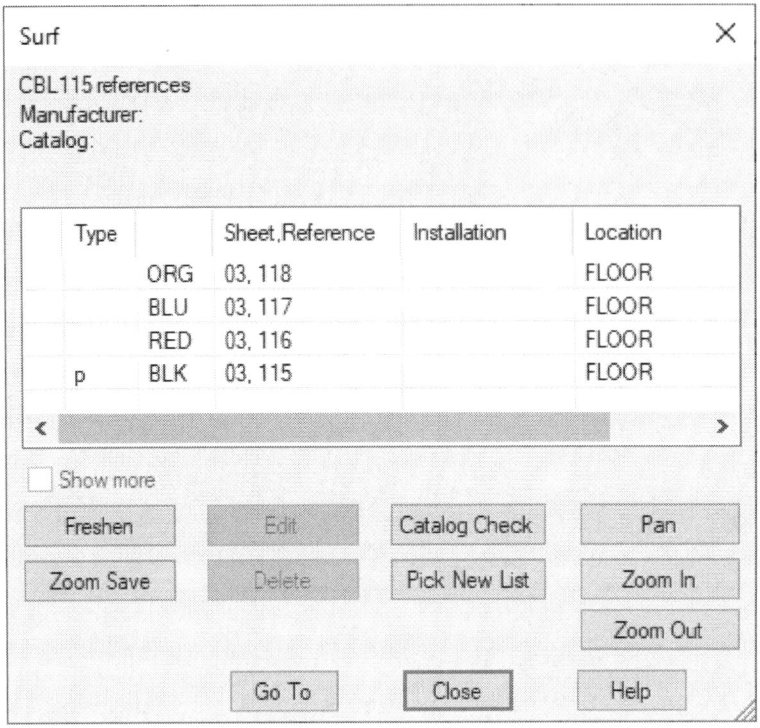

Figure 2–11

- In the *Project Manager* toolbar (*Location View* tab), click  (Display Details and Connections) to expand the view and display the details and connections information of the selected node or device.
  - You might need to further expand the expanded view to accommodate all of the columns.
  - The *Details* tab displays the details of the selected node/device, as shown in Figure 2–12.

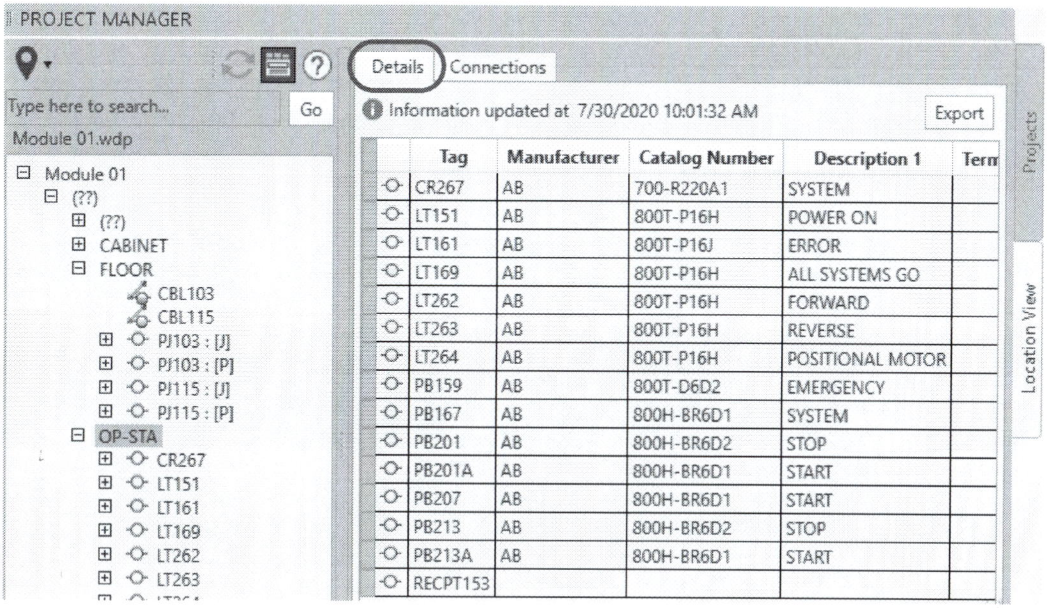

Figure 2–12

- Select the *Connections* tab to display the wiring and from/to connections of the selected node/device, as shown in Figure 2–13.

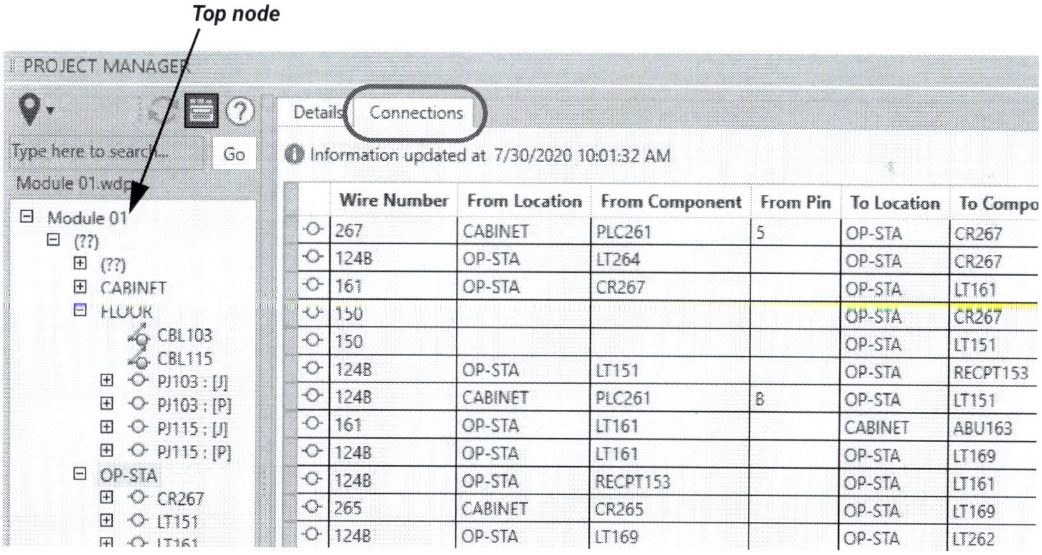

Figure 2–13

- The top node is the representation of the entire project. Selecting this node displays the details and location of all of the devices and components in the project.

2.2 Accessing Project Files

Accessing project files in the *Project Manager* (*Projects* tab) is the first step when creating a new set of electrical drawings or accessing an existing set, as shown in Figure 2–14.

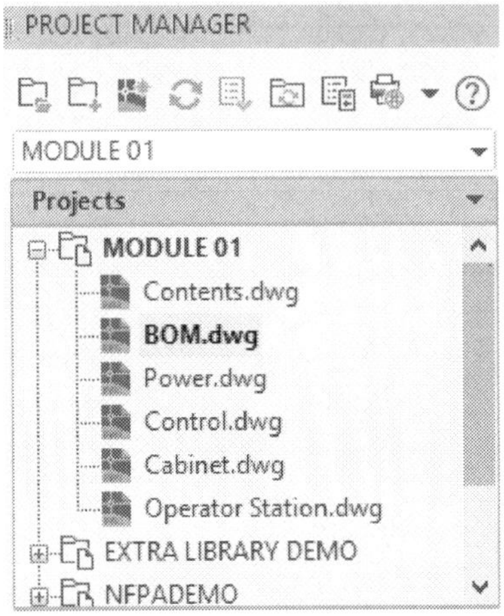

Figure 2–14

Open an Existing Project File

The **Open Project** command opens the *Select Project File* dialog box, which enables you to open an existing project.

Open Project

Drop-down list: Project Manager>**Open Project**

Shortcut menu: *(blank area of Project Manager)* **Open Project**

- To start the **Open Project** command, in the *Project Manager* toolbar (*Projects* tab), click (Open Project). You can also start the command in the *Project Manager* drop-down list or in the shortcut menu.
- When a project file is opened, it is automatically set as the active project. It displays in bold in the *Project Manager*.
- Double-click on the project file in the *Project Manager* to expand/collapse the project and display the list of drawings it contains. You can also expand/collapse the project file by clicking ⊞/⊟ on the left side of the project file.

- The drop-down list contains list of all the currently open projects and the **Recent**, **New Project**, and **Open Project** commands, as shown in Figure 2–15.

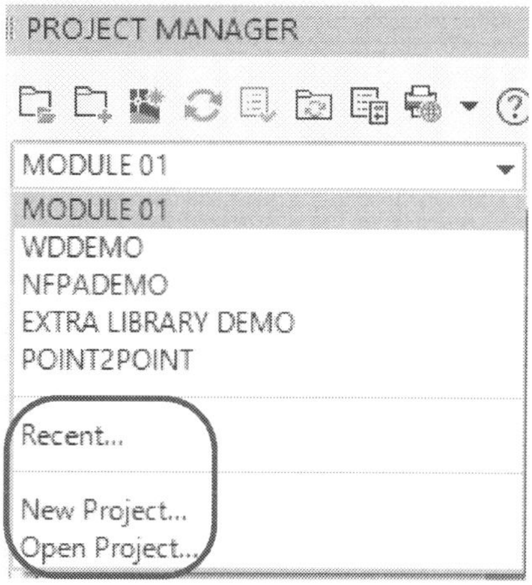

Figure 2–15

- The **Recent** command displays a list of recently opened project files.

Create a New Project File

When starting a new design, the first step is to create a new project file. Use the **New Project** command to create a project file (.WDP) and configure settings.

 **New Project**

Drop-down list: Project Manager>**New Project**

Command Prompt: acenewproject

Shortcut menu: *(blank area of Project Manager)* **New Project**

How To: Create a New Project

1. In the *Project Manager* toolbar (*Projects* tab), click  (New Project).
    - You can also start the command in the *Project Manager* drop-down list or in the shortcut menu.

2. In the *Create New Project* dialog box, type a name for the project file, as shown in Figure 2–16. The WDP extension is added automatically.

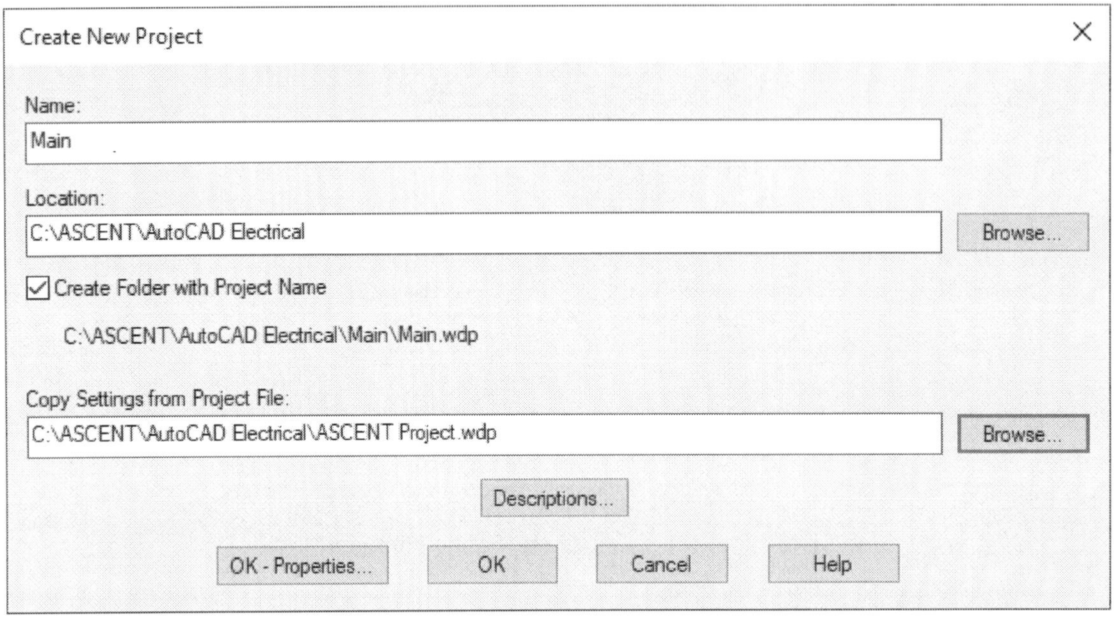

Figure 2–16

3. Enter a location in which to create the project or click **Browse...** to open the *Browse For Folder* dialog box and select the required folder for the location.
4. Select **Create Folder with Project Name**. The location and name of the new project are previewed below the checkbox.
5. (Optional) Type a name or click **Browse...** to select an existing project file from which to copy settings into the new project.

6. (Optional) Click **Descriptions...** to open the *Project Description* dialog box, as shown in Figure 2–17. Enter the project descriptions and click **OK**.

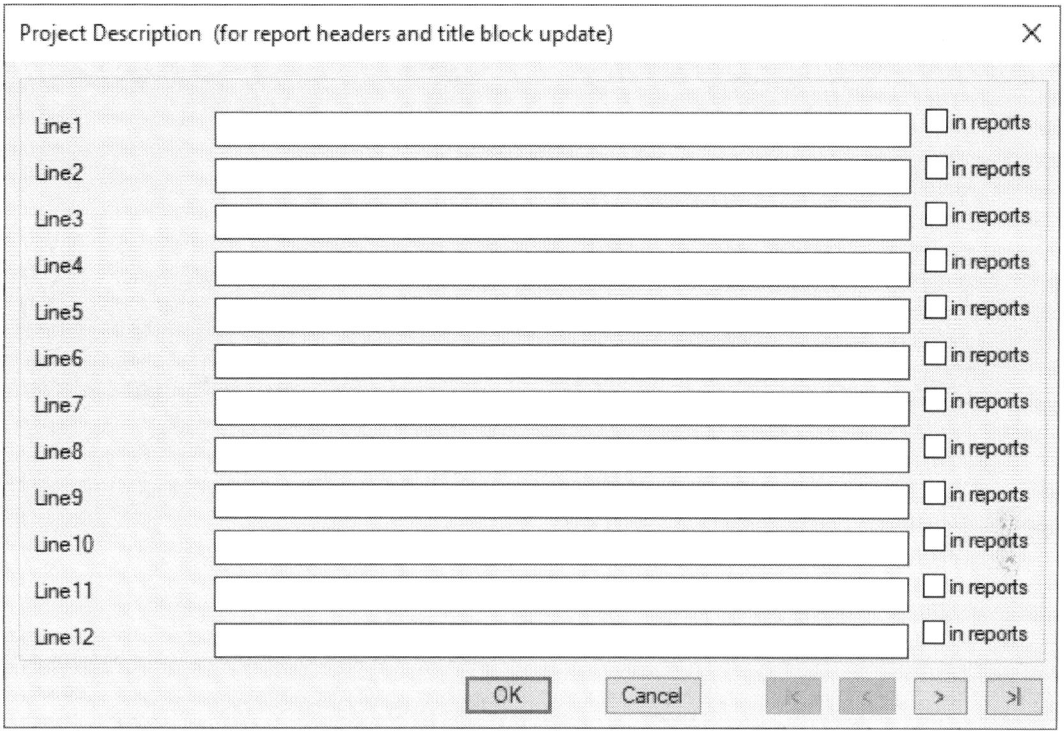

Figure 2–17

Description fields	• Can be used in reports by selecting **in reports.** • Can be used to automatically populate title blocks.
Line# labels	• Can be customized to display a more descriptive name for each line. • Can be mapped with a WDL file.

7. (Optional) In the *Create New Project* dialog box, click **OK-Properties...** to modify the project properties in the *Project Properties* dialog box, as shown in Figure 2–18. You can also create the project file without modifying the project properties and edit the project properties later, as required.

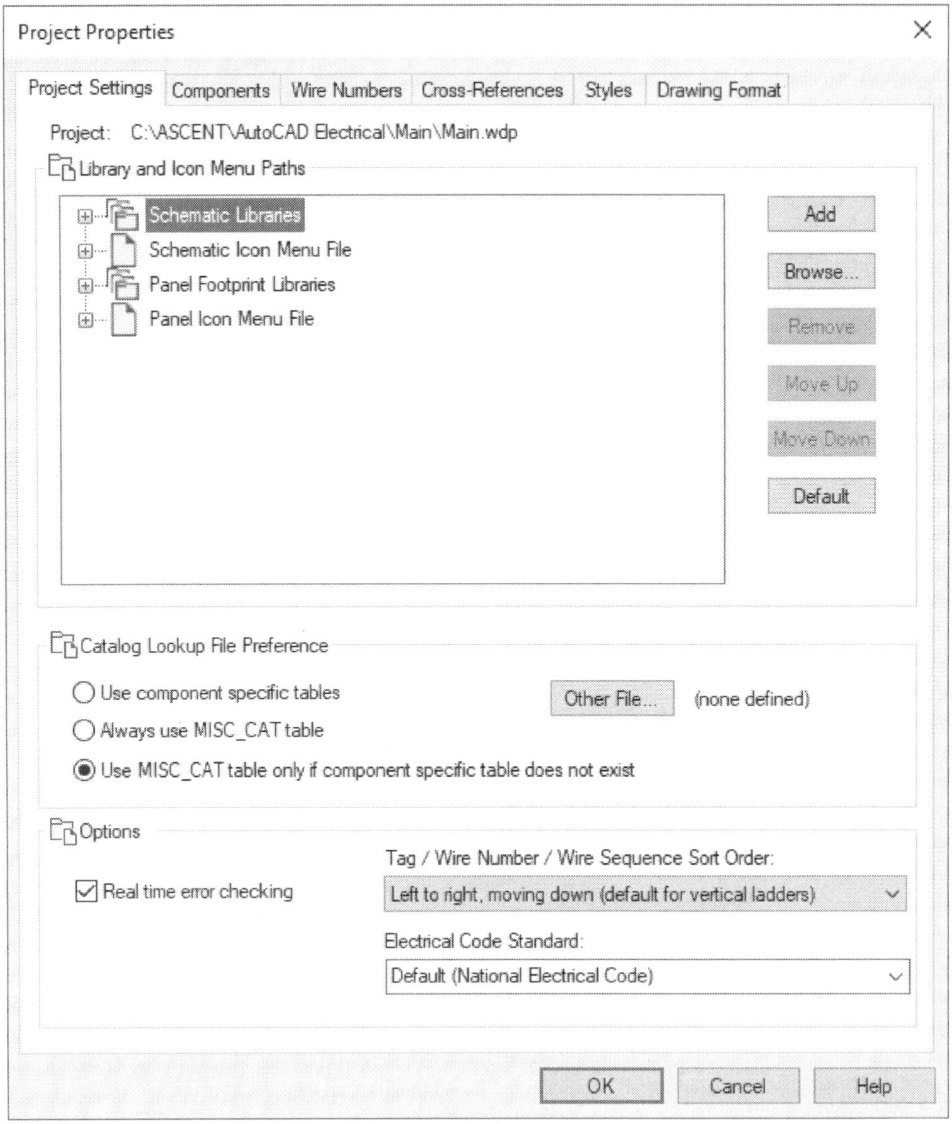

Figure 2–18

- The Project Properties become the default for new drawings created with the AutoCAD Electrical **New Drawing** command.
- When adding existing drawings to a project, you have the option of setting project properties as the default for the drawing properties or applying them to the drawing later.

Activate or Close a Project File

The active project file controls which DWG files are affected when commands are run. When running commands that affect multiple drawings, only drawings that are part of the active project file are updated. When finished working on a project, you can close it.

How To: Activate a Project File

1. In the *Project Manager* (*Projects* tab), right-click on a project file and select **Activate**, as shown in Figure 2–19. You can also select the project file in the *Project Manager* drop-down list.

- Only one project can be active at a time. The currently active project is located at the top of the list and identified in bold.
- You can work on drawings from other projects. However, you cannot update references to other drawings in that project until you have activated the project file for that drawing.

How To: Close a Project File

1. In the *Project Manager,* right-click on the project file and select **Close**, as shown in Figure 2–20.

- If you close the active project, the next project in the list is set as active.
- Closing a project removes the project file from the *Project Manager* list, but does not remove it from your hard drive.

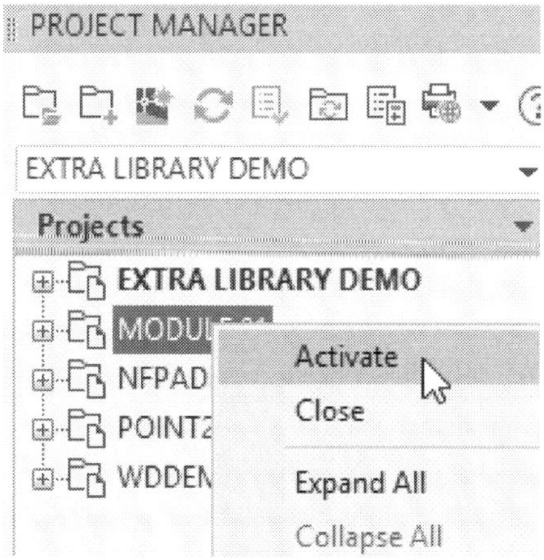

Figure 2–19

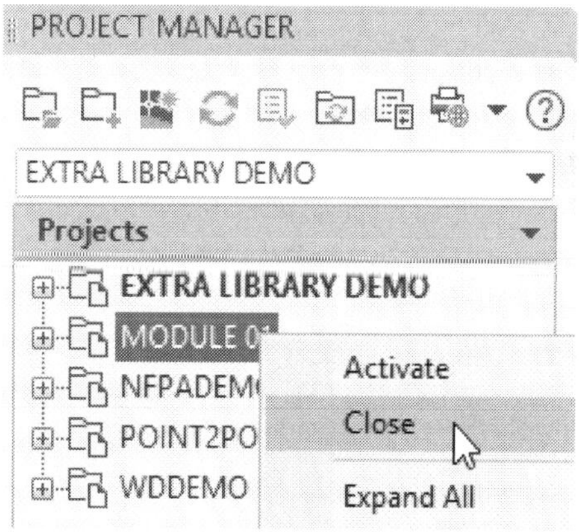

Figure 2–20

Practice 2a
Open, Close, and Create Project Files

Practice Objectives

- Open, close, and compare separate projects.
- Create a new project based on an existing project.

In this practice, you will open two project files and compare the drawing lists contained in the projects. You will also activate a project and close a project file. Finally you will create a new, blank project file, as shown in Figure 2–21.

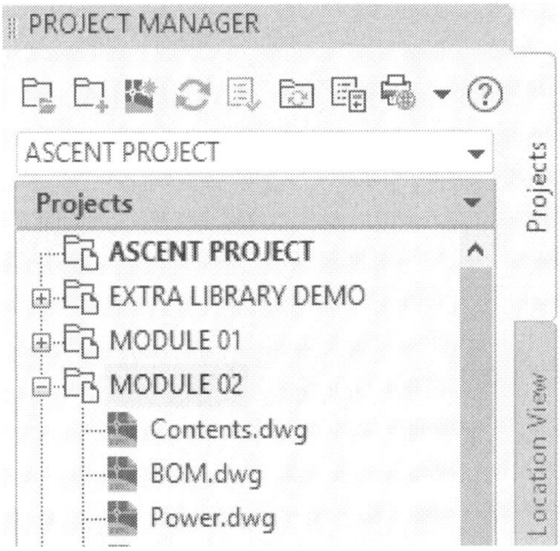

Figure 2–21

1. In the *Project Manager*, verify that the *Projects* tab is selected. In the toolbar, click (Open Project). The *Select Project File* dialog box opens.
2. In your practice files folder, in the *Module 02* folder, select **Module 02.wdp** and click **Open**. The **Module 02** project file opens and is set as the active project.
3. In the *Project Manager*, double-click on **Module 02**. The project drawing list displays in the *Project Manager*, as shown in Figure 2–22.

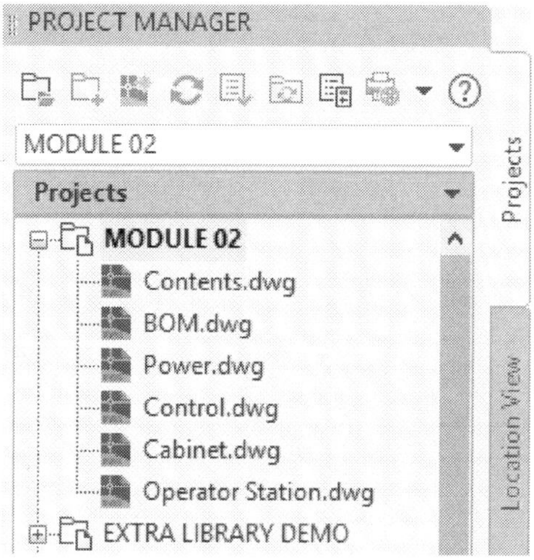

Figure 2–22

4. In the *Project Manager*, select **Control.dwg**. In the lower half of the *Project Manager*, note the information displayed in the *Details* and *Preview* areas, as shown in Figure 2–23. Click  (Preview) and  (Details) to switch between the two views.

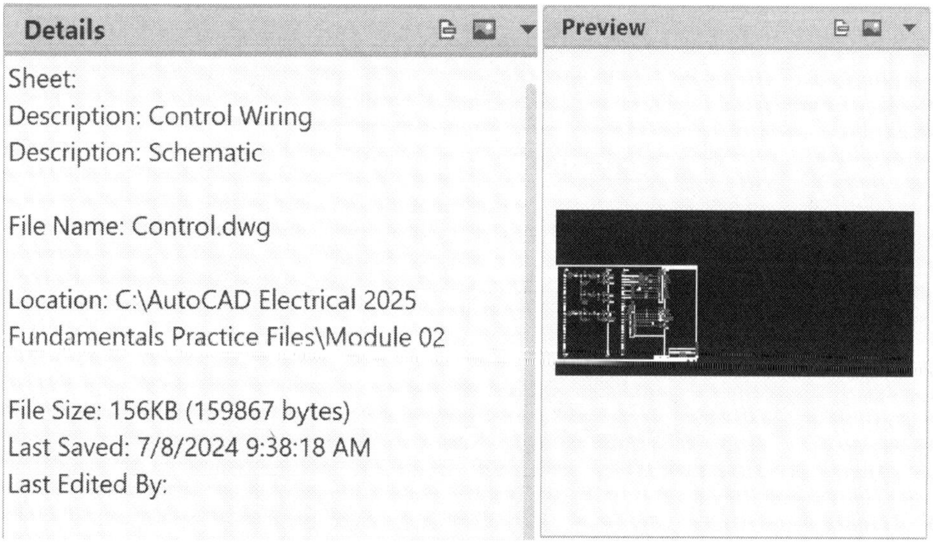

Figure 2–23

5. At the top of the *Project Manager*, just below the *Project Manager* toolbar, expand the drop-down list and select **Open Project**. The *Select Project File* dialog box opens.
6. In the *Module 02* folder, select **Different Project.wdp** and click **Open**. The *Different Project* project file is listed and set as the active project.

7. In the *Project Manager*, double-click on **Different Project**. The project drawing list displays in the *Project Manager*, as shown in Figure 2–24.

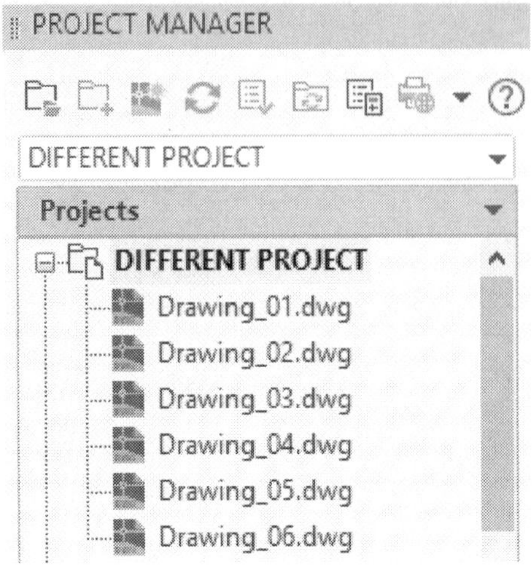

Figure 2–24

8. In the *Project Manager*, right-click on **Module 02** and select **Activate**, as shown in Figure 2–25. **Module 02** is set as the active project.

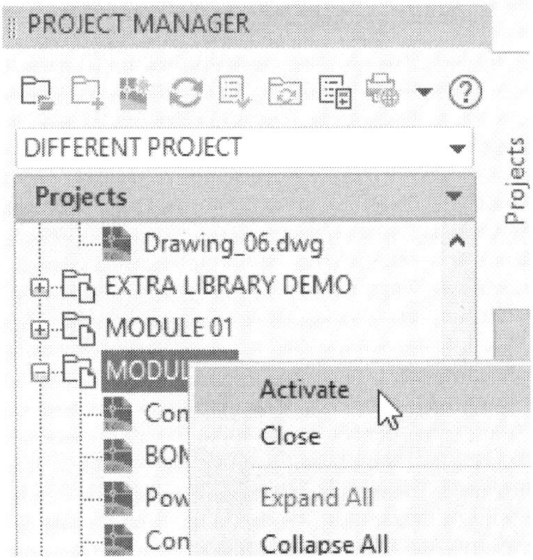

Figure 2–25

9. Right-click on **Different Project** and select **Close**.
10. In **Module 02**, double-click on **Control.dwg** to open it. To create a new project, a drawing should be open.

11. Click  (New Project) (shown in Figure 2–26) to open the *Create New Project* dialog box.

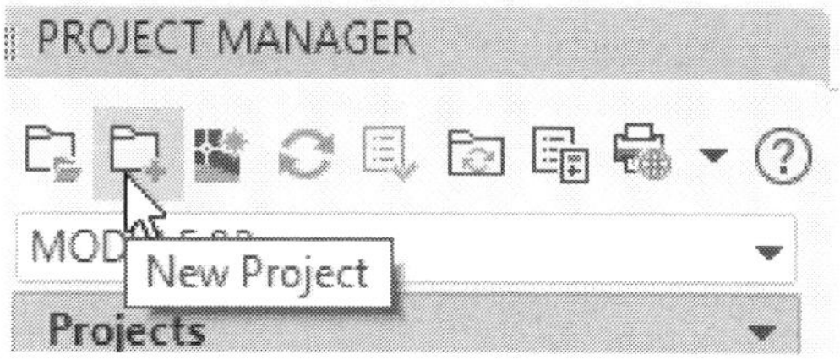

Figure 2–26

12. In the *Name* field, enter **ASCENT Project**. Next to the *Location* field, click **Browse...**, locate your practice files folder, select the *Module 02* folder and click **OK** (the path to your practice files folder and *Module 02* folder is set). Clear the **Create Folder with Project Name** option. In the *Copy Settings from Project File* field, verify that the practice files folder and *Module 02* folder path is set. If required, next to the *Copy Settings from Project File* field, click **Browse...**, locate your practice files folder, locate the *Module 02* folder, and open **Module 02.wdp**, which displays in the edit box, as shown in Figure 2–27.

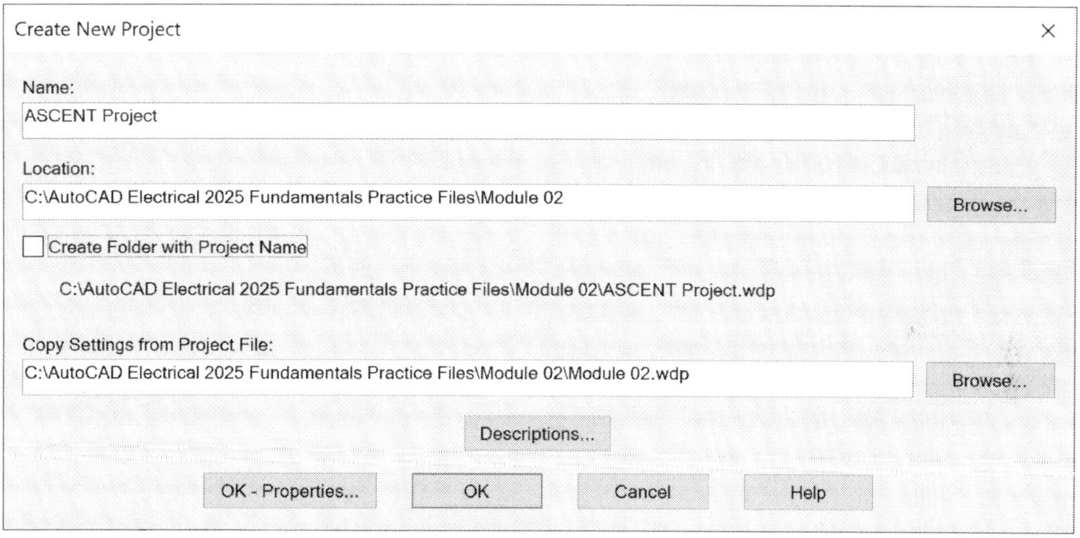

Figure 2–27

13. Click **Descriptions...**. The *Project Description* dialog box opens. Enter the following information as shown in Figure 2–28.
    - *Line1:* **ASCENT PROJECT**
    - *Line2:* Your Name
    - *Line3:* Your Company

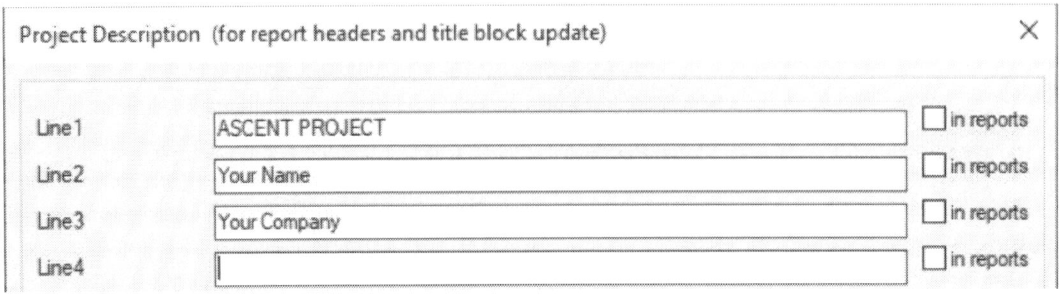

Figure 2–28

14. Click **OK** to return to the *Create New Project* dialog box.
15. Click **OK-Properties**. The *Project Properties* dialog box opens, as shown in Figure 2–29. Select the different tabs to see the available settings. Click **OK**.

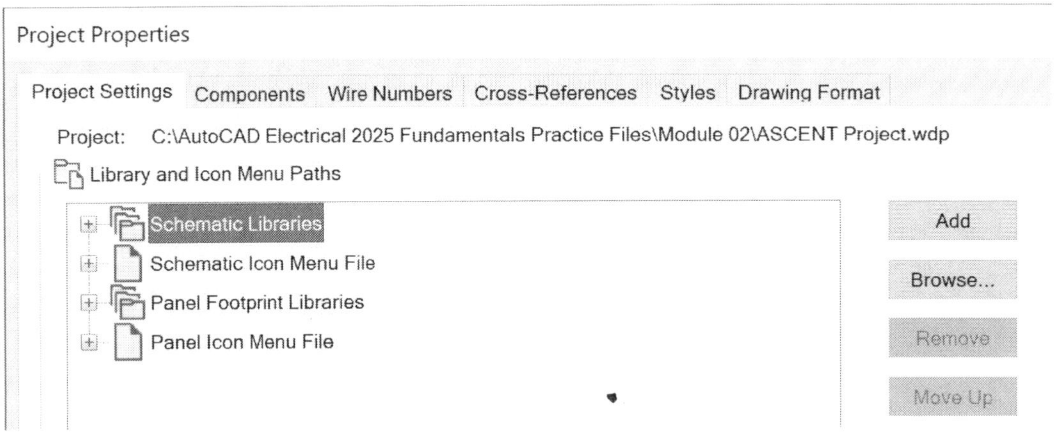

Figure 2–29

16. The **ASCENT PROJECT** project file is created and set as the active project. In the *Project Manager*, note that there is no plus icon next to **ASCENT PROJECT**, indicating that it is currently an empty project.

End of practice

2.3 Opening a Drawing

After you open a project, you can open the drawings contained in it by:

- Right-clicking on the drawing file in the *Project Manager* (*Projects* tab) and selecting **Open**, as shown in Figure 2–30.
- Double-clicking on the drawing file.
- Using standard AutoCAD methods.

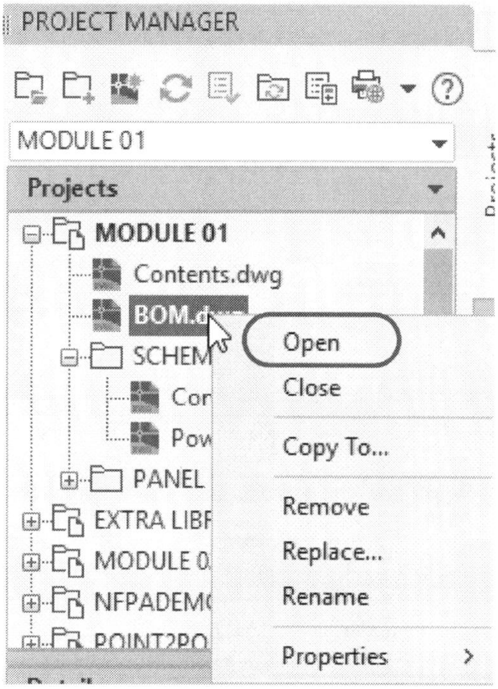

Figure 2–30

How To: Open a Drawing File from the Project Manager

1. Double-click on the project file to expand it and display the drawing files in it.
2. Double-click on the drawing or right-click on it and select **Open**.

- The AutoCAD Electrical software supports Multiple Document Interface (MDI), which permits for multiple drawings to be open during one session.

2.4 Creating a Drawing

When a new project file is created, it does not contain any drawings. You must create new drawings or add existing ones to the project. The **New Drawing** command in the *Project Manager* (*Projects* tab) (shown in Figure 2–31) creates a new drawing, adds it to the active project, and opens a dialog box which enables you to can configure the drawing properties. The standard **New** command can also be used to create a new drawing, which can then be added to the project file.

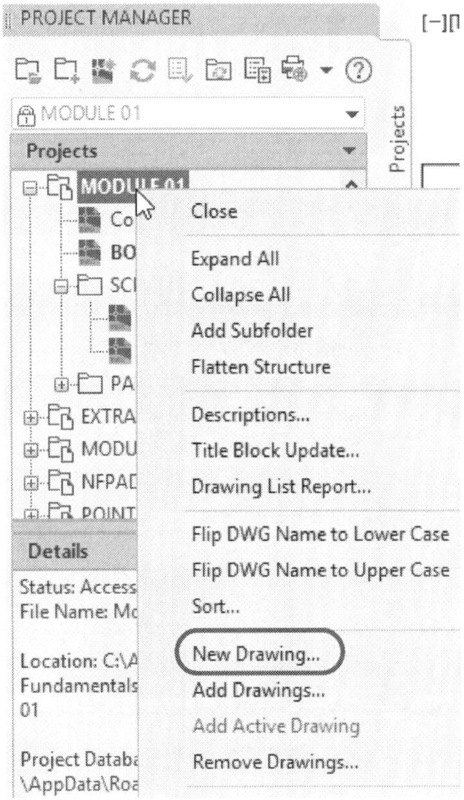

Figure 2–31

 **New Drawing**

Command Prompt: acenewdrawing

Shortcut menu: *(on a project file in Project Manager)* **New Drawing**

How To: Create a New Drawing

1. In the *Project Manager*, click  (New Drawing) or right-click on the project file and select **New Drawing**. The *Create New Drawing* dialog box opens, as shown in Figure 2–32.

   Note: *To create a new drawing in the project, another drawing should be open.*

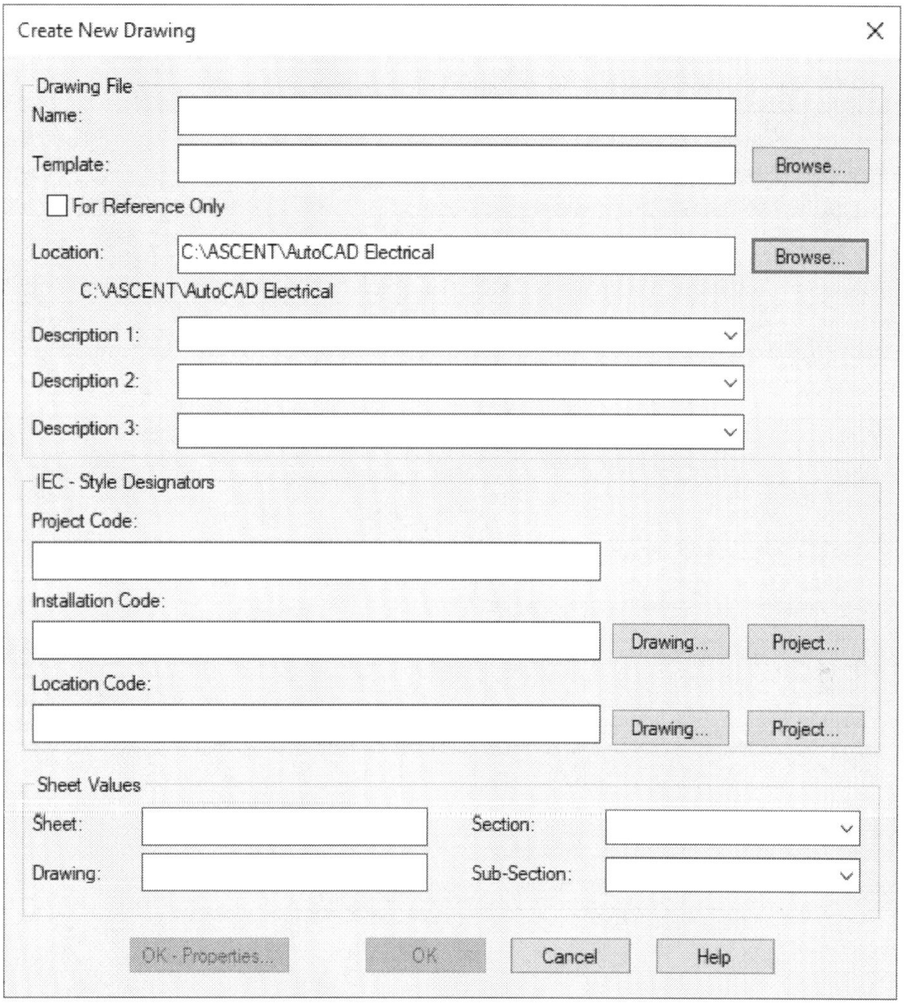

Figure 2–32

2. Type a name in the *Name* field.
3. In the *Template* field, specify a template file (DWT). You can type the path and filename or use **Browse...**.

4. If this is to be a reference file, select **For Reference Only**. Reference files are ignored during certain AutoCAD Electrical commands.
5. In the *Location* field, specify the location of the new file.
6. Fill in the *Description* fields.
7. Fill in the *IEC – Style Designators* fields.
8. Fill in the *Sheet Values* fields.
9. Click **OK** to create the file or **OK-Properties** to create the file and open the *Drawing Properties* dialog box, as shown in Figure 2–33.

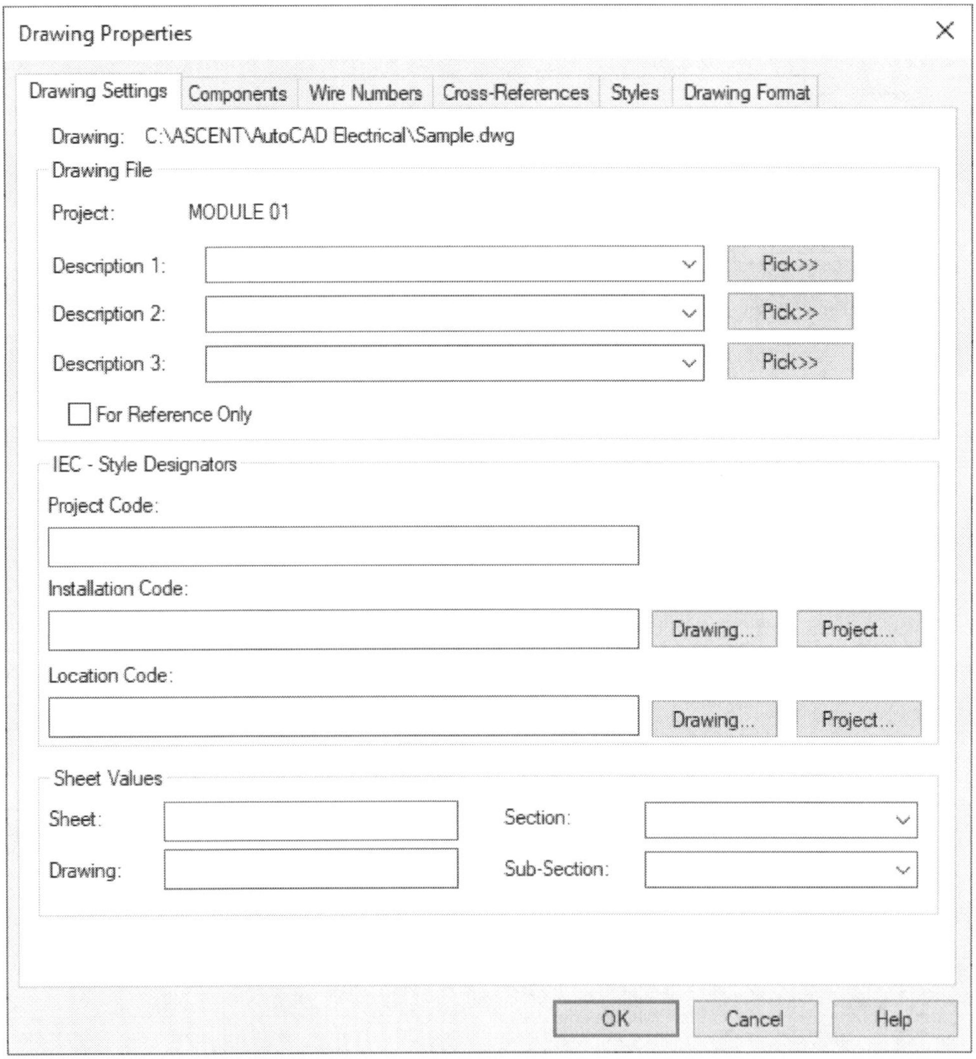

Figure 2–33

10. Configure the properties of the drawing file.

- After creating the file, you can modify all fields except for *Name*, *Location*, and *Template*. To edit the drawing properties, right-click on the drawing in the *Project Manager* and select **Properties>Drawing Properties**.
- The Description properties can be displayed in the *Project Manager* and used in reports.
- The information in the *IEC - Style Designators* field is used for IEC style symbols.
- The *Section* and *Sub-Section* codes are used to group drawings when running project-wide commands or creating reports.

2.5 Add a Drawing to a Project File

You can add an existing drawing to a project using the **Add Drawings** command, as shown in Figure 2–34.

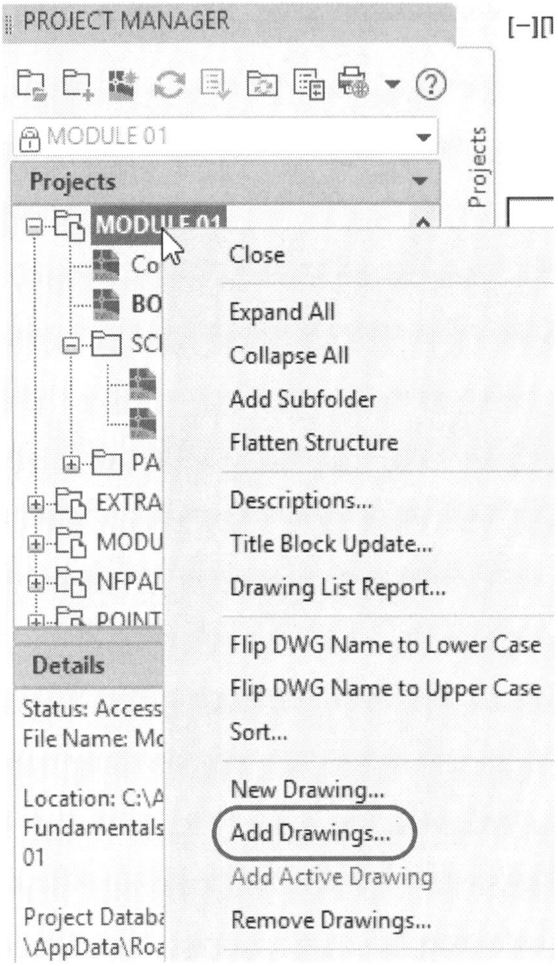

Figure 2–34

How To: Add an Existing Drawing to a Project

1. In the *Project Manager* (*Projects* tab), right-click on the project to which you want to add the drawing, and select **Add Drawings**.
2. In the *Select Files to Add* dialog box, browse to and select the drawing you want to add. You can add multiple drawings using <Ctrl> or <Shift>.

3. In the *Apply Project Defaults to Drawing Settings* warning box shown in Figure 2–35, you can select whether to apply the settings from the project file to the drawing(s) you are adding. These include the component tag, wire numbers, and other settings.

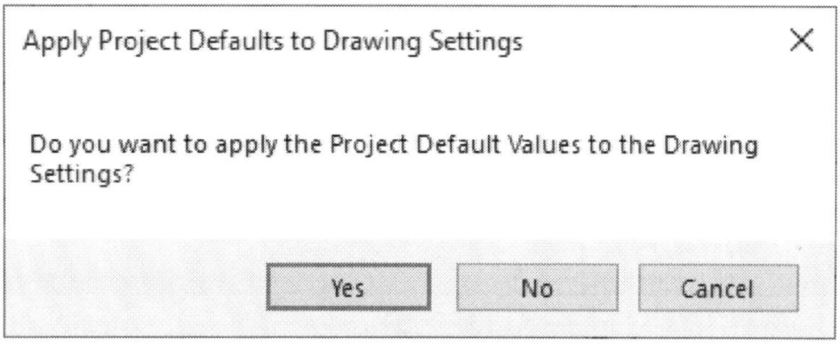
Apply Project Defaults to Drawing Settings
Do you want to apply the Project Default Values to the Drawing Settings?
Yes
No
Cancel

Figure 2–35

- You can also add the active drawing (currently open) to the project by right-clicking on the project file in the *Project Manager* and selecting **Add Active Drawing**. You are then prompted by the Apply Project Defaults to Drawing Settings.
- When drawings are added to a project, they are appended to the end of the drawing list.

2.6 Managing Drawings in Projects

When a project has been created and the drawings added, you need to manage it. Project management is done using the *Project Manager* (*Projects* tab), ribbon, or shortcut menus.

Subfolders

The list of drawings in the *Project Manager* can be divided into subfolders to organize the drawings by grouping related drawings, as shown in Figure 2–36.

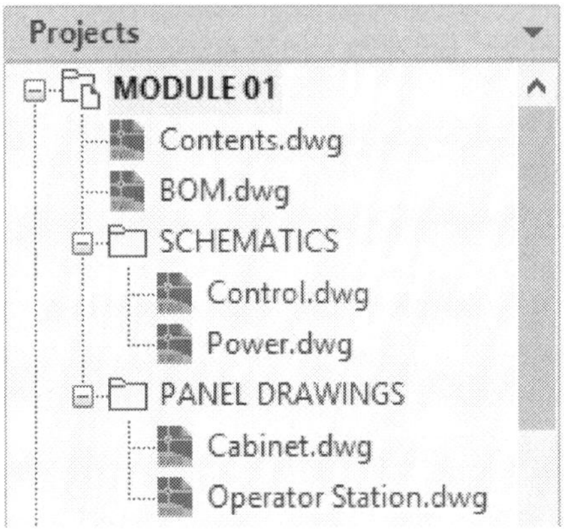

Figure 2–36

- They can be further divided into additional subfolders. There can be an unlimited number of subfolder levels.
- The subfolders in the *Project Manager* do not affect the location in which the drawings are saved.
- Commands for subfolders can be found in the shortcut menu of a project or subfolder in the *Project Manager*, as shown in Figure 2–37. When you right-click on a subfolder, the commands in the context menu only apply to that subfolder.

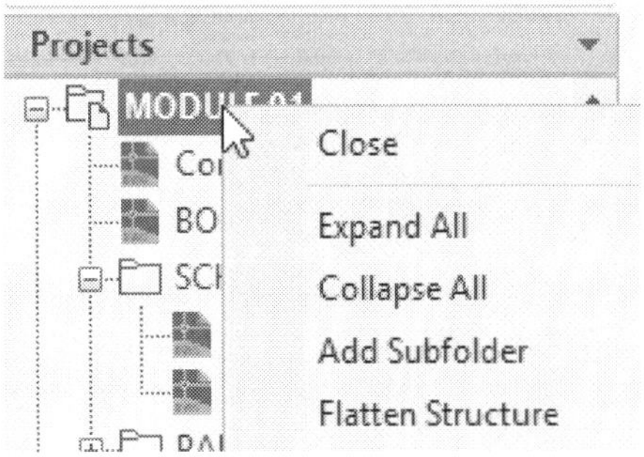

Figure 2–37

Add Subfolder	Adds a new subfolder below the selected one.
Expand All	Expands all of the subfolder nodes below, including the selected one.
Collapse All	Collapses all of the subfolder nodes below, including the selected one.
Flatten Structure	Flattens the entire project structure. All of the subfolders are removed, and all of the drawings are listed in the main list. You cannot undo these changes. This option is only available for the main project node and the active project file.

Reorder

The order of the drawings in the project is important. When running project-wide update tools and reporting tools, the drawings are processed in the order in which they are listed in the project, and continue straight through any subfolders. The drawing order can affect data, such as component tags and wire numbers.

- You can drag and drop a drawing to a new position in the *Project Manager* list.
- You can move the drawing from one subfolder to another, as shown in Figure 2–38.

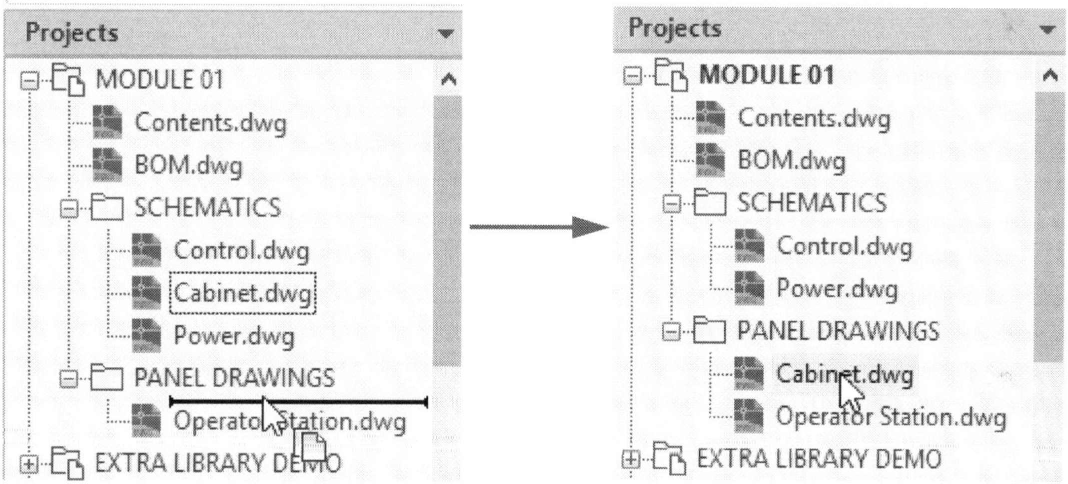

Figure 2–38

- You can also drag and drop subfolders. However, all of the drawings listed below a subfolder move with the subfolder.
- If you drop the drawing directly on a subfolder, the drawing is placed at the bottom of the subfolder.
- If a subfolder is empty, you need to drop the drawing directly on the subfolder to add the drawing to it.

Remove

Removing a drawing from the project does not affect the drawing itself. The file is removed from the project list, but is not deleted from the hard drive.

How To: Remove a Single Drawing or Subfolder from a Project

1. In the *Project Manager*, right-click on the drawing file or subfolder you want to remove.
2. In the shortcut menu, select **Remove**, as shown in Figure 2–39.

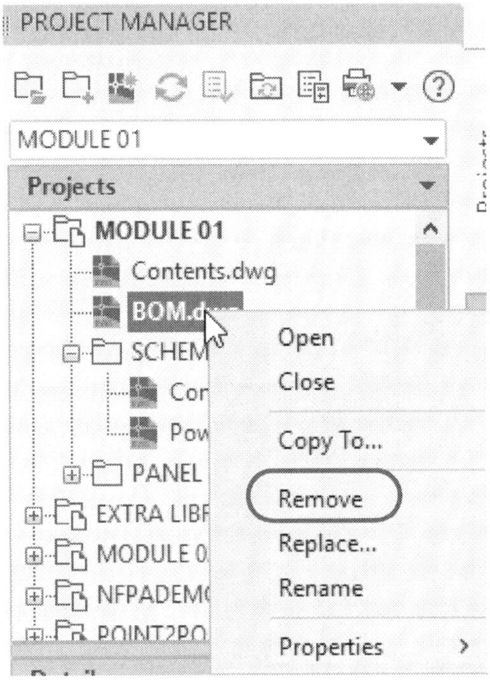

Figure 2–39

- When you remove a subfolder, all of the drawings in that subfolder node are also removed from the project.

How To: Remove Multiple Drawings from a Project

1. In the *Project Manager*, right-click on the project containing the drawings you want to remove and select **Remove Drawings**. The *Select Drawings to Process* dialog box opens, as shown in Figure 2–40.
   - You can remove drawings from active or non-active projects.

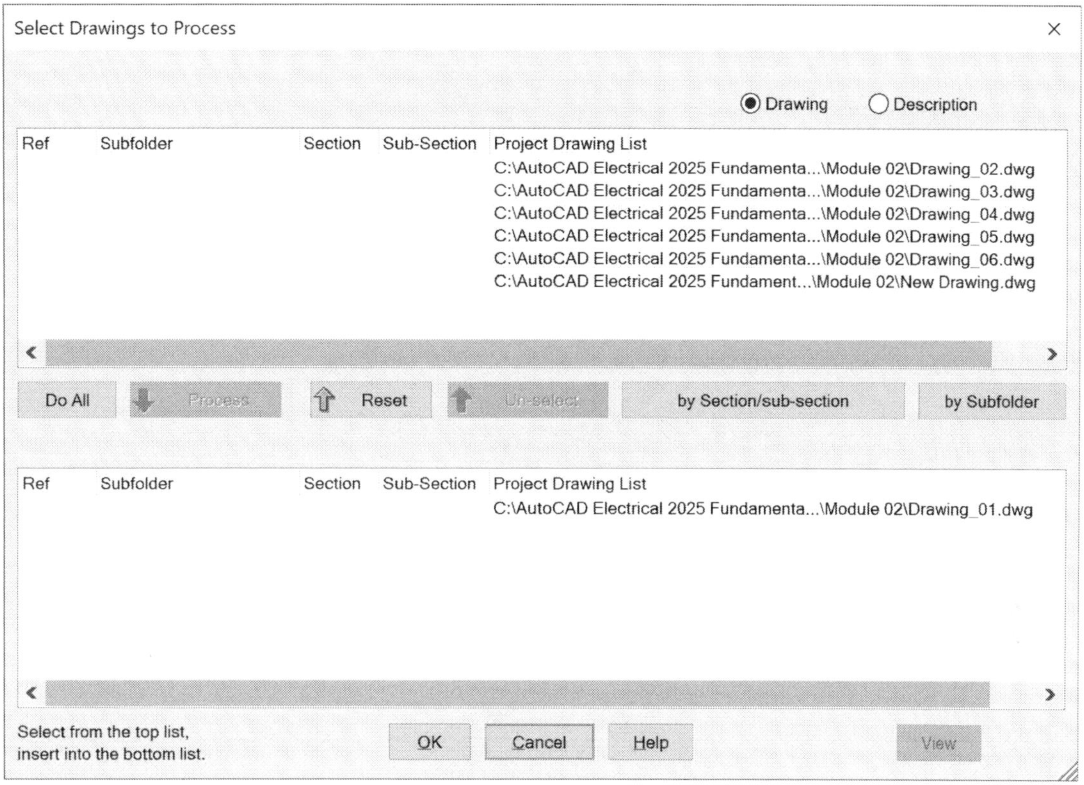

Figure 2–40

2. Click **Do All** to select all of the drawings from the project, or select individual drawings and click **Process**. This procedure moves the selected files from the upper area to the lower area of the dialog box.
3. Click **Reset** to clear the lower area, moving all of the drawings in the lower area to the upper area.
4. In the lower area, select a drawing and click **Un-select** to move it from the lower area to the upper area.
5. To move drawings from the upper area to the lower area according to their section or sub-section codes, click **by Section/sub-section**. Select the appropriate section and sub-section in the dialog box and click **OK**.
6. To move drawings from the upper area to the lower area according to their subfolder location, click **by Subfolder**. Select the appropriate subfolder in the dialog box and click **OK**.
7. Click **OK** to process the drawings. All of the drawings in the lower area are processed.

Replace

You might need to replace a drawing in a project with another one. Doing so replaces the drawing in the project list, but does not affect the drawings on your local drive.

How To: Replace a Drawing in a Project

1. In the *Project Manager*, right-click on the drawing to be replaced.
2. In the shortcut menu, select **Replace**, as shown in Figure 2–41.

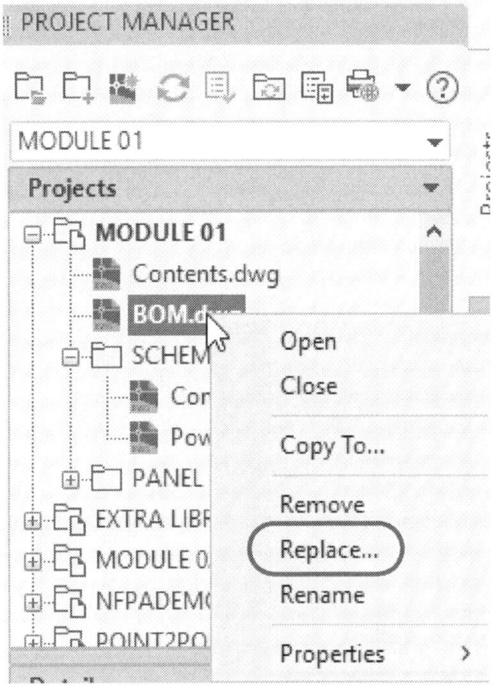

Figure 2–41

3. In the *Select Replacement Drawing* dialog box, browse to and select the drawing you want to add to the project.
4. Select whether to apply project settings to the drawing using the *Apply Project Defaults to Drawing Settings* dialog box.

Rename

You might need to rename a drawing file or subfolder in a project. It is a common practice to give drawings temporary names during the design stage, and then assign drawing numbers as the project progresses or when it is released.

How To: Rename a Drawing or Subfolder in a Project

1. In the *Project Manager*, right-click on the drawing or subfolder that you want to rename.
2. In the shortcut menu, select **Rename**.
3. In the *Project Manager*, type the new name.
4. Press <Enter> to accept the new name.

Hint: AutoCAD Electrical Rename Command

The project file references the drawings by drawing name. Therefore, it is recommended that you use the AutoCAD Electrical **Rename** command rather than Windows Explorer. The AutoCAD Electrical **Rename** command modifies the project file and changes the drawing name on the disk.

Previous/Next Drawing Command

When the drawing that is currently open is part of the active project, the **Previous Drawing** and **Next Drawing** commands can be used to browse through the drawings in the project file.

Previous Drawing

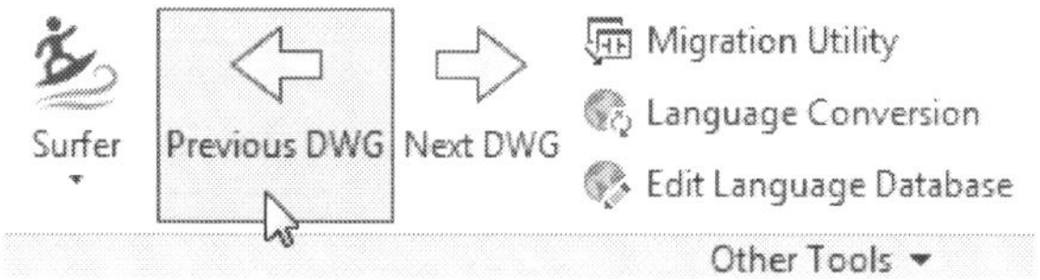

Ribbon: *Project* tab>*Other Tools* panel

Quick Access Toolbar

Next Drawing

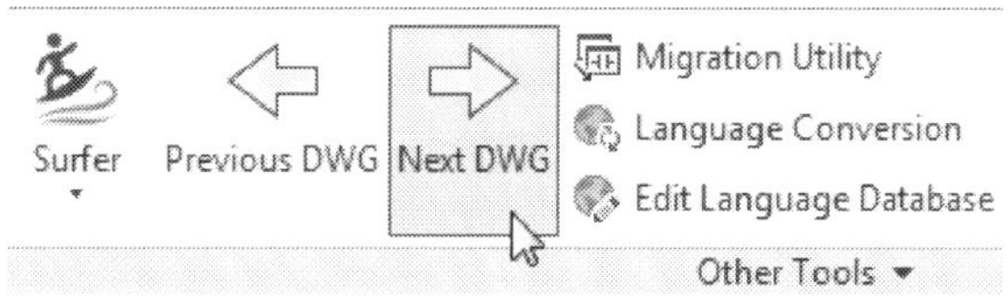

Ribbon: *Project* tab>*Other Tools* panel

Quick Access Toolbar

- The **Next Drawing** command saves and closes the currently open drawing, and then opens the next drawing in the project.
- The **Previous Drawing** command works similarly except it opens the previous drawing in the project.
- When using these commands, note that the software performs a quick save (**Qsave**) on the drawing that is currently open before closing it and opening the previous/next drawing in the list. **Qsave** is only performed if the currently open drawing has been changed.
- These commands are only available if the drawing that is currently open is part of the active project.
- You can load the **Next Drawing** and **Previous Drawing** commands in the Quick Access Toolbar by right-clicking on the command in the ribbon and selecting **Add to Quick Access Toolbar**.

Hint: Drawing Load Time

Be patient when browsing through several drawings. It can take a few seconds to load the drawing before the **Previous/Next Drawing** commands become available again.

2.7 Project Manager Drawing List

The *Project Manager* (*Projects* tab) can be customized to display different information for the drawings, as shown in Figure 2–42. Along with the Drawing filename, you can display more information, making it easier to distinguish what data exists in a drawing.

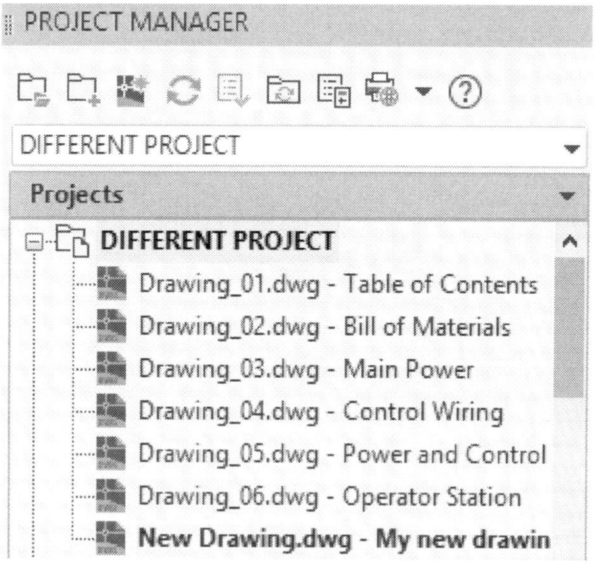

Figure 2–42

	**Drawing List Display Configuration**  **Project Manager Toolbar**

How To: Configure the Drawing List Display

1. In the *Project Manager*, click (Drawing List Display Configuration). The *Drawing List Display Configuration* dialog box opens as shown in Figure 2–43.

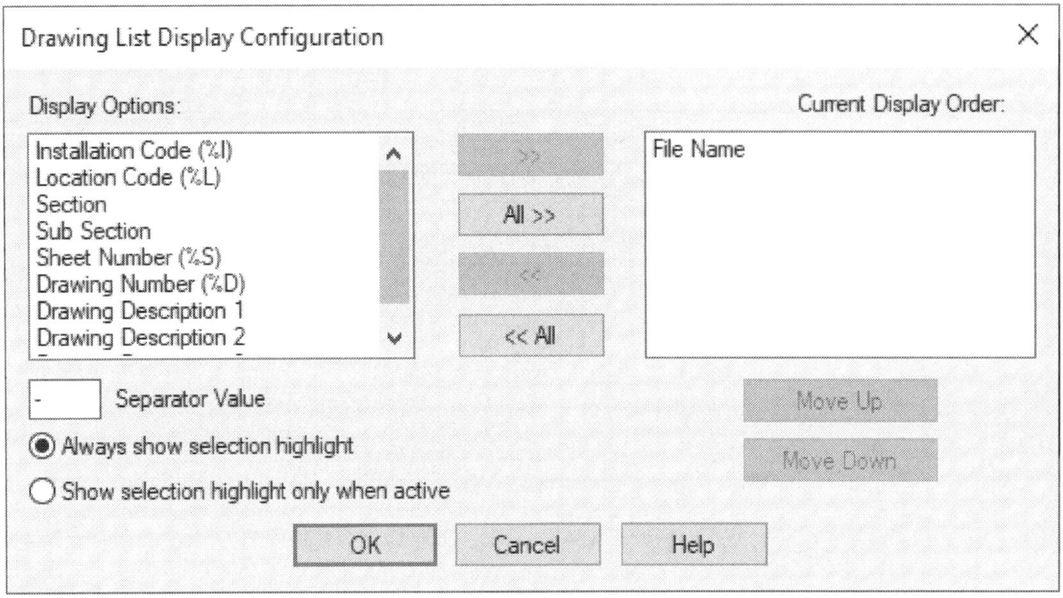

Figure 2–43

2. On the left side of the dialog box, select the property you want to add to the display and click **>>**.
3. On the right side of the dialog box, select the property you want to remove from the display and click **<<**.
4. To add all properties to the display, click **All >>**.
5. To remove all properties from the display, click **<<All**.
6. To change the order in which the properties display, select a property, and click **Move Up** or **Move Down**.
7. You can change the separator in the *Separator Value* field.
8. Click **OK** to complete the command.

- This feature is only useful if you populate drawing properties such as **Drawing Description** and **Section Code**.

Practice 2b
Projects and Drawing Files

Practice Objectives

- Navigate through the drawings in a project.
- Move a drawing to a new location in the drawing list.

In this practice, you will open a project file and use different methods to access the drawings in the project. You will then add an existing drawing to the project, reorder the drawings, and verify the new order, as shown in Figure 2–44.

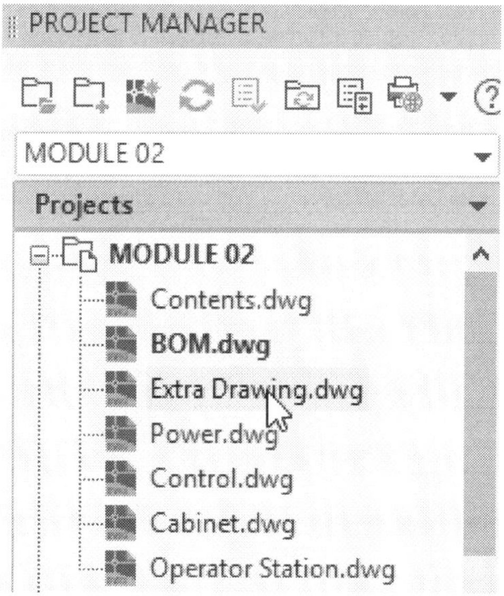

Figure 2–44

1. If **Module 02** is the active project, skip to Step 3. If it is listed in the *Project Manager* but is not active, right-click, select **Activate,** and then skip to Step 3. Otherwise, in the *Project Manager* toolbar, click (Open Project). The *Select Project File* dialog box opens.
   - Verify that the *Projects* tab is selected in the *Project Manager*.
2. In your practice files folder, in the *Module 02* folder, select **Module 02.wdp** and then click **Open**. The **Module 02** project file is opened and set as the active project.

3. If required, in the *Project Manager*, double-click on **Module 02** to display the project drawing list, as shown in Figure 2–45.

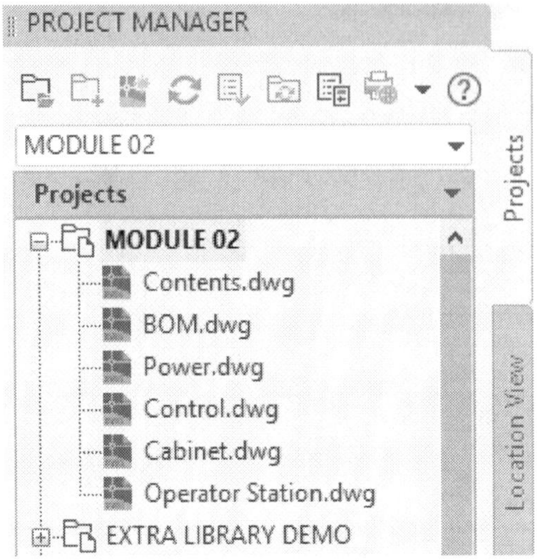

Figure 2–45

4. Verify that no drawing is open. If there is, right-click and select **Close**. Right-click on **Contents.dwg** and select **Open** to open it.

5. In the Quick Access Toolbar, click , or in the ribbon (*Project* tab>*Other Tools* panel), click  (Next DWG) to open the next drawing in the list. **Contents.dwg** is closed and **BOM.dwg** is opened.

   - If the **Next Drawing** and **Previous Drawing** tools are not displayed in the Quick Access Toolbar, you can load them by right-clicking on the command in the ribbon and selecting **Add to Quick Access Toolbar**.

6. Click  (Next DWG) again to open the next drawing in the list. **BOM.dwg** is closed and **Power.dwg** is opened.

7. Click  (Previous DWG) to open the previous drawing in the list. **Power.dwg** is closed and **BOM.dwg** is opened again.

8. Select and right-click on **Module 02** and select **Add Drawings**, as shown in Figure 2–46. The *Select Files to Add* dialog box opens.

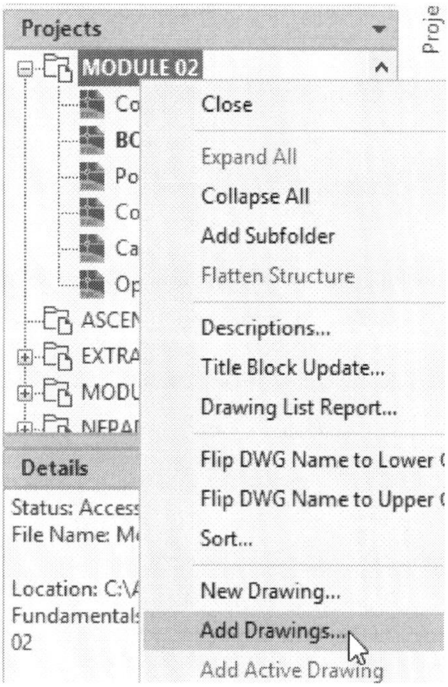

Figure 2–46

9. In your practice files folder, in the *Module 02* folder, select **Extra Drawing.dwg** and click **Add**. In the *Apply Project Defaults to Drawing Settings* dialog box, click **Yes**. **Extra Drawing.dwg** is added as the last drawing in the drawing list for **Module 02**, as shown in Figure 2–47. If the added drawing does not display in the list, click  (Refresh) in the *Project Manager* toolbar.

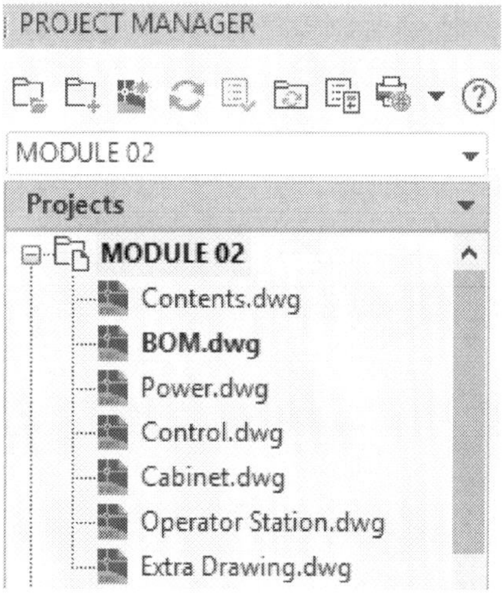

Figure 2–47

10. Right-click on **Extra Drawing.dwg** and select **Properties>Drawing Properties...**. The *Drawing Properties* dialog box opens.
11. In the *Description 1* field, type **Reports**, as shown in Figure 2–48. Click **OK**.

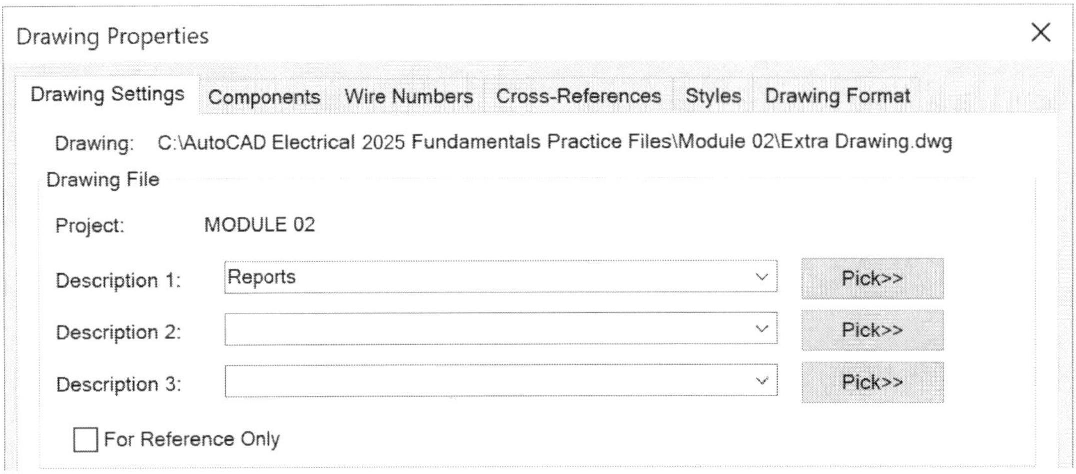

Figure 2–48

12. In the *Project Manager*, drag **Extra Drawing.dwg** directly below **BOM.dwg**, as shown on the left in Figure 2–49, and drop it there, as shown on the right in Figure 2–49. The drawing list updates in the *Project Manager*.

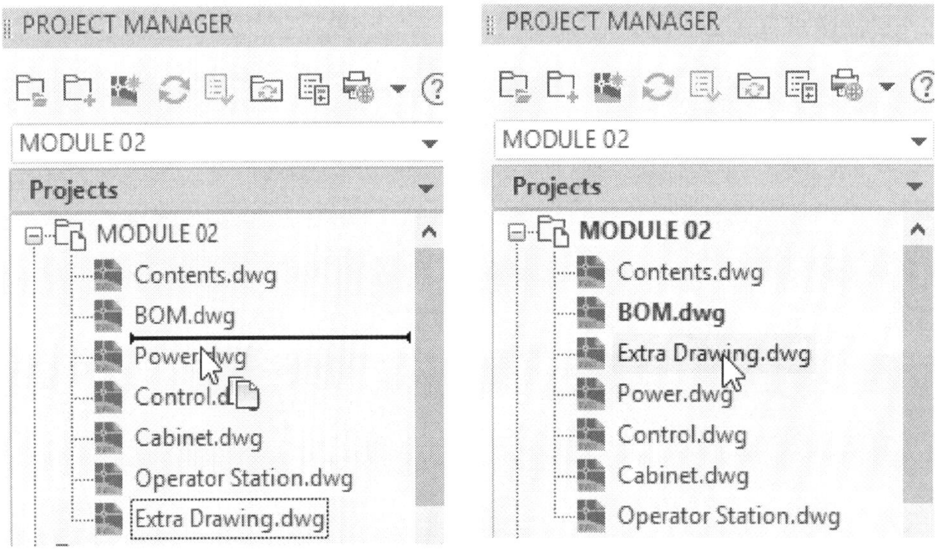

Figure 2–49

13. Verify that **BOM.dwg** is the currently open drawing. Click (Next Drawing) to open the next drawing, **Extra Drawing.dwg**. Click (Next Drawing) again to open **Power.dwg**.
14. Close **Power.dwg**.

End of practice

Practice 2c
Modify an Existing Project File

Practice Objectives

- Modify the drawing list display.
- Add new and remove existing drawings from the active project.
- Create a subfolder and move a drawing into it.

In this practice, you will open an existing project file. You will configure the drawing list to display the description for each drawing. You will then create a new drawing file for the project, remove an existing drawing from the project, and rename a drawing in the *Project Manager*. Finally, you will create a subfolder and move a drawing into it, as shown in Figure 2–50.

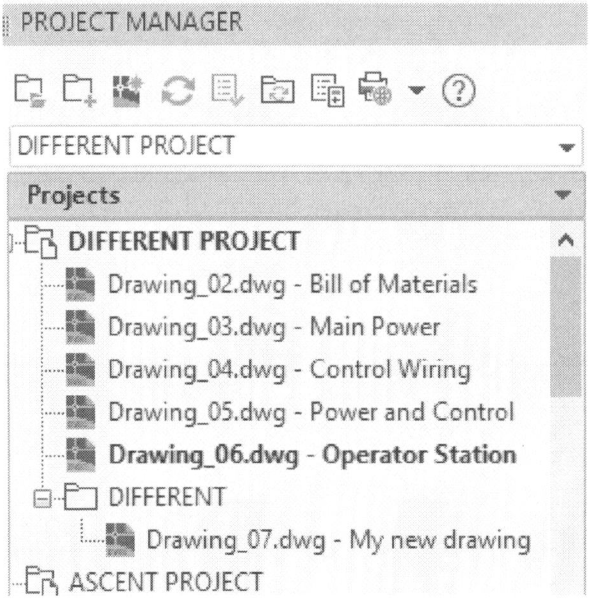

Figure 2–50

1. In the *Project Manager* toolbar, click  (Open Project). The *Select Project File* dialog box opens.
2. In your practice files folder, in the *Module 02* folder, select and open **Different Project.wdp**. The **Different Project** project file opens and is set as the active project.

3. In the *Project Manager*, double-click on **Different Project**. The drawing list displays in the *Project Manager*, as shown in Figure 2–51.

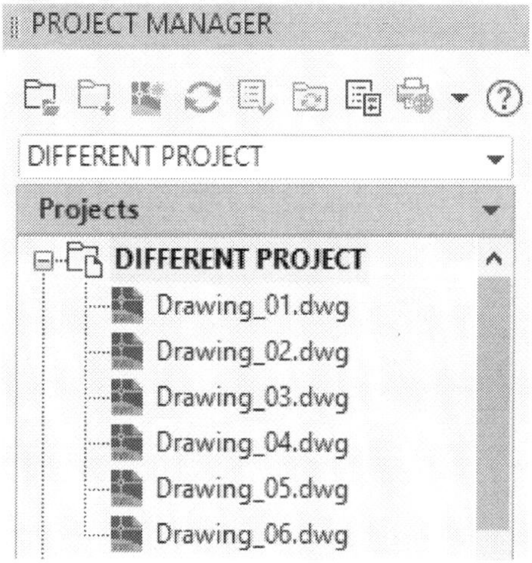

Figure 2–51

4. In the *Project Manager* toolbar, click (Drawing List Display Configuration). The *Drawing List Display Configuration* dialog box opens.
5. In the *Display Options* area, select **Drawing Description 1**, and click **>>** to move it to the *Current Display Order* area, as shown in Figure 2–52. Click **OK**. The drawing list in the *Project Manager* updates to include the drawing descriptions for each file.

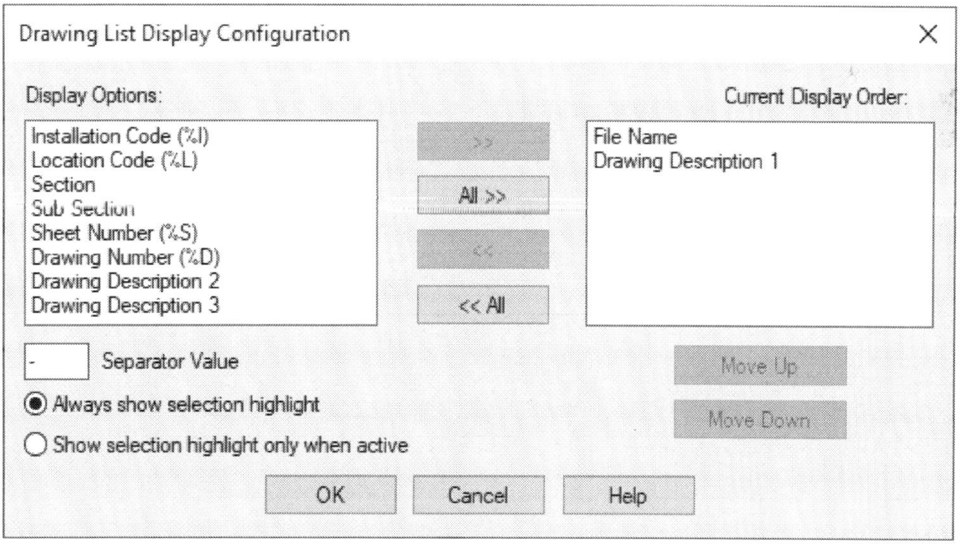

Figure 2–52

6. In the *Project Manager*, select and right-click on **Drawing_04.dwg - Control Wiring** and select **Open**.
7. In the *Project Manager*, right-click on **Different Project** and select **New Drawing...**. The *Create New Drawing* dialog box opens.
8. In the *Create New Drawing* dialog box, set the following, as shown in Figure 2–53:
   - *Name*: **New Drawing**
   - *Template*: **Electrical_template.dwt** (Use **Browse** and select **Electrical_template** from the practice files folder.)
   - *Location*: **Module 02** (Verify that it points to *Module 02* in the practice files folder or use **Browse** to set it.)
   - *Description 1*: **My new drawing**

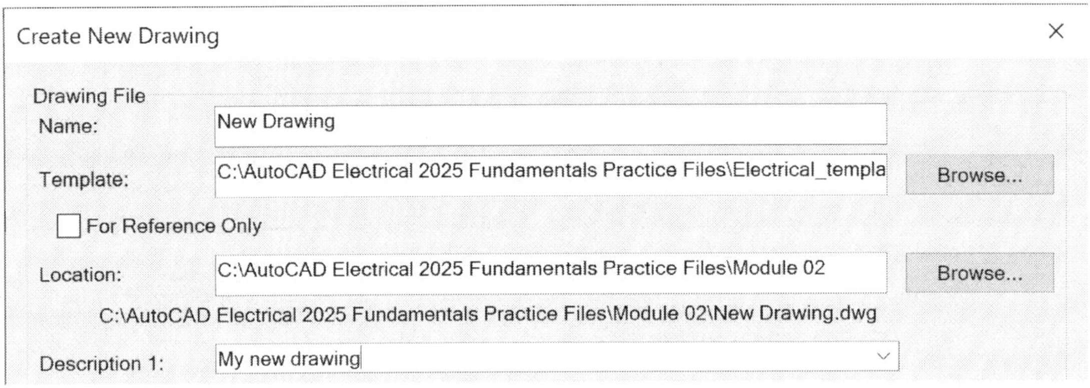

Figure 2–53

9. Click **OK**.
10. In the *Apply Project Defaults to Drawing Settings* dialog box, click **Yes**. A new file called **New Drawing** is created and added to the end of the drawing list, as shown in Figure 2–54.

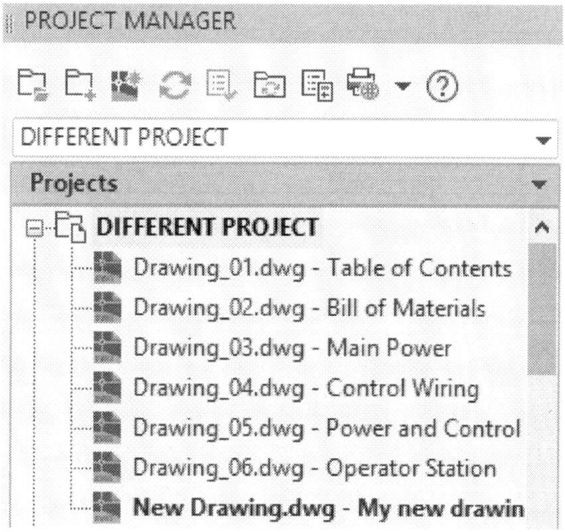

Figure 2–54

Note: *Click (Refresh) if the new drawing does not display in the list.*

11. Right-click on *Different Project* and select **Remove Drawings**. The *Select Drawings to Process* dialog box opens.
12. Select **Drawing_01.dwg** in the upper area and click **Process** to move it to the lower area, as shown in Figure 2–55.

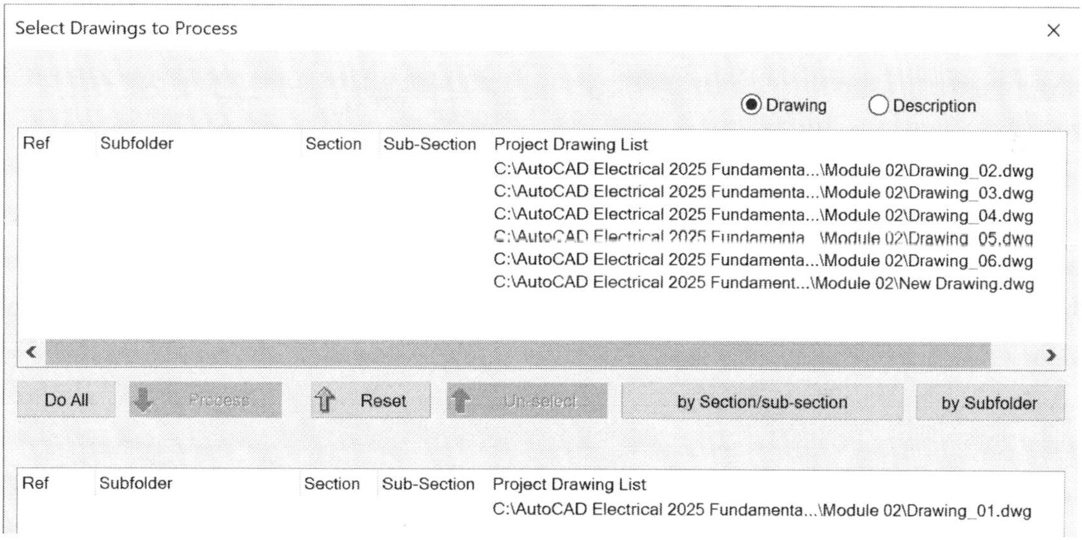

Figure 2–55

13. Click **OK**. The *Remove Drawing(s) from Project List* dialog box opens. Click **OK**. **Drawing_01.dwg** is removed from the drawing list, but not deleted from the hard drive.

14. Click (Previous Drawing) to open the previous drawing in the list. **Drawing_06.dwg** opens.

15. Right-click on **New Drawing.dwg** and select **Rename**. In the *Project Manager*, type **Drawing_07.dwg** and press <Enter>.

    Note: *Click (Refresh) to refresh the Project Manager list if the renamed drawing does not display.*

16. Right-click on *Different Project* and select **Add Subfolder**, to add a NEW FOLDER to the drawing list. In the *Project Manager*, change the *NEW FOLDER* name to **DIFFERENT**.

17. Drag and drop **Drawing_07.dwg** onto the **DIFFERENT** subfolder to add the drawing to the subfolder.

18. Save and close all of the open drawings.

End of practice

Chapter Review Questions

1. What information is stored in a project file?
    a. Project settings and a list of drawing files.
    b. Project settings and symbol attributes.
    c. Symbol attributes and a list of drawing files.
    d. File summary information and a list of drawing files.

2. How many project files can be open at one time?
    a. 1
    b. 2
    c. 64
    d. Unlimited

3. How many project files can be active at one time?
    a. 1
    b. 2
    c. 64
    d. Unlimited

4. Where can you access the **Open Project** command?
    a. Application Menu
    b. *Project* tab>Project Tools panel
    c. Project Manager palette
    d. Quick Access Toolbar

5. When you remove a drawing from a project, it is also deleted from the hard drive.
    a. True
    b. False

6. When creating a drawing using the *Project Manager*, what are the description fields used for?
    a. Displayed in the *Project Manager* and used in reports.
    b. Export to spreadsheets.
    c. Displayed in the *Project Manager* and in the schematic symbols.
    d. Placed in the project file for reference only.

7. After you have added drawings to a project, how can you change the order in which they are listed in the project file?
    a. Click **Re-order** in the *Project Manager*.
    b. Drag and drop drawing files (and subfolders) in the *Project Manager* tree list.
    c. Remove it from the project and add it again into a new location.
    d. You cannot change the order of drawings in the list.

8. How do you change the drawing name display in the *Projects* area in the *Project Manager*?
    a. Right-click on a drawing name and click **Display**.
    b. Use **Display Configuration** on the ribbon.
    c. You cannot change the drawing name display.
    d. Use **Drawing List Display Configuration** in the *Project Manager* toolbar.

9. Using the **Rename** command when right-clicking on a drawing in the *Project Manager* changes the name of the drawing on the disk and also updates the project file to use the new drawing name.
    a. True
    b. False

Command Summary

Button	Command	Location
NA	**Activate**	• **Project Manager:** (*project shortcut menu*)
NA	**Add Drawings**	• **Project Manager:** (*project shortcut menu*)
NA	**Add Subfolder**	• **Project Manager:** (*project shortcut menu*)
NA	**Close**	• **Project Manager:** (*project shortcut menu*)
	**Drawing List Display Configuration**	• **Project Manager toolbar**
	**New Drawing**	• **Project Manager toolbar**
	**New Project**	• **Project Manager toolbar**
	**Next Drawing**	• **Quick Access Toolbar** • **Ribbon:** *Project* tab>*Other Tools* panel
NA	**Open**	• **Project Manager:** (*drawing shortcut menu*)
	**Open Project**	• **Project Manager toolbar**
	**Previous Drawing**	• **Quick Access Toolbar** • **Ribbon**: *Project* tab>*Other Tools* panel
NA	**Remove**	• **Project Manager:** (*project shortcut menu*)
NA	**Reorder**	• **Project Manager:** (*drag and drop*)
NA	**Replace**	• **Project Manager**: (*drawing shortcut menu*)
NA	**Rename**	• **Project Manager:** (*drawing shortcut menu*)

Chapter 3

Schematics I - Single Wires/ Components

Ladders and wires are the foundation of schematic drawings. Knowledge of automatic ladder creation and then inserting and editing wires and rungs enables you to efficiently create clean wire networks. Knowing how to add component symbols and create parent/child relationships of these components enables you to efficiently create schematic drawings.

Learning Objectives

- Set up and identify the different types of drawing reference styles.
- Create ladders and revise existing ladder reference numbers.
- Recognize and insert wire objects.
- Modify wires and rungs.
- Create, manage, and change wire types.
- Insert wires between the rails of a ladder.
- Assign and modify wire numbers.
- Insert source and destination signal arrows and link them together.
- Add and modify component symbols in a drawing.
- Identify parent/child components and insert a child component.

3.1 Referencing

To provide intelligence, schematic drawings need a way of uniquely identifying and locating each individual wire and symbol. These wires and symbols are AutoCAD® blocks with attributes. The AutoCAD® Electrical tags each object (wire or component) by populating its specific attributes based on a reference. This reference provides the object's location in the drawing and its unique identity.

- The AutoCAD Electrical software has three different types of referencing styles: **Line Referencing**, **X-Y Grid Referencing**, and **X-Zone Referencing**.
- An individual drawing can only have one type of referencing style. However, a project can contain drawings that each use a different referencing style.
- The **X-Y Grid** and **X Zones** setups include an **Insert label** option that is available only when these are accessed through the ribbon.
- For continuity, this course mainly uses line referencing (ladder logic). However, all commands and workflows perform in the same way, regardless of reference style.

How To: Set Up a Drawing Reference Style

1. Start the **Drawing Properties** command. (Right-click on the drawing in the *Project Manager* (*Projects* tab) and select **Properties>Drawing Properties**.)
2. Switch to the *Drawing Format* tab.
3. In the *Format Referencing* area, select the required Reference style, as shown in Figure 3–1.

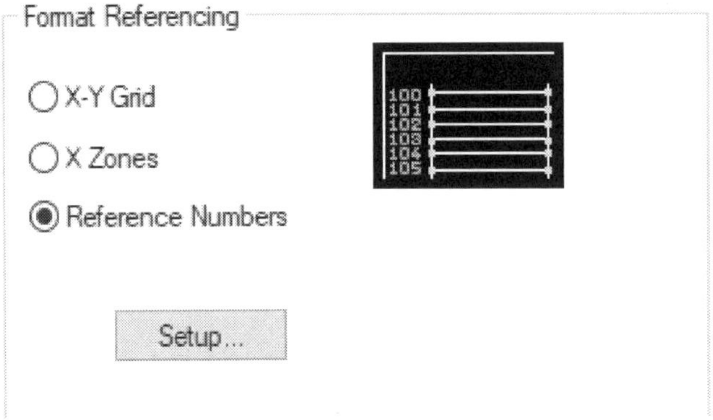

Figure 3–1

4. Click **Setup...**.
5. Adjust the settings, as required.
6. Click **OK** twice.

Line Reference

Line Reference is typically used with Ladder Logic style schematics where the wires and components are tagged based on the rung number on which they are located.

- Line reference numbers are added to the drawing during the insertion of a ladder, as shown in Figure 3–2. The *Line Reference Numbers* dialog box enables you to control the setup, as shown in Figure 3–3.

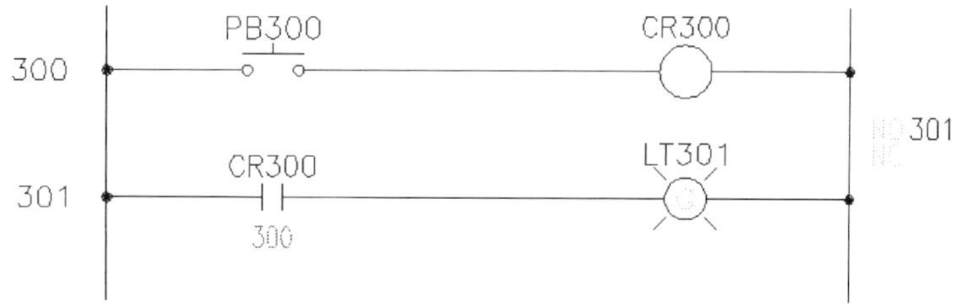

Figure 3–2

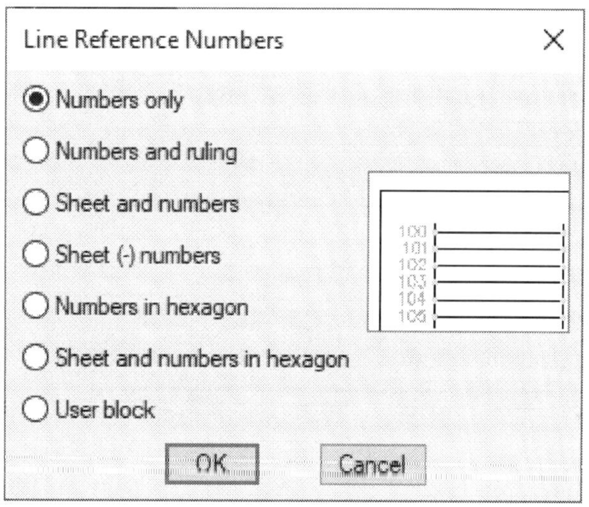

Figure 3–3

X-Y Grid Referencing

X-Y Grid Referencing is typically associated with point-to-point style schematics where the wires and components are tagged based on the X- and Y-coordinate at which they are located.

- You can set up the X-Y Grid Reference in the *Drawing Properties* dialog box, in the *Drawing Format* tab, in the *Format Referencing* area or by clicking (X-Y Grid Setup) in the *Schematic* tab>*Insert Wires/Wire Numbers* panel. A typical X-Y grid style schematic is shown in Figure 3–4, and the *X-Y Grid Setup* dialog box is shown in Figure 3–5.

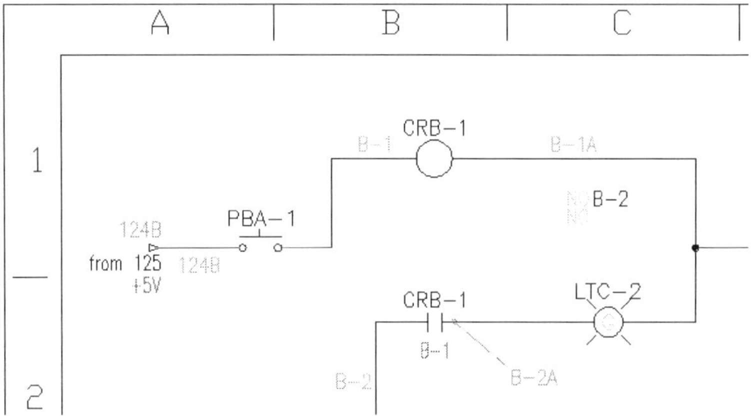

Figure 3–4

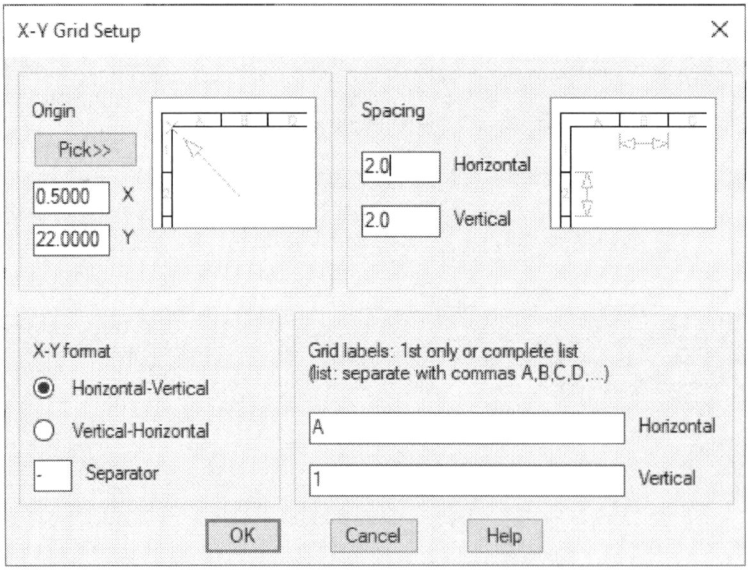

Figure 3–5

X Zones

X Zone Referencing is typically associated with point-to-point style schematics where the wires and components are tagged based on the X column zone at which they are located.

- You can set up the X Zone Reference in the *Drawing Properties* dialog box, in the *Drawing Format* tab, in the *Format Referencing* area or by clicking (X Zone Setup) in the *Schematic* tab>*Insert Wires/Wire Numbers* panel. A typical X zone style schematic is shown in Figure 3–6, and the *X Zones Setup* dialog box is shown in Figure 3–7.

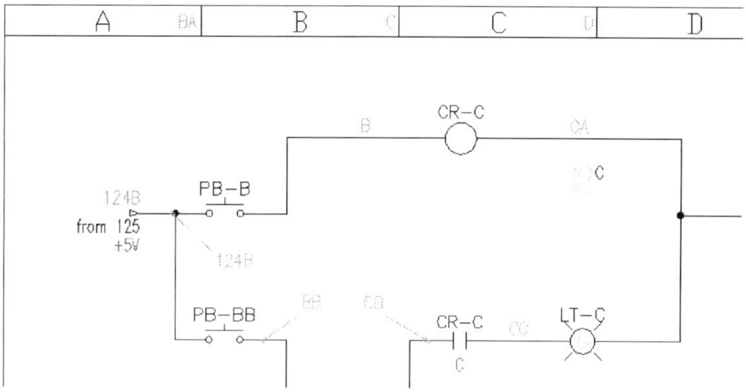

Figure 3–6

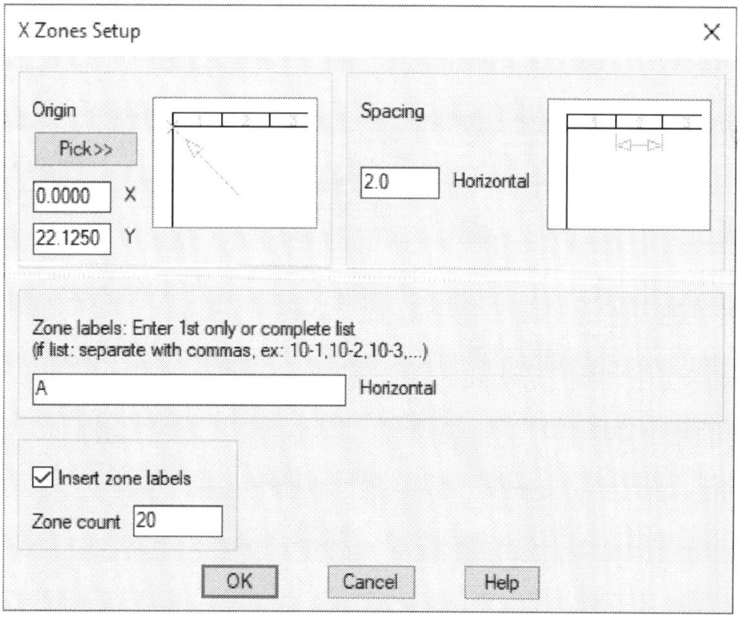

Figure 3–7

3.2 Ladders

Insert Ladders

Ladders (shown in Figure 3–8) are the foundation of schematic drawings. The software includes commands that automate the creation and modification of ladders. You can insert ladders at any point during the creation of a drawing. When inserting a ladder, you control its width, spacing, and reference numbers.

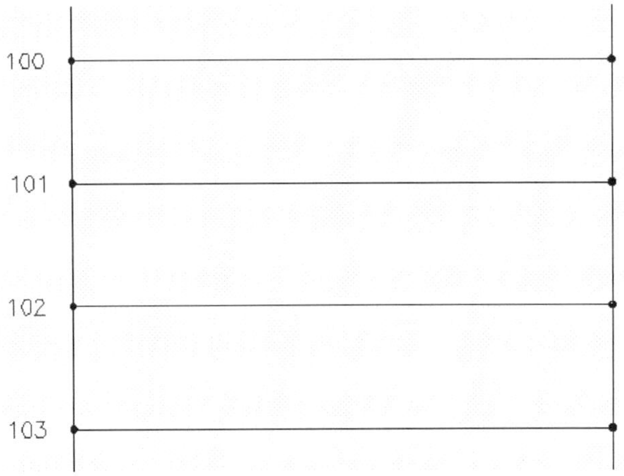

Figure 3–8

Insert Ladder

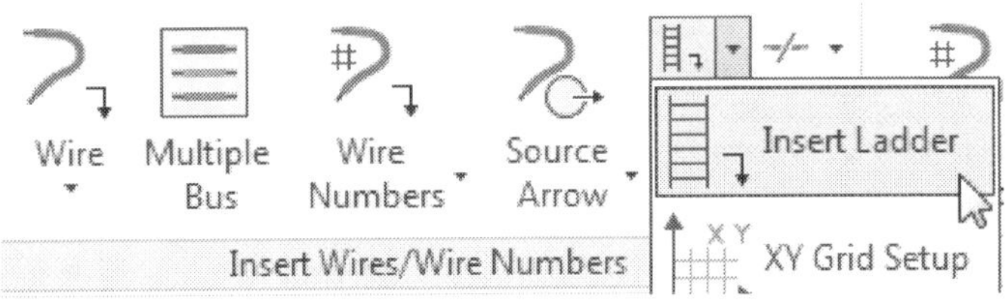

Ribbon: *Schematic* tab>*Insert Wires/Wire Numbers* panel

Command Prompt: aeladder

How To: Create a Ladder

1. Start the **Insert Ladder** command. The *Insert Ladder* dialog box opens, as shown in Figure 3–9.

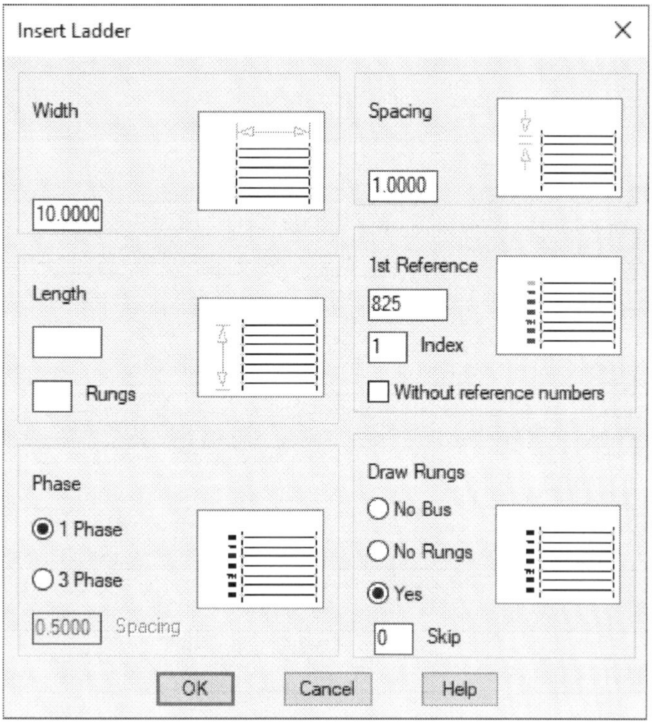

Figure 3–9

2. Use the *Width* field to control the width of the ladder.
3. Use the *Spacing* field to control the space between rungs of the ladder.
4. Use one of three options to control the length of the ladder:
   - In the *Length* field, enter a length. The number of rungs is calculated automatically.
   - In the *Rungs* field, enter the number of rungs. The length is calculated automatically.
   - Leave the *Length* and *Rungs* fields blank and pick points in the drawing window to determine the length of the ladder.
5. Use the *1st Reference* field to control the first reference number of the ladder. If a ladder already exists in the drawing, *1st Reference* displays the next available number.
   - If the drawing is set to use **X-Y Grid** or **X Zone** reference styling, the *1st Reference* area of the *Insert Ladder* dialog box is grayed out and not used.
6. Use the *Index* field to control how the reference numbers increment.

7. Select **Without reference numbers** to insert a ladder without reference numbers (i.e., when adding ladders to drawings with **X-Y Grid** or **X-Zones** reference styles).
8. Use the *Phase* area to define whether the ladder is single phase or 3-phase.
9. Use the *Draw Rungs* area to control the geometry that is included with the ladder.
   - **No Bus:** Inserts only reference numbers.
   - **No Rungs:** Inserts only reference numbers and rails.
   - **Yes:** Inserts reference numbers, rails, and rungs.
   - **Skip:** Inserts a rung and skips a defined number of references before adding another rung.
10. Click **OK** to exit the dialog box and insert the ladder.
    - (Optional) To set a wire type, type **T** or right-click and select **wireType**. In the *Set Wire Type* dialog box, select the wire type in the list of available options, as shown in Figure 3–10. Click **OK** to accept the new wire type.

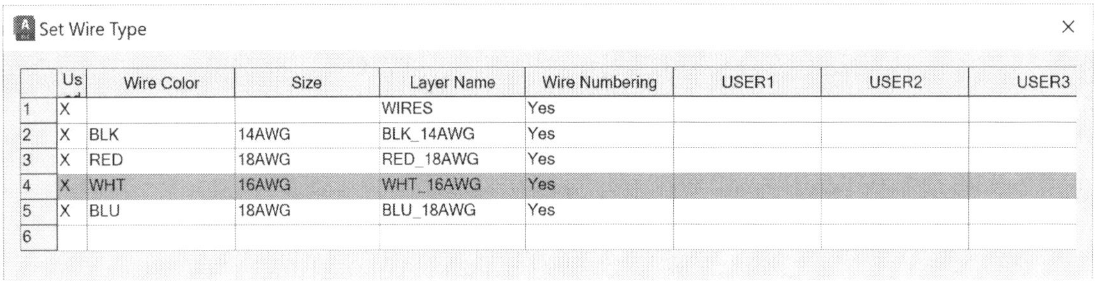

	Us	Wire Color	Size	Layer Name	Wire Numbering	USER1	USER2	USER3
1	X			WIRES	Yes			
2	X	BLK	14AWG	BLK_14AWG	Yes			
3	X	RED	18AWG	RED_18AWG	Yes			
4	X	WHT	16AWG	WHT_16AWG	Yes			
5	X	BLU	18AWG	BLU_18AWG	Yes			
6								

Figure 3–10

11. Pick the start position of the first rung. If you left the *Length* and *Rungs* fields blank, pick the position of the last rung.
    - The default settings for the ladder width and spacing can be modified in the *Drawing Settings* dialog box.
    - The ladder is inserted on the default wire layer unless a designated wire layer is set to current.
    - Do not erase the first reference number of the ladder. It is the Master Line Reference (MLR) and carries the ladder's intelligence. The other reference numbers are text fields and can be erased, as required.
    - You can have an unlimited number of ladders in a single drawing, but they cannot overlap.

Revise Ladders

Once a ladder is created, you can modify its line references using the **Revise Ladder** command, as shown in Figure 3–11. This command does not change the lines or rungs of the ladder, but updates the reference numbers along the side of the ladder.

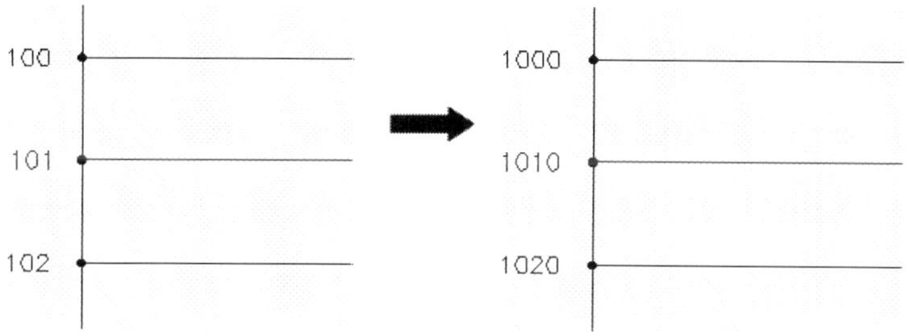

Figure 3–11

Revise Ladder

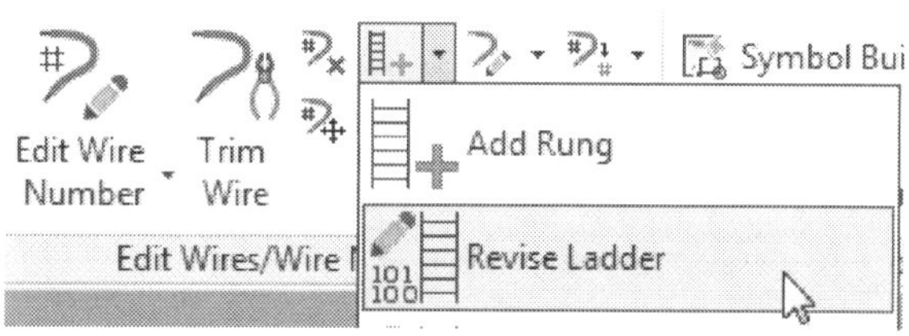

Ribbon: *Schematic* tab>*Edit Wires/Wire Numbers* panel

Command Prompt: aereviseladder

How To: Change a Ladder

1. Start the **Revise Ladder** command. The *Modify Line Reference Numbers* dialog box opens, as shown in Figure 3–12.

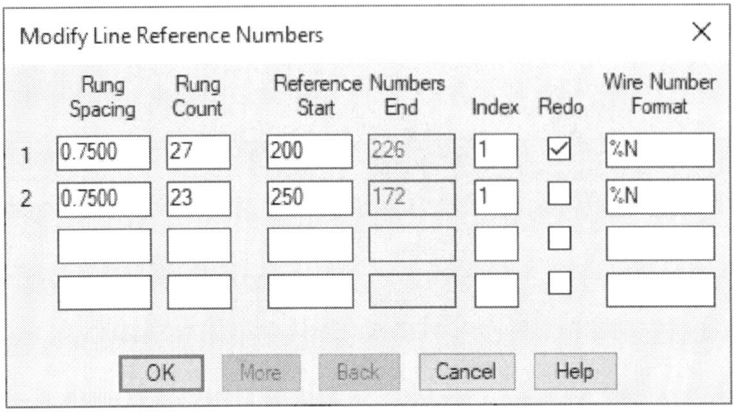

Figure 3–12

2. Change the values for the ladder you want to modify. The information for each ladder in the drawing displays in a separate row.

Rung Spacing	Controls the distance between reference numbers.
Rung Count	Controls how many reference numbers are present.
Reference Numbers Start	Controls the first reference number for the ladder.
Reference Numbers End	Displays the last reference number used for the ladder.
Index	Displays the increment between reference numbers.
Redo	Forces an update of the reference numbers.
Wire Number Format	Controls the information in the wire number. You can use the Electrical replaceable parameters or static text.
Move and **Back**	Available if there are more than 4 ladders in a drawing. Click them to display the next set of ladders in the dialog box.

3. Click **OK**.

- The **Revise Ladder** command only affects reference numbers along the side of the ladder and does not modify existing rungs. If you need to add additional rungs or remove existing rungs, you have to use separate commands to add or trim rungs after revising the reference numbers.

- You can also use other editing commands to modify the ladder, such as the AutoCAD **Stretch** command or the AutoCAD Electrical **Scoot** command.
- Changing the reference numbers does not affect component tags or wire numbers until **Project-Wide Update/Retag** or **Automatic Wire Numbers** are used to update these values.

Practice 3a
Ladders

Practice Objective

- Create ladders and revise existing ladder reference numbers.

In this practice, you will insert two different ladders into a blank drawing. You will then use the **Revise Ladder** command to change the ladders. The final drawing is shown in Figure 3–13.

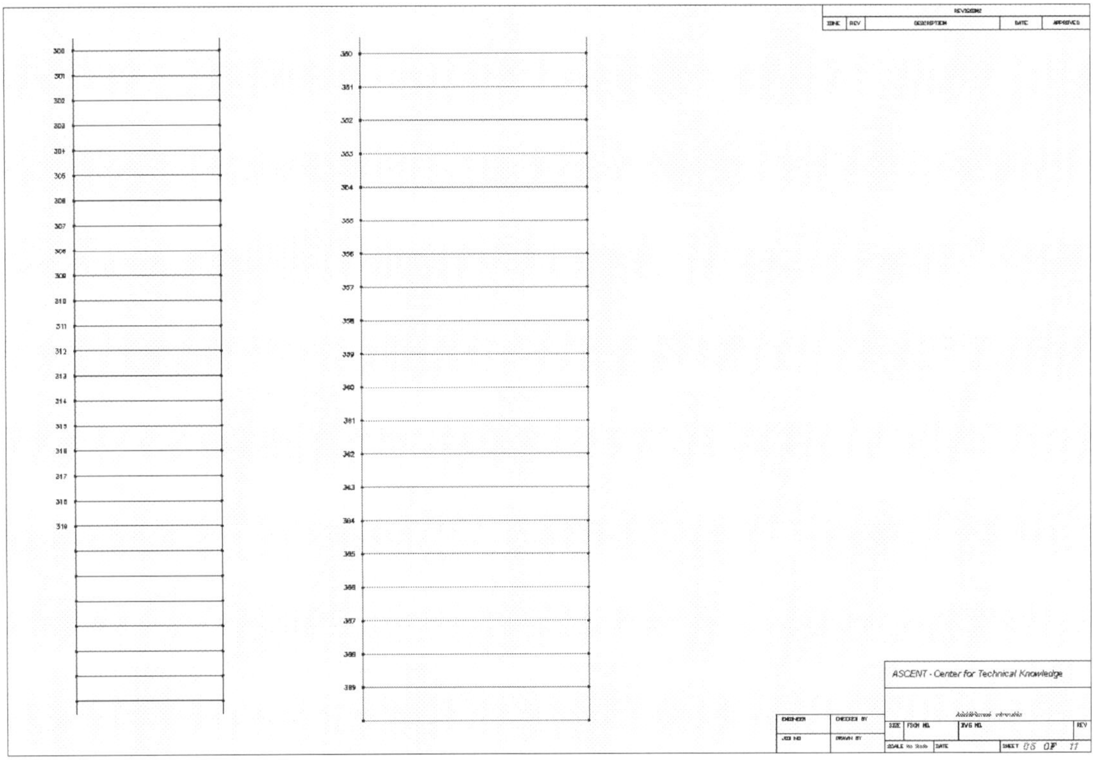

Figure 3–13

1. In your practice files folder, in the *Module 03* folder, open the **Module 03** project file.
2. In the *Project Manager*, expand the Module 03 project file, right-click on **Ladders.dwg**, and select **Open**.

   Note: *In the Project Manager, if the description is displayed along with the drawing name, you can change the display order in the Drawing List Display Configuration dialog box. Select Drawing Description* ***1*** *in the Current Display Order area, and click* ***<<*** *to move it to the Display Options area.*

3. In the *Schematic* tab>*Insert Wires/Wire Numbers* panel, click (Insert Ladder).
4. In the *Insert Ladder* dialog box that opens, set the following, as shown in Figure 3–14 (type the values in the relevant fields and press <Enter> to accept them):
   - *Length*: **15** (Press <Enter> and note that the *Rungs* are calculated based on the length and spacing.)
   - *Rungs*: **27** (Press <Enter> and note that the *Length* is updated as it is calculated based on the spacing and number of rungs.)
   - *1st Reference*: **300**

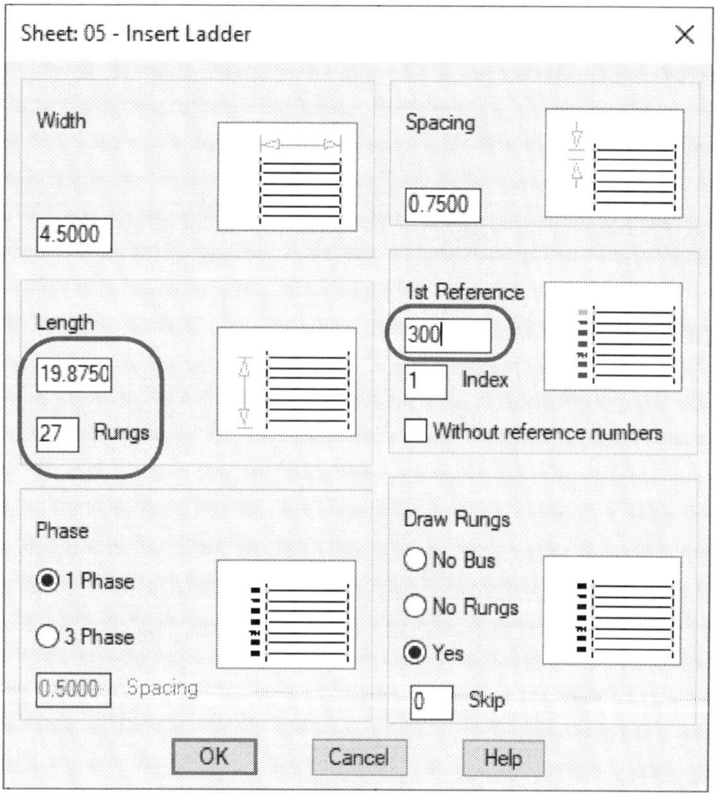

Figure 3–14

5. Click **OK**.

6. In the Status Bar (bottom right corner of the screen), expand (Customization) and select **Coordinates**. The coordinates display in the Status Bar.

7. Near the upper left corner of the drawing sheet, pick a point near **2, 21** as the start position of the ladder. The ladder is inserted based on the input in the *Insert Ladder* dialog box. Note that the reference number for the first rung is **300** and there are 27 rungs with the last rung numbered as **326**.

8. Click (Insert Ladder) to insert another ladder.

9. In the *Insert Ladder* dialog box that opens, set the following values, as shown in Figure 3–15. Note that the *1st Reference* field is automatically using the next available reference number (327).

   - *Width*: **7**
   - *Spacing*: **1**
   - *Length* and *Rungs*: leave blank

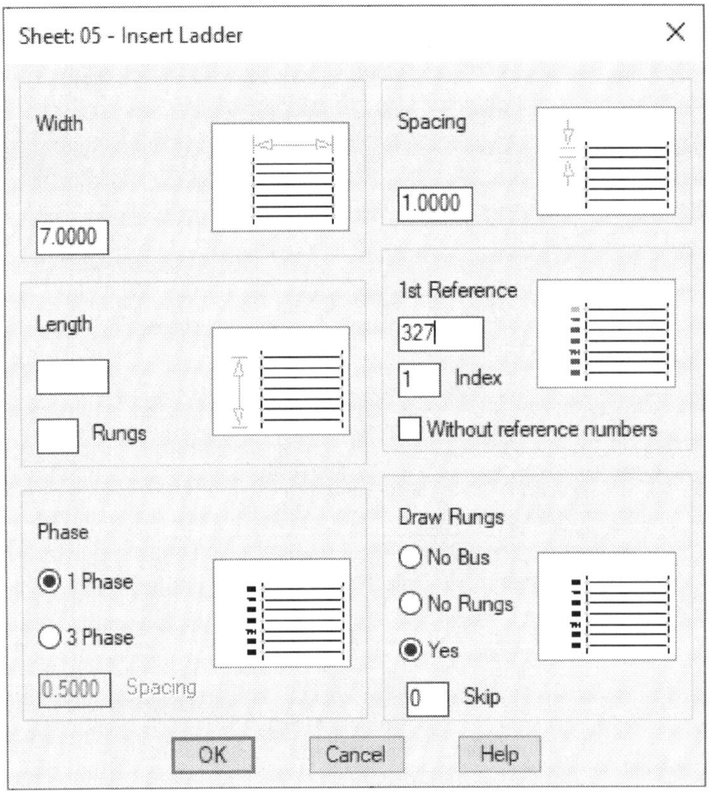

Figure 3–15

10. Click **OK**.

11. At the Command Prompt, type **T** and press <Enter>. The *Set Wire Type* dialog box opens.

12. Select the wire type **RED_14AWG**, as shown in Figure 3–16. Click **OK**.

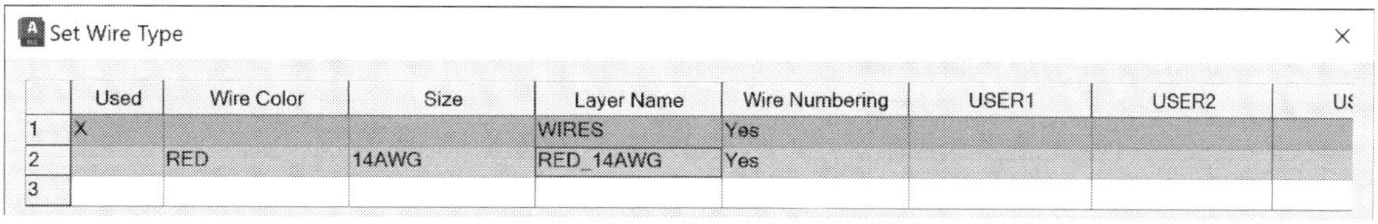

Figure 3–16

13. Pick a point near **11, 21** as the start position of the ladder. Pick a point near **11, 1** as the position of the last reference number. A second ladder is drawn based on your inputs and this time the wires are defined as red 14AWG.
    - For the endpoint of the ladder, move the cursor down and click when the **Y** value displays as **1** in the **Status Bar**. Disregard the X value displayed in the Status Bar as it is automatically confined at 11.
14. In the *Schematic* tab>*Edit Wires/Wire Numbers* panel, click (Revise Ladder).
15. In the *Modify Line Reference Numbers* dialog box that opens set the following, as shown in Figure 3–17:
    - *Rung Count* for both ladders: **20**
    - *Reference Start* for the second ladder: **350**

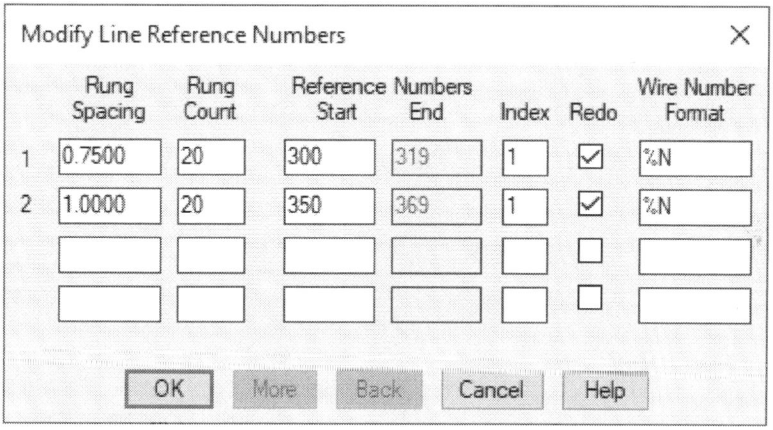

Figure 3–17

16. Click **OK**.
17. Note that the number of Reference Numbers has changed, and that the actual number of rungs on the ladder remains the same.
18. Save **Ladders.dwg**.

End of practice

3.3 Insert Wires

Wires are the AutoCAD line objects, which are placed on a layer designated as a wire layer, as shown in Figure 3–18. Any other objects on a wire layer are not considered wires. Wire layers are created using the **Create/Edit Wire Type** command.

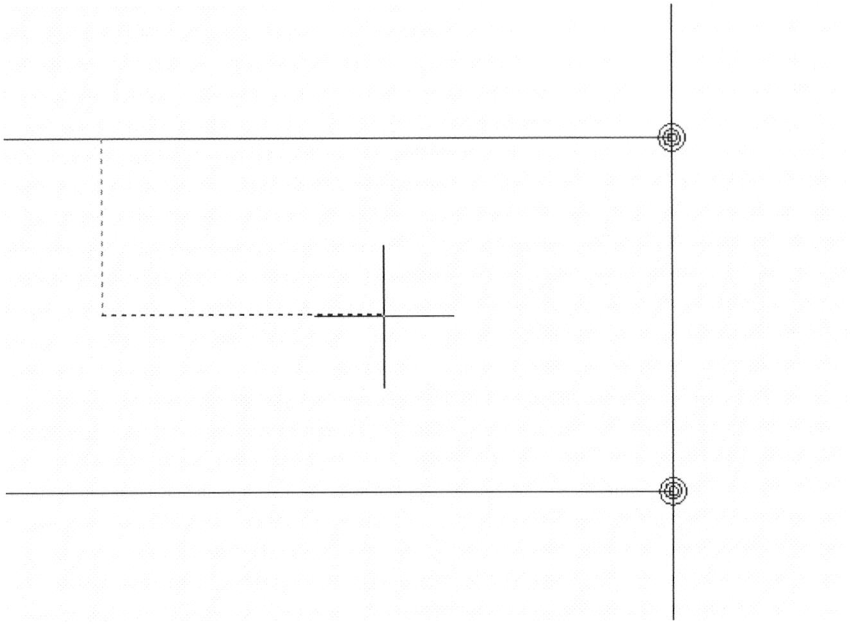

Figure 3–18

Insert Wire

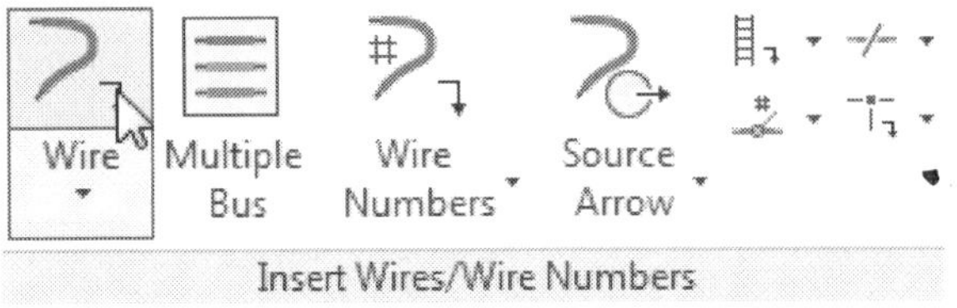

Ribbon: *Schematic* tab>*Insert Wires/Wire Numbers panel*

Command Prompt: aewire

Shortcut menu: *(on a wire)* **Insert Wire**

How To: Insert a Wire

1. Start the **Insert Wire** command.
2. (Optional) To change the type of wire to be inserted, type **T** and press <Enter> or right-click and select **wireType,** as shown in Figure 3–19.

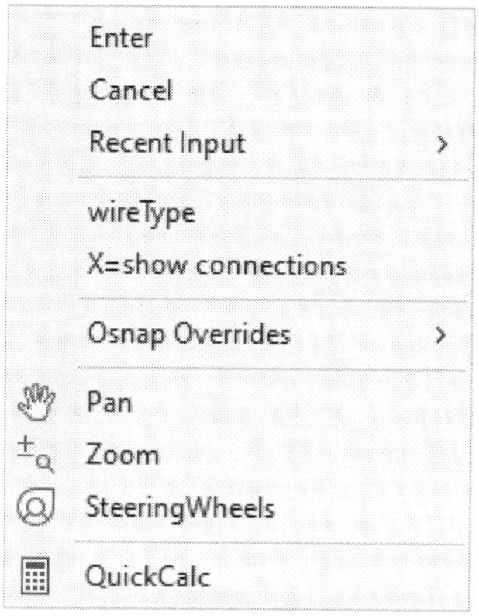

Figure 3–19

3. (Optional) To display the connection attributes of the visible components, type **X** and press <Enter> or right-click and select **X=show connections**.
4. Select the start point of the wire.
5. Use **Horizontal (H)**, **Vertical (V)**, or **Continue (C)** to force the wire to follow your intent.
6. Select the second point of the wire.
7. Continue picking points to define the wire.
8. Right-click to end the current segment and continue the **Insert Wire** command.
9. Press <Esc> to end the command.

- When inserting a wire, if you hover over an existing component, its connection points display as green X's. When you click on the component, the wire is connected to the nearest connection point.
- The software inserts connection dots where wires intersect and loops where wires cross. These indicators are controlled in the *Project Properties* or *Drawing Properties* dialog box, in the *Styles* tab>*Wiring Style* area.
- The **Insert Wire** command draws horizontal and vertical segments. Type **H** to force a horizontal start or **V** to force a vertical start.

- Angled wires can be inserted using the **22.5 Degree**, **45 Degree**, or **67.5 Degree** commands. These are located in the drop-down list in the **Insert Wire** command in the *Schematic* tab>*Insert Wires/Wire Numbers* panel, as shown in Figure 3–20.

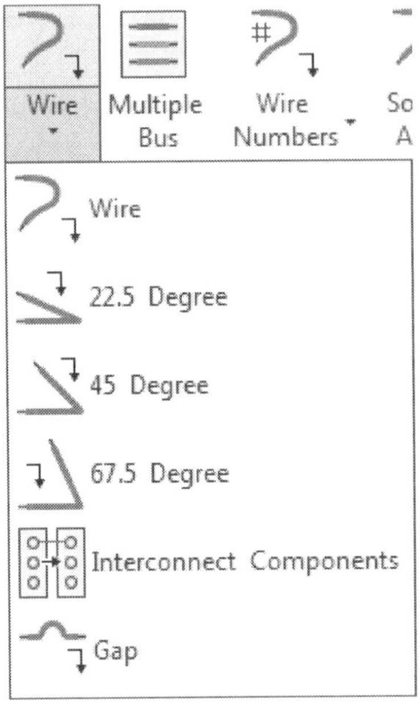

Figure 3–20

- Wire networks are any combination of wires and components that form a complete electrical conductor. This is most evident when adding wire numbers.
- Wires and components are recognized as connected if the wire is within a certain distance of the component's connection attribute. This is the wire trap distance, which is 0.025 for inch units and 0.625 for millimeter units.
- The AutoCAD **Line** command can also be used to draw wires if they are on a designated wire layer. This method does not create connection points, wire loops, etc.

3.4 Edit Wires

When the ladders and wires have been created, you might need to modify the wires and rungs. Several automated commands can be used to modify the wires and clean up the wire networks.

Trim Wire

The **Trim Wire** command trims wires back to their intersections with other wires or symbols. If no intersection is found, it erases the selected wire. Any connection dots are removed and the wire numbers are updated.

Trim Wire

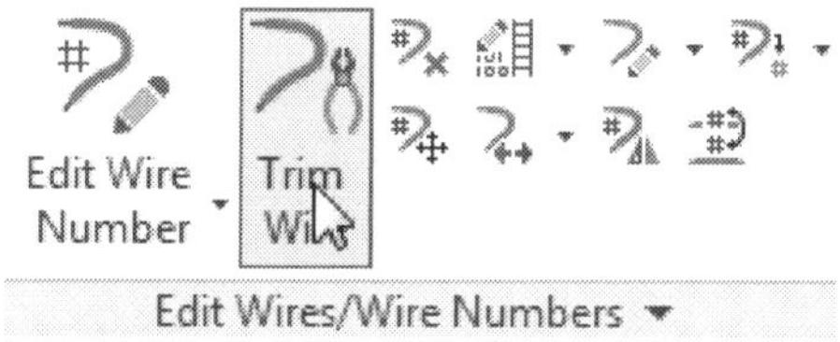

Ribbon: *Schematic* tab>*Edit Wires/Wire Numbers* panel

Command Prompt: aetrim

Shortcut menu: *(on a wire)* **Trim Wire**

How To: Trim a Wire

1. Start the **Trim Wire** command.
2. Select the wire to trim.
3. Continue selecting wires, as required.
4. Right-click or press <Esc> to end the command.

- You can also right-click on a wire and select **Trim Wire** in the Marking Menu.
- The **Trim Wire** command can also be used to erase wires if no intersections are found.
- The AutoCAD **Trim** command can also be used. However, you have to select trimming boundaries and it does not clean up the drawings (remove connection dots, update wire numbers, etc.).
- To use a fence selection, type **F** and press <Enter>.
- To use a crossing selection window, type **C** and press <Enter>.
- To use **Zoom Extents** while trimming, type **Z** and press <Enter>.

Stretch Wires

The opposite of the **Trim Wire** command is the **Stretch Wire** command. It extends a wire to the next intersecting wire or component wire connection. The **Stretch Wire** command adds connection dots and updates wire numbers where required.

Stretch Wire

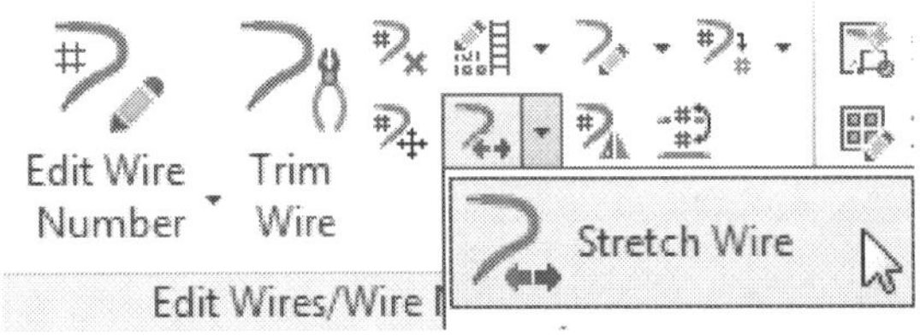

Ribbon: *Schematic* tab>*Edit Wires/Wire Numbers* panel

Command Prompt: aestretchwire

Shortcut menu: *(on a wire)* **Stretch Wire**

How To: Stretch a Wire

1. Start the **Stretch Wire** command.
2. Select the wire to extend.
3. Right-click or press <Esc> to end the command.

- You can also right-click on a wire and select **Stretch Wire** in the Marking Menu.
- **Stretch Wire** is useful when a connection needs to be extended to a component.
- The AutoCAD **Extend** command can also be used, but it does not add connection dots.

3.5 Add Rungs

The **Add Rung** command inserts wires between the rails of a ladder. The rungs are extended to the nearest connection point on the left and right sides of the rung.

Add Rung

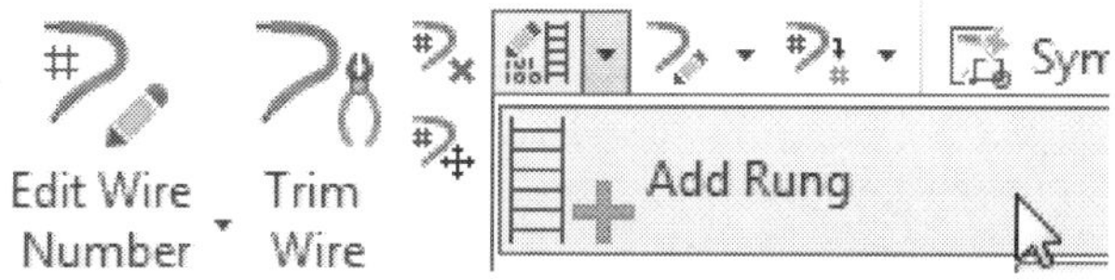

Ribbon: *Schematic* tab>*Edit Wires/Wire Numbers* panel

Command Prompt: aerung

How To: Add a Rung

1. Start the **Add Rung** command.
2. Pick the area between the rails to locate the rung.
3. Continuing picking between the rails to add more rungs.
4. Right-click and select **Enter** or press <Esc> to end the command.

- You must pick between the rails and not directly on them to add a rung.
- When you pick in the drawing window, the new rung is added at the reference number closest to your selection.
- Type **T** and press <Enter> or right-click and select **wireType** to change the wire type.
- If a drawing has either vertical or horizontal ladders with **Line Referencing**, a rung is only added at the position of a line reference. This added rung can be between any component connection point or ladder rails.
- In a drawing with **X-Y Grid** or **X-Zone** referencing, the rung is added at any point selected between two rails.

3.6 Wire Setup

You can create and modify wire types and then set a wire's type when inserting the wire or after it is inserted. Wire types are controlled by layers.

Creating Wire Types

The **Create/Edit Wire Type** command creates and manages wire types. It enables you to create new layers or designate existing layers as wire types. You can then assign the appropriate properties to the wire layers.

Create/Edit Wire Type

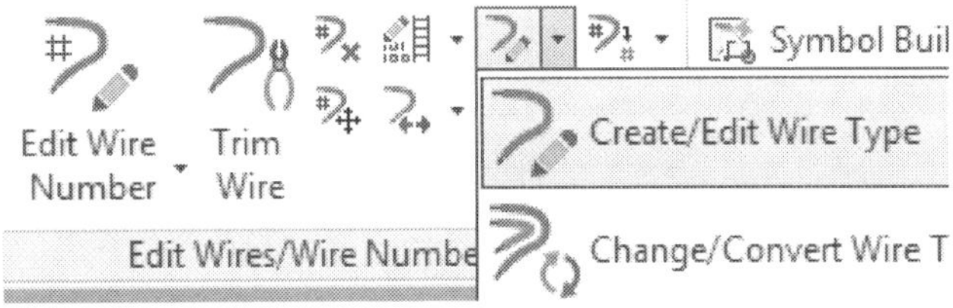

Ribbon: *Schematic* tab>*Edit Wires/Wire Numbers* panel

Command Prompt: aewiretype

The **Create/Edit Wire Type** command opens the *Create/Edit Wire Type* dialog box, as shown in Figure 3–21.

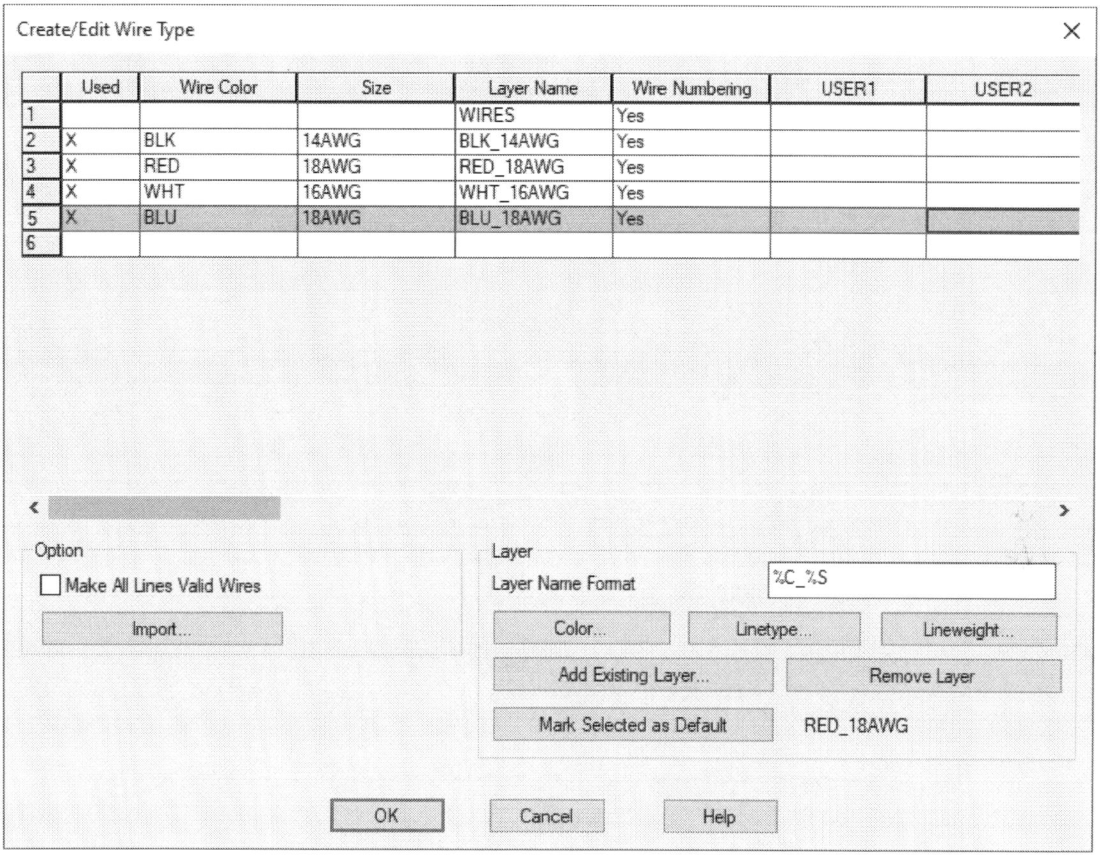

Figure 3–21

Used	An *X* in this column indicates that the wire type is used in the current drawing. If the column is blank, the layer name exists in the drawing, but there are currently no wires on that layer.
Wire Color	Wire color property for the wire type. Replaceable parameter %C in **Layer Name**.
Size	Wire size property for the wire type. Replaceable parameter %S in **Layer Name**.
Layer Name	Layer name for the wire type. Created based on the **Layer Name Format**.
Wire Numbering	Determines whether a wire receives a wire number when using the automated wire numbering command. Set to **Yes** or **No**.
User 1-5	User defined properties. Replaceable parameter %1 - %5 in **Layer Name**. Heading names can be changed in Project Properties.

User 6-20	User defined properties. Cannot be used in **Layer Name**, but can be used in some reports. Heading names can be changed in Project Properties.
Make All Lines Valid Wires	If selected, all layers in the drawing become valid wire layers and any line object is considered a wire.
Import	Imports defined wire types from other drawings. Select **Master Drawing** in the *Wire Type Import* dialog box. Select wire types in the *Import Wire Types* dialog box.
Layer Name Format	Controls the layer naming scheme. You can include any of the replaceable parameters in the dialog box or text strings. Layer names cannot include special characters, such as / \ " : ; ? * | , = ' > <.
Color, Linotype, and Lineweight	Sets the color, linetype, and lineweight for the wire layer, similar to the AutoCAD Layer Properties Manager.
Add Existing Layer	Adds an existing layer as a valid wire layer. Opens the *Layers for Line "Wires"* dialog box. You can click **Pick** to select a layer from a list of existing layers. You can also type a layer name in the *Layer Name* field.
Remove Layer	Removes the selected layer from the list of valid wire layers. Does not delete the layer from the drawing.
Mark Selected as Default	Sets the selected layer as the default wire layer. This wire type is used unless the current layer is a wire layer.

- The *User 1-20* fields are used in various AutoCAD Electrical reports. You can rename them to make them easier to use. The names can be changed in the *Project Properties* dialog box in the *Wire Numbers* tab.

How To: Create a Wire Type

1. Start the **Create/Edit Wire Type** command. The *Create/Edit Wire Type* dialog box opens.
2. Add wire layers, as required.
3. Modify rows of layer properties, as required.
4. Click **OK**.

Changing the Wire Type of a Wire

The **Change/Convert Wire Type** command enables you to change the wire type of an existing wire. You can also set the wire type while inserting a wire by right-clicking and selecting **wireType**.

Change/Convert Wire Type

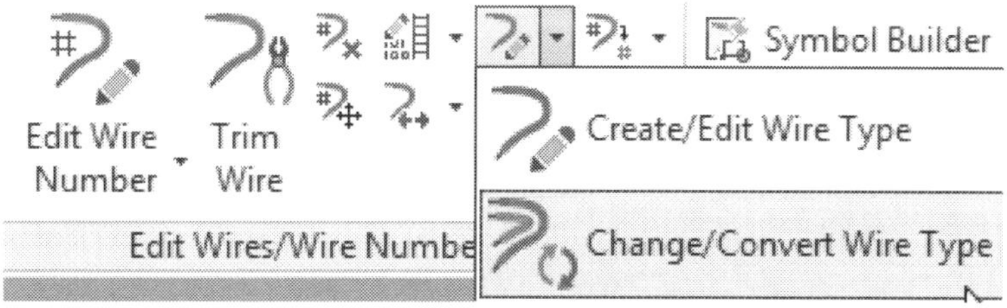

Ribbon: *Schematic* tab>*Edit Wires/Wire Numbers* panel

Command Prompt: aeconvertwiretype

Shortcut menu: *(on a wire)* **Change/Convert Wire Type**

How To: Change the Wire Type

1. Start the **Change/Convert Wire Type** command. The *Change/Convert Wire Type* dialog box opens, as shown in Figure 3–22.

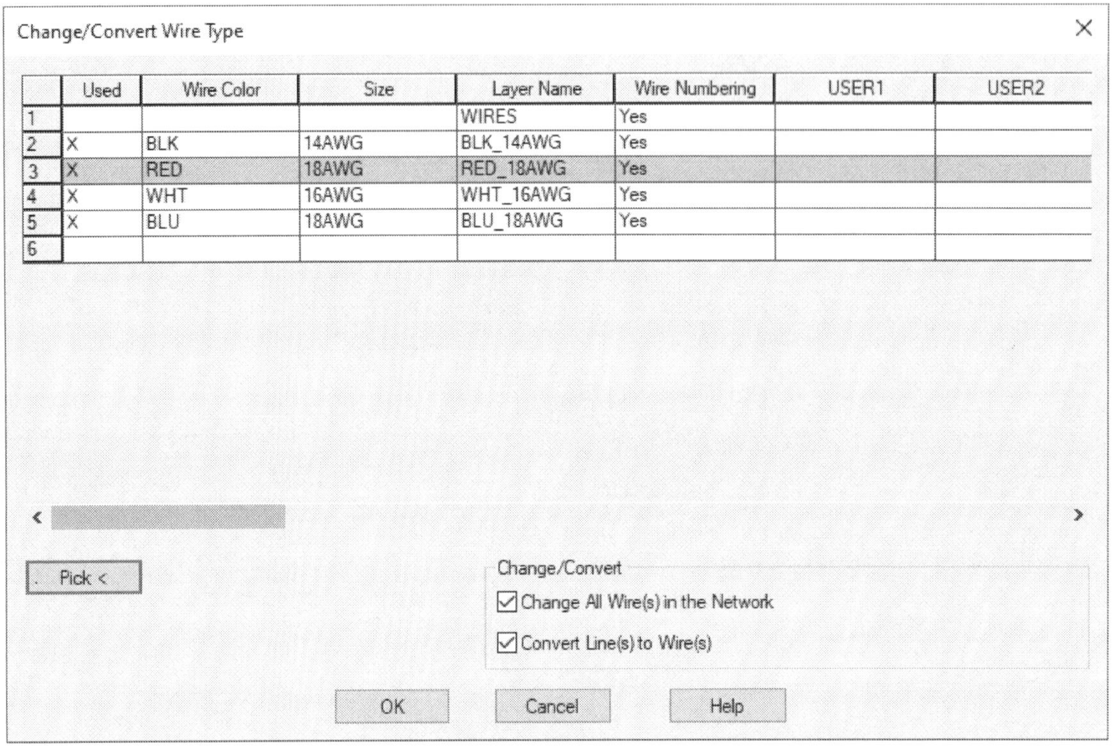

Figure 3–22

2. Select the required master wire type.
3. Click **OK**.
4. Select the wire(s) to change.
5. Right-click or press <Enter> to end the command.

- You can use the **Fence (F)** and **Crossing (C)** options when selecting wires.
- **Pick<** enables you to select an existing wire from the drawing as the master wire type.
- You can change individual segments of a wire network (instead of the entire network) when **Change All Wires(s) in the Network** is not selected.
- If a line is on a layer that is not currently designated as a wire layer, you can still convert it when the **Convert Line(s) to Wire(s)** option is selected.

3.7 Wire Numbers

Wire numbers can automatically be assigned to wires in a drawing. This can be done for individual wire networks, a single drawing, or the entire project.

Insert Wire Numbers

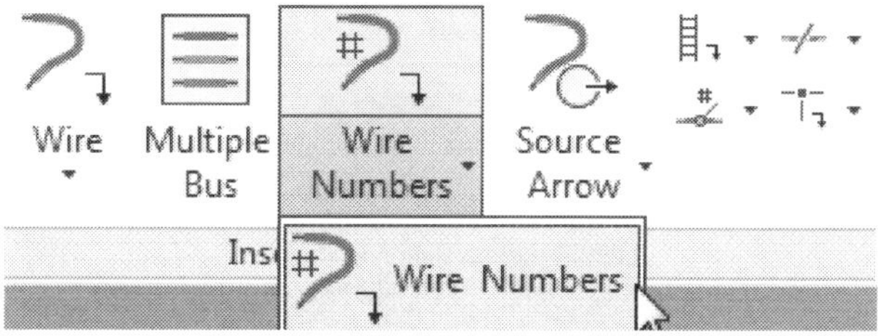

Ribbon: *Schematic* tab>*Insert Wires/Wire Numbers* panel

Command Prompt: aewireno

Shortcut menu: *(on a wire)* **Wire Numbers>Automatic Wire Numbers**

How To: Assign Wire Numbers

1. Start the **Insert Wire Numbers** command.
2. Set the options in the dialog box, as required.
3. Select the options for processing the wires (project, individual, or drawing).
   - **Project-wide:** Select drawings from the entire project to process.
   - **Pick Individual Wires:** Select individual wires to number.
   - **Drawing-wide:** Process the entire drawing.
4. Select the drawings or wires to process, depending on the option selected in Step 3.

- Wires on the same reference line are assigned a suffix. The wire number suffix is defined in the *Drawing Properties* dialog box, in the *Wire Numbers* tab, in the *Wire Number Format* area, in *Suffix Setup*.

The **Insert Wire Numbers** command opens the *Wire Tagging* dialog box, as shown in Figure 3–23.

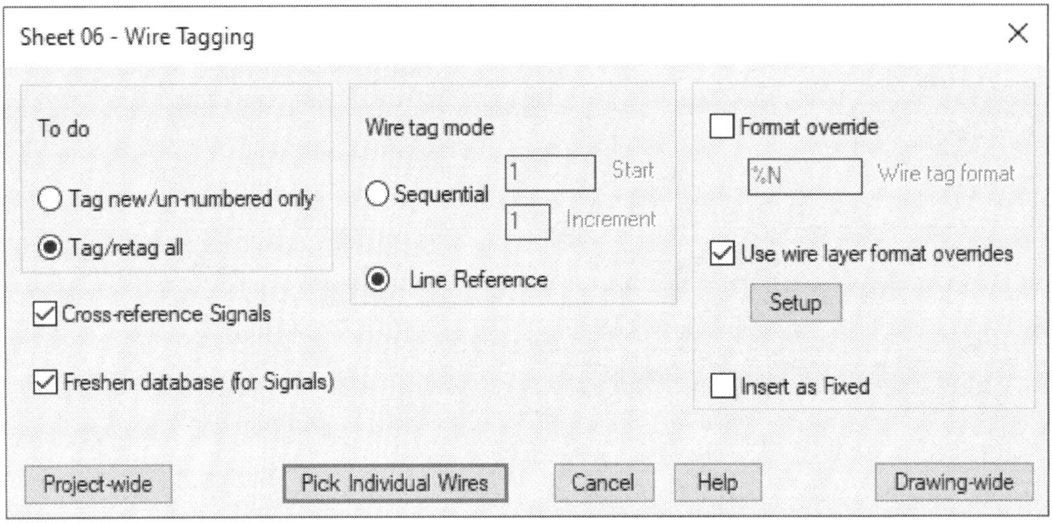

Figure 3–23

To do	• **Tag new/un-numbered only** applies wire numbers to any wire that does not already have one. • **Tag/retag all** applies wire numbers to all wires over-writing those already tagged (unless set to fixed).
Cross-reference Signals	Updates the cross-referencing text for wire source and destination symbols.
Freshen database (for Signals)	Updates the project database for wire source and destination symbols.
Wire tag mode	• **Sequential:** Assigns wire numbers sequentially, starting at the upper left corner of the drawing. You can specify the starting number and increment value. • **Line Reference:** Assigns wire numbers based on the reference number of the ladder (or the X-Y Grid or X-Zone reference number).
Format override	Sets the format for wire numbers if it is different from the default. The default format is set in the *Drawing Properties* dialog box, in the *Wire Numbers* tab, in the *Wire Number Format* area. Common overrides include: **%S** (sheet number of the drawing), **%A** (section drawing property), **%B** (sub-section drawing property), **%D** (drawing number), **%N** (sequential or reference-based number applied to the component), **%X** (suffix character position for reference-based tagging (not present = end of tag)), **%P** (IEC-style project code (default for drawing)), **%I** (IEC-style installation code (default for drawing)), **%L** (IEC-style location code (default for drawing)).

Use wire layer format overrides	Enables you to configure the wire number format for individual wire layers.
Insert as Fixed	Inserts wire numbers as fixed, which are not processed when the **Automatic Wire Numbers** command is used.

- The default wire sequencing for each wire network is defined in the *Project Properties* dialog box, in the *Project Settings* tab, *Tag/Wire Number/Wire Sequence Sort Order* drop-down list. A new wire sequence is not required to be set if a wire network already follows the default one.

Wire Number Types

Wire numbers are attributes attached to an invisible block. Only one wire is assigned to each wire network. There are four types of wire numbers: **Normal**, **Fixed**, **Extra**, and **Terminal/Signal**.

Normal	Default type for automatically inserted wire numbers. They are updated when the **Insert Wire Number** command is used.
Fixed	This wire type is locked and does not automatically update when wire numbers are updated. Wire numbers can be fixed when inserted or when edited manually.
Extra	A copy of a normal or fixed wire number. When wire numbers are initially inserted, each wire network receives one wire number. The extra wire numbers are copies of wire numbers inserted at other areas on the network.
Terminal/ Signal	Wire numbers for terminals or signal arrows.

- Each wire number type is placed on a different layer as defined in the *Drawing Properties* dialog box, in the *Drawing Format* tab, in the *Layers* area, in the **Define** option. The layers can be changed to suit your standards.

Copy Wire Numbers

When the **Insert Wire Number** command is used, only one wire number is inserted per wire network in a drawing. You might want to display a network's wire number in multiple places in the drawing. The **Copy Wire Number** command displays a wire number at the point at which the wire is selected. These are considered to be **Extra** wire numbers.

Copy Wire Number

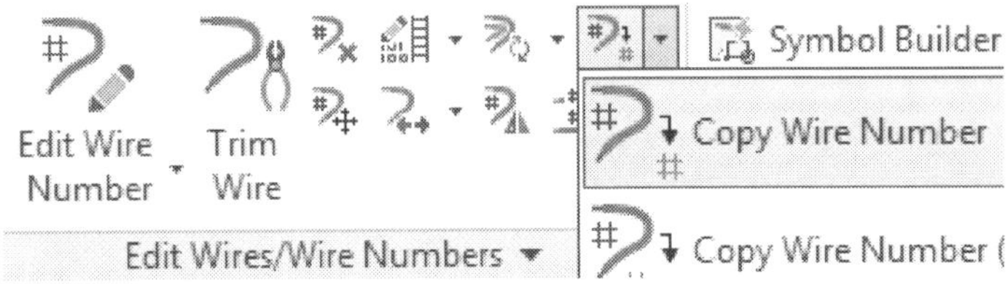

Ribbon: *Schematic* tab>*Edit Wires/Wire Numbers* panel

Command Prompt: aecopywireno

Shortcut menu: *(on a wire)* **Wire Numbers>Copy Wire Number**

How To: Copy Wire Numbers

1. Start the **Copy Wire Number** command.
2. Select the wire whose wire number you need to display.
3. Continue selecting wires to copy their wire numbers.
4. Right-click to end the command.

- The wire number displays at the selected point on the wire.

Wire Number Position

Wire numbers are automatically positioned based on the settings in *Drawing Properties* and the location selected on the wire. You might want to move wire numbers after they are placed, as shown in Figure 3–24. Several commands are included for accomplishing this action.

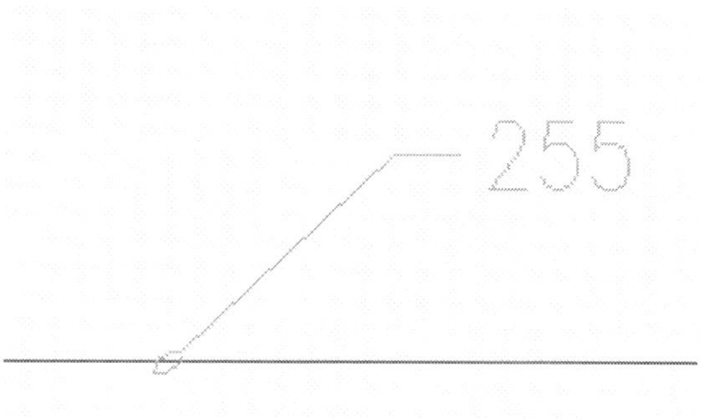

Figure 3–24

Wire Leaders

Wire leaders are lines extending from the wire number to the wire itself. They are useful if the wire number cannot be displayed where it would be placed by default.

Wire Number Leader

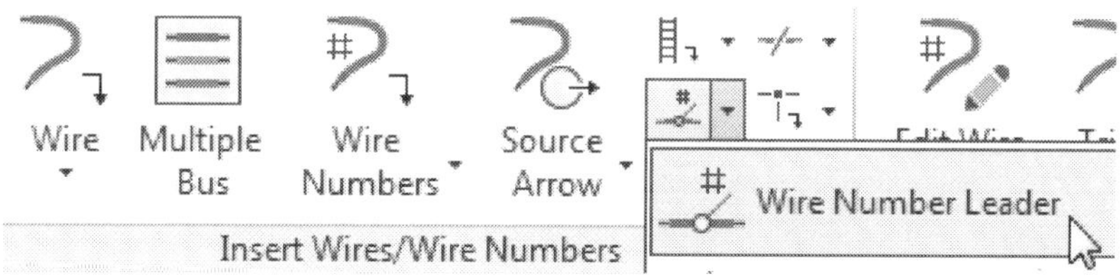

Ribbon: *Schematic* tab>*Insert Wires/Wire Numbers* panel

Command Prompt: aewirenoleader

Shortcut menu: *(on a wire)* **Wire Number Leader**

How To: Add a Wire Leader

1. Start the **Wire Number Leader** command.
2. Pick a wire number to which to add a leader.
3. Pick the position for the end of the leader line.

4. Continue picking points for the leader line and right-click or press <Enter> to end the leader.
5. Pick the next wire number to which to add a leader and right-click or press <Enter> to end the command.

- After you start the **Wire Number Leader** command, you can type **C** to collapse or remove wire leaders. Select the wire number to remove its leader.
- The software automatically adds wire leaders if a wire number does not fit between existing components.
- Wire leaders can be added to all wire numbers when they are inserted by editing *Drawing Properties*.

Move Wire Number

The **Move Wire Number** command moves a wire number to a different wire in the same network. You do not have to pick the existing number, only the wire where you want it to be displayed Wire numbers can also be flipped to the other side of a wire or placed in line with the wire by right-clicking and selecting **Flip Wire Number** or **Toggle Wire Number in Line**.

Move Wire Number

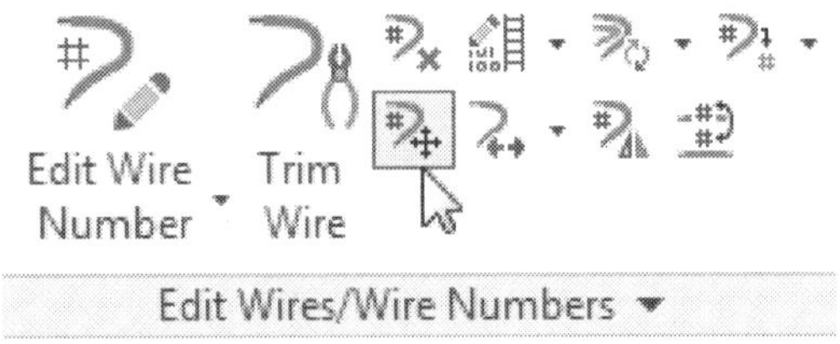

Ribbon: *Schematic* tab>*Edit Wires/Wire Numbers* panel

Command Prompt: aemovewireno

Shortcut menu: *(on a wire number)* **Move Wire Number**

How To: Move Wire Numbers

1. Start the **Move Wire Number** command.
2. Select the wire to which you want to move the wire number.
3. Right-click or press <Enter> to end the command.

Scoot

The **Scoot** command moves the wire number to a different position on the same wire.

Scoot

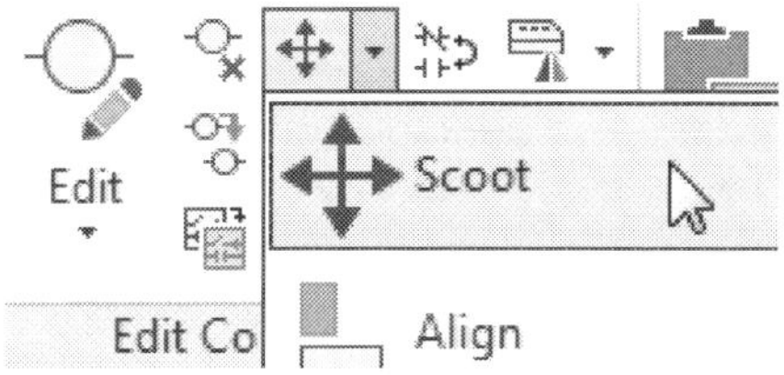

Ribbon: *Schematic tab>Edit Components* panel

Command Prompt: aescoot

Shrtcut menu: *(on a wire number)* **Scoot**

How To: Scoot Wire Numbers

1. Start the **Scoot** command.
2. Select the wire number you want to move.
3. Select the new position for the wire number.
4. Continue to move numbers, as required.
5. Right-click or press <Enter> to end the command.

- The **Scoot** command limits you to moving the wire number to positions on the existing wire.
- The **Scoot** command can be used to move other AutoCAD Electrical objects, such as symbols and wires.

Edit Wire Numbers

After wire numbers have been placed, you might want to change the value of an individual wire number.

Edit Wire Number

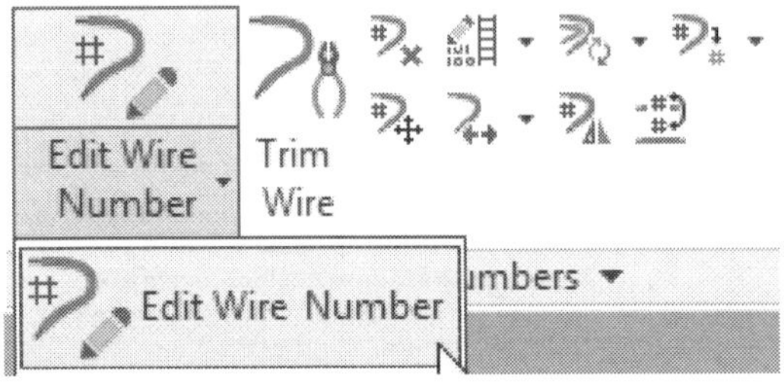

Ribbon: *Schematic* tab>*Edit Wires/Wire Numbers* panel

Command Prompt: aeeditwireno

Shortcut menu: *(on a wire number)* **Edit Wire Number**

How To: Edit a Wire Number

1. Start the **Edit Wire Number** command.
2. Select the wire number to change. The *Edit Wire Number/Attributes* dialog box opens with the current number displayed, as shown in Figure 3–25.

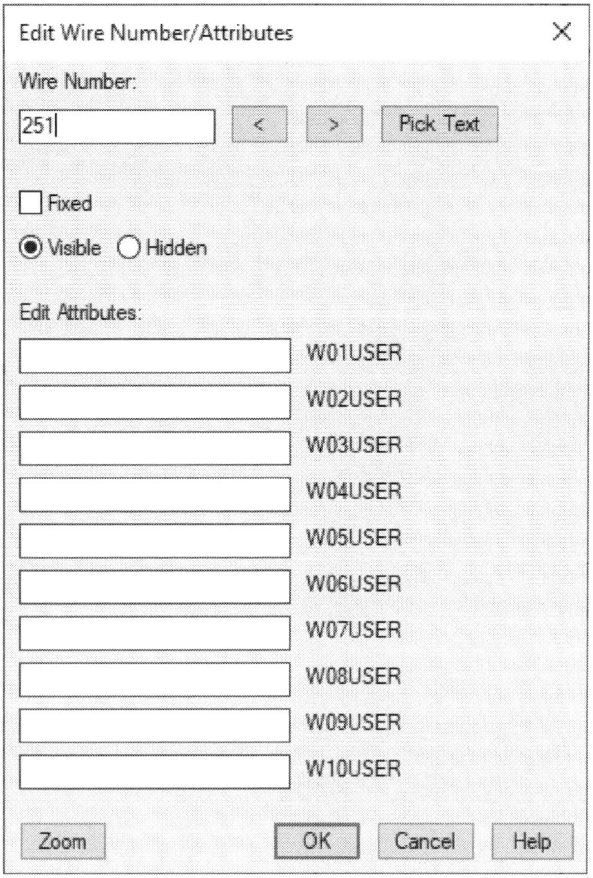

Figure 3–25

3. Use **<** and **>** to increase or decrease the wire number. You can also use **Pick Text** to select a new wire number.
4. Select **Fixed** to lock the wire number so that it is not updated when the **Insert Wire Number** command is used.
5. Use the *Edit Attributes* list to modify the 10 wire attributes. These attributes are available through various reports such as the From-to report.
6. Click **OK** to accept the new number.
7. Select the next wire number to edit.
8. Right-click or press <Enter> to end the command.

- If the number entered has already been assigned to a different wire network, a warning message box opens.

3.8 Source and Destination Signal Arrows

You might want to carry a wire's signal to a different area of the current drawing or across multiple drawings. This ability enables the same wire to be shown in different areas of a drawing. The source and destination signal arrows enable this functionality. The source and destination wire networks are linked with a user-defined code.

Source Signal Arrow

The **Source Signal Arrow** marks where the wire is coming from. The reference number indicates where the destination arrow is located. The wire number displays with the source signal arrow, as shown in Figure 3–26.

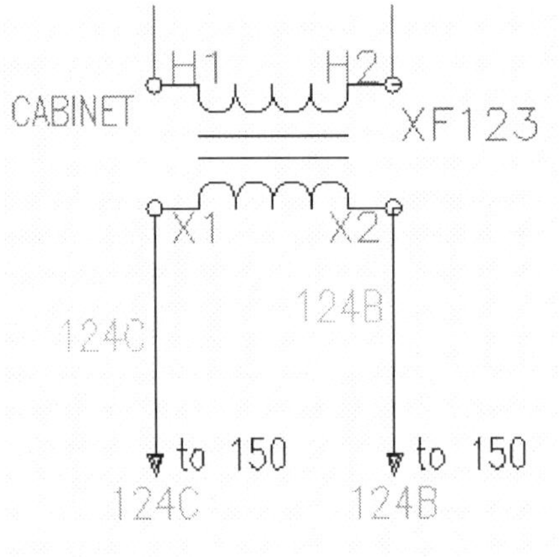

Figure 3–26

Source Arrow

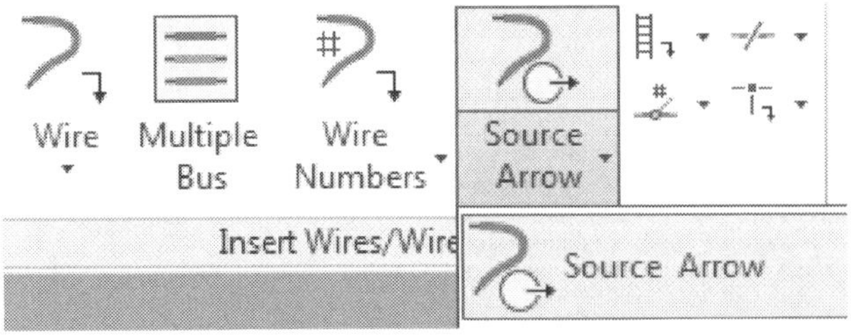

Ribbon: *Schematic* tab>*Insert Wires/Wire Numbers* panel

Command Prompt: aesource

Shortcut menu: *(on a wire)* **Source/Destination>Source Signal Arrow**

How To: Add a Source Arrow

1. Start the **Source Arrow** command.
2. Select near the end of the wire that needs a source arrow.
3. In the *Signal - Source Code* dialog box, provide the source code and any additional information.
4. To insert the source arrow, click **OK**.

- One source arrow can be linked to multiple destination arrows.
- The wire number from the source is duplicated in the destination.
- If wire numbers have not been added to the wire network, "???" displays at the source and destination arrows.

The *Signal – Source Code* dialog box (shown in Figure 3–27) is used to enter the text code that links the source and destination.

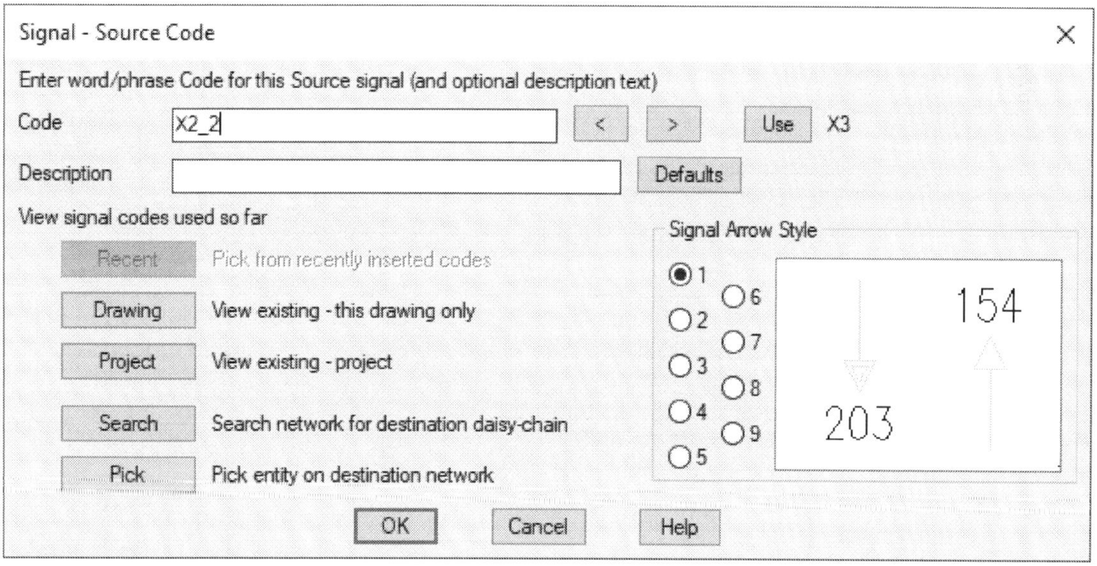

Figure 3–27

Code	Specifies the text code used to link the source wire network to the destination wire network(s). • Use a unique text/number string for each source. • Code has 32 character maximum. • Use **<** and **>** to increase or decrease the last digit of the code. • Click **Use** to populate the code with the next integer of a numbered sequence.
Description	Type a description of the source signal. This is an optional field that can aid in linking destination arrow(s).
Recent	Displays a list of recently input signal codes.
Drawing	Displays a list of source and destination codes used in the active drawing.
Project	Displays a list of source and destination codes used in the active project file. • Useful when linking wire networks between different drawings.
Search	Follows the selected wire network to find linked destination arrows. If a destination is found, its signal code is used.
Pick	Pick a wire network to search for destination arrows. If a destination is found, its signal code is used.
Signal Arrow Style	Specifies the signal arrow style to use for the source arrow. • Four predefined styles are installed and you are able to create up to five user-defined styles.

- Click **OK** to insert the source arrow and update the information on any associated destination arrows.
- After inserting the source arrow, you are prompted to insert the accompanying destination arrow. If the destination wire network is in the same drawing, you can insert it now.
- If the destination wire network is in a different drawing, this option cannot be used. You have to use the **Destination Signal Arrow** command to insert a destination arrow in a different drawing.

Destination Signal Arrow

The **Destination Signal Arrow** indicates where the wire number originates, as shown in Figure 3–28. The source wire number and the reference number where the source arrow is located display with the destination arrow.

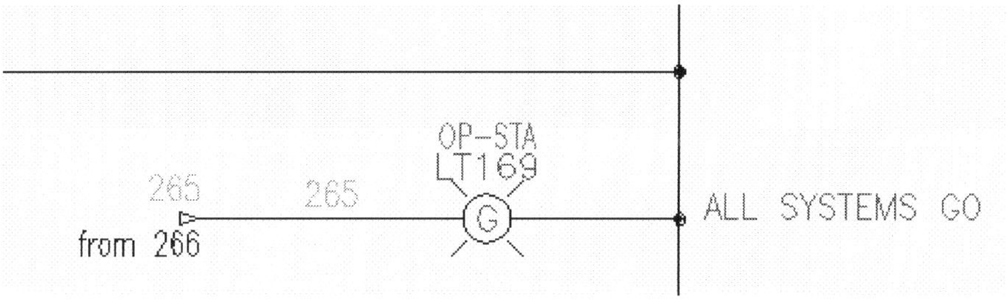

Figure 3–28

Destination Arrow

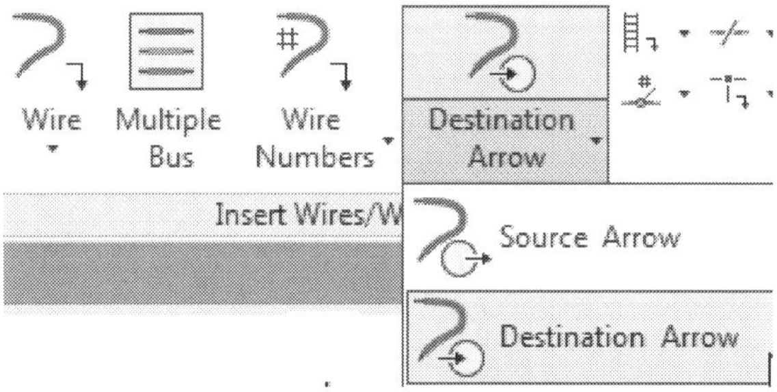

Ribbon: *Schematic* tab>*Insert Wires/Wire Numbers* panel

Command Prompt: aedestination

Shortcut menu: *(on a wire)* **Source/Destination>Destination Signal Arrow**

How To: Add a Destination Arrow

1. Start the **Destination Arrow** command.
2. Select near the end of the wire that needs a destination arrow.
3. In the *Insert Destination Code* dialog box, enter the signal code and any additional information.
4. Select **OK** to insert the destination arrow.

- A destination can only be linked to one source.

The *Insert Destination Code* dialog box (shown in Figure 3–29) is used to enter the text code that links the source and destination. It opens after you pick the location of the destination arrow.

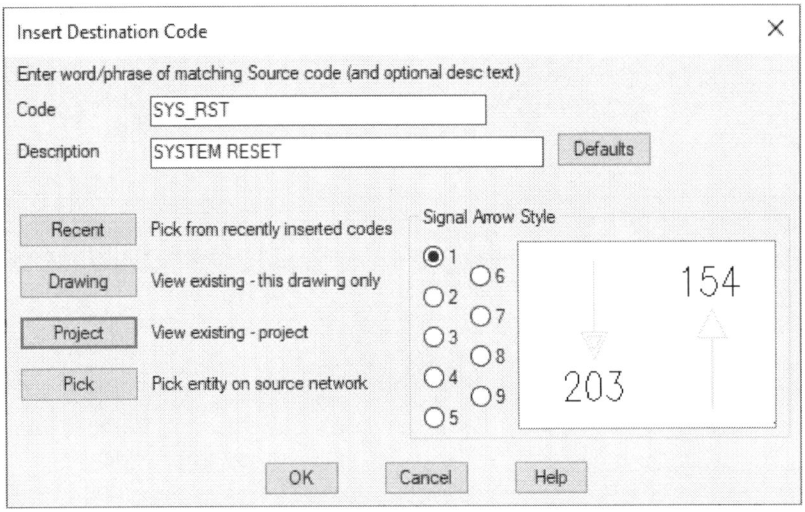

Figure 3–29

Code	Specifies the text code used to link the source wire network to the destination wire network(s). • Use a unique text/number string for each source. • Code has 32 character maximum.
Description	Type a description of the destination signal. This is an optional field that can aid in linking source arrow(s).
Recent	Displays a list of recently input source and destination codes.
Drawing	Displays a list of source and destination codes used in the active drawing.
Project	Displays a list of source and destination codes used in the active project file. Useful when linking wire networks between different drawings.
Pick	Pick a wire network to search for source arrows. If a source arrow is found, its signal code is used.
Signal Arrow Style	Specifies the signal arrow style to use for the destination arrow. • Four predefined styles are installed and you are able to create up to five user-defined styles.

- Click **OK** to insert the destination arrow and update the information on the associated source arrow.

Practice 3b
Insert and Manage Wires

Practice Objectives

- Insert and modify wires, wire rungs, and wire numbers.
- Create and change the wire type.

In this practice, you will work in an existing drawing. You will add rungs to a ladder, add individual wires, and trim wires. You will then create a new wire type and apply it to existing wires. Finally, you will add wire numbers to the drawing, as shown in Figure 3–30.

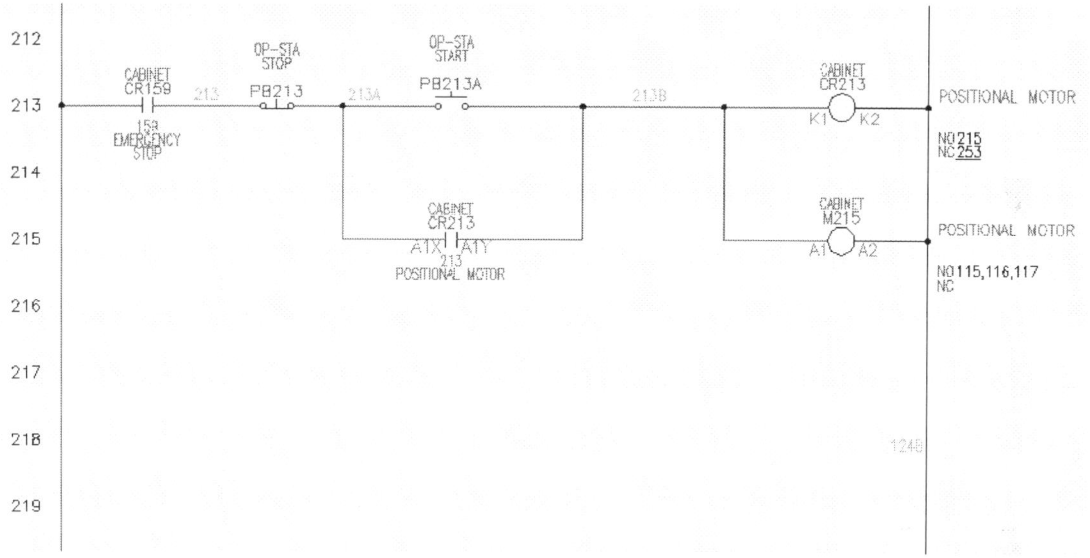

Figure 3–30

Task 1: Add rungs.

1. If the **Module 03** project is not active, open and activate it now.
2. In the *Project Manager*, expand the drawing list and double-click on **Control.dwg** to open the drawing.
3. Zoom to lines 212 through 219.
4. In the *Schematic* tab>*Edit Wires/Wire Numbers* panel, click (Add Rung).

5. Pick a point on line 215 between the symbols labeled CR213 and M215, pick a second point on line 217, and pick a third point on line 219, as shown in Figure 3–31. Note that the three rungs are created.
6. Press <Enter> to end the command.

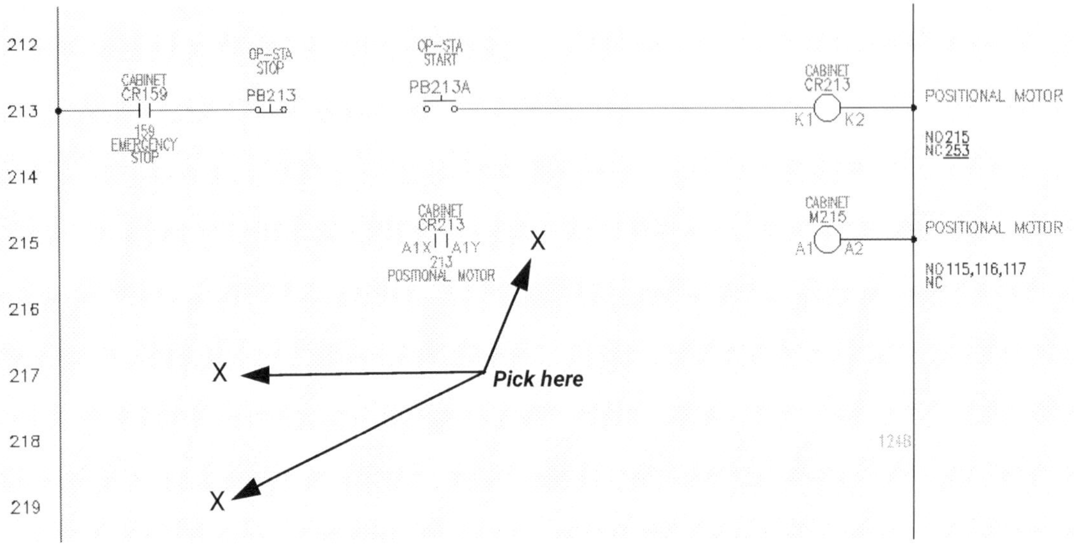

Figure 3–31

Task 2: Add and trim wires.

1. Zoom in on the symbols labeled PB213 and PB213A on line 213.
2. In the *Schematic* tab>*Insert Wires/Wire Numbers* panel, click  (Wire). Type **X** and press <Enter> to display the connection points (green crosses) on the symbols.
3. Add a wire between symbols PB213 and PB213A, ensuring that you select very near to the connection points on the symbols.
   - Toggle off **Snap** mode and toggle on **Nearest OSnap**.
4. As you are still in the **Wire** command, add two wires vertically, starting on the wire between PB213A and CR213 and ending on the wire between CR213 and M215. The circuit should display as shown in Figure 3–32. Press <Enter> to end the command.

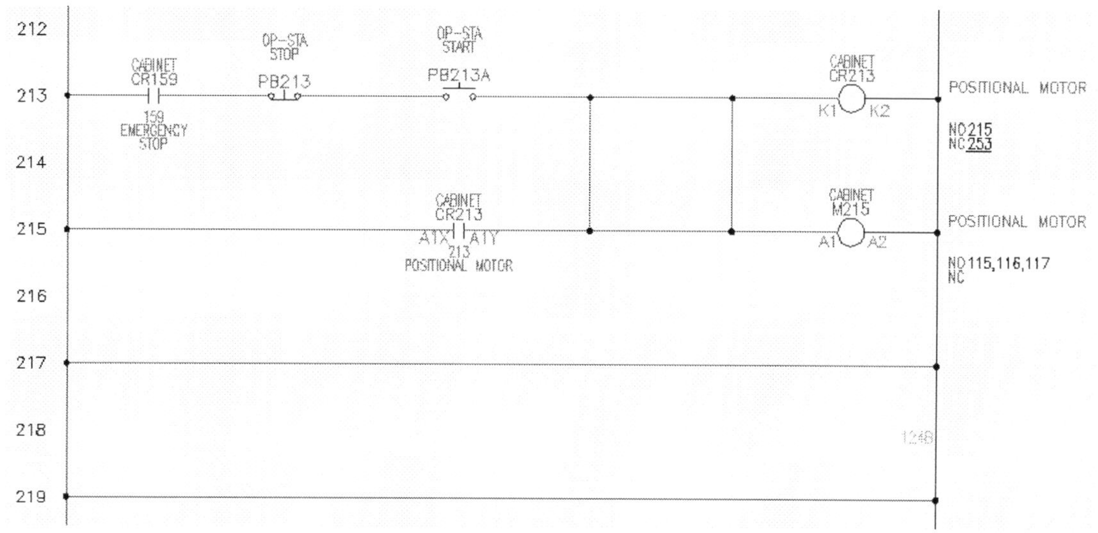

Figure 3–32

5. In the *Schematic* tab>*Edit Wires/Wire Numbers* panel, click (Trim Wire).
6. Select the wire at line 215 between CR213 and the rail, as shown in Figure 3–33.
7. Select the wire at line 215 between the two vertical wires you drew earlier, as shown in Figure 3–33.
8. Select the rungs that make a short circuit on lines 217 and 219, as shown in Figure 3–33.
9. Press <Enter> to end the command.

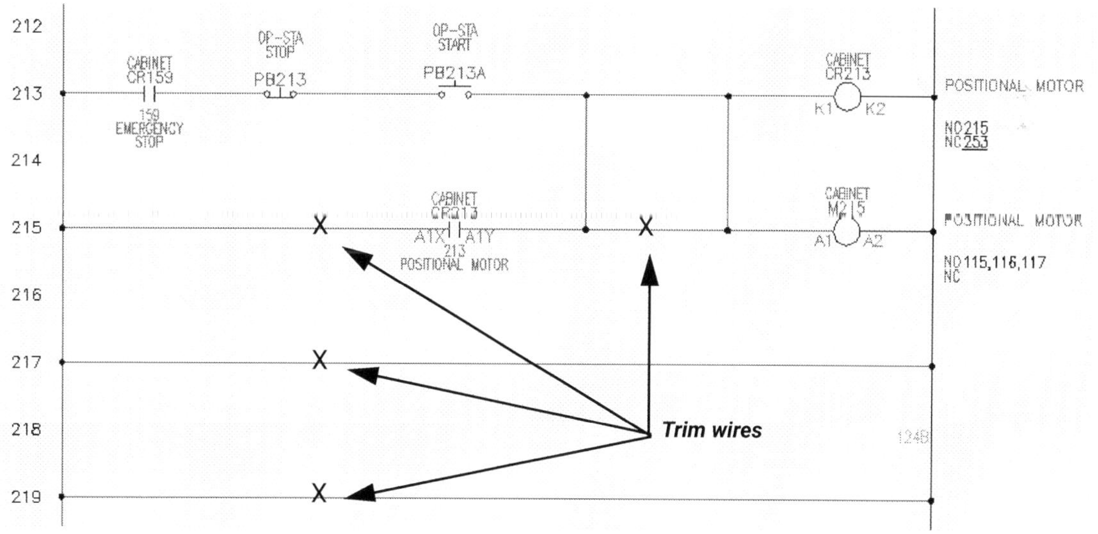

Figure 3–33

10. Click  (Wire).

11. Select a point near the midpoint of the wire between PB213 and PB213A and then hover the cursor near the left side of CR213, which displays the connection points on CR213 (as shown in Figure 3–34). As the second point, select near the left connection point on CR213.

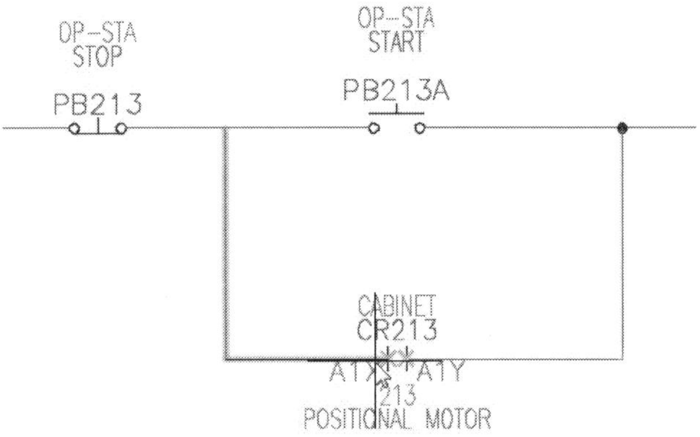

Figure 3–34

12. Press <Enter> to end the command.

Task 3: Create and change wire type.

1. In the *Schematic* tab>*Edit Wires/Wire Numbers* panel, click  (Create/Edit Wire Type). The *Create/Edit Wire Type* dialog box opens.
2. In the last blank row, select the *Wire Color* cell. For the wire color, type **BLU**. Select the *Size* cell and type **18AWG**. Press <Tab> to display the new *Layer Name*, as shown in Figure 3–35.

Create/Edit Wire Type

	Used	Wire Color	Size	Layer Name	Wire Numbering	USER1	USER2
1	X			WIRES	Yes		
2	X	BLK	14AWG	BLK_14AWG	Yes		
3	X	RED	18AWG	RED_18AWG	Yes		
4	X	WHT	16AWG	WHT_16AWG	Yes		
5		BLU	18AWG	BLU_18AWG	Yes		
6							

Figure 3–35

3. In the *Layer* area of the dialog box, click **Color**. In the *Select Color* dialog box, select **blue** as the color. Click **OK**.

4. In the *Create/Edit Wire Type* dialog box, click **OK**.
5. Right-click on the horizontal wire between PB213A and CR213 and select **Change/Convert Wire Type**. The *Change/Convert Wire Type* dialog box opens.
6. Select the wire type you just created (**BLU_18AWG**) and click **OK**. All wires in the wire network change, not just the wire that was selected.
7. Press <Enter> to end the command.

Task 4: Insert wire numbers.

1. In the *Schematic* tab>*Insert Wires/Wire Numbers* panel, click (Wire Numbers).
2. In the *Wire Tagging* dialog box, leave the default settings and click **Drawing-wide**. The AutoCAD Electrical software automatically adds wire numbers to each wire network, as shown in Figure 3–36.

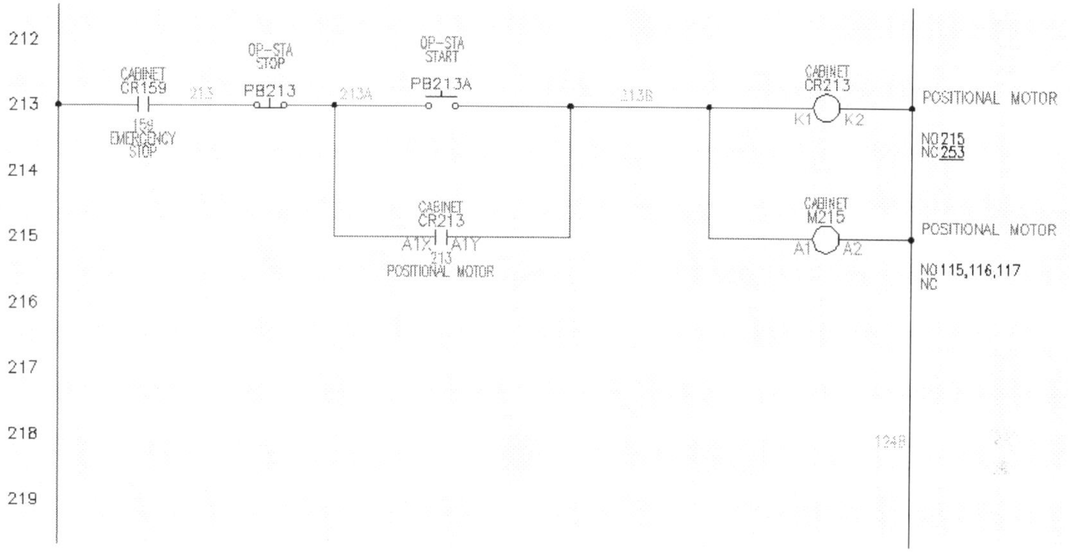

Figure 3–36

3. Save **Control.dwg**.

End of practice

Practice 3c
Insert Source and Destination Arrows

Practice Objective

- Insert source and destination signal arrows.

In this practice, you will work in an existing drawing. You will add source and destination arrows to the rails of a ladder and to wires in a circuit, as shown in Figure 3–37.

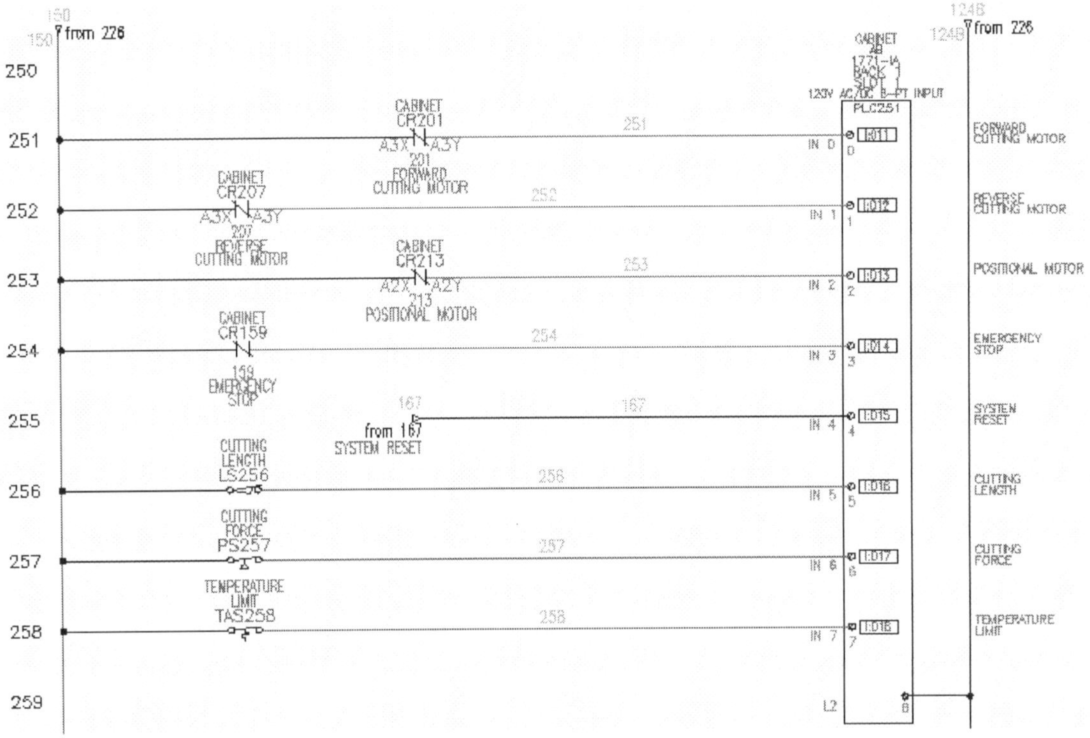

Figure 3–37

1. If the **Module 03** project is not active, open and activate it now.
2. In the *Project Manager*, expand the drawing list and double-click on **Control.dwg** to open the drawing, if it is not already open.
3. Zoom to the bottom of the ladder on the left side.
4. In the *Schematic* tab>*Insert Wires/Wire Numbers* panel, click (Source Arrow).

5. Select near the bottom of the right rail, as shown in Figure 3–38.

Figure 3–38

6. The *Signal - Source Code* dialog box opens. In the *Code* field, type **X2_2** (as shown in Figure 3–39). Click **OK**.

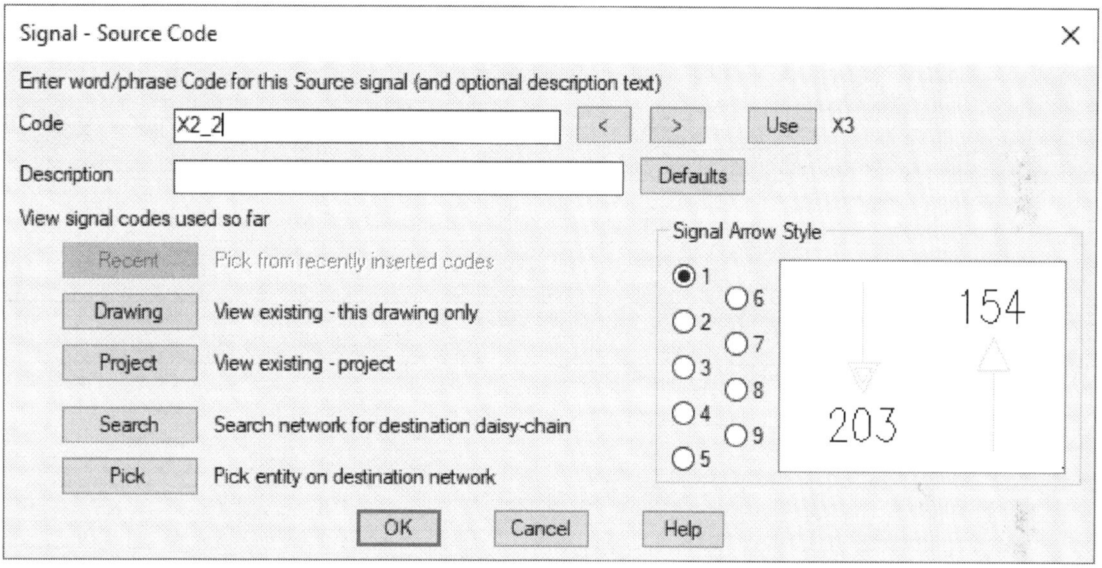

Figure 3–39

7. The *Source/Destination Signal Arrows* dialog box opens, as shown in Figure 3–40. Click **OK** to insert the destination arrow.

Figure 3–40

8. Select near the top of the right rail of the ladder on the right side, as shown in Figure 3–41. Note that **from 226** displays at the top of this rail.

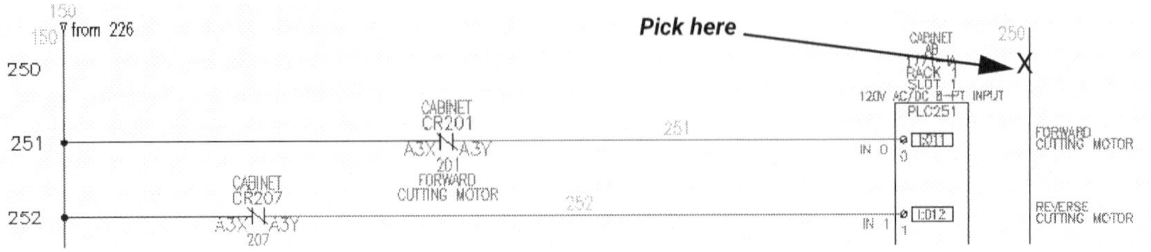

Figure 3–41

9. Click (Previous Drawing) to open the previous drawing, **Power.dwg**.
10. Zoom to line 167.
11. Click (Source Arrow).
12. Click near the right end of the wire on line 167, as shown in Figure 3–42.

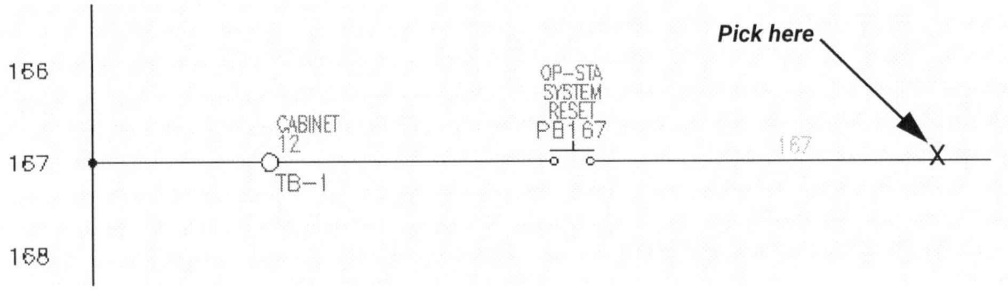

Figure 3–42

13. in the *Signal - Source Code* dialog box that opens, set the following, as shown in Figure 3–43:
    - *Code*: **SYS_RST**
    - *Description*: **SYSTEM RESET**

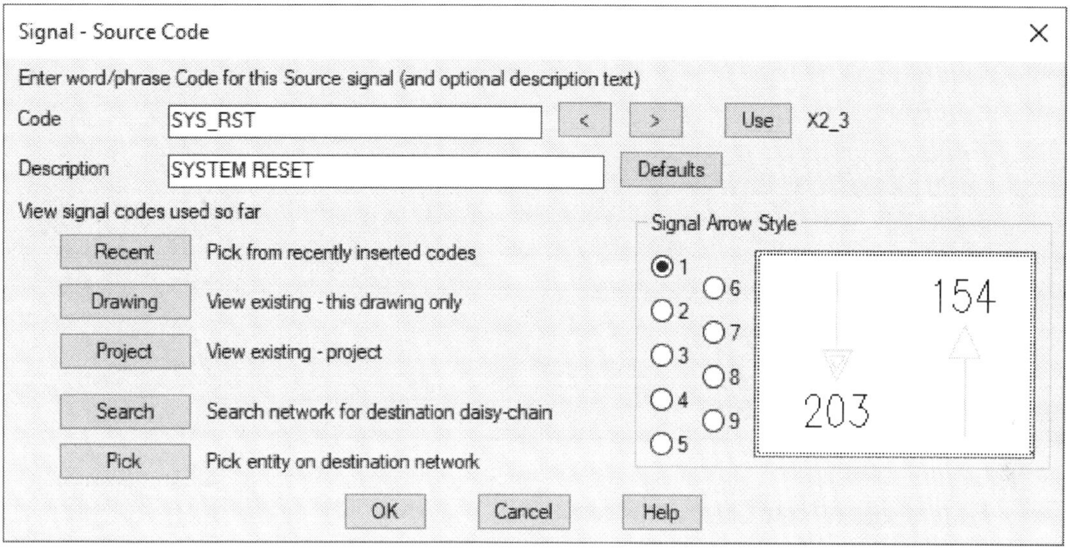

Figure 3–43

14. Click **OK**.
15. The *Source/Destination Signal Arrows* dialog box opens. Click **No**. Note that the source arrow is added to the right end of the line.
16. To insert the destination arrow into **Control.dwg**, click (Next Drawing) to open the next drawing, **Control.dwg**.
17. Zoom to line 255.
18. In the *Schematic* tab>*Insert Wires/Wire Numbers* panel, click (Destination Arrow).
19. Select near the left end of the wire on line 255 as shown in Figure 3–44.

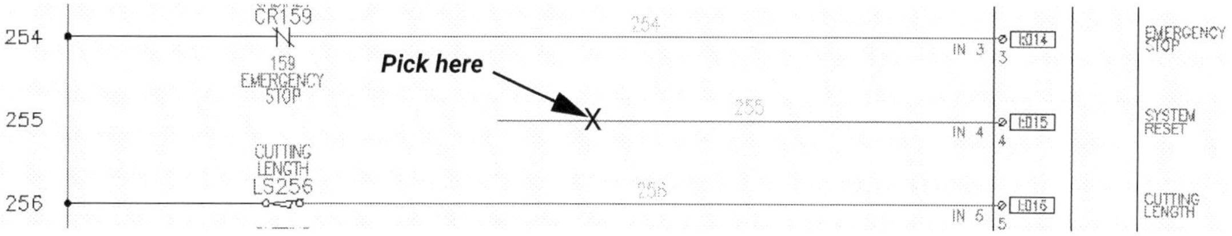

Figure 3–44

20. The *Insert Destination Code* dialog box opens. Click **Project**.
21. The *Signal codes - - Project-wide Source* dialog box opens. It lists all source signal codes in the active project. In the list, select the **SYS_RST** code that you just created, as shown in Figure 3–45. Click **OK**.
    - If SYS_RST is not displayed in the dialog box, click **Freshen** to update the list.

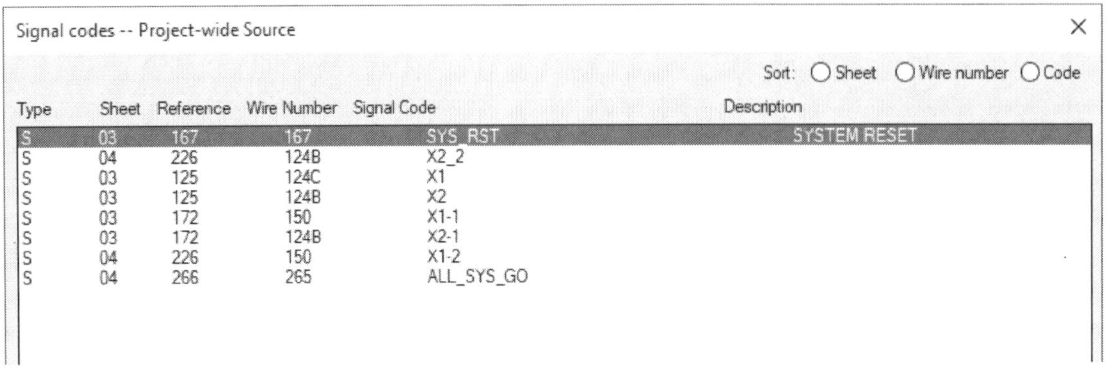

Figure 3–45

22. The *Insert Destination Code* dialog box is updated by populating the *Code* and *Description* fields, as shown in Figure 3–46. Click **OK**.

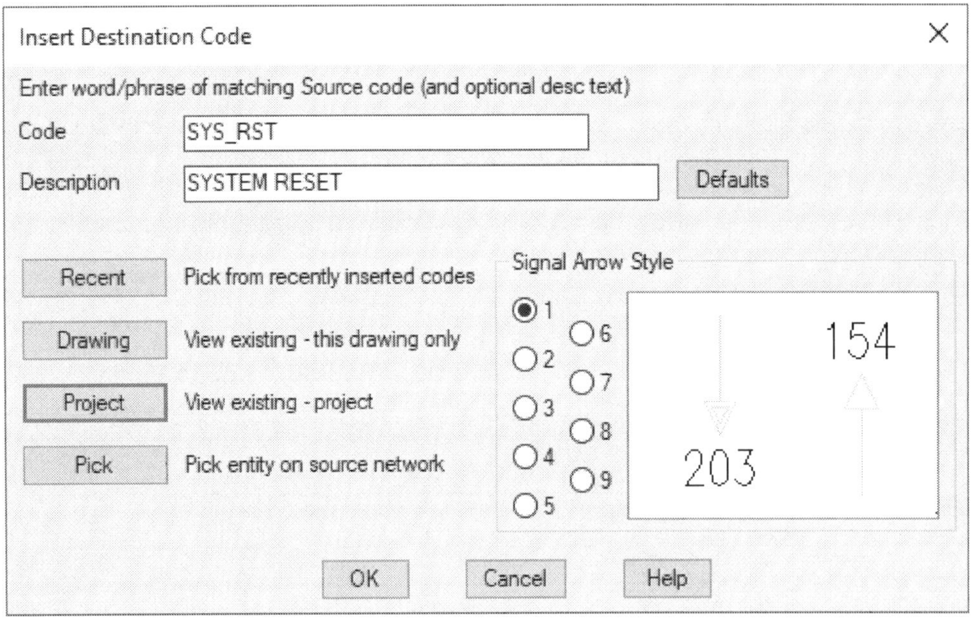

Figure 3–46

23. The *Change Destination Wire Layer?* dialog box opens. Click **Yes**. The destination arrow is inserted, as shown in Figure 3–47, and the source arrow is updated.

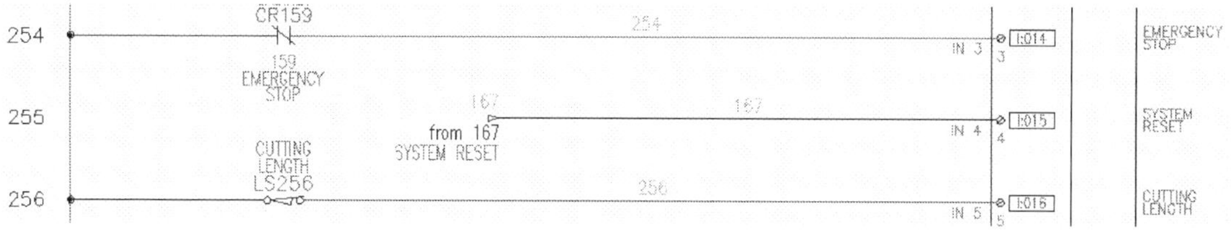

Figure 3–47

24. Click (Previous Drawing) to open the previous drawing, **Power.dwg**.
25. Zoom to the source arrow on line 167. It now displays the reference number of the destination arrow **to 255**, as shown in Figure 3–48.

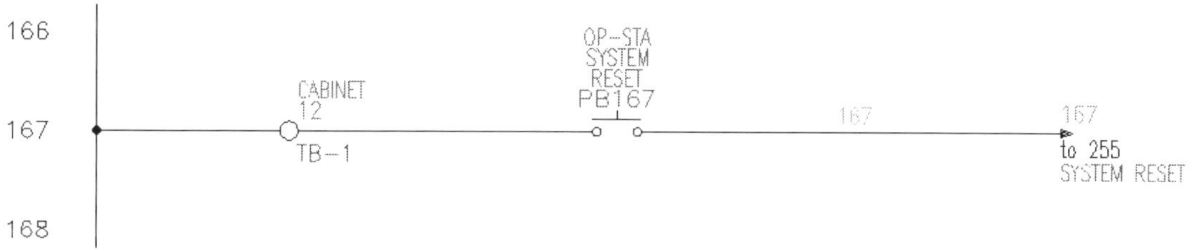

Figure 3–48

26. Save **Power.dwg**.

End of practice

3.9 Insert Component

When creating a schematic drawing (as shown in Figure 3–49), you add a ladder, add or trim wires as required, and then add component symbols to the drawing.

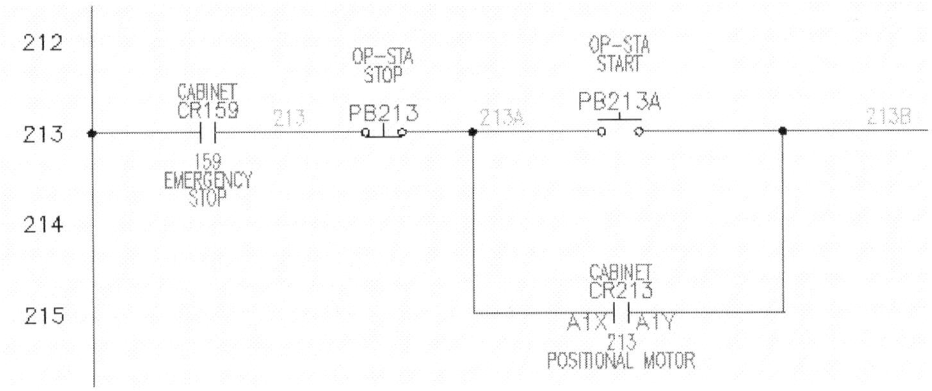

Figure 3–49

- The component symbols represent the physical components of the control system, but are not typically actual representations of the component.
- The component symbols are AutoCAD blocks with attributes and contain both visible and invisible attributes.
  - Visible attributes contain information such as component tags, pin numbers, and descriptions, depending on the symbol
  - Invisible attributes contain information such as wire connection points, and manufacturer information
- The AutoCAD Electrical software contains several symbols libraries to support different standards, including NFPA, IEC, and IEEE. These libraries can be customized to meet specific company standards.

Icon Menu

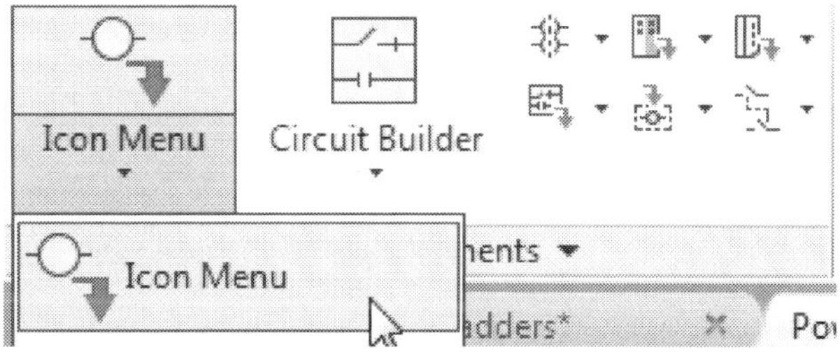

Ribbon: *Schematic* tab>*Insert Components* panel

Command Prompt: aecomponent

Shortcut menu: *(on a wire)* **Insert Component>Insert Component**

How To: Insert a Component

1. Start the **Insert Component** command.
2. In the *Insert Component* dialog box, select the component category.
3. In the submenu, select the component to insert.
4. In the drawing window, pick the location of the component. The *Insert / Edit Component* dialog box opens.
5. Edit the *Insert / Edit Component* dialog box, as required.
6. Click **OK** to complete the command or **OK-Repeat** to insert the same component again.

- Component tags are automatically assigned based on settings in Drawing Properties.
- You do not have to complete the dialog box when you insert a component. The information can be added or updated later.
- If catalog data is not assigned to a component, it does not display in the BOM report.

Insert Component Dialog Box

The *Insert Component* dialog box (shown in Figure 3–50) is used to insert component symbols. The available symbols are organized into categories.

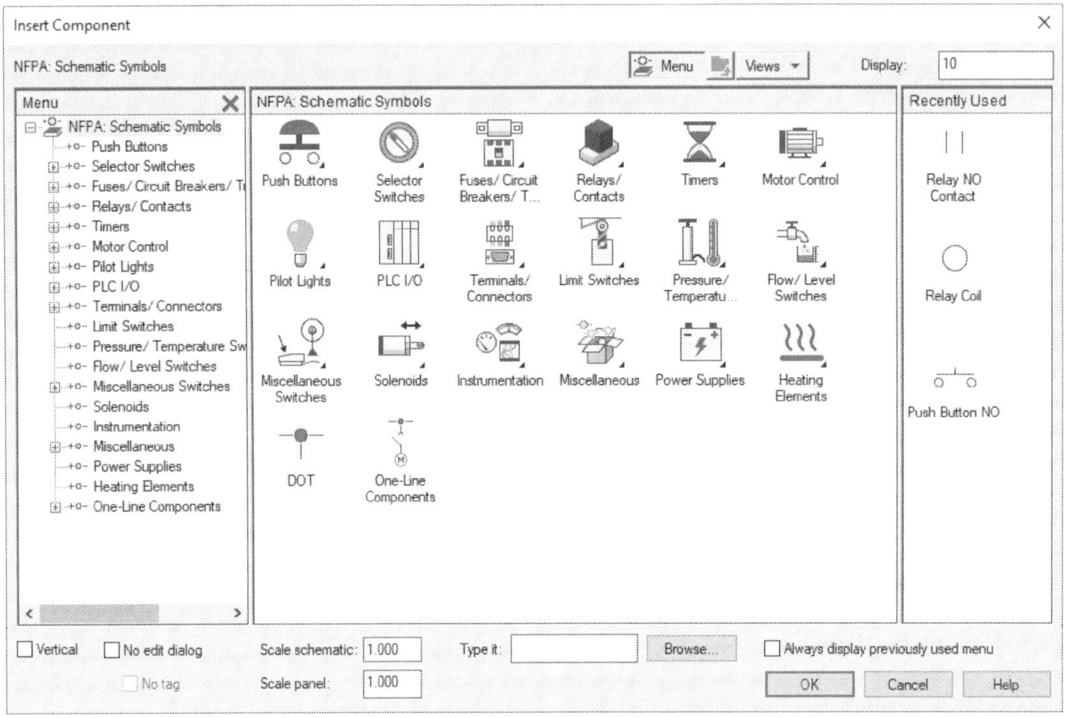

Figure 3–50

- The Menu tree view on the left contains a text list of the available categories of symbols. The view corresponds to the icon picture list.
- The middle area of the dialog box displays icons for the available categories or symbols. Select a submenu icon (small triangle in the lower-right corner) to display its submenu or a symbol icon to insert that symbol.
- The column to the right side of the symbol icons is the *Recently Used* list and is populated as you add symbols to the drawing.

The options in the *Insert Component* dialog box are described in the following table:

	Toggles the display of the Menu tree view of symbols and categories on and off.
	Navigates up one level in the menu structure.
Views	Controls the display of icons in the middle area of the dialog box. Options include: **Icon with text**, **Icon only**, and **List view**.
Display	Enter the number of symbols to display in the *Recently Used* list.
Vertical	Forces an orientation opposite to the ladder in the current drawing. If a vertical wire is selected, The AutoCAD Electrical software automatically re-orients the symbol.
No edit dialog	Inserts a component without displaying the *Edit Component* dialog box.
No tag	Inserts a component without assigning the automatic component tag. You can assign a component tag later in the *Edit Component* dialog box.
Scale: schematic	Scale at which the symbol is inserted into a schematic drawing. The default setting is controlled in the *Drawing Properties* dialog box in the *Drawing Format* tab. If the scale is changed, the value is maintained during the drawing edit session.
Scale panel	Scale at which the symbol is inserted into a panel drawing. The default setting is controlled in the *Drawing Properties* dialog box in the *Drawing Format* tab. If the scale is changed, the value is maintained during the drawing edit session.
Type it	If you know the block name of the symbol, you can type it instead of selecting it in the dialog box.
Browse...	Search for a DWG block file to use as the symbol. This is useful if you need a custom symbol that is not part of the Icon Menu.
Always display previously used menu	If selected, the sub-menu of the previously inserted symbol displays the next time the **Insert Component** command is started.

Insert / Edit Component

After you select a symbol and place it in the drawing, the *Insert / Edit Component* dialog box opens, as shown in Figure 3–51. You can fill out the information in the dialog box when you insert the symbol or you can edit it later to update the information.

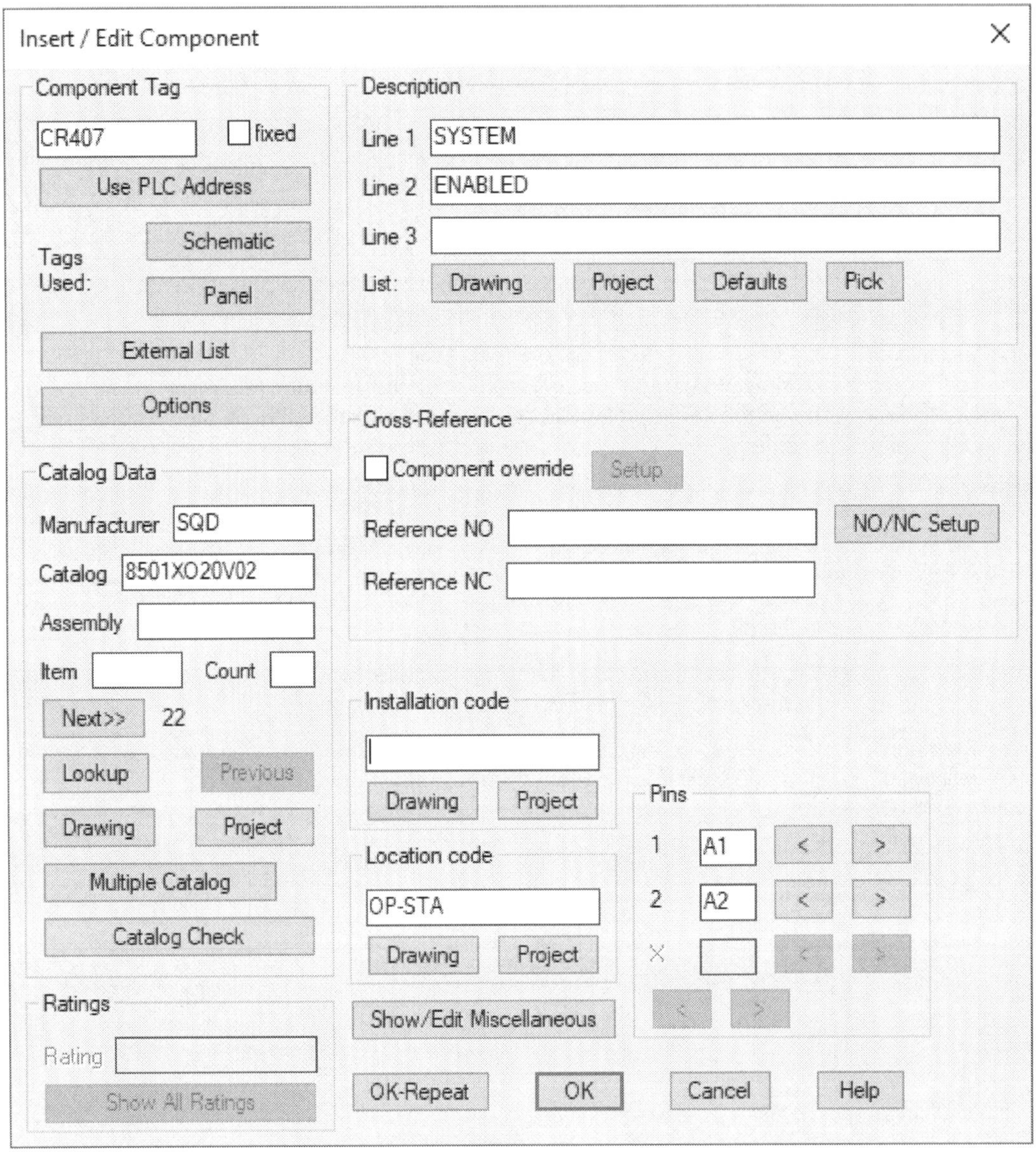

Figure 3–51

Component Tag

Displays the component tag automatically assigned to the component as defined in the *Drawing Properties* dialog box in the *Drawing Format* tab. You can override the default tag by typing in the field.

- Component tags must contain the family code and a number. The number is based on the reference number where the symbol is placed or on a sequential number.
- You can lock the component tag by selecting **fixed**. If the tag is fixed, it is not automatically updated when any of the retagging tools are used.
- Other options for the Component Tag:

Use PLC Address	Uses the PLC pin address as a Tag if directly connected to a PLC.
Schematic	Displays a list of all components in the project that use the same family code.
Panel	Displays a list of the components that have been placed in the project's panel drawings.
External List	Displays the contents of an external text file that might contain the values that you want to use.
Options	Enables you to assign a family tag override format.

You can enter up to three lines of description for a symbol. The description can be any text that describes the function or type of component.

- By default, descriptions are automatically capitalized. This can be changed in Drawing Properties.
- Click **Drawing** to display a list of descriptions used in the drawing for the same type of component.
- Click **Project** to display a list of descriptions used in the entire project for the same type of component.
- The Defaults list displays a list of default descriptions. It is based on the **wd_desc.wdd** text file.
- Click **Pick** to select a component in the current drawing and to use its description.

Catalog Data

This area controls the catalog information for the component, including the manufacturer and catalog number. This information can be used in BOM and other reports. Catalog data is stored in an Access database. The default database is **default_cat.mdb**.

Manufacturer	The manufacturer code for the component. Type the code or click **Lookup** and select the code in the Catalog Browser.
Catalog	The catalog number for the component. Type the code or click **Lookup** and select the code in the Catalog Browser.
Assembly	The assembly code used to link several BOM items to one catalog code.
Item	Unique identifier for each component.
Count	Specifies the quantity number for the part number.
Lookup	Opens the Catalog Browser. You can select the BOM information in this dialog box.
Drawing	Searches the drawing for similar components and displays a list of catalog data from those components. You can select from this list.
Project	Searches for similar components. You can specify to search in the active project, another project, or an external file (TXT or CSV). You can select from this list.
Multiple Catalog	Enables you to add other catalog numbers to the component. You can add up to ten additional catalog numbers. These display as subassembly components in the BOM and other reports.
Catalog Check	Indicates how the catalog data would be displayed in the BOM report.

Hint: Catalog Browser

The catalog data can be accessed from a *Catalog Browser*, as shown in Figure 3–52. You can open the modeless *Catalog Browser* (palette) by clicking (Catalog Browser) in the *Schematic* tab>*Insert Component* panel. It can remain open while other commands are being performed and you can use it to insert schematic components directly into a drawing. The *Catalog Browser* dialog box opens when you click **Lookup** in the *Catalog Data* area in the *Insert / Edit Component* dialog box. An input is required to exit the dialog box before performing the next step for the command. It is a search based dialog box, in which you can search for the database records in the catalog by entering a search string in the *Search* edit box and clicking . Based on your entry, all of the matching values display in the *Results* area. Only columns that display in the *Results* area are searched. You can control the columns that you want to display by right-clicking on the column header and selecting the required columns. Selecting the column header sorts the data in the column. You can also use to edit the catalog information.

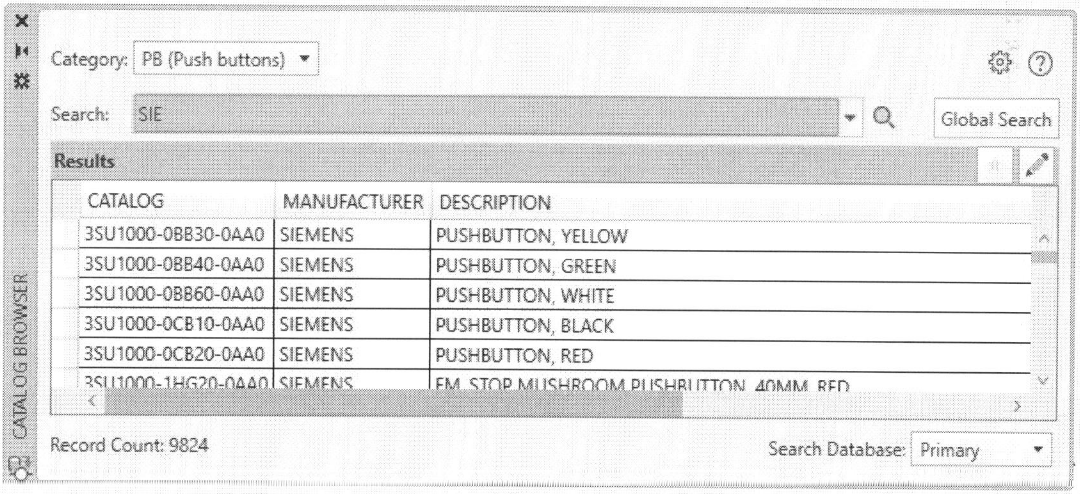

Figure 3–52

If a symbol is not associated to the catalog data entry, the *Assign Symbol to Catalog Number* dialog box opens indicating that the selected symbol needs to be mapped. Select **Map symbol to catalog number** to associate the symbol to the selected component.

Cross-Reference

Displays any references to other components (parent/child relationships). When inserting a new component, there are no current cross-references. You can enter cross-reference information here, but typically relationships are built using the *Insert / Edit Child Component* dialog box.

- Select **Component override** to override the format of the cross-reference information.
- Enter cross-reference information in the *Reference NO* and *Reference NC* fields.
- Click **NO/NCSetup** to control the maximum number of contacts and pin information for the component. If a catalog number has been selected, this data is automatically populated.

Installation/Location Codes

Codes are used to specify where a component is physically located. These can also be used to group components when running reports.

- Click **Drawing** to display a list of codes used in the current drawing.
- Click **Project** to display a list of codes used in all drawings listed in the project file.
- Default installation and location codes can be created with an AutoCAD Electrical Mapping file (.INST or .LOC).

Pins

Assign pin numbers to the component. Default pin numbers can be assigned in the pin list database.

- Use **<** and **>** to increase and decrease the pin numbers.

Ratings

Assign the rating value of the component. If the field is grayed out, the component does not have any rating attributes. A component can have up to 12 rating attributes.

Show/Edit Miscellaneous

Displays any attributes assigned to the component symbol that are not standard AutoCAD Electrical attributes.

Combined Tags

In the *Insert / Edit Component* dialog box, the *Installation* value and *Location* value are individual parameters, separate from the *Component Tag* value. This option is typically used when following the NFPA Standard.

Alternatively, the *Installation* code and *Location* code can be combined into the *Component Tag*, which can be set in the Project Properties - Component settings. This option is typically used when following the IEC Standard. The *Insert / Edit Component* dialog box is also slightly different in that the *Installation* and *Location* fields are placed in a different location in the dialog box, as shown in Figure 3–53.

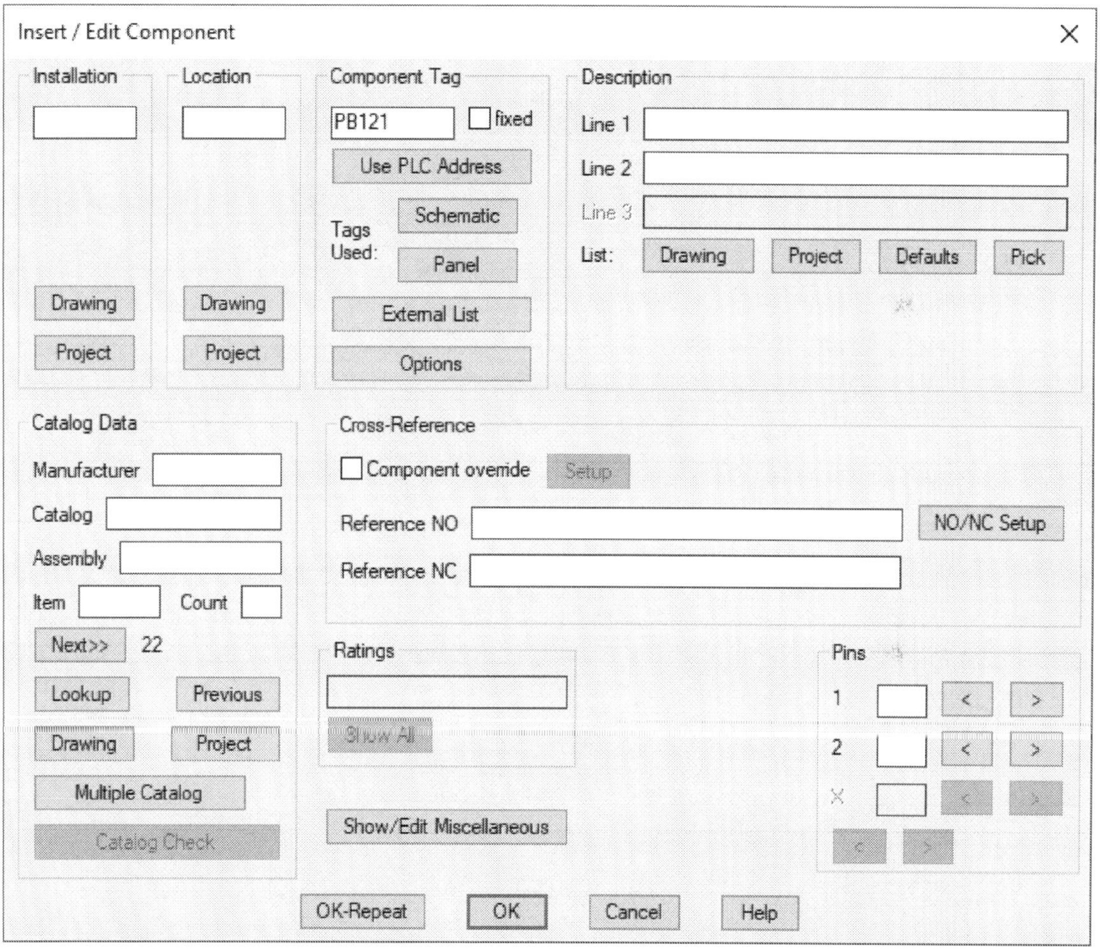

Figure 3–53

Edit Component

Existing components in a circuit can be edited using the **Edit Component** command which opens the *Insert / Edit Component* dialog box. Any value can be edited, including: tag ID, descriptions, catalog assignment, location and installation codes, ratings, and various other miscellaneous values.

Edit Component

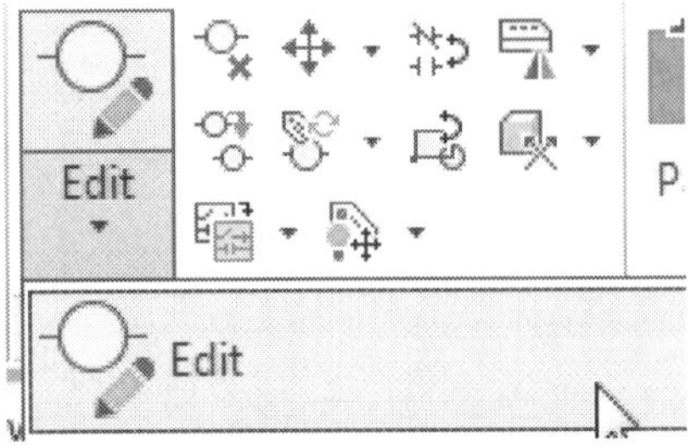

Ribbon: *Schematic* tab>*Edit Components* panel

Command Prompt: aeeditcomponent

Shortcut menu: *(on a component)* **Edit Component**

How To: Edit a Component

1. Start the **Edit Component** command.
2. Select the component you want to edit.
3. Edit any values in the *Insert / Edit Component* dialog box.
4. Click **OK** to complete the command.

3.10 Parent/Child Components

Parent/Child components are components that represent a single physical object but need to be displayed in multiple areas of a schematic drawing as separate symbols to indicate the various electrical portions of the overall physical object, as shown in Figure 3–54. The parent component contains the definition for the physical object, while the child component is linked back to the parent component for its definition. Examples of parent components are push buttons or relays. Examples of child components are contacts or other linked components.

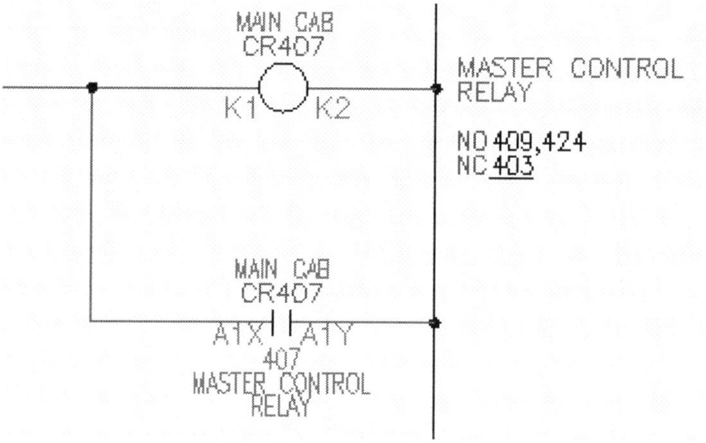

Figure 3–54

Insert / Edit Child Component Dialog Box

Parent components are inserted as normal components. Child components are inserted in a similar way to normal components, but using the *Insert / Edit Child Component* dialog box, as shown in Figure 3–55.

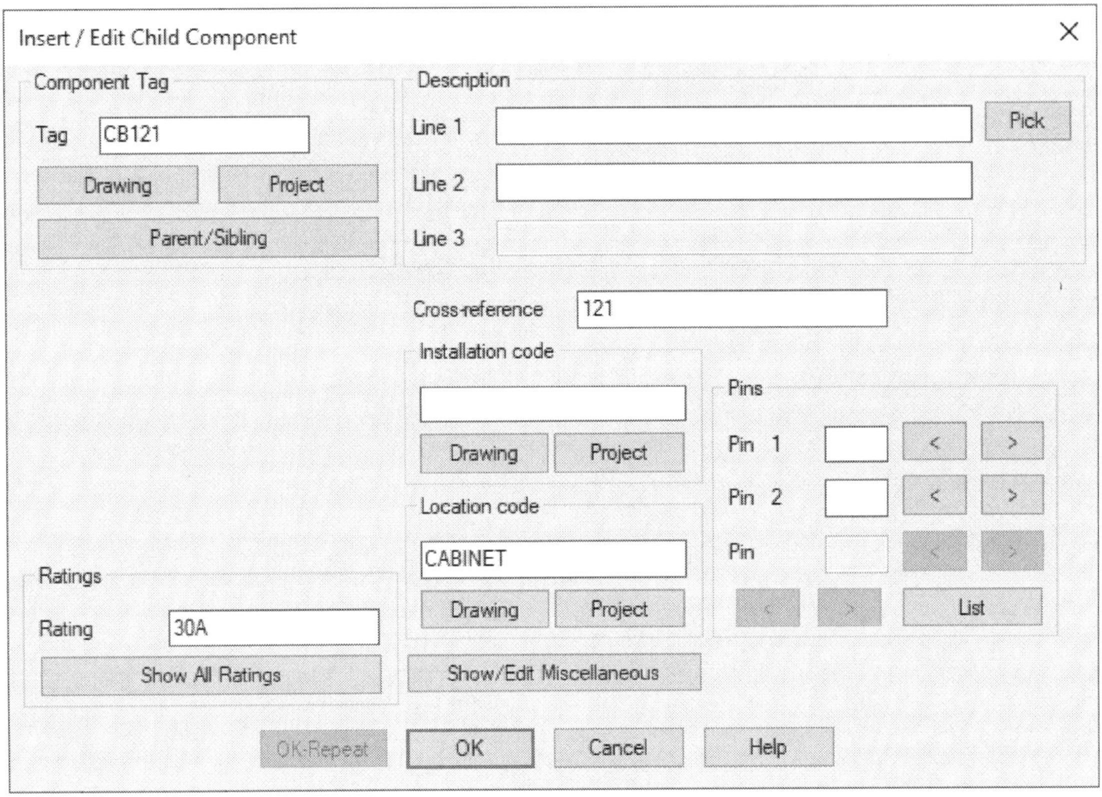

Figure 3–55

Component Tag	The component tag for a child component is initially populated with the family code of the component. The reference number is assigned based on the parent component to which the child is linked. You can type the component tag in the field or use one of the following selection methods: • **Drawing:** Displays a list of parent components from the same family located in the active drawing. • **Project:** Displays a list of parent components from the same family located in any drawing listed in the active project. • **Parent/Sibling:** Enables you to select the parent component or sibling component if they are in the same drawing.

Description	Enables you to enter a description of the component. These fields are automatically populated after selecting the parent component. You can also type the description.
Cross-reference	Automatically populated when the parent component is selected. You can also enter the cross-reference information.
Installation/ Location Codes	Automatically populated when the parent is selected. You can also enter the information.
Pins	If the pin list database is configured for the catalog number assigned to the parent, the pin numbers are automatically populated. Otherwise, you can assign pin numbers in the fields.
Ratings	Assign the rating value of the component. If the field is grayed out, the component does not have any rating attributes. A component can have up to 12 rating attributes.
Show/Edit Miscellaneous	Displays any attributes assigned to the component symbol that are not standard AutoCAD Electrical attributes.

- In the drawing, the parent contacts display only the cross-reference for those child contacts that are not directly linked to the parent. All the other child contacts are still counted and displayed in the cross-reference report.

How To: Insert a Child Component

1. Start the **Insert Component** command.
2. Select the component category.
3. In the submenu, select the child component to insert.

   Note: *Any component with* ***2nd +*** *in the name is a child component. However, note that not all child components have a* ***2nd +*** *in their names.*

4. In the drawing window, pick the location of the component. The *Insert / Edit Child Component* dialog box opens.
5. Edit the *Insert / Edit Child Component* dialog box.
6. Click **OK** to end the command or **OK-Repeat** to insert the same component again.

Practice 3d
Insert Component Symbols

Practice Objective

- Insert parent and child component symbols.

In this practice, you will work in two different drawings. You will first add a push button, then a relay and a contact. Next, you will open a different drawing in the project and add a second contact, referencing the contact in the first drawing. Finally, you will add a third contact, exceeding the maximum contacts for the relay, and receive a warning from the software. The final circuit is as shown in Figure 3–56.

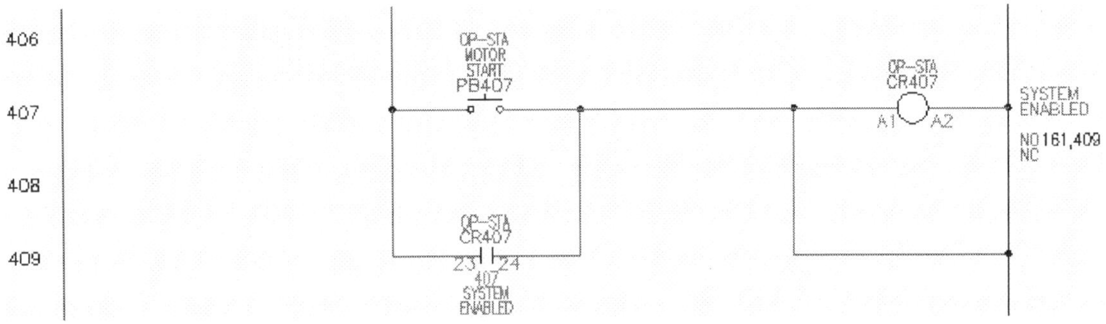

Figure 3–56

Task 1: Insert a standalone symbol.

1. If the **Module 03** project is not active, open and activate it now.
2. In the *Project Manager*, expand the drawing list and double-click on **Schematic Symbols.dwg** to open the Schematic Symbols drawing.
3. Zoom to the wires on lines 407 and 409.
4. In the *Schematic* tab>*Insert Components* panel, click (Icon Menu). The *Insert Component* dialog box opens.
5. To open the **Push Buttons** menu, click (Push Buttons).
6. To insert a Normally Open push button, click (Push Button NO).

7. Pick a point on the wire at line 407 to insert the push button, as shown in Figure 3–57.

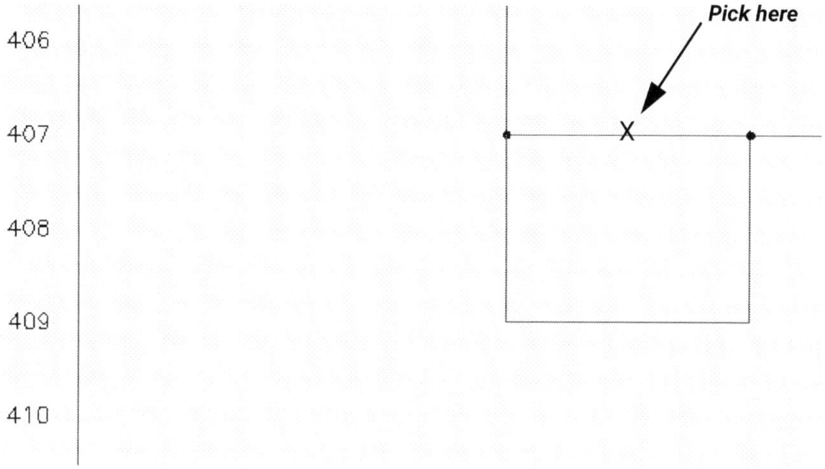

Figure 3–57

8. The *Insert / Edit Component* dialog box opens. Note that the Component Tag is assigned automatically, as shown in Figure 3–58.

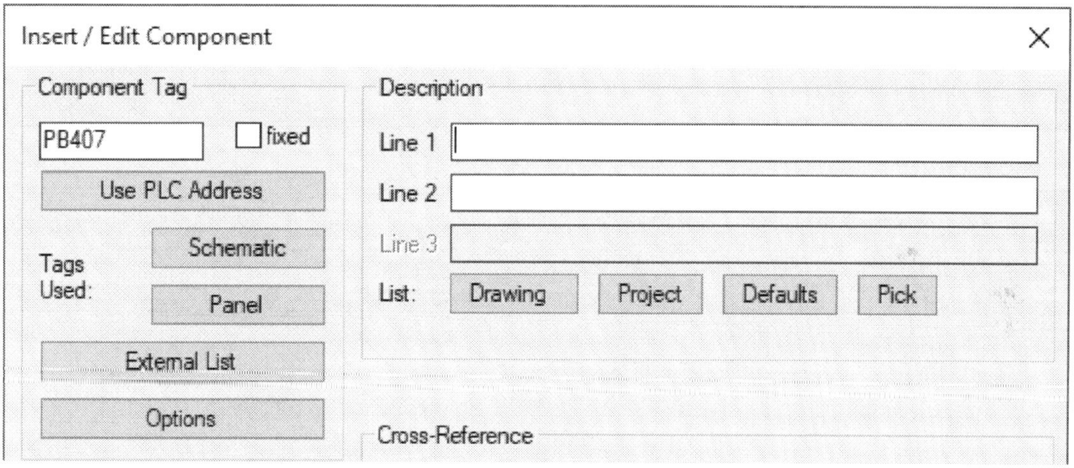

Figure 3–58

9. In the *Description* area, set the following:

   - *Line 1*: **motor**
   - *Line 2*: **start**

   The descriptions are automatically capitalized after you click in another field or press <Enter>.

10. In the *Insert / Edit Component* dialog box, in the *Catalog Data* area, click **Lookup** to open the Catalog Browser. In the *Search* edit box, type **SQD** and click . Note that the *MANUFACTURER* list only displays the items that are provided by this manufacturer. Select the *CATALOG* **KR1RH5**, and note that *TYPE* is set to **30.5mm FLUSH** and *STYLE* is set to **RED**, as shown in Figure 3–59. Click **OK**.

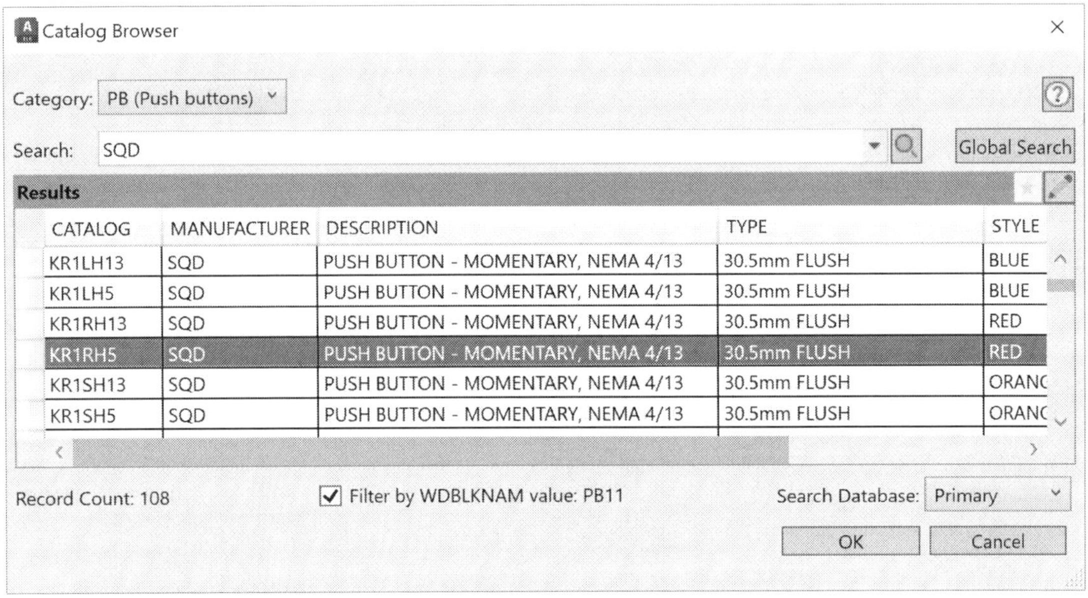

Figure 3–59

- The *Catalog Data* area of the *Insert / Edit Component* dialog box updates as shown in Figure 3–60.

11. In the *Insert / Edit Component* dialog box, in the *Location code* area, click **Project**. The *All Locations–Project* dialog box opens.
12. Select **OP-STA** and click **OK**. The *Location code* area of the *Insert / Edit Component* dialog box updates as shown in Figure 3–60. Click **OK** to insert the symbol.

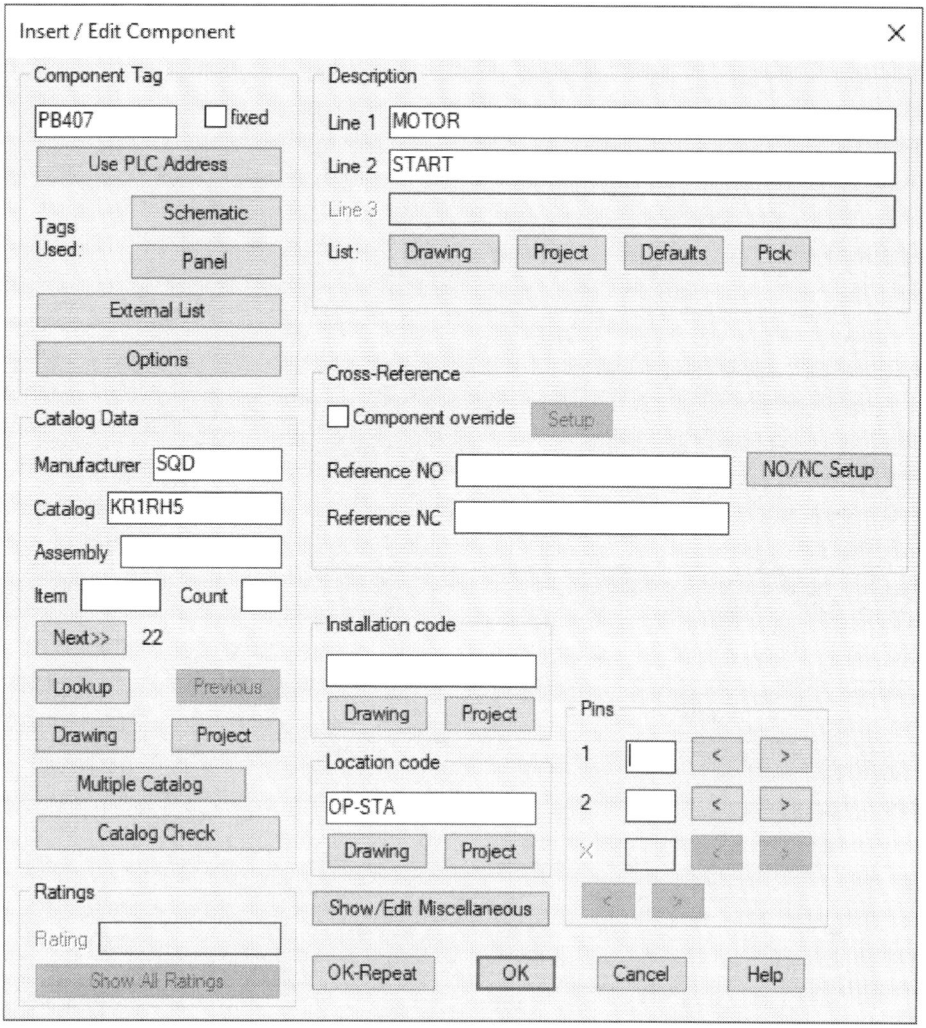

Figure 3–60

13. If the *Assign Symbol to Catalog Number* dialog box opens indicating that the selected symbol needs to be mapped, select **Map symbol to catalog number**. If the symbol has been already mapped, this dialog box does not open.

Task 2: Insert a parent symbol.

1. Click  (Icon Menu). The *Insert Component* dialog box opens.

2. Click  (Relays/Contacts) to insert the relay coil. Click  (Relay Coil) to insert a relay coil.

3. Pick a point on the wire at line 407 to insert the relay coil, as shown in Figure 3–61.

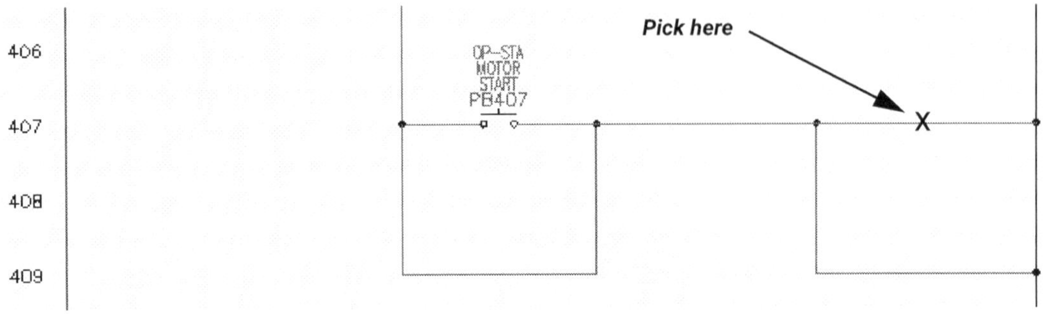

Figure 3–61

4. The *Insert / Edit* Component dialog box opens. In the *Description* area, click **Defaults** to open the *Descriptions (general)* dialog box. In the G*eneric descriptions* list, select **SYSTEM|ENABLED** and click **OK**. Note that the *Description* area updates with the selected descriptions.
5. In the *Catalog Data* area, click **Lookup** to open the Catalog Browser. In the *Search* edit box, type **SQD** and click  to search for items by this manufacturer. Select the **CATALOG** title and select the upward facing arrow to reverse the display list. For *CATALOG*, select **8501XO20V02**, as shown in Figure 3–62. Note that it has a **TYPE X, 120VAC** coil, and that this relay only has **2 NO (convertible)** contacts. Click **OK**.

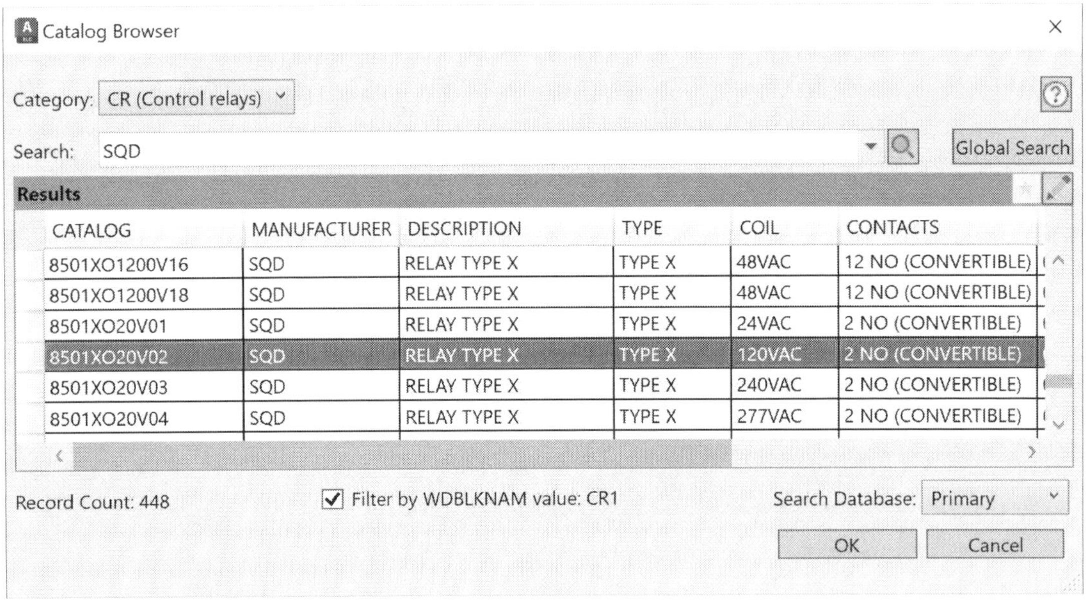

Figure 3–62

6. In the *Insert / Edit Component* dialog box, in the *Location code* area, click **Project**. The *All Locations–Project* dialog box opens. Select **OP-STA** and click **OK**. The *Insert / Edit Component* dialog box updates, as shown in Figure 3–63. Click **OK**.

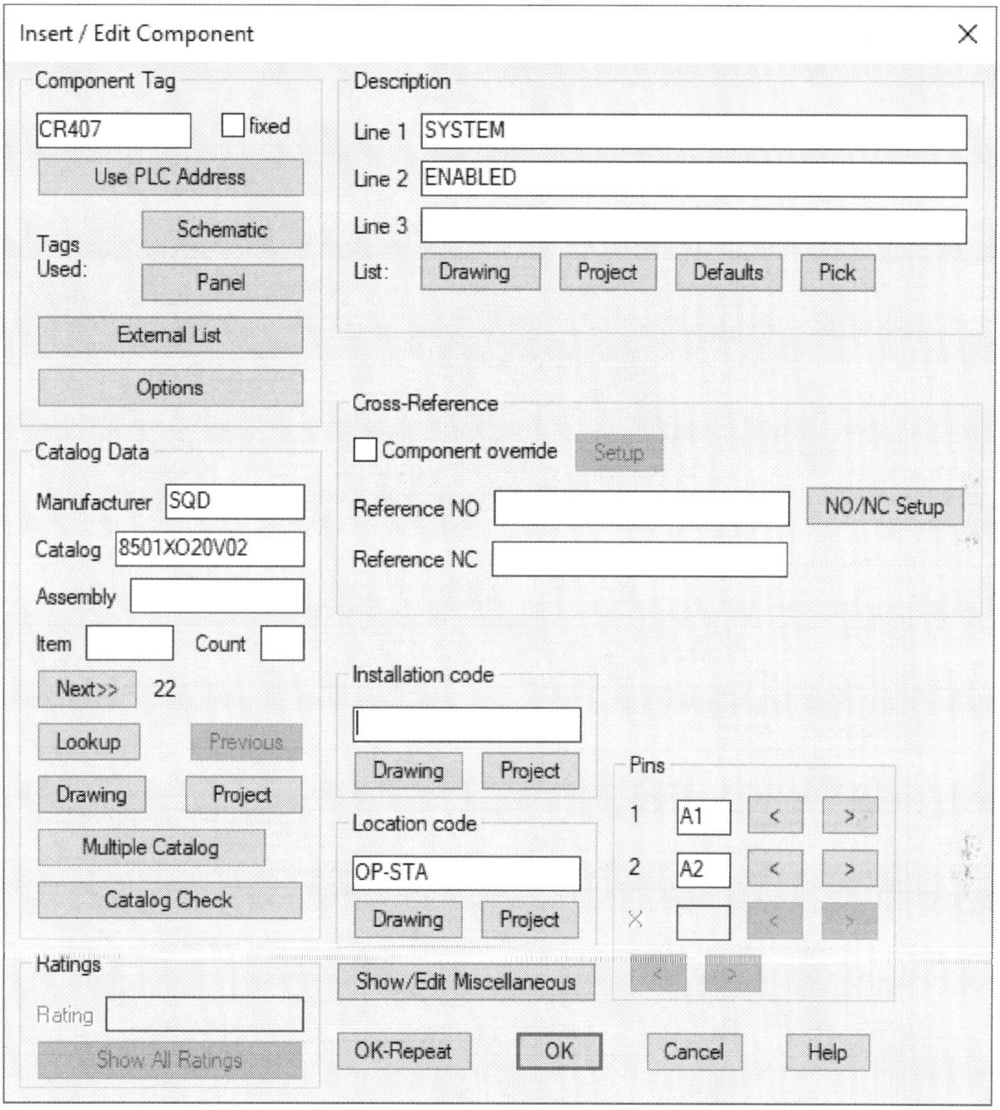

Figure 3–63

7. If the *Assign Symbol to Catalog Number* dialog box opens indicating that the selected symbol needs to be mapped, select **Map symbol to catalog number**.

Task 3: Insert child symbols.

1. Click (Icon Menu). Click (Relays / Contacts) to open the **Relays and Contacts** submenu. Click (Relay NO Contact) to insert a Normally Open (N.O.) contact.
2. Pick a point on the wire at line 409, as shown in Figure 3–64, to insert the contact. The *Insert / Edit Child Component* dialog box opens.

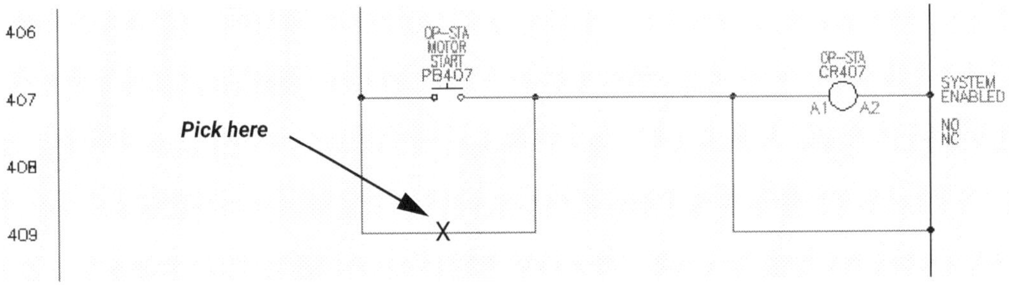

Figure 3–64

3. Click **Parent/Sibling**. Select component **CR407** to establish a parent/child relationship between the relay and contact. The dialog box is filled out based on the information from CR407. Click **OK**.

   Note: *You might need to map the symbol to the catalog number.*

4. In the **Module 03** project, open **Power.dwg**.
5. Zoom in to line 161 and click (Icon Menu). Click (Relays/Contacts) and then (Relay NO Contact) to insert a Normally Open contact. Pick a point on line 161, as shown in Figure 3–65. The *Insert / Edit Child Component* dialog box opens.

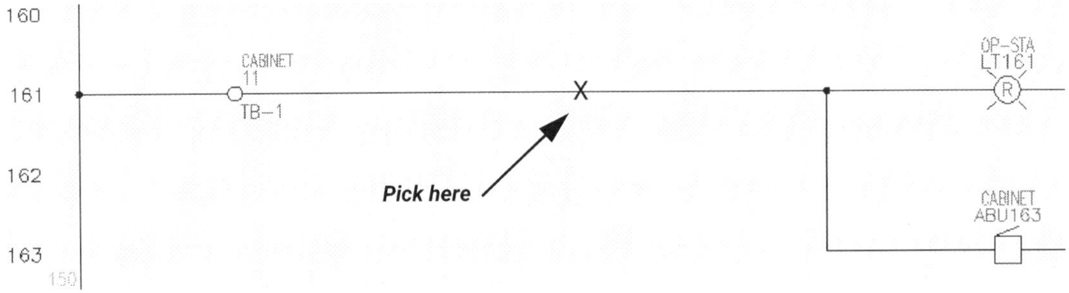

Figure 3–65

6. In the *Component Tag* area, click **Project** to open the *Complete Project list for FAMILY="CR"* dialog box. Select **CR407**, as shown in Figure 3–66. Click **OK**.

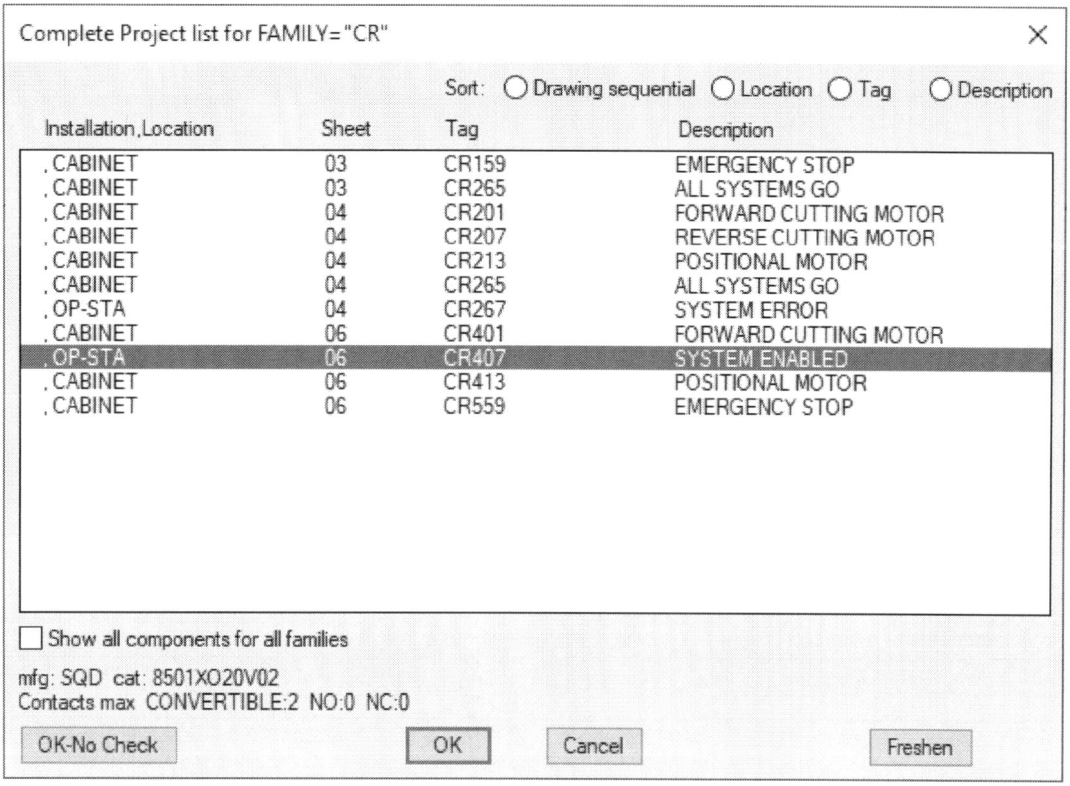

Figure 3–66

Note: *You might need to map the symbol to the catalog number.*

7. Click **OK** to close the *Insert / Edit Child Component* dialog box. The contact is now linked to the relay that was inserted into **Schematic Symbols.dwg**.

8. Open **Schematic Symbols.dwg**. Zoom to CR407. The NO references, next to the schematic symbol, have updated to display both contact line references (161 and 409).

9. Click (Icon Menu). In the *Recently Used* area, click (Relay NO Contact) to insert a Normally Open contact. Select a point on line 407, as shown in Figure 3–67. The *Insert / Edit Child Component* dialog box opens.

   - You can also use the regular method of selection by clicking (Relays/Contacts) and then clicking (Relay NO Contact).

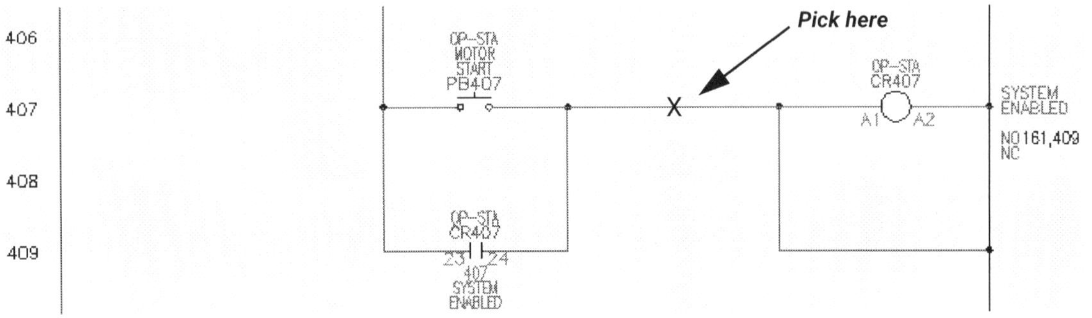

Figure 3–67

10. In the *Component Tag* area, click **Project** to open the *Complete Project list for FAMILY="CR"* dialog box. Select **CR407** and click **OK**. The *Alert: Too many contact references* dialog box opens, as shown in Figure 3–68. This is because the relay you inserted only has 2 available contacts and this is the third contact you are trying to attach to the relay.

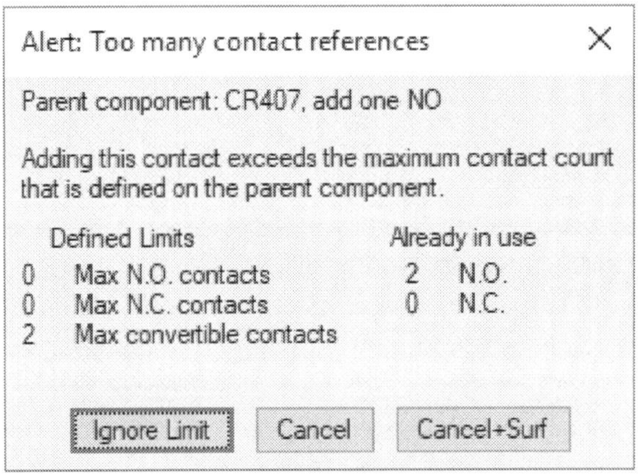

Figure 3–68

11. Click **Cancel** to cancel inserting the contact.

12. Save and close **Schematic Symbols.dwg** and any other drawing that is open.

End of practice

Chapter Review Questions

1. What information does the **Revise Ladder** command control? (Select all that apply.)
   a. Rung Count
   b. Ladder direction
   c. Ladder wire type
   d. Reference Start

2. To create wire types, use the **Create/Edit Wire Type** command to designate layers as wire layers.
   a. True
   b. False

3. Using the **Insert Wire Numbers** command, how do you add wire numbers to all wires in the active drawing?
   a. Click **All-Wires**.
   b. Click **Drawing-wide**.
   c. Click **Project-wide**.
   d. Click **Setup**.

4. How many destination signal arrows can be linked to one source signal arrow?
   a. One
   b. Two
   c. Based on the number of pins on the source signal arrow
   d. Unlimited

5. How many source signal arrows can be linked to one destination signal arrow?
   a. One
   b. Two
   c. Based on the number of pins on the destination signal arrow
   d. Unlimited

6. A parent symbol and a child symbol have different *Insert / Edit* dialog boxes.

a. True

b. False

Command Summary

Button	Command	Location
	**Add Rung**	• **Ribbon:** *Schematic* tab>*Edit Wires/Wire Numbers* panel
	**Catalog Browser**	• **Ribbon:** *Schematic* tab>*Insert Components* panel>*Icon Menu* drop-down list
	**Change/Convert Wire Type**	• **Ribbon:** *Schematic* tab>*Edit Wires/Wire Numbers* panel
	**Copy Wire Numbers**	• **Ribbon:** *Schematic* tab>*Edit Wires/Wire Numbers* panel
	**Create/Edit Wire Type**	• **Ribbon:** *Schematic* tab>*Edit Wires/Wire Numbers* panel
	**Destination Arrow**	• **Ribbon:** *Schematic* tab>*Insert Wires/Wire Numbers* panel
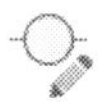	**Edit Component**	• **Ribbon:** *Schematic* tab>*Edit Components* panel
	**Edit Wire Numbers**	• **Ribbon:** *Schematic* tab>*Edit Wires/Wire Numbers* panel
	**Icon Menu**	• **Ribbon:** *Schematic* tab>*Insert Components* panel
	**Insert Ladder**	• **Ribbon:** *Schematic* tab>*Insert Wires/Wire Numbers* panel
	**Insert Wire**	• **Ribbon:** *Schematic* tab>*Insert Wires/Wire Numbers* panel
	**Insert Wire Numbers**	• **Ribbon:** *Schematic* tab>*Insert Wires/Wire Numbers* panel
	**Move Wire Number**	• **Ribbon:** *Schematic* tab>*Edit Wires/Wire Numbers* panel
	**Multiple Wire Bus**	• **Ribbon:** *Schematic* tab>*Insert Wires/Wire Numbers* panel
	**Revise Ladder**	• **Ribbon:** *Schematic* tab>*Edit Wires/Wire Numbers* panel
	**Scoot**	• **Ribbon:** *Schematic* tab>*Edit Components* panel

Button	Command	Location
	**Source Arrow**	• **Ribbon:** *Schematic* tab>*Insert Wires/Wire Numbers* panel
	**Stretch Wire**	• **Ribbon:** *Schematic* tab>*Edit Wires/Wire Numbers* panel
	**Trim Wire**	• **Ribbon:** *Schematic* tab>*Edit Wires/Wire Numbers* panel
	**Wire Leaders**	• **Ribbon:** *Schematic* tab>*Insert Wires/Wire Numbers* panel

Chapter 4

Schematics II - Multiwire and Circuits

The AutoCAD® Electrical software includes options for automating the process of building 3-phase circuits by adding a 3-phase ladder, components, multiwires, and wire numberings using single relevant commands. Knowledge of these commands saves time during the design process. Learning to save user-defined circuits for reuse at a later stage also improves efficiency.

Learning Objectives

- Create a smart line between multicontact components.
- Insert a 3-phase ladder and several wires at the same time.
- Insert a 3-phase component and set up 3-phase wire numbers.
- Insert cable markers, already saved circuits, and groups of wires.
- Save a circuit as an icon and as a .DWG file.
- Copy, paste, and move circuits.
- Copy, cut, and paste components and wires using the circuit clipboard.
- Build a circuit based on information selected in a list.

4.1 Dashed Link Lines

When creating stacked contacts for a multicontact component, the **Link Components with Dashed Line** command draws a smart line between components, as shown in Figure 4–1. The command thus creates cross-reference link for contacts and also hides attributes on the child component. This is used when creating stacked symbols, such as a selector switch. To build a selector switch, you insert the parent symbol, and then the child symbols, and finally link them together using the **Link Components with Dashed Line** command.

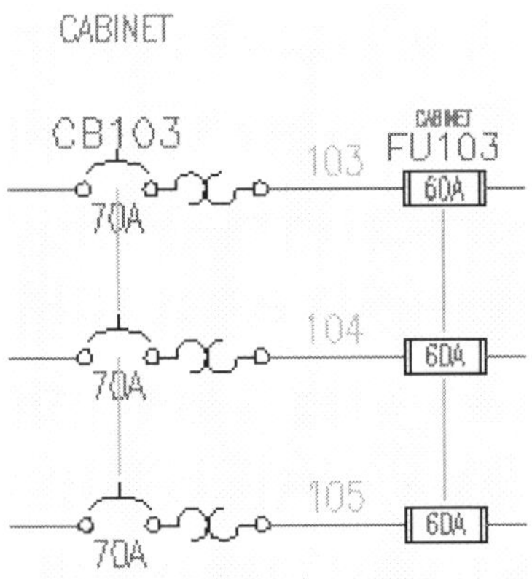

Figure 4–1

Link Components with Dashed Line

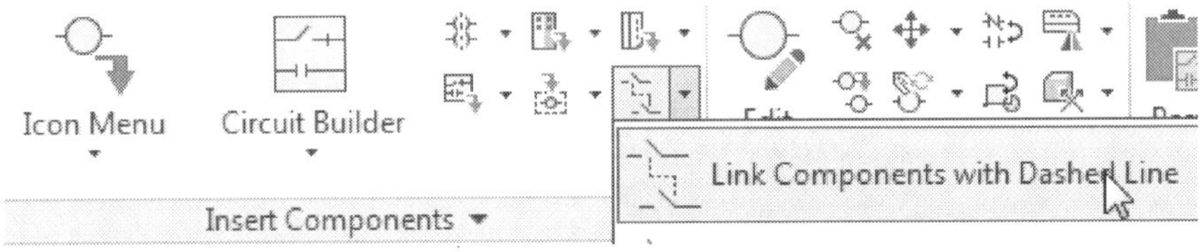

Ribbon: *Schematic* tab>*Insert Components* panel

Command Prompt: aelink

How To: Insert a Dashed Link Line

1. Start the **Link Components with Dashed Line** command.
2. Select the master component.
3. Select the child component.
4. Right-click or press <Enter> to end the command.

Practice 4a
Dashed Link Lines

Practice Objective

- Construct a 3-phase symbol by linking individual symbols.

In this practice, you will build a selector switch symbol using the **Link Components with Dashed Line** command. You will first add the individual symbols that compose the selector switch, and then link the symbols with a dashed link line. The final circuit displays as shown in Figure 4–2.

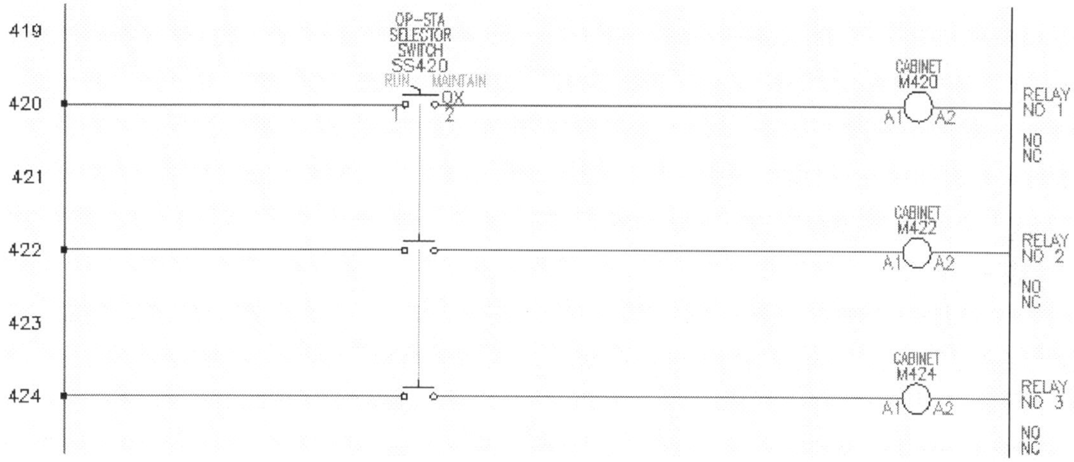

Figure 4–2

1. In the *Module 04* folder from your practice files folder, open and activate **Module 04** project file.
2. In the *Project Manager*, expand the **Module 04** project and double-click on **Schematic Symbols.dwg** to open it.
3. Zoom to lines 420 to 424.
4. In the *Schematic* tab>*Insert Components* panel, click  (Icon Menu). In the *Insert Component* dialog box, click  (Selector Switches) to open the **Selector Switches** menu. Click 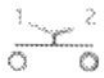 (2 Position Maintain, NO) to insert a 2 Position Maintain, N.O. selector switch.

5. Pick a point near the middle of the wire on line 420, as shown in Figure 4–3.

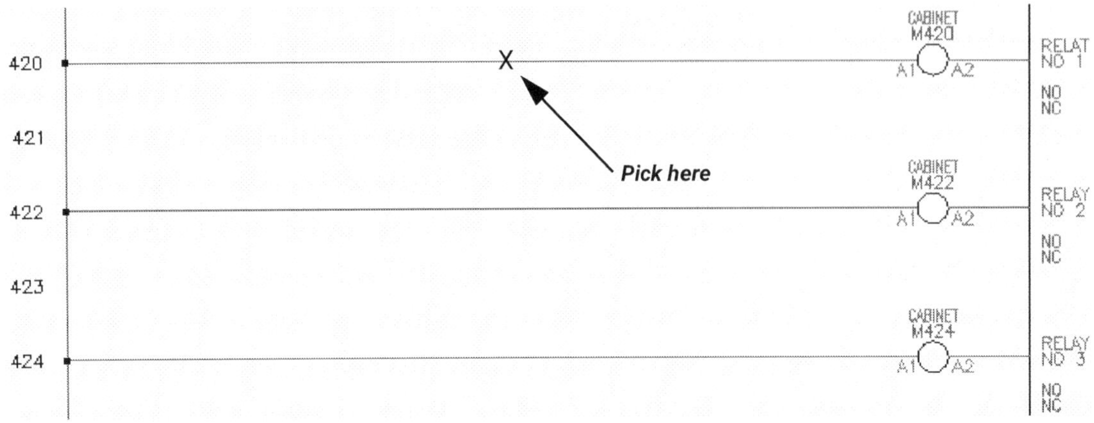

Figure 4–3

6. In the *Insert / Edit Component* dialog box that opens, set the following for the *Description*:
   - *Line 1*: **SELECTOR**
   - *Line 2*: **SWITCH**
7. In the *Catalog Data* area, click **Lookup** to open the Catalog Browser. In the *Search* field, type **800T-H** and search. Clear the **Filter by WDBLKNAM value:** option near the bottom of the Catalog Browser, if required.
8. Select **800T-H2A2** in the Results list, as shown in Figure 4–4. Note that it displays the following values:
   - *MANUFACTURER*: **AB**
   - *TYPE:* **30.5mm**
   - *STYLE*: **KNOB - WHITE INSERT**

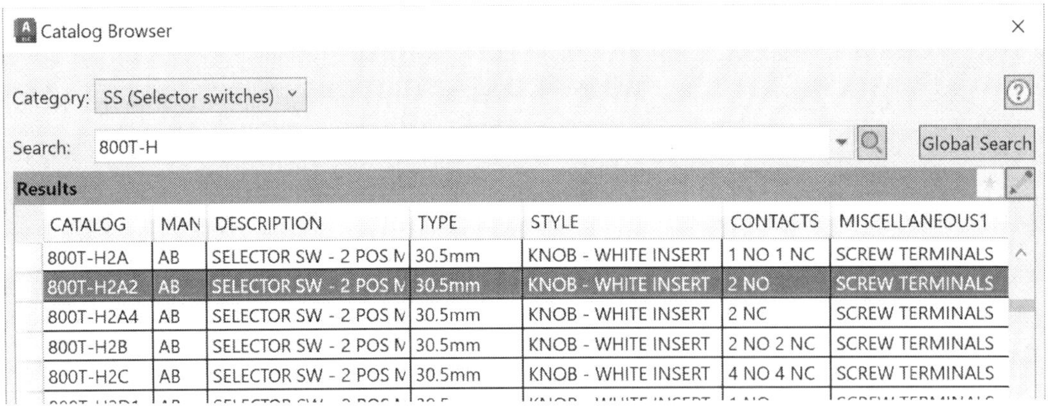

Figure 4–4

9. Click **OK**.
10. In the *Insert / Edit Component* dialog box, in the *Location code* area, click **Project**. The *All Locations–Project* dialog box opens. Select **OP-STA**, click **OK.**
11. In the *Insert / Edit Component* dialog box, set the following, as shown in Figure 4–5:
    - In the *Pins* area, *for Pin 1*, type **1**.
    - In the *Pins* area, *for Pin 2*, type **2**.
    - In the *Switch Position* area, *for Position 1*, type **RUN**.
    - In the *Switch Position* area, for *Position 2*, type **MAINTAIN**.

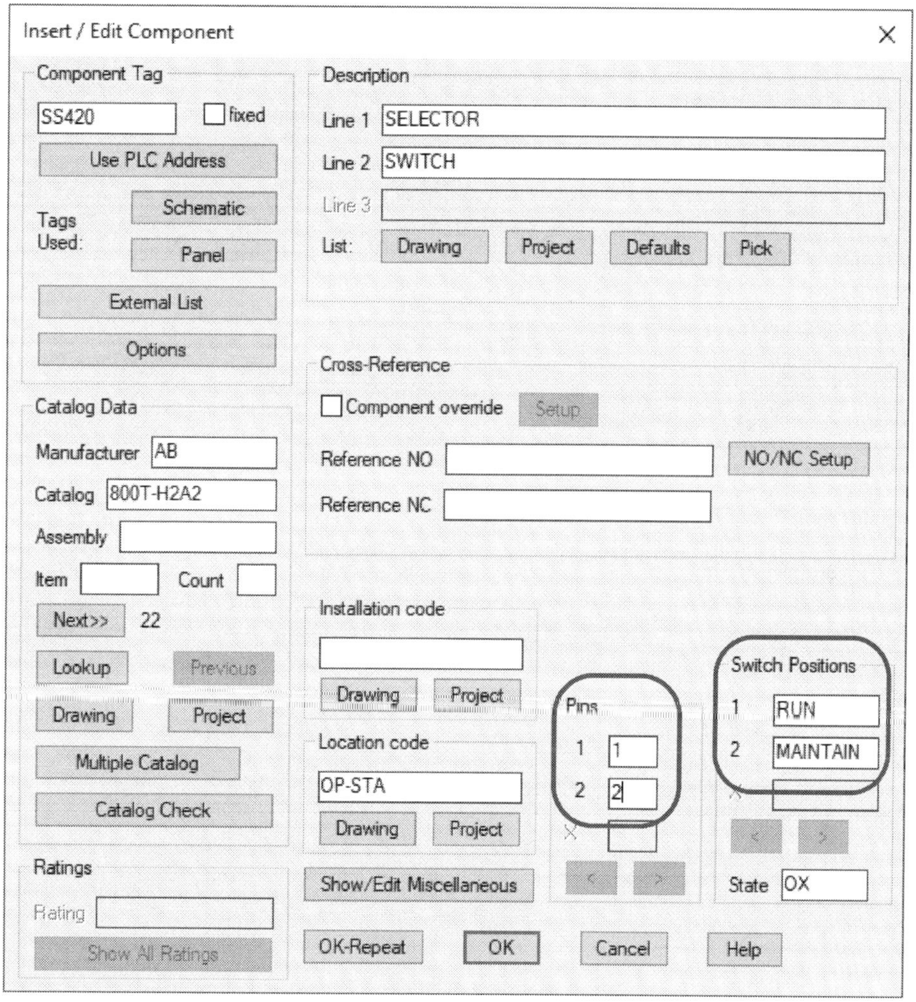

Figure 4–5

12. Click **OK**.

13. In the *Schematic* tab>*Insert Components* panel, click (Icon Menu). Click (Selector Switches) to open the **Selector Switches** menu. Click (2nd+ NO Contact) to insert a 2nd+ N.O. contact. Pick a point near the middle of the wire on line 422, directly below the switch you just inserted, as shown in Figure 4–6. The *Insert / Edit Child Component* dialog box opens.

Note: *You do not have to place the new switch exactly in line with the first switch. You will align the switches later.*

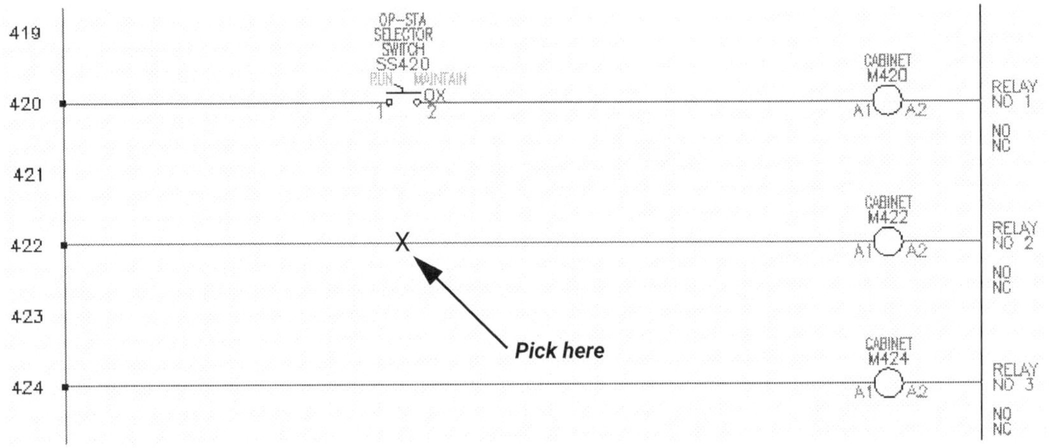

Figure 4–6

14. Click **Parent/Sibling** and pick the selector switch that you first inserted (SS420) on line 420. The dialog box is populated with the information from the parent symbol. Click **OK**.

15. Click (Icon Menu) and click (Selector Switches) again. Click (2nd+ NO Contact) to insert another 2nd+ N.O. contact. Pick a point near the middle of the wire on line 424, directly below the switch you just inserted, as shown in Figure 4–7. The *Insert / Edit Child Component* dialog box opens.

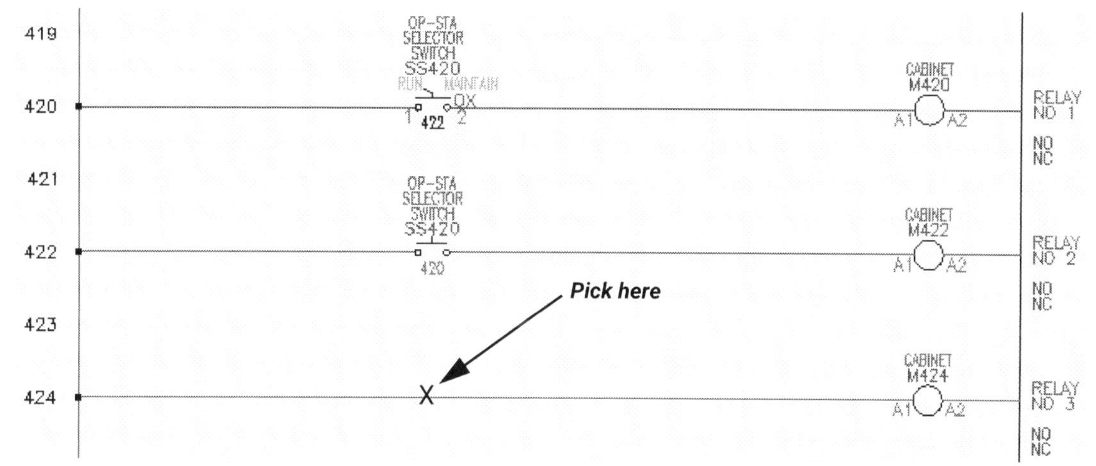

Figure 4–7

16. Click **Parent/Sibling** and click on the parent selector switch SS420 that you inserted on line 420. The dialog box is populated with the information from the parent symbol. Click **OK**.
17. If the selector switches are not placed in a straight line, align them first. In the *Schematic* tab>*Edit Components* panel, click (Align) (located in the (Scoot) drop-down list). Select the parent switch on line 420. A blue vertical line displays passing through the selected component. Select the switches on lines 422 and 424. Press <Enter> to exit the command and note that the switches are vertically placed in a straight line.
18. In the *Schematic* tab>*Insert Components* panel, click (Link Components with Dashed Line).
19. Select the selector switch on line 420 as the component from which to link.
20. Select the child selector switch on line 422 and then select the switch on line 424. Press <Enter>. Note that a link line is created between the three selected switches.
    - Using the Layer properties, you can set the linetype style as dashed for the link line.
21. Save **Schematic Symbols.dwg**.

End of practice

4.2 3-Phase Ladders

The AutoCAD Electrical software includes options for automating the process of building 3-phase circuits including a 3-phase ladder, as shown in Figure 4–8.

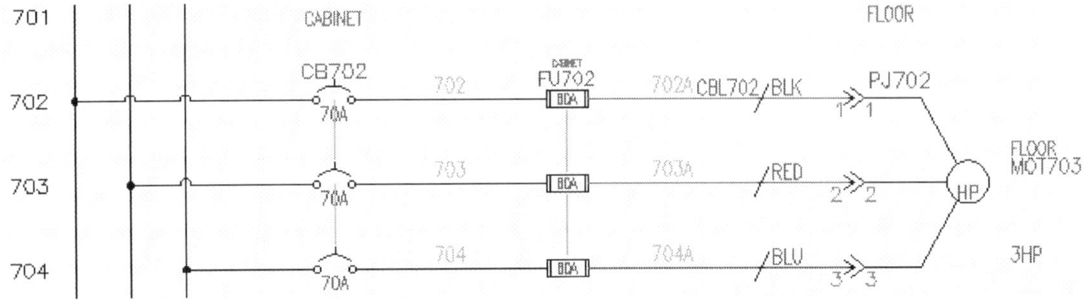

Figure 4–8

Insert Ladder

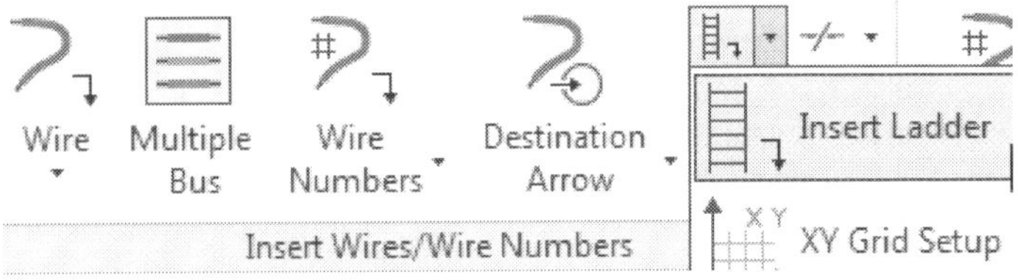

Ribbon: *Schematic* tab>*Insert Wires/Wire Numbers* panel

Command Prompt: aeladder

How To: Create a 3-Phase Ladder

1. Start the **Insert Ladder** command. The *Insert Ladder* dialog box opens.
2. In the *Insert Ladder* dialog box, in the *Phase* area, select **3 Phase**.
3. In the *Spacing* field, specify the distance between the wires in the ladder.
4. Fill in the other options, as required.
5. Click **OK**.
6. Pick the start point of the ladder.
7. If the length or number of rungs was not specified, pick the end point of the ladder.

- When you select the **3 Phase** option, the *Width* and *Draw Rungs* areas are not available in the *Insert Ladder* dialog box, as shown in Figure 4–9. Instead, the **Spacing** option in the *Phase* area becomes available, which controls the distance between the wires of the 3-phase ladder.

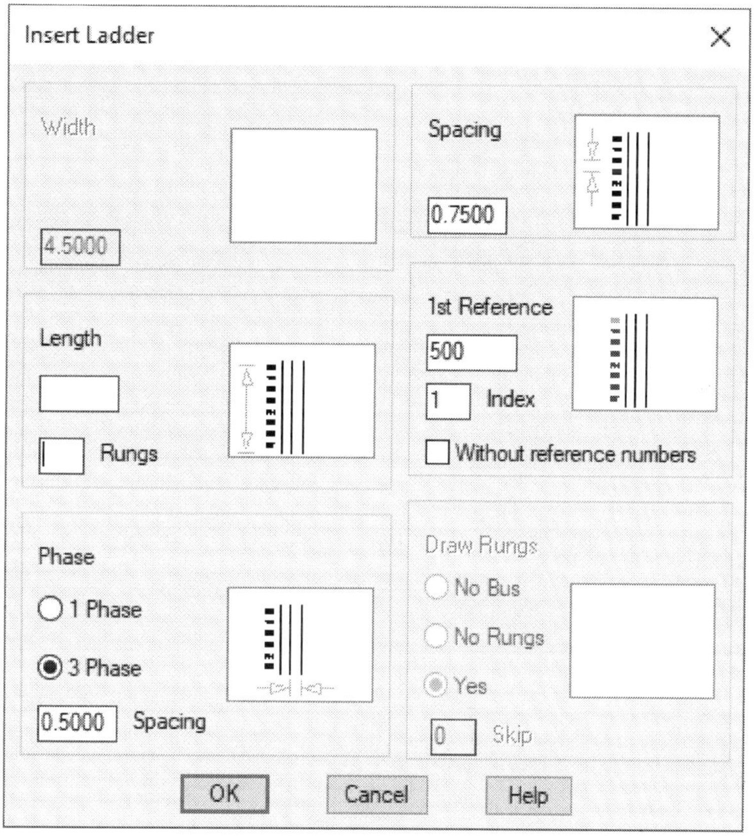

Figure 4–9

- A 3-phase ladder consists of reference numbers similar to a single phase ladder and 3 rails or wires. When inserting a 3-phase ladder, you can specify the length of the ladder, the number of rungs, or pick the approximate length in the drawing window.

4.3 Multiple Wire Bus

Inserting several wires in one command can be very useful when creating 3-phase circuits (as shown in Figure 4–10) and in point to point type drawings.

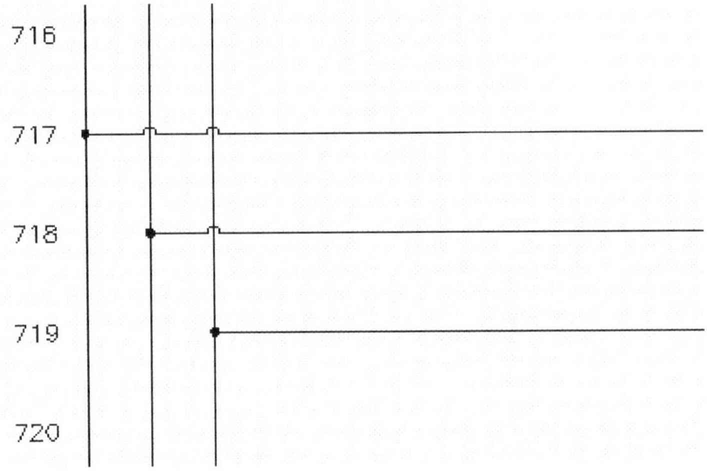

Figure 4–10

Multiple Wire Bus

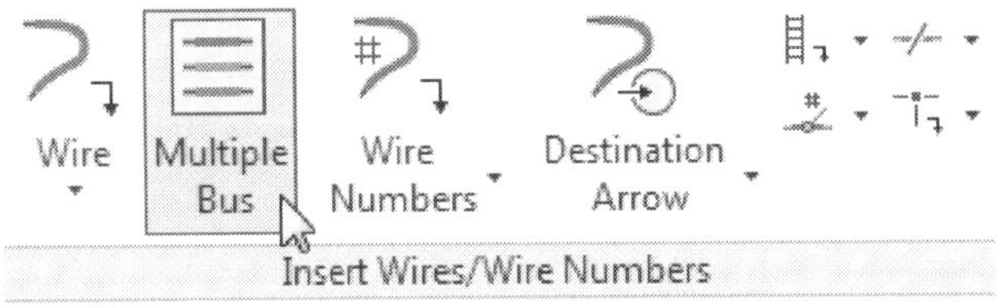

Ribbon: *Schematic* tab>*Insert Wires/Wire Numbers* panel

Command Prompt: aemultibus

How To: Insert a Multiple Wire Bus

1. Start the **Multiple Bus** command.
2. In the *Multiple wire Bus* dialog box, in the *Horizontal* and *Vertical* areas, specify the wire spacing.
3. Select the **Starting at** method of inserting the wires.
4. Specify the number of wires to insert, (not used with the **Component (Multiple Wires)** method).

5. Click **OK**.
6. Pick the start point for the wires or crossing window, depending on the method of insertion.
7. Pick the end point on the wires or the crossing window, depending on the method of insertion.
    - When prompted for the first point, type **T** to change the wire type.
    - To create multiple bends in a Multiple Wire Bus, use **Continue (C)** when placing the network.
    - When inserting wires, you can add a 90 degree bend by selecting a point above or below when the green arrows display, as shown in Figure 4–11.

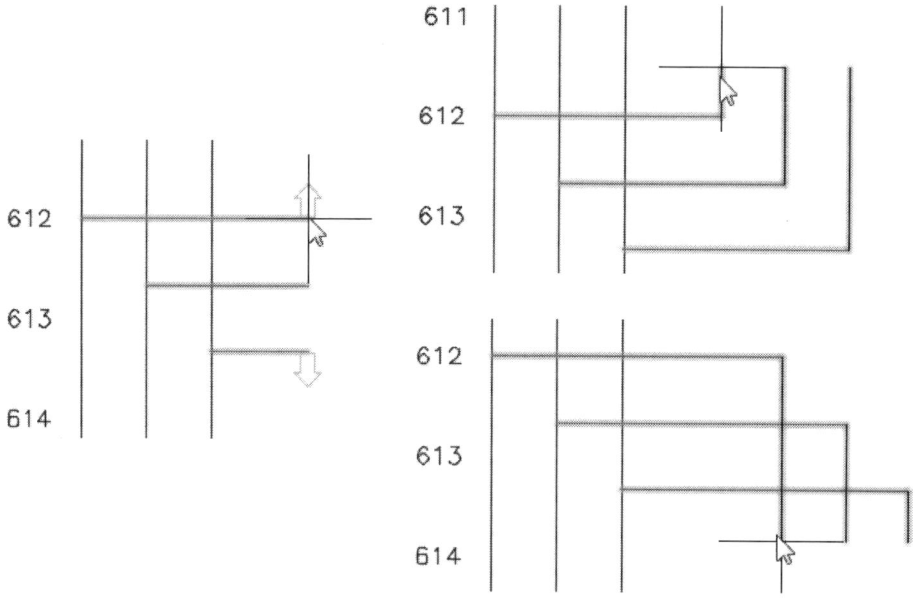

Figure 4–11

- To flip on a bend, use **Flip (F)** when placing the network, as shown in Figure 4–12.

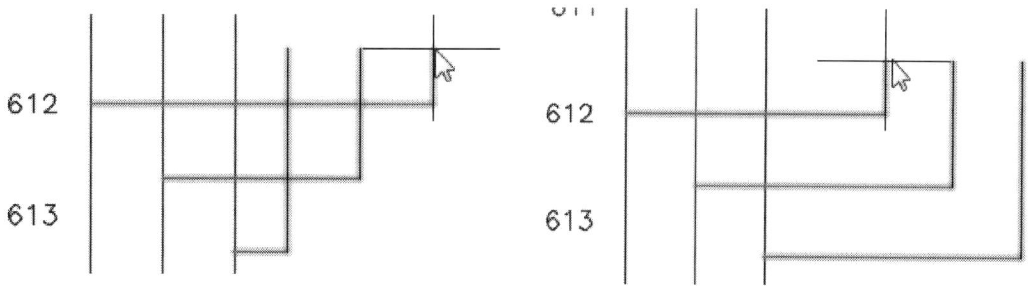

Figure 4–12

The *Multiple Wire Bus* dialog box (shown in Figure 4–13) controls various settings for multiple wire insertion.

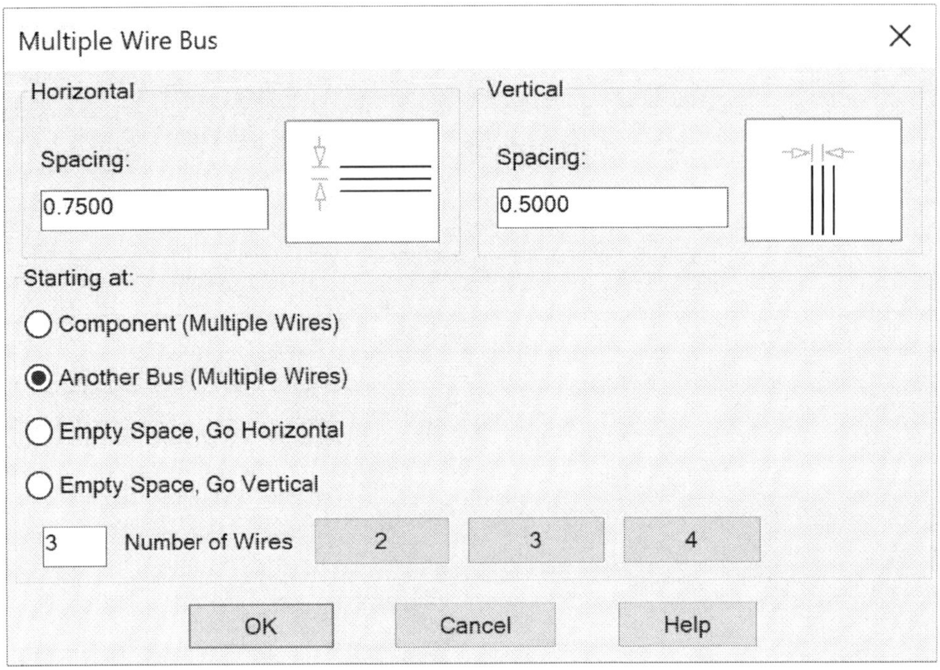

Figure 4–13

Horizontal	Controls the horizontal spacing between wires.
Vertical	Controls the vertical spacing between wires.
Starting at	Specify where you want to start the wires. • **Component (Multiple Wires):** Wires start at an existing component. Select the component's connection points using a crossing window. • **Another Bus (Multiple Wires):** Wires start on an existing bus or group of wires. The first wire of the new bus connects to your first selection. The additional wires of the bus are created as you cross the cursor over other wires. If there are more new wires than existing wires, the extra wires are added to the first wire. • **Empty Space, Go Horizontal:** Starts a horizontal bus from the point you pick. • **Empty Space, Go Vertical:** Starts a vertical bus from the point you pick. • **Number of Wires:** Specifies the number of wires to insert. There are shortcut buttons for 2, 3, or 4 wires, but you can enter any value in the dialog box.

4.4 3-Phase Components

3-phase components (as shown in Figure 4–14) are similar to single phase components and are defined as AutoCAD® blocks with attributes. 3-phase components automatically insert the second and third components on the next available wires and connect them with dashed link lines.

- Horizontal components insert symbols from top to bottom.
- Vertical components insert symbols from left to right.

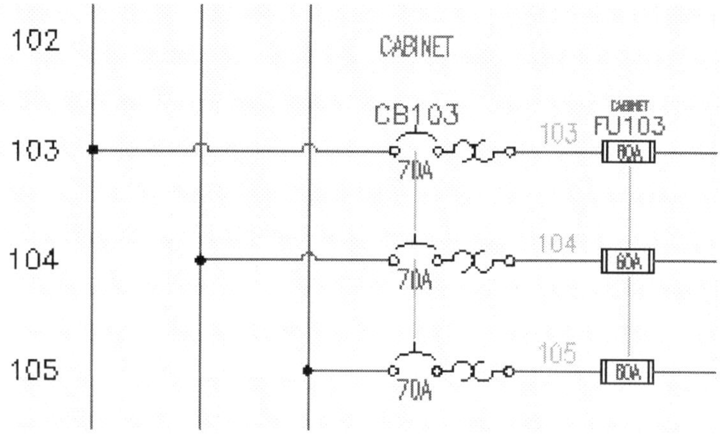

Figure 4–14

How To: Insert a 3-Phase Component

1. Start the **Insert Component** command.
2. Select the component category.
3. Select the 3-phase component to insert.
4. In the drawing window, pick the location of the component.
5. Select whether to build the component up or down.
6. Populate the *Insert / Edit Component* dialog box.
7. Click **OK** to complete the command or **OK-Repeat** to insert the same component again.

- Some components, such as 3-Phase Motors, automatically bend wires to their connection points. This might create wires that are not connected, requiring you to manually place a wire on the motor.

4.5 3-Phase Wire Numbering

You can add custom wire numbers to 3-phase circuits, as shown in Figure 4–15.

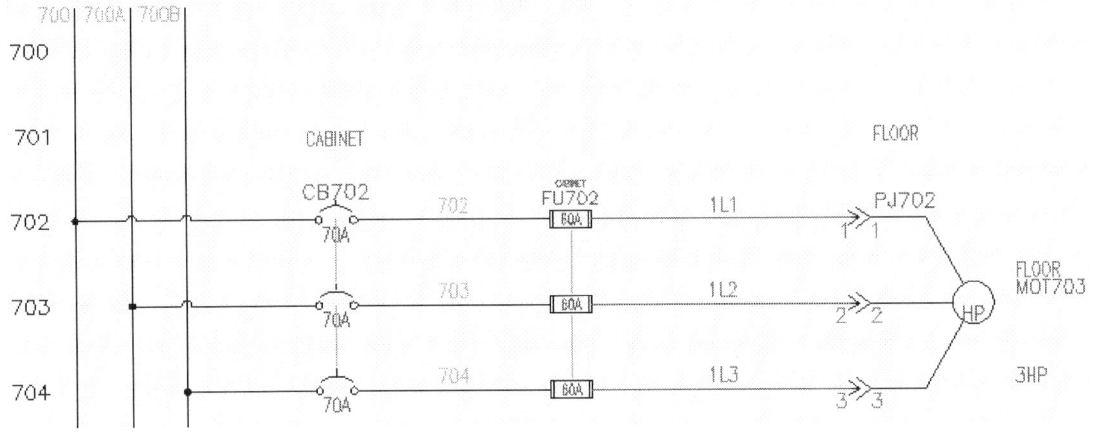

Figure 4–15

3 Phase Wire Numbers

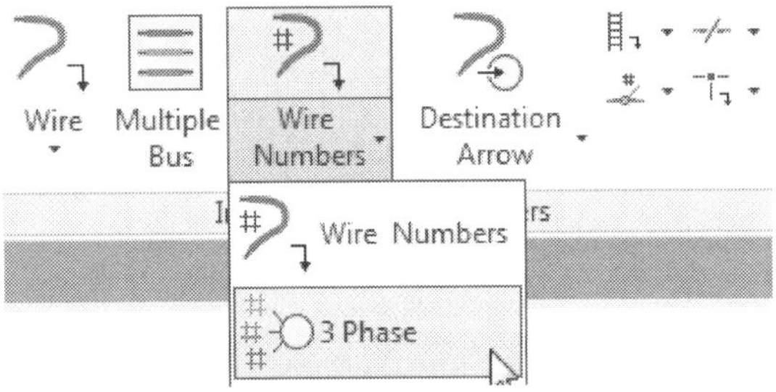

Ribbon: *Schematic* tab>*Insert Wires/Wire Numbers* panel

Command Prompt: ae3phasewireno

How To: Insert 3 Phase Wire Numbers

1. Start the **3 Phase Wire Numbers** command.
2. In the dialog box, specify the *Prefix*, *Base*, *Suffix*, and *Maximum* values. Verify the format in the *Wire Numbers* area.
3. Click **OK**.
4. Pick the wires to which to add wire numbers.

5. Change the properties for the next set of wire numbers.
6. Click **OK** to continue or **Cancel** to end the command.

- When picking wires, you can use the **Fence** option to select several wires at once.
- The 3-phase wire numbers are inserted as fixed wire numbers. They are not updated if the **Automatic Wire Number** command is used.
- You can add to the default prefix and suffix list by creating a text file and naming it **<projectname>.3ph** or **default.3ph**.

The *3 Phase Wire Numbering* dialog box (shown in Figure 4–16) contains various settings for 3-phase wire numbers.

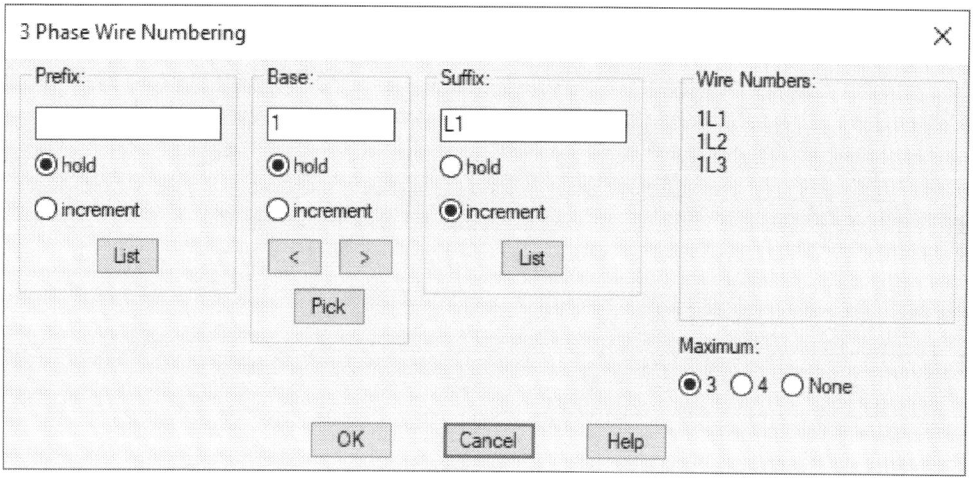

Figure 4–16

Prefix	Specify a prefix value for the wire numbers.
Base	Specify the base number for the wire numbers.
Suffix	Specify a suffix value for the wire numbers.
Wire Numbers	Displays a preview of wire numbers to be inserted.
Maximum	Specify the maximum number of wire numbers.

- **Increment:** Increments the last digit for each wire number.
- **Hold:** Keeps the prefix constant for all wire numbers.
- **Pick:** Enables you to pick an existing wire number and use its base value.
- **List:** Displays a pick list of default wire numbers.

Practice 4b
3-Phase Circuit

Practice Objective

- Build a 3-phase circuit.

In this practice, you will create a new drawing and build a 3-phase circuit, as shown in Figure 4–17. You will create a 3-phase bus and wire network. You will also insert various 3-pole component symbols and 3-phase wire numbers.

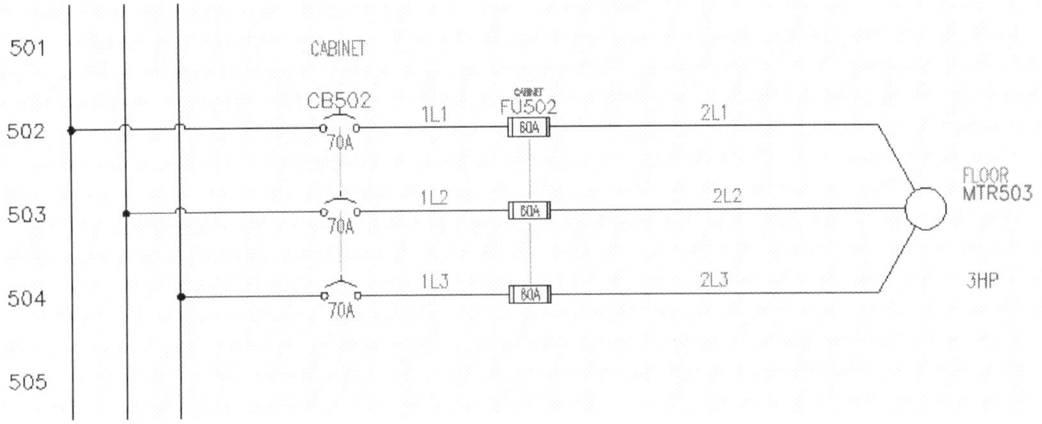

Figure 4–17

Task 1: Insert a 3-phase ladder and wires.

1. If the **Module 04** project is not active, open and activate it now.

2. In the *Project Manager* toolbar, click (New Drawing). You must have a drawing open for this command to be active.

3. In the *Create New Drawing* dialog box, verify that *Template* is set to **Electrical_template.dwt** in your practice files folder. Continue by setting the following, as shown in Figure 4–18:

   - *Name*: **3 Phase**
   - *Description 1*: **3 Phase Wiring**

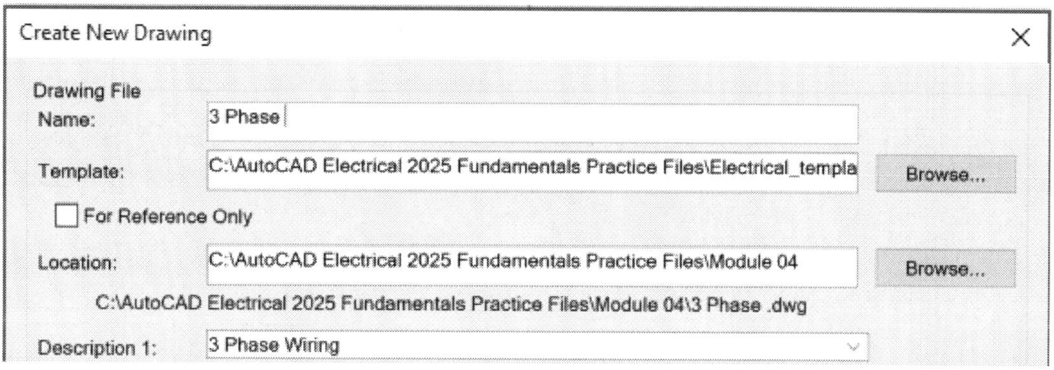

Figure 4–18

4. Click **OK**.
5. In the *Apply Project Defaults to Drawing Settings* dialog box, click **Yes**. The new **3 Phase.dwg** drawing opens.
6. In the *Schematic* tab>*Insert Wires/Wire Numbers* panel, click (Insert Ladder). The *Insert Ladder* dialog box opens.
7. In the *Phase* area, select **3 Phase**. In the *1st Reference* field, type **500** (as shown in Figure 4–19). Click **OK**.

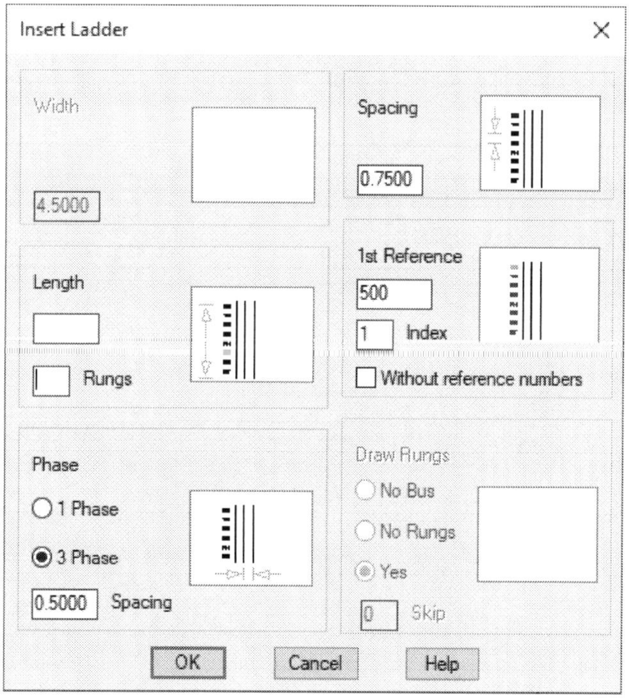

Figure 4–19

8. For the first point, pick at approximately **3, 20**. For the second point, drag your cursor down till the Y coordinate displays **10**. The X coordinate does not matter as it is controlled by the first point clicked.

   - To display the coordinates in the Status Bar, expand (Customization) and select **Coordinates**.

9. Zoom to lines 500 to 505 on the ladder.

10. In the *Schematic* tab>*Insert Wires/Wire Numbers* panel, click (Multiple Bus). The *Multiple Wire Bus* dialog box opens.

11. In the *Horizontal* area, in the *Spacing* field, type **0.7500**. Select **Another Bus (Multiple Wires)** and verify that *Number of Wires* is set to **3**, as shown in Figure 4–20. Click **OK**.

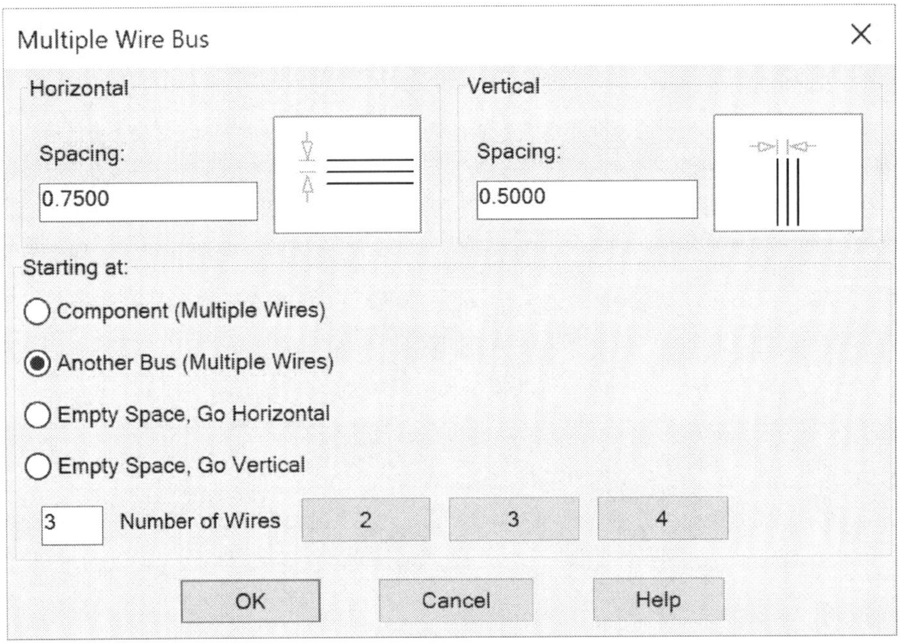

Figure 4–20

12. Select the farthest left rail near line 502. Drag your cursor to the right and for the second point, pick when the X coordinate point displays **11** in the Status Bar, as shown in Figure 4–21. Press <Enter> to complete the command.

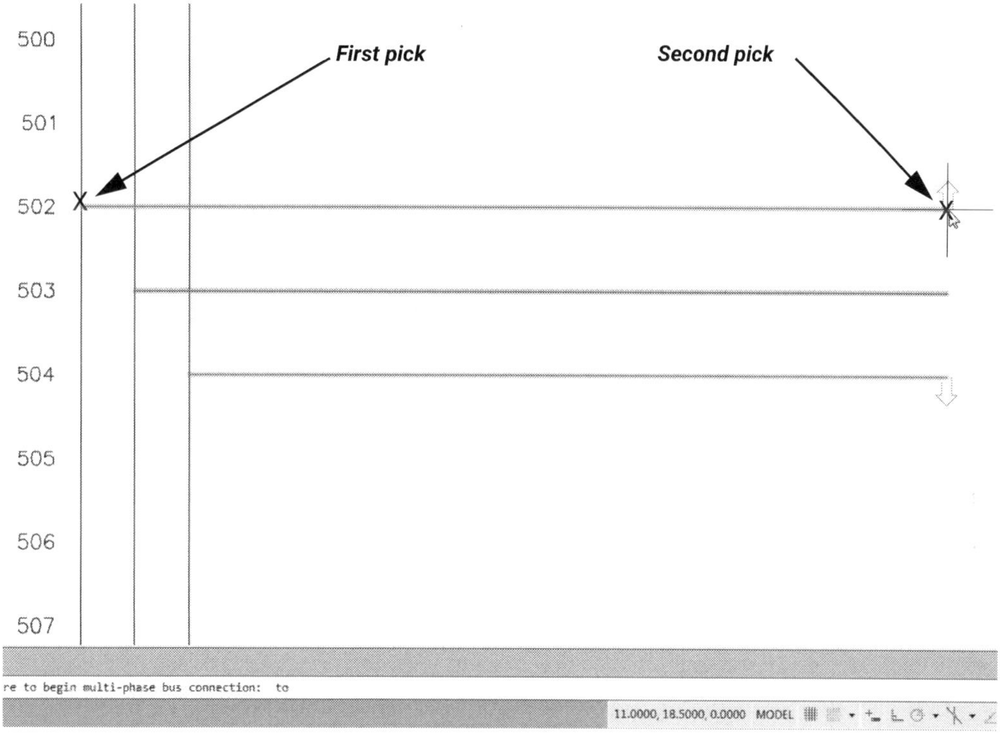

Figure 4–21

Task 2: Insert a 3-pole symbol.

1. Click  (Icon Menu). Click  (Fuses/Circuit Breakers/ Transformers) to open the *Fuses, Circuit Breakers and Transformers* menu. Click 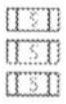 (3 Pole Fuse with Tags) to insert a 3 Pole Fuse with Tags.

2. Pick a point near the middle of the wire on line 502, as shown in Figure 4–22. In the *Build Up or Down?* dialog box, click **Down**. The *Insert / Edit Component* dialog box opens.

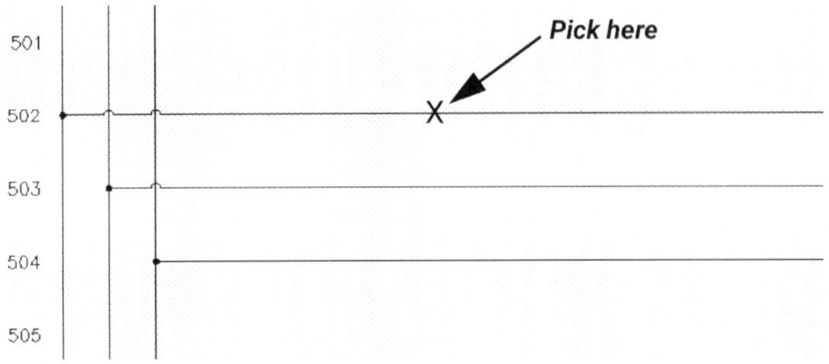

Figure 4–22

3. In the *Catalog Data* area, click **Lookup** to open the Catalog Browser. In the *Search* field, **BUSSMANN** is already displayed. Type **480** and press <Enter> to search. In the *Results* list, select **SC-60** and note that the *Manufacturer* is **BUSSMANN**, as shown in Figure 4–23. Click **OK**.

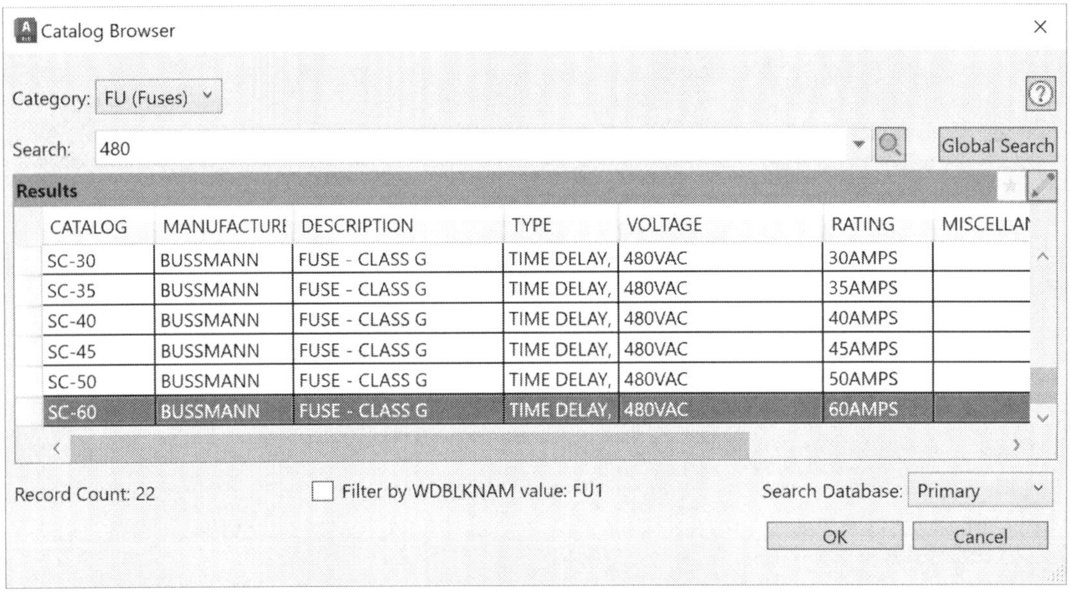

Figure 4–23

4. In the *Insert / Edit Component* dialog box, in the *Location code* area, click **Project.** Select **CABINET** and click **OK**.

5. The *Insert / Edit Component* dialog box displays as shown in Figure 4–24. Click **OK**.
   - You might be required to map the symbol to the catalog number.

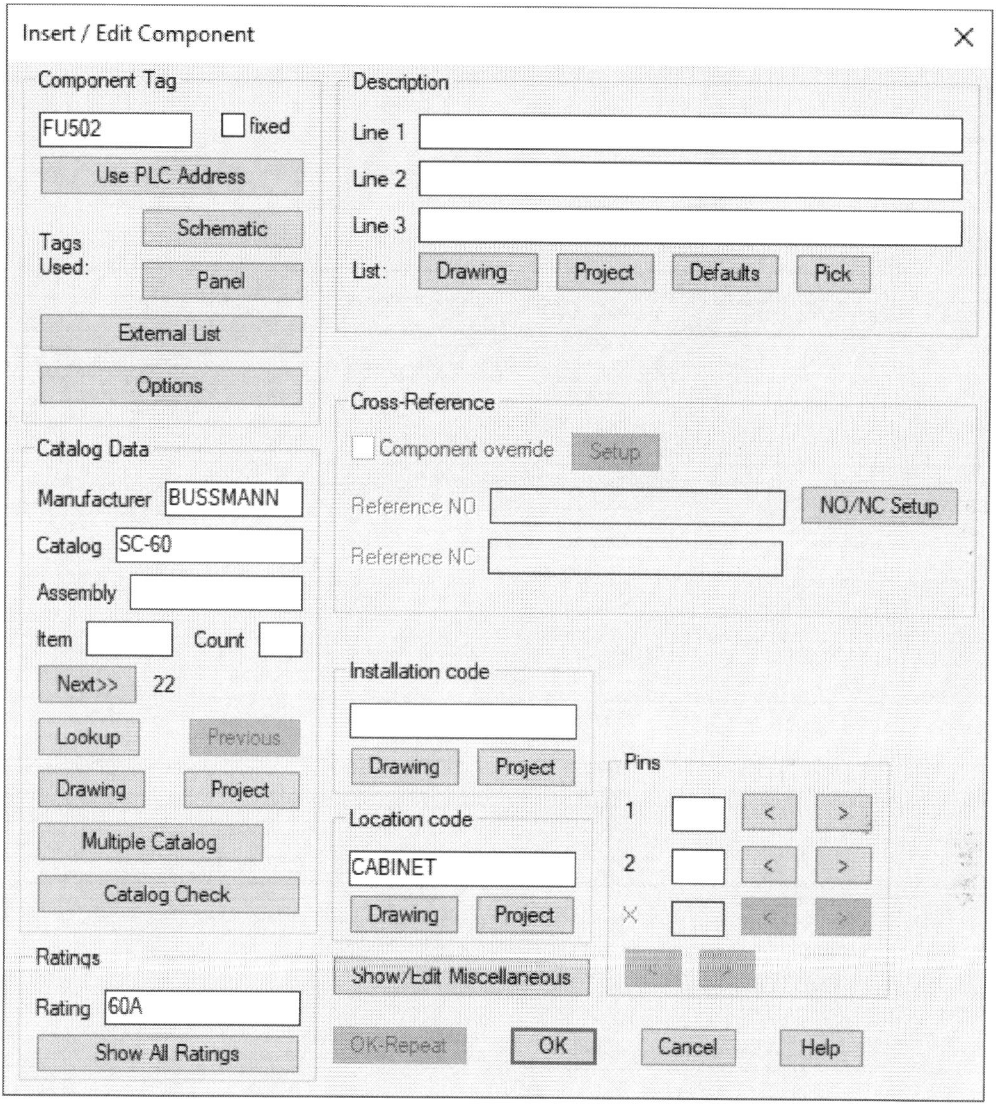

Figure 4–24

Task 3: Build a 3-pole symbol.

1. Click (Icon Menu). Click (Fuses/Circuit Breakers/ Transformers) and click (Circuit Breakers/ Disconnects). Click (Circuit Breaker 1 Pole) to insert a Circuit Breaker 1 Pole symbol.
2. Pick a point on the wire on line 502, as shown in Figure 4–25. The *Insert / Edit Component* dialog box opens.

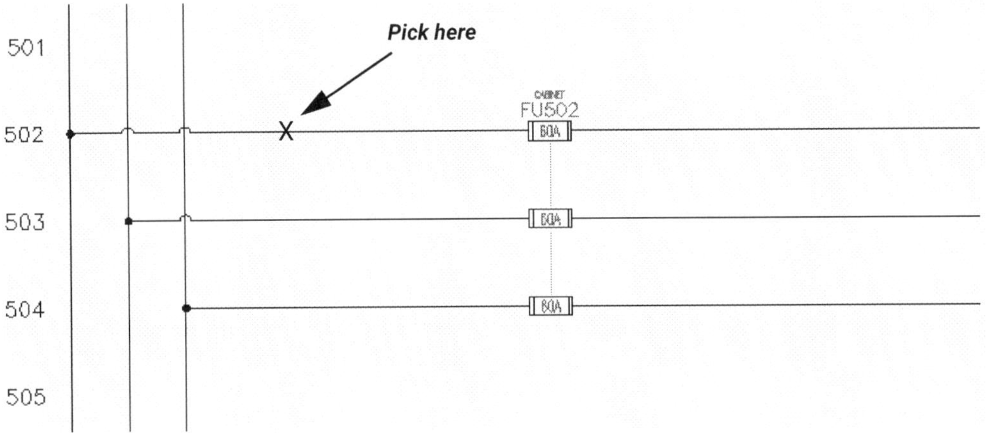

Figure 4–25

3. In the *Catalog Data* area, click **Lookup** to open the Catalog Browser. In the *Search* field, type **EATON** and press <Enter>. Select **JGS3070FAG**, which is a Eaton 70 amps 3-pole circuit breaker. Click **OK**.
4. In the *Location code* area, click **Project**. Select **CABINET** and click **OK**.

5. The *Insert / Edit Component* dialog box displays as shown in Figure 4–26. Click **OK**.
   - You might be required to map the symbol to the catalog number.

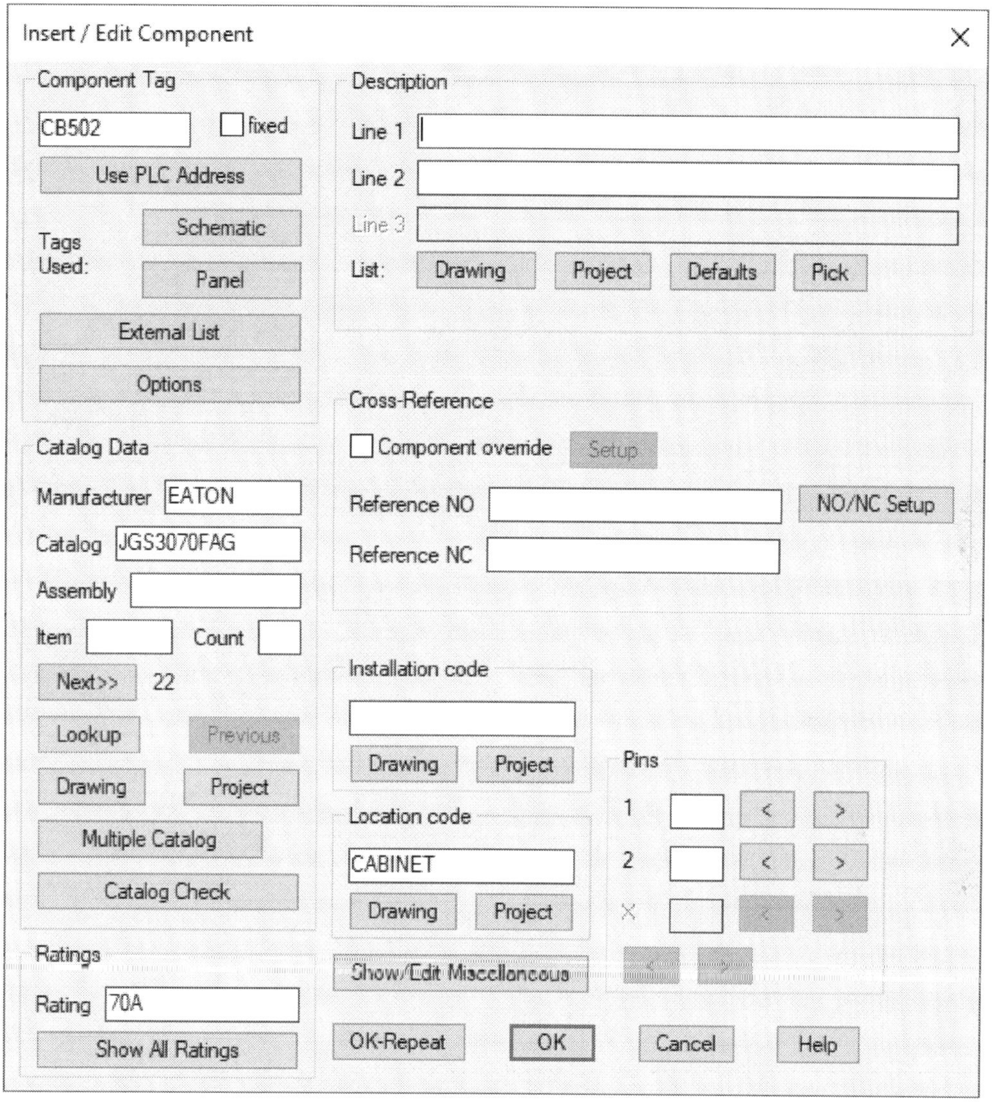

Figure 4–26

6. Click (Icon Menu). Click (Fuses/Circuit Breakers/ Transformers), then (Circuit Breakers/Disconnects), and then (2nd+ Circuit Breaker 1 Pole) to insert a 2nd+ Circuit Breaker 1 Pole symbol.

7. Select the wire on line 503 directly below the circuit breaker symbol inserted previously, as shown in Figure 4–27. The *Insert / Edit Child Component* dialog box opens.

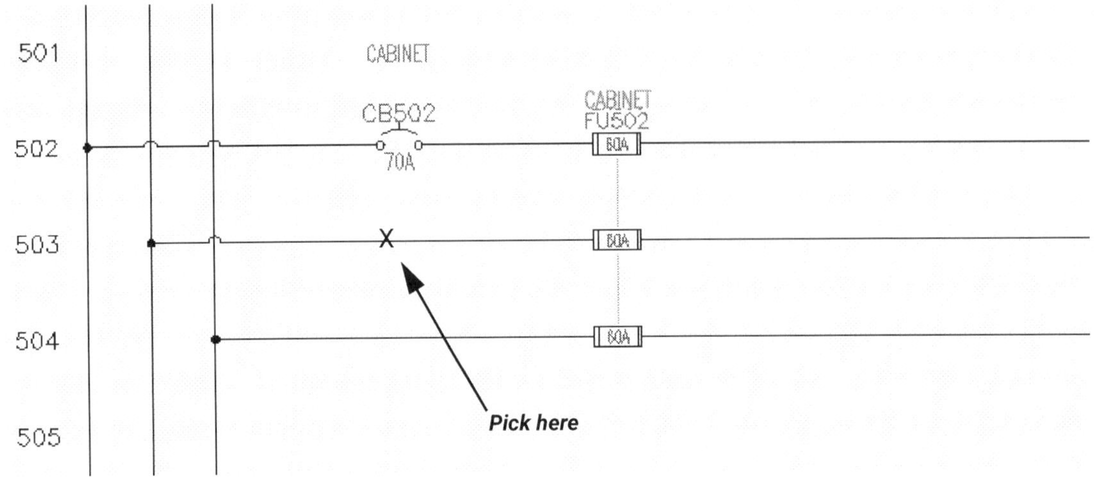

Figure 4–27

8. Click **Parent/Sibling**. Select **CB502**.
9. In the *Copy Rating Values to Child?* dialog box, click **Yes, Update Child**.
10. In the *Insert / Edit - Child Component* dialog box, click **OK**.
11. Repeat the process to insert another 2nd+ circuit breaker symbol on line 504 directly below the one you just inserted.
12. Click (Link Components with Dashed Line).
13. Select the circuit breakers on line 502, then 503, and then 504. Press <Enter> to end the command.

Task 4: Insert a 3-phase motor.

1. Click (Icon Menu), then (Motor Control), and then (3 Phase Motor) to insert a 3 Phase Motor.
2. Click a point near the end of the wire on line 503, as shown in Figure 4–28.

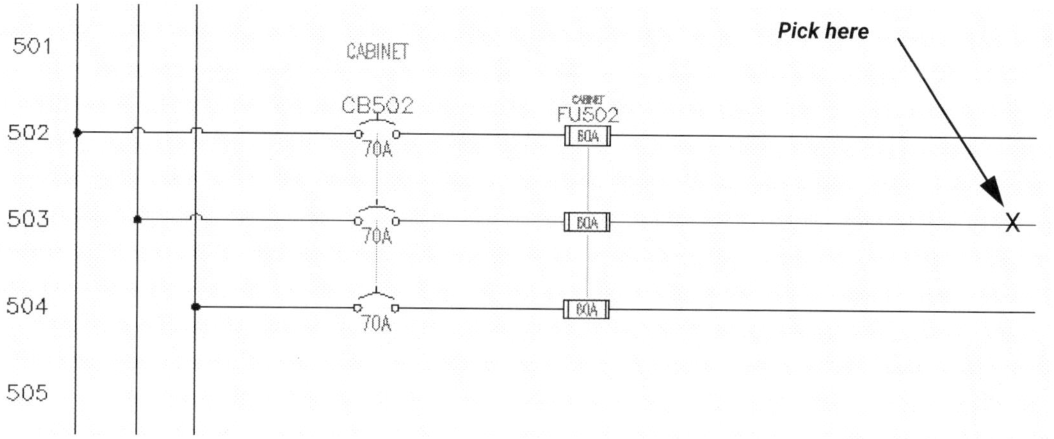

Figure 4–28

3. In the *Insert / Edit Component* dialog box under *Catalog Data*, click **Lookup**. Search in the Catalog Browser for **1329RS-ZA00318VNC -DH** and select it (it is a **AB 3HP AC motor**). Click **OK**.
4. In the *Location code* area, click **Project**. Select **FLOOR** and click **OK**.
5. In the *Insert / Edit Component* dialog box, click **OK**. A 3-phase motor is connected to the three wires.

   Note: *If the motor does not connect all three wires, place a wire manually and trim, as required.*

Task 5: Insert 3-phase wire numbers.

1. In the *Schematic* tab>*Insert Wires/Wire Numbers* panel, click (3 Phase Wire Numbers) (located in the *Wire Numbers* flyout menu).

2. Verify that the *3 Phase Wire Numbering* dialog box has the default values shown in Figure 4–29. Click **OK**.

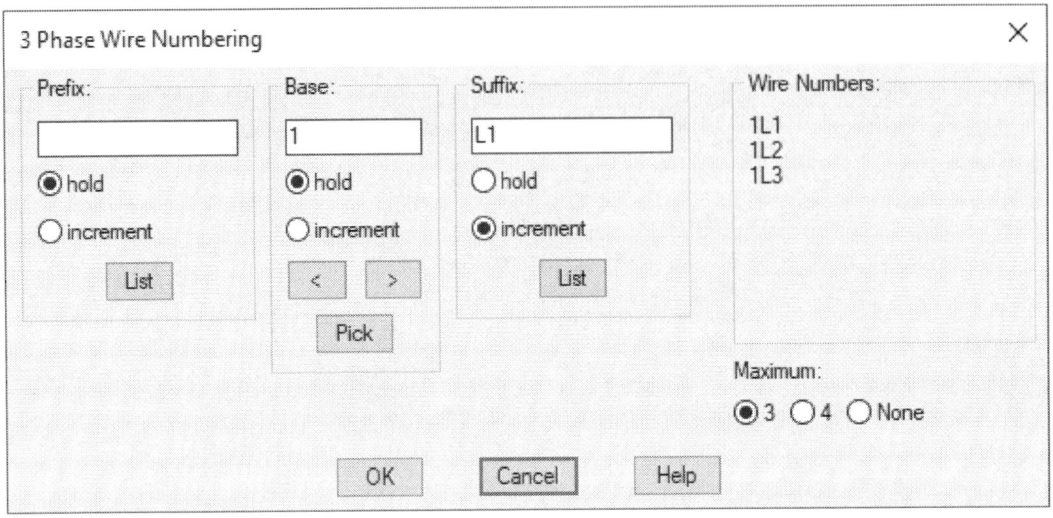

Figure 4–29

3. Select each wire between the breaker and the fuse on lines 502, 503, and then 504. The *3 Phase Wire Numbering* dialog box opens when you click on the third wire, 504.
4. The Wire Numbers preview displays 1L1, 1L2, and 1L3. Change the *Base* field value to **2** and press <Enter>. Note that the Wire Numbers preview updates to display 2L1, 2L2, and 2L3, as shown in Figure 4–30. Click **OK**.

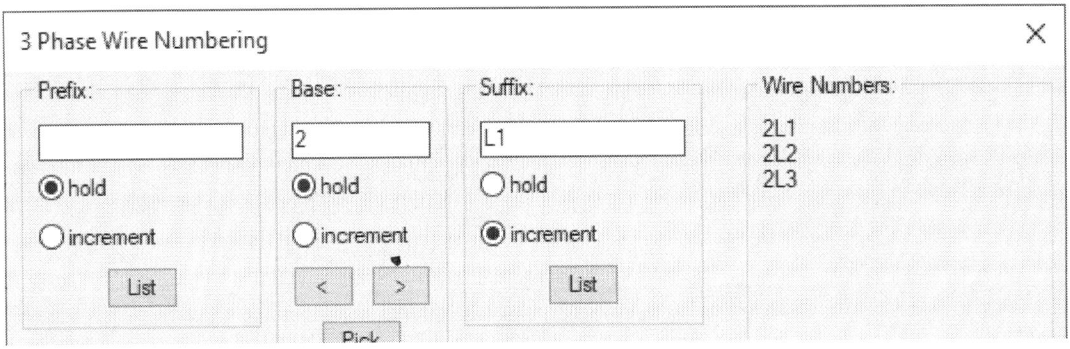

Figure 4–30

5. Click on each wire between the fuse and the motor on lines 502, 503, then 504. Click **Cancel** to end the command. The circuit displays as shown in Figure 4–31.

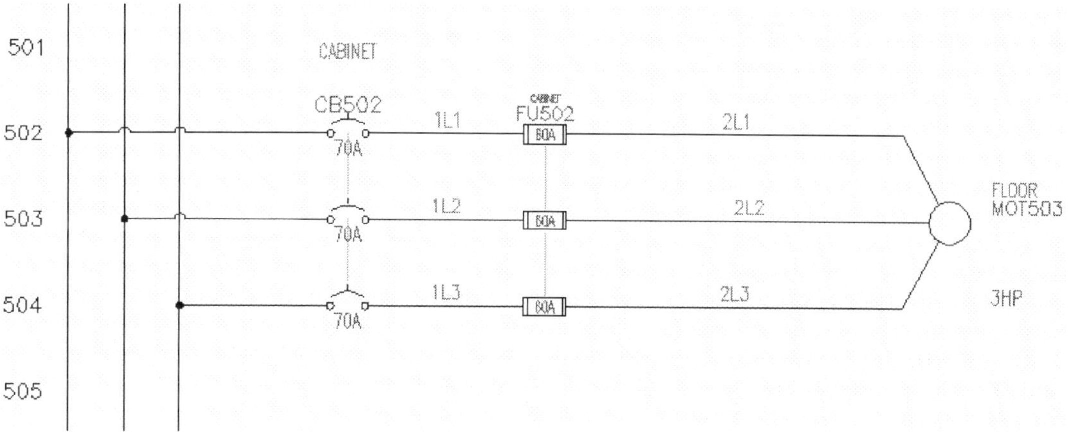

Figure 4–31

6. Use  (Align) to line up the wire numbers.
7. Save **3 Phase.dwg**.

End of practice

4.6 Cable Markers

Cable markers (as shown in Figure 4–32) are AutoCAD blocks with attributes similar to schematic components. The cable markers function as parent/child components. The first marker inserted is the parent and the additional ones are child markers.

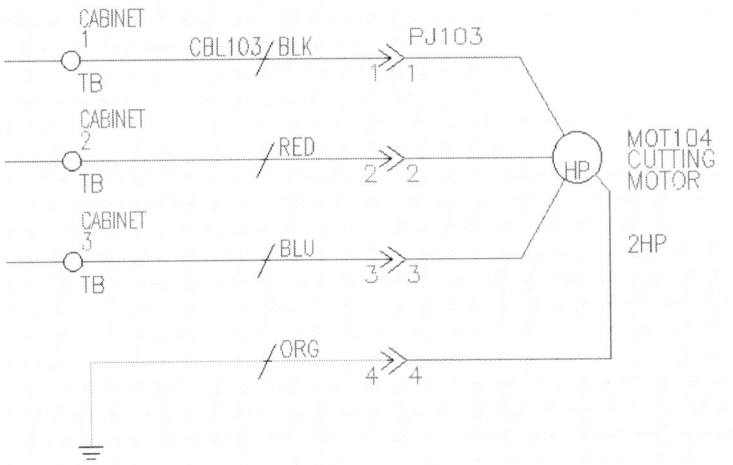

Figure 4–32

Cable Markers

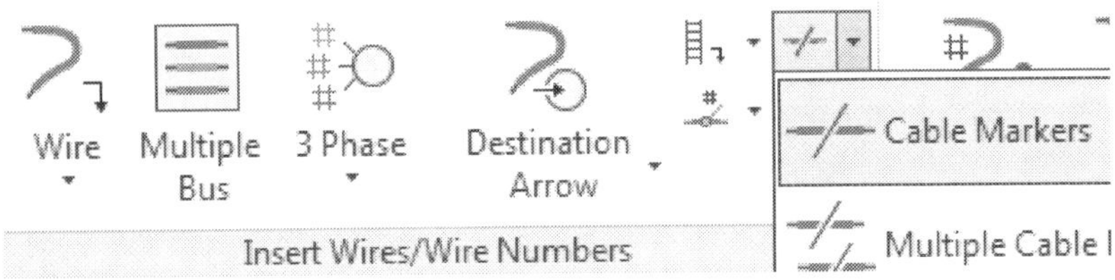

Ribbon: *Schematic* tab>*Insert Wires/Wire Numbers* panel

Command Prompt: aecablemarker

How To: Insert a Cable Marker

1. Start the **Cable Markers** command.
2. In the *Insert Component* dialog box, select **Cable Marker**.
3. Pick the insertion point for the cable.
4. Fill in the *Insert / Edit Cable Marker* dialog box.

5. Click **OK**.
6. In the *Insert Some Child Components?* dialog box, click **OK Insert Child** to add child markers or **Close** to end the command.
7. If inserting child markers, pick the location of the child marker.
8. Fill in the *Insert / Edit Child Marker* dialog box.
9. Click **OK.**
10. Pick the location for the next marker or press <Esc> to end the command.

The **Cable Markers** command opens the **Cable Markers** submenu in the *Insert Component* dialog box, as shown in Figure 4–33. You can also access it by using the **Icon Menu** command and navigating to the **Cable Markers** submenu manually.

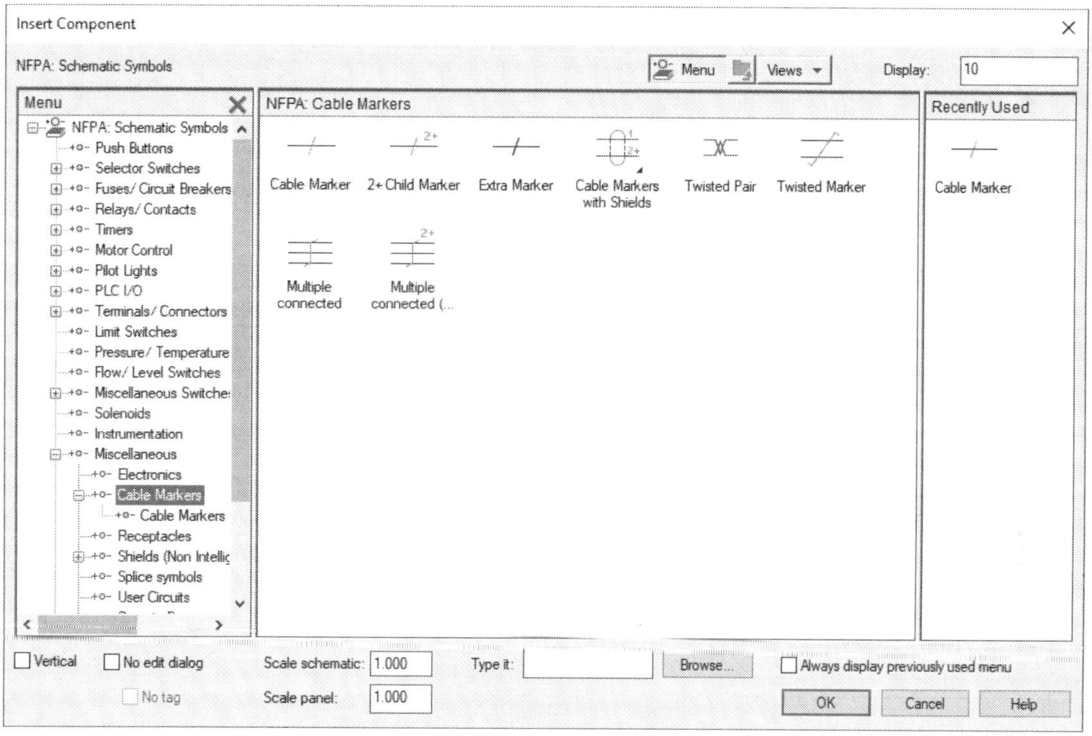

Figure 4–33

Insert / Edit Cable Marker (Parent Wire)

After the Cable Markers insertion point has been selected, the *Insert / Edit Cable Marker (Parent wire)* dialog box opens, as shown in Figure 4–34.

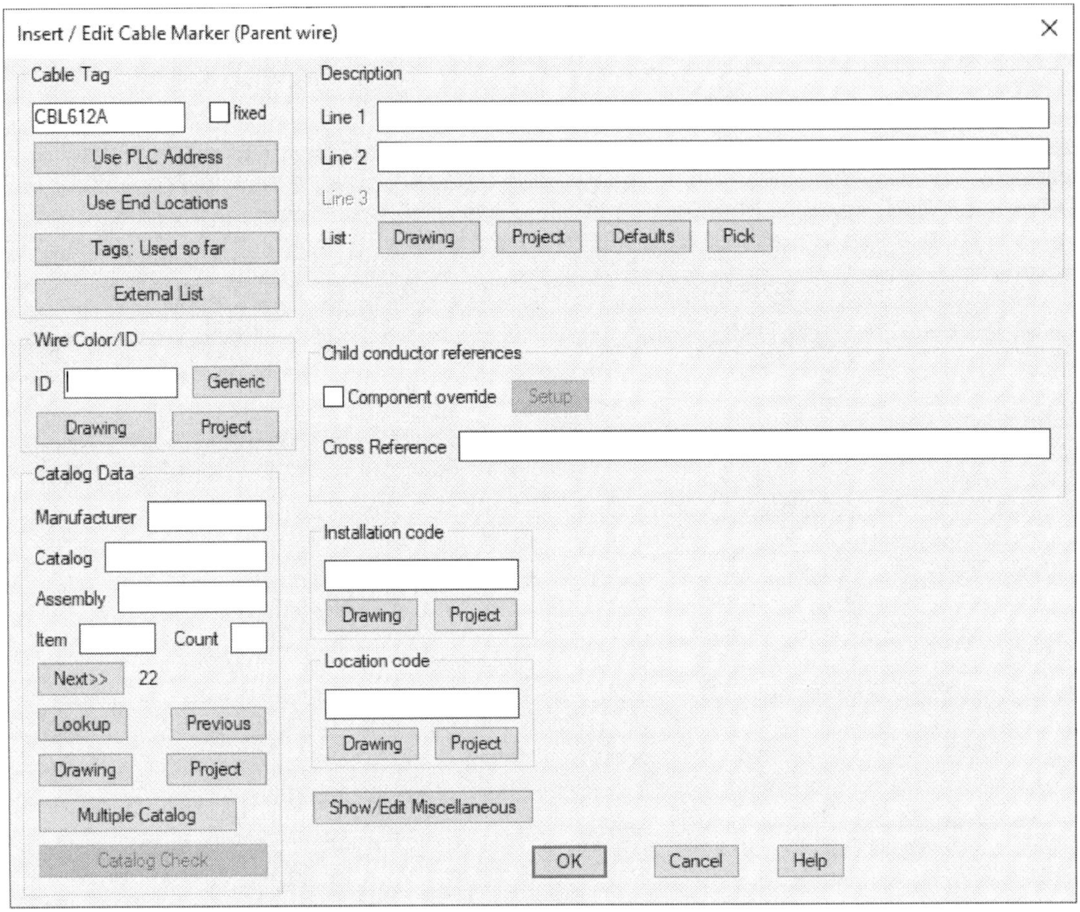

Figure 4–34

Cable Tag	Similar to a component tag, this tag is assigned automatically based on the drawing settings.
Description	You can provide up to two lines of description for the symbol. • By default, descriptions are automatically capitalized. This setting can be changed in Drawing Properties. • **Drawing** displays a list of descriptions used in the drawing for the same type of component. • **Project** displays a list of descriptions used in the entire project for the same type of component. • **Defaults** lists default descriptions. This list is based on the **wd_desc.wdd** text file. • **Pick** enables you to select a component in the current drawing and use its description.
Wire Color/ID	Specify the conductor color code. You can type the code, select from a generic list, or select from a list of codes used in the drawing or project. The generic list of cable colors is contained in the file **cblcolor.dat** and found in Windows 10: *C:\Users\<username>\AppData\Roaming\Autodesk\AutoCAD Electrical <version>\<release number>\<country code>\Support*.
Child Conductor References	You can configure the cross-reference formats using **Component Override** and **Setup**. You can specify child conductors. The information is automatically updated when you insert the child conductors.
Catalog Data	Specify the manufacturer and catalog number for the cable. This area functions like the catalog data for components.
Installation/ Location Codes	Specify the installation and location code for the cable. This area functions like the installation and location code for a component.
Show/Edit Miscellaneous	Displays any other attributes assigned to the component symbol that are not standard AutoCAD Electrical attributes.

Hint: Color Sequence for Custom Cables

In order to add color convention to the newly created custom cables, use Microsoft Access to open the database *Default_Cat.mdb*. The table that is responsible for Cable colors and color sequence is **_W0_CBLWIRES**. Add new rows in the required color sequence, adding as many rows as there are wires in the cable. The cable compiles together based on the same Catalog number and Manufacturer name, as shown in Figure 4–35.

_W0_CBLWIRES

CATALOG	MANUFACTU	CONDUCTO	GAUGE	RECNUM
2A-1002	ANIXTER	BLK	10AWG	764
2A-1002	ANIXTER	RED	10AWG	765
2A-1003	ANIXTER	BLK	10AWG	766
2A-1003	ANIXTER	RED	10AWG	767
2A-1003	ANIXTER	BLU	10AWG	768
2A-1004	ANIXTER	BLK	10AWG	769
2A-1004	ANIXTER	RED	10AWG	770

Figure 4–35

After you have inserted the first cable marker, you are prompted to insert child cable markers in the *Insert Some Child Components?* dialog box, as shown in Figure 4–36. You can hide the tag, the location text, or the description text of the child markers.

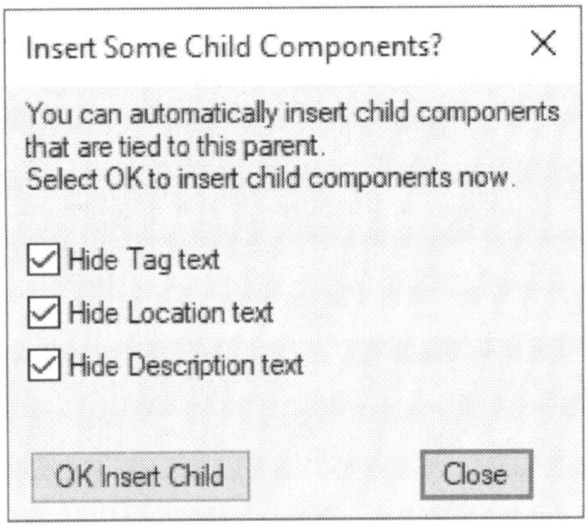
Insert Some Child Components?
You can automatically insert child components that are tied to this parent.
Select OK to insert child components now.
Hide Tag text
Hide Location text
Hide Description text
OK Insert Child
Close

Figure 4–36

Insert / Edit Cable Marker (2nd+ Wire of Cable)

You can insert child components when you insert the parent or you can insert child components using 2+ Cable Marker in the *Insert / Edit Child Marker (2nd + wire of cable)* dialog box, as shown in Figure 4–37.

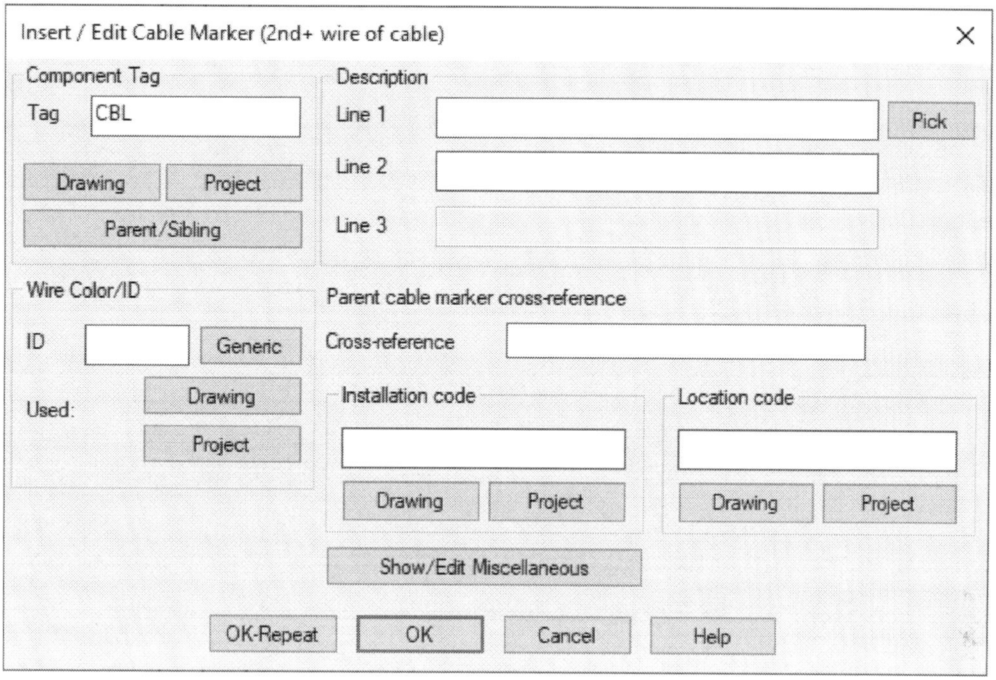

Figure 4–37

Many of the options for placing a child component are the same as for a parent. The different areas are described as follows:

Component Tag	The component tag for a child component is initially populated with the family code of the component, but is not assigned a reference number. The reference number is assigned based on the parent component to which the child is linked. You can type the component tag in the field or use the **Drawing**, **Project**, or **Parent/Sibling** options to select the parent.
Description	Populated from the parent component. You can also type it in the dialog box.
Parent Cable Marker Cross-Reference	Displays the reference number for the location of the parent cable marker. The field is populated when you select the parent marker or you can type the reference number.

How To: Insert a Child Cable Marker

1. Start the **Cable Marker** command.
2. In the *Cable Markers* dialog box, select **2+ Cable Marker**.
3. Pick the location of the child marker.
4. Populate the *Insert / Edit Child Marker (2nd + wire of cable)* dialog box.
5. Click **OK**.

4.7 Fan In/Out

The **Fan In Source** and **Fan Out Destination** commands are used to display multiple wires from a cable that come together into one wire, as shown in Figure 4–38.

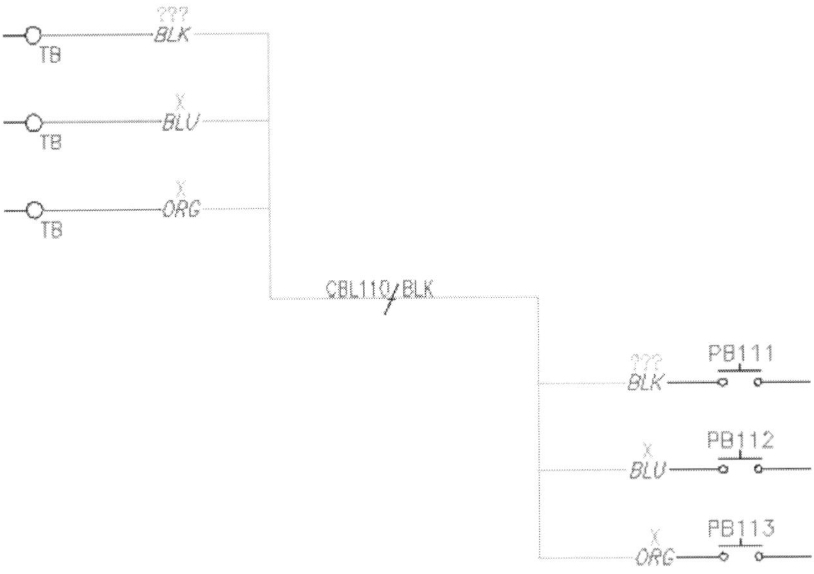

Figure 4–38

Fan In Source

Fan In Source

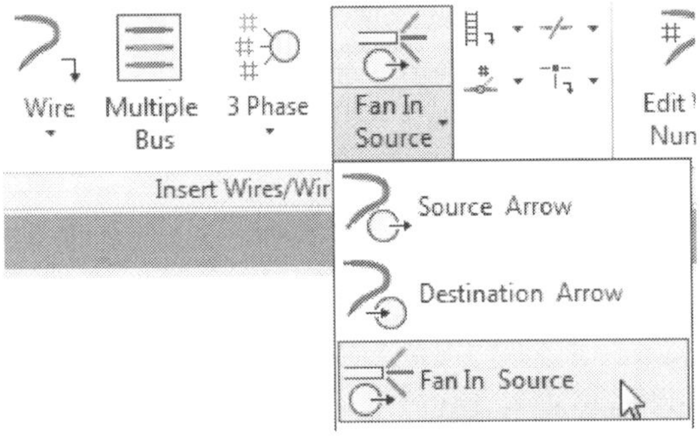

Ribbon: *Schematic* tab>*Insert Wires/Wire Numbers* panel

Command Prompt: aefaninsrc

How To: Insert a Fan-In Source Signal Marker

1. Start the **Fan In Source** command.
2. Select the style and orientation in the *Fan-In/Fan-Out Signal Source* dialog box, as shown in Figure 4–39.

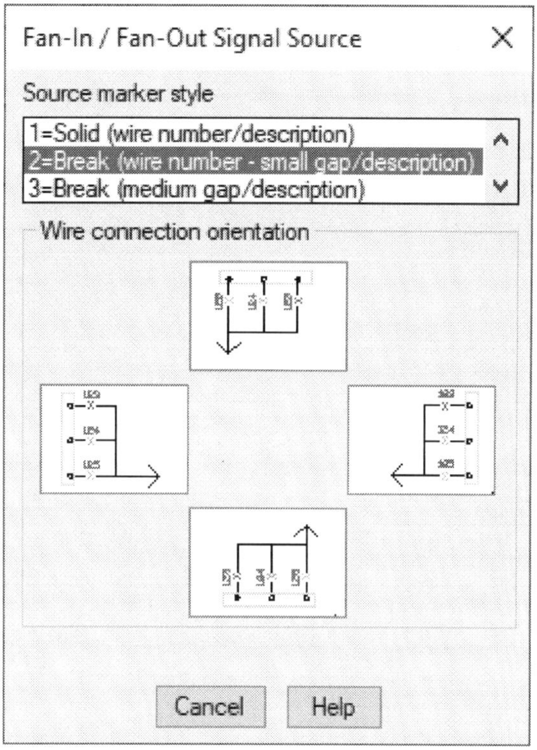

Figure 4–39

3. Select the wire where you want to place the cable marker. The symbol can be moved later, as required.

4. In the *Signal – Source Code* dialog box (shown in Figure 4–40), specify the code that links the source to the destination. Specify the *Description* that is the wire color.

   Note: *The source can be any combination of text or numbers, but they must be unique for each source.*

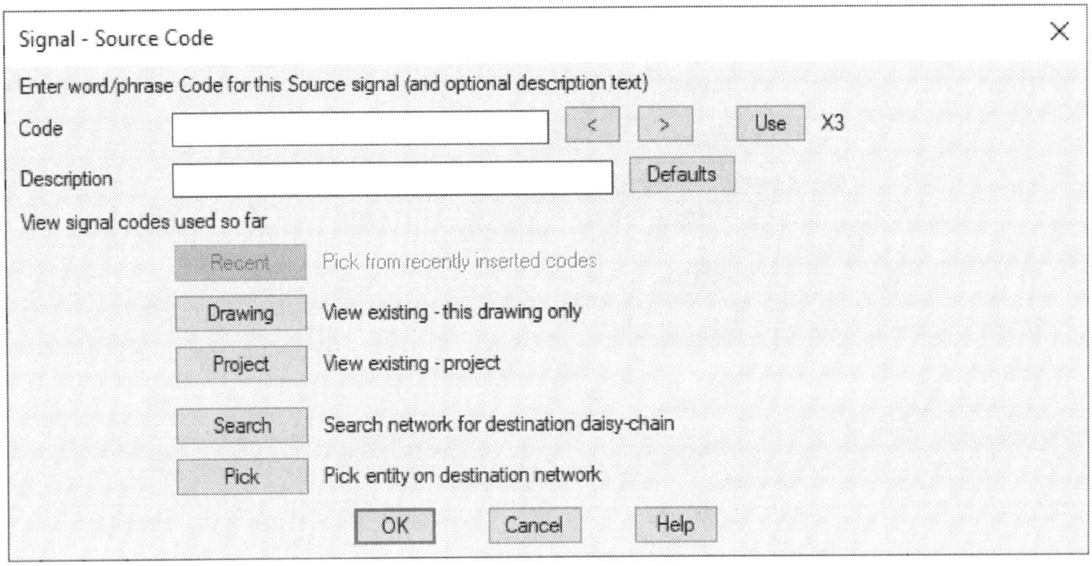

Figure 4–40

- You can click **Drawing** or **Project** to open a dialog box listing codes (as shown in Figure 4–41) used in the drawing or the entire project. You can select a code from the list.

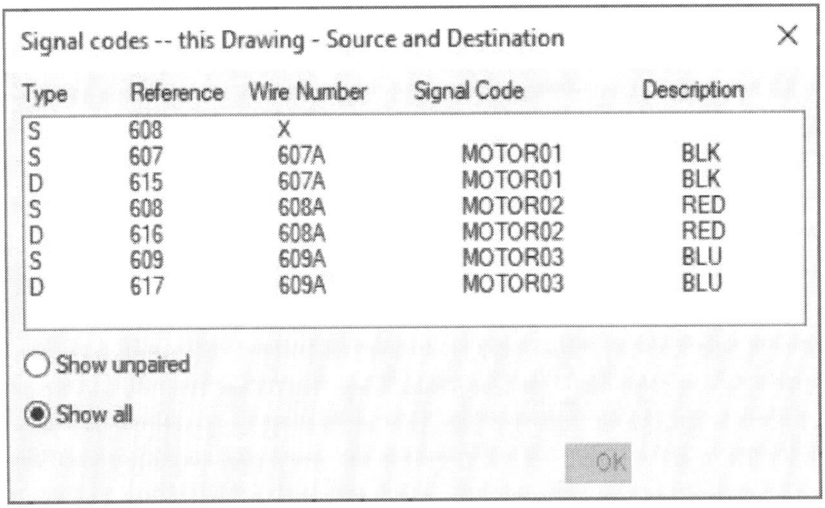

Figure 4–41

5. The *Source/Destination Signal markers (for Fan In/Out)* dialog box opens after the first source marker is inserted, as shown in Figure 4–42. In this dialog box, you can select to insert more source markers or insert a destination marker that corresponds to the source you just inserted.

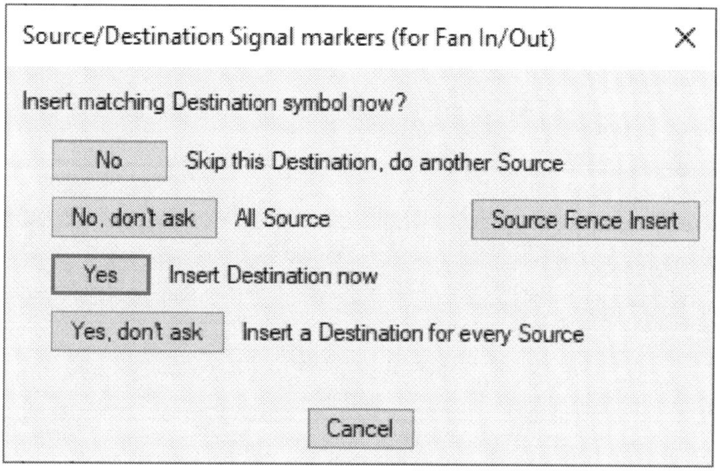

Figure 4–42

6. Continue adding sources or a destination, depending on what was selected in Step 5.
   - When you insert a Fan In/Out source marker, the wire for the cable is automatically moved to the **_MULTI_WIRE** layer. The **_MULTI_WIRE** layer is defined in Drawing Properties.
   - Use the **Match Properties** command to move all of the wire segments for the cable to the **_MULTI_WIRE** layer.

Fan Out Destination

The destination marker is where the wire is going. This could be on the same drawing as the source or you can link to a different drawing in the project.

Fan Out Destination

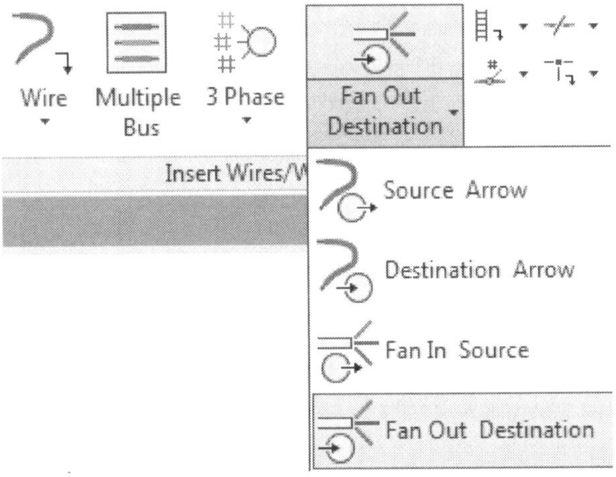

Ribbon: *Schematic* tab>*Insert Wires/Wire Numbers* panel

Command Prompt: aefanindest

How To: Insert a Fan Out Destination Signal Marker

1. Start the **Fan Out Destination** command.
2. In the *Fan-In/Fan-Out Signal Destination* dialog box, select the style and orientation.
3. Select the wire where you want to place the cable marker. The symbol can be moved later, as required.

4. Specify the signal code in the *Destination "From" Arrow (Existing)* dialog box, as shown in Figure 4–43. The signal code links the source and destination signals.

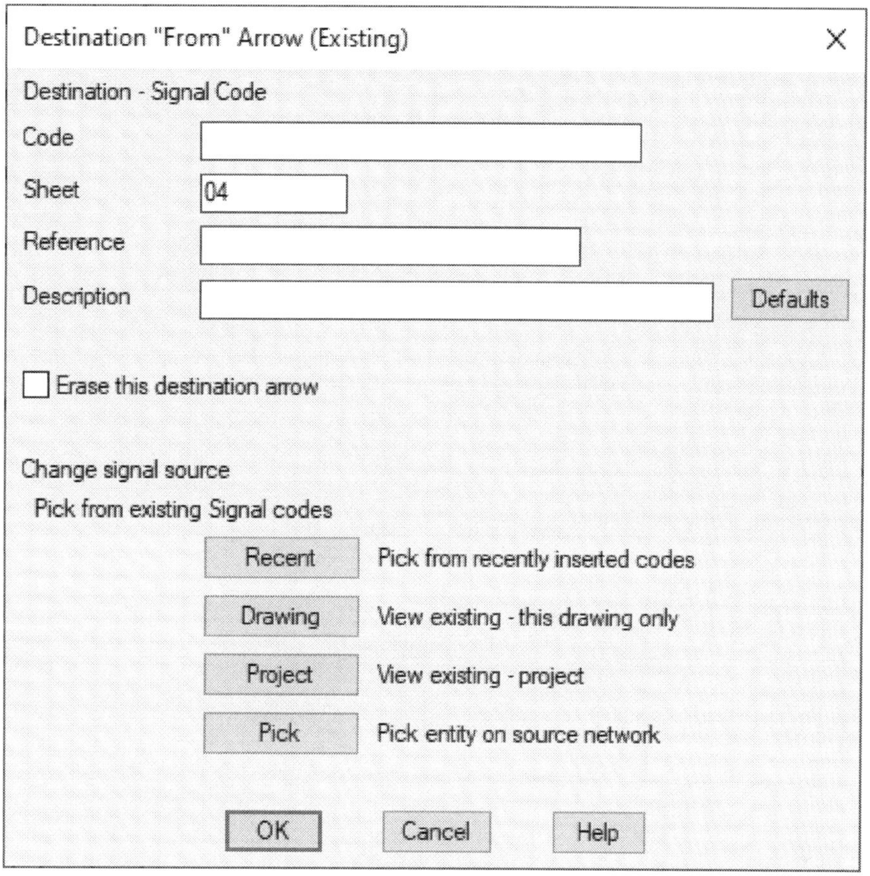

Figure 4–43

5. Pick to insert another destination marker or press <Esc> to end the command.

- After inserting the source and destination markers, you need to draw the connecting wires and add a cable marker.

Practice 4c
Cables

Practice Objective

- Insert cable markers, fan in source and fan out destination signal markers.

In this practice, you will insert cable markers on a 3-phase circuit. You will then use the **Fan In/Out** commands to insert fan in/out source and destination symbols. You will then connect the wires with a single cable. Finally, you will add wire numbers to the drawing to see the cable markers update. The completed circuit displays similar to that shown in Figure 4–44.

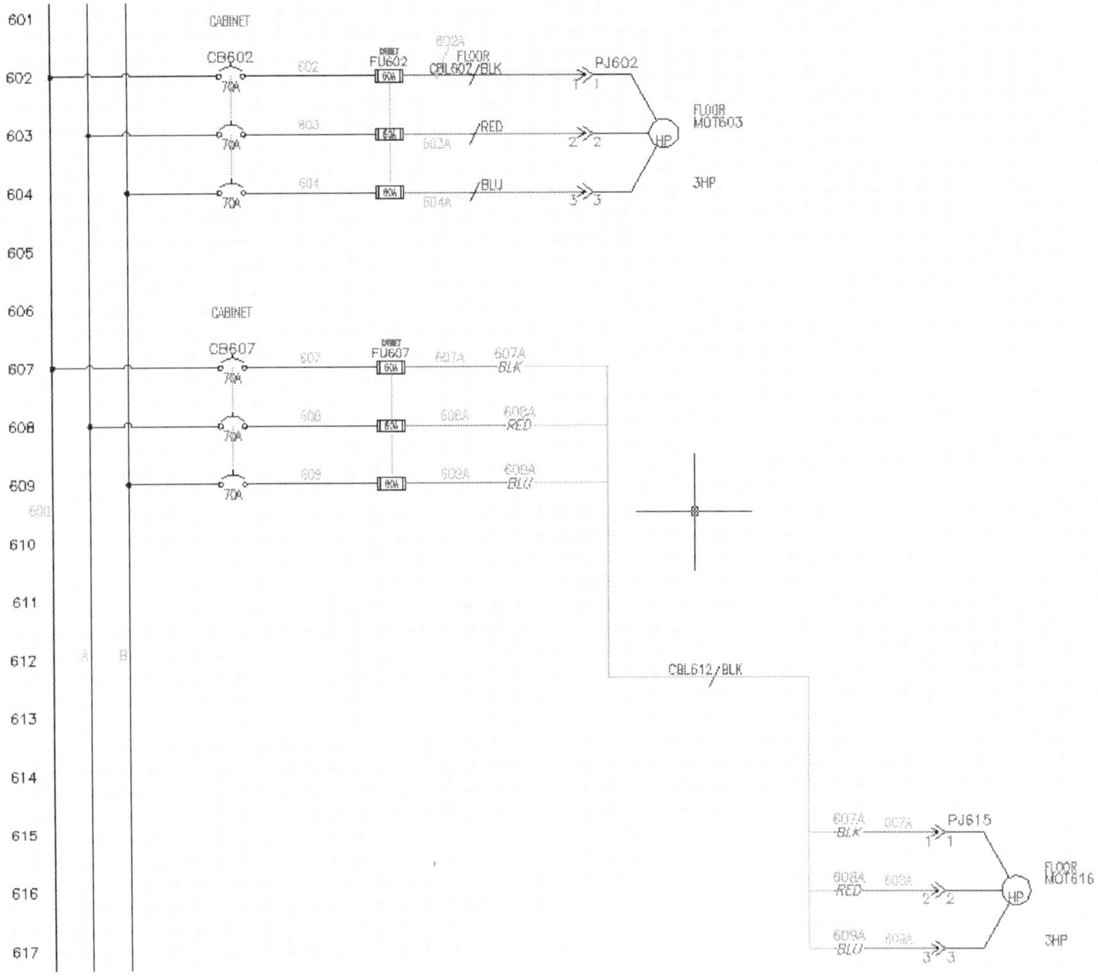

Figure 4–44

Task 1: Insert cable markers.

1. If the **Module 04** project is not active, open and activate it now.
2. In the **Module 04** project, open **Cables.dwg**.
3. Zoom in to the circuit on lines 602 to 604.
4. In the *Schematic* tab>*Insert Wires/Wire Numbers* panel, click (Cable Markers). The *Insert Component* dialog box opens, and automatically displays the **Cable Markers** submenu.
5. Click (Cable Marker) to insert a cable marker.
6. Pick the wire between fuse FU602 and connector PJ602, as shown in Figure 4–45. The *Insert / Edit Cable Marker (Parent wire)* dialog box opens.

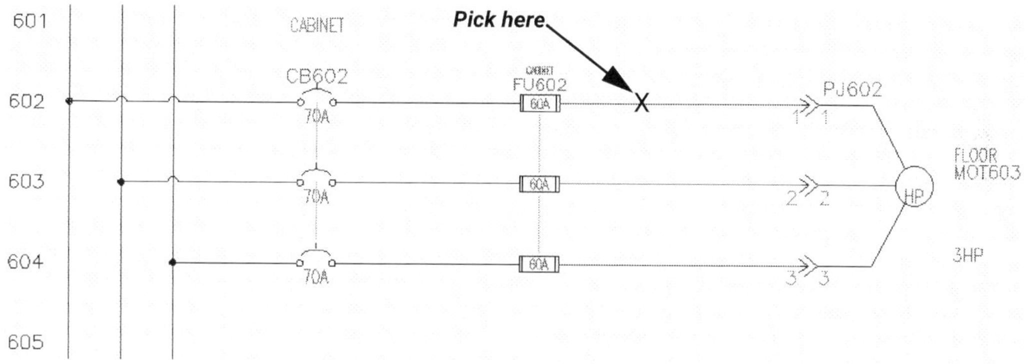

Figure 4–45

7. In the *Catalog Data* area, click **Lookup**. In the Catalog Browser, search for **2MR-1405** and select it. Note that it is the ANIXTER 14AWG EPR/CPE control cable. Click **OK**.
8. In the *Location code* area, click **Project**. In the *All Locations - Project* dialog box, select **FLOOR** and click **OK**.
9. In the *Insert / Edit Cable Marker* dialog box, click **OK**.
   - You might be required to map the symbol to the catalog number.
10. The *Insert Some Child Components?* dialog box opens. Leave all boxes checked and click **OK Insert Child**.
11. Select the red wire of rung 603, directly below the cable marker that you just placed to insert a cable marker there.
12. In the *Insert / Edit Cable Marker (2nd+ wire of cable)* dialog box, click **OK**.
13. Select the blue wire of rung 604, directly below the cable marker that you just placed and click **OK** in the dialog box.
14. Press <Esc> to end the command.

Task 2: Insert fan in/out symbols.

1. Zoom to the circuits on lines 607 to 617.

2. In the *Schematic* tab>*Insert Wires/Wire Numbers* panel, click  (Fan In Source) (located in the *Source Arrow* flyout menu).

3. In the *Fan-In/Fan-Out Signal Source* dialog box, click 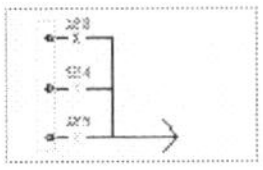.

4. Pick near the middle of the wire on right end of line 607, as shown in Figure 4–46.

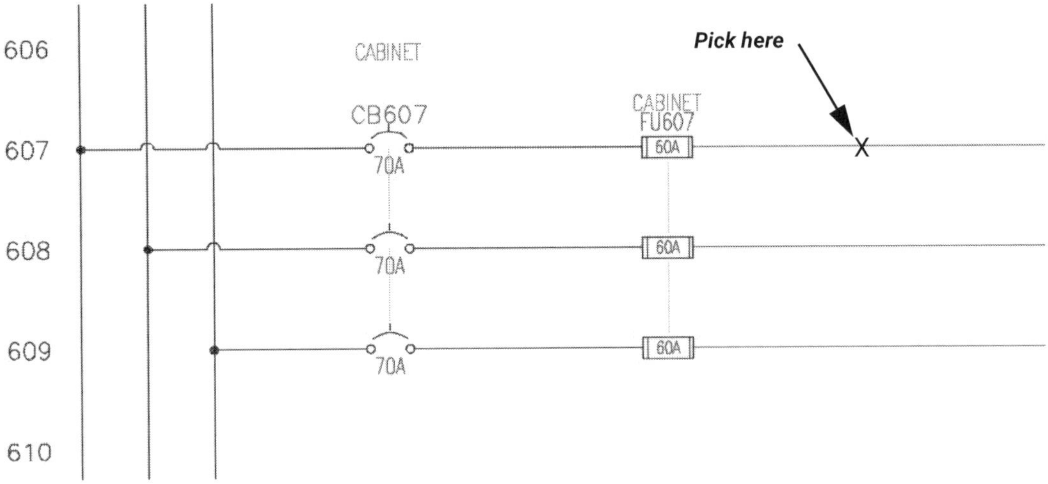

Figure 4–46

5. In the *Signal–Source Code* dialog box that opens, enter the following:
   - *Code*: **MOTOR01**
   - *Description*: **BLK**

6. Click **OK**.

7. The *Source/Destination Signal markers (for Fan In/Out*) dialog box opens. Click **Source Fence Insert**.

8. Pick a point above the middle of the wire at the right end of line 608. Pick a second point below the middle of the wire at the right end of line 609 (as shown in Figure 4–47) to create a fence line over both the wires. Press <Enter> to continue.

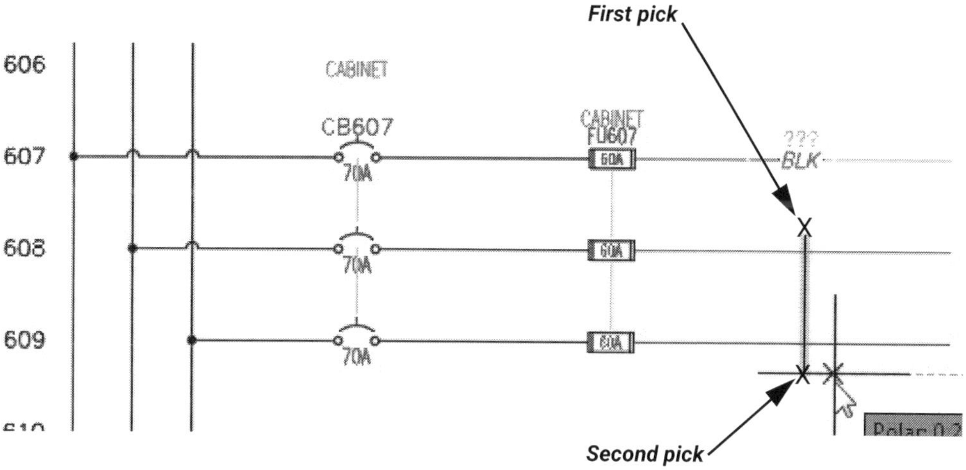

Figure 4–47

9. In the *Keep?* dialog box, verify that the **Keep this one** option is selected. Click **OK**.
10. In the *Source "To" Arrow (Existing)* dialog box, note that the number at the end of the Code is automatically incremented and now displays as **MOTOR02**. Change the *Description* to **RED** and click **OK**.
11. In the *Keep?* dialog box, click **OK**.
12. In the *Source "To" Arrow (Existing)* dialog box, note that the *Code* displays as **MOTOR03**. Change the *Description* to **BLU** and click **OK**.
13. In the *Schematic* tab>*Insert Wires/Wire Numbers* panel, click  (Fan Out Destination).
14. In the *Fan-In/Fan-Out Signal Destination* dialog box, click 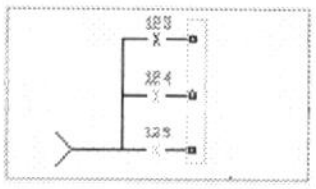.

15. Select the wire on line 615, near the left side, as shown in Figure 4–48. The *Destination "From" Arrow (Existing)* dialog box opens. Also note that a diamond shape is placed on the wire where you clicked.

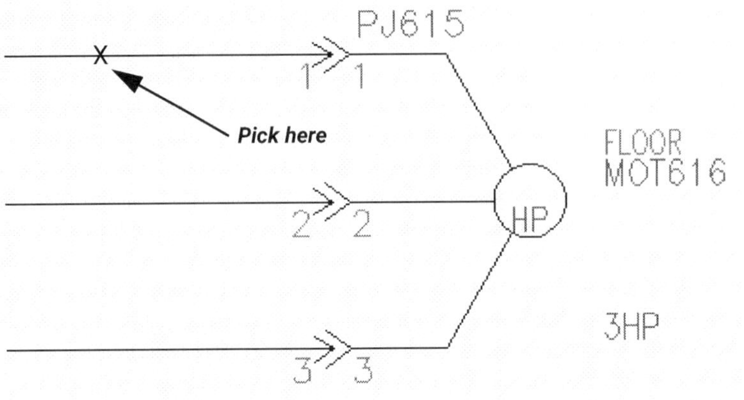

Figure 4–48

16. In the *Destination "From" Arrow (Existing)* dialog box, click **Drawing** and in the *Signal codes* dialog box, select **MOTOR01**, as shown in Figure 4–49. Click **OK**.

Signal codes -- this Drawing - Source and Destination

Type	Reference	Wire Number	Signal Code	Description
D	615	X		
S	607	???	MOTOR01	BLK
S	608	???	MOTOR02	RED
S	609	???	MOTOR03	BLU

Figure 4–49

17. The *Destination "From" Arrow (Existing)* dialog box is automatically populated. Click **OK**.
18. Select the wire on line 616, below the previous selection. A diamond shape is placed on the wire and the *Destination "From" Arrow (Existing)* dialog box opens.
19. In the *Destination "From" Arrow (Existing)* dialog box, click **Drawing** and in the *Signal codes* dialog box, select **MOTOR02**. Click **OK**.
20. In the *Destination "From" Arrow (Existing)* dialog box, click **OK**.
21. Select the wire on line 617, below the previous selection.
22. In the *Destination "From" Arrow (Existing)* dialog box, click **Drawing** and in the *Signal codes* dialog box, select **MOTOR03**. Click **OK**.
23. In the *Destination "From" Arrow (Existing)* dialog box, click **OK**.
24. Press <Esc> to end the command.

Task 3: Insert a wire and cable marker.

1. Click  (Wire).
2. Pick a point on the end of the wire on line 607, as shown in Figure 4–50.
3. Pick a second point midway between the two circuits, as shown in Figure 4–50.
4. Type **H** and press <Enter>.
5. Pick a point on the end of the wire on line 617 as shown in Figure 4–50. Press <Enter> to end the command.

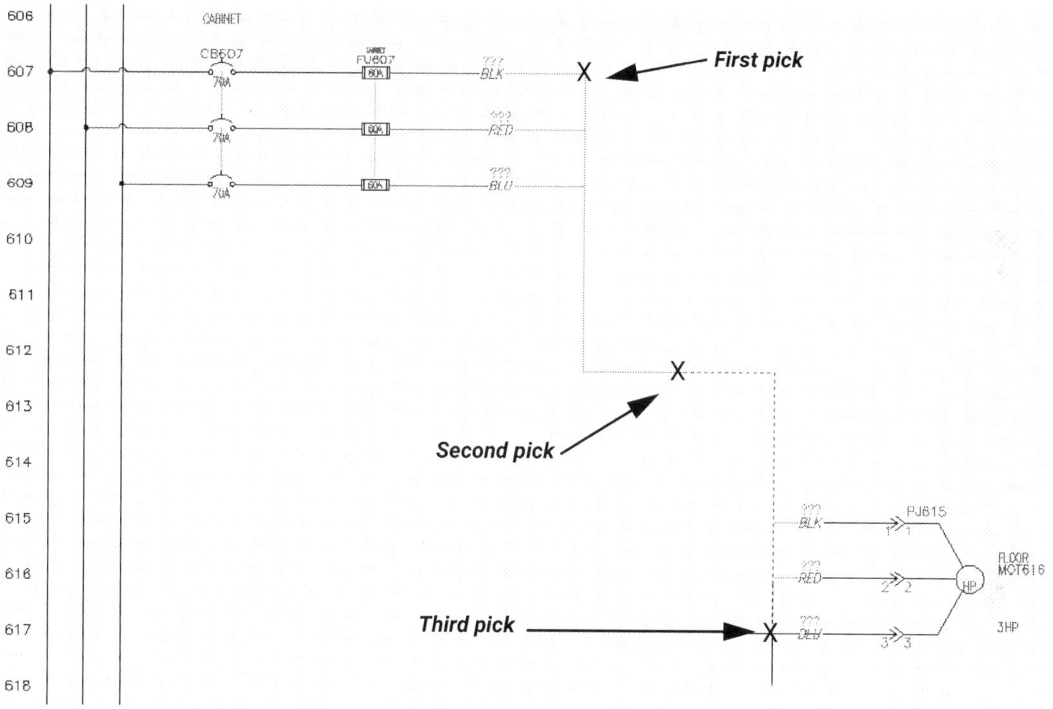

Figure 4–50

6. Right-click on the wire on line 615 between the Fan In/Out Destination Symbol and the PJ615 connector. Select **Change/Convert Wire Type** from the Marking Menu.
7. In the *Change/Convert Wire Type* dialog box, select **BLK_14AWG** as the wire type and click **OK**. Press <Enter> to end the command.
8. Repeat to change the wire on *line 616* to **RED_14AWG** and the wire on *line 617* to **BLU_14AWG**.

9. Insert an **ANIXTER 2MR-1405** cable marker on the horizontal wire between the two circuits. In the *Insert Some Child Components?* dialog box, click **Close**.
10. Add wire numbers using the defaults and **Drawing-wide**.
11. Save **Cables.dwg**.

End of practice

4.8 Insert Saved Circuits

If you have circuits that you use frequently, you can reuse them. The AutoCAD Electrical software has commands to save and insert circuits or groups of components and wires.

Insert WBlocked Circuit

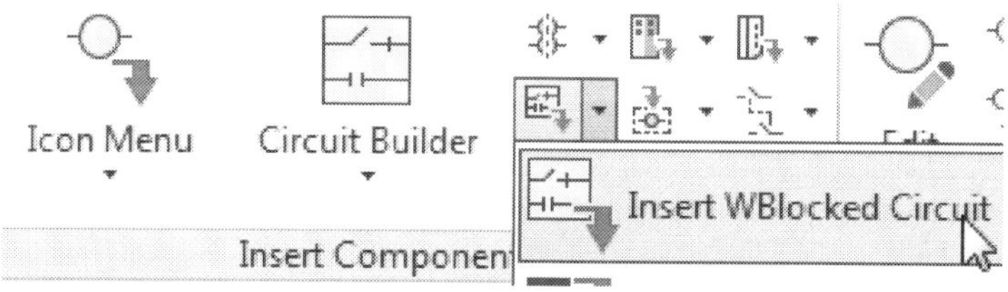

Ribbon: *Schematic* tab>*Insert Components* panel

Command Prompt: aewbcircuit

How To: Insert a WBlocked Circuit

1. Start the **Insert WBlocked Circuit** command.
2. Browse to and select the DWG file that was previously wblocked.
3. In the *Circuit Scale* dialog box, select the options.
4. Place the circuit in the drawing window.

The **Insert Wblocked Circuit** command enables you to browse to a DWG file that has been saved using the AutoCAD **Wblock** command. When the circuit is inserted, the components are retagged and the wire numbers set to "???". After you select the DWG file to insert, the *Circuit Scale* dialog box opens, as shown in Figure 4–51.

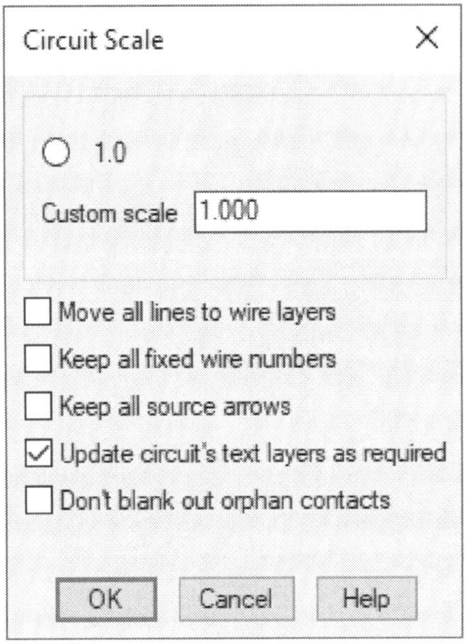

Figure 4–51

Custom scale	Specify a scale for the circuit.
Move all lines to wire layers	If selected, all line entities are moved to the default wire layer. Lines on layer **0** are not moved.
Keep all fixed wire numbers	Maintains any wire numbers that were set to fixed in the circuit.
Keep all source arrows	If selected, all source arrows are maintained when the circuit is inserted. The default is to erase the source arrows.
Update circuit's text layers as required	Updates the text layers of the circuit according to Drawing Properties.
Don't blank out orphan contacts	Maintains the tag ID for contacts even if the parent is not found.

Insert Saved Circuit

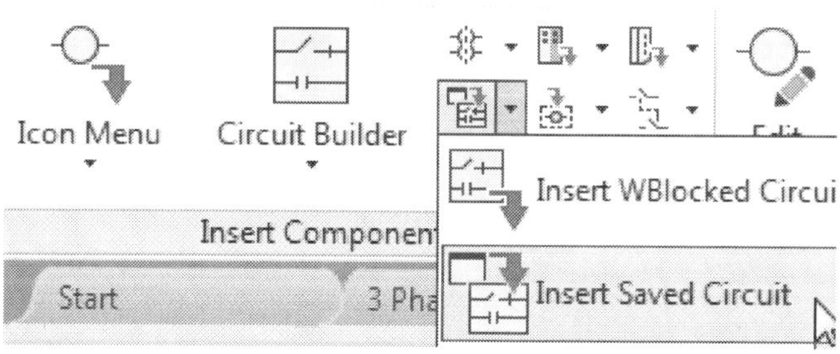

Ribbon: *Schematic* tab>*Insert Components* panel

Command Prompt: aesavedcircuit

How To: Insert a Saved Circuit

1. Start the **Insert Saved Circuit** command.
   - To use the **Insert Saved Circuit** command, you must first save circuits to the Icon Menu or the disk.

2. In the *Insert Component* dialog box, in the **Saved User Circuits** submenu (as shown in Figure 4–52), select the circuit that you want to insert.

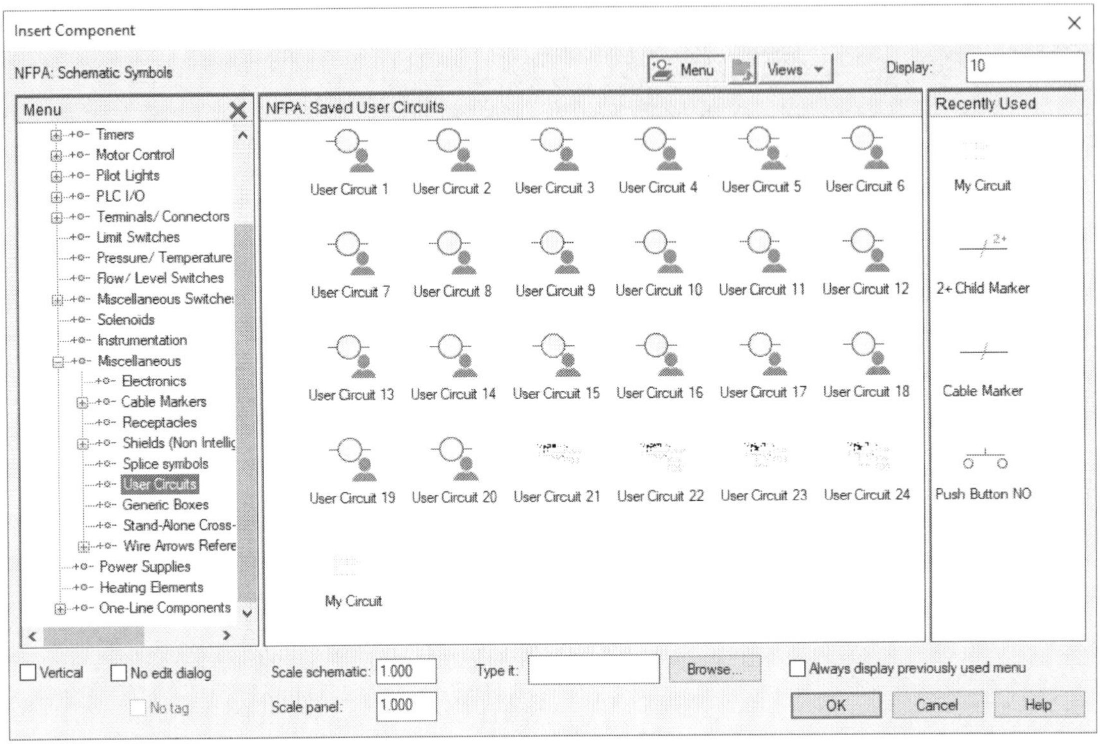

Figure 4–52

3. In the *Circuit Scale* dialog box, select the options. In the drawing window, place the circuit.
   - This is the same dialog box that is used when placing a Wblocked Circuit.

4.9 Save Circuits to Icon Menu

The **Save Circuit to Icon Menu** command saves the circuit to a DWG file and creates an icon for the Icon Menu (*Insert Component* dialog box).

Save Circuit to Icon Menu

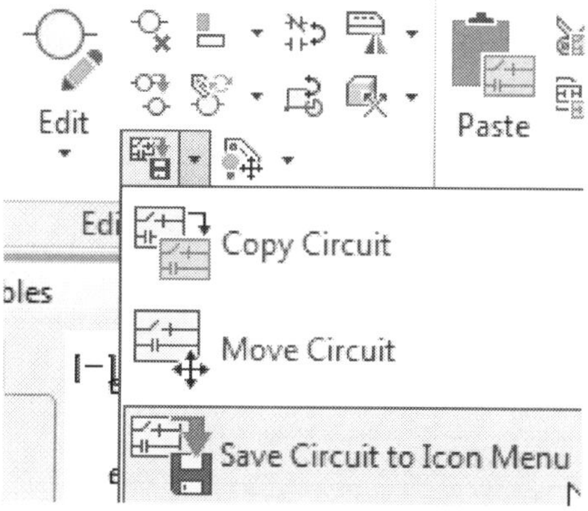

Ribbon: *Schematic* tab>*Edit Components* panel

Command Prompt: aesavecircuit

How To: Save a Circuit to the Icon Menu

1. Zoom in on the circuit.
2. Start the **Save Circuit to Icon Menu** command. The *Save Circuit to Icon Menu* dialog box opens.

3. Right-click in a blank area and select **Add icon>New circuit**, as shown in Figure 4–53.

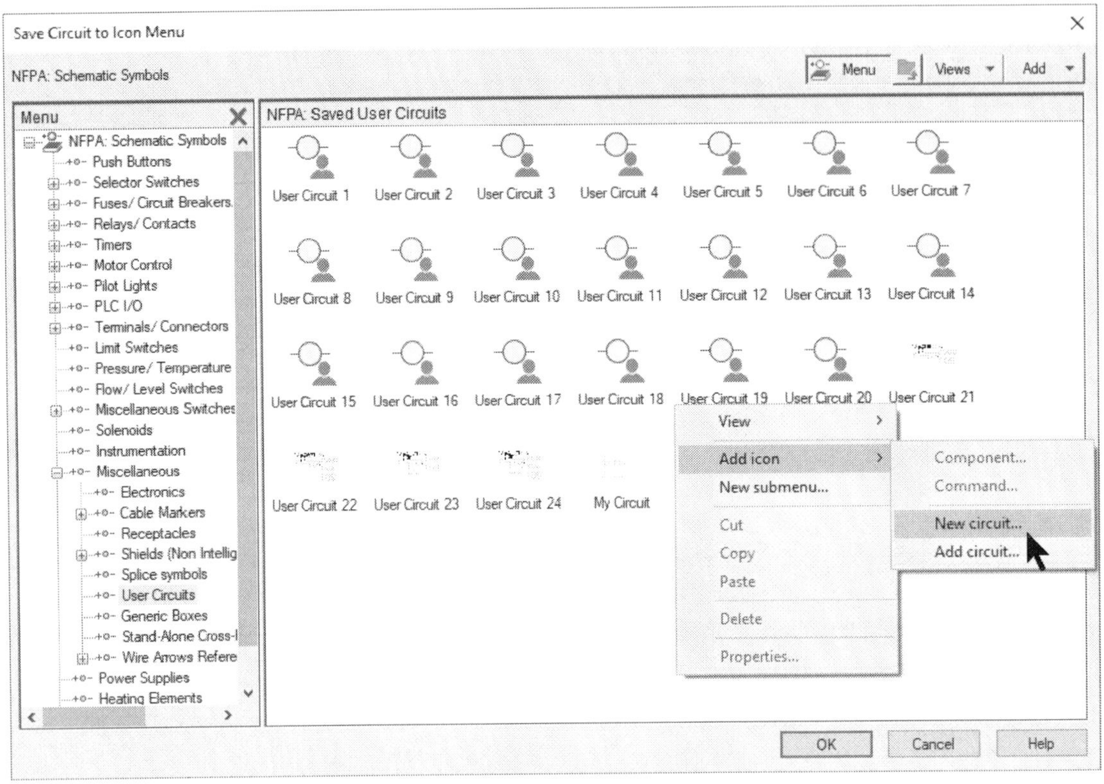

Figure 4–53

4. In the *Create New Circuit* dialog box, fill in the fields and click **OK**.
5. Select the base point for the circuit.
6. Select the circuit's components and wires and press <Enter>.
7. In the *Save Circuit to Icon Menu* dialog box, click **OK**.

To add custom circuits, in the *Save Circuit to Icon Menu* dialog box, in the *Saved User Circuits* area, right-click in a blank area, and select **Add icon>New circuit**. It opens the *Create New Circuit* dialog box (as shown in Figure 4–54), which is used to input information for the circuit.

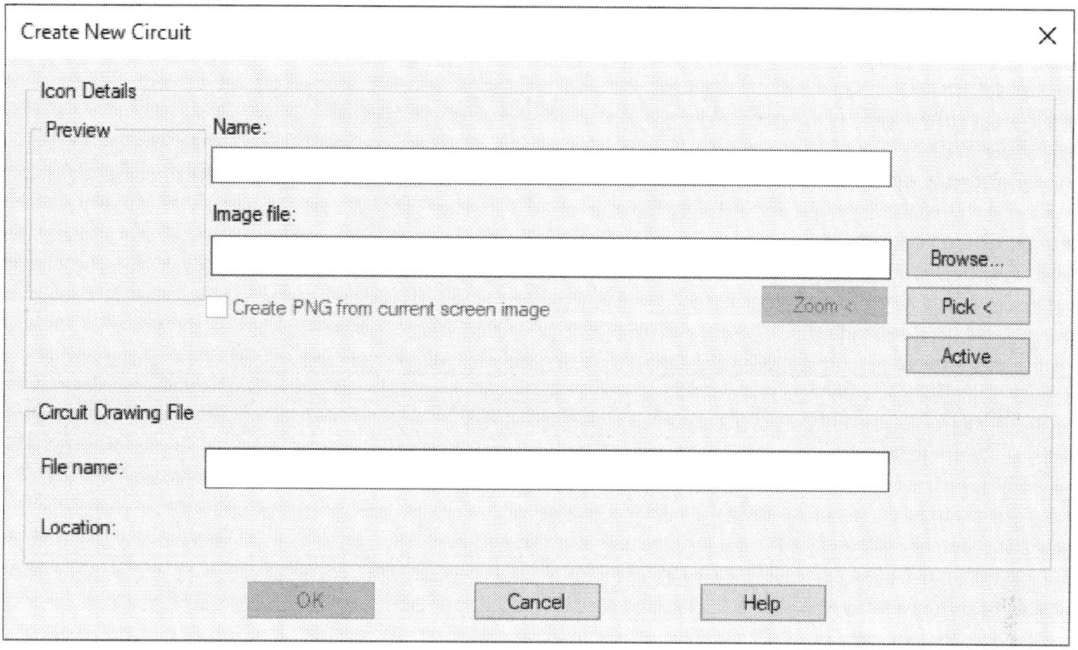

Figure 4–54

There are various options in the *Create New Circuit* dialog box.

Preview	Displays a preview of the icon to be added to the menu.
Name	Enter the name to be displayed below the icon image in the menu.
Image file	Enter the name of the image file to be used or use the buttons to populate this field.
Create PNG from current screen image	If selected, a new image file is created from the active drawing window.
Browse	Displays the *Open* dialog box used to browse to an existing image file for the icon.
Zoom<	If creating a new image file, use this button to change the active drawing window before capturing the image.
Pick	Select an existing block to use its name as the name for the image file.
Active	Click this button to use the active drawing name as the name for the new image file.
File name	Enter the name for the DWG file that contains the circuit definition. This file is created after you select the geometry to use for the circuit.
Location	Displays the path for the new DWG file.

- A screen shot of the drawing window is taken to use as the icon image. Position the drawing window correctly to create a meaningful image.
- When selecting the base point for the circuit commands, it is a good idea to use temporary OSNAPS to accurately select the point.
- Four example icons are already defined.
- To edit an existing icon, right-click on it and select **Properties**.

4.10 WBlock Circuits

You can use the AutoCAD **Wblock** command to save the circuit as its own DWG file and then use it with the **Insert Wblock Circuit** command.

Wblock

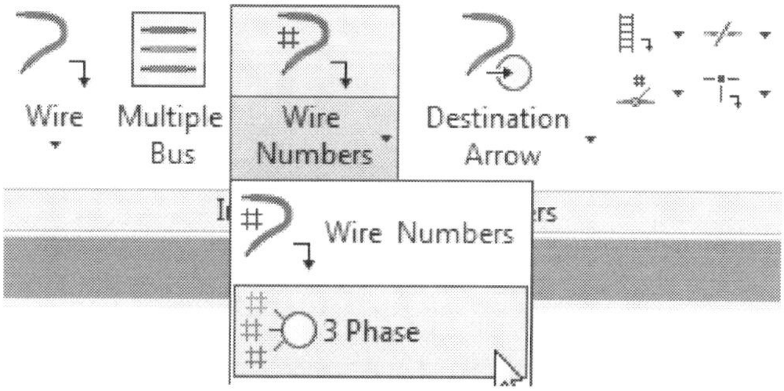

Ribbon: *Insert* tab>*Block Definition* panel
(not displayed by default so needs to be toggled on)

Command Prompt: Wblock

How To: Wblock a Circuit

1. Start the **Wblock** command. The *Write Block* dialog box opens, as shown in Figure 4–55.
2. Select the base point, and then the objects.
3. Specify the filename.
4. Click **OK**.

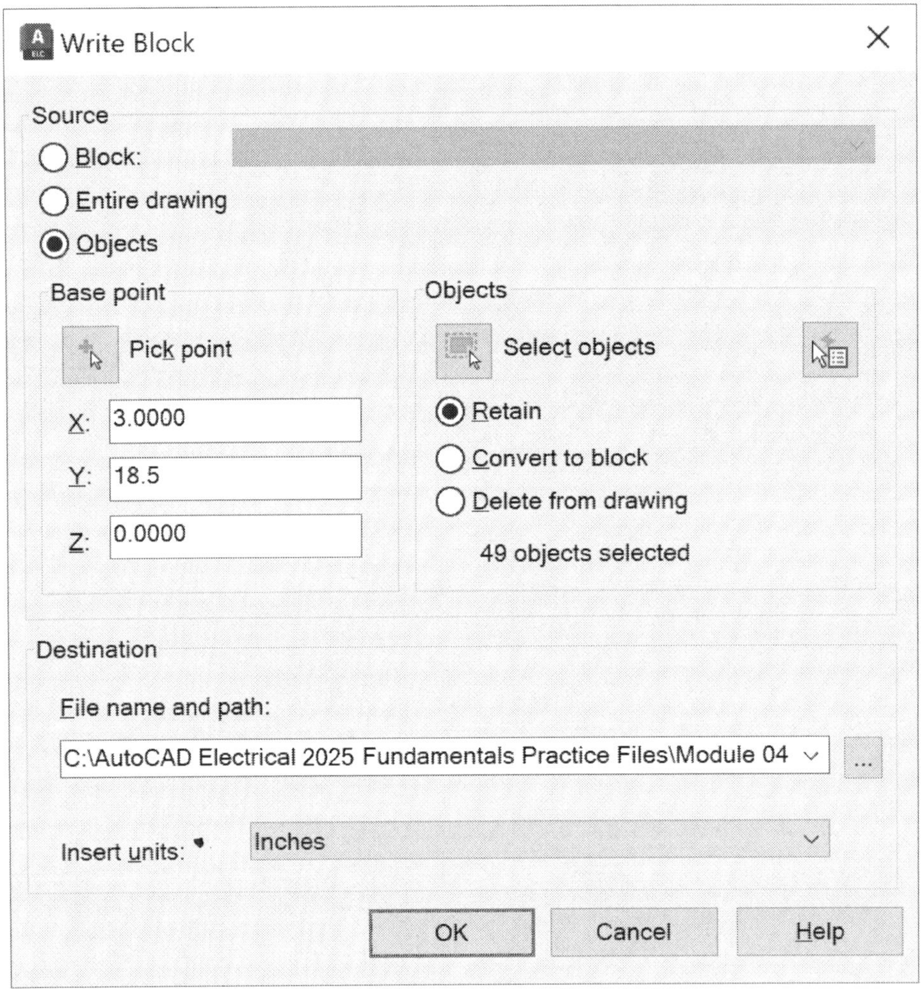

Figure 4–55

Source	• **Block:** Enables you to select an existing block to export. • **Entire drawing:** Exports the entire contents of the drawing as a block. • **Objects:** Enables you to select the block's objects.
Base point	Specify the base point for the block. You can select a point in the drawing window or type the coordinates.
Objects	Select the block's objects and what to do with the existing objects.
Destination	Specify the path and filename for the new DWG file and select the units for the block.

4.11 Copy Circuit

You can copy a circuit including components and wires in the same drawing using the **Copy Circuit** command. The copied components are retagged according to the new location.

Copy Circuit

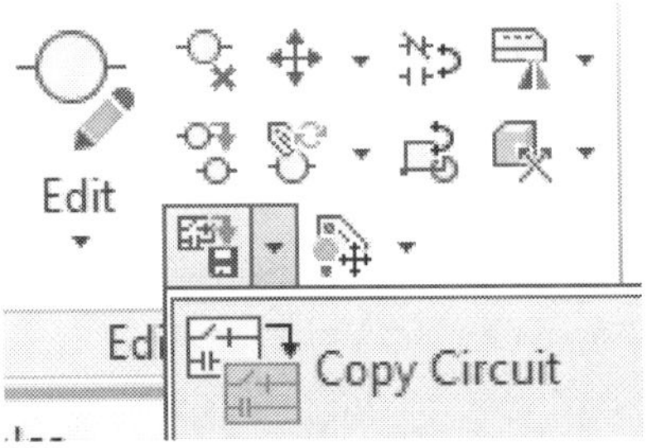

Ribbon: *Schematic* tab>*Edit Components* panel

Command Prompt: aecopycircuit

How To: Copy a Circuit

1. Start the **Copy Circuit** command.
2. Select the circuit to copy and right-click or press <Enter> to complete the selection.
3. Pick the base point.
4. Pick the location for the new circuit.

- The **Copy Circuit** command functions like the AutoCAD **Copy** command with added functionality to handle component tags and wire numbers.
- The **Multiple** option is available before selecting the base point.
- When the circuit is copied, the components are retagged and the wire numbers are set to "???".

Copy Circuit Options

When a circuit that is being copied has terminals, fixed wire numbers, or component tags, there are options available for the new circuit. After selecting the location for the new circuit, the *Copy Circuit Options* dialog box opens, as shown in Figure 4–56.

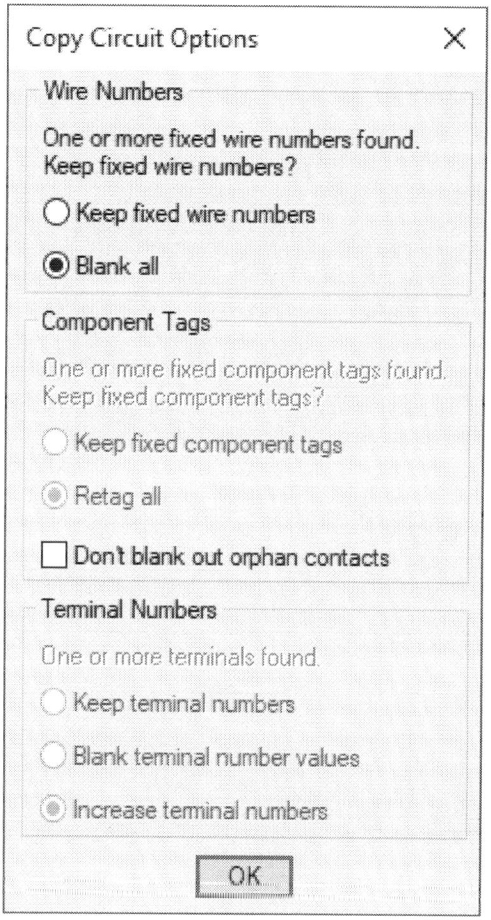

Figure 4–56

- For *Wire Numbers*, there are options for keeping the numbers set as **Fixed** or to blank them all.
- For *Component Tags*, there are options for keeping the tags set as **Fixed**, or to retag them all. Another option that can be selected is to not blank out orphan contacts.
- For *Terminal Numbers*, the options include to keep the terminal numbers, blank out their values, or increment their number.

4.12 Move Circuit

You can move a circuit from one location in a drawing to another location using the **Move Circuit** command.

Move Circuit

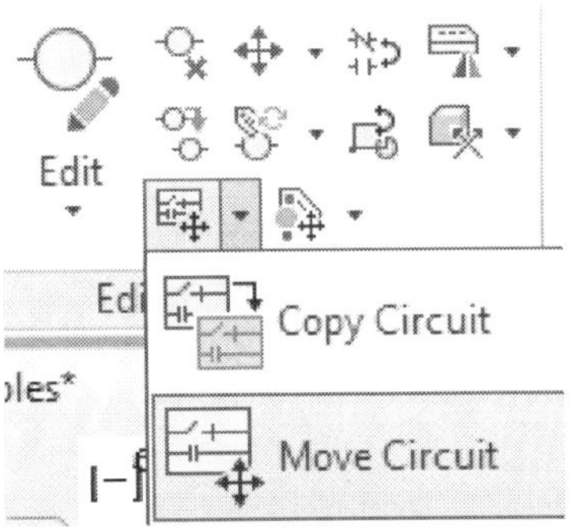

Ribbon: *Schematic* tab>*Edit Components* panel

Command Prompt: aemovecircuit

How To: Move a Circuit

1. Start the **Move Circuit** command.
2. Select the circuit to move and right-click or press <Enter> to complete the selection.
3. Pick the base point from which to move.
4. Pick the point to which to move the circuit.

- The **Move Circuit** command functions like the AutoCAD **Move** command with added functionality to handle component tags and wire numbers.
- When the circuit is moved, the components are retagged and wire numbers set to "???".

4.13 Circuit Clipboard

You can use the **Cut Circuit** and **Copy Circuit Clip** commands to cut/copy the components and wires and save them on a circuit clipboard. Use the **Paste Circuit** command to paste those objects in the same drawing or another drawing.

Copy Clip

Cut Circuit

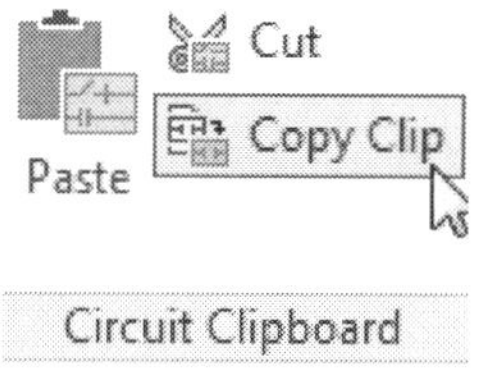

Ribbon: *Schematic* tab>*Circuit Clipboard* panel

Command Prompt: aecirccopyclip, aecirccut

How To: Cut or Copy a Circuit Reference

1. Start the **Copy Circuit Clip** or **Cut Circuit** command.
2. Select the base point to be used as an insertion point.
3. Select the circuit to copy or cut. If you use the **Cut Circuit** command, the selected objects are removed.
4. Press <Enter> to complete the command. The objects are placed on the clipboard.

Paste Circuit

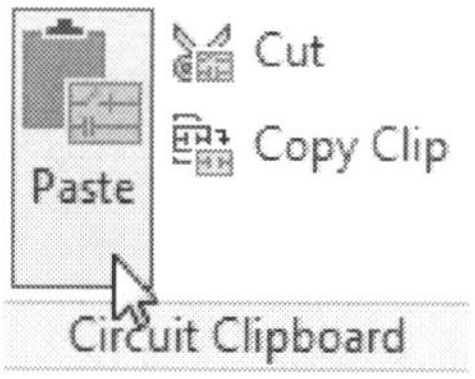

Ribbon: *Schematic* tab>*Circuit Clipboard* panel

Command Prompt: aecircpaste

How To: Paste a Circuit Reference

1. Start the **Paste Circuit** command.
2. Select the options in the *Circuit Scale* dialog box.
3. Pick the base point as an insertion point at which to paste the previously saved objects from the clipboard.

- The *Circuit Scale* dialog box (shown in Figure 4–57) provides you with the option of scaling the complete circuit and other options for the component tags and wire numbers.

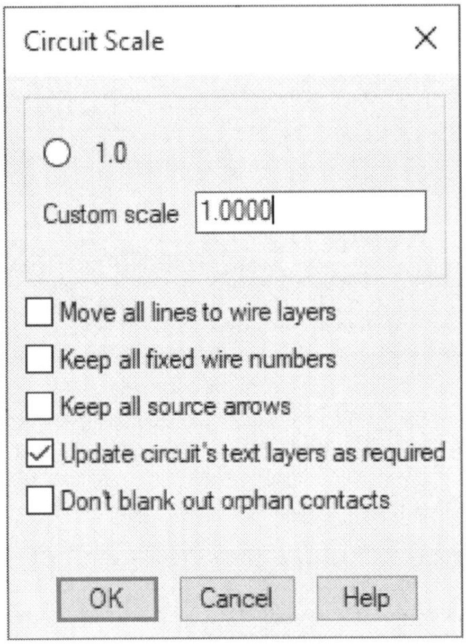

Figure 4–57

- For Wire Numbers, you can keep the numbers set as fixed, or blank them all.
- For Component Tags, you can keep them or retag them all.
- Another option that can be selected is to not blank out orphan contacts.

4.14 Circuit Builder

The **Circuit Builder** command builds a circuit based on information selected from a list. The circuit is built on-the-fly, enabling the software to adjust for rung spacing, wires between components, and annotation.

Circuit Builder

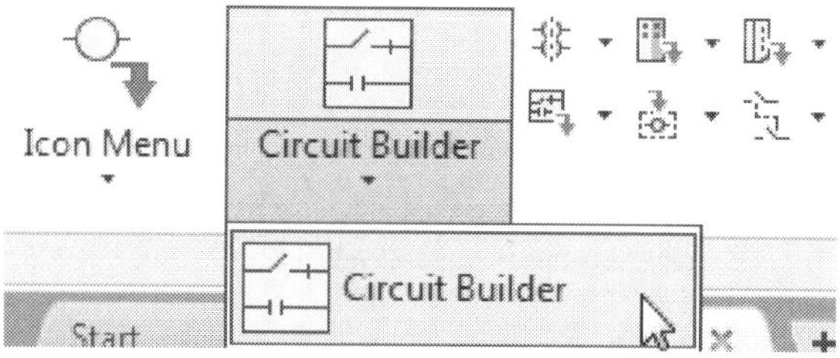

Ribbon: *Schematic* tab>*Insert Components* panel

Command Prompt: aecircbuilder

How To: Insert a Circuit Using Circuit Builder

1. Start the **Circuit Builder** command.
2. In the *Circuit Selection* dialog box, select the circuit to insert.
3. Click **Insert** to insert using default settings or **Configure** to insert the circuit and customize the settings.
4. Select the insertion point for the circuit.

- A spreadsheet called **ace_circuit_builder.xls** is used to define the available circuits, circuit types, and default values. The default location for the spreadsheet is *C:\Users\Public\Documents\Autodesk\Acade <version>\Support* for Windows 10.
- Drawing templates are used to define the placement of components and wire types for a circuit. The default location for drawing templates is *C:\Users\Public\Documents\Autodesk\Acade <version>\Libs\<library>* for Windows 10.
- You can create custom circuits by modifying the spreadsheet and creating DWG files to use as templates.

The *Circuit Selection* dialog box (shown in Figure 4–58) has the following options:

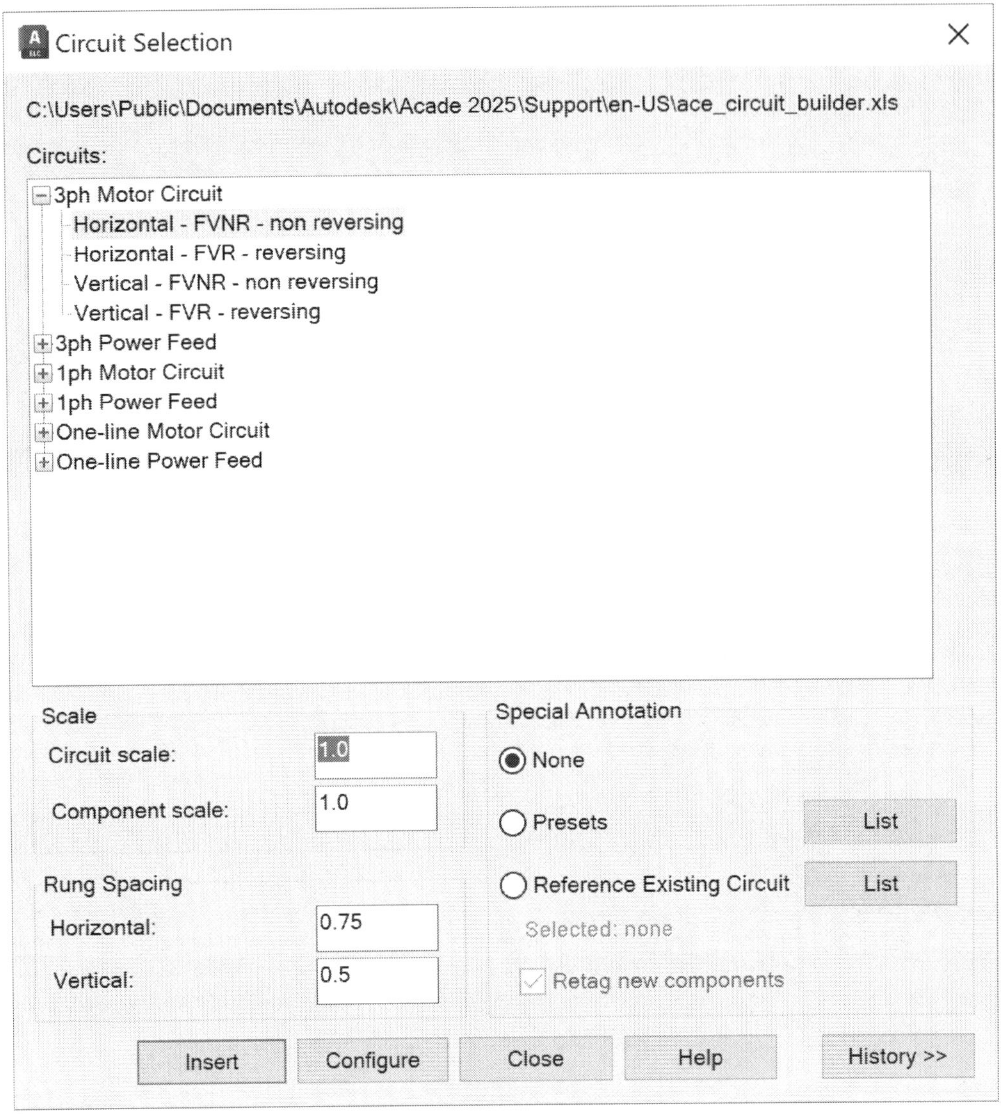

Figure 4–58

Circuits	Displays a selectable list of predefined circuits.
Scale	Set a scale for the overall circuit or for individual components.
Rung Spacing	Set the horizontal and vertical rung spacing.
Presets	Defines preset descriptions for circuit components before insertion. Click **List** to open the *Annotation Presets* dialog box.

Reference Existing Circuit	References data (descriptions, values, and Tag ID's) in an existing circuit in the active project. Click **List** to open the *Existing Circuits* dialog box. (When a reference circuit has been selected, the **Retag new components** option becomes available.)
Retag new components	• When toggled **On**, new components receive new Tag IDs. • When toggled **Off**, Circuit Builder attempts to reuse the referenced circuits' Tag IDs. • Available when the **Reference Existing Circuit** option is selected.
Insert	Inserts the circuit using the default settings.
Configure	Customizes the settings, such as annotation values, for the circuit. Opens the *Circuit Configuration* dialog box.
History	Toggles on/off the display of the *History* area where the information about the selected circuit displays.

The *Annotation Presets* dialog box (shown in Figure 4–59) enables you to select individual rows and enter their preset value. You can also click on **Drawing** or **Project** for a list of previously used values.

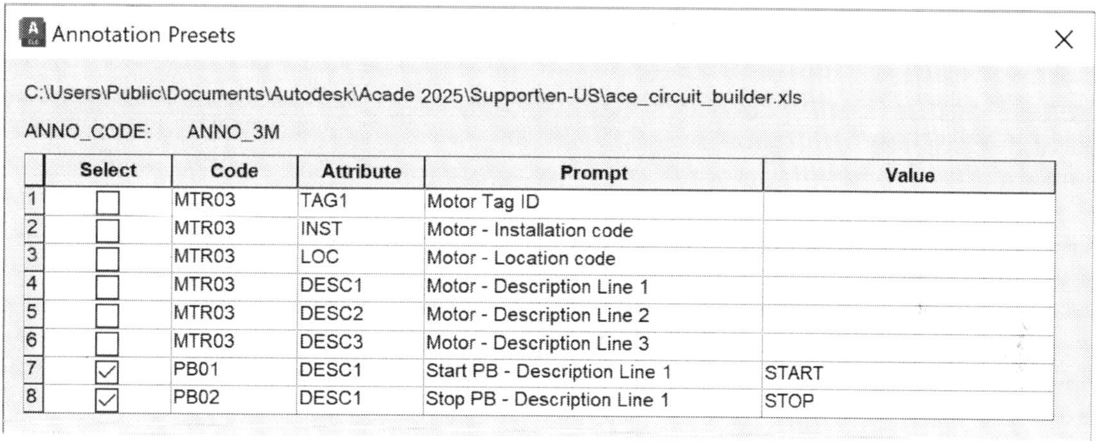

Figure 4–59

The *Existing Circuits* dialog box (shown in Figure 4–60) displays a list of all previously inserted circuits in the active project. You can select any circuit in the list to reference.

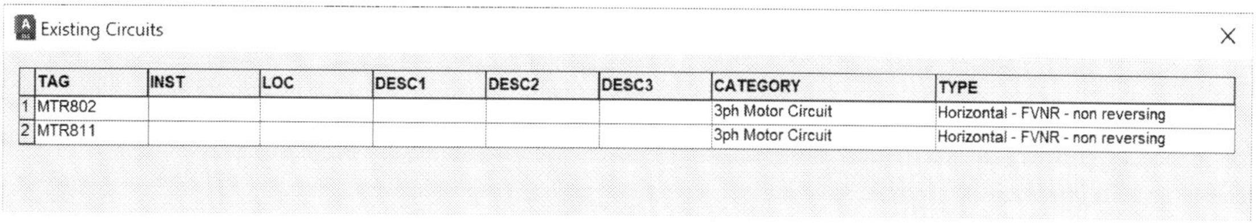

Figure 4–60

The *Circuit Configuration* dialog box (shown in Figure 4–61) is used to customize the settings for the circuit. You can configure physical devices and device annotation values.

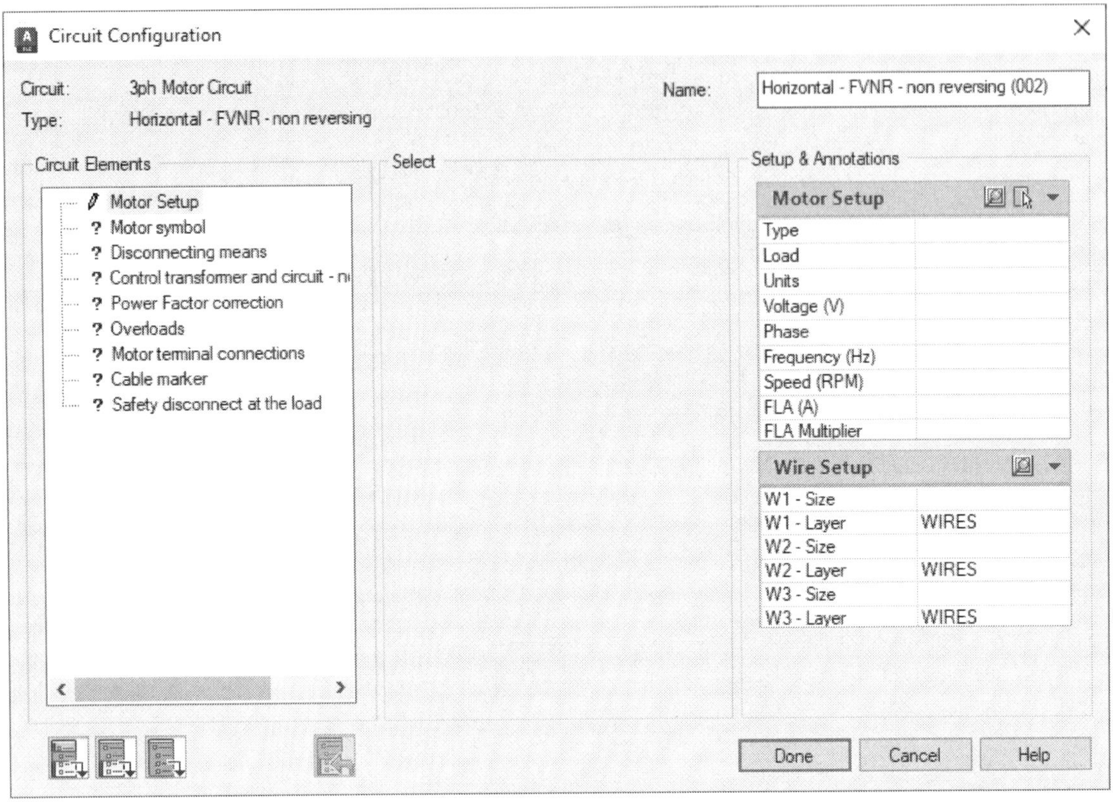

Figure 4–61

Name	Displays in the *History* area in the *Circuit Selection* dialog box for future insertions.
Circuit Elements	Displays the circuit elements for the selected circuit. The list is built based on the circuit template. Select an element to configure it.
Select	Select the options for the highlighted circuit element. They are based on the circuit spreadsheet.
Setup & Annotations	Configures the circuit elements, including device annotation values, rung spacing, and wire type. • Select a field and use the drop-down list to change settings or click to display a dialog box or click to select an existing symbol.

	Inserts the selected circuit element.
	Inserts the circuit elements up to and including the selected element.
	Inserts all circuit elements.
	Undoes the last element insertion.

Practice 4d
Reuse Circuits

Practice Objectives

- Copy, move, and paste circuit segments.
- Save a circuit segment and then insert it.

In this practice, you will work with an existing circuit. You will copy the circuit and then move it. You will also copy and paste the circuit references using the **Circuit Clipboard** commands. Finally, you will save the circuit to the Icon Menu and **Wblock** it to insert it into the drawing. The final circuit displays as shown in Figure 4–62.

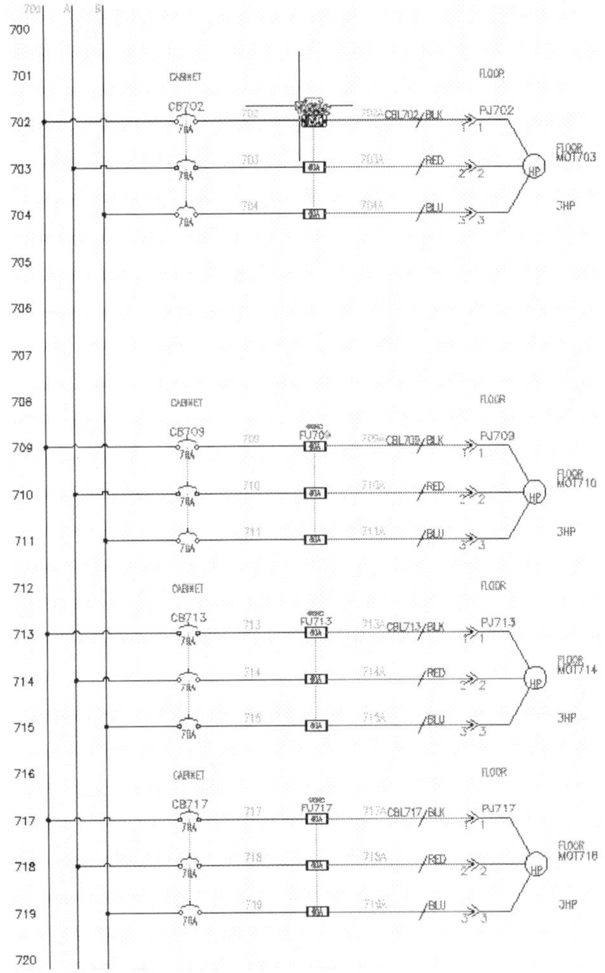

Figure 4–62

Task 1: Copy a circuit.

1. If the **Module 04** project is not active, open and activate it now.
2. Open **User Circuits.dwg** in the Module 04 project.
3. Zoom to the 3 phase circuit near the top of the drawing.
4. In the *Schematic* tab>*Edit Components* panel, click  (Copy Circuit).
5. Window around the 3 phase circuit at the top of the ladder, as shown in Figure 4–63. Be sure the rail numbers are not included in the selection set. Press <Enter> to continue the command.

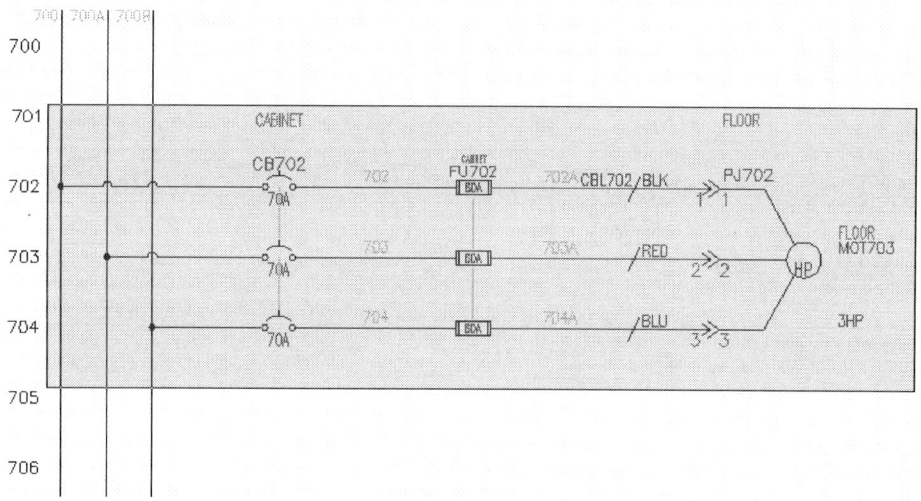

Figure 4–63

6. Use the **Endpoint** OSNAP to select the wire connection point on line 702 as the base point, as shown in Figure 4–64.

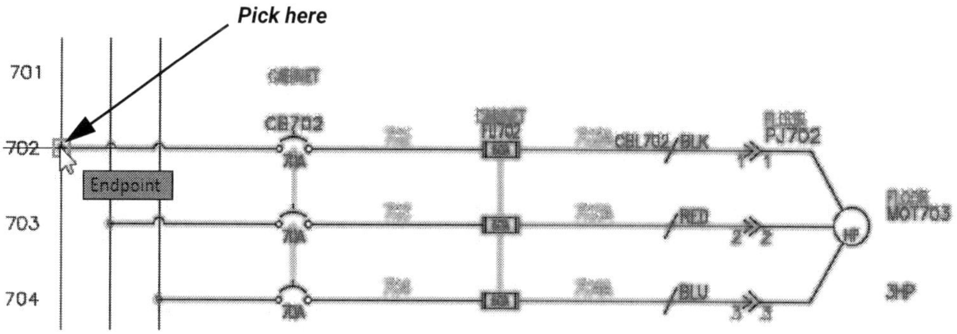

Figure 4–64

7. Select the farthest left rail on line 707 as the second point of displacement, as shown in Figure 4–65. Press <Enter> to complete the command.

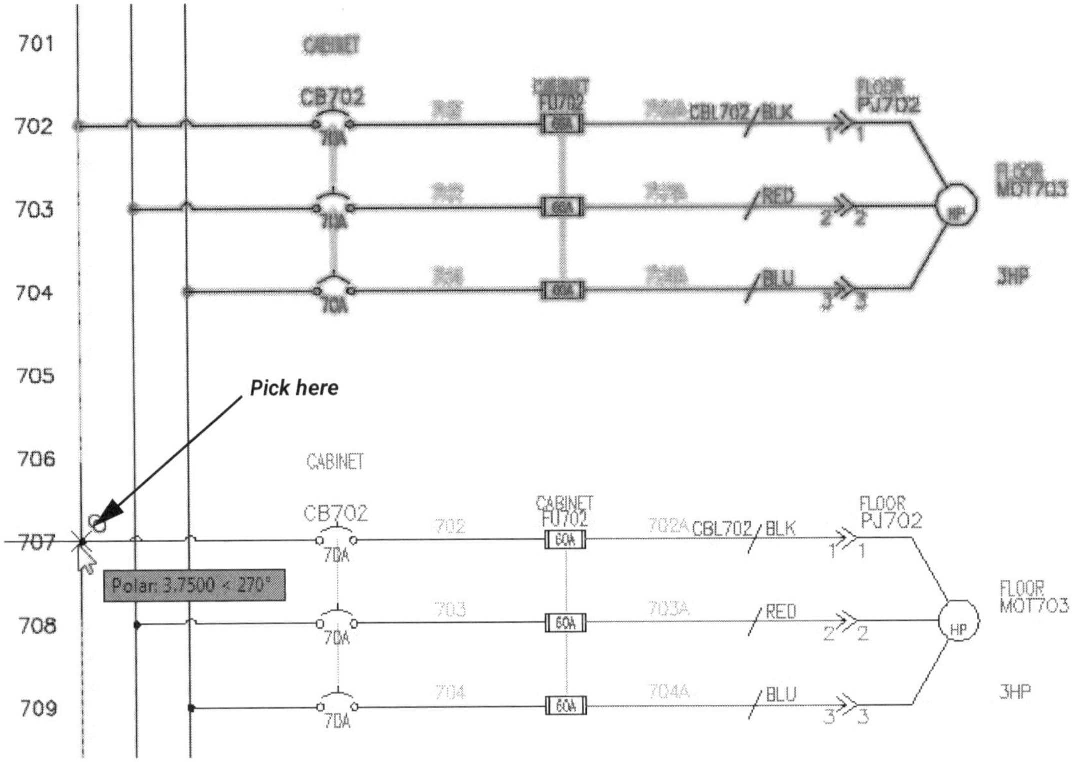

Figure 4–65

8. Note that all of the components are retagged with the exception of wire numbers that display as ???. Run the **Wire Numbers** command using **Drawing-wide**.

Task 2: Move a circuit.

1. In the *Schematic* tab>*Edit Components* panel, click (Move Circuit).
2. Window around the 3 phase circuit starting at line 707, as shown in Figure 4–66. Do not include the rail numbers. Press <Enter> to continue.

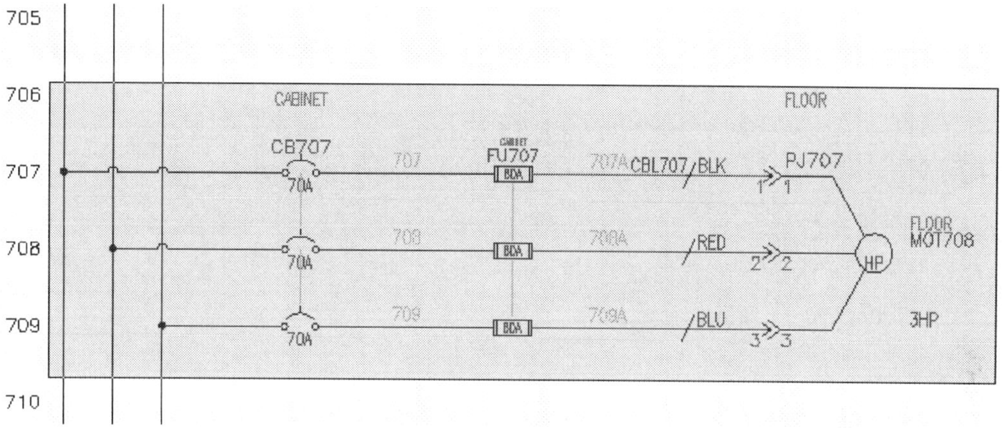

Figure 4–66

3. Select the wire connection point at line 707 as the base point, as shown in Figure 4–67.

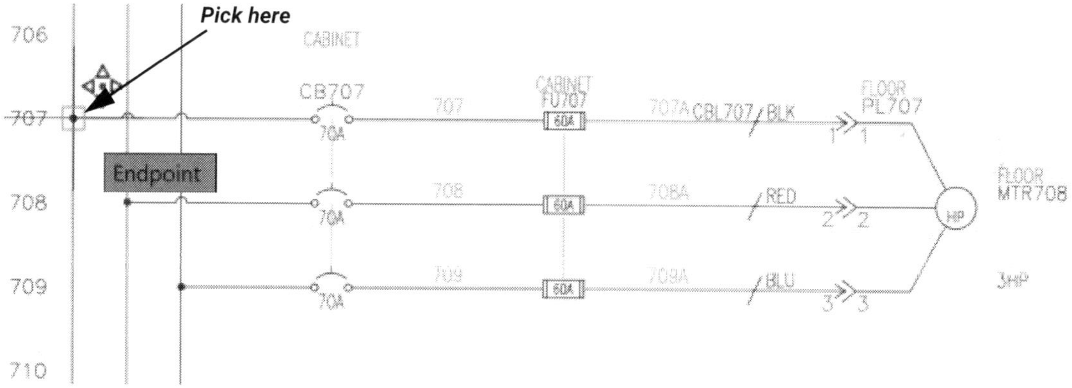

Figure 4–67

4. Select on the farthest left rail at line 709 as the second point of displacement, as shown in Figure 4–68.

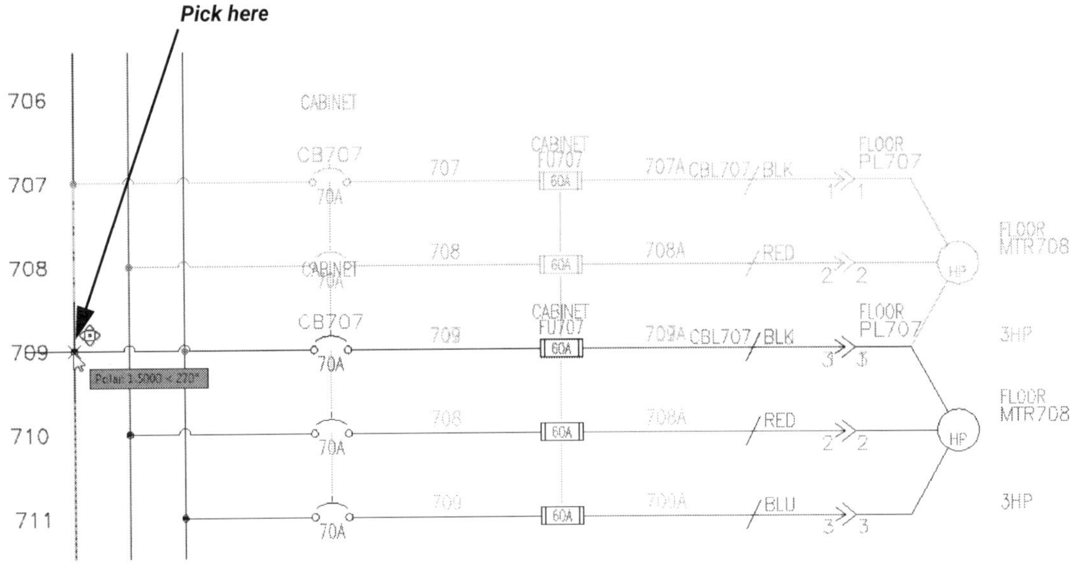

Figure 4–68

5. In the *Update Related Components* dialog box, click **Yes-Update**. Note that the wire numbers are updated automatically.

Task 3: Copy and paste circuit references using the clipboard.

1. Zoom to lines 701 to 705.
2. In the *Schematic* tab>*Circuit Clipboard* panel, click  (Copy Clip).
3. Select the wire connection point on line 702 as the base point.
4. Window around the 3-phase circuit on line 702. Ensure that the rail numbers are not included in the selection set. Press <Enter> to complete the command.
5. Open **User Circuits 2.dwg** in the Module 04 project.
6. Toggle off **Osnap** in the Status Bar.
7. Zoom to lines 710 to 716.
8. In the *Schematic* tab>*Circuit Clipboard* panel, click  (Paste). The *Circuit Scale* dialog box opens.
9. In the *Circuit Scale* dialog box, verify that only **Update circuit's text layers as required** is selected. Click **OK**.

10. Select the wire connection point on the farthest left rail at line 712 as the base point, as shown in Figure 4–69.
    - You might need to clear the **Endpoint Osnap** selection, otherwise it will paste it to the bottom endpoint.

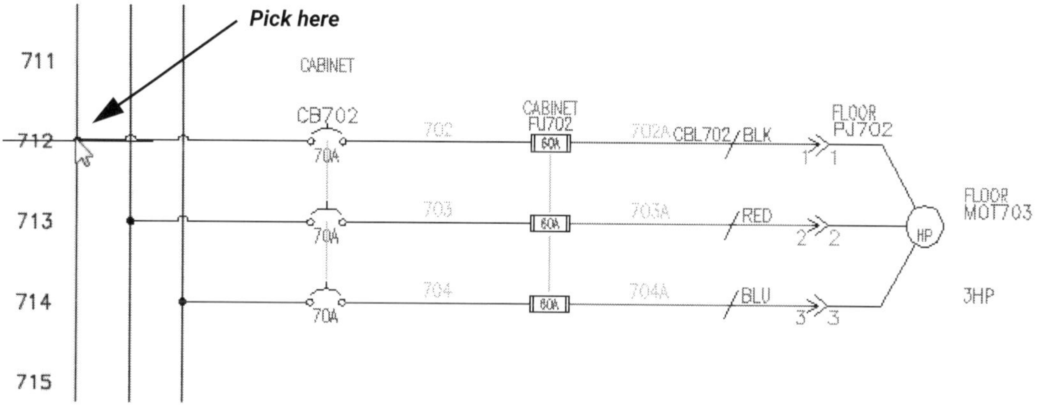

Figure 4–69

11. Note that the wire numbers display as ???. Run the **Wire Numbers** command using **Drawing-wide**.

Task 4: Save a circuit to the Icon Menu.

1. Open **User Circuits.dwg** in the Module 04 project.
2. In the *Schematic* tab>*Edit Components* panel, click  (Save Circuit to Icon Menu). The *Save Circuit to Icon Menu* dialog box opens.
3. In the *Saved User Circuits* area that displays the icon previews, right-click in a blank area and select **Add icon>New circuit**. The *Create New Circuit* dialog box opens.

4. In the *Name*, *Image file*, and *File name* fields, type **My Circuit**. Verify that **Create PNG from current screen image** is selected, as shown in Figure 4–70. Click **OK**.
   - If prompted, click **OK** to overwrite the existing files.

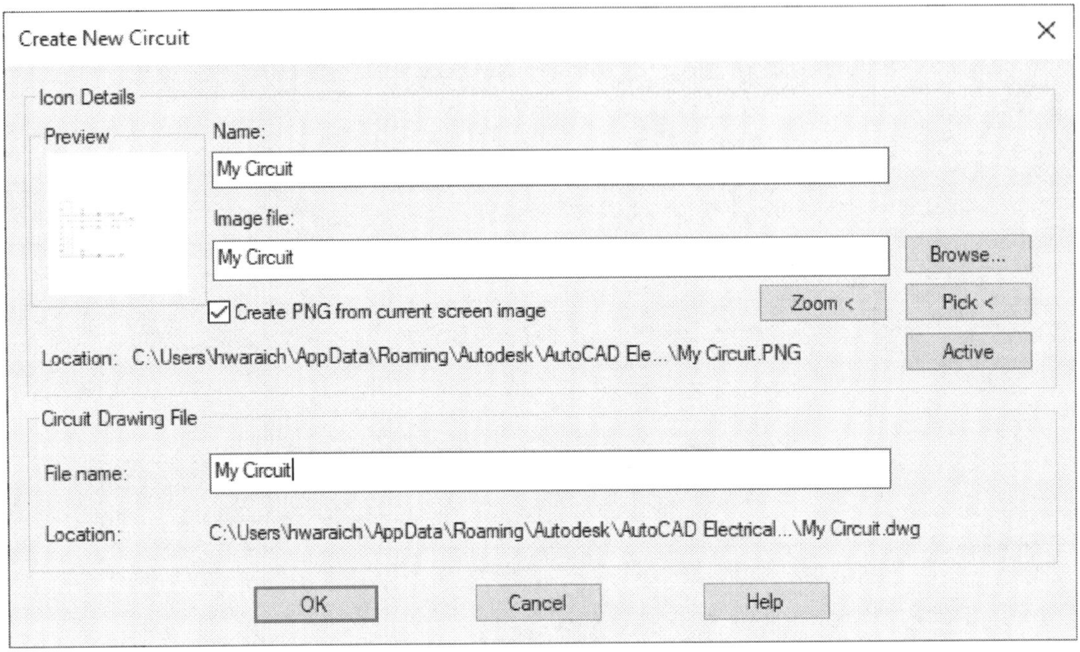

Figure 4–70

5. Pick the wire connection point on line 702 as the base point as you did with the **Copy Circuit** command.
6. Window around the circuit at lines 702 to 704. Press <Enter> to continue.
7. The *Save Circuit to Icon Menu* dialog box opens with **My Circuit** added as a new saved circuit. Click **OK**.
   - The circuit is saved and an icon is created from the current screen image.
8. Zoom to lines 713 to 715.
9. In the *Schematic* tab>*Insert Components* panel, click 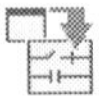 (Insert Saved Circuit).
10. In the *Insert Component* dialog box, click My Circuit (My Circuit) to insert your circuit.
11. The *Circuit Scale* dialog box opens. Leave the defaults and click **OK**.
12. Pick a point on the farthest left rail on line 713 for the insertion point.

Task 5: WBlock a circuit.

1. Zoom to lines 701 to 705.
2. At the Command Prompt, type **WBLOCK** and press <Enter>. The *Write Block* dialog box opens.
3. In the *Base point* area, click (Pick point) to select the base point. Select the wire connection point at line 702.
4. In the *Objects* area, click (Select objects) to select the objects. Window around the 3-phase circuit on line 702 as done in previous steps. Press <Enter> to return to the dialog box.
5. In the *Destination* area, click (Browse) to browse for the drawing location. Browse to the *Module 04* folder in your practice files folder. Leave the *File name* as the default **new block.dwg**. Click **Save**.
6. The *Write Block* dialog box should display similar to that shown in Figure 4–71. Click **OK**.

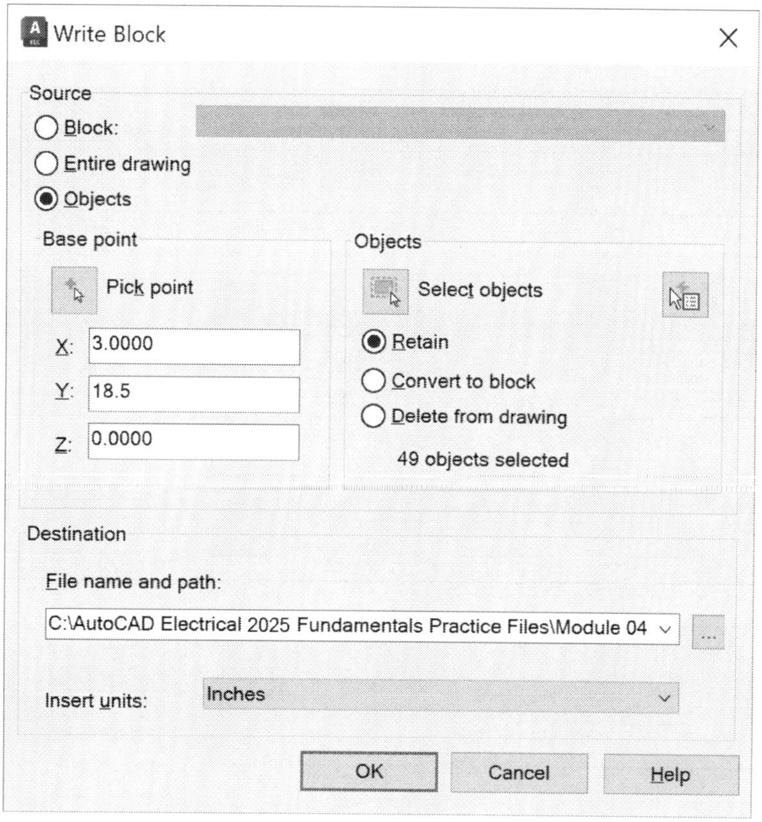

Figure 4–71

7. Zoom to lines 716 to 720.
8. In the *Schematic* tab>*Insert Components* panel, click  (Insert WBlocked Circuit).
   - If the dialog box does not display, type **FILEDIA** at the Command Prompt, press <Enter>, type **1**, and press <Enter> again.
9. In the *Insert WBlocked Circuit* dialog box, browse to the **new block.dwg** file in the *Module 04* folder in your practice files folder. Click **Open**.
10. In the *Circuit Scale* dialog box, click **OK**.
11. Pick a point on the farthest left rail at line 717.
12. Run the **Wire Numbers** command using **Drawing-wide**.
13. Save **User Circuits.dwg**.

End of practice

Practice 4e
Circuit Builder

Practice Objective

- Build and insert a circuit.

In this practice, you will insert two circuits using the Circuit Builder. The first circuit is inserted using the default settings. The second circuit is inserted with customized settings. The final circuit displays as shown in Figure 4–72.

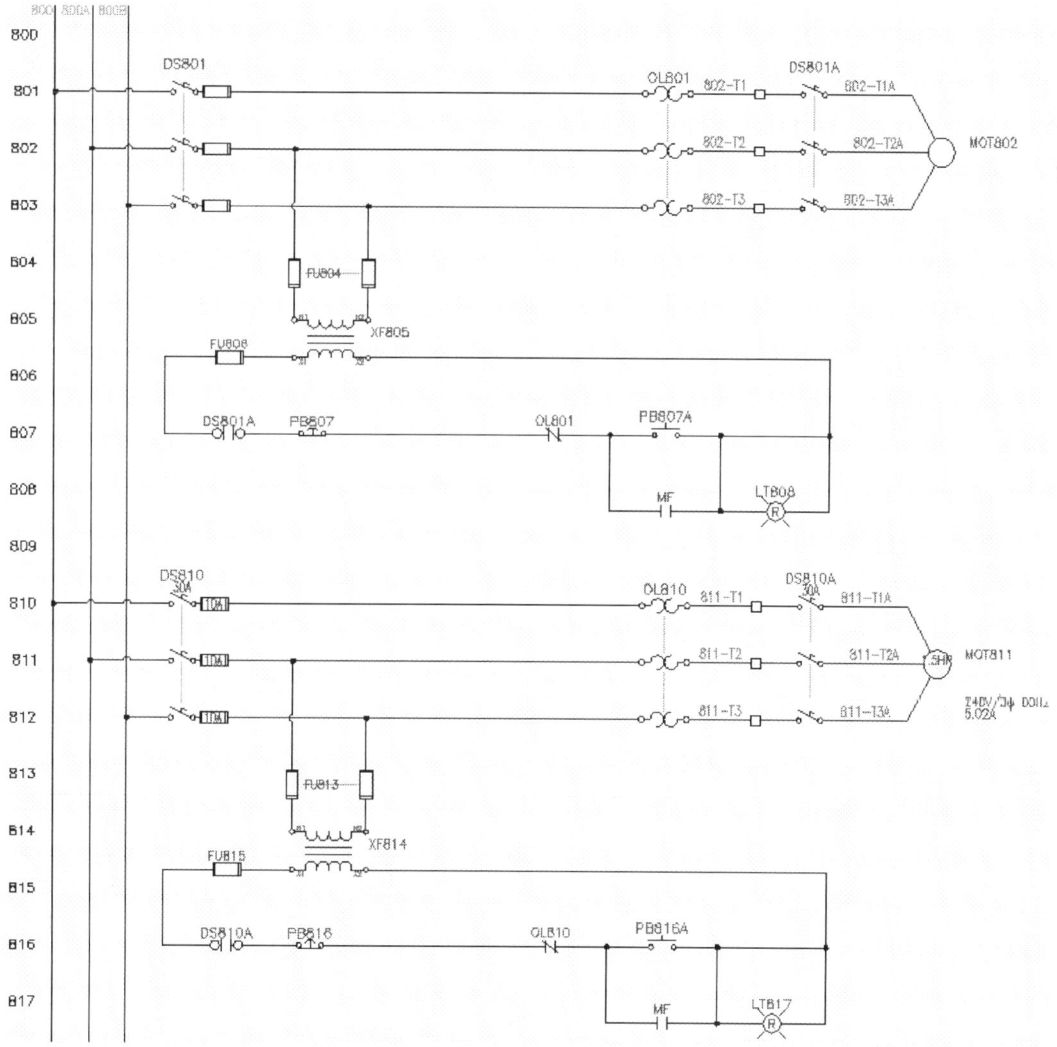

Figure 4–72

Task 1: Insert a circuit with default settings.

1. If the **Module 04** project is not active, open and activate it now.
2. In the **Module 04** project, open **Circuit Builder.dwg**.
3. Zoom to lines 800 to 810.
4. In the *Schematic* tab>*Insert Components* panel, click  (Circuit Builder). The *Circuit Selection* dialog box opens.
5. In the *Circuits* area, select **3ph Motor Circuit>Horizontal FVNR – non reversing**, and click **Insert**.
6. Pick a point on the farthest left rail on line 801 for the insertion point. Note that the entire circuit is inserted with the default values.

Task 2: Insert a circuit with customized settings.

1. Zoom to lines 810 to 820.
2. Click  (Circuit Builder). The *Circuit Selection* dialog box opens.
3. In the *Circuits* area, select **3ph Motor Circuit>Horizontal FVNR – non reversing**, and click **Configure**.
4. Pick a point on the farthest left rail on line 810 for the insertion point. The template for the circuit is inserted and the *Circuit Configuration* dialog box opens.
5. In the *Setup & Annotations* area, in the *Motor Setup* title bar, click  to open the *Select Motor* dialog box.
6. At the top of the dialog box, using the appropriate drop-down lists, set the following:
   - *Type*: **Induction**
   - *Voltage*: **240**
   - *Frequency*: **60**

7. Select the **1.5 HP, 3 Phase, 1800 RPM** motor, as shown in Figure 4–73.

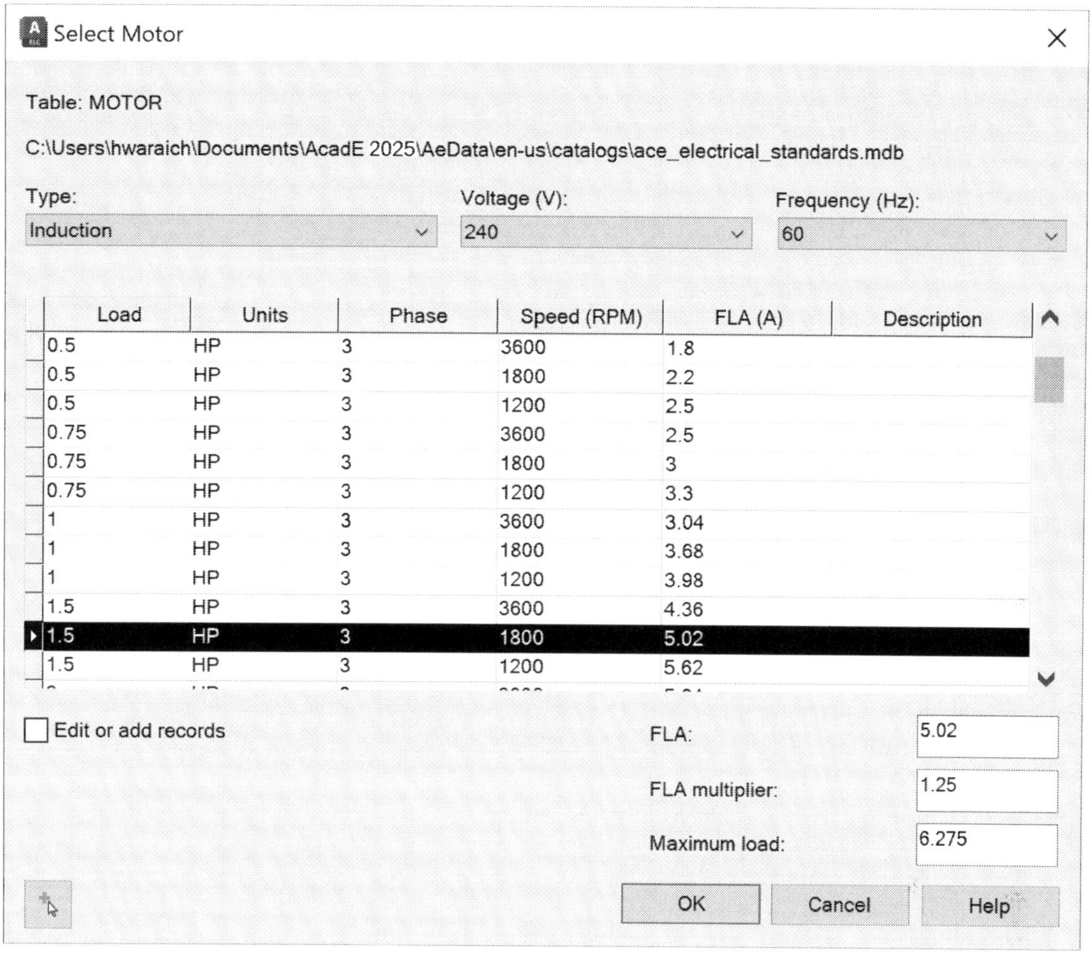

Figure 4–73

8. Click **OK**. Note that in the *Circuit Configuration* dialog box, the *Motor Setup* list values are populated with the relevant data.
9. In the *Circuit Configuration* dialog box, in the *Wire Setup* title bar, click to open the *Wire Size Lookup* dialog box.
10. Select **12AWG** and click **OK**. The information in the *Wire Setup* list updates to match the selected wire size.

11. In the bottom left corner of the dialog box, click (the leftmost icon), as shown in Figure 4–74, to only insert the highlighted circuit element with the customized values.

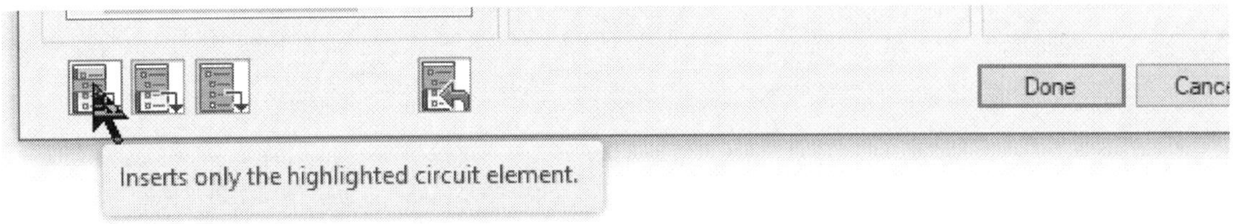
Done
Inserts only the highlighted circuit element.

Figure 4–74

12. In the *Circuit Elements* area, select **Disconnecting means** and click (the leftmost icon) to only insert the highlighted circuit element with the default values.
13. In the *Circuit Elements* area, select **Control transformer and circuit – non-reversing** and click (the leftmost icon) to only insert the highlighted circuit element with the default values. This circuit element is a nested circuit. Therefore, when the *Circuit Configuration* dialog box opens again, in the *Circuit Elements* area, note that the node is expanded to display the components in this circuit, as shown in Figure 4–75.
14. Select **Power Factor correction** and click (the middle icon) to insert all the elements up to the selected element, as shown in Figure 4–75. Note that all the elements up to and including **Power Factor correction** have a blue checkmark.

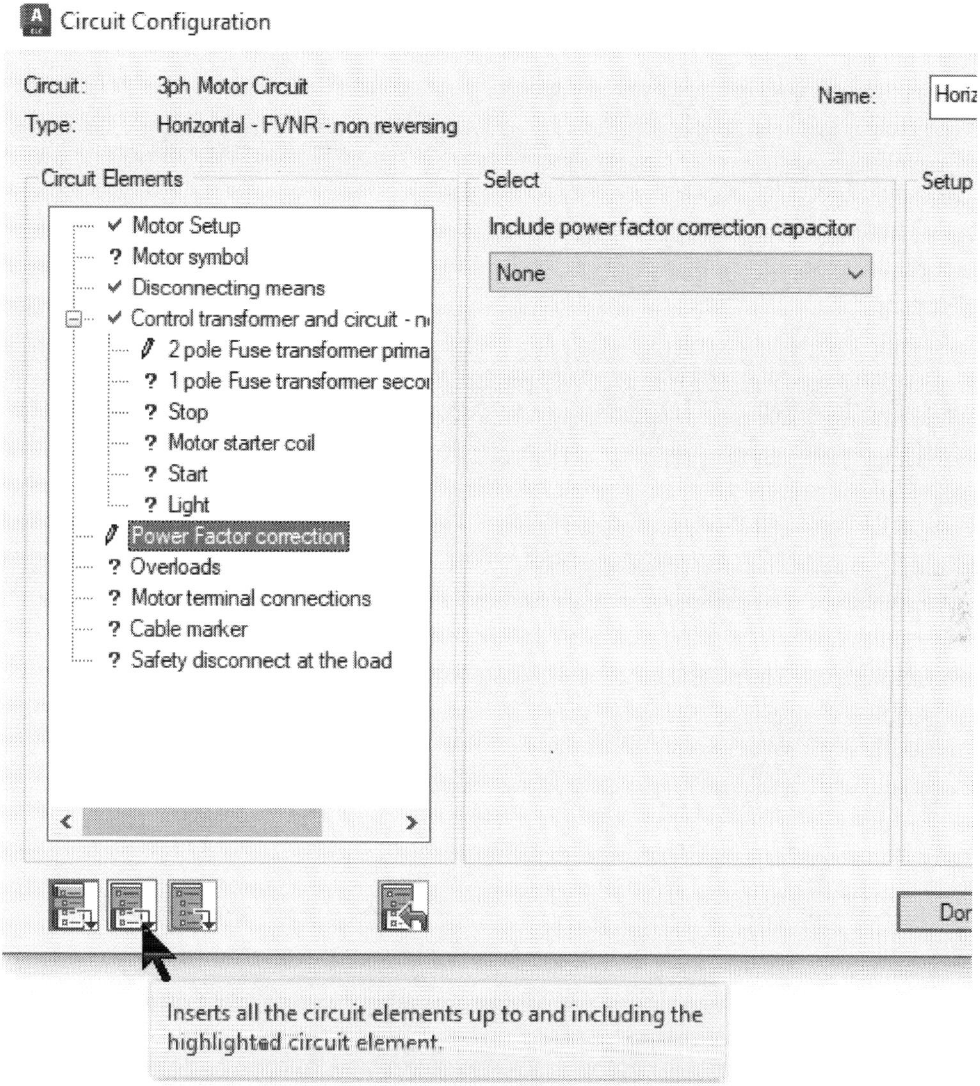

Figure 4–75

15. Click (the third icon) to insert the rest of the circuit. Note that all the elements now have a blue checkmark.
16. Click **Done** to close the dialog box.
17. Save and close all the open drawings.

End of practice

Chapter Review Questions

1. What is the purpose of the dashed link lines?
    a. Create cross-reference link for contacts in a multicontact component.
    b. Link components that have the same description.
    c. Link similar components for easy identification.
    d. Convert solid lines to dashed lines.

2. Do wire numbers inserted using the **3-phase Wire Number** command automatically update when the **Automatic Wire Number** command is used?
    a. Yes
    b. No

3. Where is the generic cable color information stored for the *Insert / Edit Cable Marker* dialog box?
    a. In the default project file.
    b. In a template file.
    c. In the file **cblcolor.dat**.
    d. In the file **genericcablecolor.dwg**.

4. What is the benefit of using the AutoCAD Electrical **Copy Circuit** and **Move Circuit** commands versus the AutoCAD **Copy** and **Move** commands?
    a. The AutoCAD Electrical commands do not work with the non-AutoCAD Electrical components.
    b. The AutoCAD Electrical commands retag components and reset wire numbers.
    c. The AutoCAD Electrical commands use fewer mouse clicks.
    d. The AutoCAD Electrical commands associate the commands within the project.

5. When using the Circuit Builder, how can you customize the annotation values of the components in the circuit?

   a. Select the circuit in the *Circuit Selection* dialog box and click **Customize**.

   b. Select the circuit in the *Circuit Selection* dialog box and click **Annotation**.

   c. Select the component, right-click and select **Edit**.

   d. Select the circuit in the *Circuit Selection* dialog box and click **Configure**.

Command Summary

Button	Command	Location
	**3 Phase Wire Numbers**	• **Ribbon:** *Schematic* tab>*Insert Wires/Wire Numbers* panel
	**Cable Markers**	• **Ribbon**: *Schematic* tab>*Insert Wires/Wire Numbers* panel
	**Circuit Builder**	• **Ribbon**: *Schematic* tab>*Insert Components* panel
	**Copy Circuits**	• **Ribbon:** *Schematic* tab>*Edit Components* panel
	**Copy Clip Circuit**	• **Ribbon:** *Schematic* tab>*Circuit Clipboard* panel
	**Cut Circuit**	• **Ribbon:** *Schematic* tab>*Circuit Clipboard* panel
	**Fan In Source**	• **Ribbon**: *Schematic* tab>*Insert Wires/Wire Numbers* panel
	**Fan Out Destination**	• **Ribbon:** *Schematic* tab>*Insert Wires/Wire Numbers* panel
	**Insert Saved Circuit**	• **Ribbon:** *Schematic* tab>*Insert Components* panel
	**Insert Wblocked Circuit**	• **Ribbon:** *Schematic* tab>*Insert Components* panel
	**Link Components with Dashed Line**	• **Ribbon**: *Schematic* tab>*Insert Components* panel
	**Move Circuit**	• **Ribbon:** *Schematic* tab>*Edit Components* panel
	**Multiple Bus**	• **Ribbon:** *Schematic* tab>*Insert Wires/Wire Numbers* panel
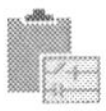	**Paste Circuit**	• **Ribbon:** *Schematic* tab>*Circuit Clipboard* panel
	**Save Circuit to Icon Menu**	• **Ribbon**: *Schematic* tab>*Edit Components* panel
	**Scoot**	• **Ribbon**: *Schematic* tab>*Edit Components* panel
NA	**WBLOCK**	• **Command Prompt:** WBLOCK
	**Wire Leaders**	• **Ribbon**: *Schematic* tab>*Insert Wires/Wire Numbers* panel

Chapter 5

Editing Commands

The AutoCAD® Electrical software provides you with a variety of editing commands that enable you to efficiently modify the components in a schematic drawing. Additional commands are also provided that enable you to modify the attributes in symbols. The effective use of these commands saves time when making changes to your designs and components.

Learning Objectives

- Edit parent or child components.
- Update the referenced components in other drawings.
- Move a component on its current wire or anywhere in the current drawing.
- Copy and automatically retag a component.
- Align multiple components vertically or horizontally.
- Delete a component from a drawing.
- Browse through a component's relationships and navigate to their locations.
- Assign the same catalog information to multiple components.
- Assign the same installation or location code to multiple components.
- Modify the attributes of an individual component.

5.1 Edit Component

You can edit components using the **Edit Component** command.

Edit Component

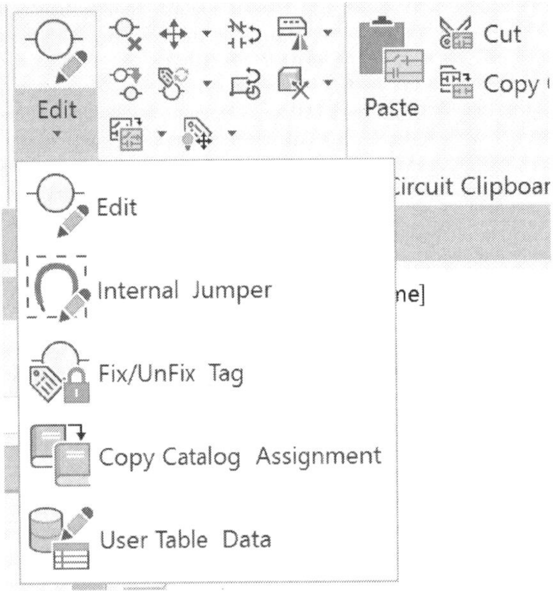

Ribbon: *Schematic* tab>*Edit Components* panel

Command Prompt: aeeditcomponent

Shortcut menu: *(on a component)* **Edit Component**

How To: Edit a Component

1. Start the **Edit Component** command.
2. Select the component to edit. The *Insert / Edit Component* dialog box opens.
   - The options in the dialog box vary and are based on the type of component selected for editing.
3. Modify the required information in the dialog box.
4. Click **OK**.

- Double-clicking a component opens the *Enhanced Attribute Editor*. It only modifies attribute values and has limited functionality.

Edit Parent Component

The *Insert / Edit Component* dialog box (shown in Figure 5–1) displays when a parent component is inserted into a drawing and is also used when editing it. The dialog box enables you to edit various information such as the Installation code, Location and Catalog information, etc. Child components are automatically updated with the new information.

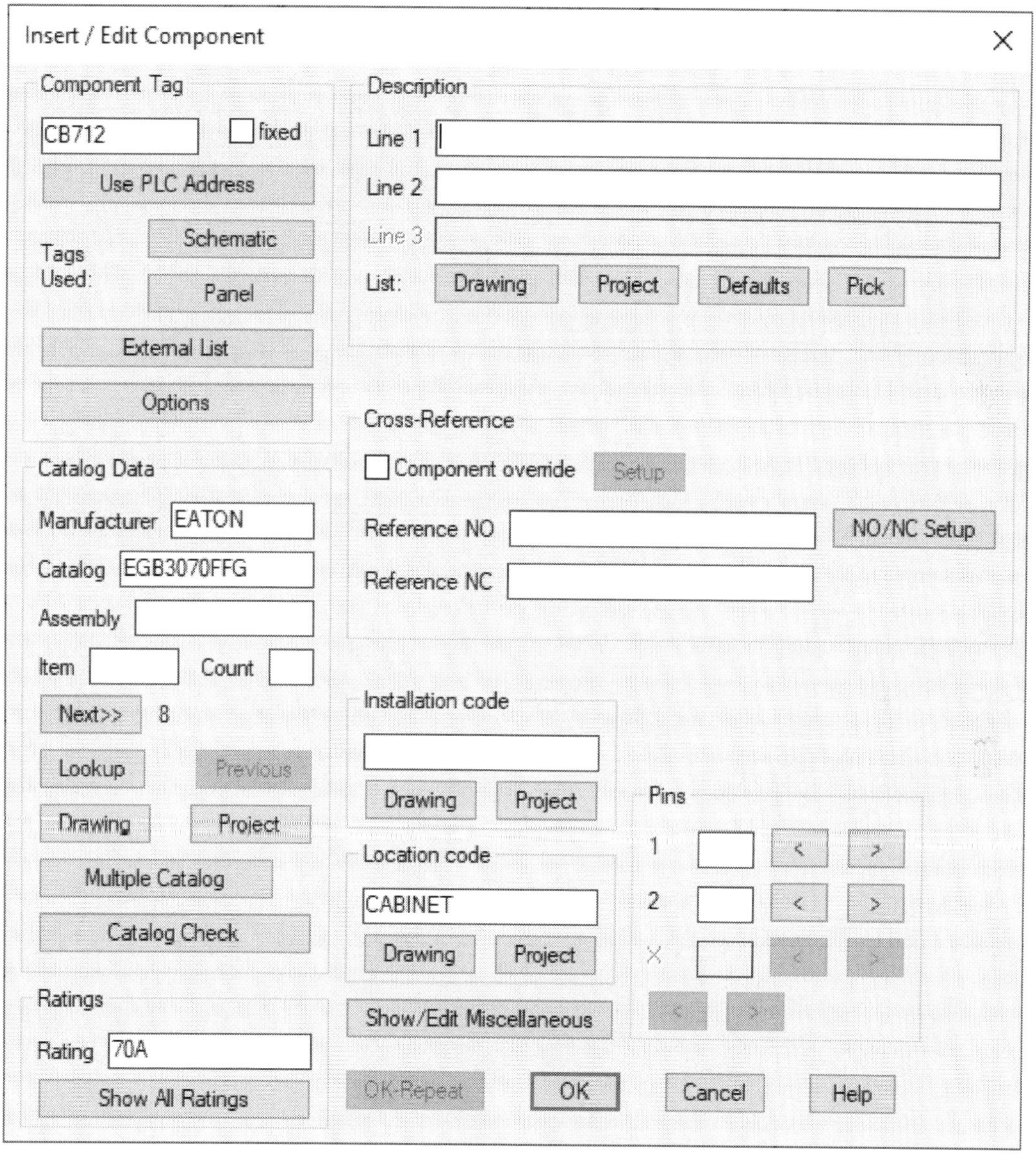

Figure 5–1

Edit Child Component

The *Insert / Edit Child Component* dialog box (shown in Figure 5–2) displays when a child component is inserted into a drawing and is also used when editing it. You can change the information for the child component, but the parent component does not update.

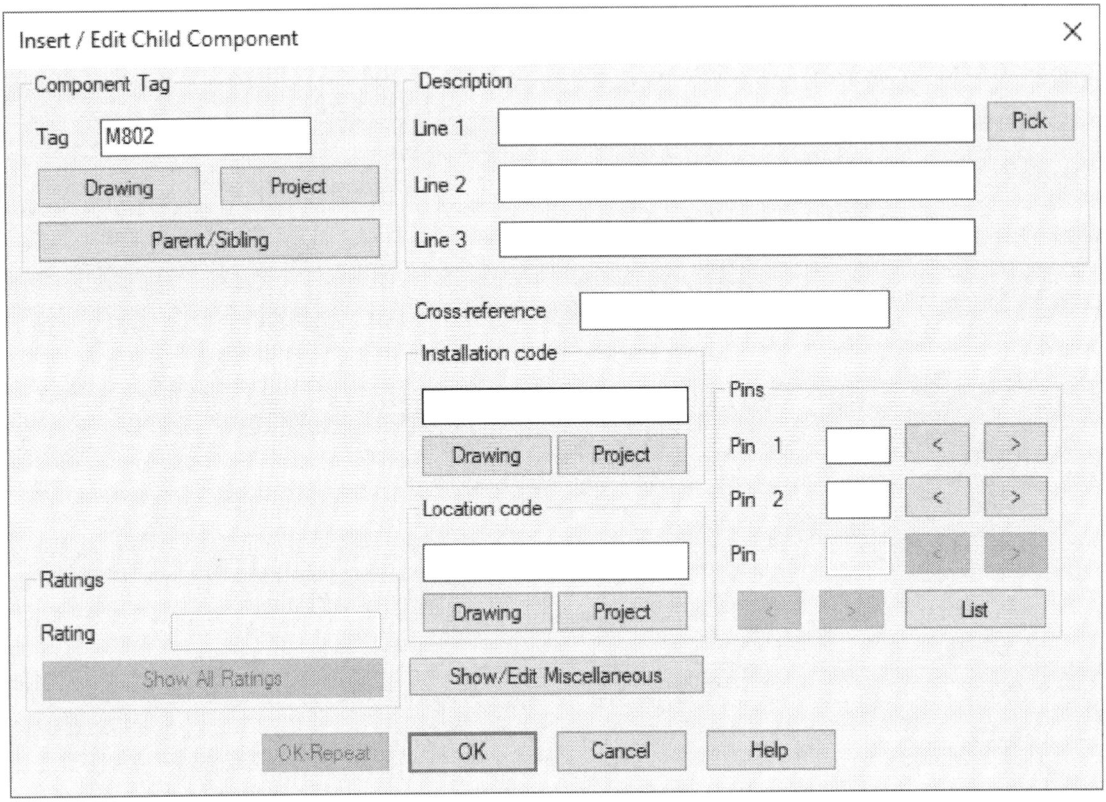

Figure 5–2

5.2 Updating Drawings

When editing components, any related components are also updated. If they are located in another drawing, you have the option of updating them immediately or adding them to the task list for updating later.

The software enables you to select when the reference updates are to be completed, using the *Update other drawings?* dialog box, as shown in Figure 5–3.

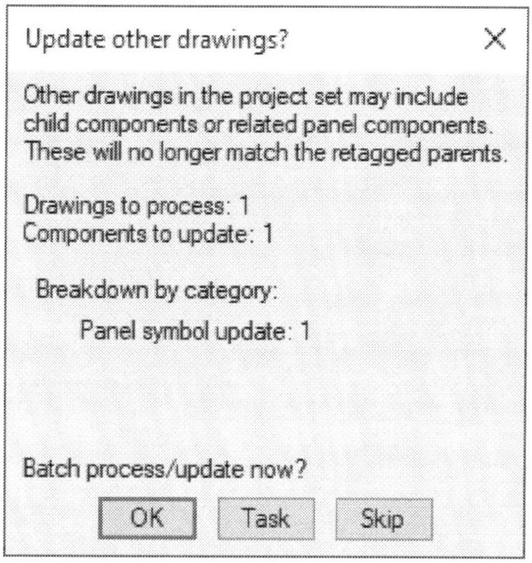

Figure 5–3

OK	Performs the update immediately. Saves the current drawing first, then opens, updates, and saves the appropriate drawing(s) before returning to the drawing you were originally editing.
Task	Saves the required information to the project task list. Enables you to perform the update later or perform several updates at the same time.
Skip	This option does not perform any updates.

If you add the required update to the task list, the information is saved to the project task list to be run at a later time.

Project Task List

Project Manager Toolbar

How To: Use the Task List

1. When prompted, save tasks to the project task list.
2. Start the **Project Task List** command.
   - The **Project Task List** is active only if there are saved tasks in the project.
3. In the *Task List* dialog box, select the tasks to perform.
4. Click **OK**.

The *Task List* dialog box (shown in Figure 5–4) lists all information on the saved tasks. It displays the login name of the user that made the changes, the filename of the affected files, and the details on the change that needs to be made.

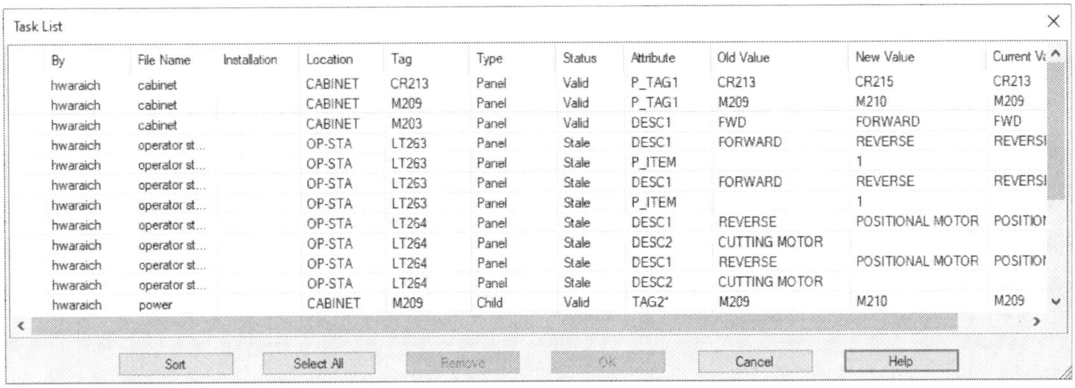

Figure 5–4

- The *Installation* and *Location* columns display codes for the components that need to be updated.
- The *Status* column displays as **Valid** if an attribute is up to date or **Stale** if it requires updating.
- The *Attribute* column displays attributes that need to be updated. The *Old Value*, *New Value*, and *Current Value* columns display the previous, new, and current values for the attribute.
- You can sort by any of the fields in the dialog box.
- When you select a task, an **X** displays in the first column.

5.3 Scoot

The **Scoot** command is a specialized version of the **Move** command. It limits the movement of the component to the wire it is currently located on. It also heals the wires to which the component is connected to.

Scoot

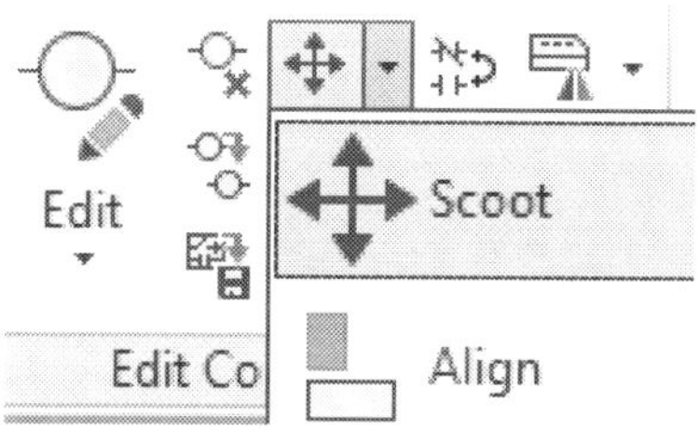

Ribbon: *Schematic* tab>*Edit Components* panel

Command Prompt: aescoot

Shortcut menu: *(on a component or wire)* **Scoot**

How To: Scoot a Component

1. Start the **Scoot** command.
2. Select the component to move.
3. Move the cursor over the same wire and pick the new location for the component.
4. Select another component to move or right-click or press <Enter> to end the command.

5.4 Move Component

The **Move Component** command moves and retags a component and attempts to clean up any wires that were affected by the move. This command enables you to move a component anywhere in the current drawing.

Move Component

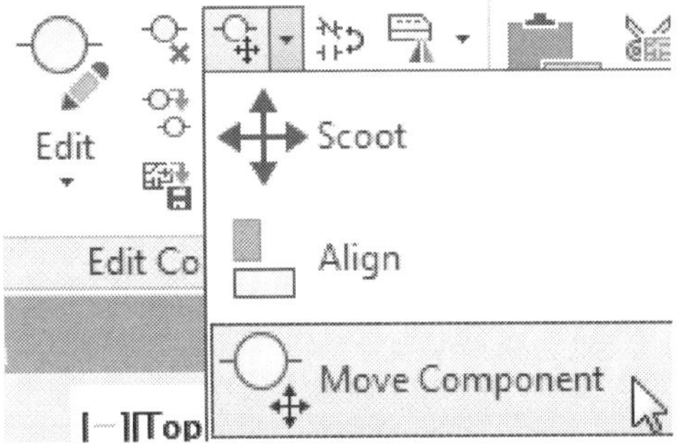

Ribbon: *Schematic* tab>*Edit Components* panel

Command Prompt: aemove

Shortcut menu: *(on a component)* **Move Component**

How To: Move a Component

1. Start the **Move Component** command.
2. Select the component to move.
3. Pick the location to which to move the component.
4. If displayed, select options in the *Component(s) Moved* dialog box.
5. If displayed, select options in the *Update Related Components?* dialog box.
6. If displayed, select options in the *Update other drawings?* dialog box.
7. If you update other drawings, select the **Qsave** option.

- Depending on where the component is moved, the *Component(s) Moved* dialog box might be displayed, as shown in Figure 5–5. It controls whether the component is retagged. If the component is not to be retagged, you have the option of updating any child components.

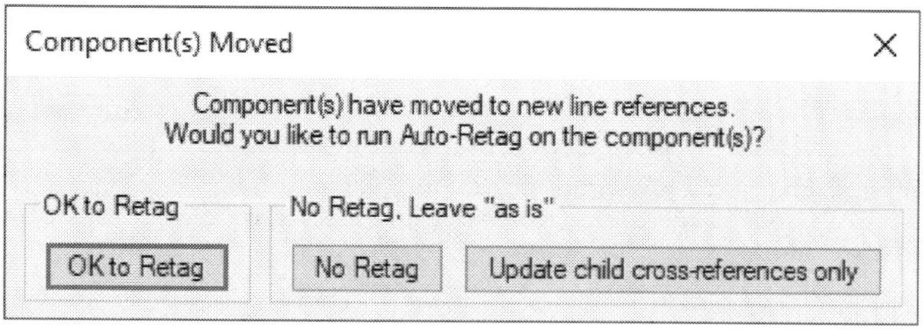
Component(s) Moved
Component(s) have moved to new line references.
Would you like to run Auto-Retag on the component(s)?
OK to Retag
No Retag, Leave "as is"
OK to Retag
No Retag
Update child cross-references only

Figure 5–5

- If there are related components in the active drawing, the *Update Related Components?* dialog box opens as shown in Figure 5–6. You can update the components now or skip updating them.

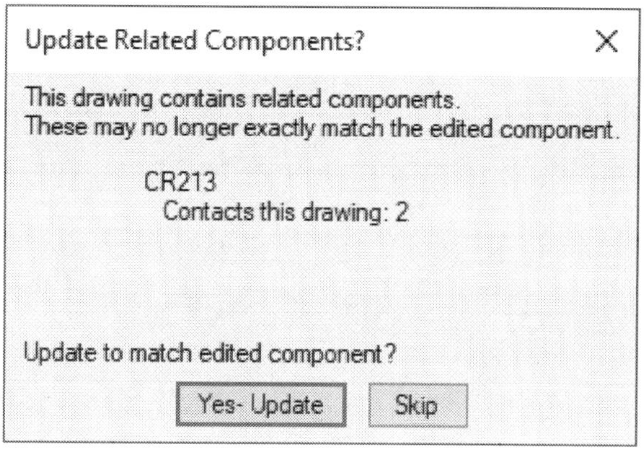
Update Related Components?
This drawing contains related components.
These may no longer exactly match the edited component.
CR213
Contacts this drawing: 2
Update to match edited component?
Yes- Update
Skip

Figure 5–6

- If there are related components in other drawings in the project, the *Update other drawings?* dialog box displays as shown in Figure 5–7. You can update now, add the updates to the project task list, or skip the updates. If you click **OK**, you are prompted to **Qsave** the current drawing.

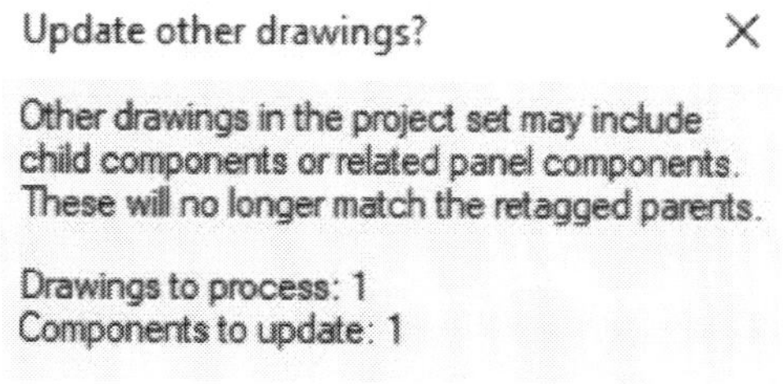
Update other drawings?
Other drawings in the project set may include
child components or related panel components.
These will no longer match the retagged parents.
Drawings to process: 1
Components to update: 1

Figure 5–7

Note: *The AutoCAD* ***Move*** *command can also be used, but it does not have the option to retag and the wires are not healed.*

5.5 Copy Component

The **Copy Component** command copies the selected component in the current drawing. After the new location is selected, the *Insert / Edit Component* dialog box opens. The new component is automatically retagged and wire numbers are updated where appropriate.

 **Copy Component**

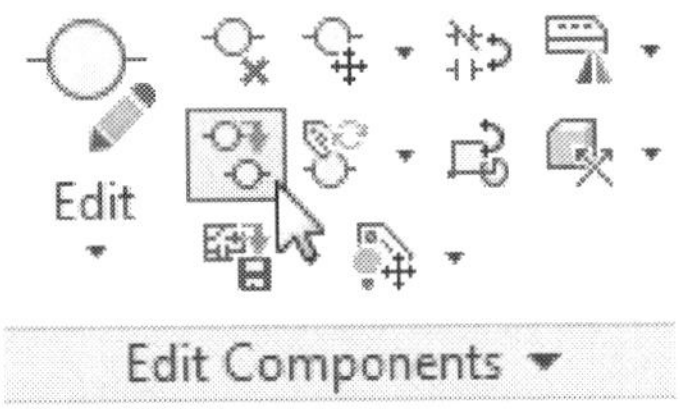

Ribbon: *Schematic* tab>*Edit Components* panel

Command Prompt: aecopycomp

Shortcut menu: *(on a component)* **Copy Component**

How To: Copy a Component

1. Start the **Copy Component** command.
2. Select the component to copy.
3. Pick the location for the new component.
4. In the *Insert / Edit Component* dialog box, change any required fields.
5. Click **OK**.

__Note:__ The AutoCAD __Copy__ command can also be used, but it does not have the option to retag and wires are not healed.

5.6 Align

The **Align** command aligns components vertically or horizontally. You are prompted to select the master component with which to align.

 **Align**

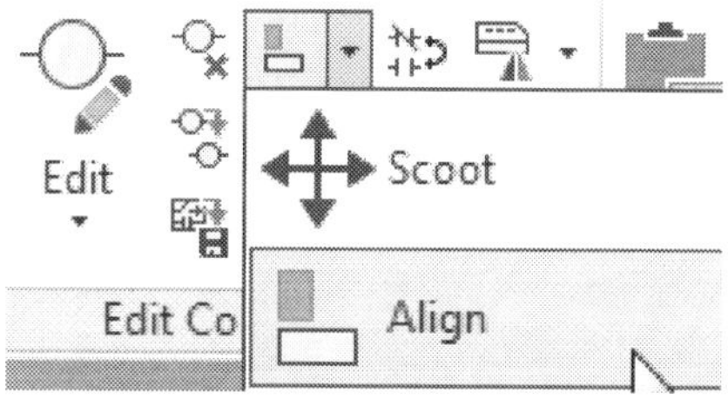

Ribbon: *Schematic* tab>*Edit Components* panel

Command Prompt: aealign

Shortcut menu: *(on a component)* **Align**

How To: Align Components

1. Start the **Align** command.
2. Select the master component to align with.
3. Select the components to align.
4. Right-click or press <Enter> to align the selected components.

- Type **H** and press <Enter> for horizontal alignment or type **V** and press <Enter> for vertical alignment after you start the **Align** command.
- You can use a crossing window, fence, or other selection options to select the components to align.

5.7 Delete Component

The **Delete Component** command removes components from the drawing. It also heals related wires and updates wire numbers.

Delete Component

Edit
Edit Components

Ribbon: *Schematic* tab>*Edit Components* panel

Command Prompt: aeerasecomp

Shortcut menu: *(on a component)* **Delete Component**

How To: Delete a Component

1. Start the **Delete Component** command.
2. Select the component(s) to delete.
3. Right-click or press <Enter> to delete the selected components.
4. If prompted, click **OK** to surf to related components.
5. Click **OK** to **Qsave** the drawing.

If a parent component is deleted you are prompted to surf to its child components in the *Search for / Surf to Children?* dialog box, as shown in Figure 5–8. If you click **OK**, the *Surf* dialog box provides the option of deleting the child component or editing the child to change its parent.

Search for / Surf to Children?
LT263
This Parent device was deleted.
Do you want to search for and Surf to
its child/peer device contacts (if any)?
OK
No

Figure 5–8

Note: *The AutoCAD* ***Erase*** *command can also be used, but the wires are not healed, nor are the wire numbers updated.*

Practice 5a
Edit Components

Practice Objectives

- Edit components and wires.
- Update the referenced components.

In this practice, you will use various editing tools to modify an existing drawing. You will use **Move Component**, **Scoot**, and **Align** to adjust the position of symbols and wires. You will also delete, copy, and edit symbols. Finally, you will use the **Task List** to update other drawings in the project. The final circuit displays as shown in Figure 5–9.

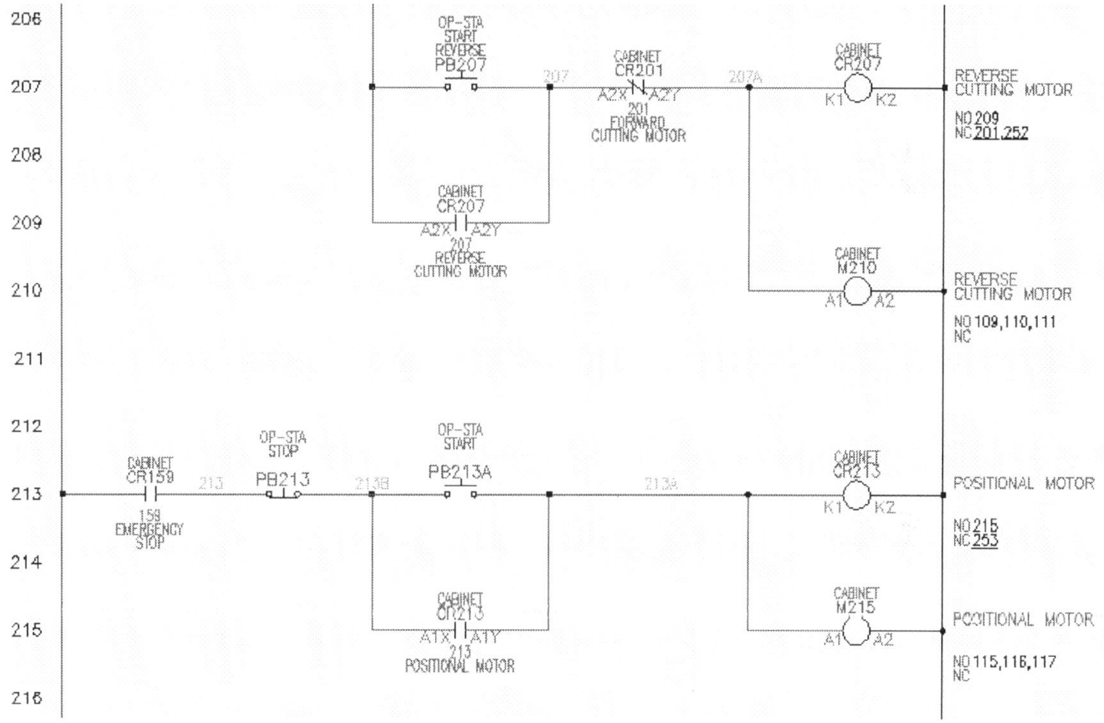

Figure 5–9

1. In your practice files folder, in the *Module 05* folder, open the **Module 05** project file.
2. In the **Module 05** project, open **Control.dwg**.
3. Zoom to lines 206 to 216.

   Note: *The contact CR213 on line 209 is part of the relay CR213 on line 213. The symbol on line 213 displays a N.O. contact on line 209.*

4. In the *Schematic* tab>*Edit Components* panel, click (Move Component).
5. Select contact **CR213** on line 209 as the component to move. Select the empty wire on line 215 as the insertion point, as shown in Figure 5–10.

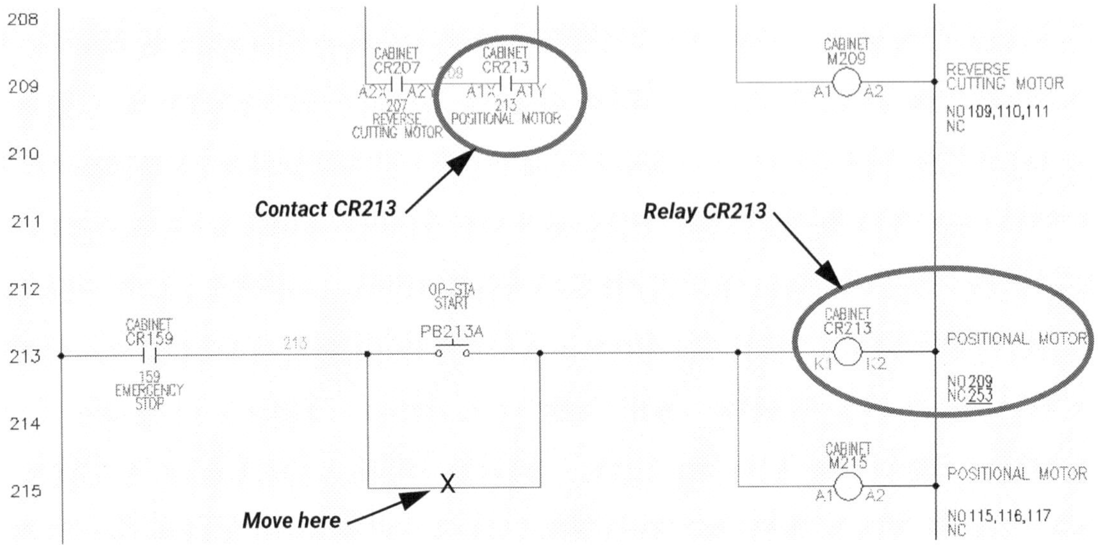

Figure 5–10

- Note that the Relay on CR213 on line 213 updates to show a N.O. contact on line 215, as shown in Figure 5–11.

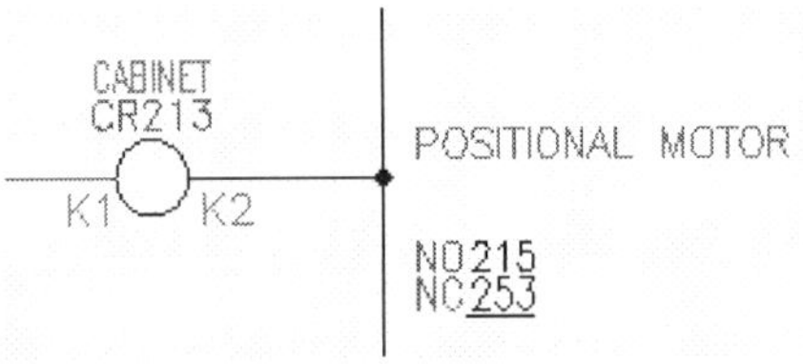

Figure 5–11

6. On line 207, right-click on PB207A and select **Move Component** in the Marking Menu.

7. Select on wire 213 between CR159 and PB213A for the insertion point, as shown in Figure 5–12.

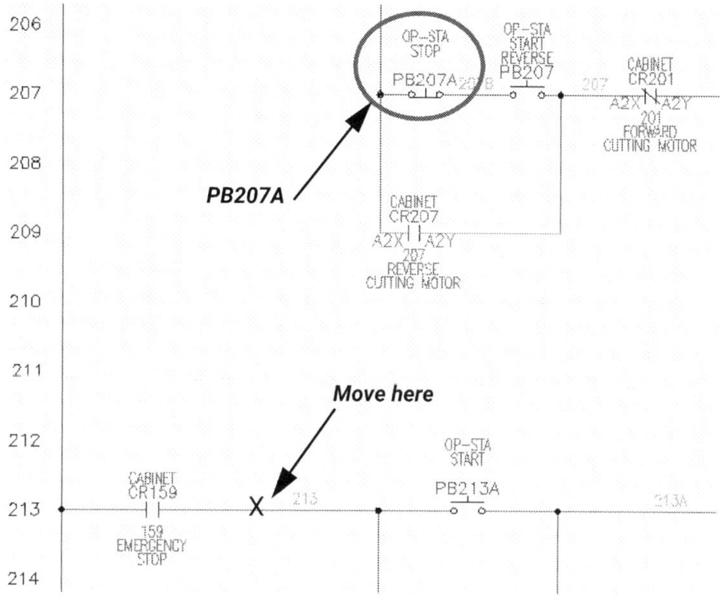

Figure 5–12

- If you placed the component too close to the wire number (213), the software automatically moves the wire number, as shown in Figure 5–13.

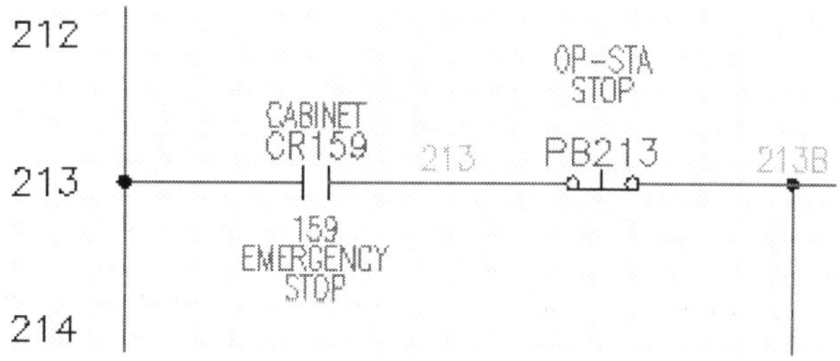

Figure 5–13

8. In the *Component(s) Moved* dialog box, click **OK to Retag**. The component needs a new component tag because it was moved to a different line number.
9. In the *Update other drawings?* dialog box, click **OK**. Other symbols in different drawings are linked to this symbol.
10. In the *QSAVE* dialog box, click **OK**. Note that **Operator Station.dwg** is opened where the linked panel components are updated, and you are returned to **Control.dwg**.

11. On wire 207, right-click on PB207 and select **Scoot** in the Marking Menu. The cursor changes into a box enclosing the symbol. Scoot the symbol (the box cursor) near the left end of the wire so that it is closely aligned with contact CR207 below, as shown in Figure 5–14. Press <Enter>.

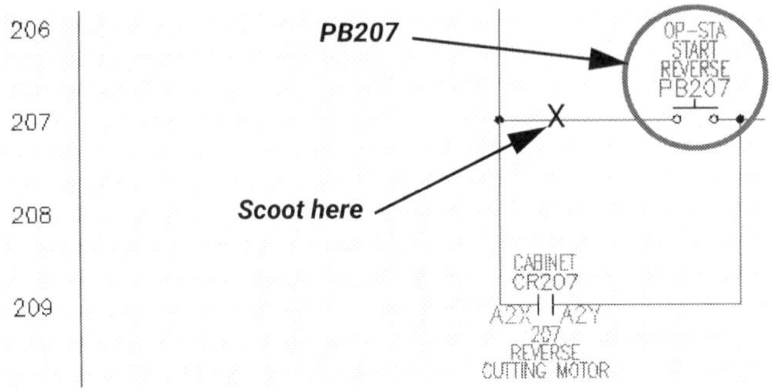

Figure 5–14

12. Zoom to lines 200 to 210.

13. In the *Schematic* tab>*Edit Components* panel, click (Align). Pick contact **CR201** on line 203 as the component to align with. A temporary vertical line displays passing through the contact CR201. Select **PB207** and **CR207** as the components to align, as shown in Figure 5–15. Press <Enter> to align and end the command. Note that **PB207** and **CR207** are aligned with **CR201**.

- If the align line still displays near the components, zoom in or out to remove it.

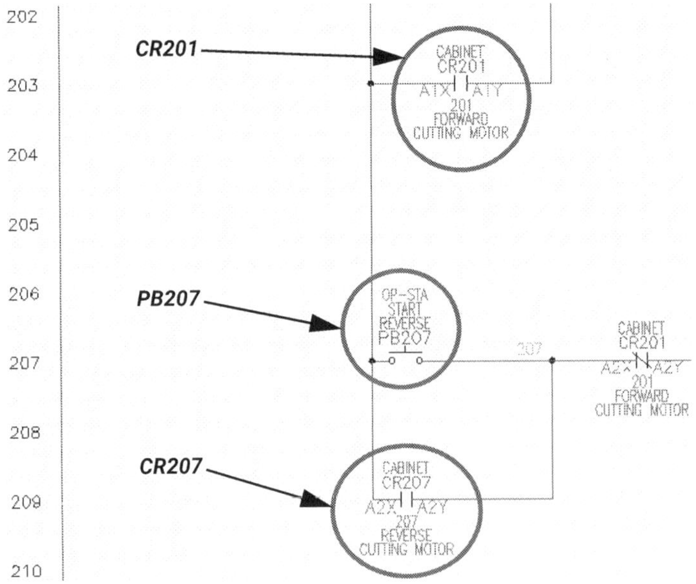

Figure 5–15

14. In the *Schematic* tab>*Edit Components* panel, click (Scoot). Pick the wire on line 209 that contains M209. The cursor changes into a box enclosing the wire. Move the box cursor down and select a point on line 210, as shown in Figure 5–16.

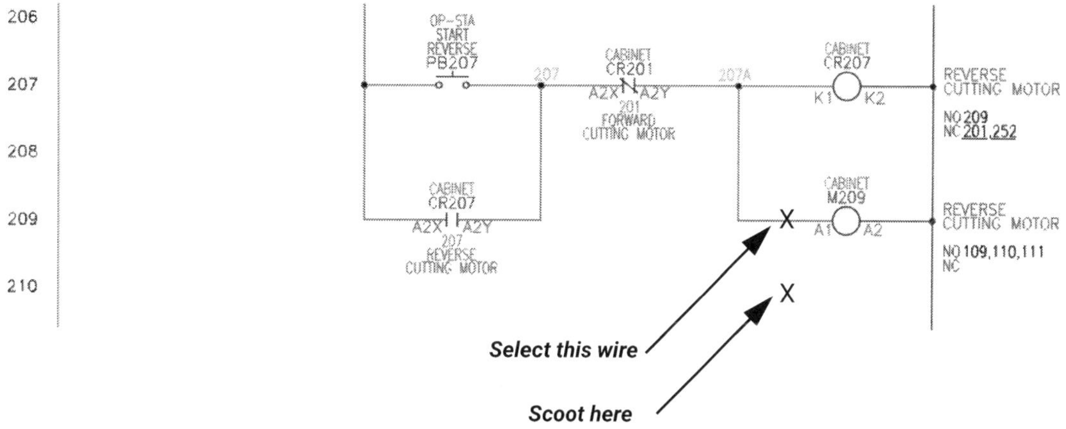

Figure 5–16

15. In the *Component(s) Moved* dialog box, click **OK to Retag**.
16. In the *Update other drawings?* dialog box, click **Task** to save it in the *Task List* for later update.
17. Zoom to lines 260 to 268.
18. In the *Schematic* tab>*Edit Components* panel, click (Delete Component). On wire 263, select **LT263** and press <Enter>. The LT263 is removed from the drawing and the *Search for/Surf to Children?* dialog box opens. Click **No**.
19. Right-click on LT264 and select **Delete Component** in the Marking Menu. In the *Search for/ Surf to Children?* dialog box, click **No**.
20. In the *Schematic* tab>*Edit Components* panel, click (Copy Component). Select **LT262** as the component to copy. Select a point on line 263 below LT262 as the insertion point.
21. In the *Insert / Edit Component* dialog box, set *Line 1* of the Description to **REVERSE** and click **OK-Repeat**.
22. In the *Update other drawings?* dialog box, click **Task**.
23. Pick a point on line 264 below LT263 as the insertion point. In the *Insert / Edit Component* dialog box, set *Line 1* of the Description to **POSITIONAL MOTOR** and clear *Line 2*. Click **OK**.
24. In the *Update other drawings?* dialog box, click **Task**.
25. Zoom to lines 200 to 208.

26. In the *Schematic* tab>*Edit Components* panel, click (Edit) and on line 203, select **M203** as the component to edit.
27. In the *Insert / Edit Component* dialog box, set *Line 1* of the *Description* to **FORWARD** and click **OK**.
28. In the *Update other drawings?* dialog box, click **Task**.
29. In the *Project Manager*, click (Project Task List) to run the tasks that have been saved.
30. In the *Task List* dialog box, note *Old Value*, *New Value*, and *Current Value* for the edited attributes, as shown in Figure 5–17. The *File Name* column also displays the affected drawing files. Click **Select All** to select all listed tasks. This is indicated by an **X** in the first column of all of the rows. Click **OK**.

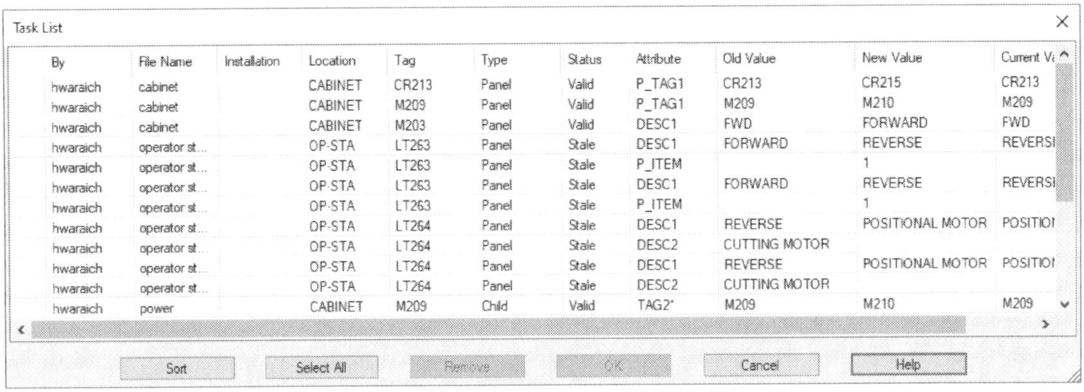

By	File Name	Installation	Location	Tag	Type	Status	Attribute	Old Value	New Value	Current Va
hwaraich	cabinet		CABINET	CR213	Panel	Valid	P_TAG1	CR213	CR215	CR213
hwaraich	cabinet		CABINET	M209	Panel	Valid	P_TAG1	M209	M210	M209
hwaraich	cabinet		CABINET	M203	Panel	Valid	DESC1	FWD	FORWARD	FWD
hwaraich	operator st...		OP-STA	LT263	Panel	Stale	DESC1	FORWARD	REVERSE	REVERSI
hwaraich	operator st...		OP-STA	LT263	Panel	Stale	P_ITEM		1	
hwaraich	operator st...		OP-STA	LT263	Panel	Stale	DESC1	FORWARD	REVERSE	REVERSI
hwaraich	operator st...		OP-STA	LT263	Panel	Stale	P_ITEM		1	
hwaraich	operator st...		OP-STA	LT264	Panel	Stale	DESC1	REVERSE	POSITIONAL MOTOR	POSITIOI
hwaraich	operator st...		OP-STA	LT264	Panel	Stale	DESC2	CUTTING MOTOR		
hwaraich	operator st...		OP-STA	LT264	Panel	Stale	DESC1	REVERSE	POSITIONAL MOTOR	POSITIOI
hwaraich	operator st...		OP-STA	LT264	Panel	Stale	DESC2	CUTTING MOTOR		
hwaraich	power		CABINET	M209	Child	Valid	TAG2*	M209	M210	M209

Figure 5–17

31. In the *QSAVE* dialog box, click **OK**. The software opens the affected drawings (listed in the *File Name* column), updates the affected symbols, saves and closes those drawings, and returns to the originally open drawing, which is **Control.dwg**.
32. Save **Control.dwg**.

End of practice

5.8 Surfer Command

The **Surfer** command browses through related components. These can be parent/child components, schematic and panel components, information in reports, source and destination arrows, or any related symbols.

Surfer

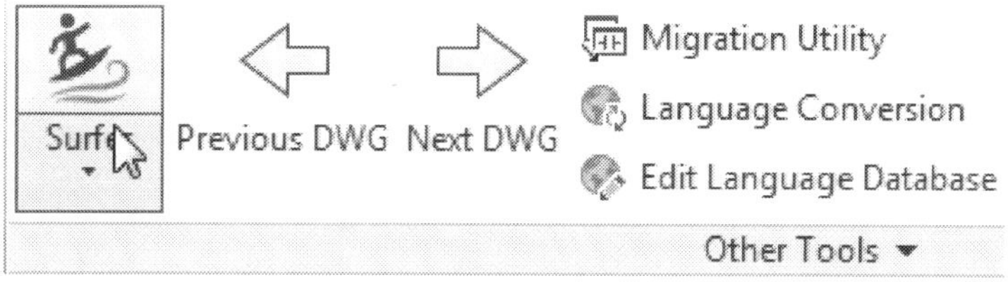

Ribbon: *Project* tab>*Other Tools* panel

Command Prompt: aesurf

Shortcut menu: *(on a component)* **Surfer**

How To: Use the Surfer Command

1. Start the **Surfer** command.
2. Select the component to surf.
3. Select the component to work with in the *Surf* dialog box.
4. Use the buttons in the dialog box to make modifications.
5. Click **Close** to end the command.

The *Surf* dialog box (shown in Figure 5–18) contains commands for browsing and modifying symbols. The top portion of the dialog box displays the component tag, manufacturer, and catalog number of the selected symbol. The *Surf* dialog box looks different when surfing source and destination symbols.

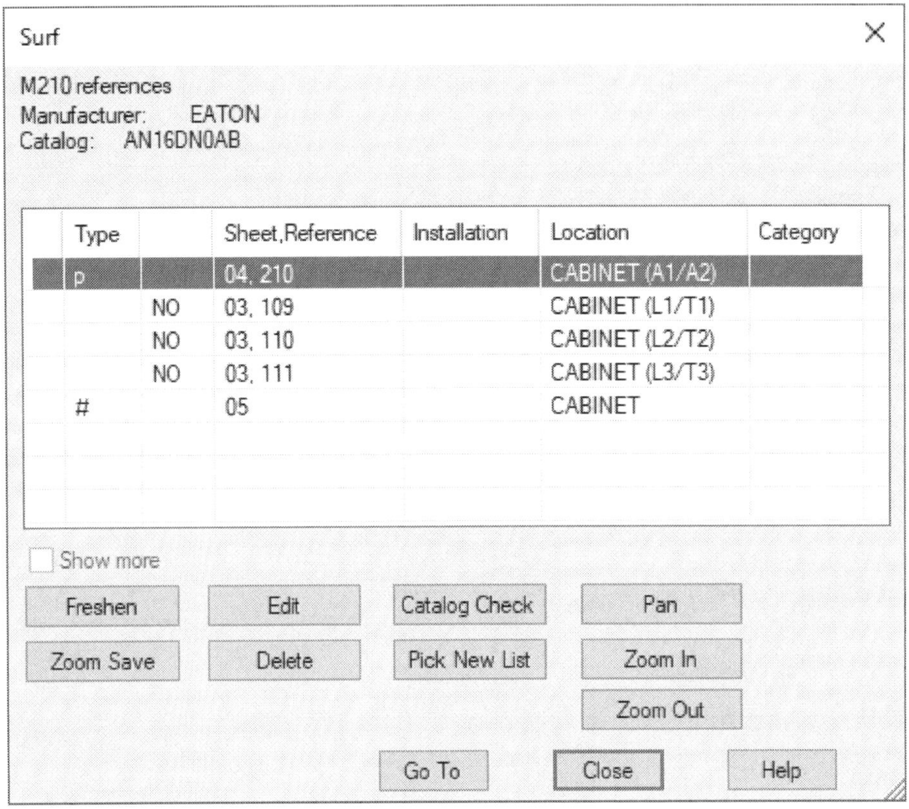

Figure 5–18

The columns and buttons in the dialog box contain the following information:

Type	The *Type* column displays different codes for different types of symbols. They include:	
	c: Component symbol	**# np:** Panel nameplate
	p: Parent symbol	**NO:** Normally open contact
	t: Terminal symbol	**NC:** Normally closed contact
	w: Wire number	**Dst:** Destination arrow
	#: Panel symbol	**Src:** Source arrow
Sheet, Reference	Displays the sheet number and line reference number for the component.	
Installation, Location	Displays the installation, location, and pin attribute values.	

Freshen	Refreshes the *Surf* dialog box with changes to the current drawing.
Edit	Edits the selected component. Similar to the **Edit Component** command.
Catalog Check	Opens the *Bill of Materials Check* dialog box. Displays the catalog information as shown in a BOM report.
Pan	Moves the view in the active drawing.
Zoom Save	Saves the current zoom factor to the drawing.
Zoom In	Zooms in on the active drawing.
Zoom Out	Zooms out of the active drawing.
Delete	Deletes the active component. Similar to the **Delete Component** command.
Pick New List	Pick a new component to surf.
Go To	Zooms to the selected component. If the component is in a different drawing, the current drawing is saved, the drawing containing the component is opened, and the drawing window is zoomed to the selected component.

Practice 5b
Surfer

Practice Objective

- Navigate to a component's relationships.

In this practice, you will use the **Surfer** command to browse between related components, as shown in Figure 5–19.

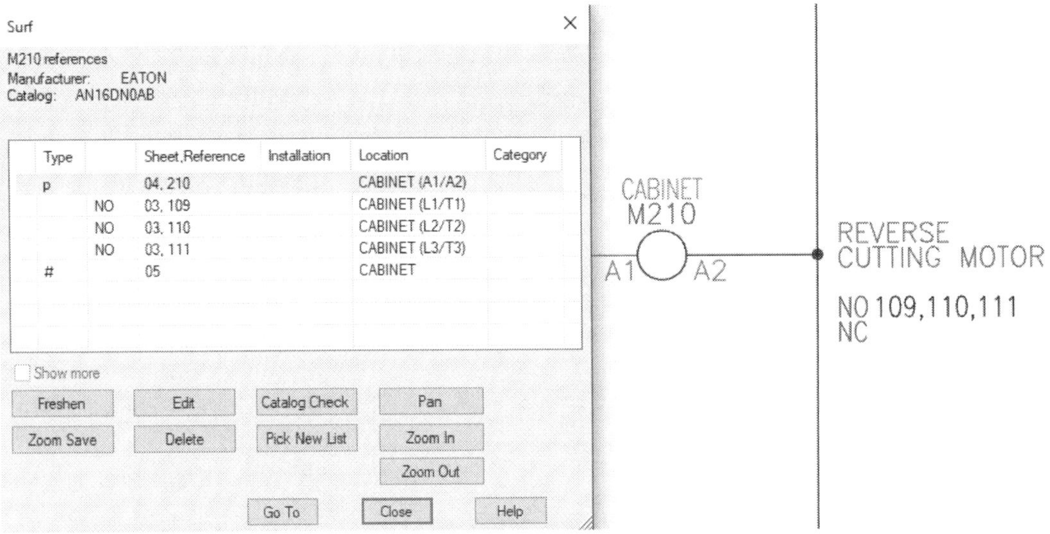

Figure 5–19

1. If the **Module 05** project is not active, open and activate it now.
2. Open **Control.dwg** in the **Module 05** project.
3. Zoom to lines 206 to 211.
4. In the *Project* tab>*Other Tools* panel, click  (Surfer). The **Surfer** tool is also located in the Quick Access Toolbar.
5. Pick **M210** on line 210. The *Surf* dialog box opens, as shown in Figure 5–20.

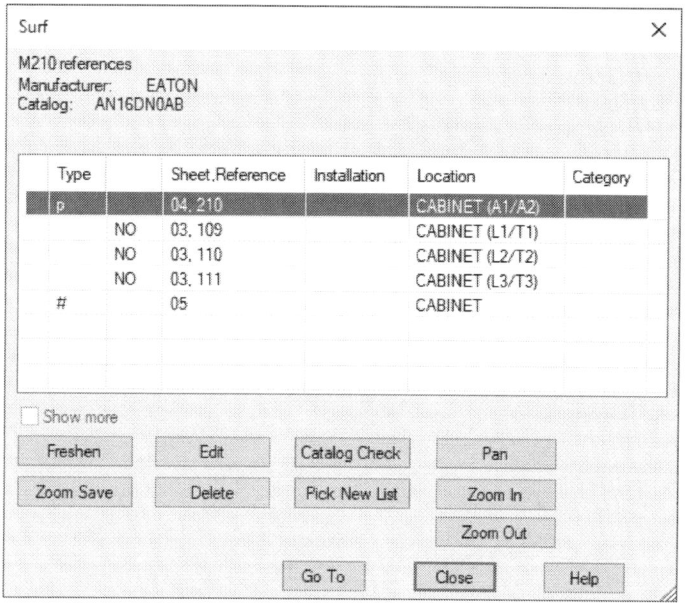

Figure 5–20

6. Select the row for the normally open contact on sheet 03, line 111 (*Sheet,Reference* column displays **03,111**) and click **Go To**. **Power.dwg** is opened and zoomed to the symbol with the *Surf* dialog box still open.
7. In the dialog box, click **Zoom Out** twice to see the other components. The other contacts for the motor starter are positioned above/below the selected contact, as shown in Figure 5–21.
   - If the *Surf* dialog box is blocking the view in the drawing, move it to the side, as required.

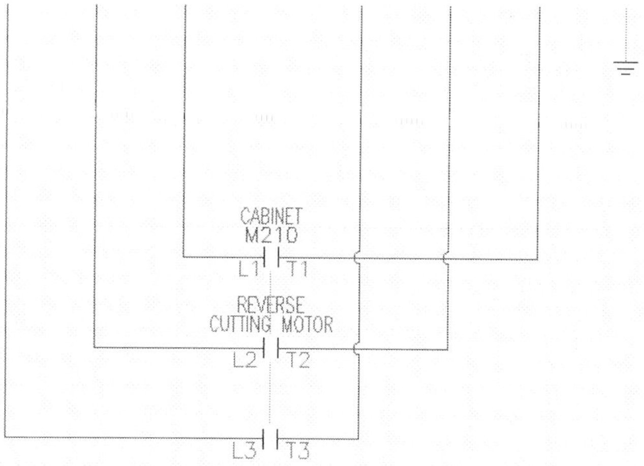

Figure 5–21

8. In the *Surf* dialog box, double-click on the row displaying **04,210** in the *Sheet,Reference* column. **Control.dwg** is opened and zoomed to the symbol.
9. Click **Close** in the *Surf* dialog box to exit the command.
10. In the **Module 05** project, open **BOM.dwg**.
11. Zoom to the last few rows along the left of the table. Note 5 LT tags are listed in one of the bottom rows of the table.
12. Click  (Surfer).
13. In the report (table), select **LT151**. The *Surf* dialog box opens listing references (all 5 LT tags) to LT151, LT169, LT262, LT263, and LT264, as shown in Figure 5–22.

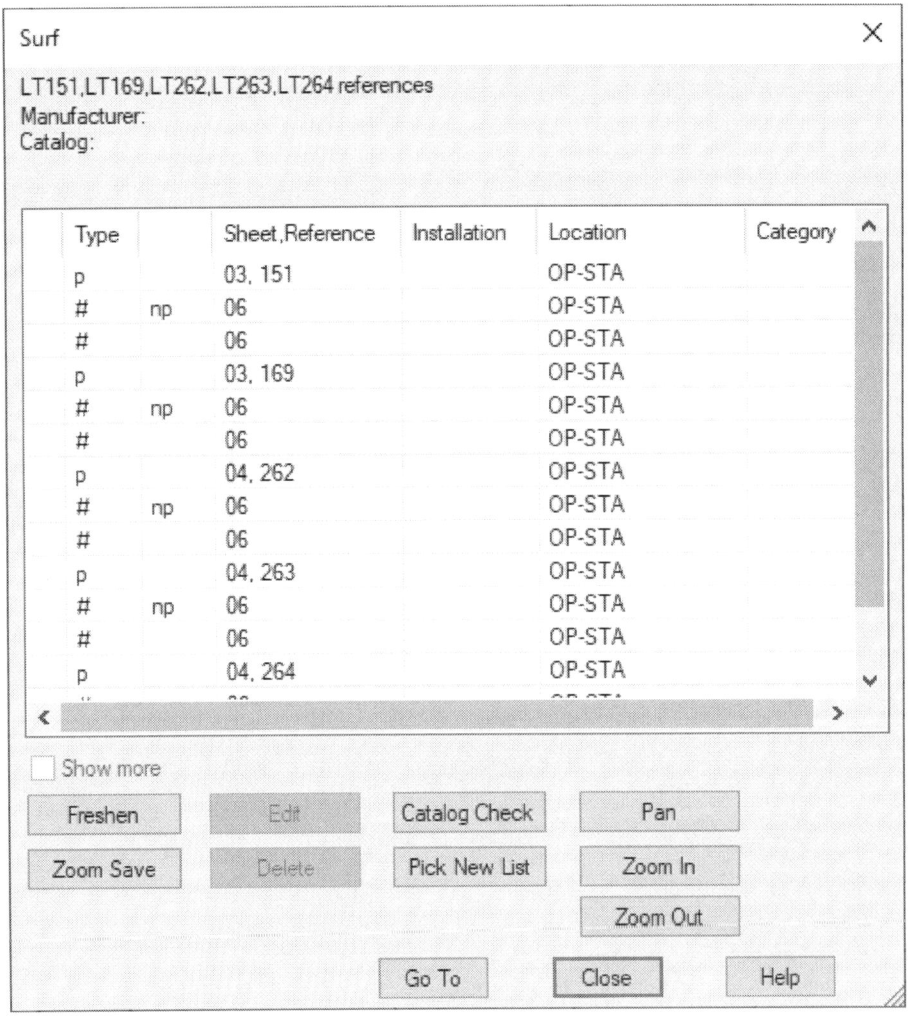

Figure 5–22

14. Select the first row for *Sheet,Reference* **03, 151** and click **Go To**. **Power.dwg** is opened and zoomed to the symbol for LT151. In the dialog box, note a **x** for 03,151, as shown in Figure 5–23.

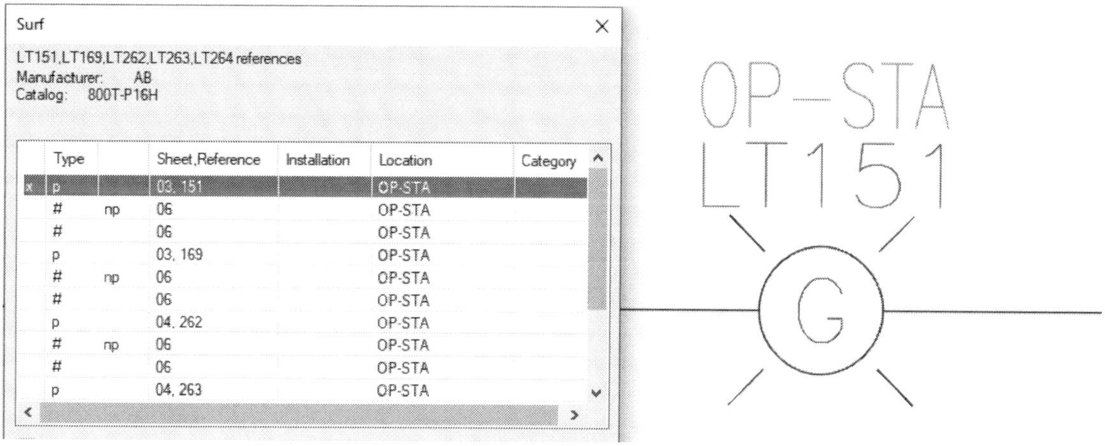

Figure 5–23

15. In the dialog box, select the next row (*Sheet,Reference* is **06**) and click **Go To**. **Operator Station.dwg** is opened and zoomed to the nameplate for LT151. The nameplates are included because you are surfing based on the component tag.

16. Click **Close** in the *Surf* dialog box to exit the command.

17. In the **Module 05** project, open **BOM.dwg**.

18. Zoom to the last few rows of the table on the left.

19. Click (Surfer).

20. In the table, in the *Catalog* column, select **800T-P16H**. The *Surf* dialog box opens listing all references to the catalog number, as shown in Figure 5–24. The list does not include the name plates because you are surfing based on the catalog number and the nameplates have a different catalog number.

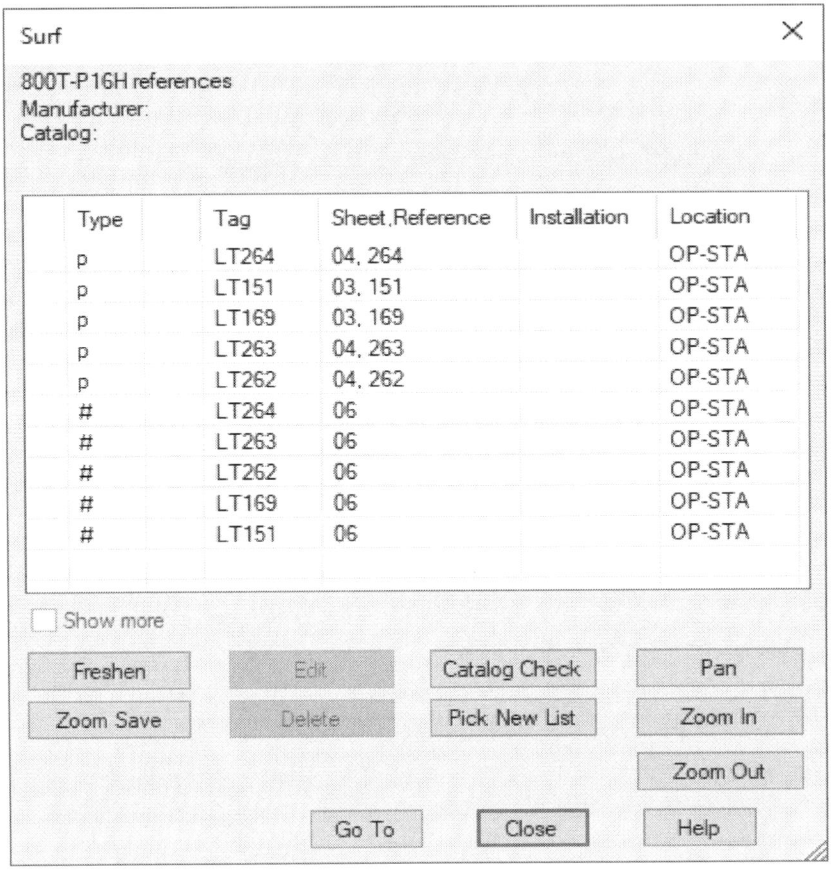

Figure 5–24

21. Click **Close**.
22. Save and close all the open drawings.

End of practice

Practice 5c
Additional Surfer Practice

Practice Objective

- Navigate to a component's relationships.

In this practice, you will delete a symbol and use the **Surfer** command to browse to and delete related symbols. The final drawing displays as shown in Figure 5–25.

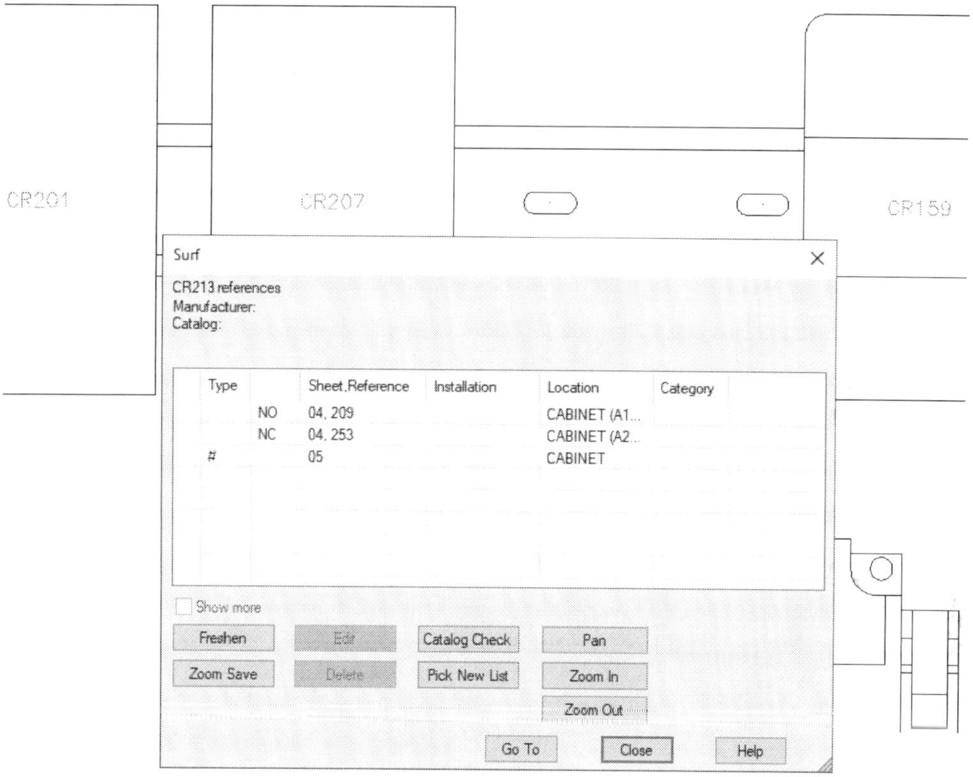

Figure 5–25

1. If the **Module 05** project is not active, open and activate it.
2. In the **Module 05** project, open **Control.dwg**.
3. Zoom to lines 212 to 217.
4. Use **Delete Component** command to delete CR213 on line 213. (Right-click and select **Delete Component** or use  (Delete Component) in the *Schematic* tab>*Edit Components* panel.)

5. In the *Search for/Surf to Children?* dialog box, click **OK**. In the *Qsave* dialog box, click **OK**. The *Surf* dialog box opens (as shown in Figure 5–26), displaying the list of symbols related to CR213.

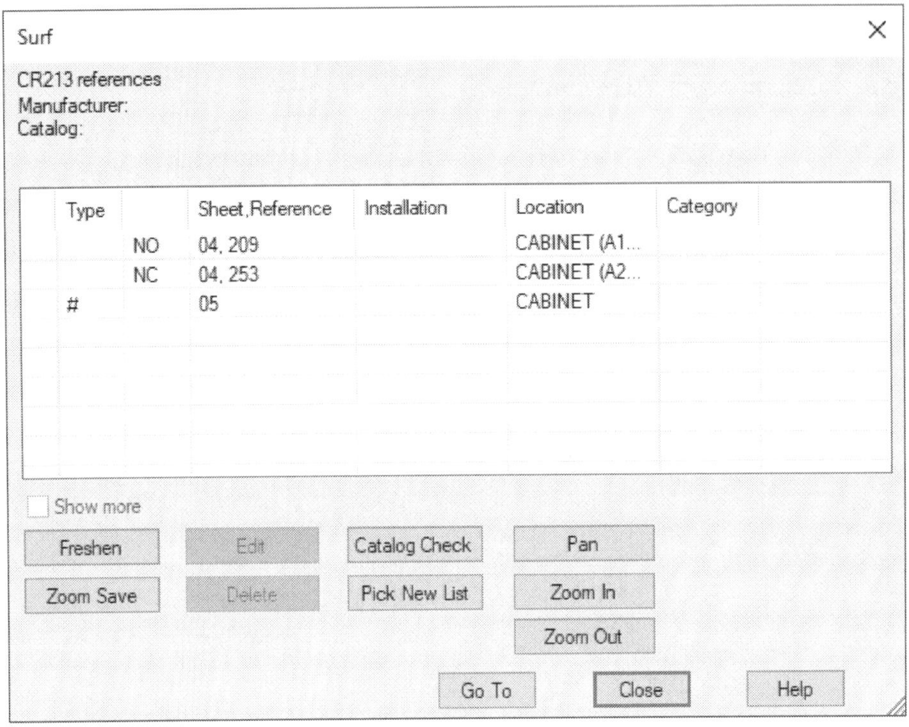

Figure 5–26

6. Select the **NO** contact on *Sheet,Reference* **04, 215** and click **Go To**.
7. In the *Surf* dialog box, click **Delete**. In the *Delete: Are you sure?* dialog box, click **OK-Delete It**.
8. The *Surf* dialog box opens again. Select the **NC** contact on *Sheet,Reference* **04, 253** and click **Go To**. In the *Surf* dialog box, click **Delete** and **OK-Delete It** in the *Delete: Are you sure?* dialog box.
9. Select the panel footprint (marked with "#") on *Sheet* **05** and click **Go To**.
10. **Cabinet.dwg** is opened and zoomed to the footprint.
11. Click **Zoom Out** twice. Click **Delete** and **OK-Delete It** in the *Delete: Are you sure?* dialog box.
12. Click **Close** in the *Surf* dialog box.
13. Save and close **Cabinet.dwg** and **Control.dwg**.

End of practice

5.9 Copy Catalog Assignment

The **Copy Catalog Assignment** command copies the manufacturer, catalog, assembly, and multiple catalog attributes from one component to another. This command is useful when assigning the same catalog information to multiple components or when changing the catalog information for multiple components.

Copy Catalog Assignment

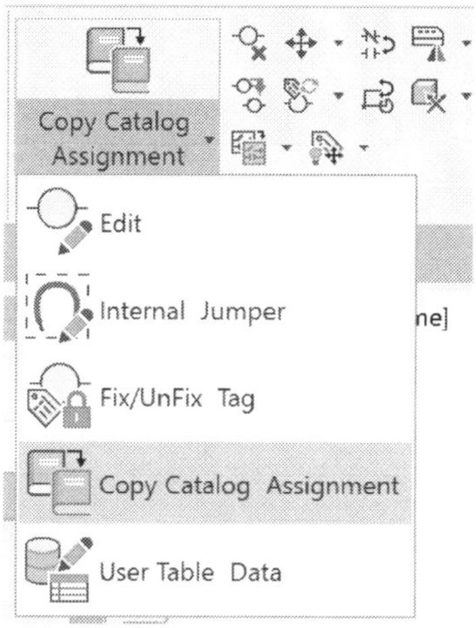

Ribbon: *Schematic* tab>*Edit Components* panel

Command Prompt: aecopycat

How To: Copy a Catalog Assignment

1. Start the **Copy Catalog Assignment** command.
2. Select the component from which to copy the catalog assignment.
3. In the *Copy Catalog Assignmen*t dialog box, verify the information.
4. Click **OK**.
5. Select the components to which to copy the attributes. Use the AutoCAD selection options to select which components to copy to.
6. In the *Caution: Existing Data on Target* dialog box, click **Overwrite**.
7. If prompted with the *Update Related Components?* dialog box, click **Yes-Update**.
8. If prompted with the *Update other drawings?* dialog box, click **OK** to add the updates to the task list.

- If you attempt to copy the catalog data to a different symbol type (e.g., copy push button information to a relay coil), a warning dialog box enables you to cancel the command.

The *Copy Catalog Assignment* dialog box, as shown in Figure 5–27, displays the catalog information that is to be copied to the components.

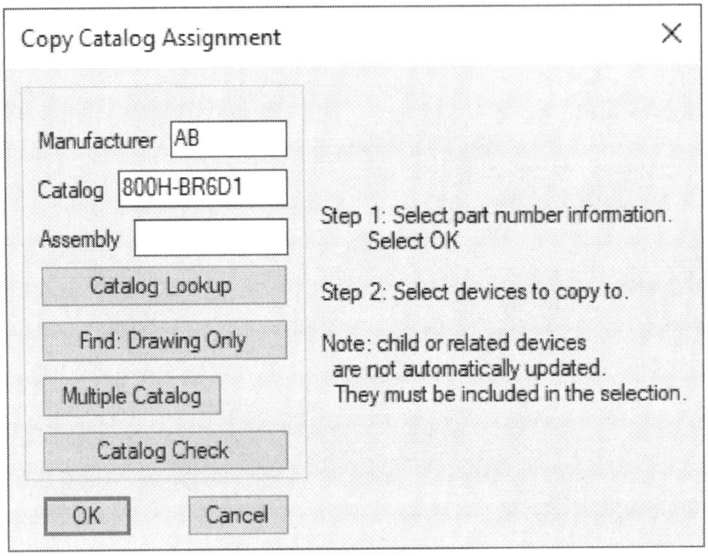
Copy Catalog Assignment
Manufacturer
AB
Catalog
800H-BR6D1
Assembly
Catalog Lookup
Find: Drawing Only
Multiple Catalog
Catalog Check
OK
Cancel
Step 1: Select part number information.
Select OK
Step 2: Select devices to copy to.
Note: child or related devices
are not automatically updated.
They must be included in the selection.

Figure 5–27

The buttons in the *Copy Catalog Assignment* dialog box are described as follows.

Catalog Lookup	Opens the *Catalog Browser* in which you can change the catalog information for the master component.
Find Drawing Only	Searches the active drawing for symbols of the same family and displays their catalog information. You can change the catalog information for the master component here.
Multiple Catalog	Opens the *Multiple Bill of Material* dialog box. You can verify the current extra catalog assignments or add more. The number of extra catalog assignments displays on the right side of the button.
Catalog Check	Opens the *Bill of Materials Check* dialog box. Use it to verify the catalog information assigned to the selected component.

After you select the component(s) to which to copy, the *Caution: Existing Data on Target* dialog box opens if the catalog information is already assigned and is different from the source catalog assignment, as shown in Figure 5–28. You can overwrite the data or cancel the command.

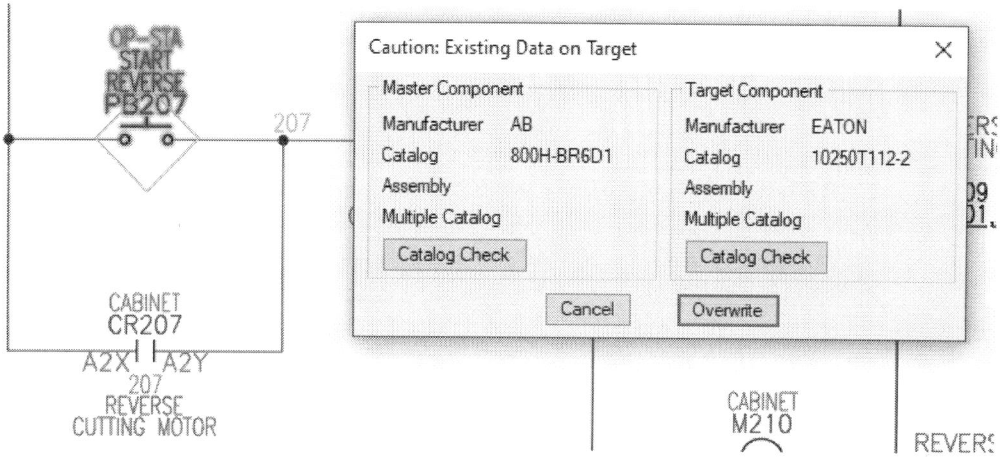

Figure 5–28

5.10 Copy Installation/Location Code Values

The **Copy Installation/Location Code Values** command copies installation and location attribute values to symbols.

Copy Installation/Location Code Values

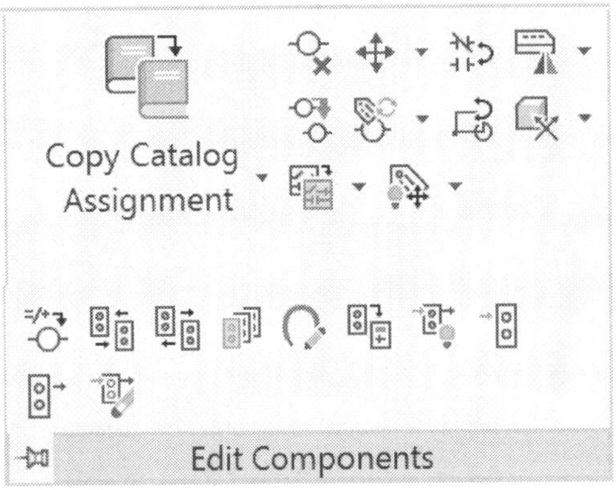

Ribbon: *Schematic* tab>expanded *Edit Components* panel

Command Prompt: aecopyinstloc

How To: Copy an Installation or Location Code

1. Start the **Copy Installation/Location Code Values** command. The *Copy Installation/Location to Components* dialog box opens as shown in Figure 5–29.

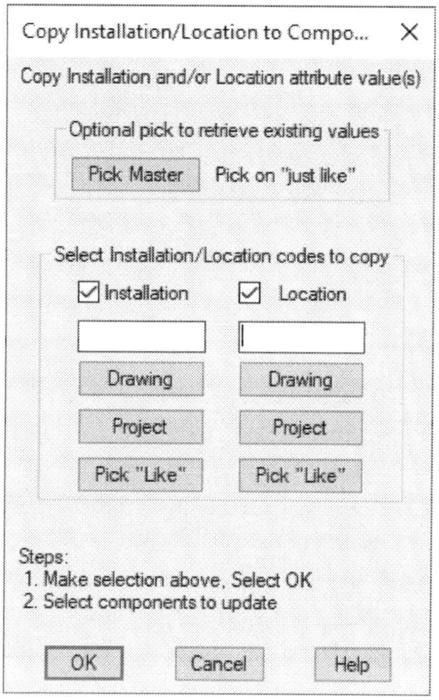

Figure 5–29

2. Select **Installation**, **Location**, or both to copy them.
3. Populate the code to copy using one of the selection options or type the value in the field.
4. Click **OK**.
5. Select the symbols to which to copy the attribute values. Use the AutoCAD selection options to select which components to copy to.
6. Right-click or press <Enter> to end the command.

- Unlike in the *Copy Catalog Assignment* dialog box, you do not see a warning if the attributes are already populated. They are overwritten.

The buttons in the *Copy Installation/Location to Components* dialog box are described as follows.

Pick Master	Pick the master symbol from which to copy the attributes. It copies the installation and location codes from that symbol, depending on what is selected in the *Select Installation/Location codes to copy* area. You can type a value in the *Installation* and *Location* fields rather than using the selection options.
Drawing	Displays a list of installation or location codes used in the active drawing. Select the attribute value from this list.
Project	Displays a list of installation or location codes used in the active project. Select the attribute value from the list.
Pick "Like"	Pick the master symbol from which to copy the attribute value.

5.11 Attribute Editing Commands

The AutoCAD Electrical software has several commands that modify attributes. They modify the selected symbol(s) and do not modify the block definition. The modification commands include:

- Move/Show Attribute
- Edit Selected Attribute
- Hide Attribute (Single Pick)
- Hide Attribute (Window/Multiple)
- Unhide Attribute (Window/Multiple)
- Add Attribute
- Rename Attribute
- Squeeze Attribute/Text
- Stretch Attribute/Text
- Change Attribute Size
- Rotate Attribute
- Change Attribute Justification
- Change Attribute Layer

Attribute Utilities

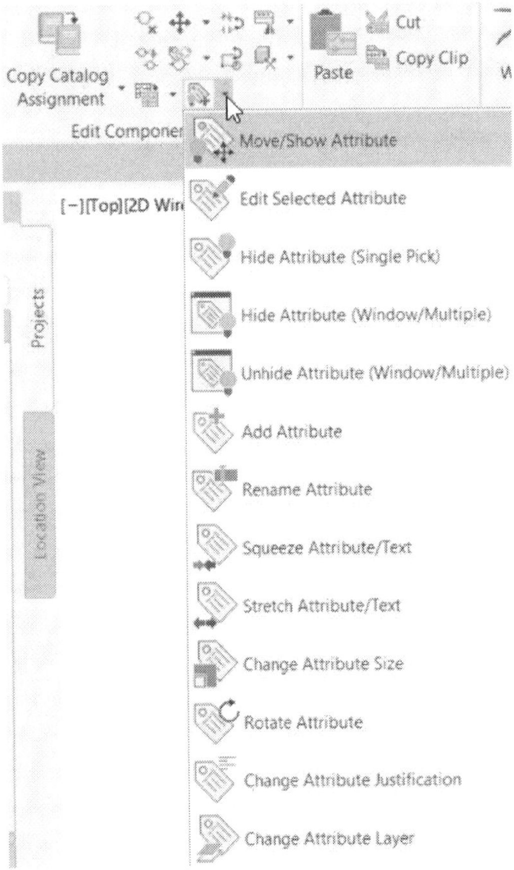

Ribbon: *Schematic* tab>*Edit Components* panel

How To: Modify Attributes

1. Start any of the **Attribute Editing** commands to make the required change.
2. Follow the dialog box or prompts in the Command Prompt to make the changes.

   Note: *There is also a Project-wide Attribute Editing control for Attribute Text Style and Attribute Size. It is located in the* ***Project Wide Utilities*** *command.*

Practice 5d
Copy AutoCAD Electrical Data

Practice Objective

- Copy catalog data and the location code from one component to another.

In this practice, you will first copy catalog data from one symbol to several other symbols. You will then copy the location code from one symbol to several other symbols. The final circuit displays as shown in Figure 5–30.

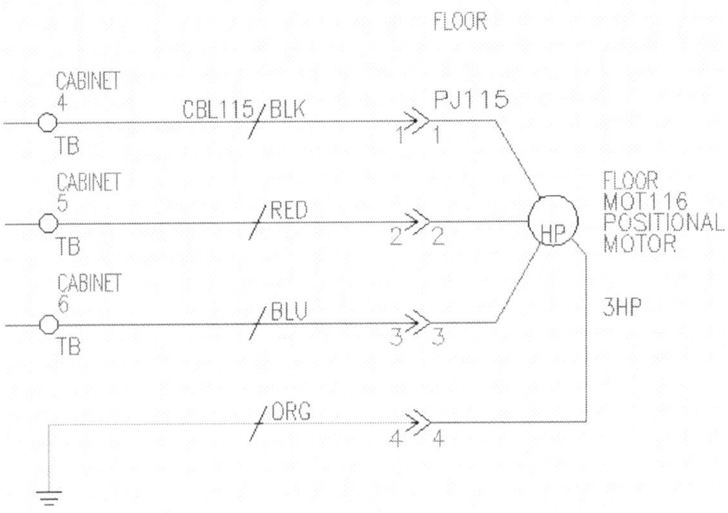

Figure 5–30

1. If the **Module 05** project is not active, open and activate it now.
2. In the **Module 05** project, open **Control.dwg**.
3. Zoom to lines 206 to 216.

4. On wire 213, edit PB213A. (Right-click and select **Edit Component** or click (Edit) in the *Schematic* tab>*Edit Components* panel.) Note that in *Catalog Data* area, no component information is available indicating that no data has been assigned, as shown in Figure 5–31. Click **Cancel** to close the *Insert / Edit Component* dialog box.

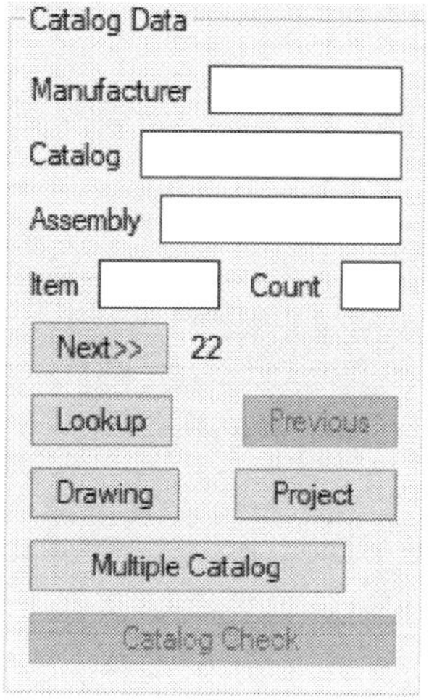

Figure 5–31

5. On wire 207, edit PB207. In the *Catalog Data* area, note this component is an Eaton push button, as shown in Figure 5–32. Click **Cancel** to close the *Insert / Edit Component* dialog box.

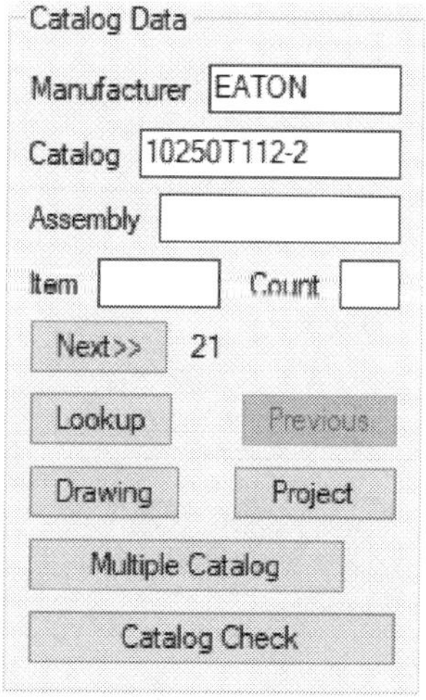

Figure 5–32

6. Zoom to lines 200 to 213.

7. In the *Schematic* tab>*Edit Components* panel, click (Copy Catalog Assignment). On wire 201, select **PB201A** as the Master component. The *Copy Catalog Assignment* dialog box opens, as shown in Figure 5–33. This component is an Allen-Bradley push button. Click **OK**. Ensure that PB201A is still selected.

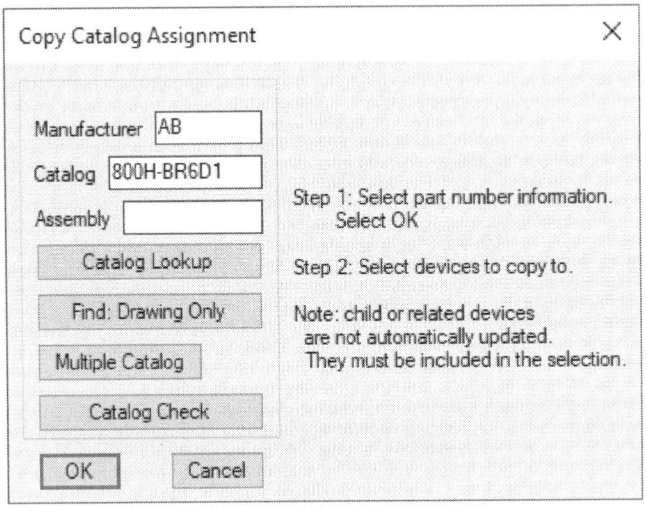

Figure 5–33

8. In addition, select **PB207**, **PB213**, and **PB213A** and press <Enter>. The *Caution: Existing Data on Target* dialog box opens, as shown in Figure 5–34. It displays the catalog data for PB201A (Master Component) and PB207 (Target Component). There is a green diamond around the component to be changed (PB207 in this case), as shown in Figure 5–34.

   - You might need to move the dialog box to display the symbol in the drawing window.

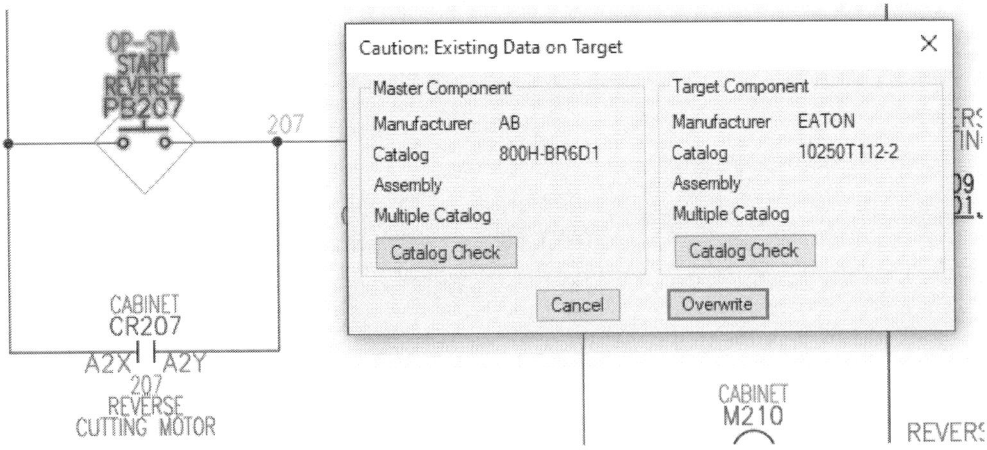

Figure 5–34

9. In the dialog box, click **Overwrite**. The *Different symbol block names* dialog box opens. It displays for PB213, as shown in Figure 5–35.

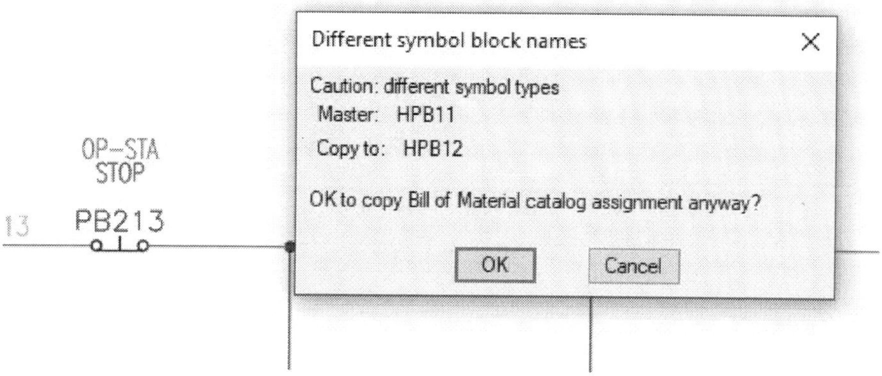

Figure 5–35

10. In the *Different symbol block names* dialog box, click **Cancel**. A warning dialog box is not displayed for PB213A because it did not have any catalog data assigned to it.
11. In the *Update other drawings?* dialog box, click **OK**. In the *QSAVE* dialog box, click **OK**.
12. Using the **Edit Component** command, edit PB213A and PB207. Note that the catalog data has been updated (Allen-Bradley) for both the components, as shown in Figure 5–36 (it was originally empty for PB213A and was EATON for PB207). Click **Cancel**.

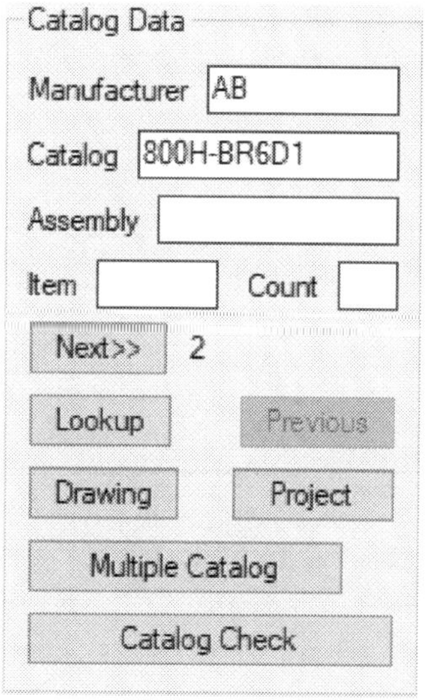

Figure 5–36

13. Click  (Previous Drawing) to close **Control.dwg** and open **Power.dwg**.

14. Zoom to MOT104 (3 phase motor) on line 104 and note that a location code (FLOOR) has been assigned to it, as shown in Figure 5–37.

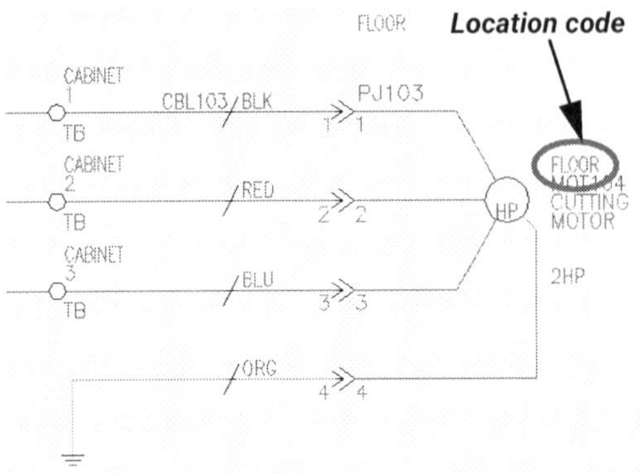

Figure 5–37

15. Zoom to MOT116 and PJ115. Note that they do not have location codes assigned to them.

16. In the *Schematic* tab>expanded *Edit Components* panel, click (Copy Installation/Location Code Values). The *Copy Installation/Location to Components* dialog box opens.

17. In the dialog box, click **Pick Master**. Select **MOT104** as the Master. The location code (FLOOR) displays in the dialog box with no installation code, as shown in Figure 5–38. Click **OK**.

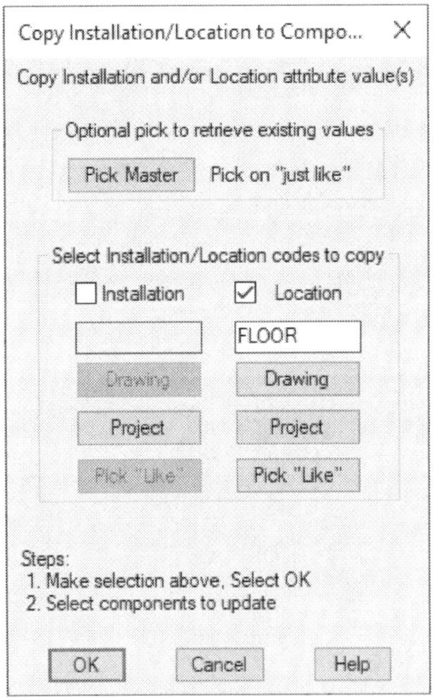

Figure 5–38

18. Select **MOT116** and **PJ115** and press <Enter>. In the *Update Related Components?* dialog box, click **Yes-Update**. No warning dialog boxes display because component type does not affect the location code assignment. MOT116 and PJ115 now have location codes, as shown in Figure 5–39.

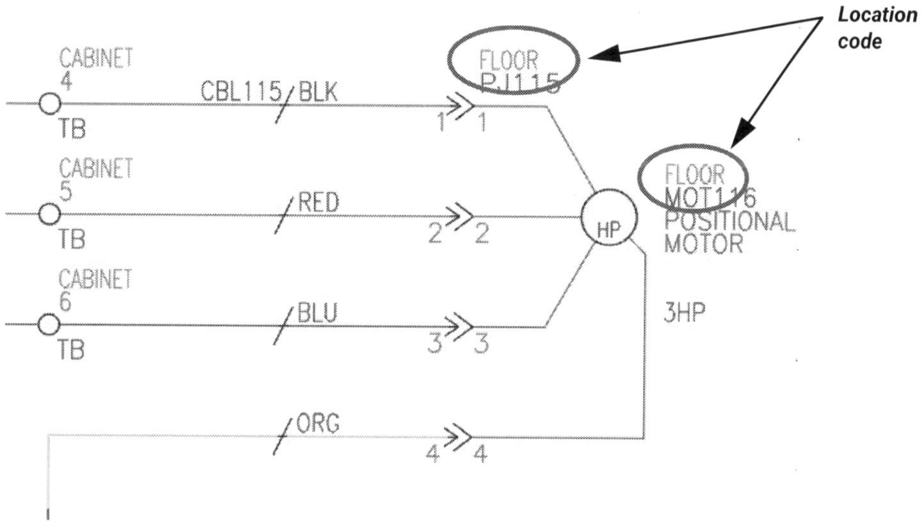

Figure 5–39

19. Save **Power.dwg**.

End of practice

Practice 5e
Attribute Editing Tools

Practice Objective

- Modify the visibility and position of attributes.

In this practice, you will edit the visibility and position of attributes on a single symbol. You will first hide attributes, and then toggle the visibility of some of them back on. Finally, you will move a single attribute. The final circuit displays as shown in Figure 5–40.

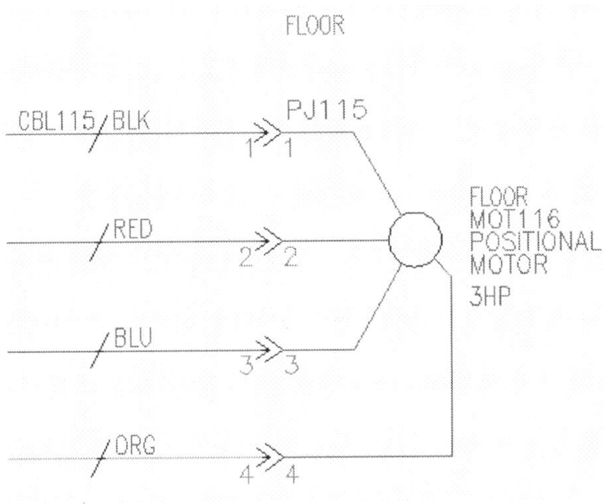

Figure 5–40

1. If the **Module 05** project is not active, open and activate it now.
2. In **Module 05**, open **Power.dwg** if it is not already open.
3. Zoom to MOT116.

4. In the *Schematic* tab>*Edit Components* panel, click (Hide Attribute (Single Pick)). Select **HP** inside the circle, and **POSITIONAL** and **MOTOR** on the right, as shown in Figure 5–41. As you select the attribute, note that it is hidden. Press <Enter> to end the command.

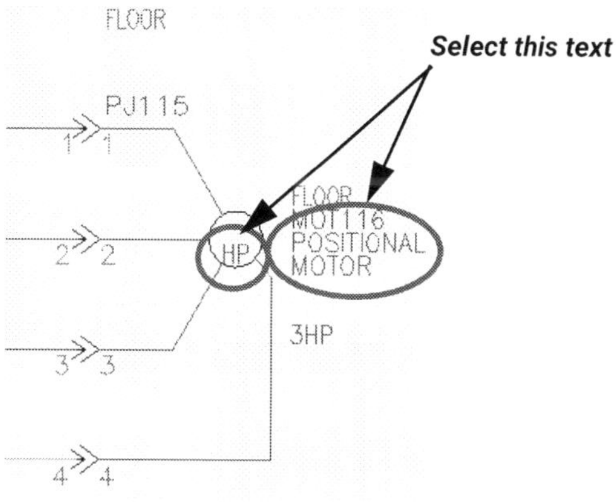

Figure 5–41

5. In the *Schematic* tab>*Edit Components* panel, click (Move/Show Attribute). Click on the circle representing MOT116 (where HP is hidden). The *SHOW / HIDE Attributes* dialog box opens, as shown in Figure 5–42. Note that **DESC1** and **DESC2** do not display a * (star) next to them. Select **DESC1** and **DESC2** and note that * is now displayed next to them indicating that these attributes will be displayed in the drawing.

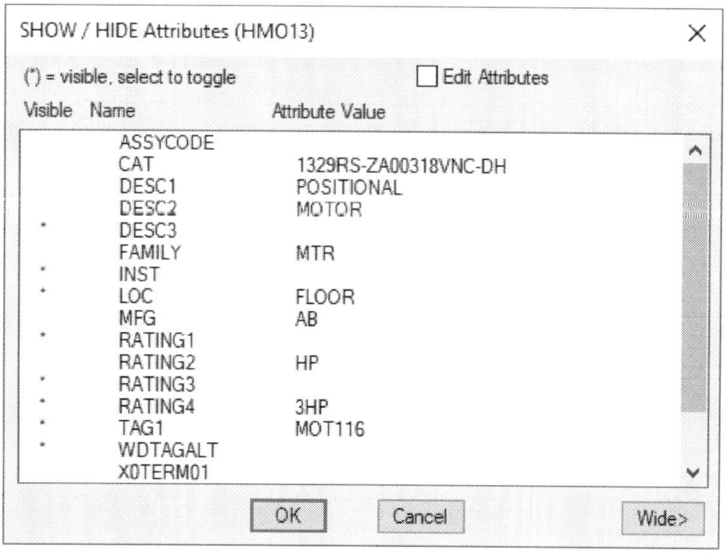

Figure 5–42

6. Click **OK**. Note that **POSITIONAL** and **MOTOR** are now displayed. Press <Enter> to end the command.

7. Click  (Move/Show Attribute).

8. Pick the **3HP** text for MOT116, as shown in Figure 5–43. Press <Enter> then click near the lower left corner of the text for the base point. Move the text up, just under the text **MOTOR** by clicking a new point. Press <Enter>.
   - Use Snap to keep the attributes aligned.

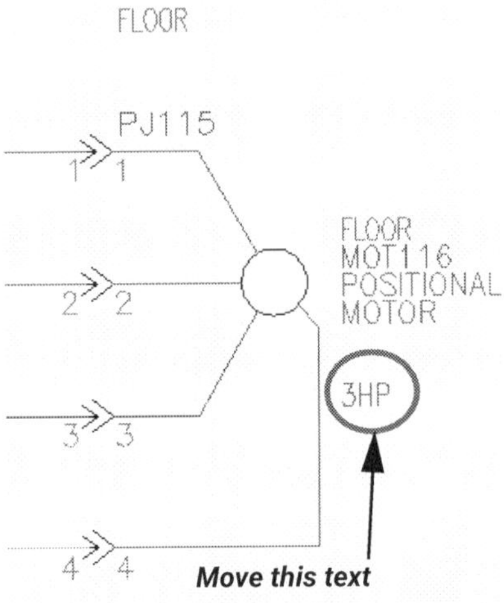

Figure 5–43

9. Zoom to MOT104. The block has not changed. The attribute editing commands only affect the block instance being modified.

10. Save and close **Power.dwg**.

End of practice

Chapter Review Questions

1. How do you modify the catalog information assigned to a symbol?
   a. Use the **Catalog** command.
   b. Use the **Edit Component** command.
   c. Use the **Copy Catalog** command.
   d. You cannot modify the catalog information.

2. What is the benefit of using the project task list?
   a. It records each task for later review.
   b. You can move to previously conducted tasks.
   c. You can process tasks from any non-active project.
   d. You can batch process updates to several components.

3. What is the difference between the **Scoot** command and the **Move Component** command?
   a. The **Scoot** command limits the movement of the symbol to the wire on which it is located, while the **Move Component** command enables the symbol to be moved anywhere in the active drawing.
   b. The **Move Component** command limits the movement of the symbol to the wire on which it is located, while the **Scoot** command enables the symbol to be moved anywhere in the active drawing.
   c. The **Scoot** command only moves symbols one snap space at a time, while the **Move Component** command moves symbols at any distance.
   d. There is no difference between the **Scoot** command and the **Move Component** command.

4. What does the **Copy Component** command do in addition to copying the component?
   a. It retags the component and renumbers wires where appropriate.
   b. It identifies it as a copied component.
   c. It deletes the original and renumbers wires where appropriate.
   d. It updates the project file.

5. When you use the **Delete Component** command to erase symbols, what happens to the wires where the symbol was located?
    a. The wires are automatically deleted.
    b. The wires are reconnected and healed.
    c. The wires maintain the deleted components location with a gap.
    d. The wires are moved to a new wire layer.

6. In the *Surf* dialog box, how can you tell where a symbol is located?
    a. The coordinates of its insertion point display.
    b. Its nearest component displays.
    c. The sheet and reference number display.
    d. It does not tell you where, it only takes you there.

7. When using the **Surfer** command, what does **Go To** do?
    a. It shows a preview of the location.
    b. It only opens the drawing containing the symbol.
    c. It opens the drawing containing the symbol and zooms to the symbol.
    d. It goes back to the previous location.

8. How can you copy the catalog attributes from one component to multiple other components?
    a. Use the **Copy Installation/Location Values** command.
    b. Use the **Copy Catalog Assignment** command.
    c. Use the **Change Attribute Layer** command.
    d. Use the **Copy Component** command.

9. When using the **Copy Installation/Location Values** command, how can you copy only a location code?
    a. Clear the **Installation** option and select **Location**.
    b. Clear the **Location** option and select **Installation**.
    c. Leave the *Installation* value field blank.
    d. You must enter both the *Installation* and *Location* values.

10. How would you modify the size of an attribute of the symbol?
    a. Use the **Edit Selected Attribute** command.
    b. Use the **Rename Attribute** command.
    c. Use the **Stretch Attribute/Text** command.
    d. Use the **Change Attribute Size** command.

11. You can modify the block definitions while using AutoCAD Electrical attribute editing commands.
    a. True
    b. False

Command Summary

Button	Command	Location
	**Align**	• **Ribbon:** *Schematic* tab>*Edit Components* panel
	**Copy Catalog Assignment**	• **Ribbon:** *Schematic* tab>*Edit Components* panel
	**Copy Component**	• **Ribbon:** *Schematic* tab>*Edit Components* panel
	**Copy Installation/ Location Values**	• **Ribbon**: *Schematic* tab>expanded *Edit Components* panel
	**Delete Component**	• **Ribbon:** *Schematic* tab>*Edit Components* panel
	**Edit Component**	• **Ribbon:** *Schematic* tab>*Edit Components* panel
	**Hide Attributes (Single Pick)**	• **Ribbon:** *Schematic* tab>*Edit Components* panel
	**Move Component**	• **Ribbon:** *Schematic* tab>*Edit Components* panel
	**Move/Show Attribute**	• **Ribbon:** *Schematic* tab>*Edit Components* panel
	**Project Task List**	• **Project Manager Toolbar**
	**Scoot**	• **Ribbon:** *Schematic* tab>*Edit Components* panel
	**Surfer**	• **Ribbon:** *Project* tab>*Other Tools* panel • **Quick Access Toolbar**

Chapter

6

Panel Drawings

Panel footprints are components to be placed in a panel and the AutoCAD® Electrical software provides you with various methods to insert them. Additionally, learning to assign Item Numbers and balloons to these component footprints on a panel layout enables you to tie the footprints to the catalog data and Bill of Materials report.

Learning Objectives

- Insert a panel footprint from the Icon Menu and from a schematic component list.
- Insert a component's schematic symbol using a list of previously inserted panel footprints.
- Edit a panel footprint.
- Assign item numbers to footprints.
- Attach a balloon and a leader to a panel footprint.

6.1 Insert Footprint (Icon Menu)

Panel footprints function like schematic symbols. They are AutoCAD® blocks with attributes and xdata. Xdata is invisible data added to a block.

- Panel footprints represent the component as it would be placed in a panel. The footprint symbols are full-scale representations of the components.

Insert Footprint (Icon Menu)

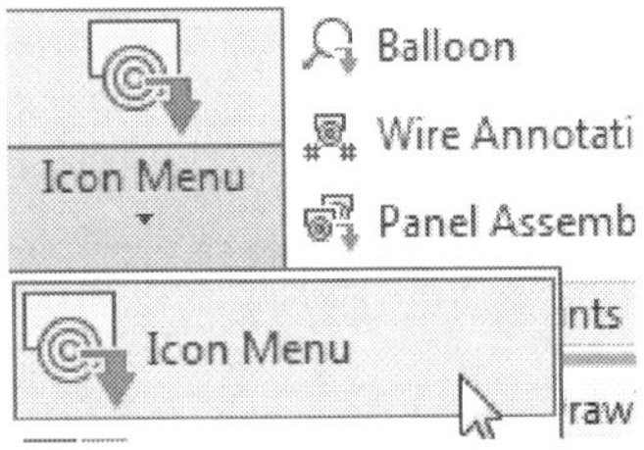

Ribbon: *Panel* tab>*Insert Component Footprints* panel

Command Prompt: aefootprint

How To: Insert a Footprint from the Icon Menu

1. Start the **Insert Footprint (Icon Menu)** command.
2. In the *Insert Footprint* dialog box, select the component type to insert.
    - Note that the Icon Menu used to insert panel footprints is similar to the Icon Menu used to insert schematic symbols.
3. If a submenu displays, pick a specific footprint to insert.
4. In the *Footprint* dialog box, select **Choice A** to assign the catalog data or **Choice B** to pick a block or geometry to use.
5. For **Choice A**, click **OK**.
6. For **Choice B**, pick in the drawing window to place the symbol.
7. In the *Panel Layout – Component Insert / Edit* dialog box, fill in the required information.
8. Click **OK**.

- The **Insert Footprint (Icon Menu)** command is used if the panel layout is being designed before the schematic or if the component has not yet been added to the schematic drawings.
- The **Insert Footprint (Icon Menu)** command should be used to insert enclosures and nameplates.

Footprint Database

When inserting a footprint, you enter a catalog part number that is used to select a block. The panel footprint lookup database is used to match Catalog Numbers to block names.

- The default footprint lookup database is **footprint_lookup.mdb** and is located in *C:\Users\<user>\Documents\Acade <version>\Aedata\<language>\Catalogs* for Windows 10.
- The database contains different tables for each manufacturer and specifies the footprint block to be used based on the catalog part number.
- When searching for a match in the footprint lookup database, the software first searches for an exact match by Catalog Number. If an exact match is not found, the last character on the right side of the Catalog Number is dropped and the search is performed again. This procedure is continued until a match is found. For example, if a Catalog Number is 123X, the database is searched for 123X, then 123, then 12, etc. This method enables one block to be assigned to multiple Catalog Numbers.

Inserting Footprint

Select a footprint to insert in the *Insert Footprint* dialog box, as shown in Figure 6–1.

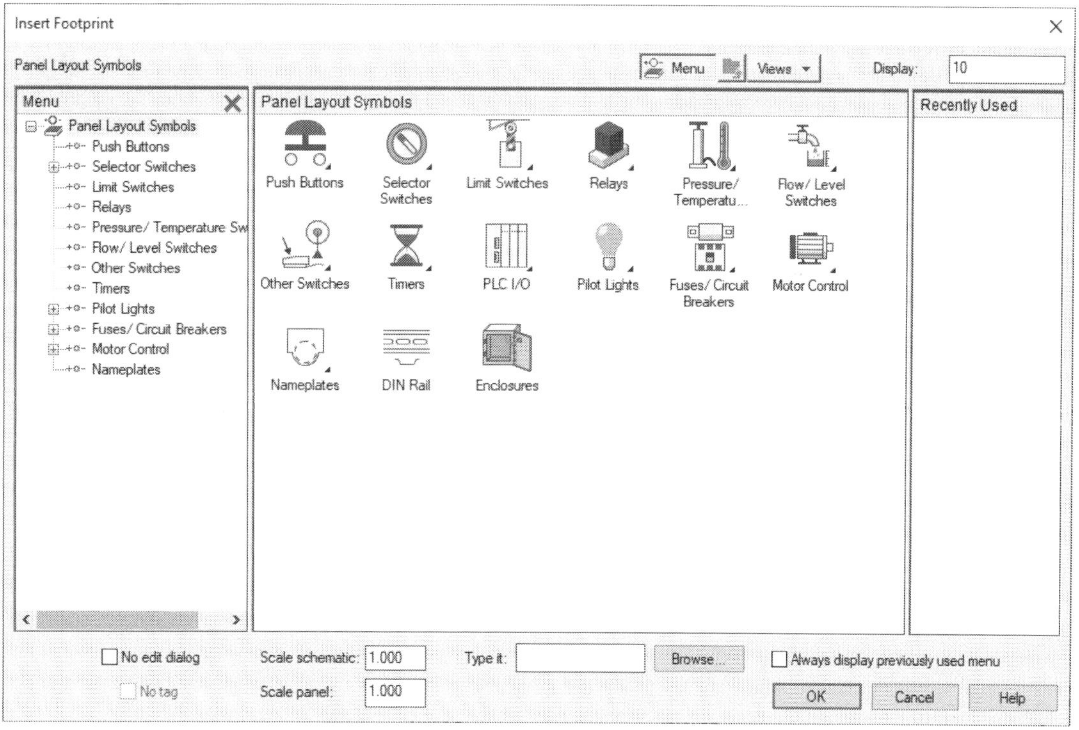

Figure 6–1

After selecting the footprint, the *Footprint* dialog box opens. You can select the manufacturer and Catalog Number in the *Choice A* area or manually select a footprint using the *Choice B* area, as shown in Figure 6–2.

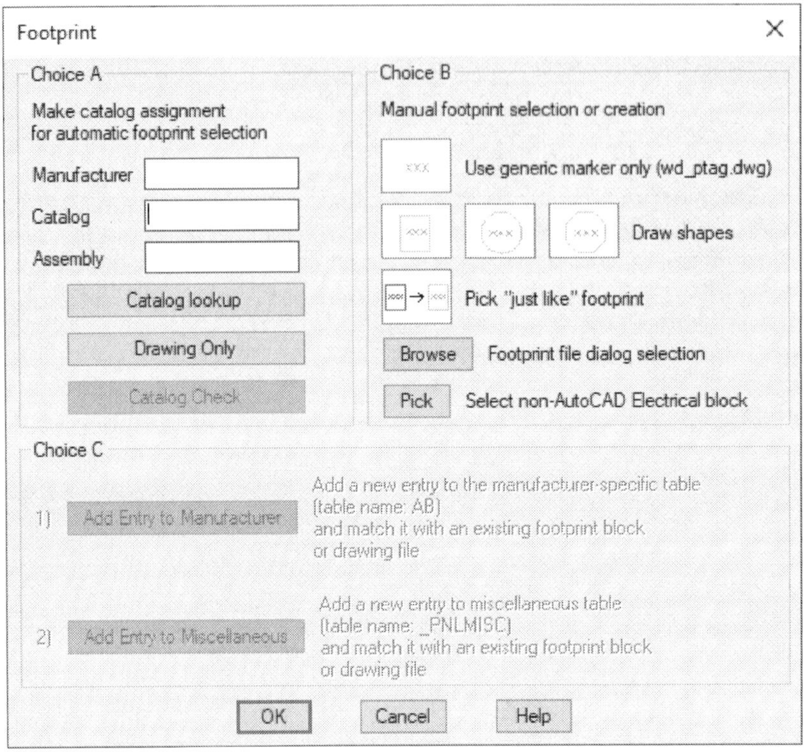

Figure 6–2

Choice A

Catalog lookup	Opens the Catalog Browser for the selected footprint type.
Drawing Only	Opens the *Catalog Values* dialog box, listing components in the drawing of the same type.

Choice B

	Inserts a block with attributes only and without any geometry. The attributes contain the component tag, description, and other properties.
	Draws generic shapes with attributes and xdata. You can draw a rectangle, circle, or octagon. Specify the size by picking in the drawing window.
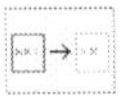	Pick a footprint in the drawing window.

Browse	Opens the standard *Browse* dialog box. Select a DWG file to use as the footprint.
Pick	Pick a standard block in the drawing to convert it to an intelligent AutoCAD Electrical footprint.

After you select a block to use and pick its placement in the drawing window, the *Panel Layout – Component Insert/Edit* dialog box opens as shown in Figure 6–3.

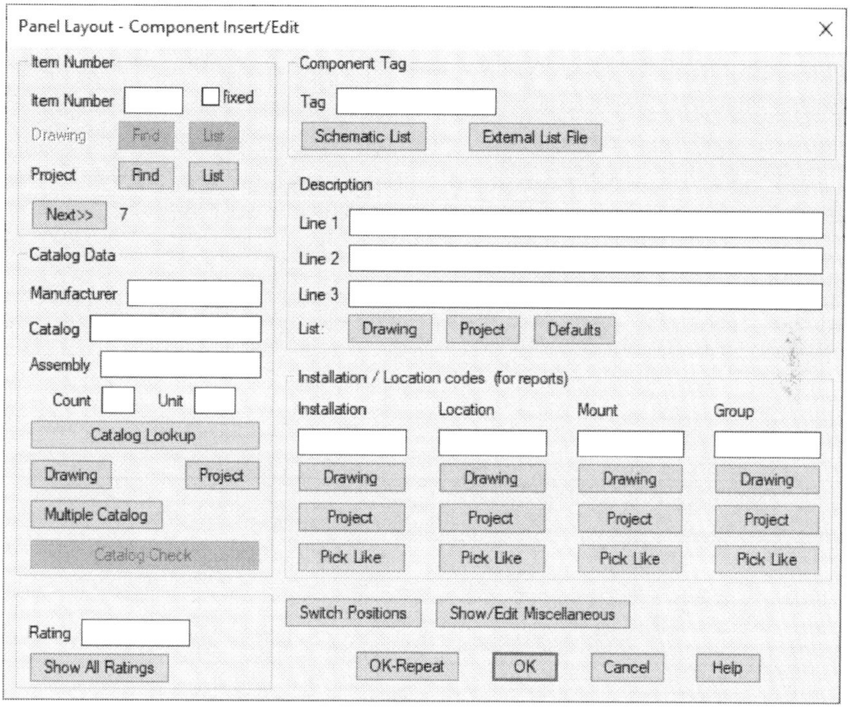

Figure 6–3

Item Number	Enter an Item Number for the component. The Item Number is linked to the component's catalog data and used in reports and balloons. You can lock the Item Number by selecting **Fixed**. If the Item Number is **Fixed**, it is not automatically updated when the **Resequence Item Numbers** tool is used.
Component Tag	Assign a component tag to a footprint.
Catalog Data	Assign catalog data to a footprint.
Description	Enter a description for a footprint.
Installation/ Location Codes	Assign installation, location, group, and mounting attributes. The group and mount attributes are specific to panel symbols and can be used in reports.
Rating	Assign rating values to the component.

Most of the buttons in the *Panel Layout – Component Insert/Edit* dialog box are the same as those used in the *Insert Component* dialog box when creating schematic drawings.

The following buttons are different:

- **Schematic List:** Displays a list of component tags from the schematic drawings in the active project. If you select a tag from the list, the information from the schematic symbol is linked to the panel footprint.
- **External List File:** Opens a *Browse* dialog box where you can select a text file that contains a list of component tags for selection.
- **Switch Positions:** Displays the switch position information assigned to a selector switch if the footprint has been linked to a schematic symbol. If the footprint has not been linked, you enter the switch position information here.

When using a combined installation and location code with the tag of a component, the *Panel Layout - Component Insert/Edit* dialog box opens, as shown in Figure 6–4.

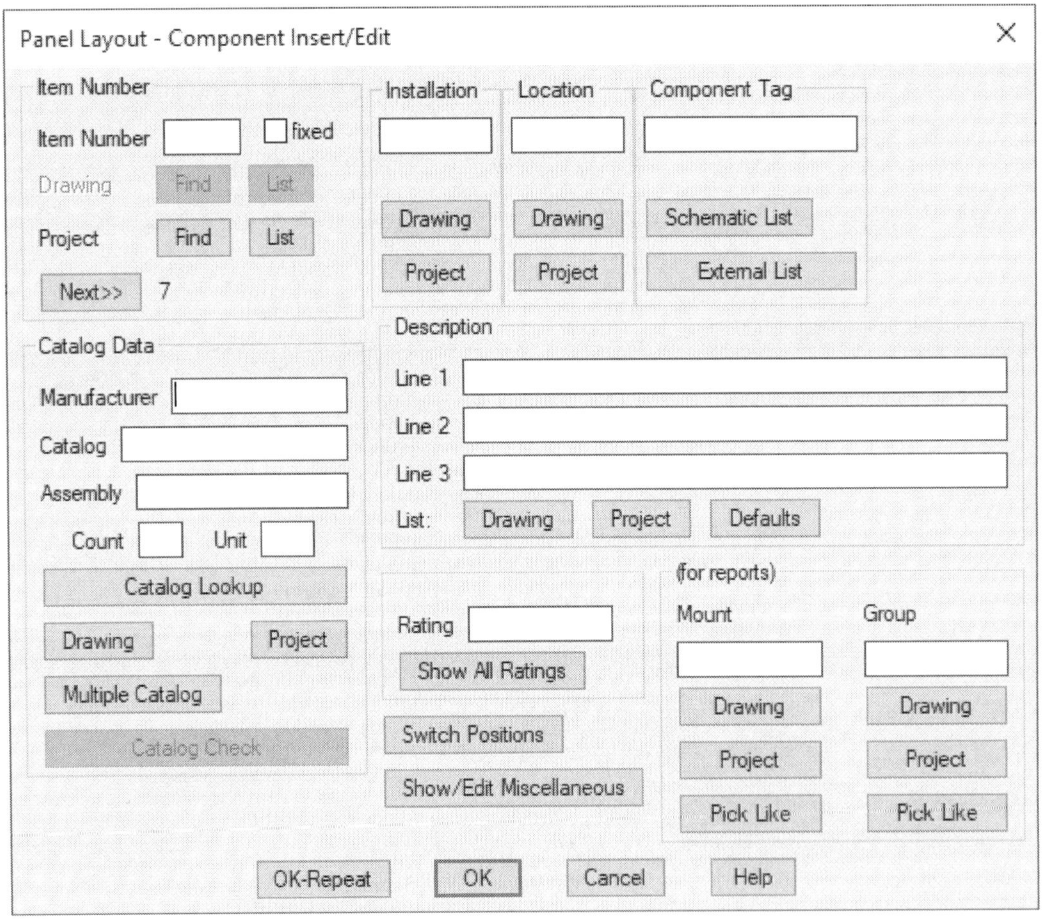

Figure 6–4

6.2 Insert Footprint (Schematic List)

The **Insert Footprint (Schematic List)** command displays a list of symbols that have already been inserted into the schematic drawings of the active project. You can insert footprints into the panel drawing using this list.

- When using this command, the panel footprint is linked to the schematic symbol using the component tag. The information attached to the schematic symbol is automatically applied to the panel footprint.

Insert Footprint (Schematic List)

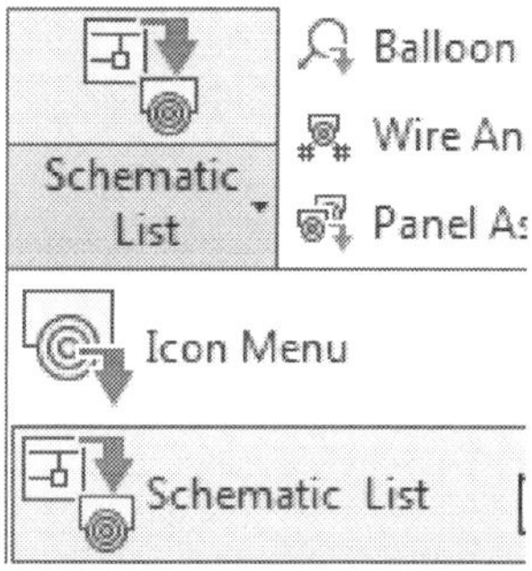

Ribbon: *Panel* tab>*Insert Component Footprints* panel

Command Prompt: aefootprintsch

How To: Insert a Footprint from the Schematic List

1. Start the **Insert Footprint (Schematic List)** command.
2. In the *Schematic Component List --> Panel Layout Insert* dialog box, set the options.
3. Click **OK**.
4. In the *Select Drawings to Process* dialog box, select the drawings to process if you are searching the project.
5. Click **OK**.
6. In the *Schematic Components* dialog box, select the component to insert.
7. Select the method to use to determine the block that represents the footprint: **Manual**, **Insert**, or **Convert Existing**.
8. Pick in the drawing window to place the footprint.
9. Pick in the drawing window to set the rotation.

10. In the *Panel Layout – Component Insert/Edit* dialog box, verify the information or enter any new data.
11. Click **OK**.
12. Repeat Steps 6 to 11 for any additional footprints.
13. Click **Close** to end the command.
14. In the *Update Other Drawings?* dialog box, click **OK**, **Task**, or **Skip**.

- The first time the command is used, the AutoCAD Electrical software searches drawings in the project to build the schematic list. During the continued session, the same list is used. Click **Reload** to regenerate the list.

The first time the command is run in the current session of the software, the *Schematic Component List --> Panel Layout Insert* dialog box opens, as shown in Figure 6–5.

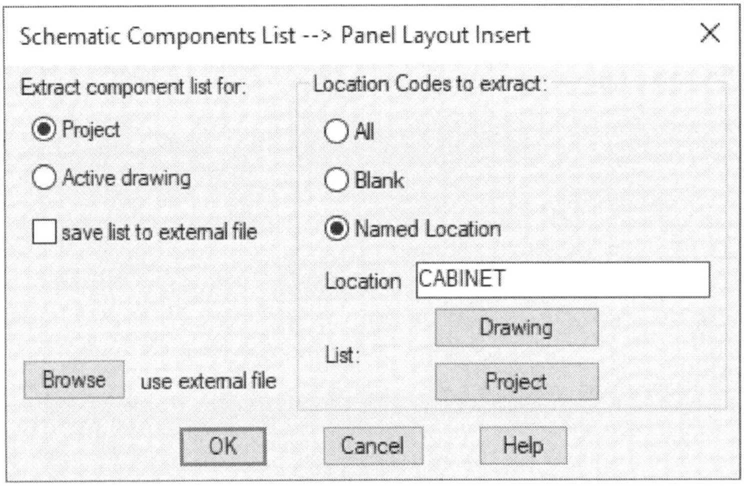

Figure 6–5

- In the *Extract component list for:* area, you can select the option to search the **Project** or **Active drawing** for existing schematic components.
- You can also **save the list to an external file**. If saving to an external file, you can save as a .WD1 or .CSV file. These extensions are types of comma delimited text files.
- **Browse...** opens the already saved file as the source for a list of schematic components.
- In the *Location Codes to extract* area, you can select to extract information for symbols that have specific location attributes.
- **All** extracts information for every schematic symbol that is part of the drawing selection set.
- **Blank** and **Named Location** extracts information for components. You can specify the code by typing it in the field, selecting it from a drawing (**Drawing**), or selecting it from a project list (**Project**).

After the source drawing(s) are searched, the *Schematic Components* dialog box opens, as shown in Figure 6–6. It displays a list of all of the symbols in the schematic drawings that meet the criteria in the *Schematic Component List --> Panel Layout Insert* dialog box.

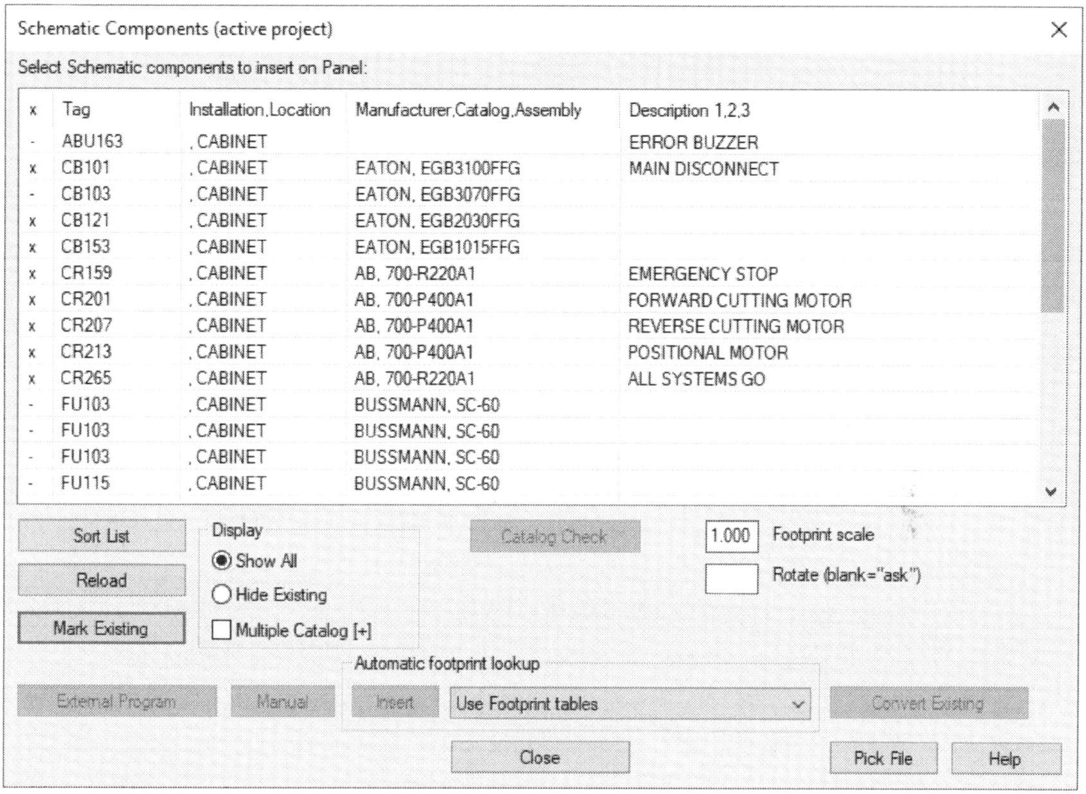

Figure 6–6

- The values in the *X* column indicate as:
  - **X –** Footprint has been inserted for that component. You might need to click **Mark Existing** for the *X* column to update.
  - **O –** Footprint has been inserted that matches the component tag, but that the manufacturer or catalog data differs between the schematic and panel symbols.
  - **A –** Footprint has not been inserted for that component.
- The other columns list the component tag, installation/location codes, manufacturer, catalog, assembly, and description.

- The options in the lower area of the dialog box are:

Sort List	Controls the sorting of the list. You can sort by up to four fields.
Reload	Returns to the *Schematic Component List --> Panel Layout Insert* dialog box to refresh the list.
Mark Existing	Puts an **X** or **O** in the left column next to components that already have footprints inserted into the panel.
Catalog Check	Displays the BOM information for the selected component.
External Program	Uses an external user routine to compile the list of components.
Manual	Inserts the footprint for the selected component. Opens the *Footprint* dialog box in which you can select how to determine the block or geometry used to represent the footprint.
Insert	Inserts the footprint for the selected component. Uses the **footprint_lookup.mdb** database to determine which block to use.
Convert Existing	Converts an existing AutoCAD block into a smart AutoCAD Electrical block and inserts the information for the selected component.
Pick File	Returns to the *Schematic Component List --> Panel Layout Insert* dialog box to refresh.

- *Display* area controls the information that displays in the list.
- **Show All** displays all schematic components in the project in the schematic list.
- **Hide Existing** removes any components from the schematic list that have already been inserted into a panel drawing. It is recommended that you use **Hide Existing** to avoid inserting multiple footprints for the same component, as already inserted components are hidden.
- **Multiple Catalog [+]** displays components with multiple Catalog Numbers assigned as individual line items.

After selecting the footprint to be inserted and the method to be used for inserting the component, you can chose in the drawing window to place it and set its rotation. When the footprint has been inserted, the *Panel Layout – Component Insert/Edit* dialog box opens, which is automatically populated with data from the schematic symbol, as shown in Figure 6–7.

> ***Note:*** *The automation helps to prevent typos or incorrect data from being added to the footprint.*

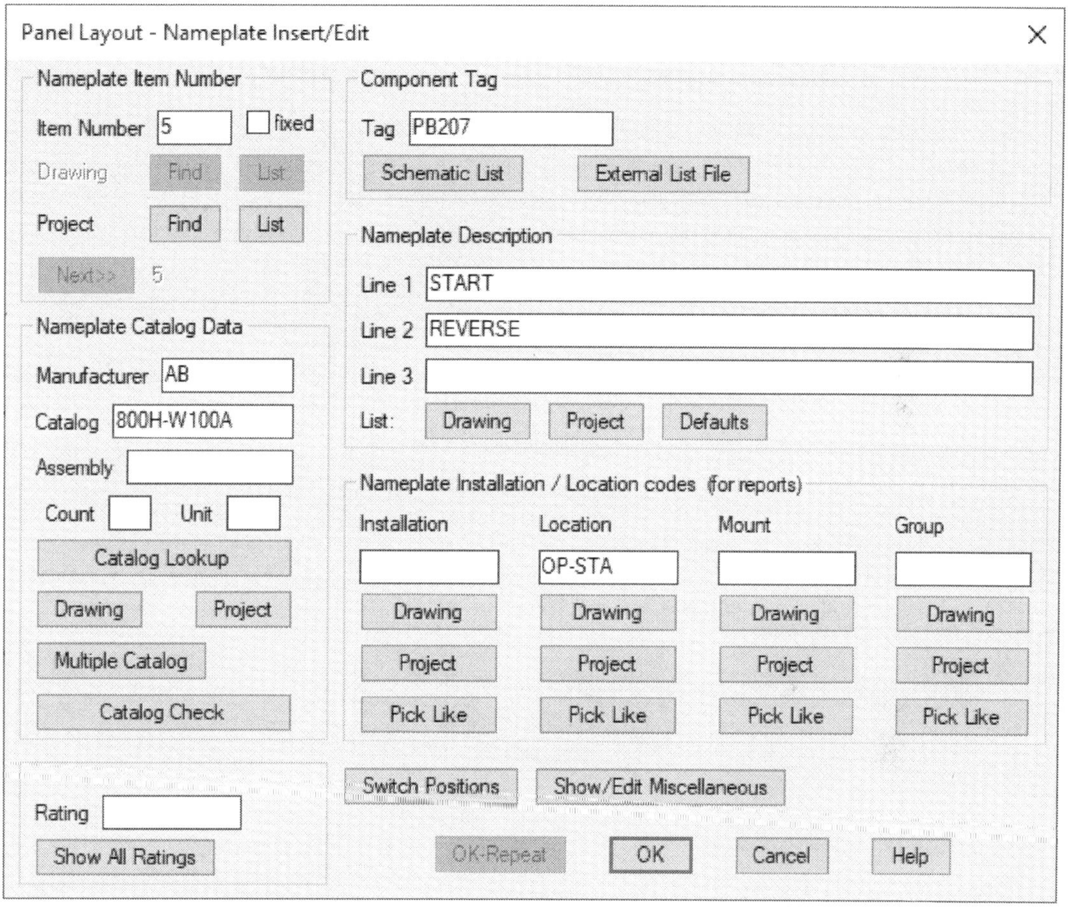

Figure 6–7

After you have verified the data attached to the footprint and inserted it, you are returned to the *Schematic Components* dialog box where you can continue to insert footprints. Click **Close** to complete the command. After you have completed the command, the *Update Other Drawings?* dialog box opens. You can perform the update immediately, add the update to the project task list to perform several updates at once at a later time, or skip the update entirely.

6.3 Insert Component (Panel List)

If you create panel drawings first, before their schematic, you can insert component symbols onto the schematic using the **Insert Component (Panel List)** command. It displays a list of footprints that have already been inserted into the panel drawings of the active project. The command links the schematic symbol to the panel footprint using the component tag. It also uses the information from the panel footprint to populate the attributes in the schematic symbol.

Insert Component (Panel List)

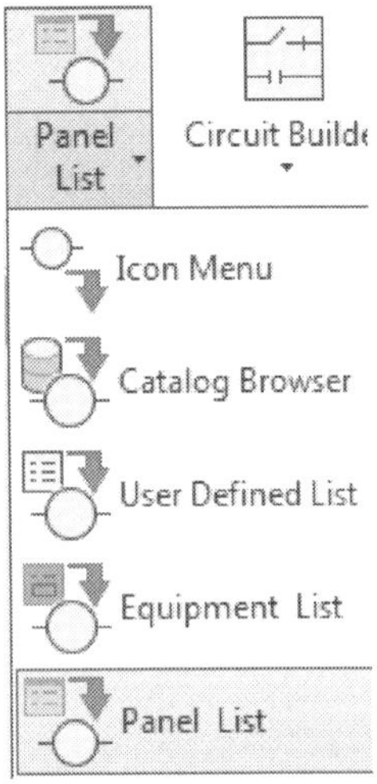

Ribbon: *Schematic* tab>*Insert Components* panel

Command Prompt: aecomponentpnl

How To: Insert a Component from a Panel List

1. Start the **Insert Component (Panel List)** command.
2. In the *Panel Layout List --> Schematic Components Insert* dialog box, set the options.
3. Click **OK**.
4. In the *Select Drawings to Process* dialog box, select the drawings to process if searching the project.
5. Click **OK**.
6. In the *Panel Components* dialog box, select the component to insert.
7. Click **Insert**.

8. In the *Insert <component>* dialog box, select the block to use.
9. Pick in the drawing window to place the footprint.
10. In the *Insert / Edit Component* dialog box, verify the information and enter any new data.
11. Click **OK**.
12. Repeat Steps 6 to 11 for any additional schematic symbols.
13. Click **Close** to end the command.
14. In the *Update Other Drawings?* dialog box, click **OK**, **Task**, or **Skip**.

The first time the command is run in the current session, the panel list of components is created. In the *Panel Layout List --> Schematic Components Insert* dialog box (shown in Figure 6–8), you can select the options to search.

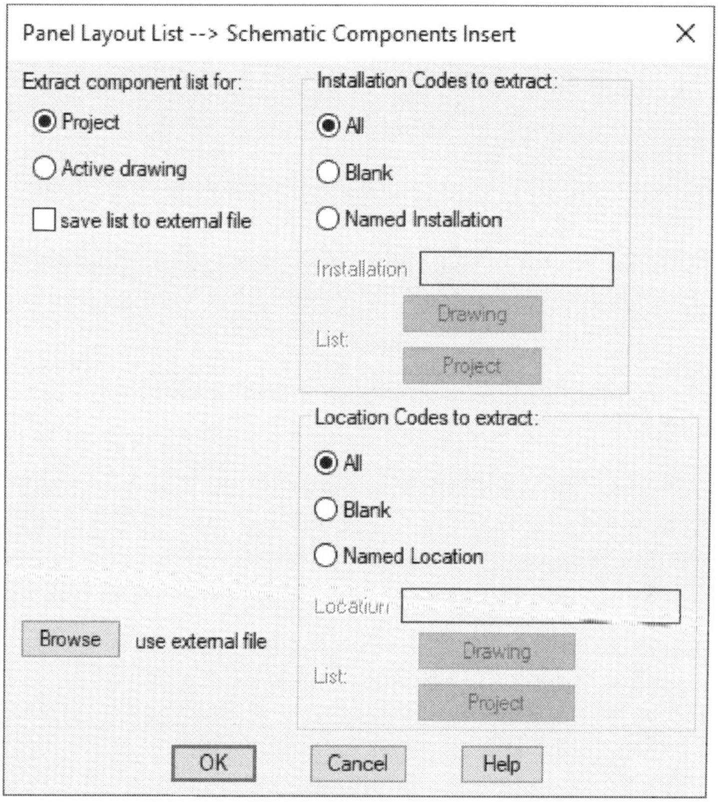

Figure 6–8

This *Panel Layout List --> Schematic Components Insert* dialog box is similar to the *Schematic Component List --> Panel Layout Insert* dialog box that is opened using the **Insert Footprint (Schematic List)**. If saving to an external file, you can save as a WD3 or CSV file.

Note: For more information about the dialog box, refer to the Insert Footprint (Schematic List) section.

After the source drawing(s) are searched, the *Panel Components* dialog box opens, as shown in Figure 6–9. It is similar to the *Schematic Components* dialog box with additional options in the *Tag Options* area.

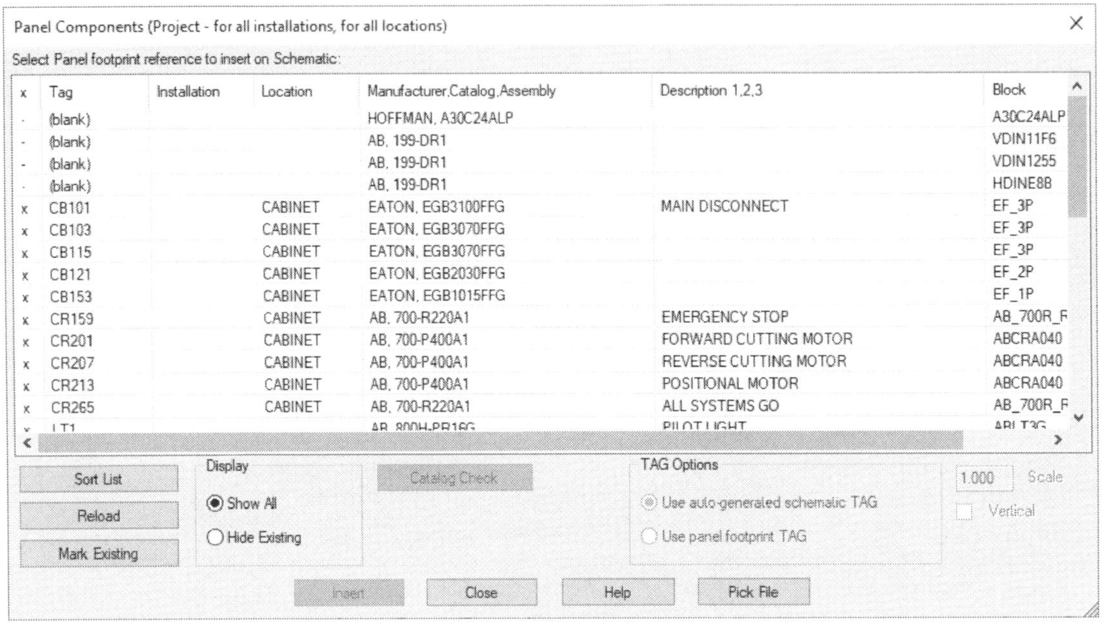

Figure 6–9

- The *X* column designates whether the component has already been inserted into a schematic drawing and can have **X**, **O**, and **A** values.
- The other columns list the component tag, installation/location codes, manufacturer, catalog, assembly, descriptions, and footprint block.
- The options in the lower part of the *Panel Components* dialog box work similar to the options in the *Schematic Components* dialog box in the *Insert Footprint (Schematic List)* section.
- The **Tag Options** are specific to the *Panel Components* dialog box. Select **Use auto-generated schematic TAG** or **Use panel footprint TAG**. These auto-generated options retag the component based on the settings in Drawing Properties and update the panel footprint with the new tag.

When you have selected the symbol to insert and the method of inserting the component, the *Insert <component>* dialog box opens. The **schematic_lookup.mdb** table is queried to determine which valid schematic symbols to use for the selected footprint. The default **schematic_lookup.mdb** file is located in *C:\Users\<user>\Documents\Acade <version>\Aedata\<language>\Catalogs* for Windows 10.

The query is based on the manufacturer and Catalog Number assigned in the panel.

Select from the displayed list (as shown in Figure 6–10), from the Icon Menu, or pick an existing symbol in the drawing window to use its block. Once the block is selected, the attributes are populated with information from the footprint.

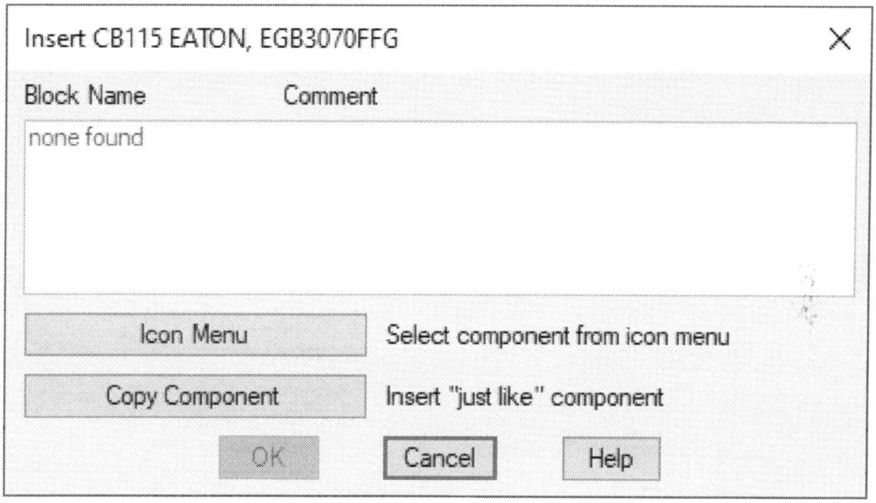

Figure 6–10

Icon Menu	Opens the *Insert Component* dialog box. Select a symbol in the Icon Menu.
Copy Component	Pick a block in the drawing window.

After the block is selected, pick in the drawing window to place the symbol. Once placed, the *Insert / Edit Component* dialog box opens, which is automatically populated with data from the footprint, as shown in Figure 6–11.

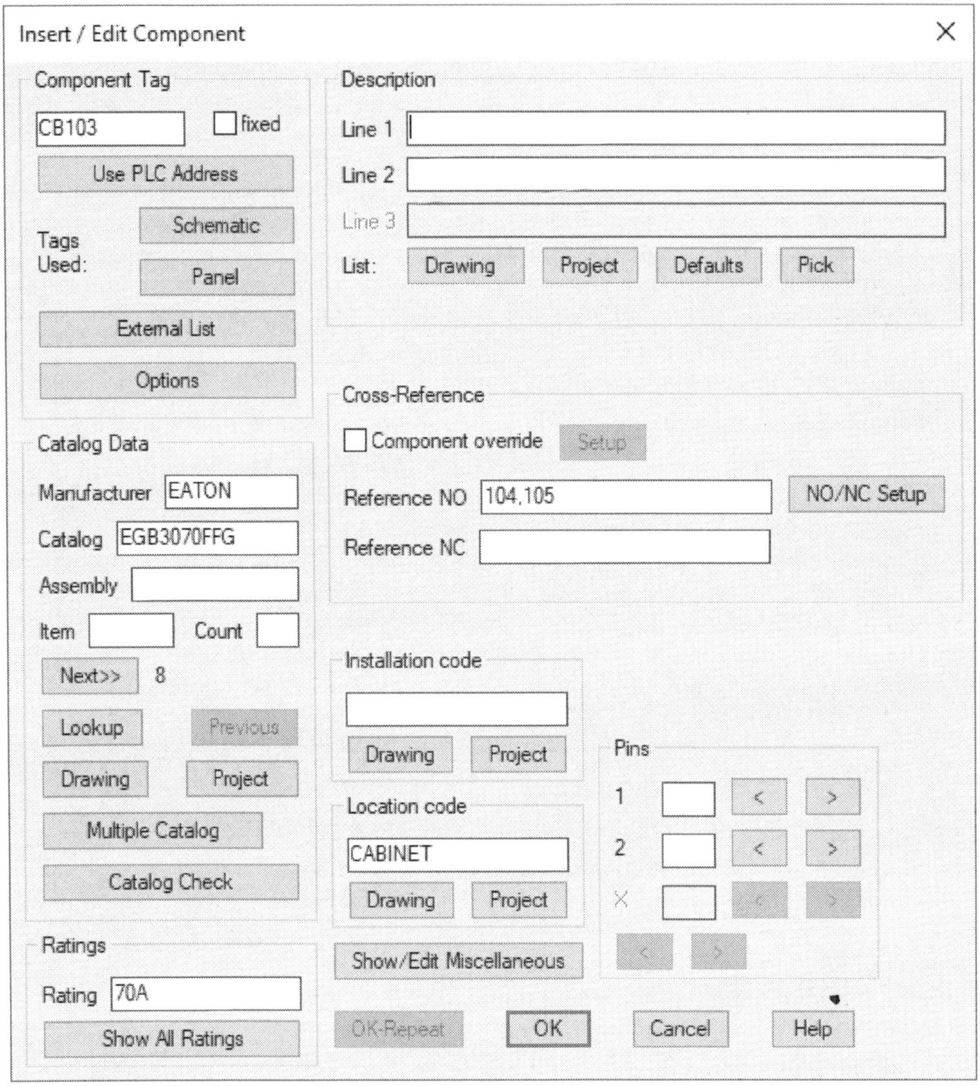

Figure 6–11

After you have verified the data attached to the schematic component and inserted it, you are returned to the *Panel Components* dialog box where you can continue to insert schematic symbols. Click **Close** to complete the command. After you have completed the command, the *Update Other Drawings?* dialog box opens. You can perform the update immediately, add the update to the project task list to perform several updates at once at a later time, or skip the update entirely.

6.4 Edit Footprint

The **Edit Footprint** command opens the *Panel Layout – Component Insert/Edit* dialog box for a selected footprint where you can edit the information associated with the footprint.

Edit Footprint

Ribbon: *Panel* tab>*Edit Footprints* panel

Command Prompt: aeeditfootprint

Shortcut menu: *(on footprint)* **Edit Footprint**

How To: Edit a Footprint

1. Start the **Edit Footprint** command.
2. Select the footprint to edit.
3. In the *Panel Layout – Component Insert/Edit* dialog box, modify the required information.
4. Click **OK**.

The *Panel Layout – Component Insert/Edit* dialog box (shown in Figure 6–12) opens where you can edit the footprint. The dialog box is also displayed when a footprint is inserted into a panel drawing.

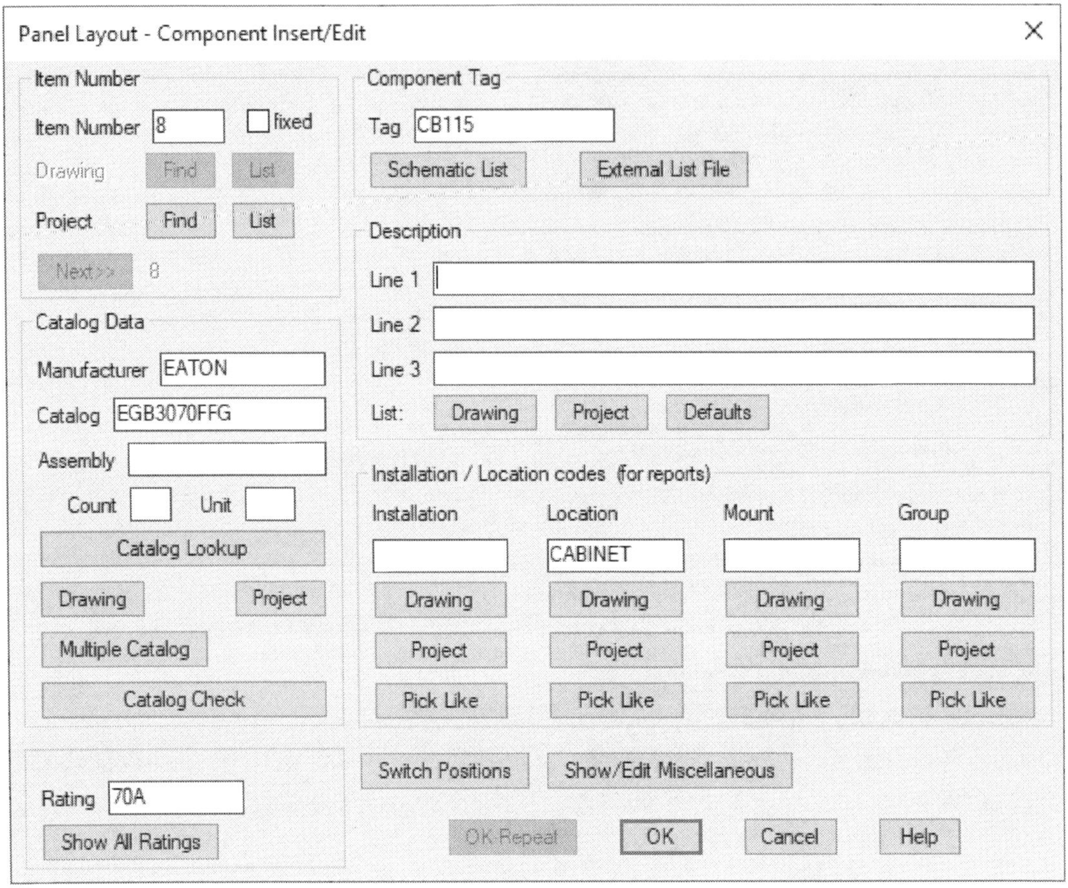

Figure 6–12

- The various **Attribute Editing** commands found in the *Schematic* tab>*Edit Components* panel, can also be used to modify a footprint. These commands control the size and position of the attributes of a single block.

Practice 6a
Insert Footprint (Icon Menu)

Practice Objectives

- Populate a new panel drawing with component footprints.
- Populate a new schematic drawing with schematic symbols.

In this practice, you will create a new drawing and insert an enclosure to use for the panel. You will then insert footprints using the Icon Menu, add nameplates to the footprints, and then add their schematic symbols to a ladder. The final drawings display as shown in Figure 6–13.

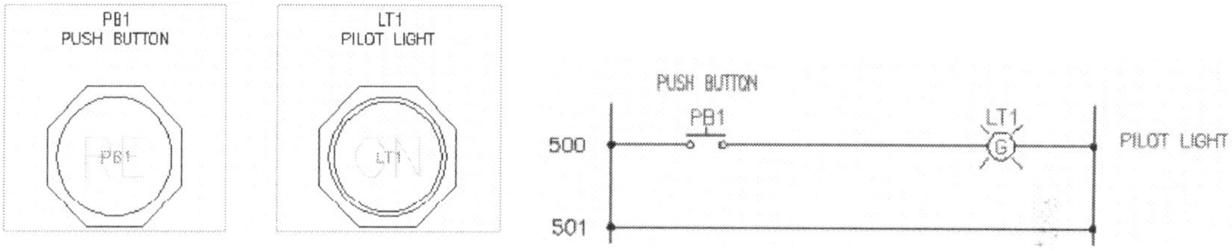

Figure 6–13

Task 1: Insert an Enclosure.

1. In your practice files folder, in the *Module 06* folder, open the **Module 06** project file.
2. Open any drawing in the Module 06 project. You need to have a drawing open to create a new drawing.

3. In the *Project Manager* toolbar, click (New Drawing). In the *Create New Drawing* dialog box, enter the information below, as shown in Figure 6–14.
   - *Name*: **Panel**
   - *Template*: Select **Electrical_template.dwt** from the practice files folder.
   - *Description 1:* **Panel Drawing**

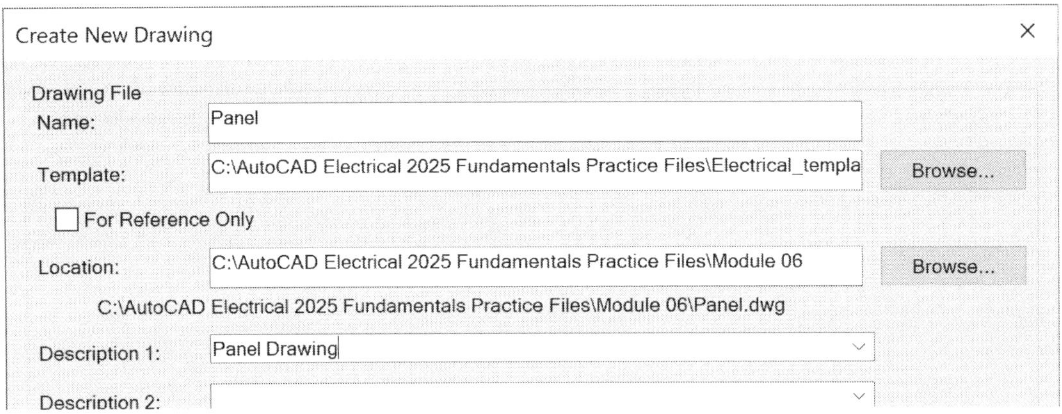

Figure 6–14

4. Click **OK**.
5. In the *Apply Project Defaults to Drawing Settings* dialog box, click **Yes**. The **Panel.dwg** is created and opened.
6. In the *Panel* tab>*Insert Component Footprints* panel, click (Insert Footprint [Icon Menu]). The *Insert Footprint* dialog box opens.
7. Click (Enclosures) to insert an enclosure. The *Footprint* dialog box opens.
8. In *Choice A* area, click **Catalog lookup** to open the Catalog Browser. Search for **HOFFMAN** and then enter the second search for **A20C**. Select **A20C16ALP** for the enclosure. In the Catalog Browser, click **OK**. Note that the *Footprint* dialog box is populated by the information. Click **OK**.
9. Note that the enclosure is attached to the cursor (note that it is bigger than the drawing sheet). Select a point near **6,1** (near the bottom of the drawing sheet) for the insertion point and press <Enter> to accept the rotation. The *Panel Layout – Component Insert/Edit* dialog box opens.
10. In the *Description* area, in *Line 1*, type **PANEL ENCLOSURE**. Click **OK**.
11. Erase the two views on the right side, leaving one enclosure on the drawing sheet.

Task 2: Insert footprints and add nameplates.

1. Click (Insert Footprint [Icon Menu]). The *Insert Footprint* dialog box opens.
2. Click (Push Buttons) and then click (Push Button NO). The *Footprint* dialog box opens.
3. Click **Catalog lookup** to open the Catalog Browser. If not already searched by default, search for the following:
   - *Manufacturer*: **AB**
   - *Type:* **30.5mm EXTENDED**
   - *Style:* **RED**

   Select **800H-BR6A** and click **OK**. Note that the *Footprint* dialog box is populated. Click **OK**.
4. Pick a point near **9,18** as the insertion point, as shown in Figure 6–15. Press <Enter> to accept the rotation.

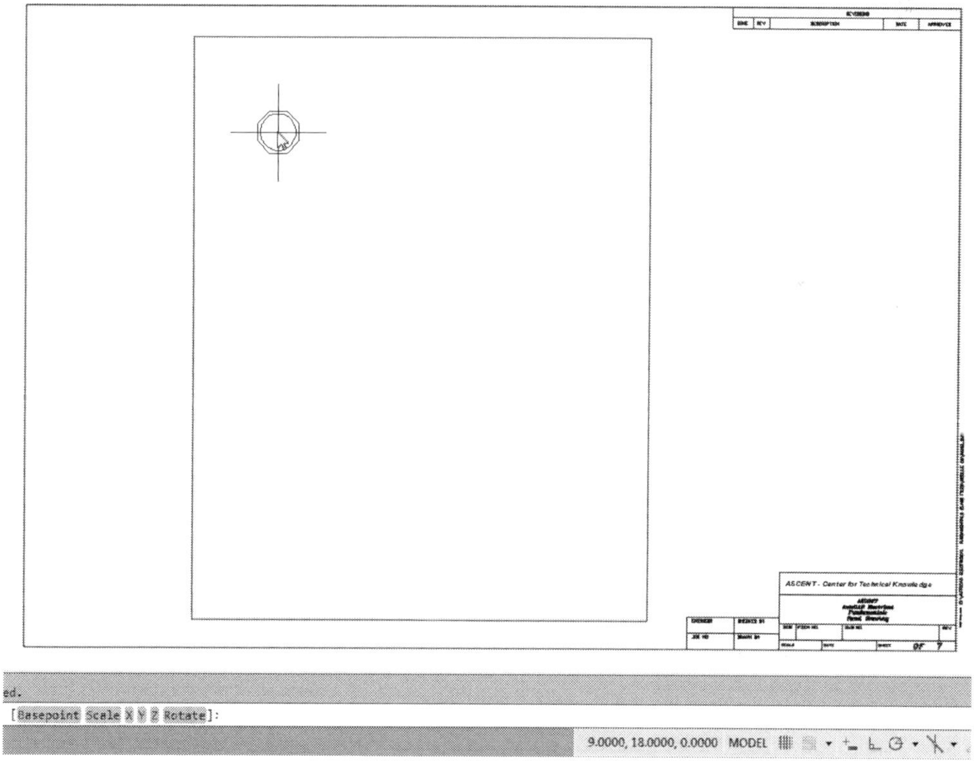

Figure 6–15

5. The *Panel Layout – Component Insert/Edit* dialog box, in the *Component Tag* area, set the following, as shown in Figure 6–16:
   - *Tag*: **PB1**
   - *Description, Line 1:* **PUSH BUTTON**

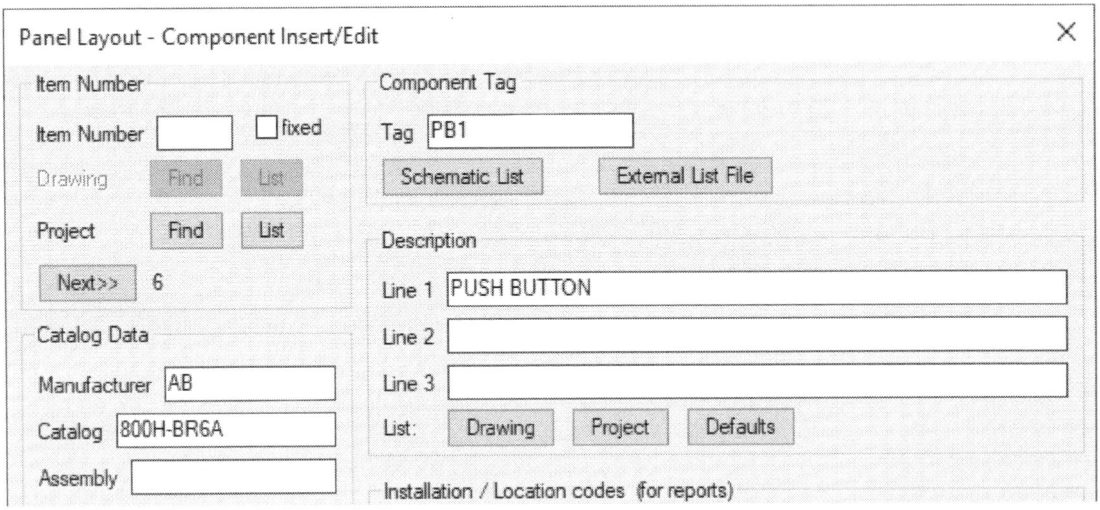

Figure 6–16

6. Click **OK**.

7. Click  (Insert Footprint [Icon Menu]). The *Insert Footprint* dialog box opens.

8. Click  (Pilot Lights) and then click  (Green Lights). The *Footprint* dialog box opens.

9. Click **Catalog lookup** to open the Catalog Browser. Search for *Manufacturer* **AB 30.5mm "120 VAC XFMR"** (if required) and select **800H-PR16G**, as shown in Figure 6–17. Click **OK**.

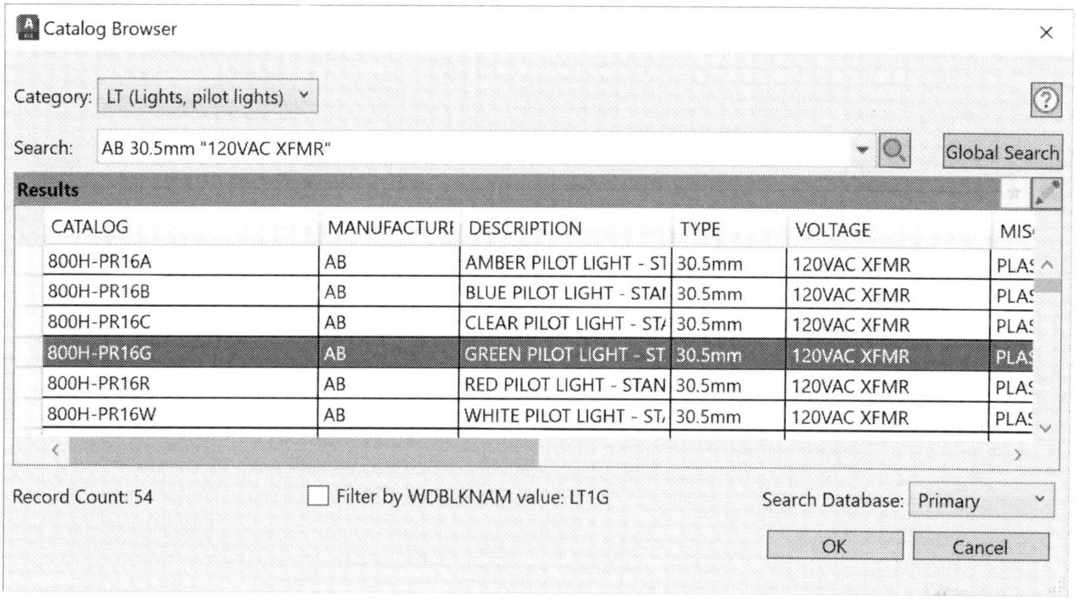

Figure 6–17

10. Note that the *Footprint* dialog box is populated. Click **OK**.
11. Pick a point near **12,18** as the insertion point. Press <Enter> to accept the rotation.
12. In the *Panel Layout-Component Insert/Edit* dialog box, set the following, as shown in Figure 6–18:
    - *Tag*: **LT1**
    - *Description, Line 1*: **PILOT LIGHT**

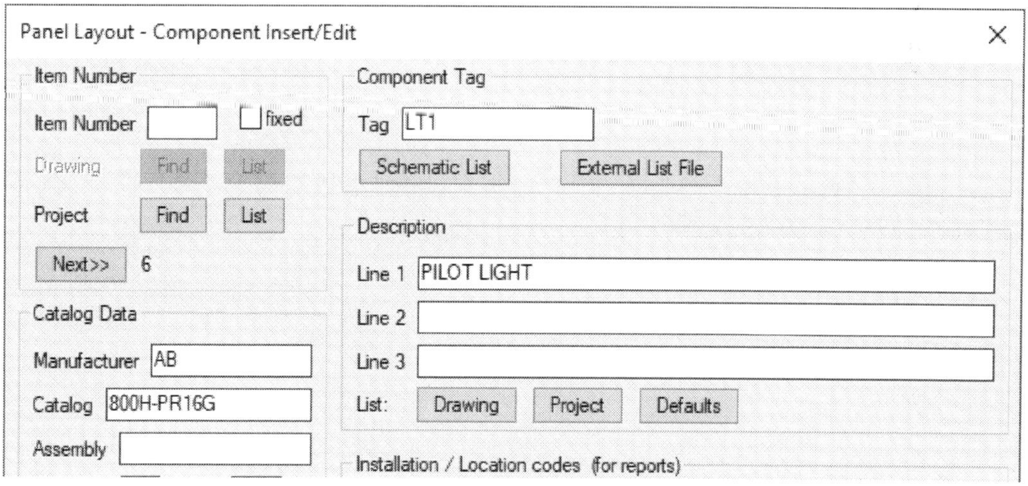

Figure 6–18

13. Click **OK**.
14. Click (Insert Footprint [Icon Menu]). The *Insert Footprint* dialog box opens.
15. Click (Nameplates) and click (Nameplate Catalog Lookup) The *Nameplate* dialog box opens.
16. Using **Catalog lookup**, search for **AB "800H AUTOMOTIVE"** in the Catalog Browser, if required. Select **800H-W500A** and click **OK**.
17. Note that the *Nameplate* dialog box is populated. Click **OK**.
18. At *Select objects* prompt, window around both the push button and the light that you inserted previously and press <Enter>.
19. The *Panel Layout – Nameplate Insert/Edit* dialog box opens for **LT1**. Click **OK**.
20. The *Panel Layout – Nameplate Insert/Edit* dialog box opens for **PB1**. Click **OK**.
21. Save **Panel.dwg**.

Task 3: Add schematic symbols to a ladder.

1. Click (New Drawing) to create a new drawing for the project with the following information:
    - *Name*: **Schematic**
    - *Description 1:* **Schematic Drawing**
    - *Template*: Verify it is set to **Electrical_template.dwt** in the practice files folder.
2. Click **OK** and click **Yes** in the *Apply Project Defaults to Drawing Settings* warning box. A new drawing **Schematic.dwg** opens.
3. In the *Schematic* tab>*Insert Wires/Wire Numbers* panel, click (Insert Ladder) to insert a ladder.

4. In the *Insert Ladder* dialog box, set the following, as shown in Figure 6–19:
    - *Rungs*: **14**
    - *1st Reference*: **500**

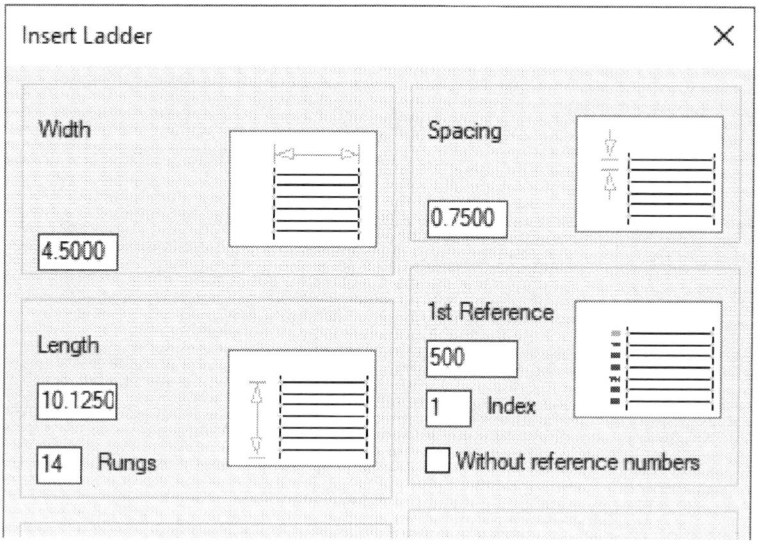

Figure 6–19

5. Click **OK**.
6. Click a point near **3,20** to insert the ladder.
7. In the *Schematic* tab>*Insert Components* panel, click (Icon Menu). Click (Push Buttons) and then click (Push Button NO).
8. Insert it near the left end of line 500. The *Insert / Edit Component* dialog box opens.
9. In the *Component Tag* area, click **Panel**. The *Panel Tag List* opens for the **Module 06** project.

10. Select **PB1** in the list as shown in Figure 6–20 and click **OK**. In the *Copy Tag* dialog box, click **OK**. The fields in the *Insert / Edit Component* dialog box are populated based on the information in the panel footprint. Click **OK**. Update and save the related drawings.

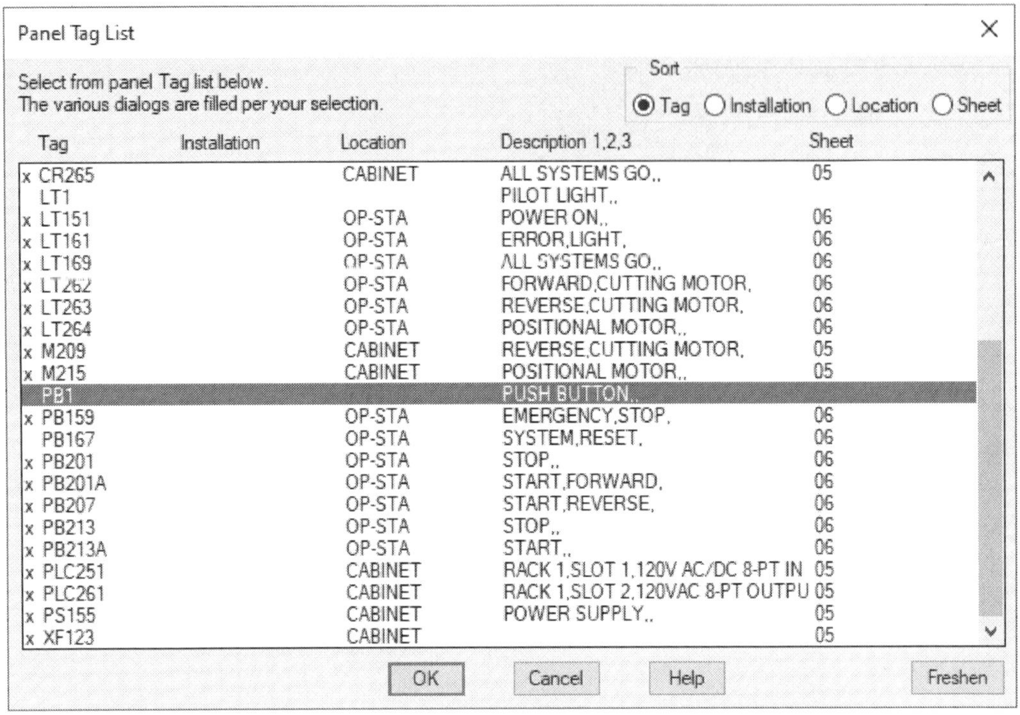

Figure 6–20

11. In the *Schematic* tab>*Insert Components* panel, click  (Icon Menu). Click  (Pilot Lights) and then click  (Green Standard) to insert a Green Standard light.
12. Click a point near the right end of line 500. The *Insert / Edit Component* dialog box opens.
13. In the *Component Tag* area, click **Panel**. The *Panel Tag List* opens for the **Module 06** project.

14. Select **LT1** in the list as shown in Figure 6–21, and click **OK**. In the *Copy Tag* dialog box, click **OK**. In the *Insert / Edit Component* dialog box, click **OK**. Update and save the drawing.

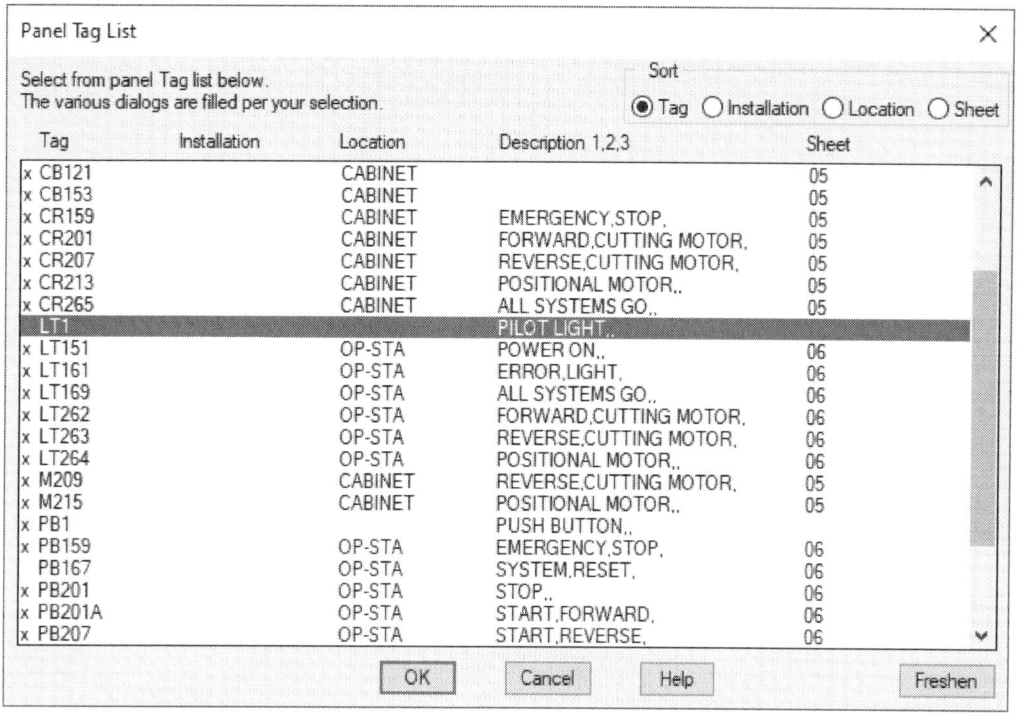

Figure 6–21

15. Save and close **Schematic.dwg**.

End of practice

Practice 6b
Insert Footprint (Schematic List)

Practice Objective

- Insert panel footprints.

In this practice, you will use the **Insert Footprint (Schematic List)** command. You will insert the footprint for a circuit breaker and a motor starter coil. The final panel drawing displays as shown in Figure 6–22.

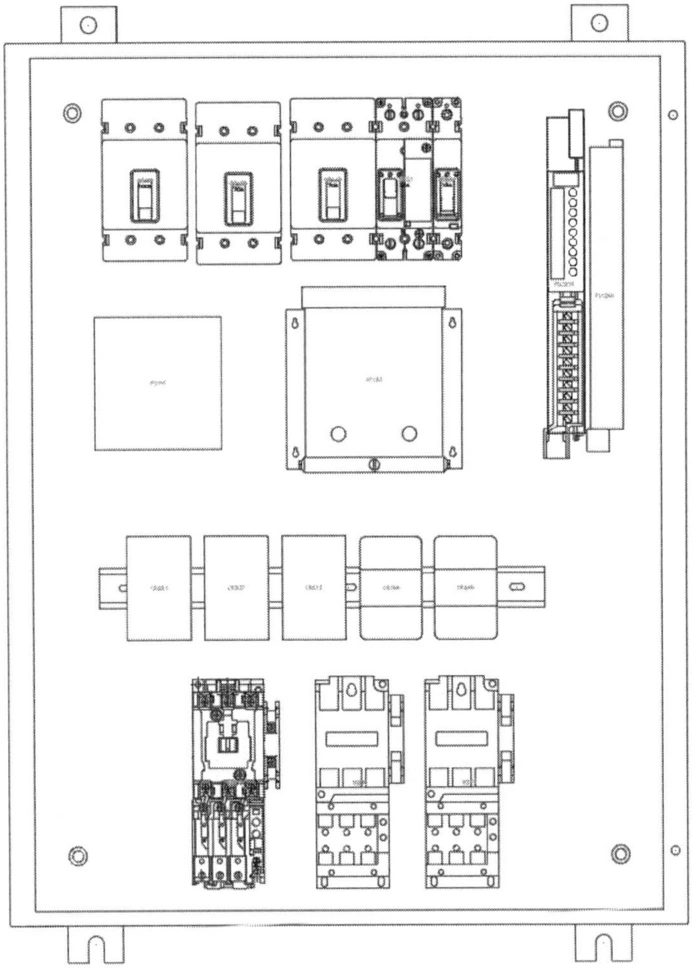

Figure 6–22

1. If the **Module 06** project is not active, open and activate it now.
2. In the **Module 06** project, open **Power.dwg**.
3. Zoom to **CB103**. Edit the component and note the information in the *Insert / Edit Component* dialog box as shown in Figure 6–23. Note that the *Location code* displays **CABINET**. The footprint for the component is going to be inserted into the Cabinet drawing. Click **Cancel**.

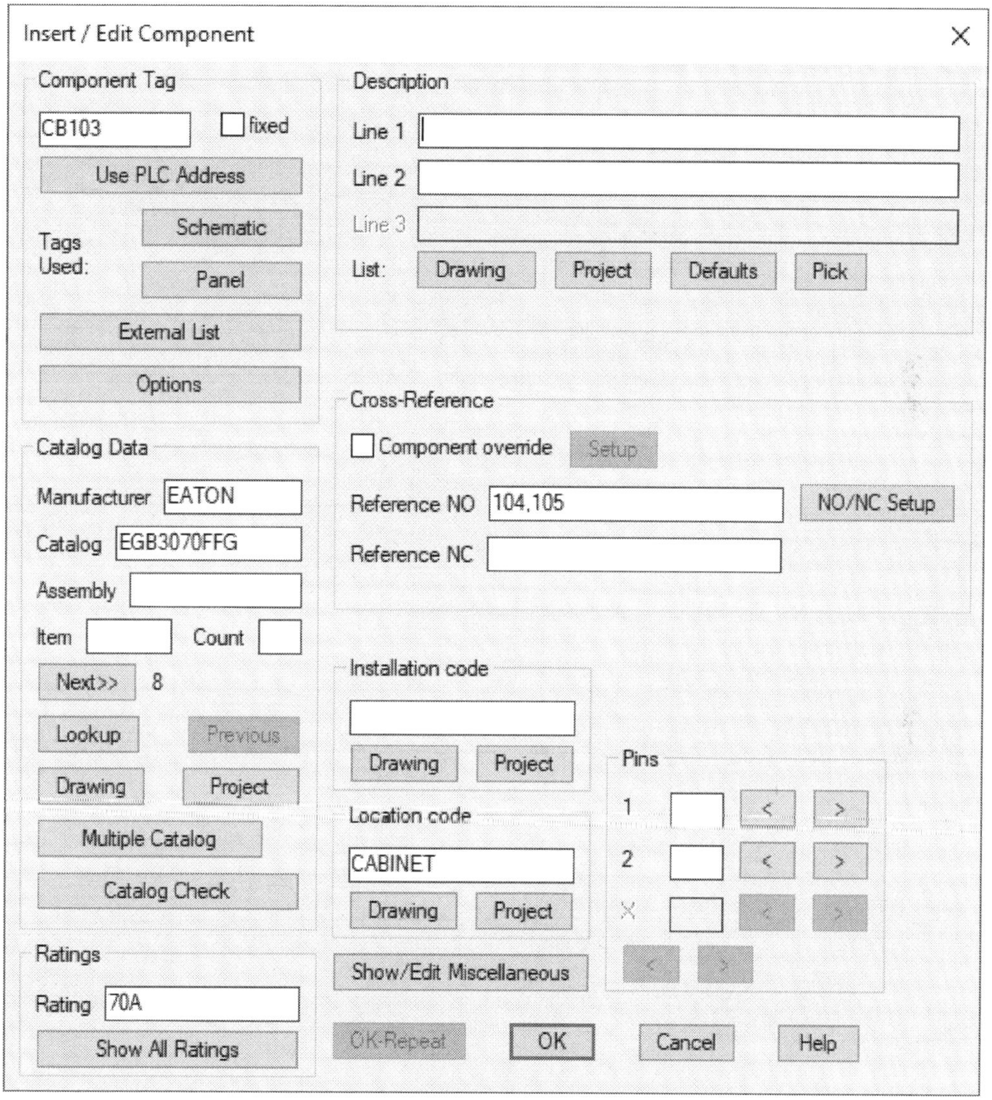

Figure 6–23

4. Click  (Next Drawing) to close **Power.dwg** and open **Control.dwg**.

5. Zoom to **M203**. Edit the component and note the information in the *Insert / Edit Component* dialog box as shown in Figure 6–24. Note that the *Location code* also displays **CABINET**. The footprint for the component is going to be inserted into the Cabinet drawing. Click **Cancel**.

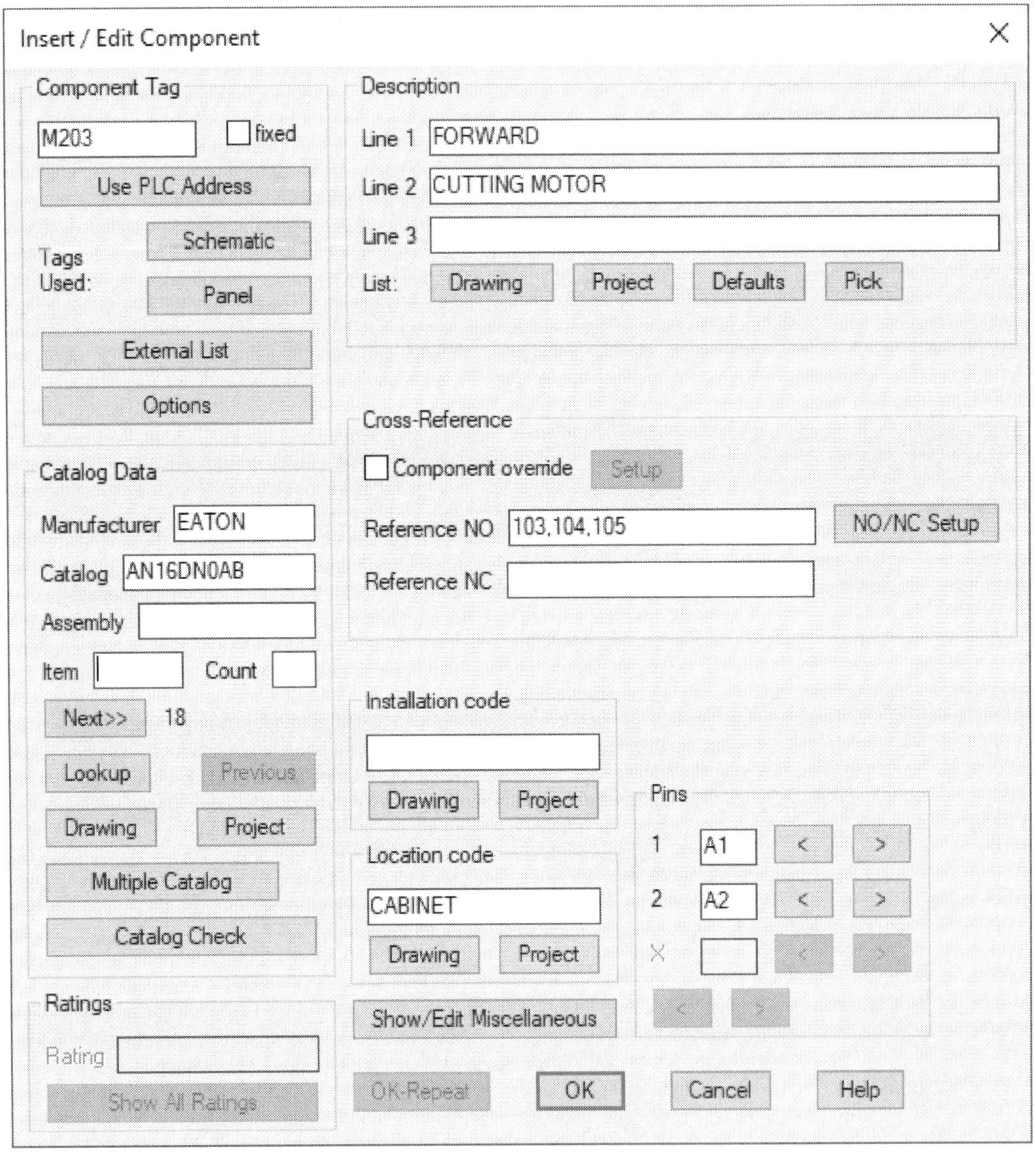

Figure 6–24

6. Click  (Next Drawing) to open **Cabinet.dwg**.
7. Zoom to the circuit breakers at the top of the cabinet.

8. In the *Panel* tab>*Insert Component Footprints* panel, click (Schematic List). The *Schematic Component List --> Panel Layout Insert* dialog box opens.

   - After clicking (Schematic List), if the *Schematic Components (active drawing)* dialog box opens, select the **Reload** option to open the *Schematic Components List -- > Panel Layout Insert* dialog box.

9. In the *Location Codes to extract* area, select **Named Location**. Click **Project**.
10. The *All Locations – Project* dialog box opens. Select **CABINET** and click **OK**.
11. In the *Schematic Component List --> Panel Layout Insert* dialog box, *Location* updates to display **CABINET**, as shown in Figure 6–25. Click **OK**. The *Select Drawings to Process* dialog box opens.

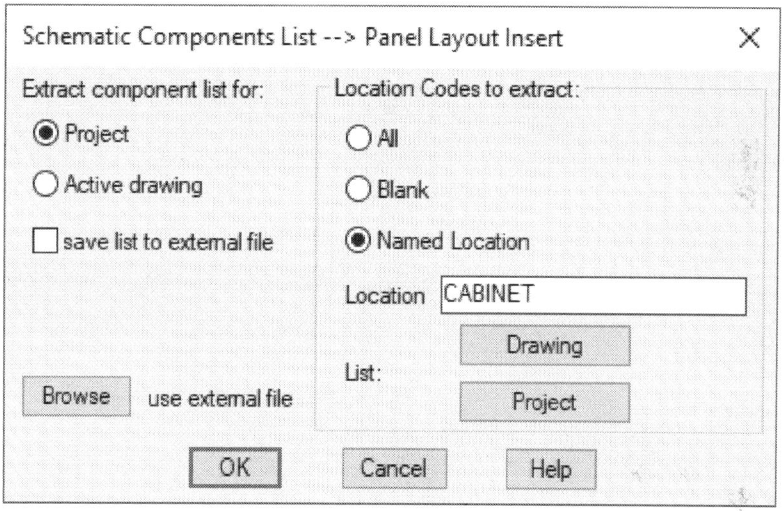

Figure 6–25

12. All of the drawings in the project are listed in the upper area of the dialog box. Click **Do All** and note that all of the drawings are moved to the lower section (as shown in Figure 6–26) so that all of the drawings in the project are processed. Click **OK**. The *Schematic Components (active project)* dialog box opens.

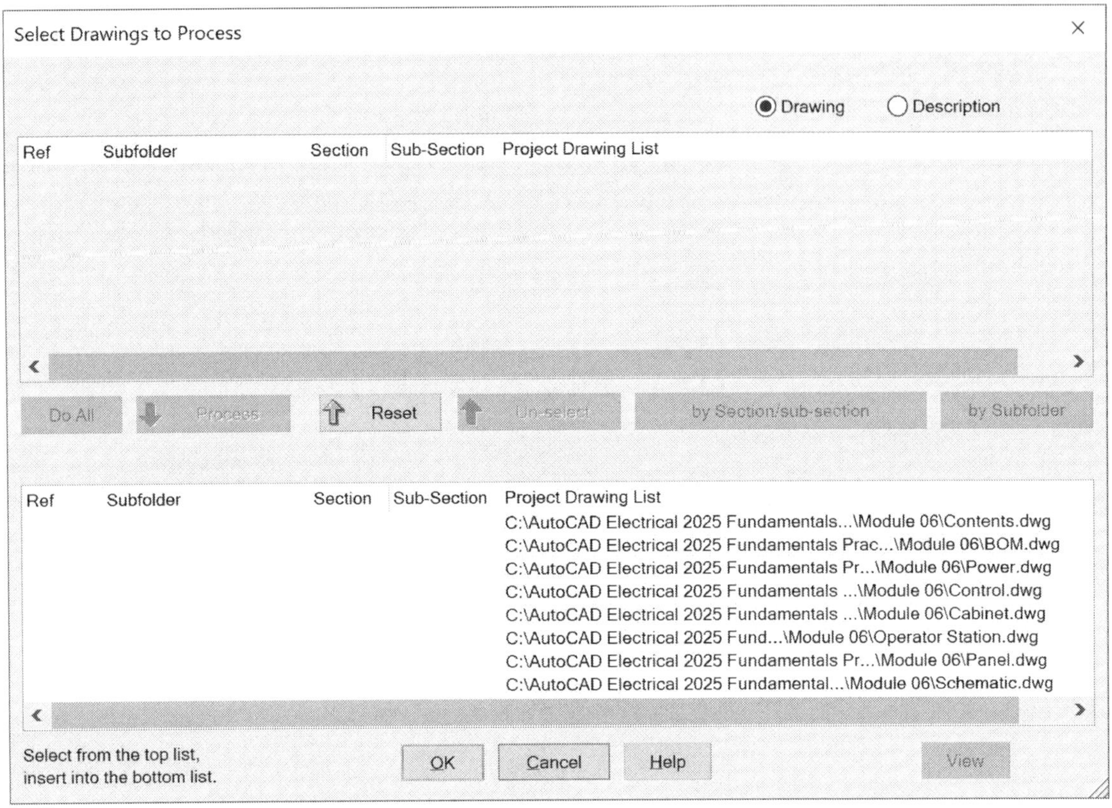

Figure 6–26

13. Click **Sort List**. In the *Sort* dialog box, in the *Primary sort* field, select **TAGNAME** from the drop-down list. Click **OK**.

14. In the *Schematic Components* dialog box, click **Mark Existing**. An **X** is placed next to each component that has already been inserted into a panel drawing as shown in Figure 6–27.

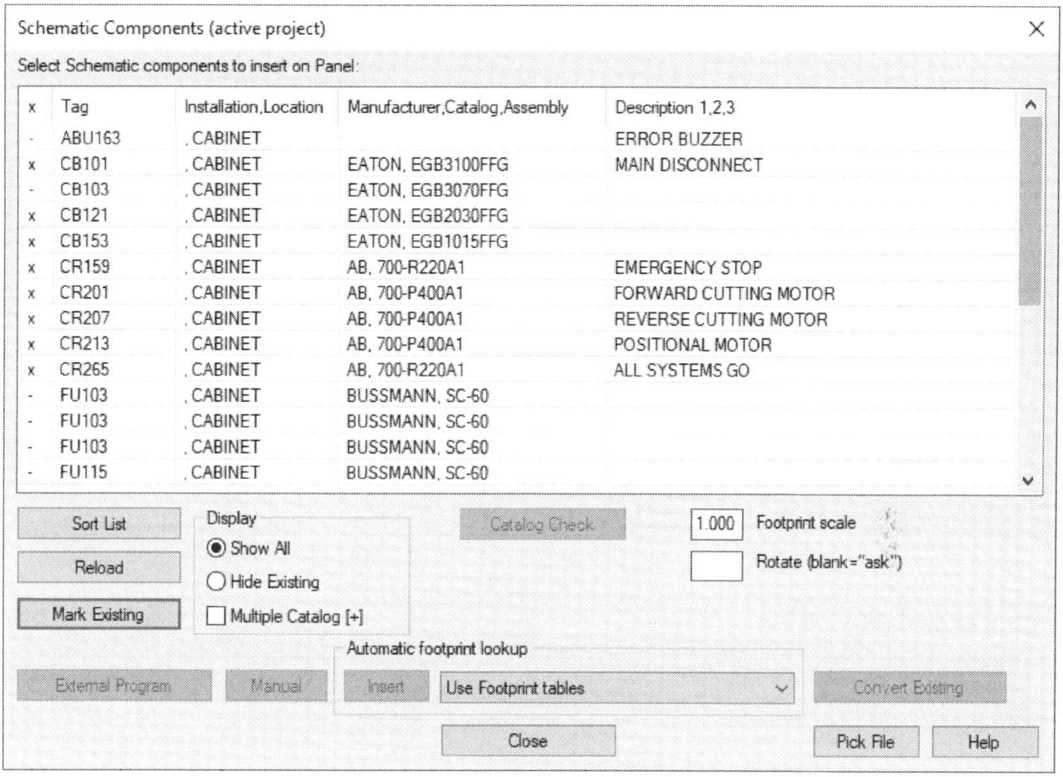

Figure 6–27

15. In the *Display* area, select **Hide Existing**. All components that were marked with an **X** in the previous step are hidden. This option eliminates the possibility of inserting multiple footprints for the same component.

16. In the list, select **CB103** and click **Insert**.

17. Pick a point between CB101 and CB115 as the insertion point, as shown in Figure 6–28. Press <Enter> to accept the rotation. The *Panel Layout – Component Insert/Edit* dialog box opens and the information is the same as in the schematic drawing. Click **OK**.

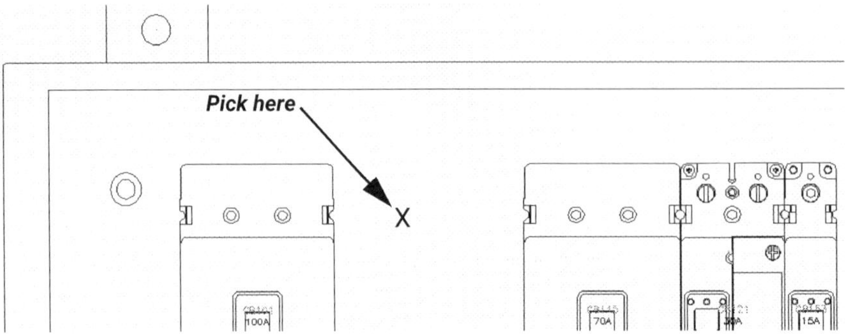

Figure 6–28

- The *Schematic Components (active project)* dialog box opens. Note that CB103 no longer displays in the list (as shown in Figure 6–29) because it is now marked as existing and currently hidden.

18. In the list, select **M203** (as shown in Figure 6–29) and click **Insert**.

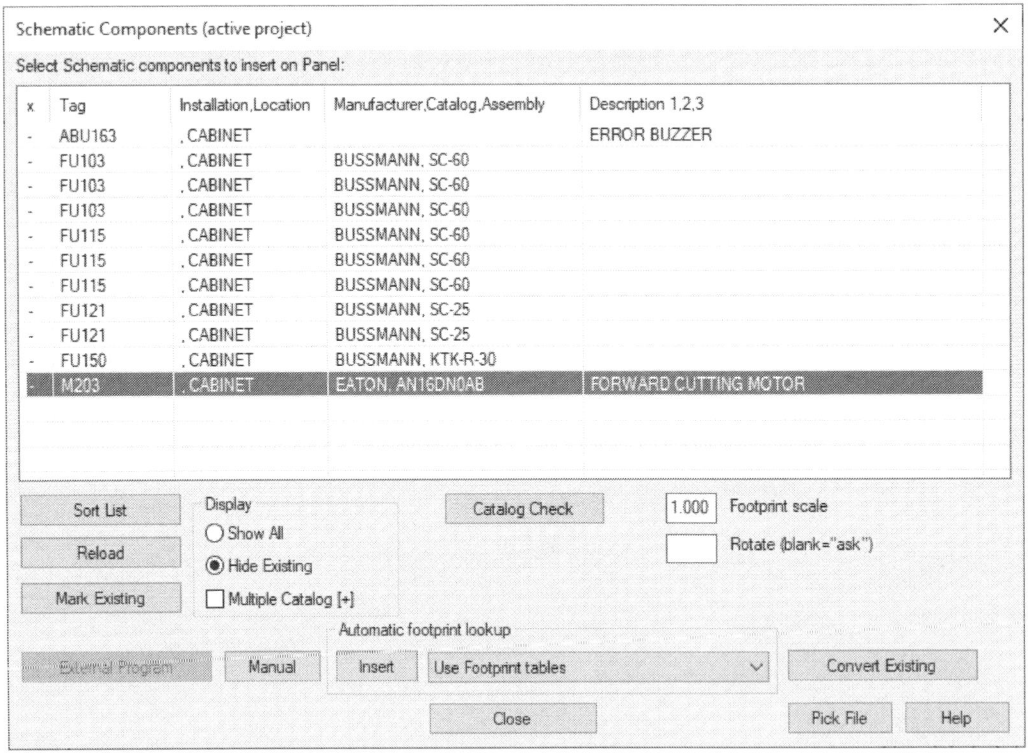

Figure 6–29

19. Zoom out and pan to the bottom of the drawing. Pick a point to the left side of M209 as the insertion point as shown in Figure 6–30. Press <Enter> to accept the rotation. The *Panel Layout – Component Insert/Edit* dialog box opens. The information is the same as in the schematic drawing. Click **OK**. The *Schematic Components (active project)* dialog box opens and M203 is no longer visible in the list.

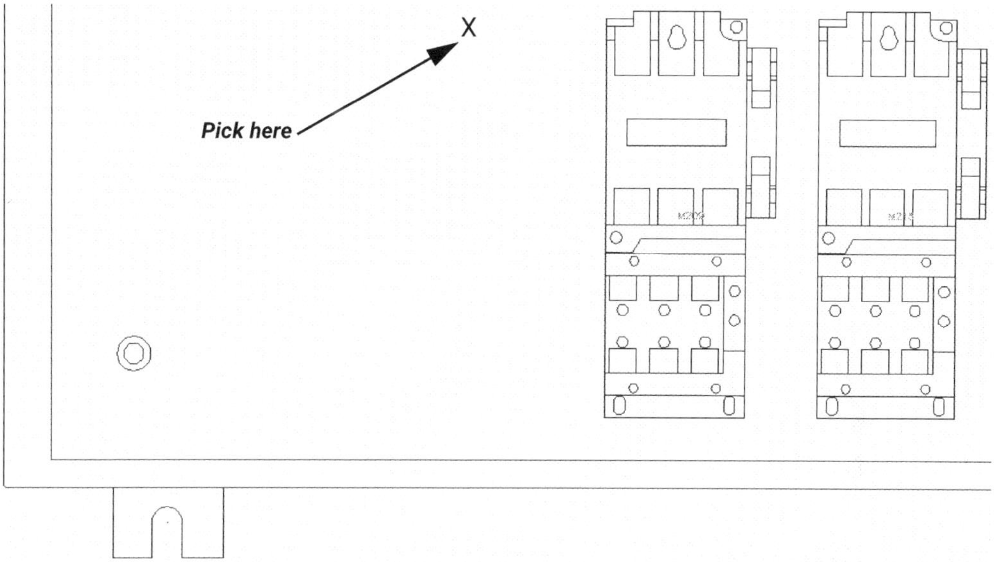

Figure 6–30

20. In the *Schematic Components (active project)*, click **Close**.

21. Click **OK** to update and save the related drawings.

22. Close **Cabinet.dwg**. Save and close the other open drawings.

End of practice

Practice 6c
Insert Component (Panel List)

Practice Objective

- Insert schematic component symbols.

In this practice, you will insert symbols into a schematic drawing from a list of panel footprints. The final circuit displays as shown in Figure 6–31.

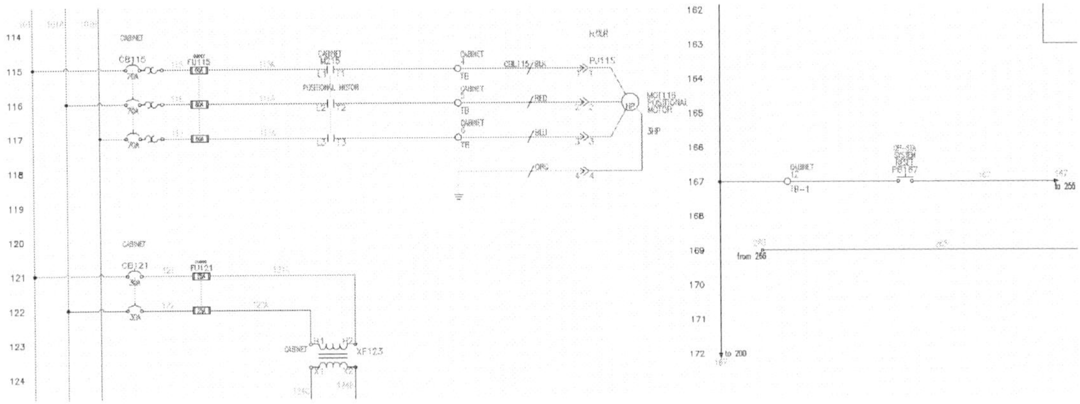

Figure 6–31

1. If the **Module 06** project is not active, open and activate it now.
2. In the **Module 06** project, open **Cabinet.dwg**.
3. Zoom to CB115 near the top of the cabinet.

4. In the *Panel* tab>*Edit Footprints* panel, click  (Edit). Select **CB115** and note the information in the *Panel Layout – Component Insert/Edit* dialog box as shown in Figure 6–32. Click **Cancel** to close the dialog box.

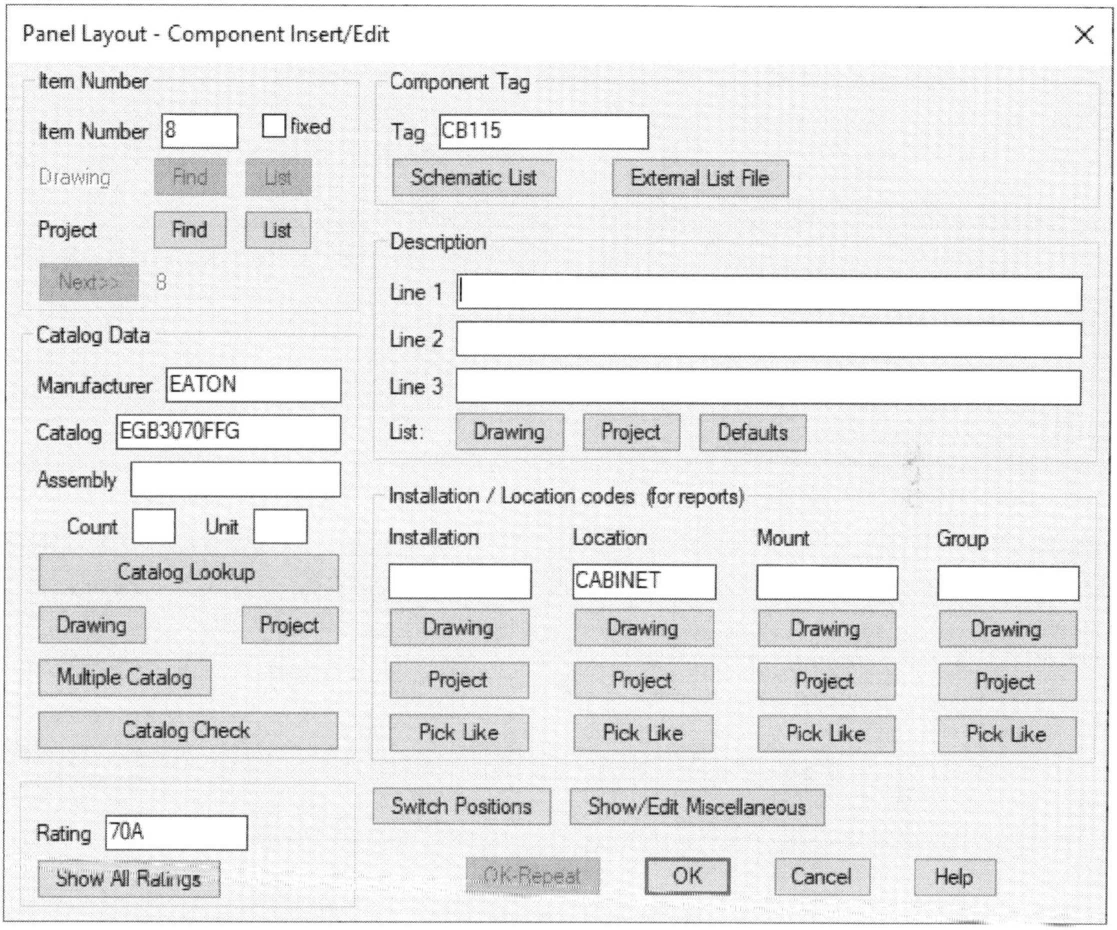

Figure 6–32

5. In the **Module 06** project, open **Power.dwg**.

6. Zoom to lines 113 to 118.

7. In the *Schematic* tab>*Insert Components* panel, click  (Insert Component [Panel List]). The *Panel Layout List --> Schematic Components Insert* dialog box opens as shown in Figure 6–33.

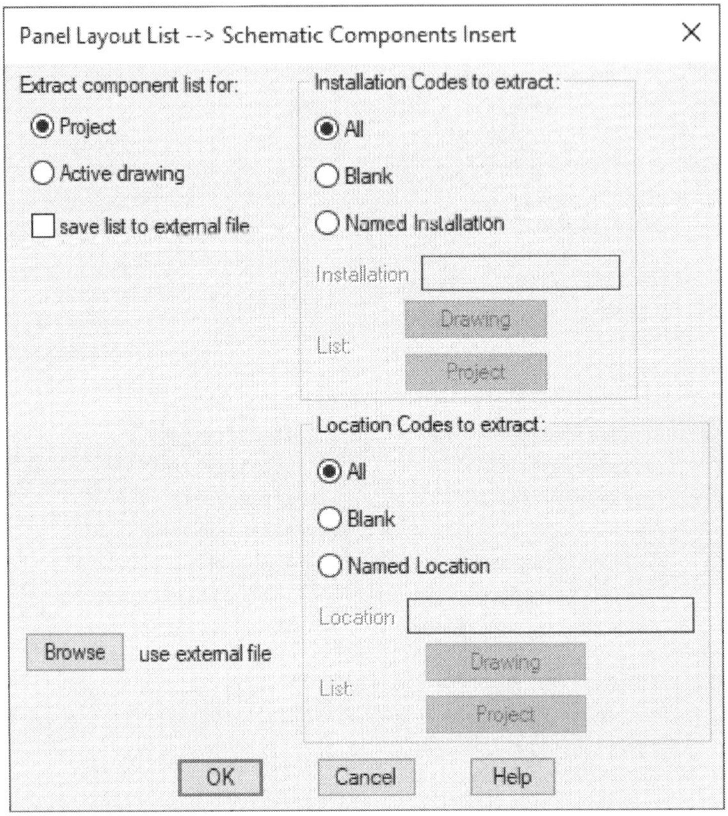

Figure 6–33

8. Leave the default settings and click **OK**. The *Select Drawings to Process* dialog box opens.
9. Click **Do All** and then click **OK**. The *Panel Components (Project – for all installations, for all locations)* dialog box opens.
10. Click **Sort List**. The *Sort* dialog box opens. In the *Primary sort* area, select **TAGNAME**. Click **OK**.
11. Click **Mark Existing**. All components that have already been inserted into a schematic drawing are marked with an **X**.
12. In the *Display* area, select **Hide Existing**. All components marked with an **X** are hidden from the list.
13. Select **CB115** and click **Insert**. The *Insert CB115 EATON, EGB3070FFG* dialog box opens, as shown in Figure 6–34. Note that **none found** displays in the *Block Name* area, indicating that no blocks are currently assigned.

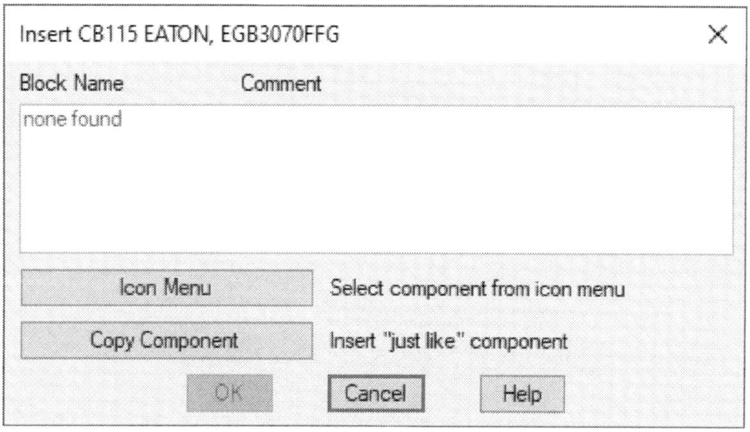

Figure 6–34

14. In the dialog box, click **Icon Menu**. The *Insert Component* dialog box opens. Click (Motor Control), click . (Breakers/Disconnects), and then click (3 Pole Thermal Circuit Breaker) to insert a 3 Pole Thermal Circuit Breaker.
15. Pick a point on line 115 next to FU115 (before it) as the insertion point, as shown in Figure 6–35.

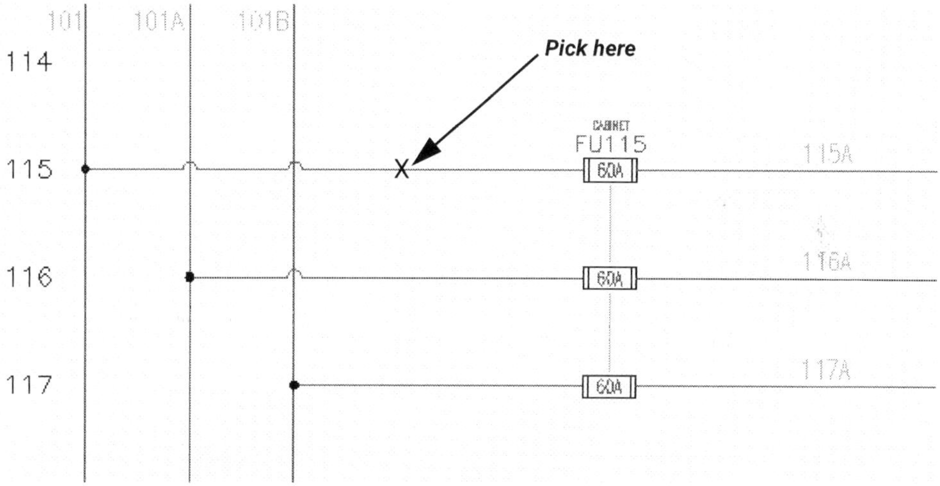

Figure 6–35

16. In the *Build Up or Down?* dialog box, click **Down**.
17. In the *Insert / Edit Component* dialog box, the information is the same as that in the panel drawing. Click **OK**.
    - You might have to map the symbol to the catalog number.
18. Zoom into lines 165 to 170.

19. In the *Schematic* tab>*Insert Components* panel, click 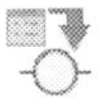 (Insert Component [Panel List]). The *Panel Components (Project–for all installations, for all locations)* dialog box opens.
20. Click **Sort List**. The *Sort* dialog box opens. In the *Primary sort* area, select **TAGNAME**. Click **OK**.
21. In the *Panel Components (Project–for all installations, for all locations)* dialog box, click **Mark Existing** and then click **Hide Existing**. Note that CB115 no longer displays in the list.
22. Select **PB167** and click **Insert**. The *Insert PB167 AB, 800H-BR6D1* dialog box opens. Select **HPB11 Push Button - N.O. contact** and click **OK**.
23. Pick a point near the middle of wire 167, as shown in Figure 6–36.

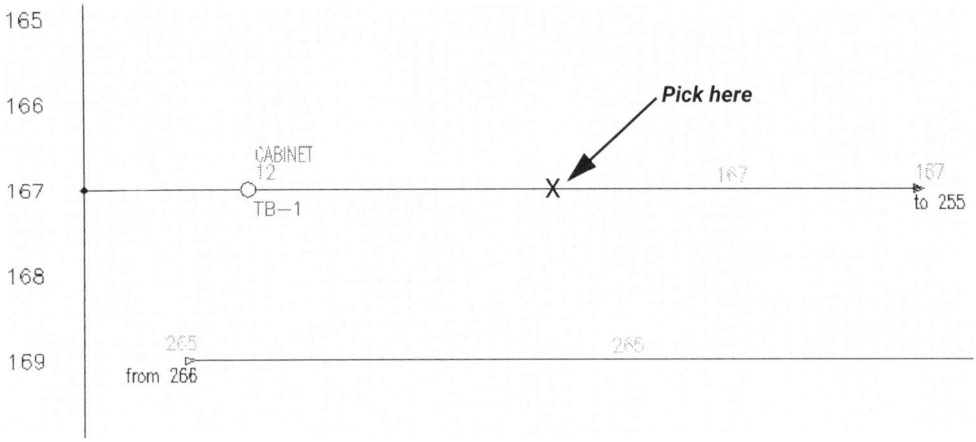

Figure 6–36

24. In the *Insert / Edit Component* dialog box that opens, click **OK**. The *Panel Components (Project–for all installations, for all locations)* dialog box opens and PB167 is no longer visible.
25. Click **Close**.
26. Click **OK** to update and save the drawing.
27. Save and close all the open drawings.

End of practice

6.5 Assign Item Numbers

Item Numbers are used in various AutoCAD Electrical reports and in balloons. You can assign Item Numbers in the *Item Number* area in the *Panel Layout – Component Insert/Edit* dialog box (as shown in Figure 6–37) when components are inserted or edited. The Item Numbers are tied to catalog data so that any components with the same catalog data have the same Item Number.

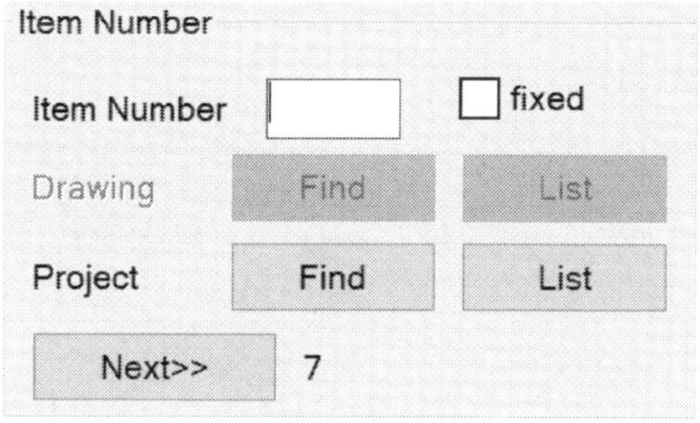

Figure 6–37

- Item Numbers are kept synced between panel and schematic symbols of the same Catalog Number.

How To: Assign Item Numbers to Footprints

1. Start the **Edit Footprint** command.
2. Pick the footprint to edit. The *Panel Layout – Component Insert/Edit* dialog box opens.
3. Assign the Item Number.
4. Click **OK**.

The *Item Number* area contains various options for selecting the footprints Item Number, as follows:

Find	Searches the drawing or project for a matching Catalog Number and uses the Item Number from that component.
List	Displays a list of Item Numbers and Catalog Numbers for footprints in the drawing or project.
Next>>	Uses the next available Item Number. The number used displays next to the button.
fixed	Locks the Item Number. The Item Number is not automatically updated when the **Re-Sequence Item Numbers** command is implemented.

If you click **Find** and no matching catalog data is found, the *No Item Number Match for this Catalog Part Number* dialog box opens with options for assigning an Item Number, as shown in Figure 6–38.

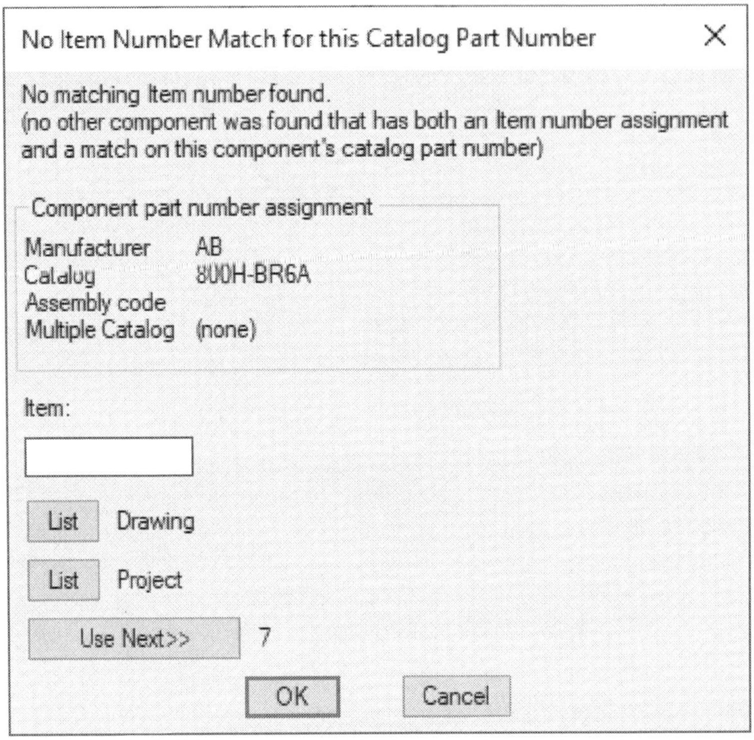
No Item Number Match for this Catalog Part Number
No matching Item number found.
(no other component was found that has both an Item number assignment and a match on this component's catalog part number)
Component part number assignment
Manufacturer AB
Catalog 800H-BR6A
Assembly code
Multiple Catalog (none)
Item:
List Drawing
List Project
Use Next>> 7
OK
Cancel

Figure 6–38

Item	Enter the Item Number to assign.
List	List of Item Numbers assigned in active drawing or entire project, depending on selection.
Use Next>>	Uses next available Item Number. The number used displays next to the button.

- For a schematic symbol, in the *Catalog Data* area in the *Insert / Edit Component* dialog box, if you assign a Catalog Number to that schematic symbol and then click the Item Number's **Next>>**, an appropriate Item Number is inserted. If the specific Catalog Number already has an Item Number assigned elsewhere in the project, the same Item Number is assigned or the next available number is assigned.
- If you assign an Item Number that is already assigned to a different Catalog Number, the *Duplicate Item Number* dialog box opens, as shown in Figure 6–39. It displays the Catalog Number assigned to that Item Number and the one you are attempting to reassign it to. You can overwrite it, or cancel and select a different Item Number.

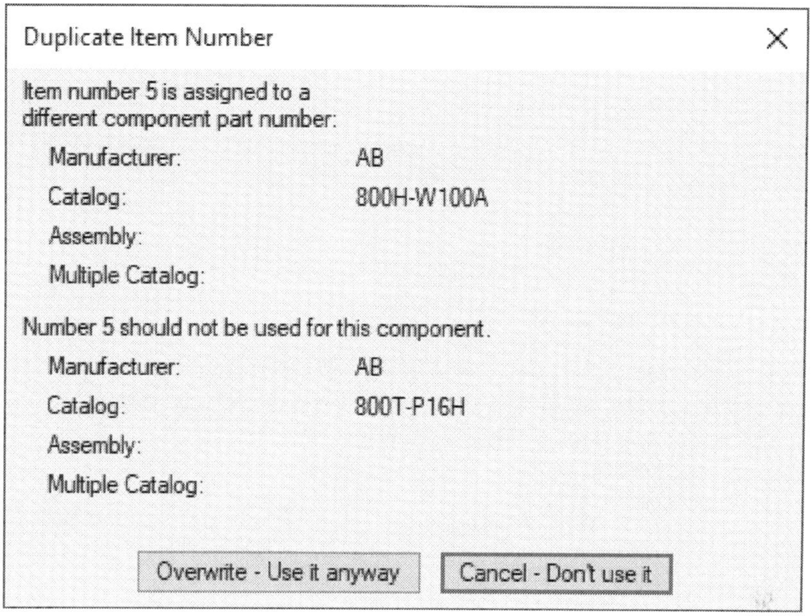

Figure 6–39

- If you assign an Item Number to a Catalog Number to which an Item Number has already been assigned, the *Mismatch Item Number Found* dialog box opens, indicating that a possible Item Number mismatch has been found. It prompts you to run the **Resequence Item Numbers** command to correct any possible mismatches.

Resequence Item Numbers

The **Resequence Item Numbers** command assigns or resequences Item Numbers starting with a value that you provide.

Resequence Item Numbers

Ribbon: *Panel* tab>*Edit Footprints* panel

Command Prompt: aeresequence

The Resequence Item Numbers command opens the *Resequence Item Numbers* dialog box, as shown in Figure 6–40.

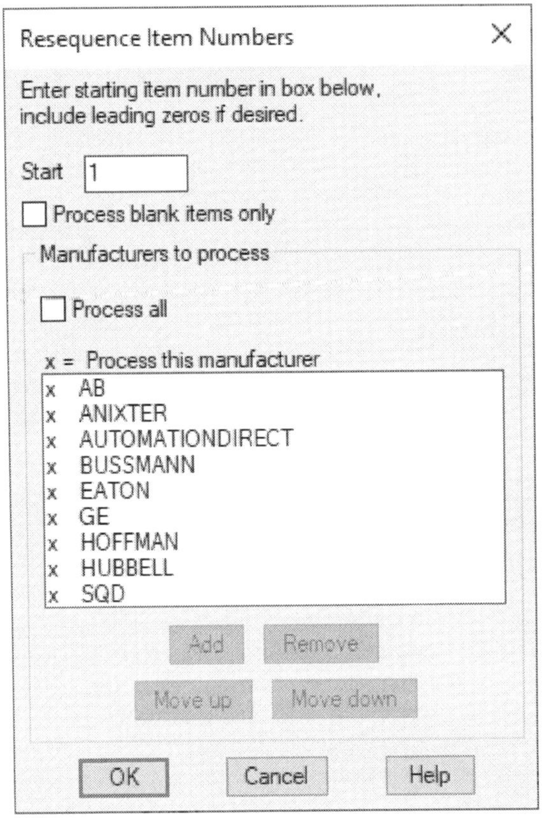

Figure 6–40

- In the *Resequence Item Numbers* dialog box, you can:
  - Set a starting value
  - Select the manufacturers to be processed
  - Select the order in which the manufacturers are going to be processed
- The entire project is processed, keeping the item numbers in sync for components that have the same catalog.
- Components are updated in a specific order as follows:
  - Panel footprint components.
  - Schematic symbol components that have an associated panel footprint (therefore, they have the same Item Number).
  - Schematic symbol components that do not have an associated panel footprint.

6.6 Add Balloons

Balloons are used to tie the footprints in the drawing to the Bill of Materials report. Balloons typically consist of a number and a leader (as shown in Figure 6–41), although the AutoCAD Electrical software does not require a leader for balloons.

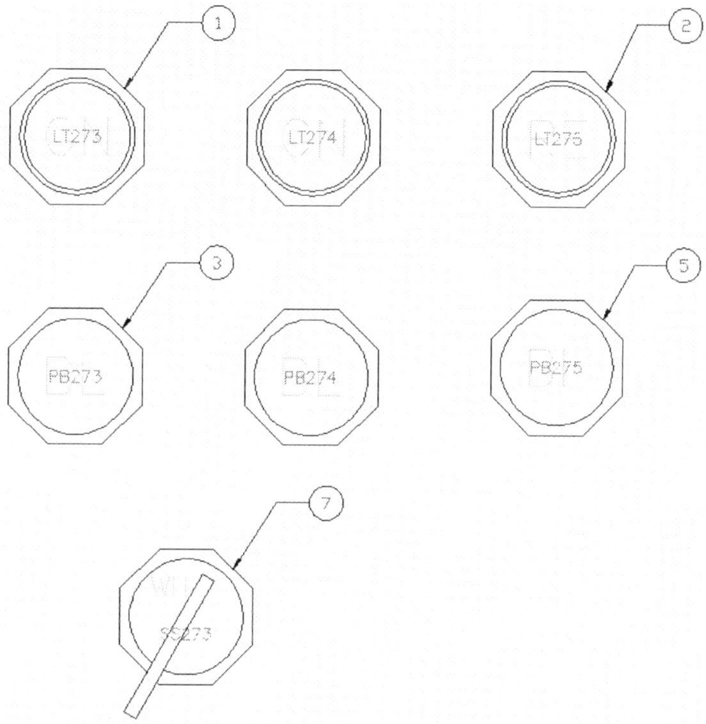

Figure 6–41

The **Balloon** command inserts balloons into a panel drawing.

Balloon

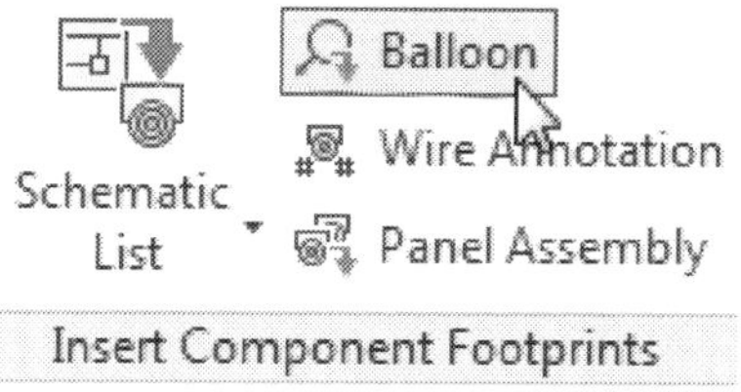

Ribbon: *Panel/WD* tab>Insert Component *Footprints* panel

Command Prompt: aeballoon

How To: Add a Balloon to a Footprint

1. Start the **Balloon** command.
2. Pick the footprint to balloon.
3. Pick the start point of the leader.
4. Pick any additional points for the leader. The last point is where the Item Number is placed.
5. Item number is required before adding a balloon to a footprint. Right-click or press <Enter> to place the balloon.
    - If an Item Number has not been assigned to the footprint, assign one in the *No Item Number Match for this Catalog Part Number* dialog box.
6. Select another footprint to balloon, right-click, or press <Enter> to end the command.

Practice 6d
Item Numbers and Balloons

Practice Objective

- Assign an Item Number to a panel footprint and attach a balloon.

In this practice, you will open an existing panel drawing, assign Item Numbers, and then add balloons to the drawing. The final panel drawing displays as shown in Figure 6–42.

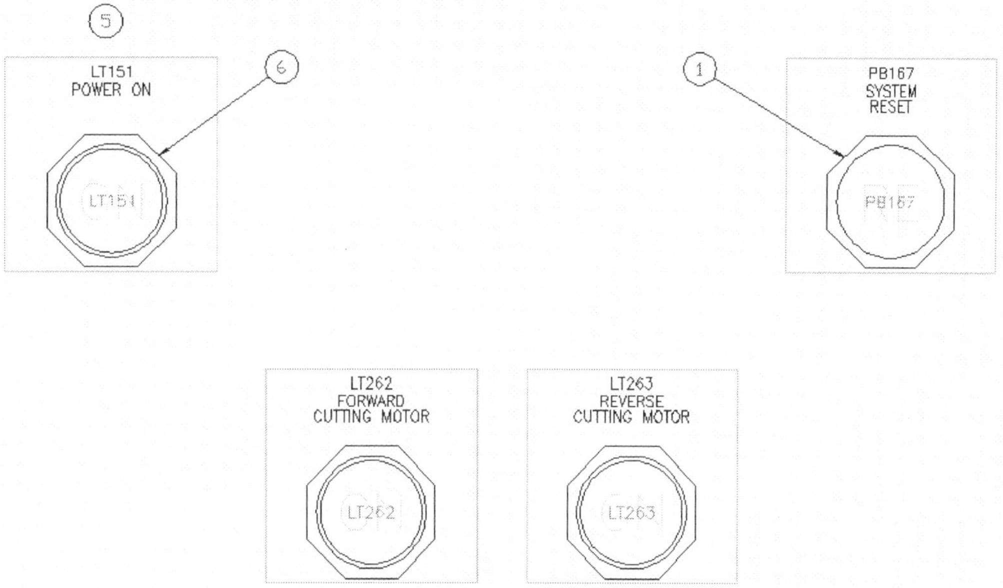

Figure 6–42

1. If the **Module 06** project is not active, open and activate it now.
2. In the **Module 06** project, open **Operator Station.dwg**.
3. Zoom to the top row of footprints in the panel.
4. In the *Panel* tab>*Edit Footprints* panel, click  (Edit).
5. Select the **LT151** geometry. (Make sure to click somewhere on the geometry and not the nameplate [outer square and text].) The *Panel Layout – Component Insert/Edit* dialog box opens.
6. Note that the *Item Number* field is blank. However, the next number to use is listed as **6**.
7. For the *Item Number*, type **5**. Click **OK**.
8. The *Duplicate Item Number* dialog box opens indicating that 5 is currently assigned to a different component part number. Click **Cancel - Don't use it**.

9. In the *Item Number* area, click **Next>>** and note that **6** is displayed in the *Item Number*. Click **OK**.
10. The *Update Related Components?* dialog box opens. Click **Yes-Update**.
11. Update and save the related drawings.
12. In the *Panel* tab>*Insert Component Footprints* panel, click  (Balloon).
13. Select **LT151** as the component. (Select the component and not the outer green square.) Note that it highlights in blue. You are now required to select two points for the start and end of the leader. Select a point on the edge of LT151 and select the second point away from the footprint, as shown in Figure 6–43. Press <Enter> to place the balloon.

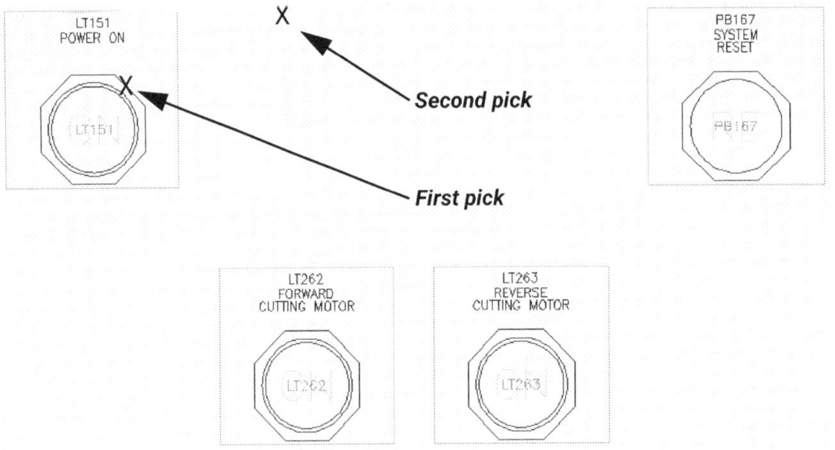

Figure 6–43

14. Select **PB167** as the component. For the starting point, select a point on the edge of PB167. For the second point, select a point away from the footprint, as shown in Figure 6–44. Press <Enter> to place the balloon.

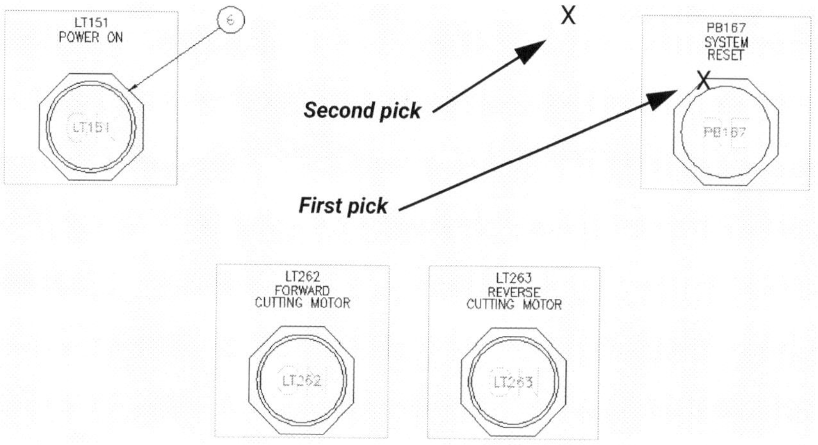

Figure 6–44

15. Select the text **LT151 POWER ON** to select the nameplate component. Note that the text and green outer square is highlighted in blue. Select a point above the nameplate as shown in Figure 6–45. Press <Enter> to place the balloon without a leader and press <Enter> again to end the command.

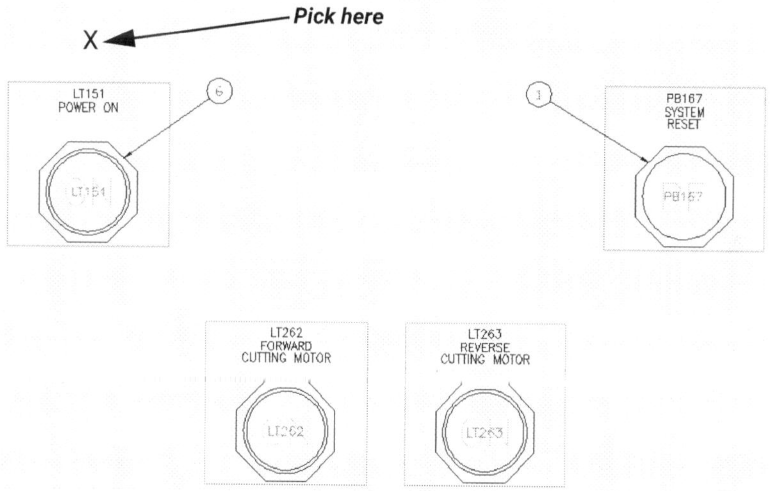

Figure 6–45

16. Save and close **Operator Station.dwg** and all other open drawings, if required.

End of practice

Chapter Review Questions

1. How does the AutoCAD Electrical software determine which block to use for a footprint?
   a. It searches **footprint_lookup.mdb** for a matching manufacturer and catalog number and links it to a block name.
   b. It searches **footprint_lookup.mdb** for a matching description and links it to a block name.
   c. It uses the previously used block.
   d. It navigates to the default directory and prompts you to select the required one.

2. What is the advantage of **Insert Footprint (Schematic List)** over **Insert Footprint (Icon Menu)**?
   a. Insert Footprint (Schematic List) enables the immediate insertion of multiple footprints at once.
   b. Insert Footprint (Schematic List) reuses the data from schematic drawings in the project to eliminate errors.
   c. Insert Footprint (Schematic List) is only a different workflow and has no advantage.
   d. Insert Footprint (Schematic List) automatically populates all attributes based on nearby schematic components.

3. Which attribute links the schematic symbol to a panel footprint?
   a. Catalog Number
   b. Item Number
   c. Component Tag
   d. Description

4. In the *Schematic Components* dialog box, for the **Insert Footprint (Schematic List)** command, how do you hide items that have already been inserted into a panel drawing?
   a. Items that have already been inserted into a panel drawing cannot be hidden.
   b. Select all items that have already been inserted, right-click, and select **Hide from all layers**.
   c. Click **Mark Existing**, then select **Show Existing** in the *Display* area.
   d. Click **Mark Existing**, then select **Hide Existing** in the *Display* area.

5. To insert schematic symbols into a drawing from a list of footprints that have already been inserted into the panel drawing of the active project, which command would you use?
    a. Insert Component (Icon Menu)
    b. Insert Component (Catalog List)
    c. Insert Component (Panel List)
    d. Insert Component (Equipment List)

6. Where are Item Numbers used in the AutoCAD Electrical software?
    a. Project files
    b. Reports only
    c. Balloons and reports
    d. Titleblocks

7. How do you search all panel drawings in a project for matching catalog data to which to assign an Item Number?
    a. In the *Panel Layout-Component Insert/Edit* dialog box, next to Project, click **Find**.
    b. In the *Panel Layout-Component Insert/Edit* dialog box, next to Project, click **Search**.
    c. In the *Panel Layout-Component Insert/Edit* dialog box, next to Item Number, click **Go To**.
    d. You cannot search all panel drawings in a project for matching data to which to assign an Item Number.

8. Which attribute must be populated before you can add a balloon to a footprint?
    a. Component Tag
    b. Item Number
    c. Catalog Number
    d. Description

Command Summary

Button	Command	Location
	Balloon	• **Ribbon**: *Panel* tab>*Insert Component Footprints* panel
	Edit Footprint	• **Ribbon:** *Panel* tab>*Edit Footprints* panel
	Insert Component (Panel List)	• **Ribbon:** *Schematic* tab>*Insert Components* panel
	Insert Footprint (Icon Menu)	• **Ribbon:** *Panel* tab>*Insert Component Footprints* panel
	Insert Footprint (Schematic List)	• **Ribbon:** *Panel* tab>*Insert Component Footprints* panel
	Resequence Item Numbers	• **Ribbon:** *Panel* tab>*Edit Footprints* panel

Chapter 7

Terminals

Terminal symbols are fundamental parts of an electrical drawing. Learning to insert terminal symbols and link them to form a single terminal strip is important in creating electrical drawings. Additionally, learning to use the Terminal Strip Editor enables you to manage terminal symbols and place terminals on panel drawings in either a graphical or tabular style.

Learning Objectives

- Insert and link terminal symbols to convert them into multiple level (or stacked) terminals.
- Insert multiple instances of the same component on multiple wires.
- Add jumpers to terminals and manage their relationship.
- Recognize the jumper column symbolism in a terminal table.
- Modify terminals inserted into schematic drawings.
- Insert a graphical or tabular representation of entire terminal strips into a panel drawing.
- Insert DIN rail symbols with catalog data.

7.1 Insert Terminal Symbols

Terminal symbols function similar to source and destination arrows: they are schematic symbols that are linked together by user-defined codes. In the case of terminals, the **Tag Strip**, **Installation**, and **Location** codes are used to link individual terminal symbols into a single terminal strip. To insert terminals, use the **Icon Menu (Insert Component)** command in the *Schematic* tab>Insert Components panel.

How To: Insert a Terminal

1. Start the **Icon Menu (Insert Component)** command.
2. Click 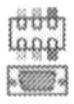 (Terminals/Connectors). The *Terminals and Connectors* submenu opens.
3. Select a terminal symbol to insert.
4. Pick the insertion point for the symbol. The *Insert / Edit Terminal Symbol* dialog box opens, as shown in Figure 7–1.
   - *The Insert / Edit Terminal Symbol* dialog box contains the same information as the *Insert / Edit Component* dialog box, with a few exceptions for handling information specific to terminals.

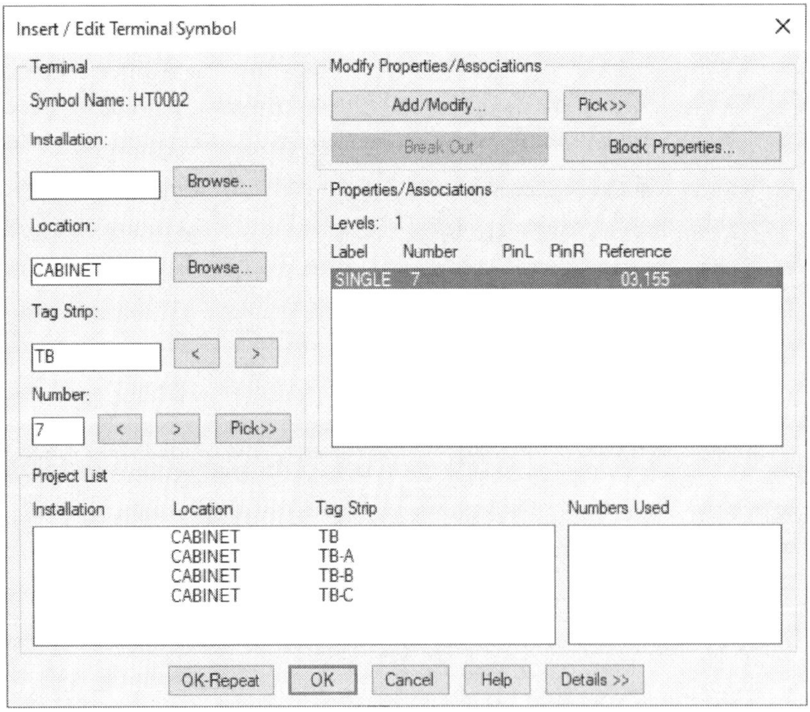

Figure 7–1

5. In the *Insert / Edit Terminal Symbol* dialog box, enter the **Tag Strip** and other information.
6. Click **OK**.

The options available in the *Insert / Edit Terminal Symbol* dialog box are described as follows:

Terminal	Enter the **Installation** code, **Location** code, **Tag Strip**, and **Number** for the terminal block.
Modify Properties/ Associations	Use these commands to modify the properties and associations of the terminal symbol. Terminal symbols can be associated to other terminal symbols to form multiple level terminals or to panel footprints.
Properties/Associations	List the associations for the terminal being inserted/edited.
Project List	List the **Tag Strip**, **Installation**, and **Location** codes used in the active project.
Details	Expands or collapses the dialog box. When expanded, you can enter catalog data, and descriptions for the terminal, as shown in Figure 7–2.

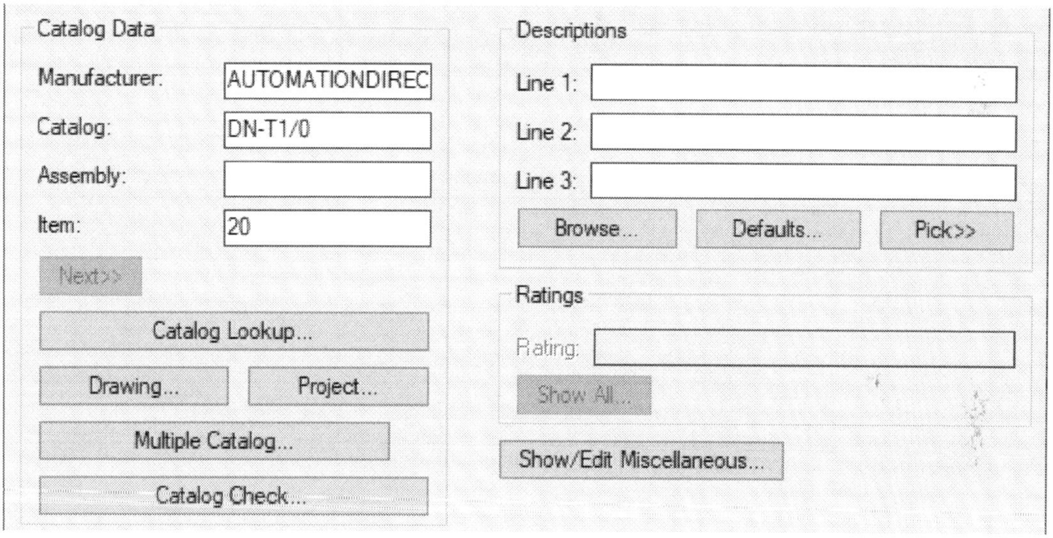

Figure 7–2

The AutoCAD® Electrical software has different shapes available for terminal symbols containing different information and functions. Some terminal symbols cause the wire numbers to change across the symbol, where as some terminal symbols do not permit this change. The information and function of a symbol can be determined from its description in the text list in the Terminals/Connectors submenu, as shown in Figure 7–3.

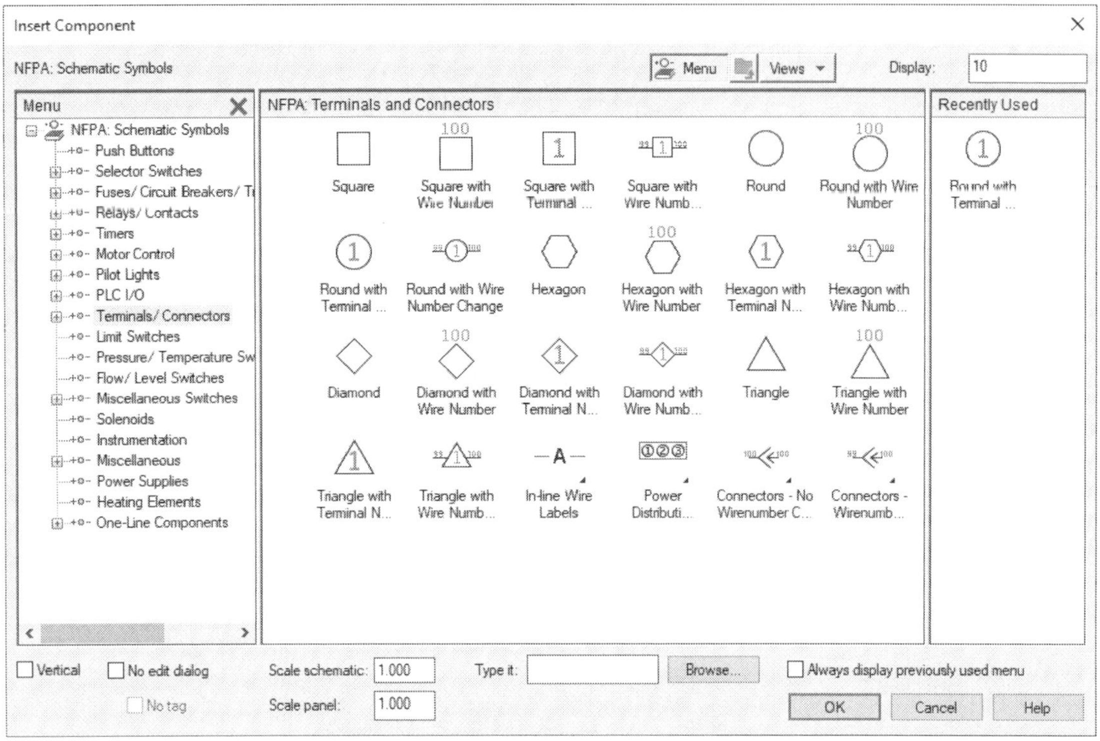

Figure 7–3

When inserting terminal symbols, the values in the *Insert / Edit Terminal Symbol* dialog box default to the values used for the previously inserted terminal symbol.

7.2 Multiple Level Terminals

The AutoCAD Electrical software supports the documentation of multiple level or stacked terminals. The information regarding the associations is stored in attributes if they are present in the terminal block symbol, however, if they are not present, the information is stores in xdata. Use the *Modify Properties/Associations* area in the *Insert / Edit Terminal Symbol* dialog box to manage the linked terminals.

How To: Associate a Terminal Using Add/Modify

1. Edit the terminal symbol you want to associate.
2. In the *Insert / Edit Terminal Symbol* dialog box, click **Add/Modify...**. The *Add / Modify Association* dialog box opens.
3. In the *Select Association* area, for *Terminal Strips*, expand the terminal strip that contains the terminal to which you want to associate.
4. Select the terminal.
5. In the *Select Association* area, in the table on the right, select the level of the terminal to which you want to associate.
6. Click **Associate**. If the button is not available, the selected level is already associated with a terminal symbol.
7. Click **OK** to close the *Add / Modify Association* dialog box.
8. Click **OK** to close the *Insert / Edit Terminal Symbol* dialog box.

How To: Associate a Terminal Using Pick

1. Edit the terminal symbol you want to associate.
2. In the *Insert / Edit Terminal* Symbol dialog box, click **Pick>>**.
3. In the drawing window, select the terminal to which you want to associate.
4. Click **OK** to close the *Insert / Edit Terminal Symbol* dialog box.

In the *Insert / Edit Terminal Symbol* dialog box, the *Modify Properties/Associations* area (shown in Figure 7–4) contains various options for associating to other terminals in the project.

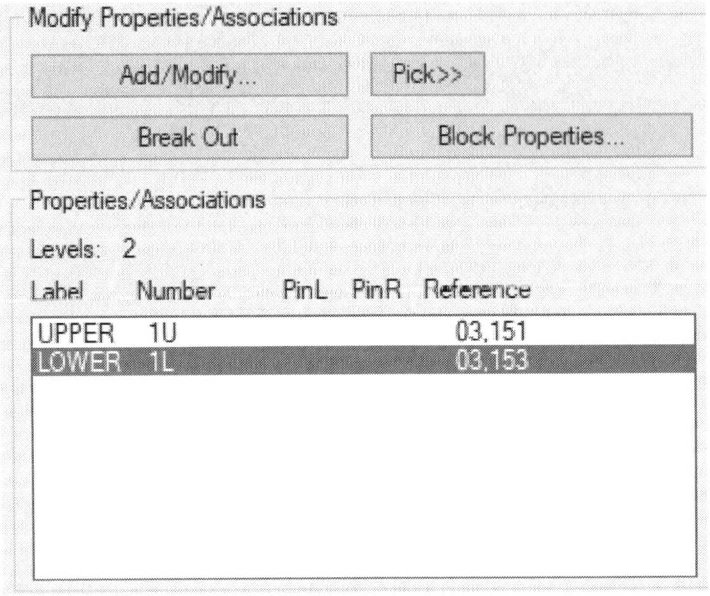

Figure 7–4

Add/Modify...	Opens the *Add / Modify Association* dialog box to associate the edited terminal block to another terminal.
Break Out	Removes the edited terminal block from the associations. All properties of the terminal are maintained.
Pick>>	In the drawing window, this option enables the selection of a terminal block to which to associate.
Block Properties...	Opens the *Terminal Block Properties* dialog box, which displays the number of levels and properties for each level. Edit the properties in this dialog box.

The *Add / Modify Association* dialog box (shown in Figure 7–5) is used to link the edited terminal to another terminal symbol to create a multiple level terminal.

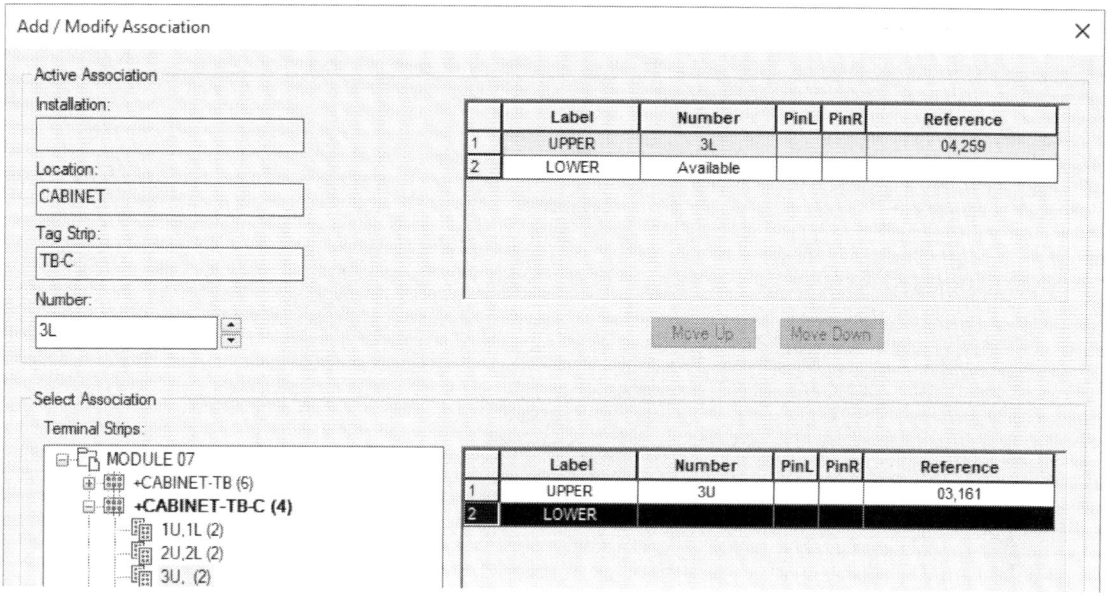

Figure 7–5

Active Association	Lists the information pertaining to the current association for the edited terminal. You can edit the terminal number here and change the order of the terminals in the table.
Active Association Table	Lists the information for the terminals that are associated to the edited terminal. If the schematic terminal symbol is associated to a panel footprint, the table has a Panel row.
Move Up/Move Down	Moves the terminal up/down one row in the table.
Select Association	The Terminal Strips tree view lists all terminal strips in the active project. Expand the terminal strip node to see a list of terminals linked to the strip. The terminal strip nodes display the **Installation**, **Location**, and **Tag Strip** values. The terminal nodes display the terminal numbers and number of levels defined for the terminal. Select a terminal to which to associate from this list.
Select Association Table	When a terminal is selected in the Terminal Strips tree, the information for that terminal is listed here. Select a row in this table to associate the edited terminal to the selected terminal.
Associate	Associates the active terminal to the selected terminal. Available only if the selected row does not have a terminal assigned to it.

The *Terminal Block Properties* dialog box (shown in Figure 7–6) is used to manage the number of levels for the terminal being edited. The default number of levels is controlled by the catalog number assigned to the terminal if there is a matching entry in the Terminal Properties database. The *Manufacturer*, *Catalog Number*, and *Assembly Code* display at the top of the dialog box.

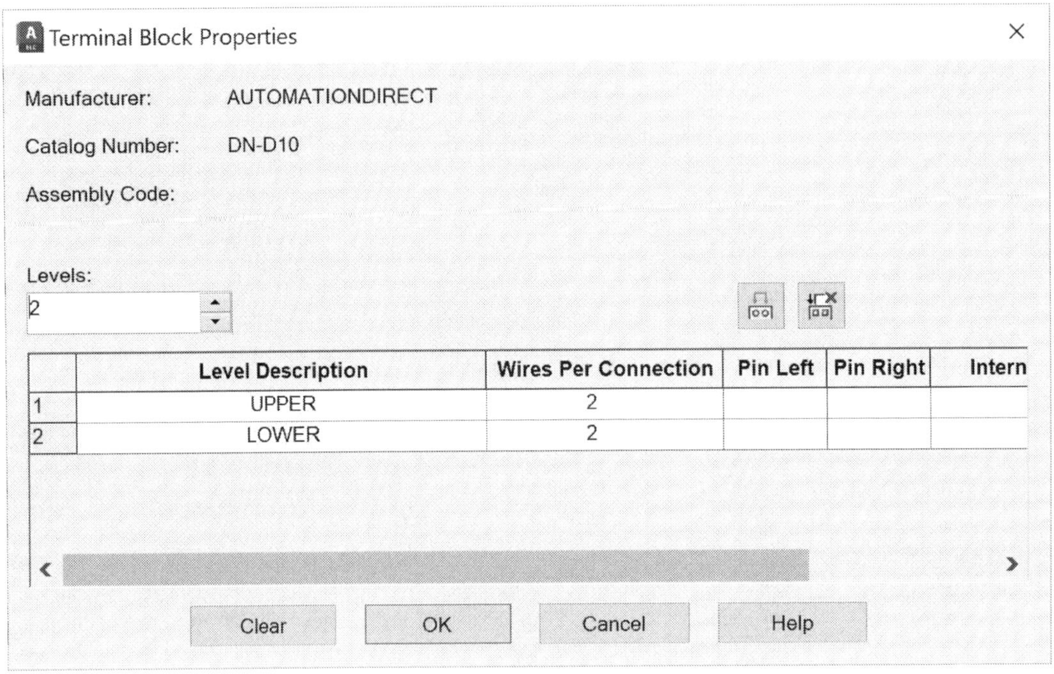

Figure 7–6

Levels	Modifies the number of levels. Type a value in the field or use the arrows to increment the value.
Table	Enter the information for each level in the table. Values include *Level Description*, *Wires Per Connection*, and numbers for *Pin Left* and *Pin Right*.
	**Assign Jumper:** Assigns a jumper to the highlighted levels (rows in the table).
	**Delete Jumper:** Deletes the jumper to the highlighted level (row in the table).

7.3 Multiple Insert Component Command

The **Multiple Insert Component** command inserts multiple instances of the same component on selected rungs. You can insert multiple terminals or add multiple components to schematic or PLC drawings.

Multiple Insert Component

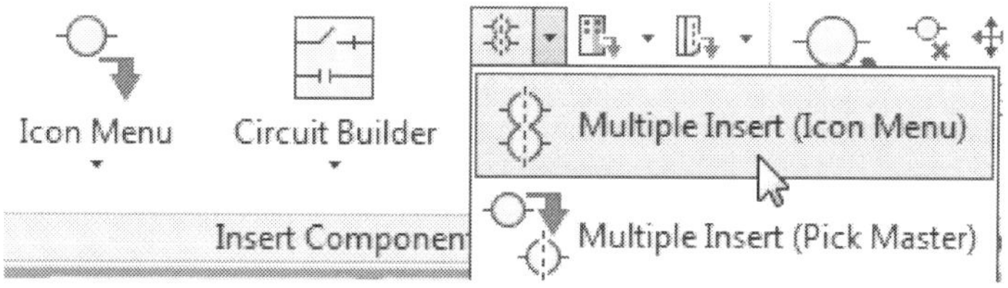

Ribbon: *Schematic* tab>*Insert Components* panel

Command Prompt: aemulti

How To: Insert Multiple Components

1. Start the **Multiple Insert Component** command. The *Icon Menu (Insert Component)* dialog box) opens.
   - The **Multiple Insert Component** command has similar functionality to the **Insert Component (Icon Menu)** command, with the difference that instead of selecting a single rung, you draw a fence or line to select multiple rungs and wires.
2. Select the type of component to insert. The submenu for that category opens.
3. In the submenu, select the symbol to insert.
4. Select multiple rungs or wires by drawing a fence or a line.
5. Right-click or press <Enter> to finish selection.
6. Use the options in the *Keep?* dialog box to insert symbols and click **OK**. The *Insert / Edit* dialog box for the symbol opens.
7. Fill in the information in the *Insert / Edit* dialog box and click **OK**.
8. Repeat Steps 6 and 7 for each wire intersection.

For each wire that the fence intersects, the *Keep?* dialog box opens. When first prompted, the *Keep?* dialog box (as shown in Figure 7–7) gives you the options to either keep the terminal or skip to the next one. For the subsequent terminals, the *Keep?* dialog box (as shown in Figure 7–8) provides you with the additional options listed below.

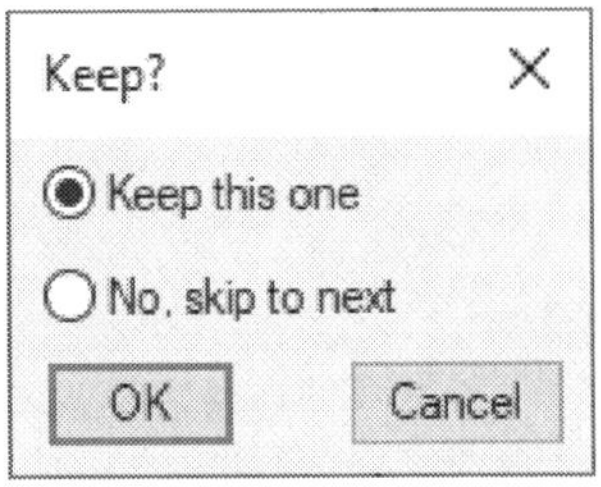

Figure 7–7

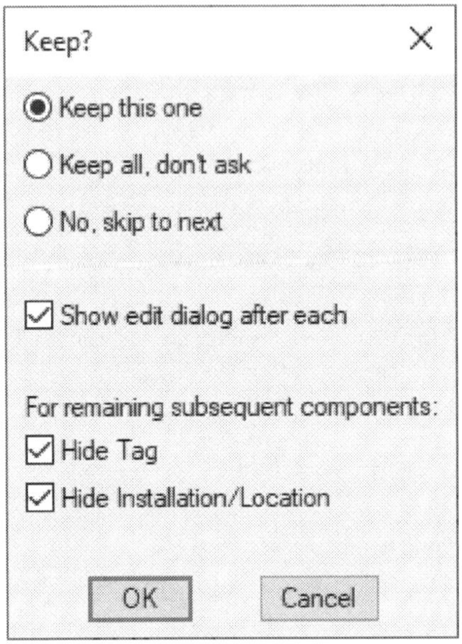

Figure 7–8

Keep this one	Inserts the symbol on this wire.
Keep all, don't ask	Inserts a symbol on each and every wire that intersects the fence.
No, skip to next	Skips the current wire and moves to the next wire that intersects the fence.
Show edit dialog after each	If selected, the appropriate *Insert / Edit* dialog box opens for each symbol that is inserted.
Hide Tag	Hides or displays the Tag Strip along with the terminal in the drawing.
Hide Installation/Location	Hides or displays the **Installation** and **Location** attributes along with the terminal in the drawing.

- The information entered in the *Insert / Edit* dialog box is maintained for each subsequent symbol inserted with the **Multiple Insert Component** command. This automation makes it easy to assign the same Tag-ID or catalog information to all of the inserted symbols.

7.4 Insert Jumpers

In the software, you can jumper two or more terminals together. Use the **Edit Jumper** command to jumper terminals and manage the relationship. The terminals can be in the same drawing or multiple drawings in the active project.

Edit Jumper

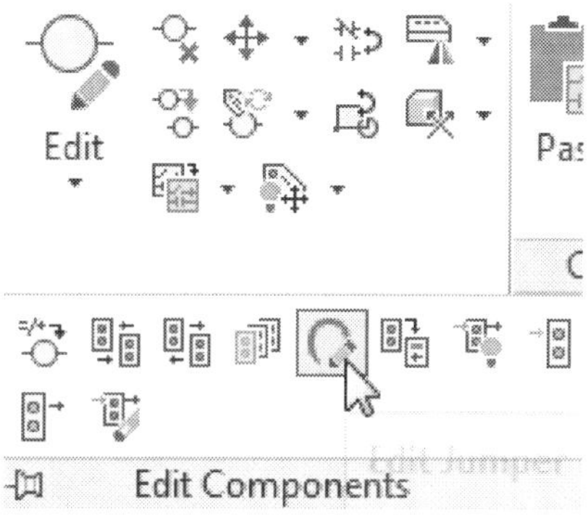

Ribbon: *Schematic* tab>expanded *Edit Components* panel

Command Prompt: aejumper

Shortcut menu: *(on a component)* **Terminals>Edit Jumper**

How To: Jumper Terminals

1. Start the **Edit Jumper** command.
2. In the graphics window, select the first terminal to jumper.
3. In the graphics window, select subsequent terminals. Alternatively, in the *Select Terminals To Jumper* dialog box, you can select using the **Browse** option.
4. Press <Enter> or right-click and select **Enter**. The *Edit Terminal Jumpers* dialog box opens.
5. Assign catalog data to the jumper.
6. Click **OK** to create the jumper.

When you start the **Edit Jumper** command, there are four options:

a. Select terminals to jumper in the graphics window.

b. Select **Browse** to open a Selection dialog box in which to select terminals in the active project.

c. Select **Edit** to edit the existing jumpers on the selected terminal.

d. Select **Show** to display a temporary line representing the current jumpers on the selected terminal.

- The options can be invoked from the Command prompt or the shortcut menu. You must first select a terminal to use the **Show**, **Edit**, and **Browse** options.

The *Edit Terminal Jumpers* dialog box (shown in Figure 7–9) opens after all terminals are selected or when the **Edit** option is selected. Use the dialog box to associate catalog information to the jumper or to delete terminals from the jumper.

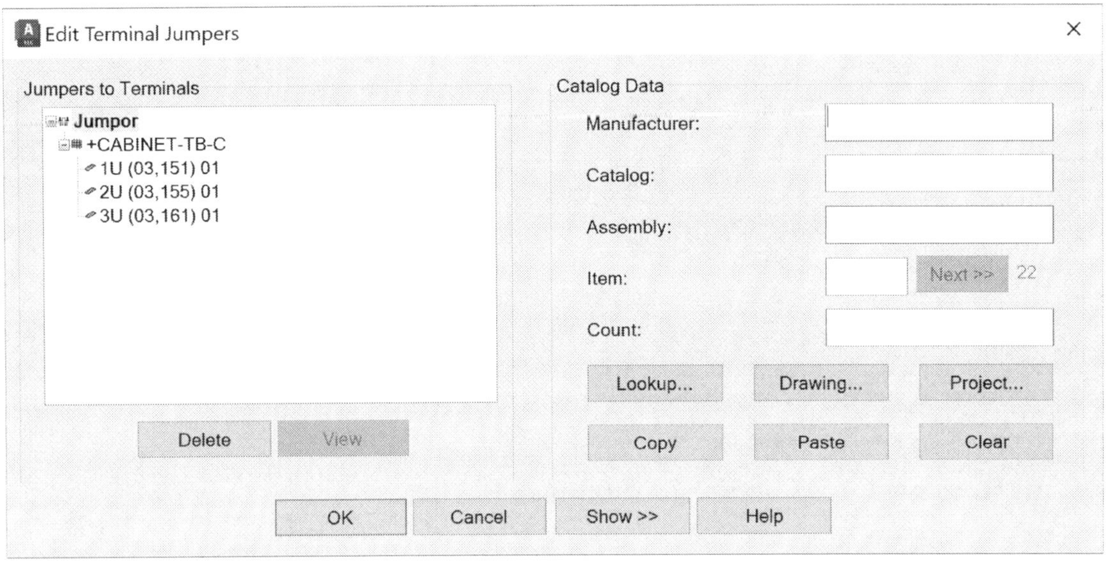

Figure 7–9

Jumpers to Terminals	Displays the jumpers associated to the selected terminal. Select a jumper to which to associate catalog data or select a terminal to view or delete the terminal from the jumper.
Catalog Data	Displays the catalog data for the jumper selected in the Jumpers to Terminals tree. You can associate data using the buttons or by entering information in the fields. Additional buttons enable you to quickly **Copy**, **Paste**, or **Clear** the current *Catalog Data* fields.
Delete	Deletes the selected terminal from the jumper or deletes the jumper depending on what is selected in the Jumpers to Terminals tree.
View	Displays the selected terminal in the lower portion of the dialog box.
Show>>	Expands the dialog box to display the selected terminal. If the dialog box is already expanded, the button changes to **<<Hide**.

The *Select Terminals To Jumper* dialog box (shown in Figure 7–10) opens when you select the **Browse** option. All terminal strips in the active project are listed in the Schematic Terminals tree.

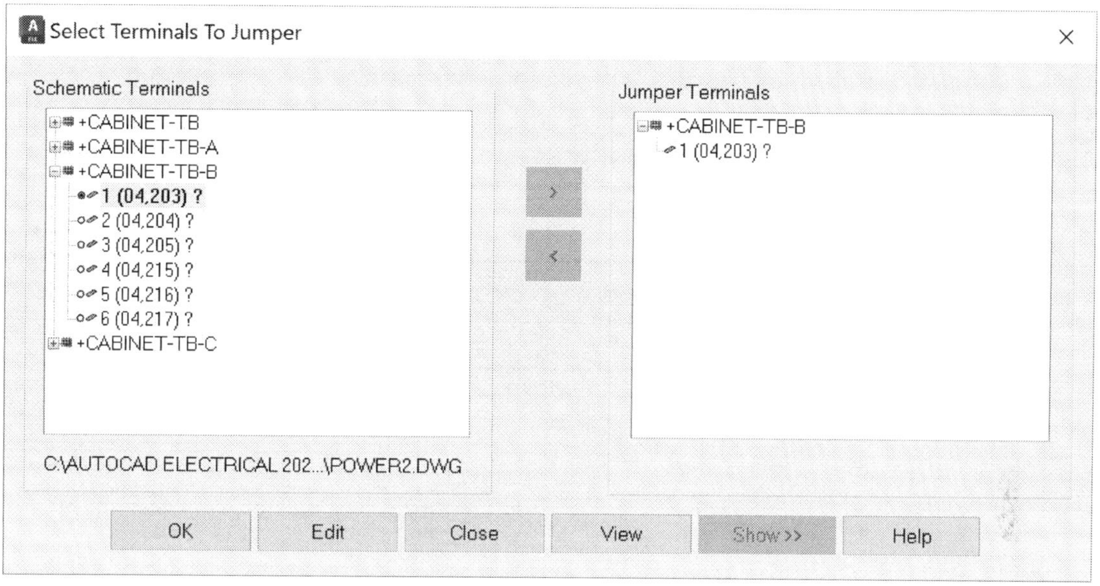

Figure 7–10

Schematic Terminals	Displays the terminal strips and terminals in the active project. Select a terminal here to add it to the jumper.
Jumper Terminals	Displays the jumper and all associated terminals.
	Adds the selected terminal to the jumper.
	Removes the selected terminal from the jumper.
Edit	Displays the *Edit Terminal Jumpers* dialog box.
View	Displays the selected object in the lower part of the dialog box. If a terminal is selected, the terminal symbol displays. If a terminal strip is selected, a table containing the information for the terminals and a jumper column displays.
Show>>	Expands the dialog box to display the selected terminal. If the dialog box is already expanded, the button changes to **<<Hide**.

7.5 Terminal Strip Editor

The Terminal Strip Editor is used in panel drawings to document terminals that are inserted into schematic drawings, as shown in Figure 7–11. The terminal strip editor searches the project file for terminal symbols and groups them by the values for **Tag Strip**, **Installation**, and **Location**. The *Terminal Strip Editor* dialog box enables you to make changes to the terminals before inserting the strip into a drawing.

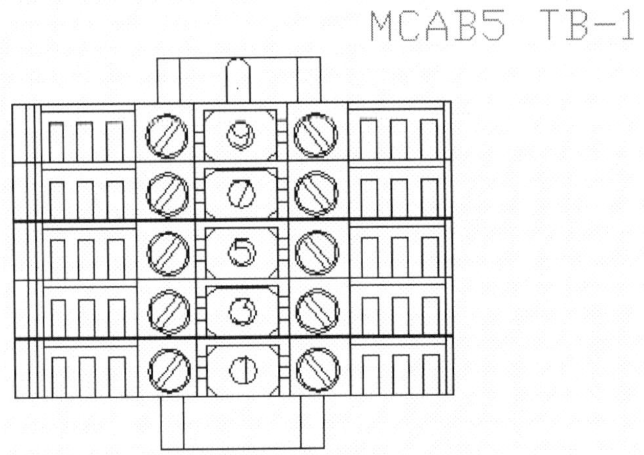

Figure 7–11

Terminal Strip Editor

Ribbon: *Panel* tab>*Terminal Footprints* panel

Command Prompt: aetse

How To: Edit a Terminal Strip

1. Start the **Terminal Strip Editor** command. The *Terminal Strip Selection* dialog box opens.
2. Select the terminal strip that you want to insert and click **Edit**. The *Terminal Strip Editor* dialog box opens.
3. In the *Terminal Strip*, *Catalog Code Assignment*, and *Cable Information* tabs, verify and modify the data.
4. In the *Layout Preview* tab, select the format and layout for the terminal strip. Click **Insert**. The terminal strip is attached to the cursor.
5. Pick the insertion point for the terminal strip.
6. Click **OK**. The *Terminal Strip Editor* opens.
7. Click **OK**. The *Terminal Strip Selection* dialog box opens.
8. Select the next terminal strip that you want to insert/edit and click **Edit** or click **Done** to end the command.

When you start the command, the software gathers all of the **Terminal Strip**, **Installation**, and **Location** values for the project in the *Terminal Strip Selection* dialog box, as shown in Figure 7–12.

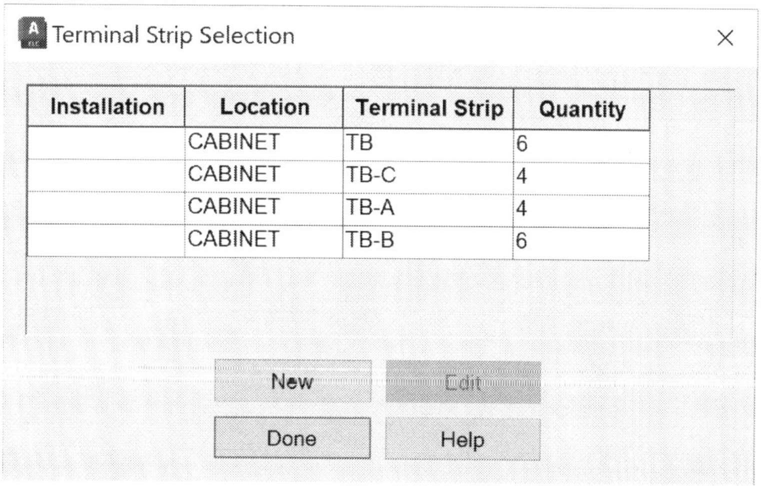

Figure 7–12

- Click **Edit** to open the *Terminal Strip Editor* and modify the selected terminal strip.
- Click **New** to create a new terminal strip to insert into the panel. You can insert the schematic symbols later.

The *Terminal Strip Editor* contains four tabs.

Terminal Strip Tab

Information for each terminal displays in the *Terminal Strip* tab, as shown in Figure 7–13. You can sort the terminals by selecting any of the column headings. The bold lines in the dialog box are used to separate the terminals in the grid. The column on the far-left of the grid indicates the different levels for a multiple level terminal (L1, L2, L3, etc.). You can select multiple terminals by holding <Ctrl> or <Shift>.

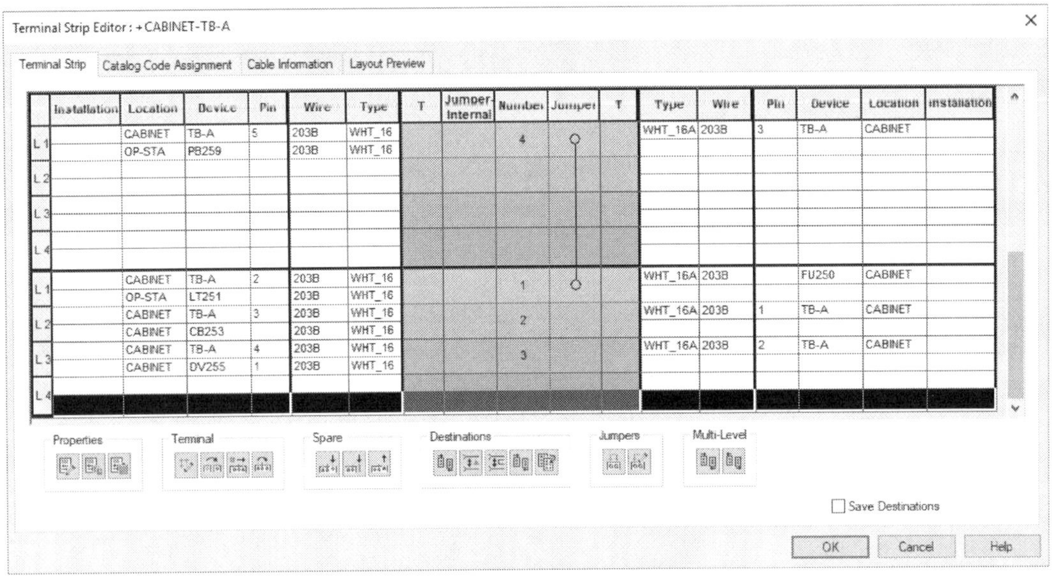

Figure 7–13

The tools (buttons) located at the bottom of the dialog box are described as follows:

Properties	Commands to edit, copy, and paste the Terminal Block properties. Clicking  opens the *Terminal Block Properties* dialog box.
Terminal	Commands to edit the terminal attributes (**Installation**, **Location**, **Tag Strip**, and **Number**), reassign the terminal to another strip, renumber the terminal strip, and move terminals.
Spare	Commands to insert spare terminals, delete terminals, and insert accessories, such as barriers, dividers, and jumper bars.
Destinations	Commands to toggle and modify **Installation** and **Location** values.
Jumpers	Commands to assign and edit jumpers in the terminal strip.
Multi-Level	Commands to associate and break apart multiple-level terminals.

Catalog Code Assignment Tab

You can modify the catalog data assigned to terminals in the *Catalog Code Assignment* tab, as shown in Figure 7–14. All of the areas (tools) are the same as the *Terminal Strip* tab, except for the *Catalog* area.

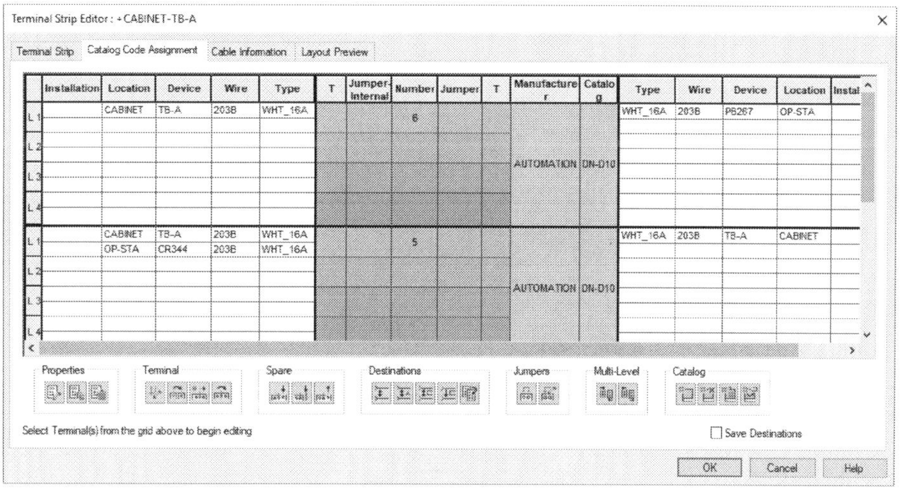

Figure 7–14

- **Catalog:** Assign, copy, paste, and delete catalog information.

Cable Information Tab

The *Cable Information* tab displays cable information that is associated to terminals in the terminal strip, as shown in Figure 7–15.

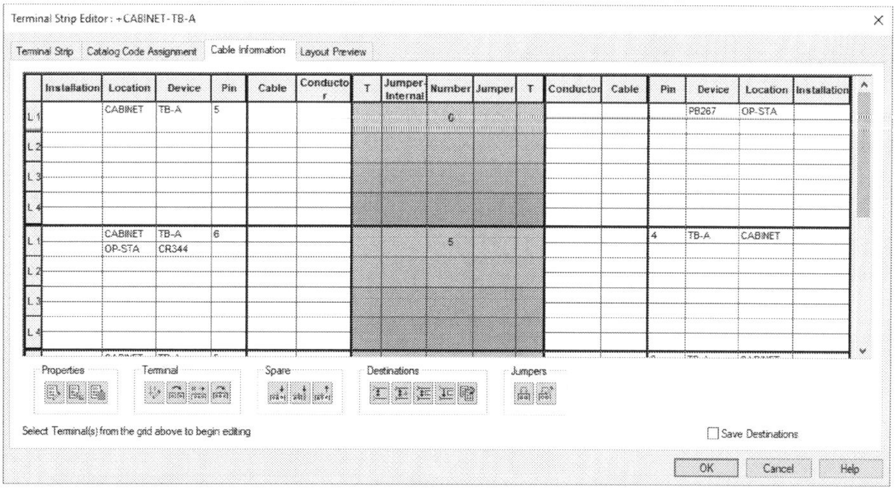

Figure 7–15

Layout Preview Tab

The *Layout Preview* tab displays a preview of the terminal strip, as shown in Figure 7–16.

- **Graphical Terminal Strip** enables you to insert AutoCAD blocks to represent the terminal strip.
- **Tabular Terminal Strip (Table Object)** enables you to insert the data as an AutoCAD table. In the *Graphical Layout* or *Tabular Layout* area, select the attributes to display with the terminal strip, depending on the selected output type. You can also set the scale and angle of the terminal strip.
- **Jumper Chart (Table Object)** enables you to insert a table with the terminal number and jumper information.

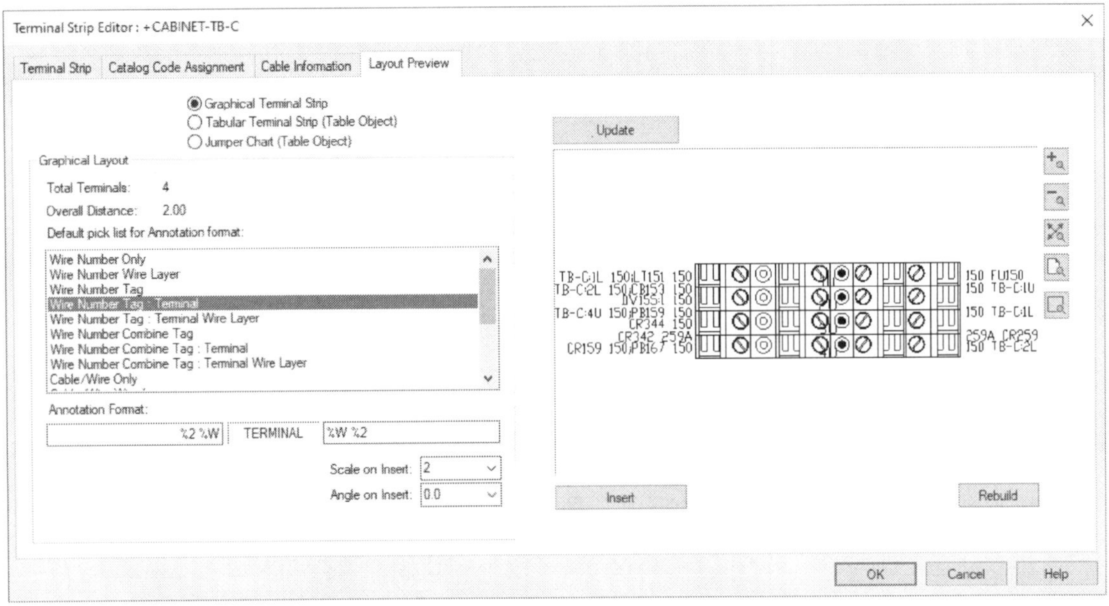

Figure 7–16

Update	Updates the preview window.
Insert	Inserts the terminal into the drawing.
Rebuild	If the terminal strip exists in the project, **Rebuild** deletes the terminal strip and recreates it.
Refresh	Available with the *Tabular Terminal Strip (Table Object)* output type. Updates the data in the table without deleting the table.

Hint: Jumper Column

When a terminal strip is added to a drawing using the **Tabular Terminal Strip (Table Object)** option, a jumper column is added to the table. The jumper column contains a series of circles for each terminal in the terminal strip, as shown in Figure 7–17. A bold line connects the circles to represent the jumper. The circle is filled in if the jumper is connected to that terminal.

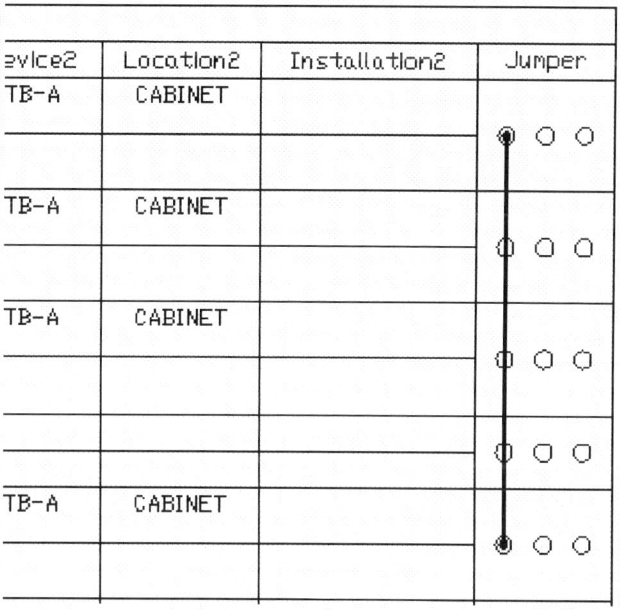

Figure 7–17

7.6 DIN Rail Command

The AutoCAD Electrical software can insert DIN rail symbols with catalog data. Use the **Insert Footprint (Icon Menu)** command to access the DIN Rail symbols.

How To: Insert a DIN Rail

1. Start the **Insert Footprint (Icon Menu)** command.
2. In the *Insert Footprint* dialog box, click  (DIN Rail). The *Din Rail* dialog box opens, as shown in Figure 7–18.
3. Select the DIN Rail that you want to insert. Enter the required information in the *Origin and Length* area and set the other options. Click **OK**. The *Panel Layout – Component Insert/Edit* dialog box opens.
4. Enter the required information in the *Panel Layout – Component Insert/Edit* dialog box.
5. Click **OK**.

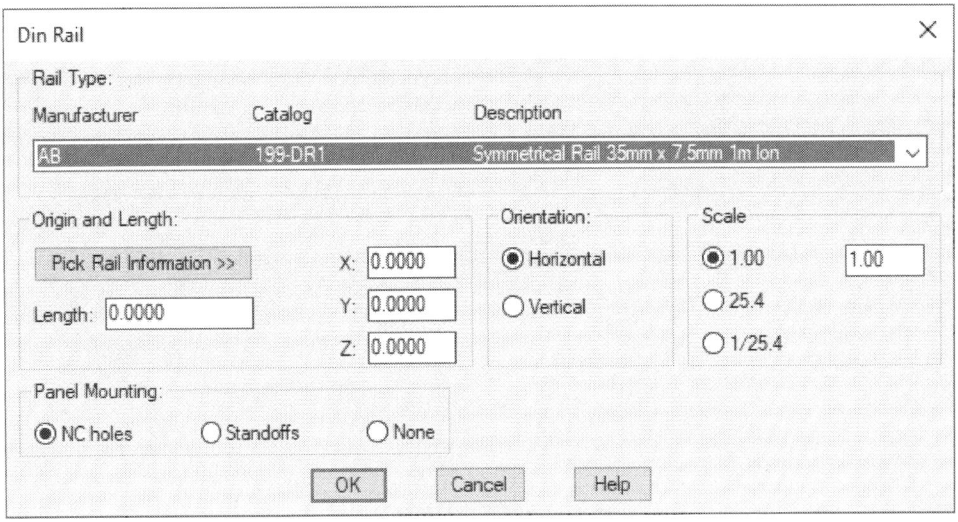

Figure 7–18

Rail Type	Select the DIN Rail type in the drop-down list.
Origin and Length	Specify the coordinates and length for the DIN Rail using the fields or click **Pick Rail Information>>** and select in the drawing.
Orientation	Specify horizontal or vertical rail.
Scale	Select a scale from the default radio buttons or enter a scale in the field.
Panel Mounting	Specify whether to mount the rail at NC holes, standoffs, or none.

- The DIN Rail information is stored in the **Wddinrl.xls** spreadsheet. By default, it is stored in *C:\Users\<user>\ Documents\Acade <version>\Aedata\<language>\Catalogs* for Windows 10. You can modify this spreadsheet to add terminals or create a custom spreadsheet.
- Most terminal symbols contain wipeouts in the block. This feature hides the DIN rail behind the terminal blocks. If the DIN rail is not hidden, use the **Draw Order** commands in the Tools drop-down list to place the rail behind the terminal strip.

Practice 7a
Insert Terminal Symbols

Practice Objective

- Insert and associate terminals to create a multiple-level terminal and jumper terminals together.

In this practice, you will insert terminal symbols into an existing schematic drawing. You will then associate terminals to create a multiple-level terminal. To complete the practice, you will jumper several terminals together and create a jumper chart, as shown in Figure 7–19

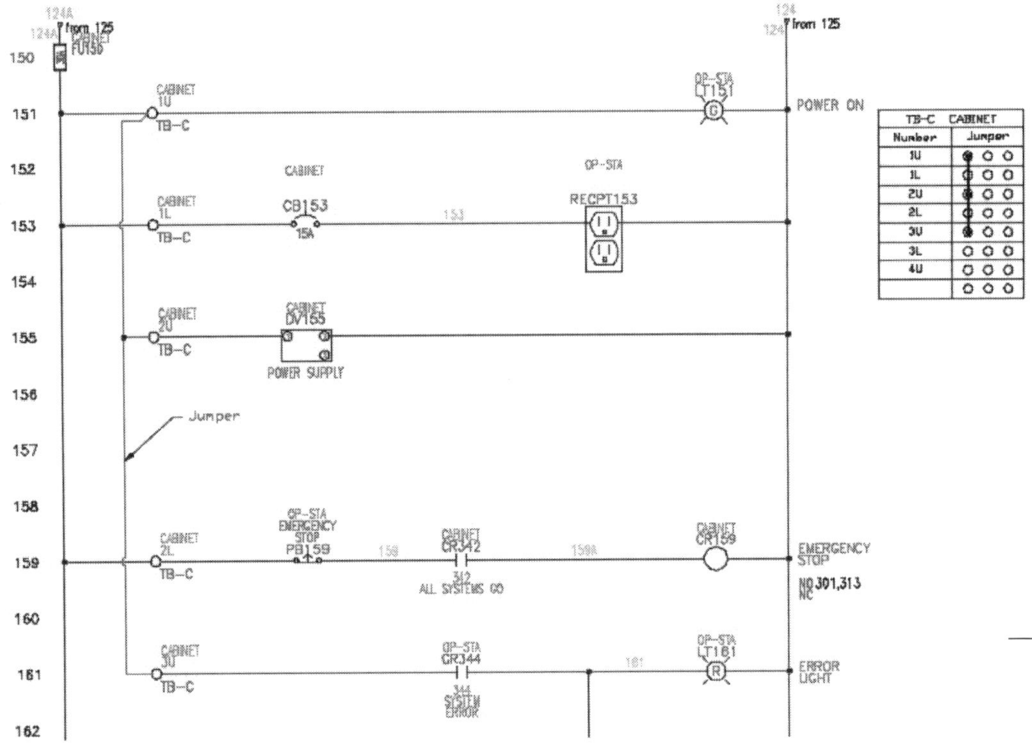

Figure 7–19

Task 1: Insert terminals in a schematic drawing.

1. Open and activate the **Module 07** project from your practice files folder.
2. In the **Module 07** project, open **Power.dwg**.
3. Zoom to the right side of the drawing on wires 150 to 167.

4. In the *Schematic* tab>*Insert Components* panel, click (Multiple Insert (Icon Menu)).

5. The *Insert Component* dialog box opens. Click (Terminals/Connectors).

6. In the **Terminals and Connectors** submenu, click (Round with Terminal Number).

7. Pick a point above the wire on line 151. Pick a second point below the wire on line 167, making sure that the line is vertical (as shown in Figure 7–20). (Toggle **Ortho** on to create a vertical line.) Press <Enter> to continue the command.

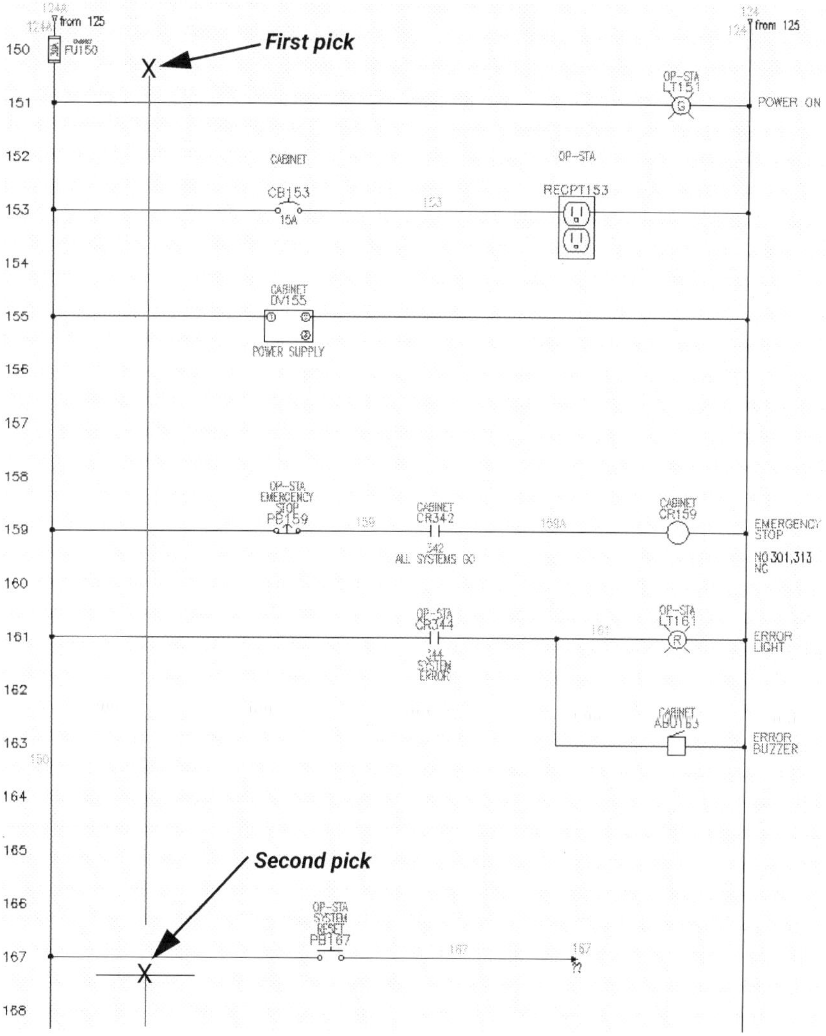

Figure 7–20

8. In the *Keep?* dialog box, verify that the **Keep this one** option is selected. Click **OK**.

9. The *Insert / Edit Terminal Symbol* dialog box opens. In the *Terminal* area, set the following options, as shown in Figure 7–21:
   - *Location*: **CABINET**
   - *Tag Strip*: **TB-C**
   - *Number*: **1**
10. In the *Catalog Data* area, enter **21** in the *Item* field and click **Catalog Lookup**, as shown in Figure 7–21. You might be required to click **Details>>** to expand the dialog box.

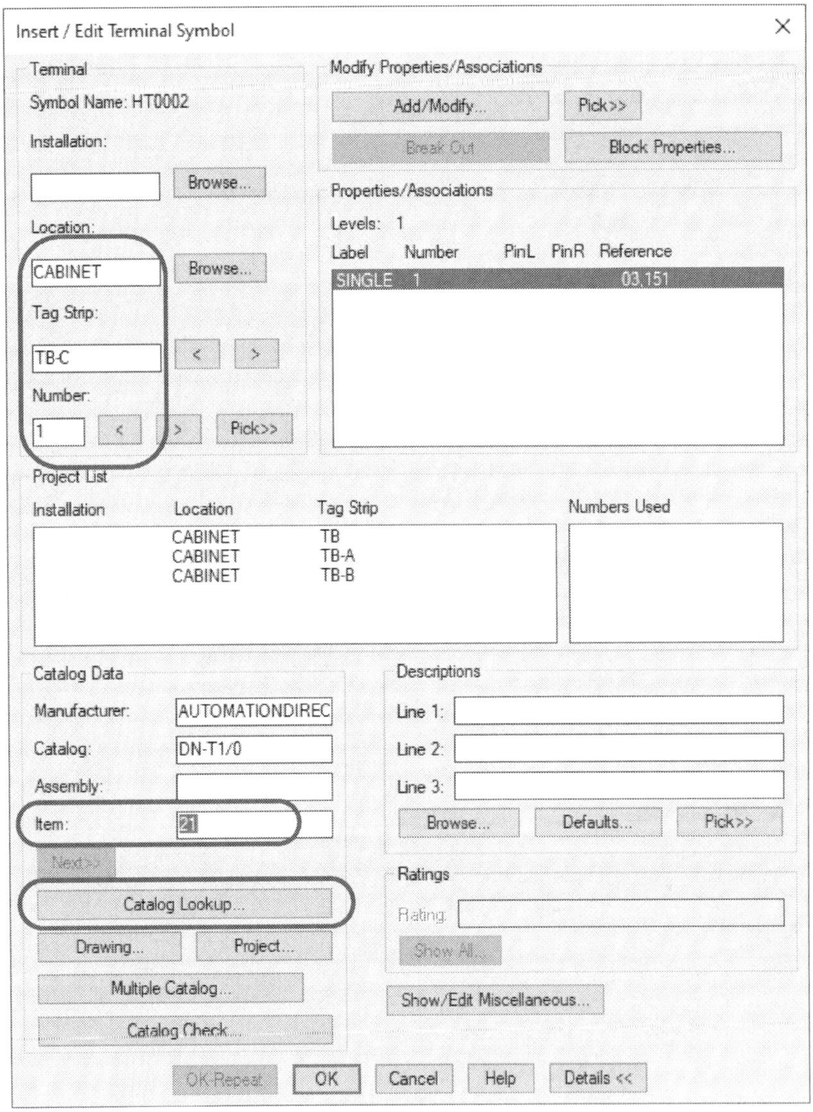

Figure 7–21

11. In the Catalog Browser, search for **DN-D10.** Select **DN-D10** and click **OK**. In the *Insert / Edit Terminal Symbol* dialog box, note that the *Catalog Data* is populated and that the *Properties/ Associations* displays two levels: **UPPER** and **LOWER**. Click **OK**.
    - You might be required to map the symbol to the catalog number.
12. The *Keep?* dialog box opens. Set the options as follows, as shown in Figure 7–22:
    - Select **Keep all, don't ask**.
    - Clear **Show edit dialog after each**.
    - Clear **Hide Tag**.
    - Clear **Hide Installation/Location**.
    - Click **OK**.

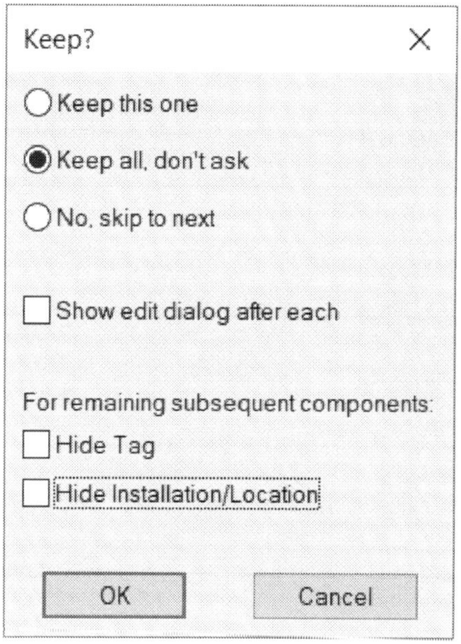

Figure 7–22

- The terminals are inserted into the drawing (on the fence selected lines), as shown in Figure 7–23.

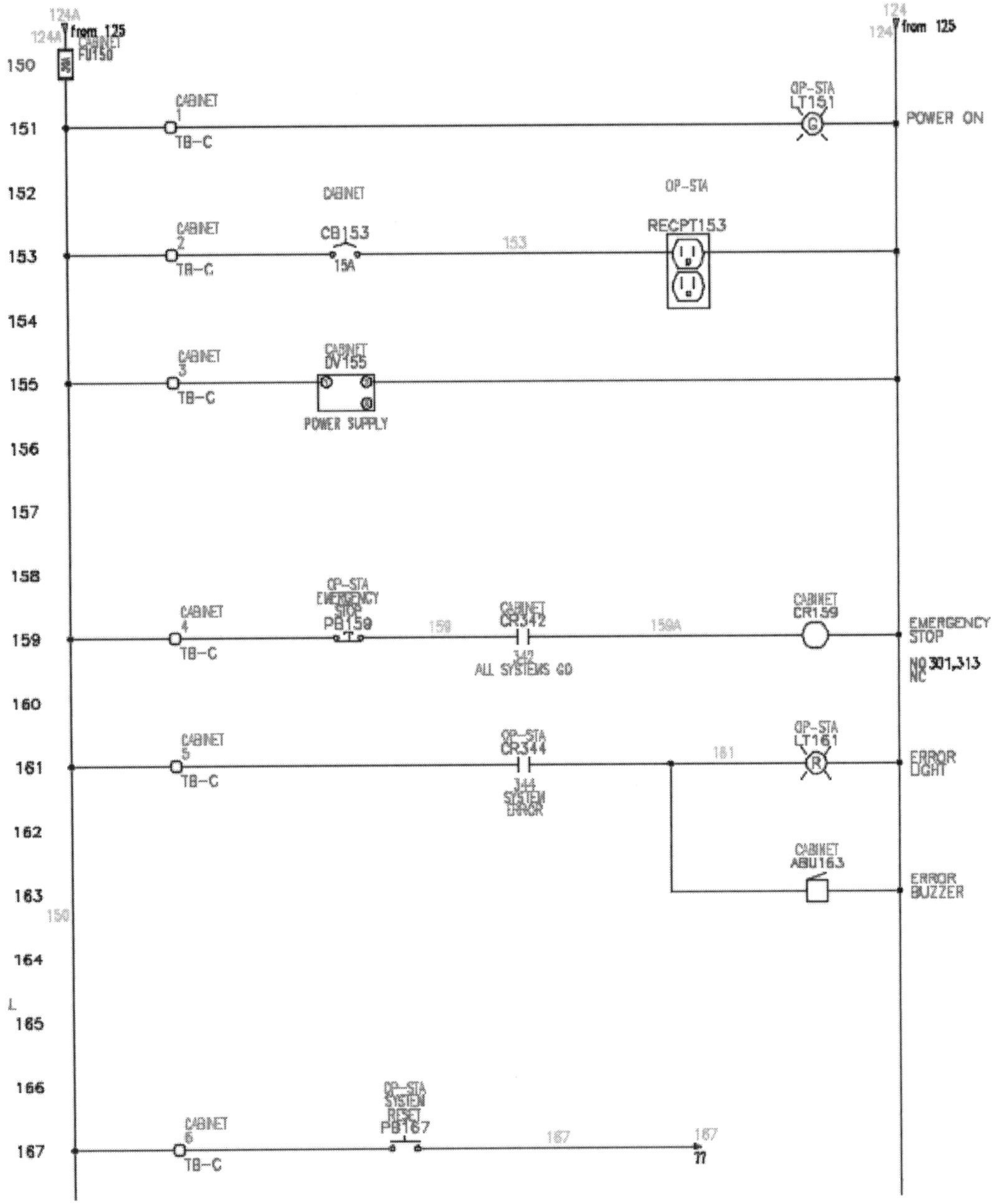

Figure 7–23

Task 2: Associate terminals into a multiple-level terminal.

1. Right-click on terminal **1**, which is located on line **151**, and select **Edit Component**. The *Insert / Edit Terminal Symbol* dialog box opens.
2. In the dialog box, in the *Project List*, note that **TB-C** is selected. Verify that in the *Properties/ Associations* area, **UPPER** is selected. In the *Number* field, type **1U**, as shown in Figure 7–24. Click **OK**.

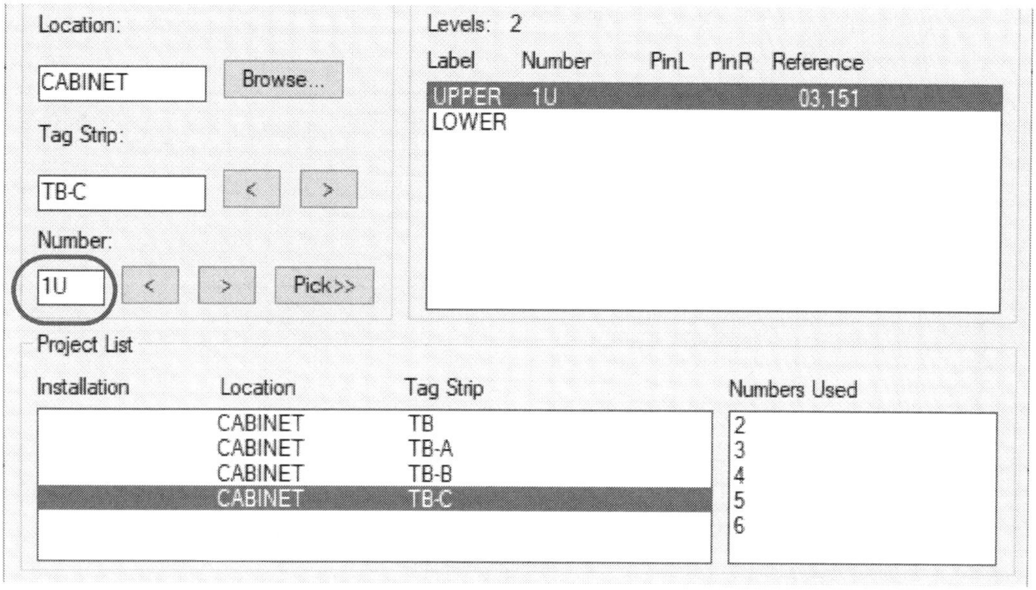

Figure 7–24

3. Right-click on terminal **2**, which is located on line **153**, and select **Edit Component**.

4. In the *Insert / Edit Terminal Symbol* dialog box, in the *Number* field, type **1L.** In the *Properties/Associations* area, verify that **UPPER** is still selected. To associate it with 1U, in the *Modify Properties/Associations* area, click **Pick>>** and select the terminal **1U** in the drawing. The dialog box is updated automatically and **LOWER 1L** is selected in the *Properties/Associations* area, as shown in Figure 7–25. Click **OK**.

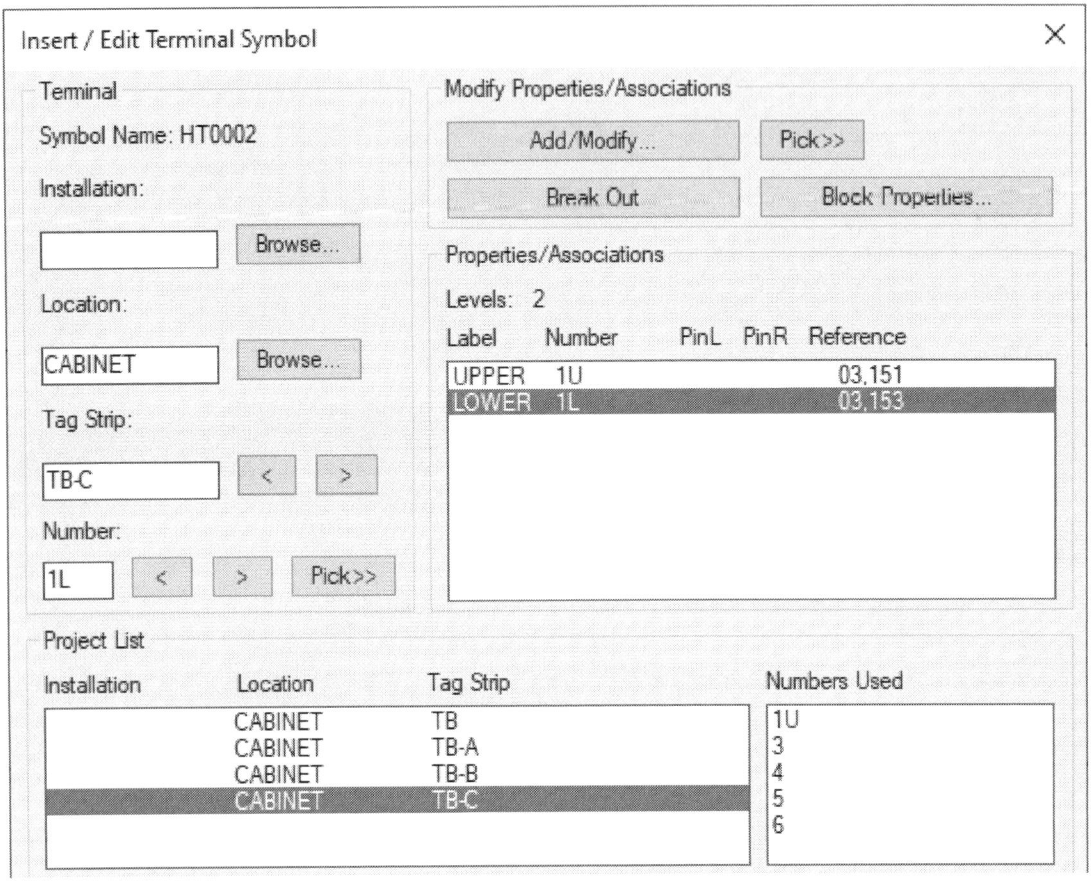

Figure 7–25

5. Right-click on terminal **3**, which is located on line **155**, and select **Edit Component**.
6. In the *Insert / Edit Terminal Symbol* dialog box, in the *Number* field, type **2U**, and click **OK**.

7. Right-click on terminal **4**, located on line **159**, and select **Edit Component**. In the *Insert / Edit Terminal Symbol* dialog box, set *Number* as **2L**. Associate 2L with 2U by clicking **Pick>>** and selecting terminal **2U** on line **155** in the drawing. The dialog box is updated automatically with **LOWER 2L** selected, as shown in Figure 7–26. Click **OK**.

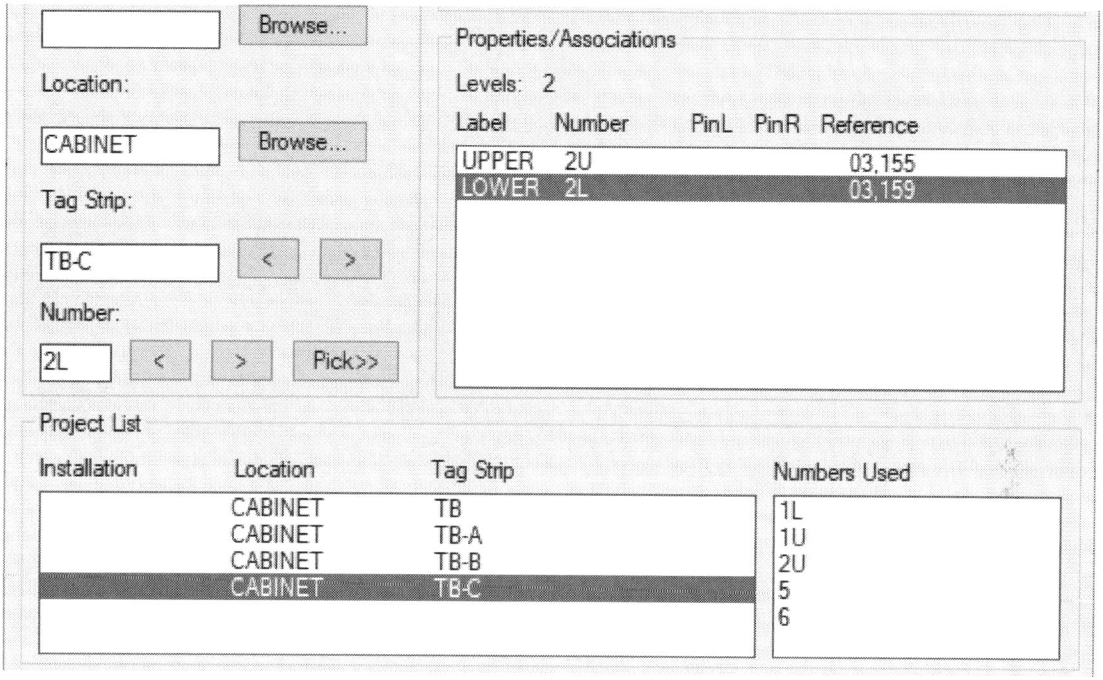

Figure 7–26

8. Right-click on terminal **5**, located on line **161**, and select **Edit Component**. In the *Insert / Edit Terminal Symbol* dialog box set *Number* to **3U**, and click **OK**.

9. Similarly using **Edit Component,** set the *Number* for terminal **6** (located on line **167**) to **4U**.

10. In the *Panel* tab>*Terminal Footprints* panel, click (Editor). If prompted, save the changes. The *Terminal Strip Selection* dialog box opens. Note that the TB-C terminal strip has four terminals (as shown in Figure 7–27), because **1U** and **1L** are counted as a single terminal as are **2U** and **2L**. **3U** and **4U** are the other two terminals, bringing the total to four. Click **Done**.

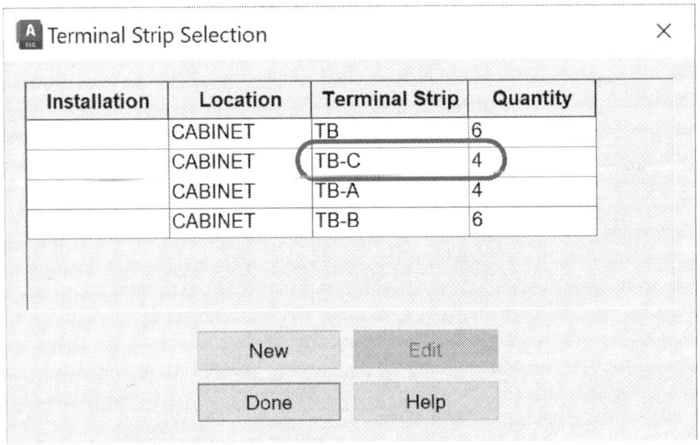

Figure 7–27

Task 3: Associate terminals in different drawings.

1. Click (Next Drawing) to open the next drawing, **POWER2.DWG**.
2. Zoom to wire number 259A on line 259.
3. In the *Schematic* tab>*Insert Components* panel, click (Icon Menu). In the *Insert Component* dialog box, click (Terminals/Connectors) and click (Round with Terminal Number). Pick a point on the line below the line number **259A** (as shown in Figure 7–28), to insert a Round with Terminal Number symbol.

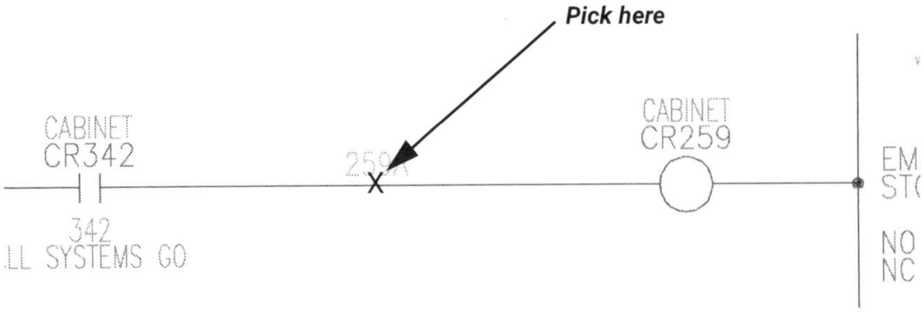

Figure 7–28

4. The *Insert / Edit Terminal Symbol* dialog box opens. In the *Project List* area, select **TB-C**, if required. Note that in the *Tag Strip* field TB-C is automatically displayed. In the *Number* field, type **3L** and press <Enter>. In the *Modify Properties/Associations* area, note that the UPPER number changes to *3L*, as shown in Figure 7–29.

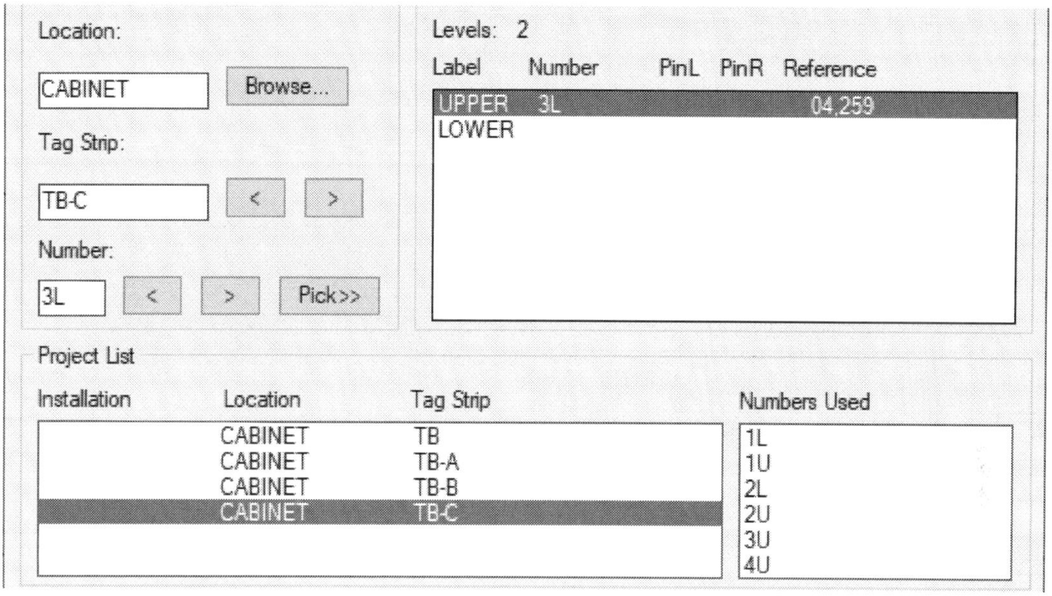

Figure 7–29

5. In the *Modify Properties/Associations* area, click **Add/Modify**. The *Add / Modify Association* dialog box opens.
6. In the *Select Association* area, expand **+CABINET-TB-C (4)** and select the branch for **3U, (2)**. Note that in the *Select Association* area table, *UPPER* has **3U** as its number whereas *LOWER* is empty, as shown in Figure 7–30.
7. Select the blank row labeled **LOWER**, as shown in Figure 7–30.

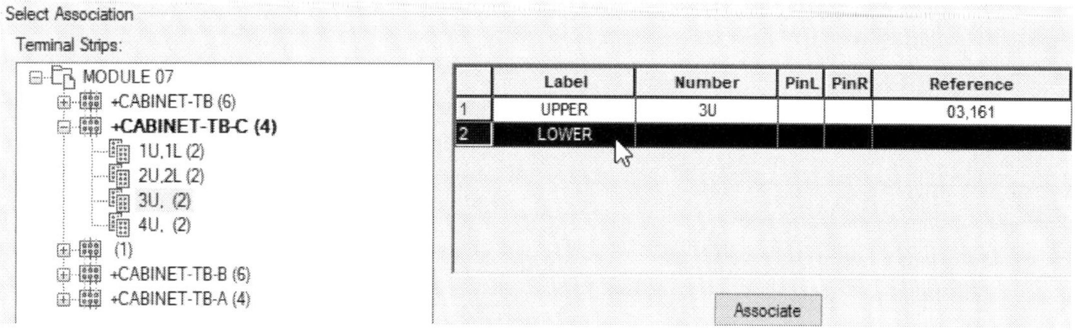

Figure 7–30

8. Click **Associate**. Terminal (3L) is associated to the multiple-level terminal (3U). The table in the *Active Association* area is updated to reflect the change, as shown in Figure 7–31.

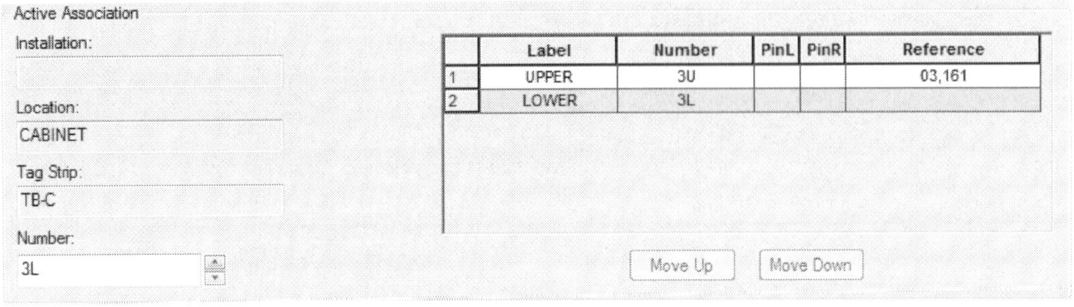

Figure 7–31

9. Click **OK** to close the *Add / Modify Association* dialog box.
10. Click **OK** to close the *Insert / Edit Terminal Symbol* dialog box.
11. If prompted, in the *Update other drawings* dialog box, click **Skip**.
    - If a *Mismatch Item Number* dialog box is opened, click **OK** to exit it.

Task 4: Jumper terminals.

1. Click (Previous DWG) to open the previous drawing, **Power.dwg**.

2. In the *Schematic* tab>*Edit Wires/Wire Numbers* panel, click (Trim Wire). Trim the wire portions of wires 155 and 161 on the left side of terminals 2U and 3U. Press <Enter> to exit the command.

3. Right-click on terminal 1U, which is located on line 151, and select **Terminals>Edit Jumper**, as shown in Figure 7–32.

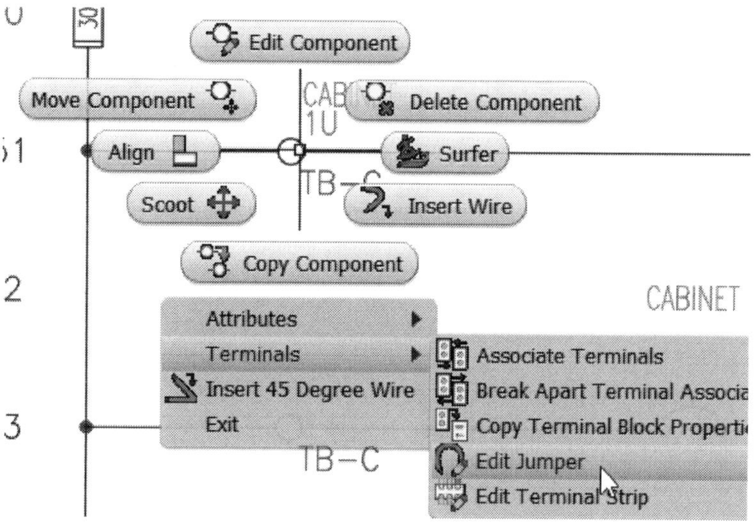

Figure 7–32

4. Select terminal **1U** on line 151, terminal **2U** on line 155, and terminal **3U** on line 161. Press <Enter>. The *Edit Terminal Jumpers* dialog box opens, as shown in Figure 7–33. Note that the jumpers are added for **CABINET-TB-C**. Click **OK**.

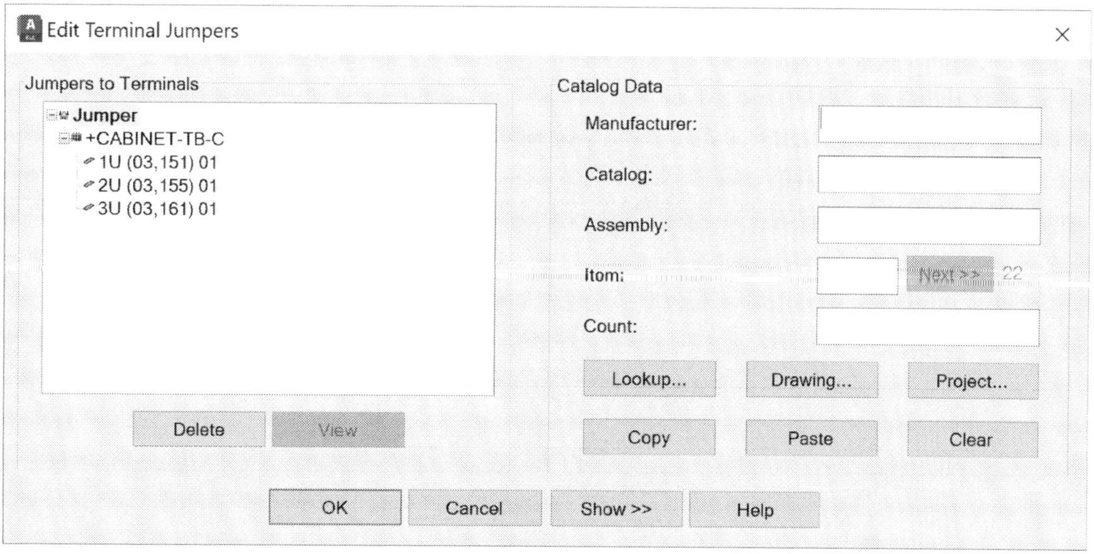

Figure 7–33

5. Right-click on terminal 1U and select **Terminals>Edit Jumper**.

6. Select terminal **1U** in the drawing. At the Command Prompt, type **S** and press <Enter>. A blue highlighted line is drawn, indicating the jumpers, as shown in Figure 7–34. This is a temporary display.

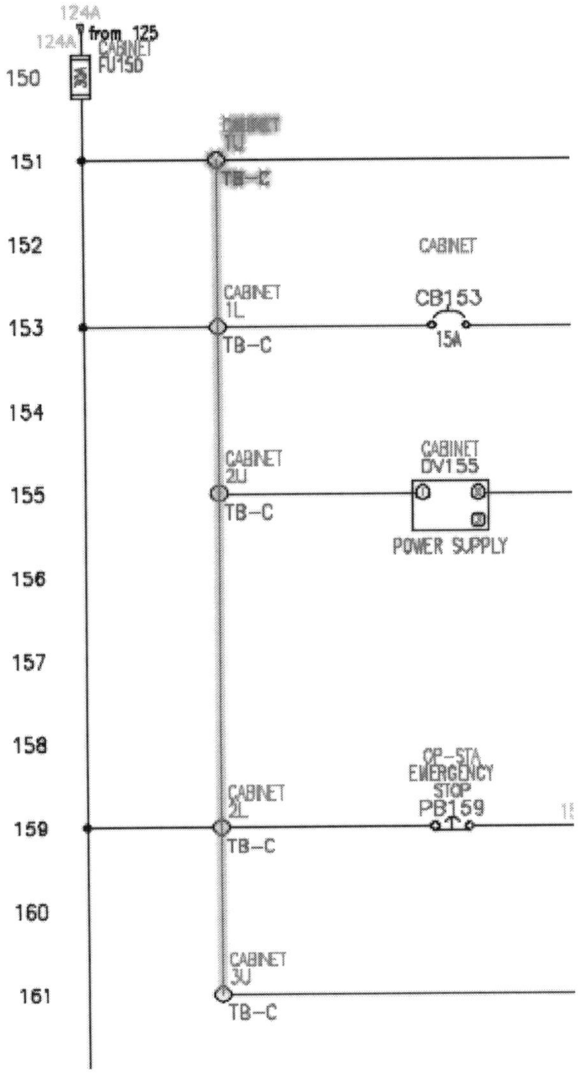

Figure 7–34

7. Press <Esc> to end the command. Zoom or pan to remove the line from the screen.

Task 5: Create a jumper chart.

1. In the *Panel* tab>*Terminal Footprints* panel, click 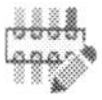 (Editor). Click **OK** to save and update the changes. The *Terminal Strip Selection* dialog box opens. (If the *Terminal Strip Editor* opens instead, exit the dialog box and restart the command again.) Select the **TB-C** terminal strip and click **Edit**.

2. The *Terminal Strip Editor* dialog box opens. (Verify that it is for the TB-C terminal strip.) Select the *Layout Preview* tab, select **Jumper Chart (Table Object)**, and click **Update**. The jumper chart displays in the preview area in the dialog box, as shown in Figure 7–35. Note that the jumper chart does not have a title heading.

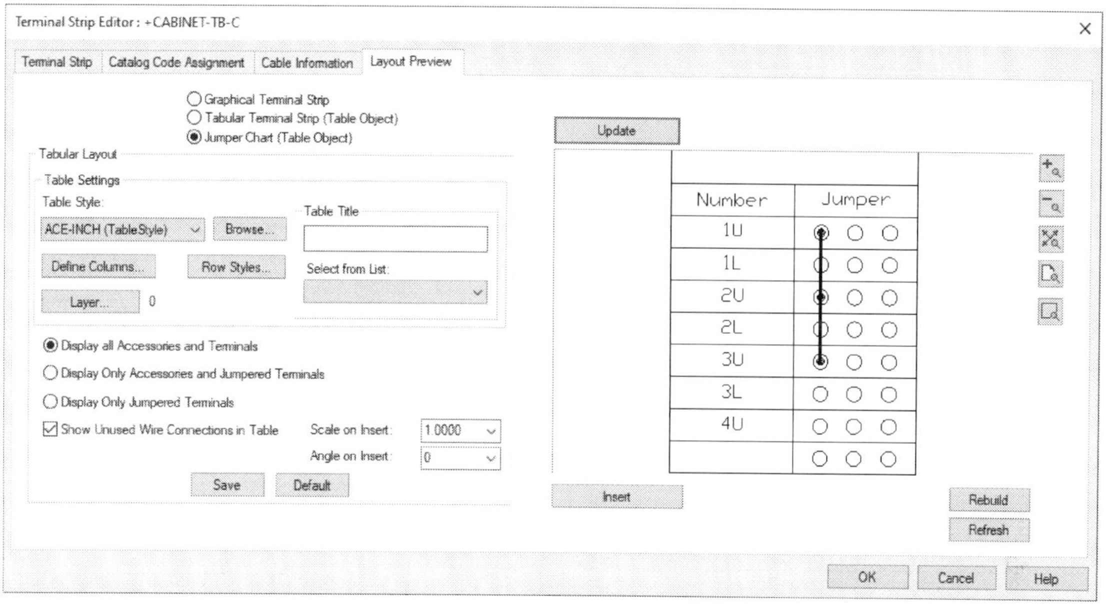

Figure 7–35

3. In the *Table Title* area, expand the *Select from List* drop-down list, and select **Terminal Strip ID (%T)**. Note that **%T** is placed in the *Table Title* field. In the *Select from List* drop-down list, select **Location (%L)**, as shown in Figure 7–36. Note that **%L** is placed after **%T** in the *Table Title* field.

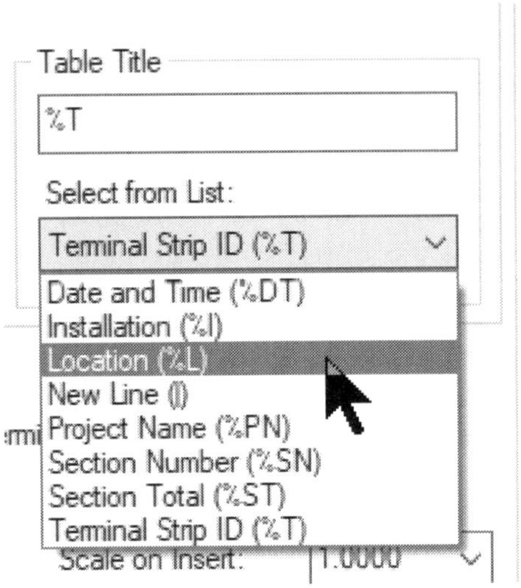

Figure 7–36

4. Click **Update**. The jumper chart is updated with the title in the preview area in the dialog box, as shown in Figure 7–37.

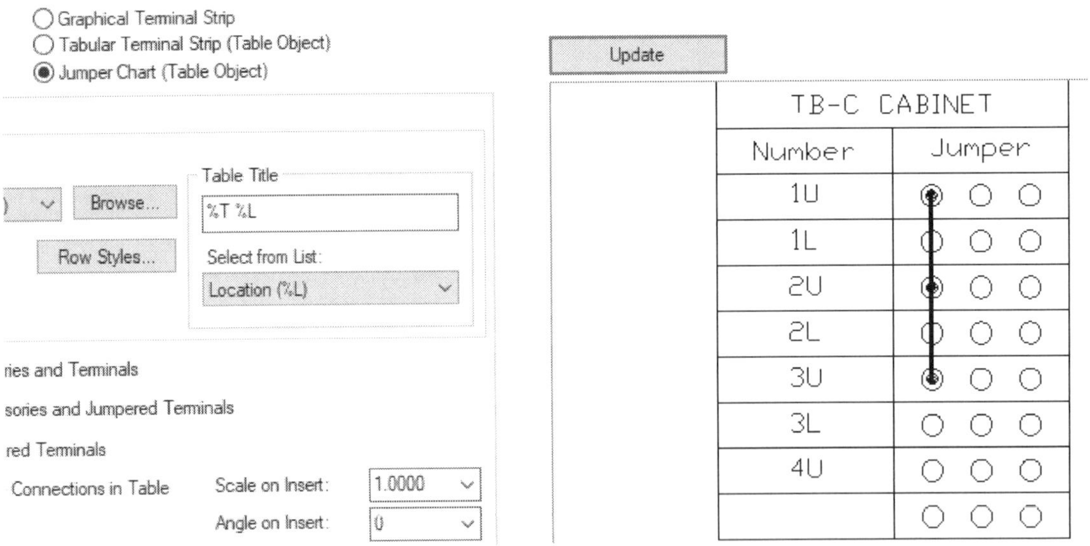

Figure 7–37

5. Click **Insert** and place the jumper chart in the empty area near the right side of the ladder that has the jumper terminals, as shown in Figure 7–38. Click **OK** in the *Terminal Strip Editor* dialog box and click **Done** in the *Terminal Strip Selection* dialog box.

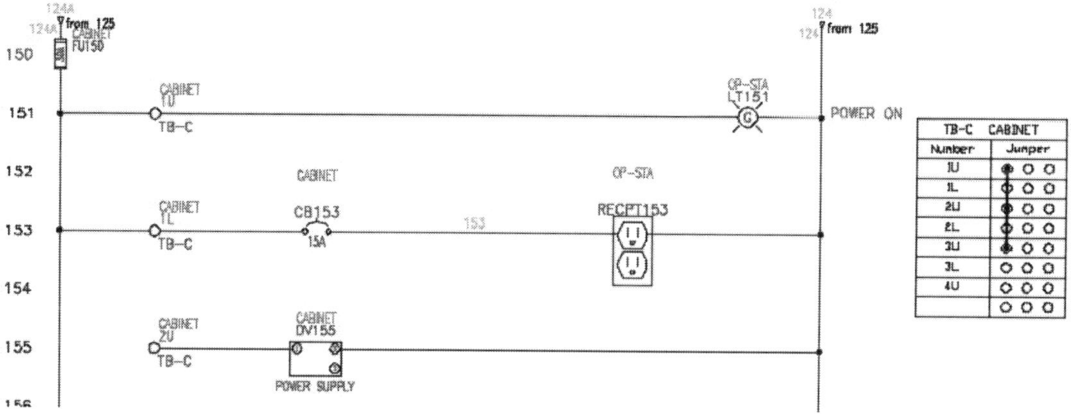

Figure 7–38

6. In the *Schematic* tab>*Edit Wires/Wire Numbers* panel, click (Create/Edit Wire Type) and create a new wire type with the following settings, as shown in Figure 7–39:

- *Layer Name*: **JUMPER**
- *Wire Numbering*: **No**
- *Size*: **14AWG**
- *Wire Color*: **BLU** (select the color blue in the *Layer* area)

Once you enter the required settings, click **OK** in the dialog box.

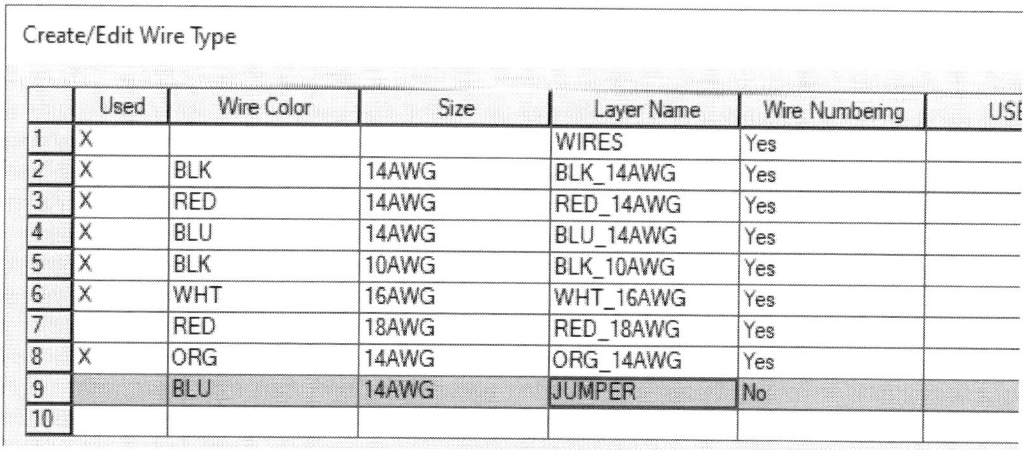
Create/Edit Wire Type

	Used	Wire Color	Size	Layer Name	Wire Numbering	USE
1	X			WIRES	Yes	
2	X	BLK	14AWG	BLK_14AWG	Yes	
3	X	RED	14AWG	RED_14AWG	Yes	
4	X	BLU	14AWG	BLU_14AWG	Yes	
5	X	BLK	10AWG	BLK_10AWG	Yes	
6	X	WHT	16AWG	WHT_16AWG	Yes	
7		RED	18AWG	RED_18AWG	Yes	
8	X	ORG	14AWG	ORG_14AWG	Yes	
9		BLU	14AWG	JUMPER	No	
10						

Figure 7–39

7. Using (Wire), add a jumper cable starting from the left quadrant of **1U** terminal to the left quadrant of **3U** terminal. (Use **Quadrant** Osnap to snap to the quadrants of the jumper.) Add a connecting wire to the **2U** terminal and press <Enter>. Right-click on the jumper wire that is created and select **Change/Convert Wire Type**. In the dialog box, select the wire type **JUMPER** and click **OK**. The whole wire changes to blue color, and the drawing displays as shown in Figure 7–40. Press <Enter>.

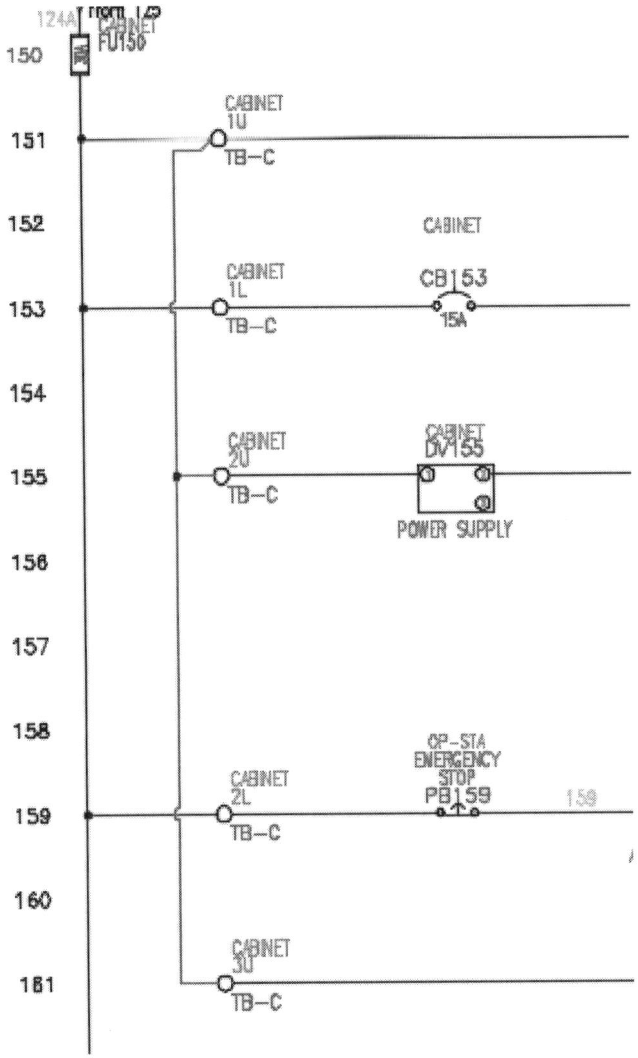

Figure 7–40

8. Right-click on the jumper wire and select **Wire Color/Gauge Labels**. In the *Insert Wire Color/ Gauge Labels* dialog box, click **Setup**.

9. In the *Wire label color/gauge setup* dialog box, select **JUMPER**, and set the following, as shown in Figure 7–41:

   * Text string to be used as label: **Jumper**. Click **OK**.
   * *Leader* area>*Text Size*: **0.125**
   * *Leader* area>*Arrow Size*: **0.125**

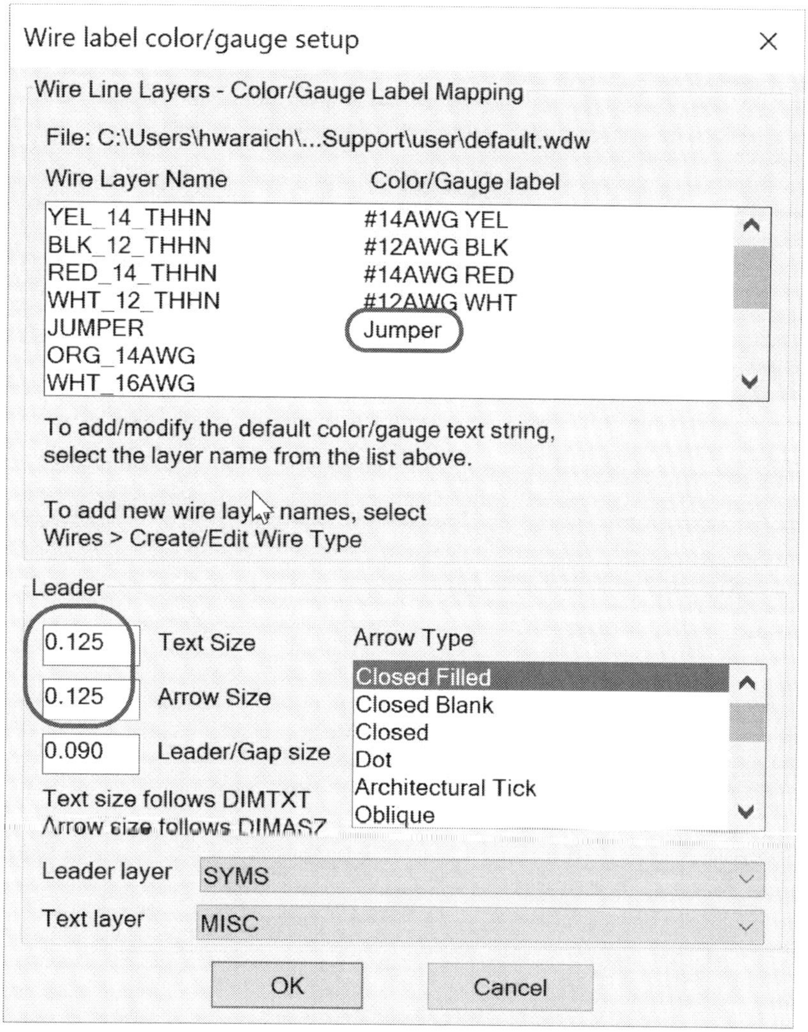

Figure 7–41

10. Click **OK**.
11. In the *Insert Wire Color/Gauge Labels* dialog box, in the *With leader* area, click **Manual**.

12. In the drawing, pick a point on the jumper wire between 2U and 2L and then pick another point anywhere to the right. Press <Enter>. The leader and the label **Jumper** are placed, as shown in Figure 7–42. Press <Esc> to exit the command.

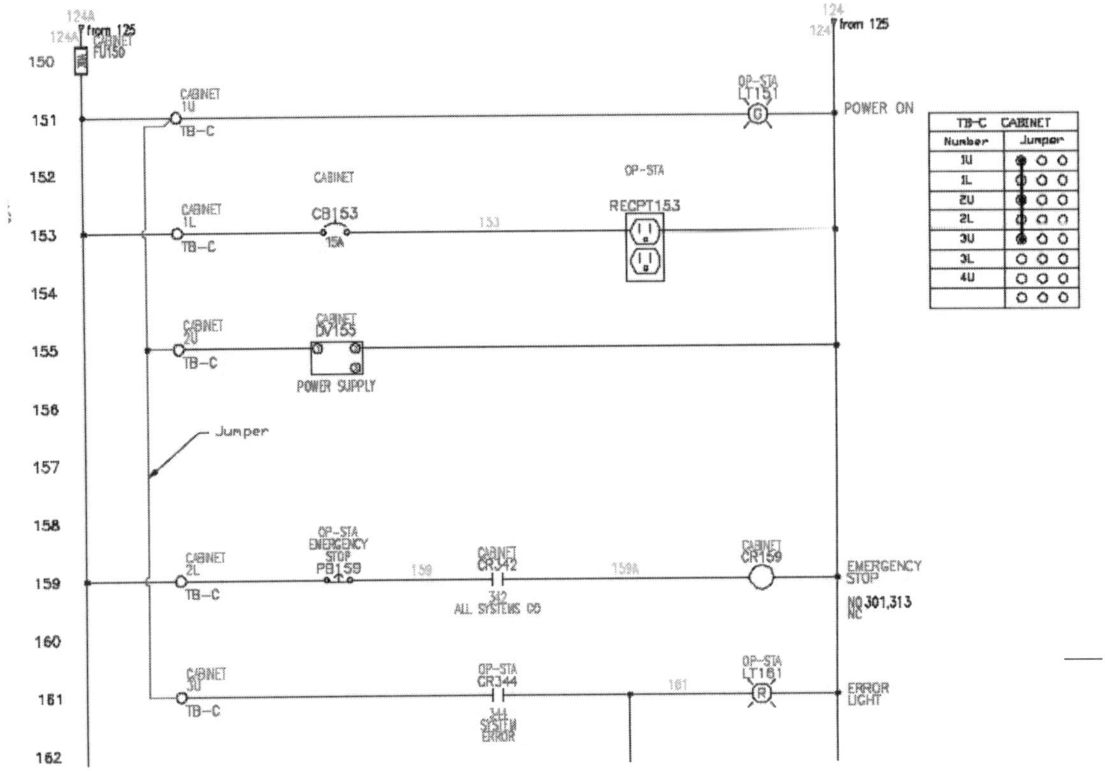

Figure 7–42

13. Save and close all of the drawings.

End of practice

Practice 7b
Insert Terminal Footprints

Practice Objective

- Insert a DIN rail and a terminal strip's graphical and tabular representations.

In this practice, you will insert a DIN rail into a panel drawing. You will then insert a terminal strip on the rail based on the terminals in the schematic drawing, as shown in Figure 7–43. Finally, you will create a terminal strip table, as shown in Figure 7–43.

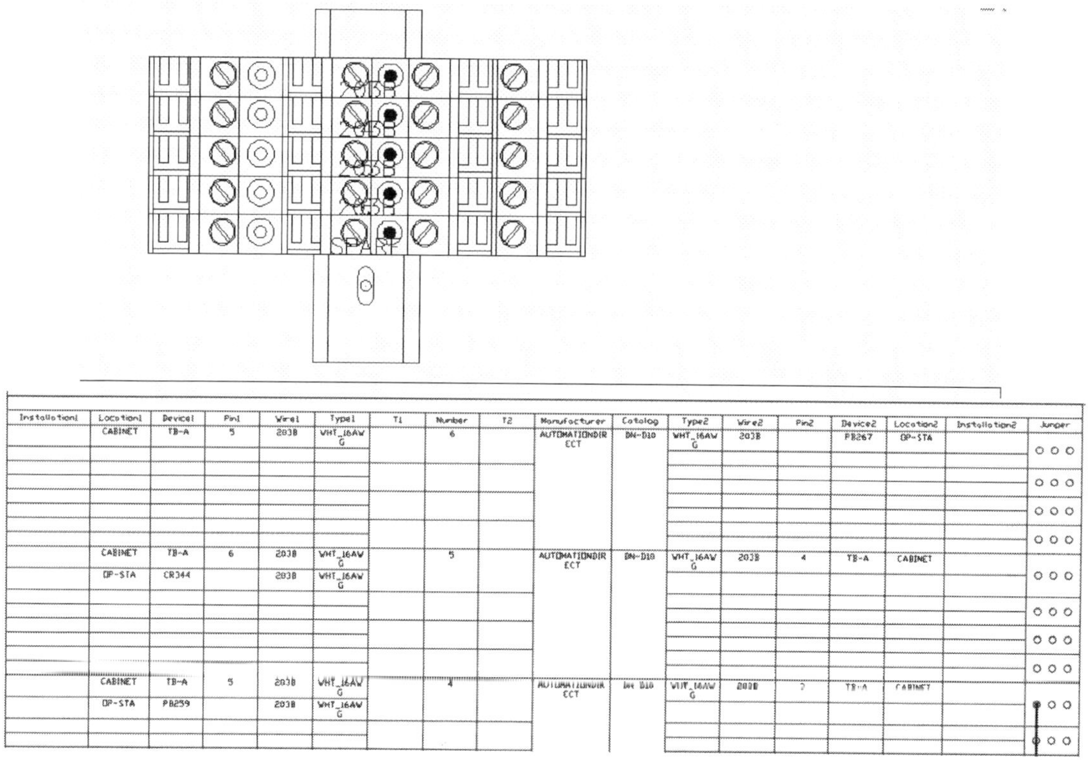

Figure 7–43

Task 1: Insert a DIN rail into a panel drawing.

1. If the **Module 07** project is not active, open and activate it now.
2. In the **Module 07** project, open **Cabinet.dwg**.
3. Zoom to the upper right portion of the titleblock near the existing terminal block.

4. In the *Panel* tab>*Insert Component Footprints* panel, click  (Insert Footprint [Icon Menu]).

5. In the *Insert Footprint* dialog box, click  (DIN Rail).

6. The *Din Rail* dialog box opens. Note that the *Rail Type* is set as **AB, 199-DR1**. Set the following, as shown in Figure 7–44:

   - *Length:* **4.5**
   - *X*: **54**
   - *Y*: **36**
   - *Orientation*: **Vertical**

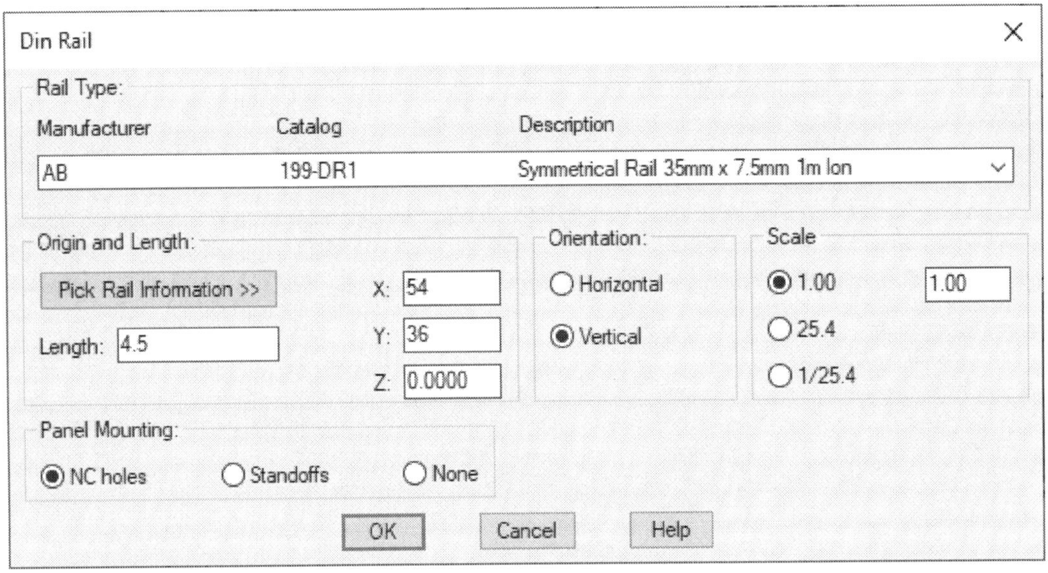

Figure 7–44

7. Click **OK**. Note that a DIN rail is inserted in the drawing at the location specified in the *Din Rail* dialog box.

Task 2: Insert a terminal strip into a panel drawing.

1. In the *Panel* tab>*Terminal Footprints* panel, click  (Editor). If prompted, save and update the drawing.

2. In the *Terminal Strip Selection* dialog box, select **TB-A** (as shown in Figure 7–45) and click **Edit**.

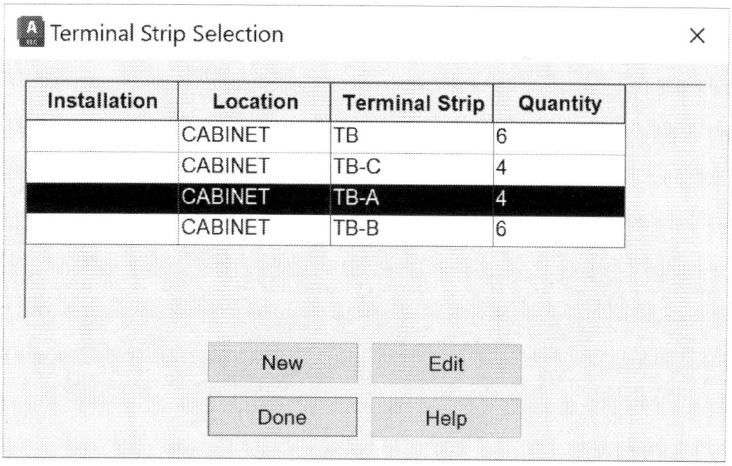

Figure 7–45

3. The *Terminal Strip Editor: +CABINET-TB-A* dialog box opens. Scroll down in the list and select the last row in the dialog box, as shown in Figure 7–46. In the *Spare (toolbar)* area, click  (Insert Spare Terminal), as shown in Figure 7–46.

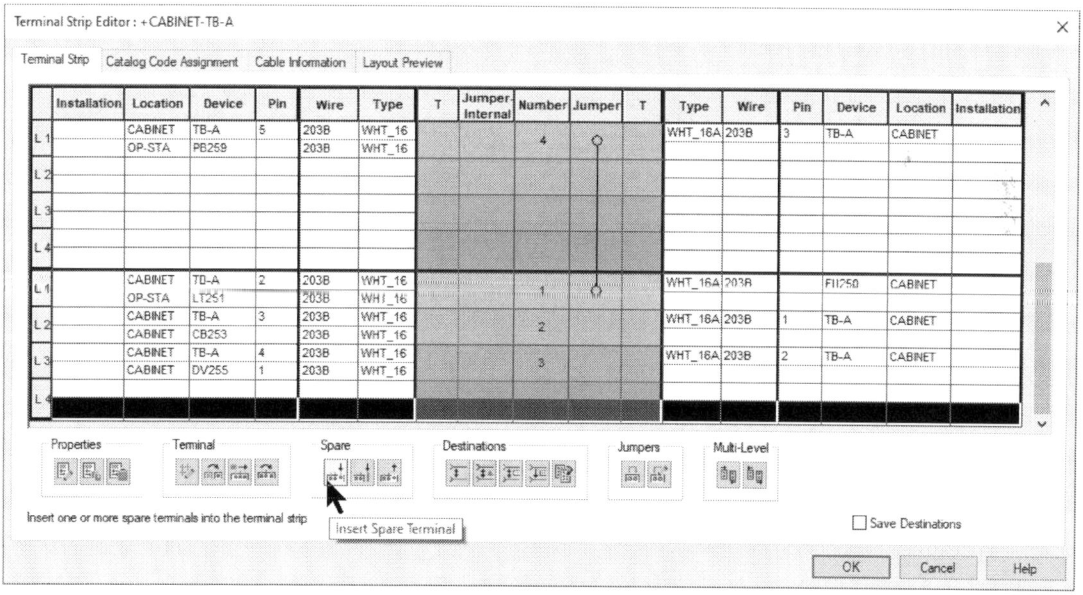

Figure 7–46

4. In the *Insert Spare Terminal* dialog box, click **Insert Below**.

5. In the *Terminal Strip Editor* dialog box, select the *Catalog Code Assignment* tab. Select any row for terminal 6, and in the *Catalog (toolbar)* area, click (Copy Catalog Number), as shown in Figure 7–47.

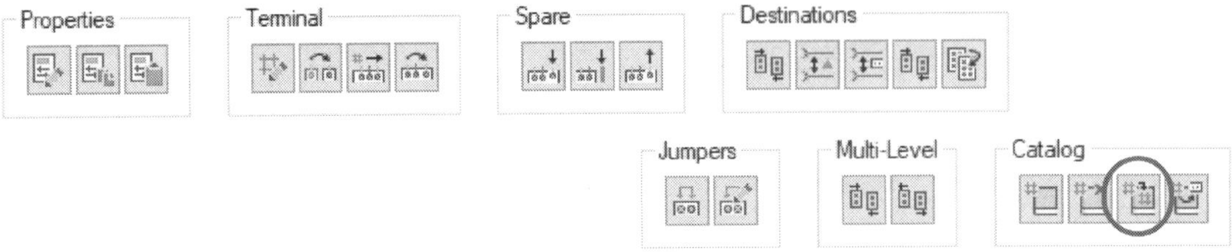

Figure 7–47

6. Scroll down and select the row for the SPARE terminal. In the *Catalog (toolbar)* area, click (Paste Catalog Number), as shown in Figure 7–48. Scroll down and note that the *Terminal Strip Editor* dialog box is updated and displays as shown in Figure 7–48.

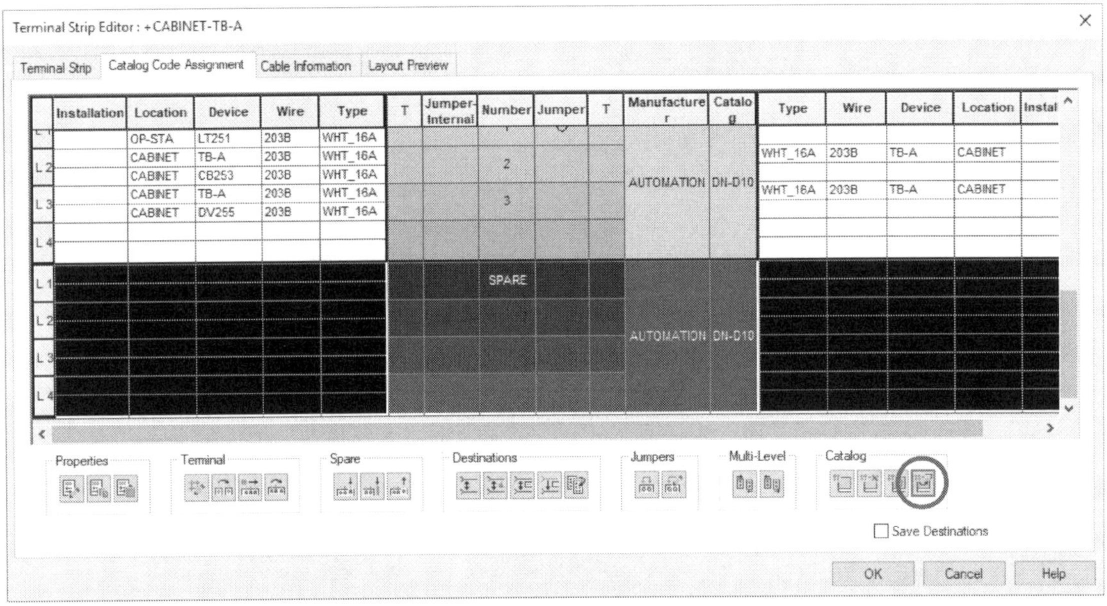

Figure 7–48

7. Select the *Layout Preview* tab. In the *Graphical Layout* area, select **Wire Number Only** and click **Update**. Note that in the dialog box, the preview displays the wire numbers, as shown in Figure 7–49.

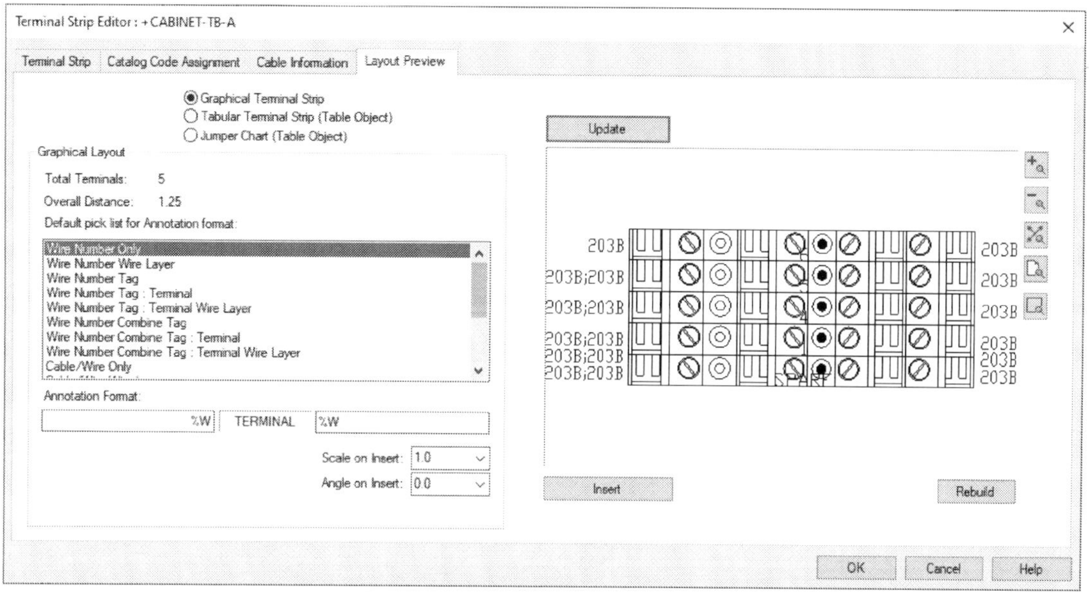

Figure 7–49

8. In the *Graphical Layout* area, select **Wire Number Combine Tag** and click **Update**. In the dialog box, the preview updates to display the tags, as shown in Figure 7–50.

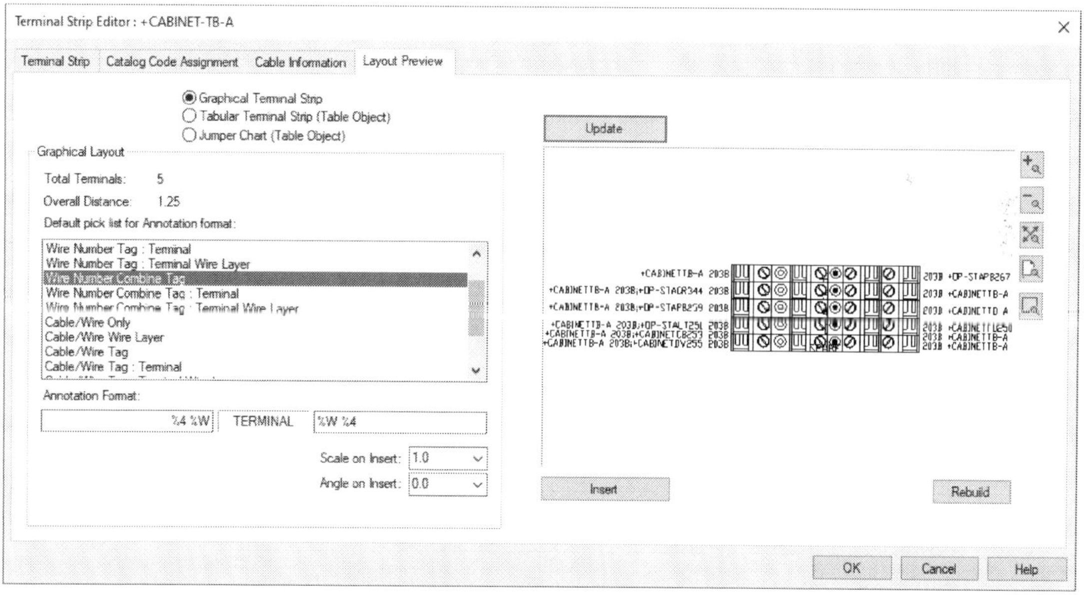

Figure 7–50

9. In *Annotation Format* area, clear both fields on either side of TERMINAL and click **Update**. The preview should display the symbol without any text.

10. In the *Scale on Insert* field, type **2**, as shown in Figure 7–51. Click **Insert**.

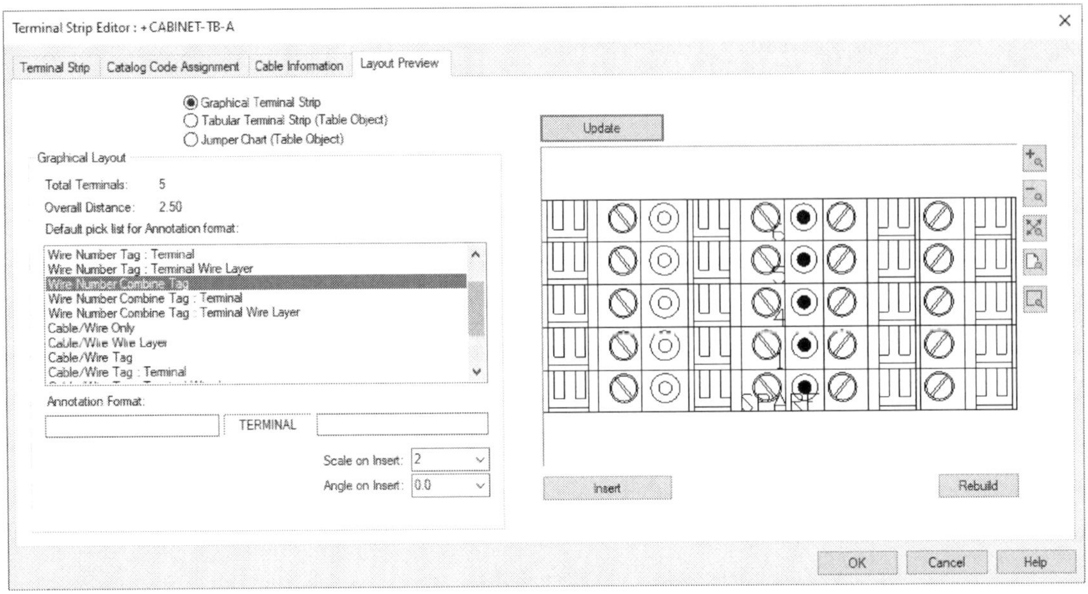

Figure 7–51

11. Note that the strip is attached to the cursor. Pick a point near the top center of the new din rail that was created to place the strip, as shown in Figure 7–52.

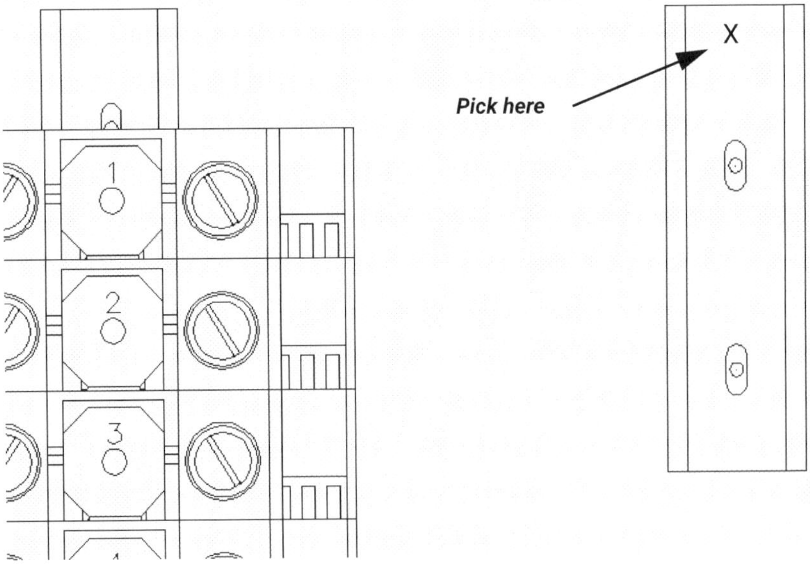

Figure 7–52

12. The *Terminal Strip Editor* opens again. Select the **Tabular Terminal Strip (Table Object)** option and click **Update**. The dialog box displays as shown in Figure 7–53. (The preview might look different depending on your current settings.)

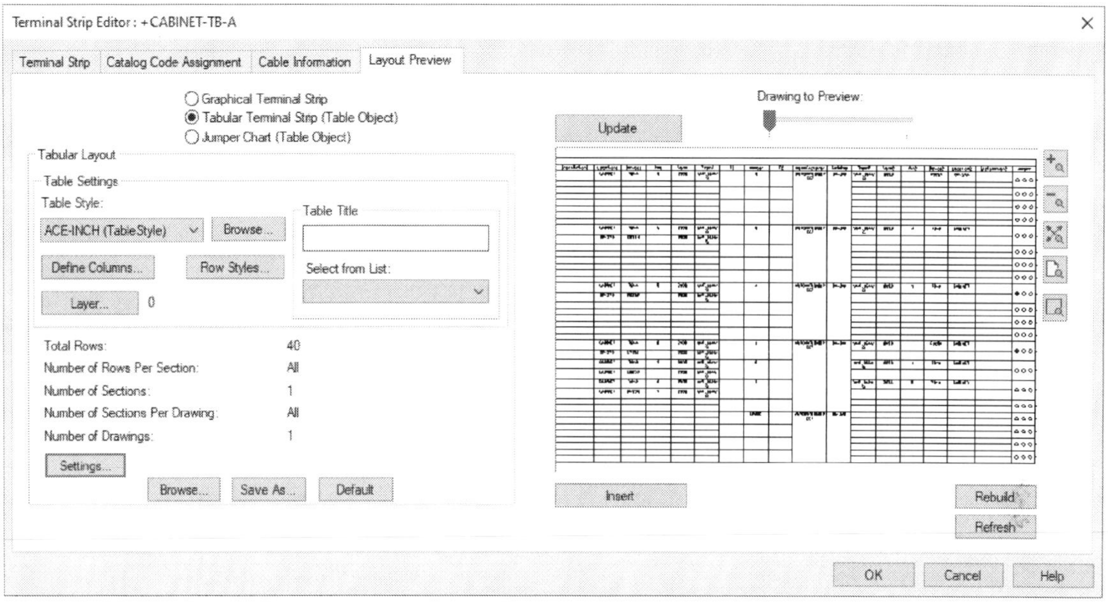

Figure 7–53

13. In the *Tabular Layout* area, click **Settings...** to open the *Terminal Strip Table Settings* dialog box.

14. In the *Terminal Strip Table Settings* dialog box, set the following options, as shown in Figure 7–54.
    - Select **Insert Multiple Sections Per Drawing**.
    - For *First Drawing Name*, use **Browse** and save it as **Table_Object_01.dwg** in the *Module 07* folder in the practice files folder.
    - For *Template*, use **Browse** to select the **Electrical_template.dwt** from your practice files folder.

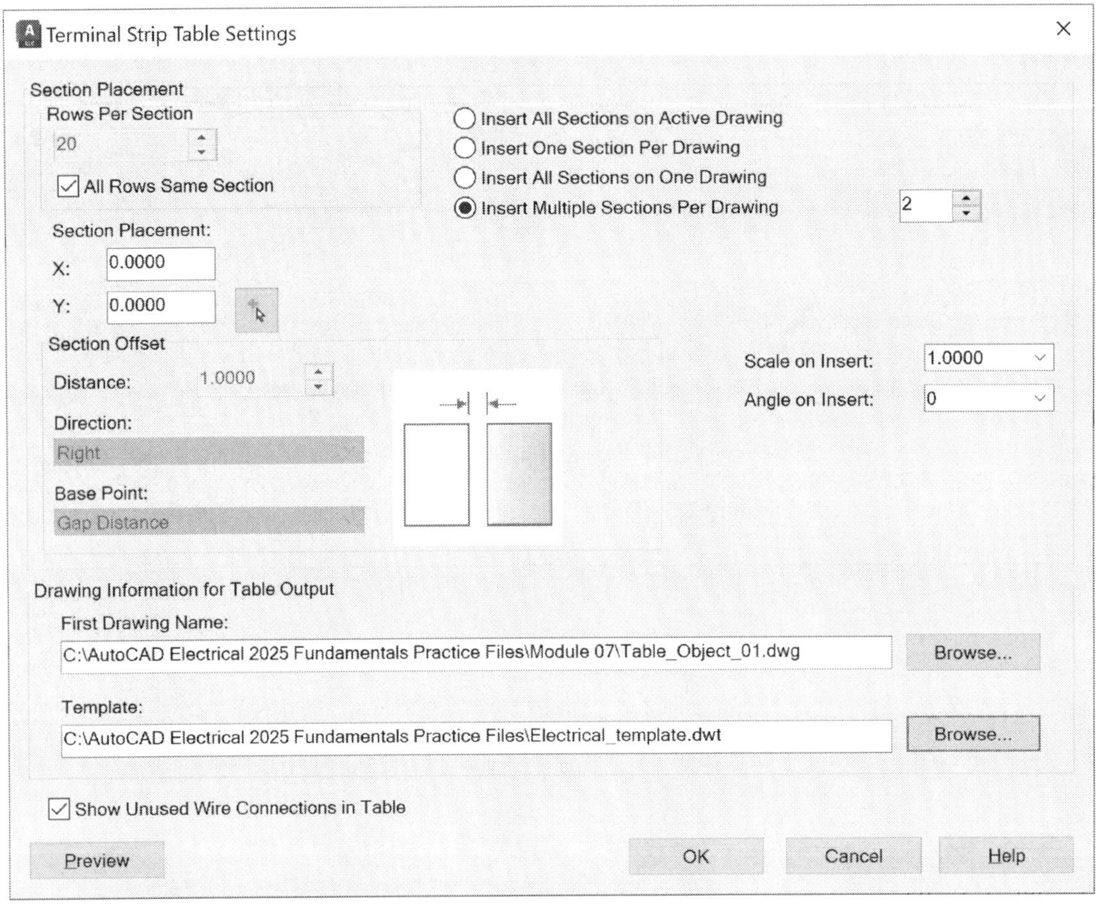

Figure 7–54

15. Click **Preview** to view the changes. Click **Done** to close the *Preview* dialog box.
16. Click **OK** to accept the settings.
17. Click **Update** to update the preview and then click **Insert** to create the drawing and insert the tables.
18. In the *Table(s) Inserted* dialog box, click **OK**.

19. In the *Terminal Strip Editor,* click **OK**.
20. In the *Terminal Strip Selection* dialog box, click **Done**. Save and update the drawing.
21. In the *Project Manager* toolbar, open **Table_Object_01.dwg** to display the tables.
    - If the **Table_Object_ 01.dwg** does not display in the Project list, in the *Project Manager* toolbar, click (Refresh).
22. Save and close all of the drawings.

End of practice

Chapter Review Questions

1. Which attributes on terminal symbols are used to link individual symbols to a terminal strip?
   a. Tag Strip, Number, Catalog
   b. Item, Catalog, Tag Strip
   c. Tag Strip, Installation, Location
   d. Installation, Location, Item

2. Which command would you use to insert multiple terminal symbols at fence crossing points on wires?
   a. Insert Component
   b. Multiple Insert Component
   c. Terminal (Panel List)
   d. Icon Menu Wizard

3. Does the wire number change across terminal symbols?
   a. Yes
   b. No
   c. It depends on the terminal symbol used, as some permit it, while others do not.
   d. It depends on the wire number change option setting in the *Wire Number Properties* dialog box.

4. When using the **Multiple Insert Component** command, how do you select the rungs on which to insert components?
   a. Fence Crossing selection
   b. Individual selection
   c. Window selection
   d. All are automatically selected

5. When using the *Terminal Strip Editor*, if you want to insert a table containing terminal data rather than inserting geometry representing the terminals, which option would you use?

   a. **Jumper Chart** option in the *Layout Preview* tab.

   b. **Graphical Terminal Strip** option in the *Layout Preview* tab.

   c. Enter **TABLE** in the *Annotation Format* field of the *Graphical Layout* area.

   d. **Tabular Terminal Strip** option in the *Layout Preview* tab.

6. How do you control the insertion coordinates when inserting a DIN rail? (Select all that apply.)

   a. Specify the coordinates and length in the *DIN Rail* dialog box.

   b. Specify the coordinates before you select the DIN rail in the *Insert Footprint* dialog box.

   c. Use the **Pick Rail Information >>** in the *DIN Rail* dialog box to get the coordinates from the drawing window.

   d. You cannot control the insertion coordinates when inserting a DIN rail.

Command Summary

Button	Command	Location
	**Edit Jumper**	• **Ribbon:** *Schematic* tab>*Edit Components panel* flyout
	**Multiple Insert Component**	• **Ribbon:** *Schematic* tab>*Insert Components* panel
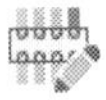	**Terminal Strip Editor**	• **Ribbon:** *Panel* tab>*Terminal Footprints* panel

Chapter

8

PLC Symbols

PLC modules function like any other schematic component and are required to be inserted in a drawing. You can add them using various methods, such as a variable parametric style, static full unit style, or individual I/O point style. Also, when using similar drawings in multiple designs, it is efficient to save data in a spreadsheet and then use the saved information to generate multiple drawings.

Learning Objectives

- Insert a parametric PLC module into a drawing.
- Insert a PLC component as a single component.
- Insert individual PLC I/O points in different areas of a drawing.
- Tag components and wires connected to PLC I/O points.
- Generate multiple drawings documenting PLC modules and their connecting components.

8.1 Insert PLC (Parametric)

PLC modules can be documented by inserting individual I/O points or by inserting the entire module as one symbol. PLC modules function like any other schematic components. They are AutoCAD® blocks with attributes for tagging, connection points, catalog information, and other data, as shown in Figure 8–1.

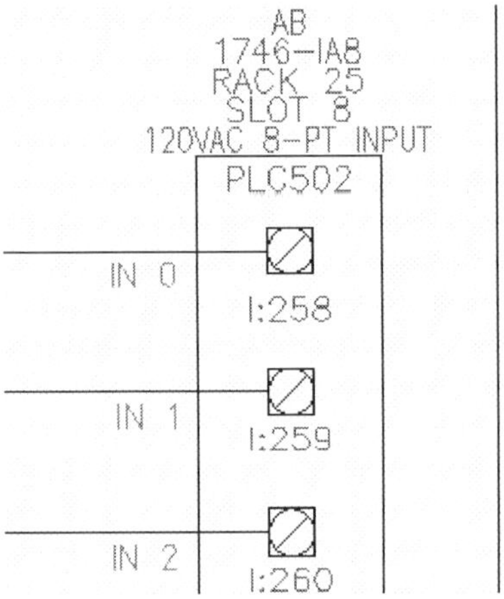

Figure 8–1

The **Insert PLC (Parametric)** command automates the insertion of an entire PLC module. Each I/O point is a block inserted on a rung of an existing ladder. After an I/O point is inserted, the command searches down the ladder for the next rung and inserts the next I/O point, thereby adjusting the spacing between I/O points to meet the rung spacing.

Insert PLC (Parametric)

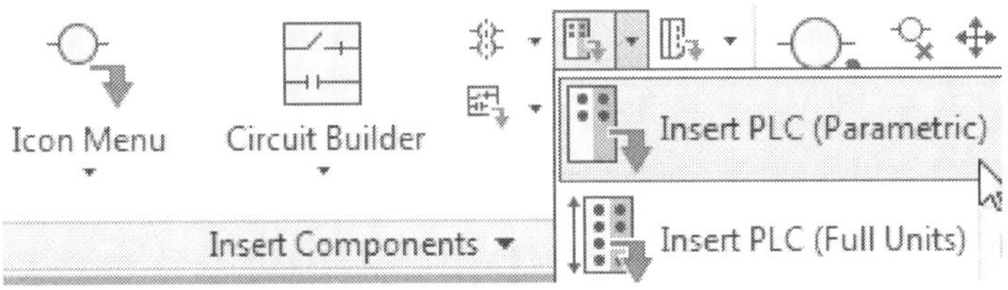

Ribbon: *Schematic* tab>*Insert Components* panel

Command Prompt: aeplcp

How To: Insert a Parametric PLC Module

1. Start the **Insert PLC (Parametric)** command. The *PLC Parametric Selection* dialog box opens.
2. Select the module and graphics style to use. Click **OK**.
3. Pick a rung in the drawing window to place the module. The *Module Layout* dialog box opens.
4. Specify the spacing to use between I/O points and whether to include spacers, breaks, and unused/extra connections. Click **OK**. The *I/O Point* dialog box opens.
5. Enter the rack number and slot number for the module. Click **OK**. The *I/O Address* dialog box opens.
6. Set the address for the first I/O point. Click **OK**.

- When the dialog boxes have been completed, the PLC is built on the selected ladder. If the PLC contains more than eight addressable points, you are prompted to use octal, decimal, or hexadecimal addressing for the remaining I/O points.
- A database file (**ace_plc.mdb**) contains the PLC manufacturer information, the number of I/O points for a module, and the blocks required to use for each I/O point. The default location of the file is *C:\Users\<user>\Documents\Acade <version>\ AeData\<language>\Plc* for Windows 10. This database can be edited using the **PLC Database File Editor** command to add PLC modules.

PLC Parametric Selection Dialog Box

The *PLC Parametric Selection* dialog box is shown in Figure 8–2.

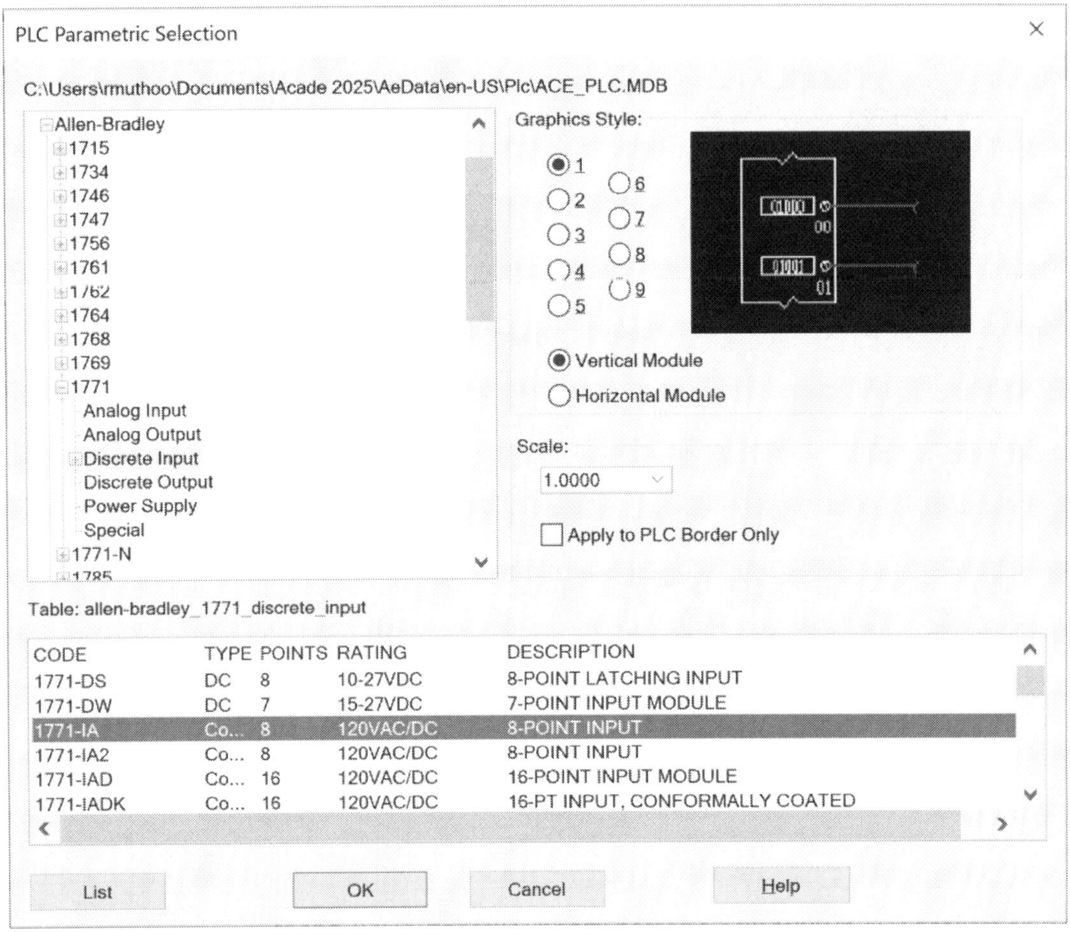

Figure 8–2

- In the *Manufacturer tree* area on the left side of the dialog box, select the manufacturer, series, series type, and code.
- In the *Graphics Style* area, select the graphic style to use with its preview displayed to control the appearance of I/O points. The software has five predefined styles and four empty styles for user-defined styles.
- In the *Scale* area, specify the scale to use for the module.
- Clicking **List** displays a report of PLC modules used in the project. Use it to determine the module types used or the slot numbers in which they are placed.
- The information for the selected module displays in the *Table* area of the dialog box.

Module Layout Dialog Box

After selecting the rung for the module, the *Module Layout* dialog box opens, as shown in Figure 8–3.

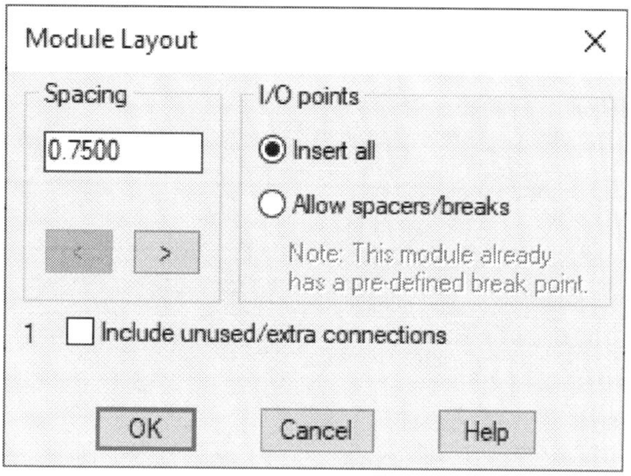

Figure 8–3

- Set the spacing between the I/O points. It defaults to the space between rungs for the selected ladder. Use **<** and **>** to step the spacing up or down.
- In the *I/O points* area, specify whether to insert all I/O points or enable spacers or breaks.
- If the **Include unused/extra connections** option is selected, the extra I/O points are included in the module, increasing its size.

I/O Point Dialog Box

After you populate the *Module Layout* dialog box and click **OK**, the *I/O Point* dialog box opens, as shown in Figure 8–4. The fields might vary depending on the type of module you are inserting.

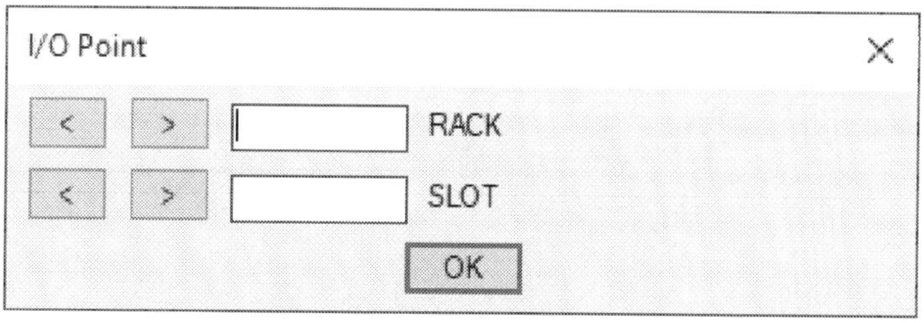

Figure 8–4

Enter values for RACK and SLOT. The information you input here populates attributes on the PLC symbol and can be used in the AutoCAD Electrical reporting tools.

I/O Address Dialog Box

The Rack and Slot values are used to build the *Quick picks* list in the *I/O Address* dialog box, as shown in Figure 8–5. Set the address for the first I/O point by selecting it from the *Quick picks* list or by entering an address in the *Beginning address* field. The addresses for the other I/O points are incremented from there.

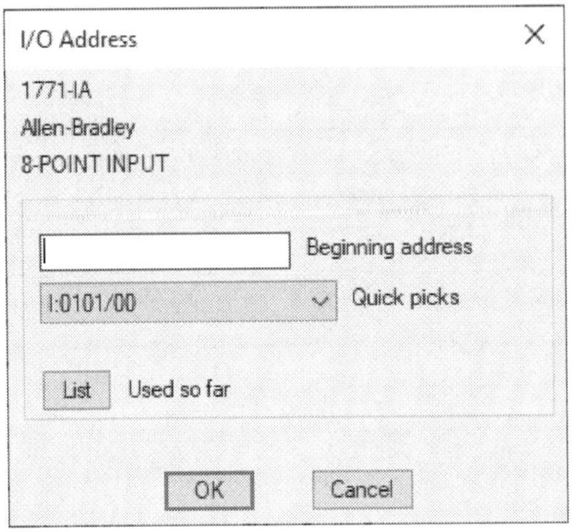

Figure 8–5

Spacers or Breaks

- Spacers skip the next rung in the ladder and is useful when more room is required to insert symbols or special wiring.
- Breaks continue the insertion of the PLC module at a different point in the drawing. This is useful when inserting large PLCs that do not fit on one ladder. You can also break a PLC and continue it in a different drawing.
- To use these options, you must select the **Allow spacers/breaks** option in the *Module Layout* dialog box. The *Custom Breaks/Spacing* dialog box opens at the possible I/O point, as shown in Figure 8–6.

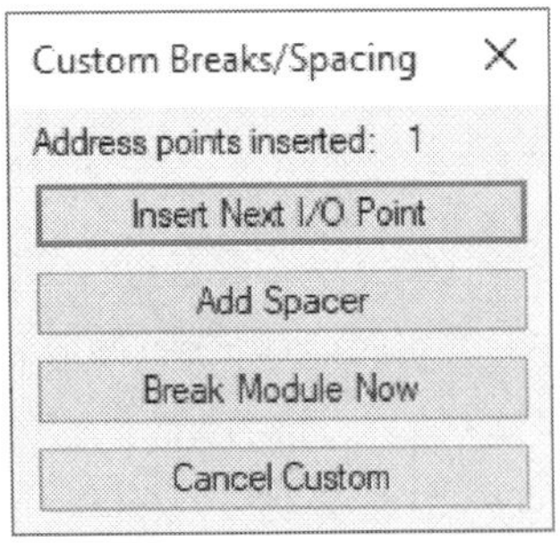

Figure 8–6

Insert Next I/O Point	Inserts the next I/O point on the rung.
Add Spacer	Skips that rung and moves to the next rung on the ladder.
Break Module Now	Breaks the module at the current I/O point.
Cancel Custom	Inserts the rest of the PLC module.

How To: Break a PLC and Continue in a Different Drawing

1. In the *Custom Breaks/Spacing* dialog box, click **Insert Next I/O Point** until you get to the I/O point where you want to break the module.
2. Click **Break Module Now** to break the module.
3. Press <Esc>. This saves the information for the module. This saving of data enables you to continue the module in another drawing.
    - If you want to insert the rest of the module in the same drawing, pick to place it instead of pressing <Esc>.
4. In the *Data Saved* dialog box, click **OK**.
5. Open the drawing into which you want to place the rest of the module.
6. Start the **Insert PLC (Parametric)** command. The *Continue "Broken" Module* dialog box opens.
    - You can continue the module here or start a new one. If you start a new module, the saved information for the previous module is discarded. The warning dialog box does not open.
7. In the *Continue "Broken" Module* dialog box, click **Continue Module**.
8. Select a rung to place the PLC module. The *Module Layout* dialog box opens.
9. Insert the rest of the I/O points of the module including any spacers or breaks.

- When a PLC module is inserted, it is a single block object. If you need to increase the spacing between two I/O points after a module is inserted, use the **Stretch PLC Module** command. It enables you to stretch the module at an I/O point.
- If you need to break a module after it is inserted, use the **Split PLC Module** command. It breaks the module at the selected point.

8.2 Insert PLC (Full Units)

The **Insert PLC (Full Units)** command inserts a PLC module as a single symbol. It does not adjust the spacing between I/O points as the **Insert PLC (Parametric)** command does. It breaks wires on ladder rungs if they intersect a connection point, as shown in Figure 8–7.

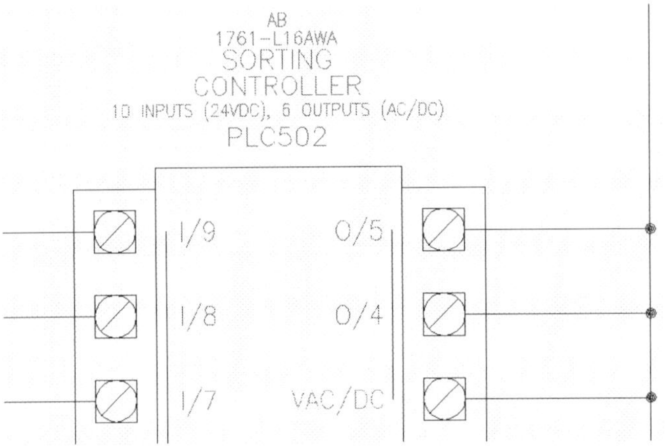

Figure 8–7

Insert PLC (Full Units)

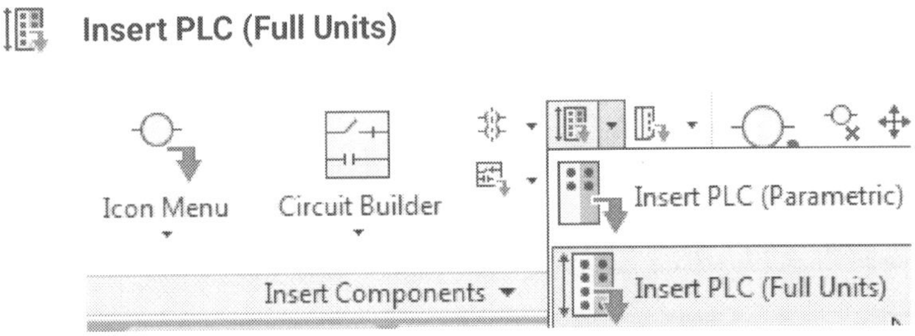

Ribbon: *Schematic* tab>*Insert Components* panel

Command Prompt: aeplc

How To: Use the Insert PLC (Full Units) Command

1. Start the **Insert PLC (Full Units)** command. The *Insert Component* dialog box opens; set to the **PLC Fixed Units** submenu.
2. Select the module category.
3. Select the module to insert.
4. Pick the insertion point for the module. The *Edit PLC Module* dialog box opens.

5. Fill in the fields in the *Edit PLC Module* dialog box.
6. Click **OK**.

- Use the **Edit Component** command to modify the attribute information attached to a PLC module. It opens the *Edit PLC Module* dialog box. This command works with PLC modules inserted using the **Parametric** and **Full Units** commands.

The **Insert PLC (Full Units)** command is similar to inserting a schematic component from the Icon Menu. In the PLC Fixed Units submenu in the *Insert Component* dialog box, select the PLC type to insert, as shown in Figure 8–8. A submenu opens. Select the module to insert from this menu.

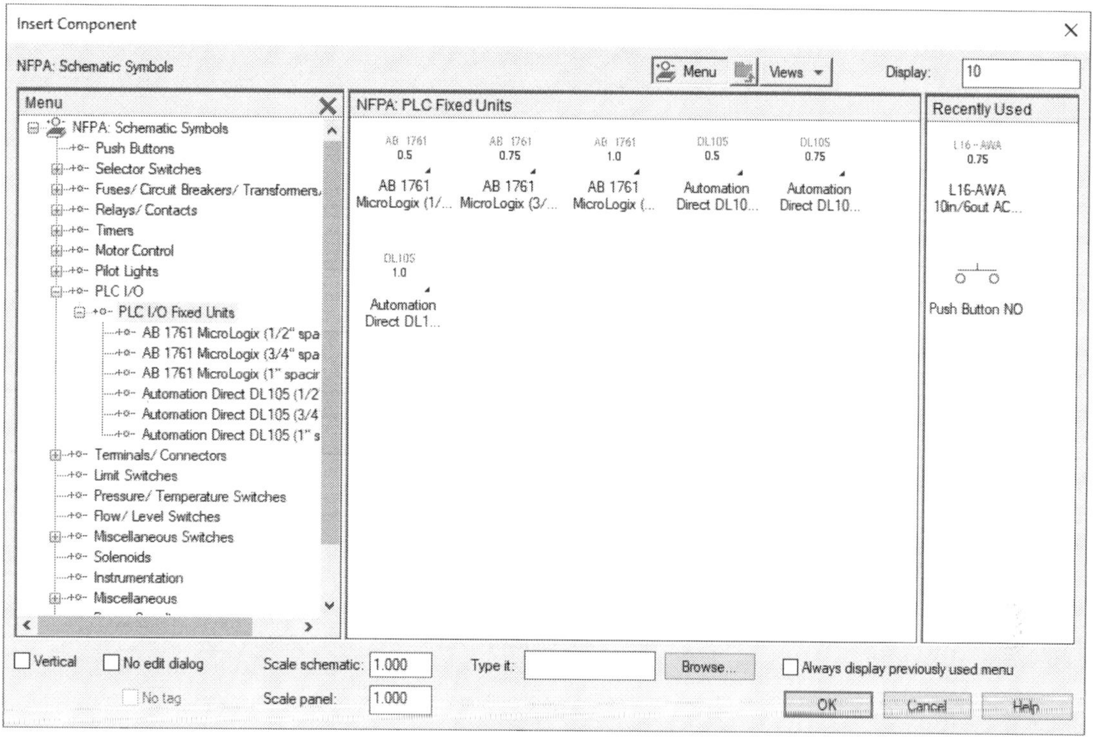

Figure 8–8

After you pick the insertion point for the module, the *Edit PLC Module* dialog box opens, as shown in Figure 8–9. It is similar to the *Insert / Edit Component* dialog box used for schematic symbols. You can insert a description for each I/O point by selecting the address in the *Addressing* area and then typing the descriptions in the *I/O Point Description* area.

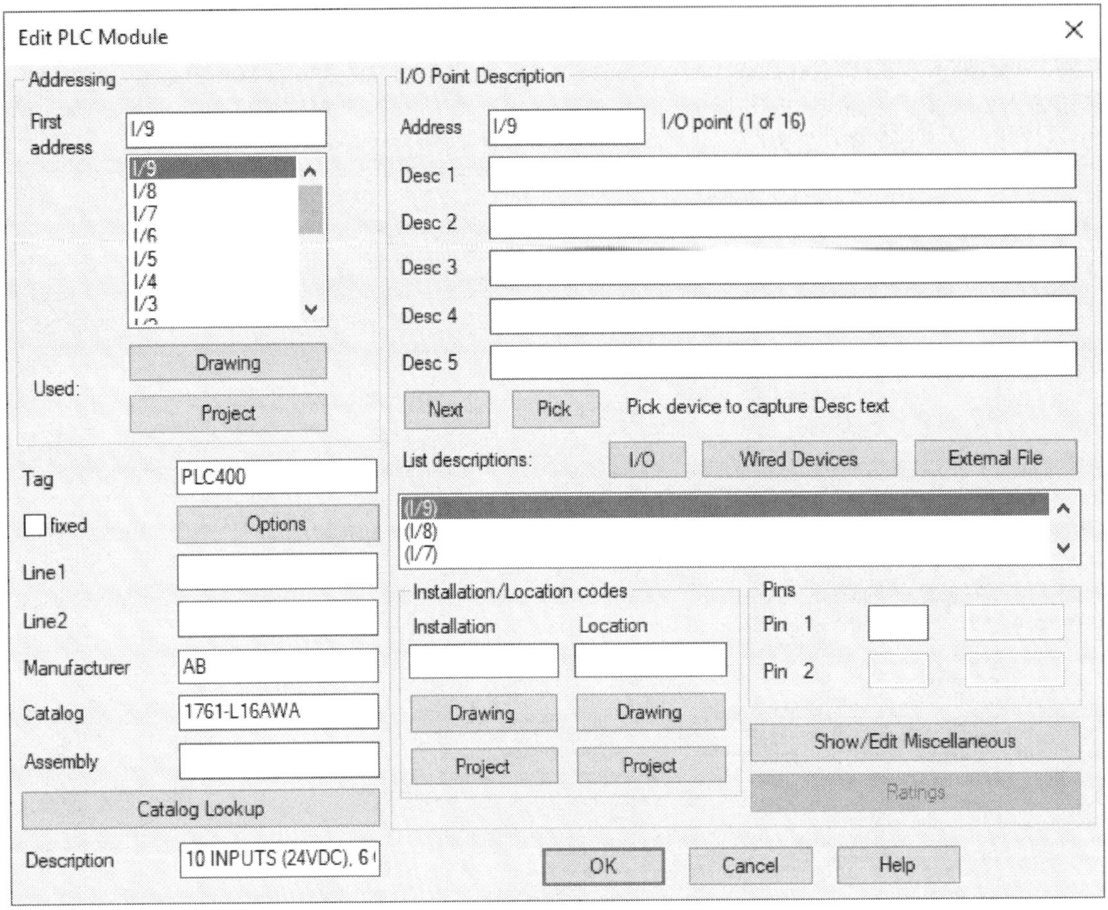

Figure 8–9

8.3 Insert Individual PLC I/O Points

You can insert individual I/O points in different areas of the drawing as shown in Figure 8–10 or even in different drawings. The PLC I/O points are parent/child schematic symbols. The parent symbol displays a list of reference numbers for the child symbols and contains the catalog information for the PLC module. The child symbol displays the reference number of the parent symbol.

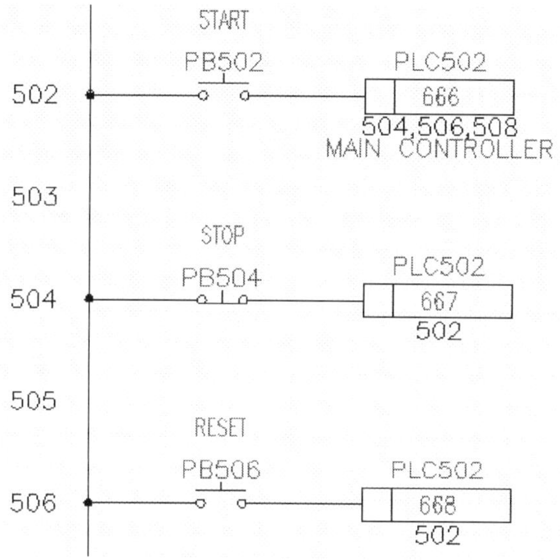

Figure 8–10

How To: Insert Individual I/O Points

1. Click  (Icon Menu (Insert Component)). The *Insert Component* dialog box opens.
2. In the icon area, click 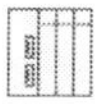 (PLC I/O) or, in the menu area, select **PLC I/O**. The **PLC I/O** submenu opens.
3. Select the symbol to insert.
4. Select the insertion point for the I/O symbol. The *Edit PLC I/O Point* dialog box opens.
5. Fill in the fields in the *Edit PLC I/O Point* dialog box. If inserting a child I/O point, be sure to link to a parent symbol.
6. Click **OK**.

Use the **Icon Menu (Insert Component)** command to insert individual I/O points. These points can be found in the **PLC I/O** submenu in the *Insert Component* dialog box, as shown in Figure 8–11. The symbols marked 1st point are the parent symbols and the symbols marked 2nd+ are the child symbols.

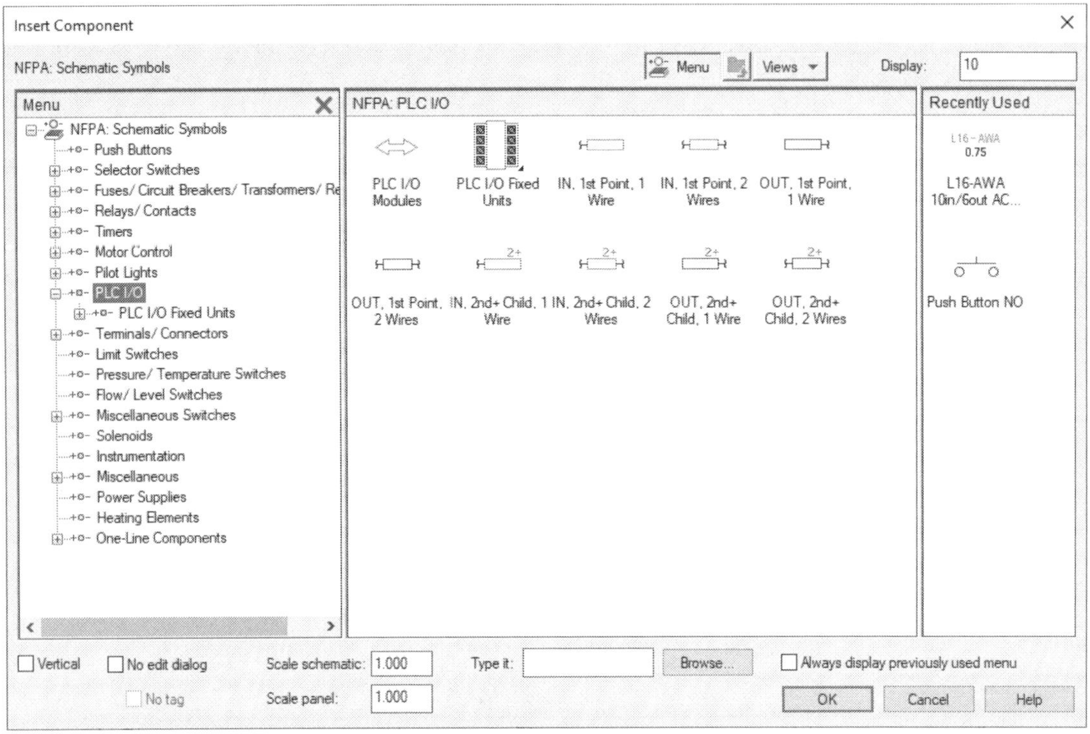

Figure 8–11

After placing an I/O point symbol, the *Edit PLC I/O Point* dialog box opens as shown in Figure 8–12.

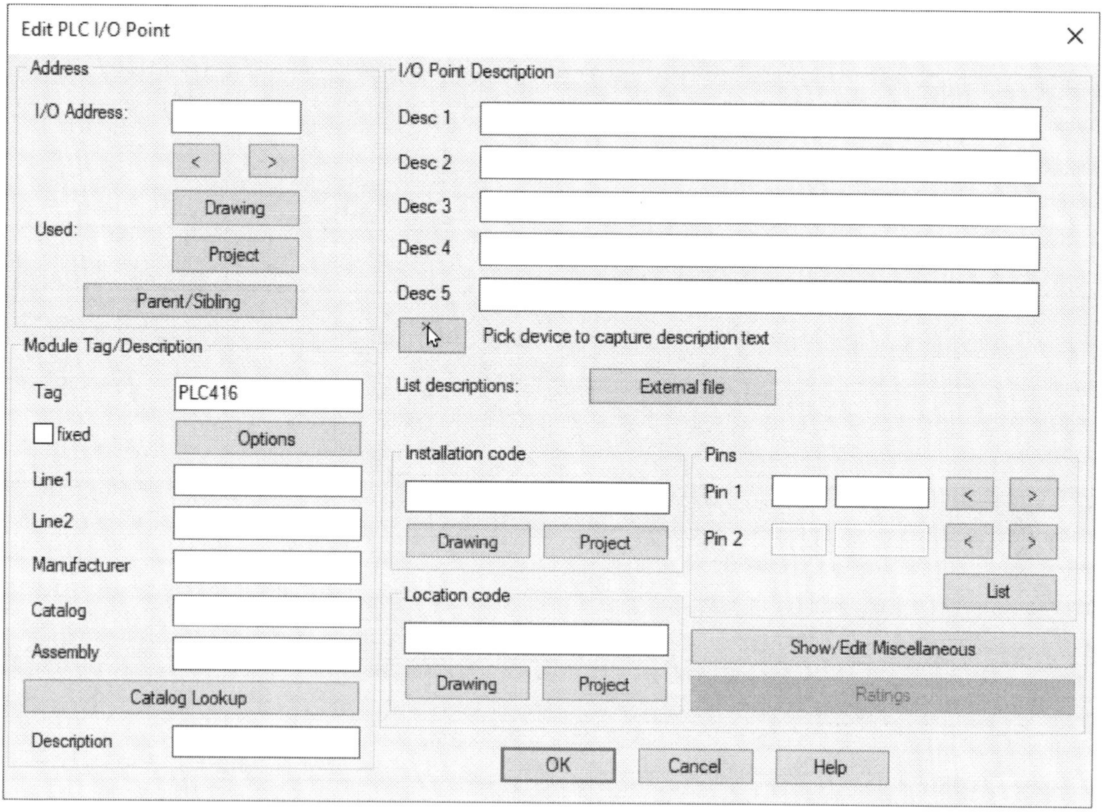

Figure 8–12

- For the parent symbol, enter the I/O Address and assign the catalog information.
- For the child symbols, assign the I/O Address and link to the parent component.
- Click **Parent/Sibling** to pick the parent or sibling symbol in the drawing.
- Click **Drawing** or **Project** to display a list of PLC modules and select from the list to link the child symbol.
- The parent symbol carries the catalog information in the attributes. Child symbols do not have the catalog option available.

8.4 PLC Based Tagging

Component tags and wire numbers can use the PLC address instead of the ladder reference number as shown in Figure 8–13. For both, it can be set in the *Drawing Properties* dialog box. If the option is set, the software checks whether the symbol or wire is connected to an I/O point. If it is, the I/O address is used. If not, the ladder reference number is used.

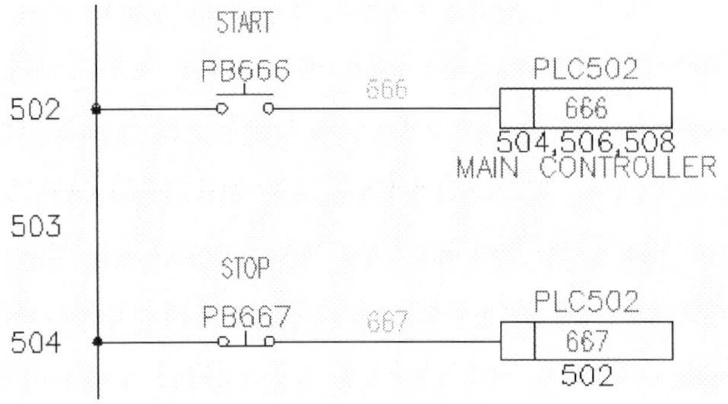

Figure 8–13

Drawing Properties

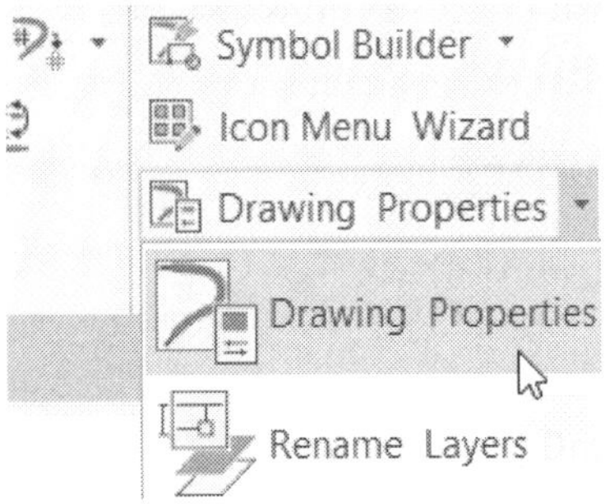

Ribbon: *Schematic* tab>*Other Tools* panel

Command Prompt: aeproperties

How To: Set the Search for PLC I/O Points on Insert Option

1. Start the **Drawing Properties** command. The *Drawing Properties* dialog box opens.
2. Select the *Components* tab.
3. In the *Component TAG Format* area, select **Search for PLC I/O address on insert**, as shown in Figure 8–14.

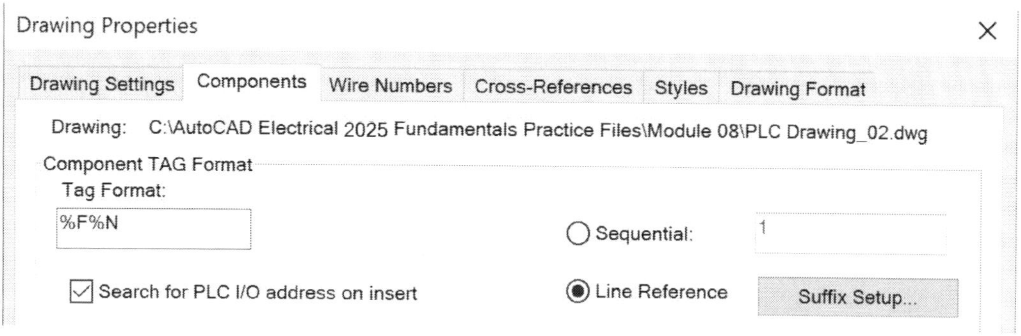

Figure 8–14

4. Select the *Wire Numbers* tab.
5. In the *Wire Number Format* area, select **Search for PLC I/O address on insert**.
   - Selecting this option adds time to component tagging and wire numbering, as the I/O point for each one needs to be checked while it is inserted. Depending on the size of your project, this process might or might not be noticeable.
6. Click **OK**.
7. If there are existing symbols or wire numbers, run the **Retag Components** and **Insert Wire Number** commands.

- Component tags can be set to use the PLC address on an individual symbol basis. When inserting or editing a symbol, click **Use PLC Address** in the *Insert / Edit Component* dialog box, as shown in Figure 8–15.

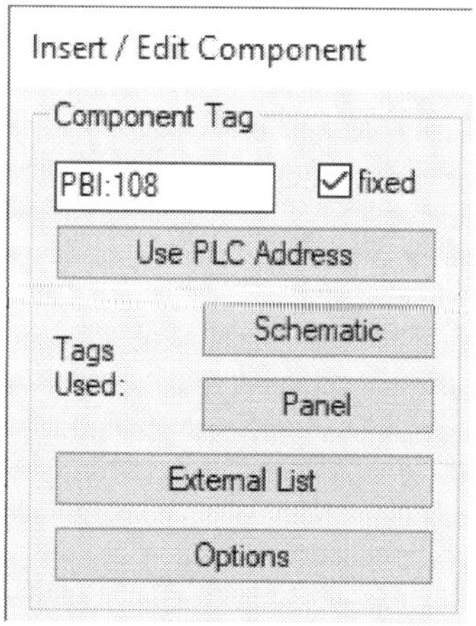

Figure 8–15

The PLC address check is only performed when symbols or tags are initially inserted. If the **PLC address** option in Drawing Properties is changed after the symbols and wire numbers have been inserted, they need to be retagged using the **Insert Wire Numbers** or **Retag Components** commands.

Practice 8a
Insert Parametric PLC Modules

Practice Objectives

- Insert parametric PLC modules.
- Insert components and connect them to PLC I/O points.

In this practice, you will insert a PLC module using the **Insert PLC (Parametric)** command. You will then insert a ladder into the drawing. You will also use the **Insert PLC (Parametric)** command to insert a PLC module that includes spacers and a break. Finally, you will insert two push button symbols: one using a referenced based component tag and the other using a PLC address based component tag. The final schematic displays as shown in Figure 8–16.

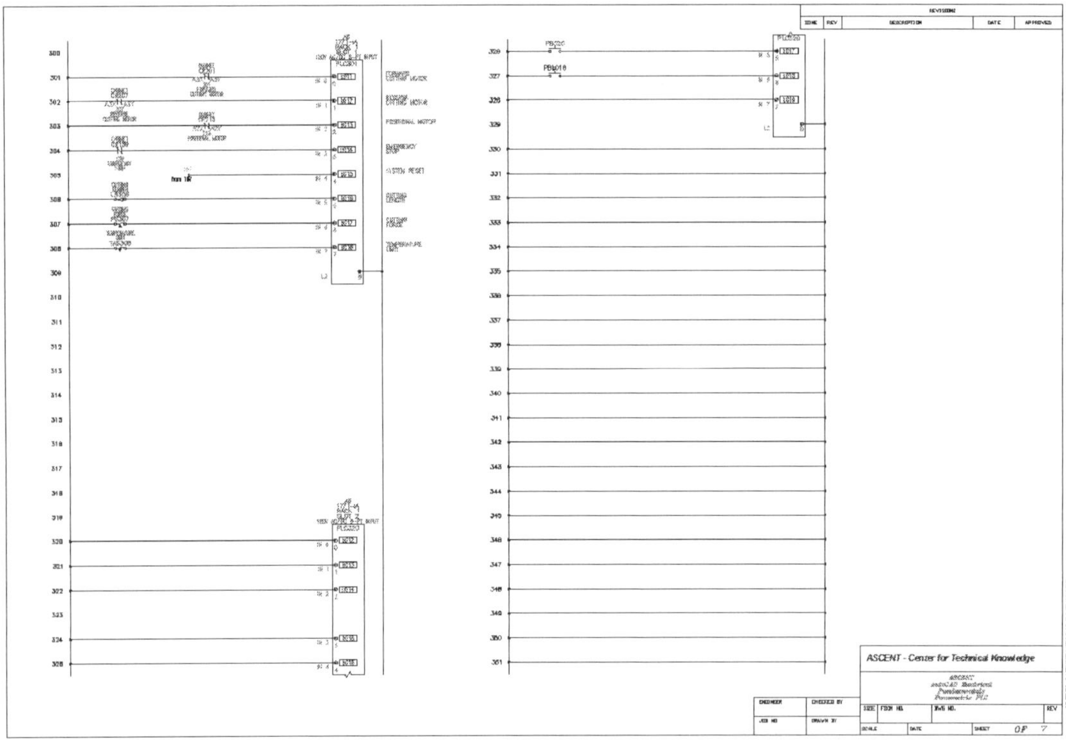

Figure 8–16

Task 1: Insert a PLC module.

1. In your practice files folder, in the *Module 08* folder, open the **Module 08** project file.
2. In the **Module 08** project, open **PLC Drawing.dwg**.
3. Zoom to the top portion of the ladder (lines 300 to 306).
4. In the *Schematic* tab>*Insert Components* panel, click  (Insert PLC (Parametric)).
5. The *PLC Parametric Selection* dialog box opens. Expand **Allen-Bradley**, **1771**, and **Discrete Input**. Select **1771-IA** in the lower portion list, as shown in Figure 8–17. Click **OK**.

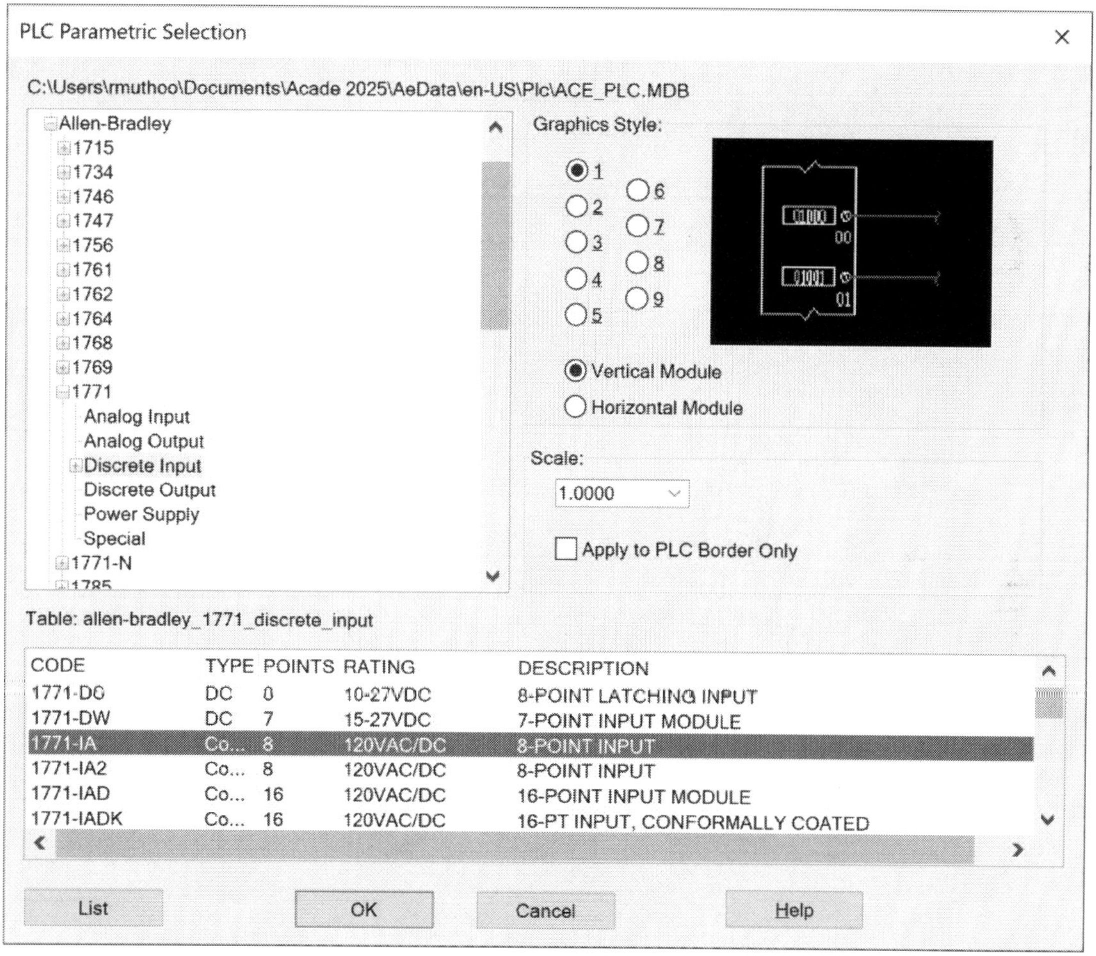

Figure 8–17

6. Pick a point on wire 301 near the right end, as shown in Figure 8–18.

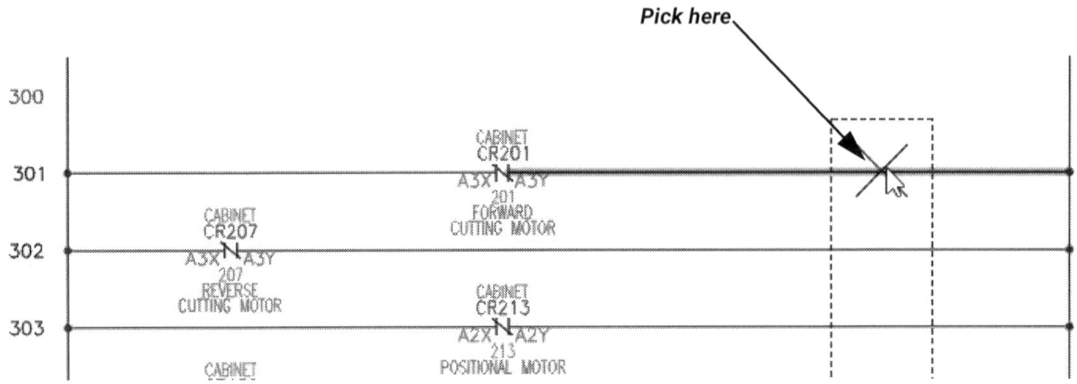

Figure 8–18

7. The *Module Layout* dialog box opens. Click **OK**.
8. In the *I/O Point* dialog box that opens, set the following (as shown in Figure 8–19), and then click **OK**:
   - *RACK*: **1**
   - *SLOT*: **1**

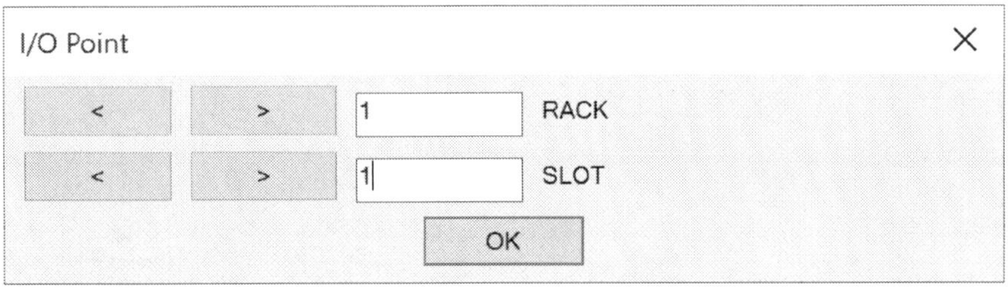

Figure 8–19

9. The *I/O Address* dialog box opens. In the *Quick picks* drop-down list, select **I:011**. Note that the *Beginning address* field automatically updates, as shown in Figure 8–20. Click **OK**.

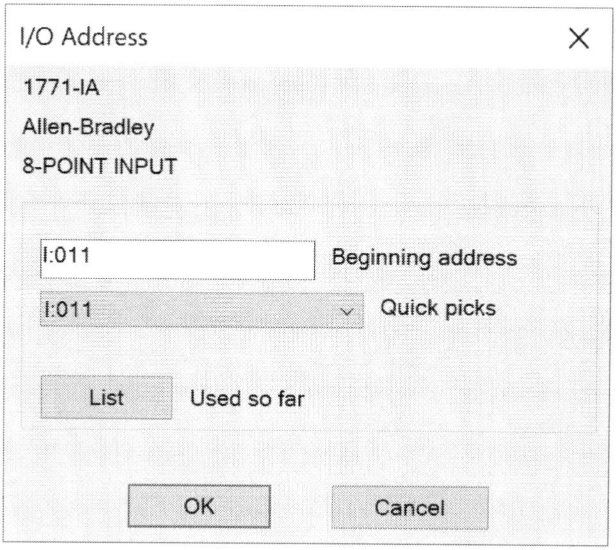

Figure 8–20

10. The *I/O Addressing* dialog box opens as shown in Figure 8–21. Click **Decimal**. The PLC module is inserted into the drawing.

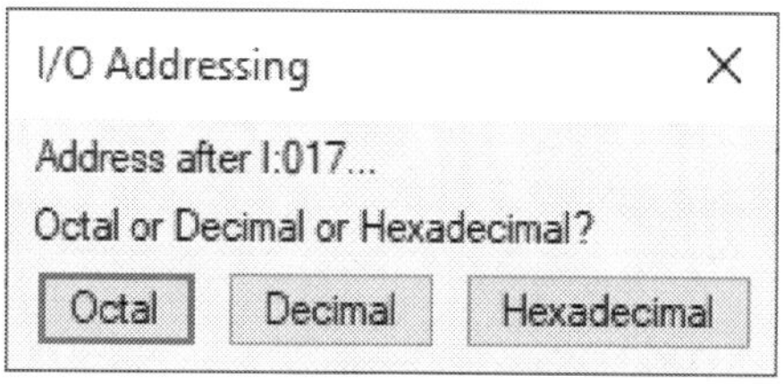

Figure 8–21

Task 2: Edit a PLC module.

1. Right-click on the PLC module you just inserted and select **Edit Component**.
2. The *Edit PLC Module* dialog box opens. In the *I/O Point Description* area, for *List descriptions*, click **Wired Devices**. The descriptions of the devices wired to the PLC are listed, as shown in Figure 8–22.

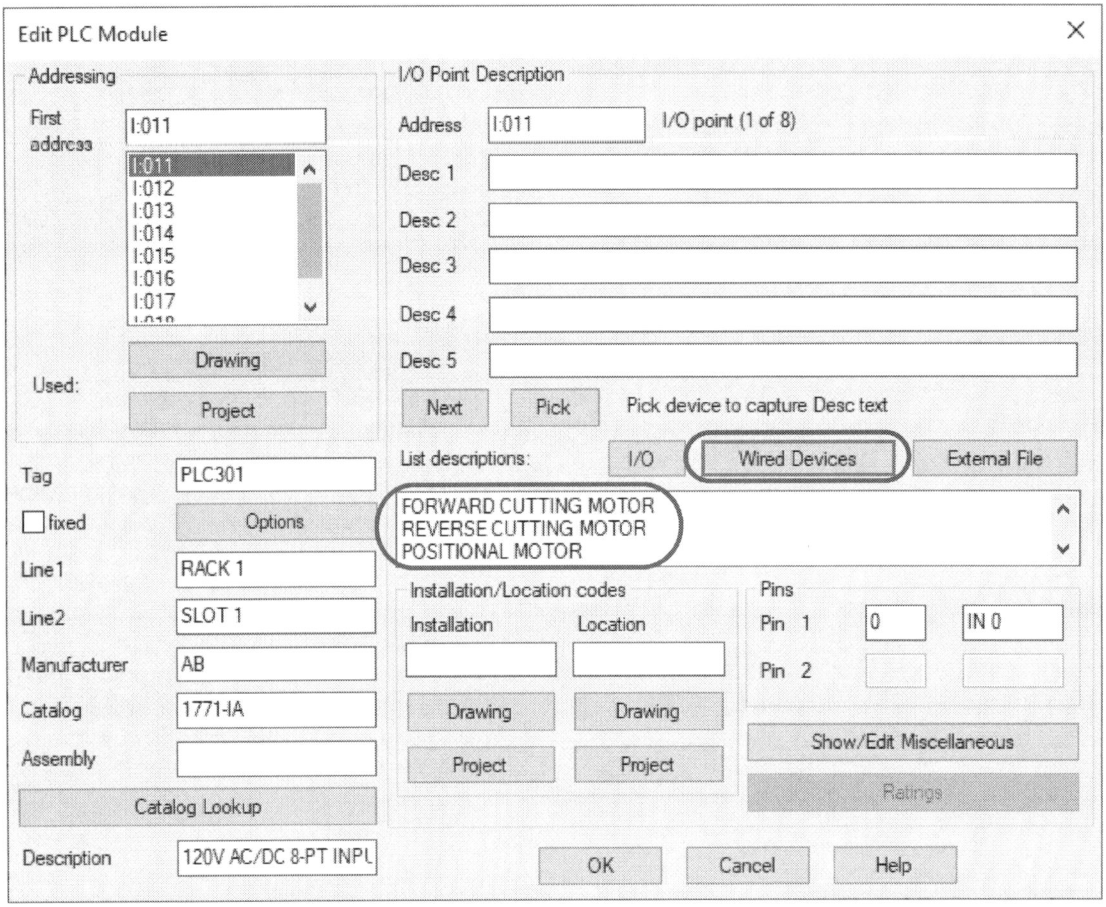

Figure 8–22

3. In the *Addressing* area, verify that **I:011** is selected. In the *List descriptions* area, select the first description, **FORWARD CUTTING MOTOR**.

4. In the *CONFIRMATION* dialog box, note that **FORWARD** displays in *Description 1* and **CUTTING MOTOR** displays in *Description 2*, as shown in Figure 8–23. Click **OK**. Note that the descriptions are automatically filled in the required fields in the *I/O Point Description* area.

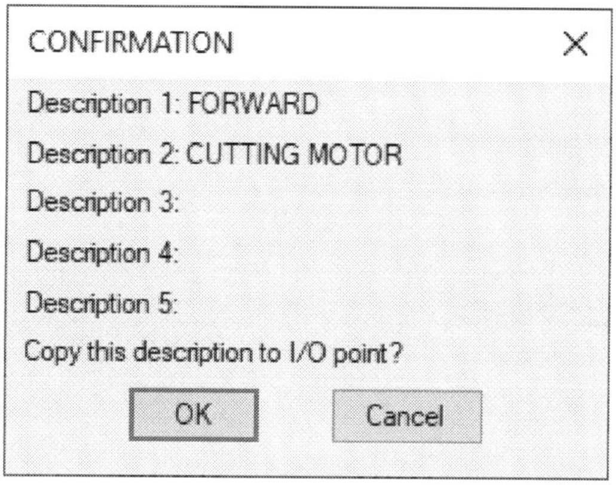

Figure 8–23

5. In the *Edit PLC Module* dialog box, repeat for each I/O Point by selecting the next address, such as **1:012** in the *Addressing* area. The corresponding description is highlighted in the list, such as **REVERSE CUTTING MOTOR** for **1:012**. Explicitly click on the highlighted **REVERSE CUTTING MOTOR** description to open the CONFIRMATION dialog box and click **OK**. This automatically enters the required information in the *I/O Point Description* fields.
   - Similarly, enter the descriptions for **1:013** and **1:014**.
   - For **I:015**, note that its corresponding highlighted description is **I:015**, indicating that it does not have a corresponding description. For **I:015**, in the *Desc 1* field, type **SYSTEM RESET**.
   - Continue until the descriptions have been entered for the last I/O Point, which is **1:018**.

6. Click **OK** in the *Edit PLC Module* dialog box and note the descriptions listed next to each I/O Point in the PLC module in the drawing, as shown in Figure 8–24.

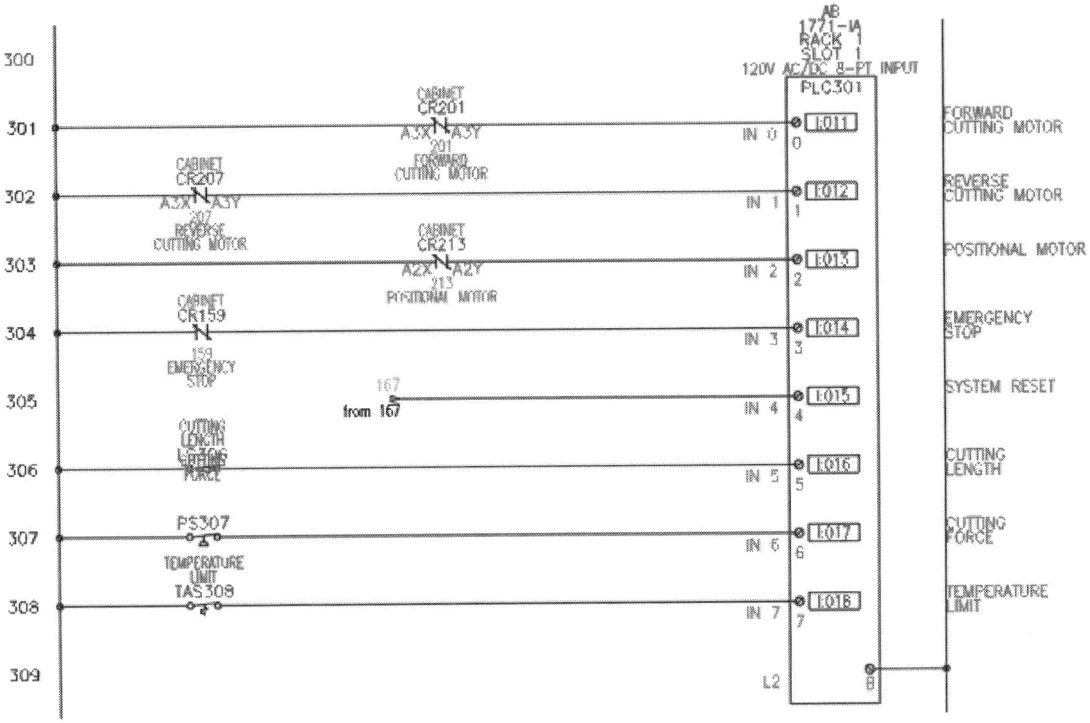

Figure 8–24

Task 3: Insert a PLC module with spacers and breaks.

1. In the ladder, use the **Trim Wire** command to trim the wires from lines 314 to 319.
   - Use the **Fence** option to speed up the process.
2. Insert a second ladder with **26** rungs, on the right side of the current ladder. Leave the other settings as default, click **OK** and pick **16,21** as the insertion point (on the right side of the original ladder). Note that the first wire of the ladder starts from number 326.
3. Zoom to wires 320 to 325 in the first ladder.
4. In the *Schematic* tab>*Insert Components* panel, click (Insert PLC (Parametric)).
5. The *PLC Parametric Selection* dialog box opens. Verify that the PLC module that you previously inserted (**Allen Bradley**, **1771**, **Discrete Input**, and **1771-IA**) is still selected. Click **OK**.

6. Pick a point on wire 320 near the right end, as shown in Figure 8–25.

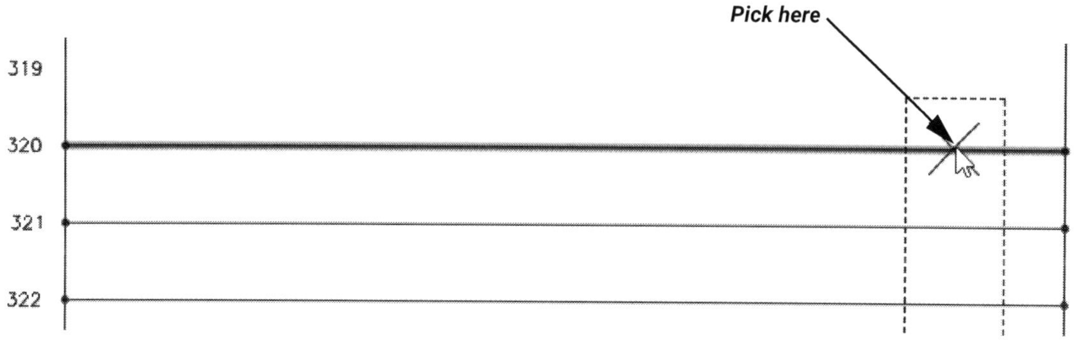

Figure 8–25

7. In the *Module Layout* dialog box, in the *I/O points* area, select **Allow spacers/breaks** (as shown in Figure 8–26), and click **OK**.

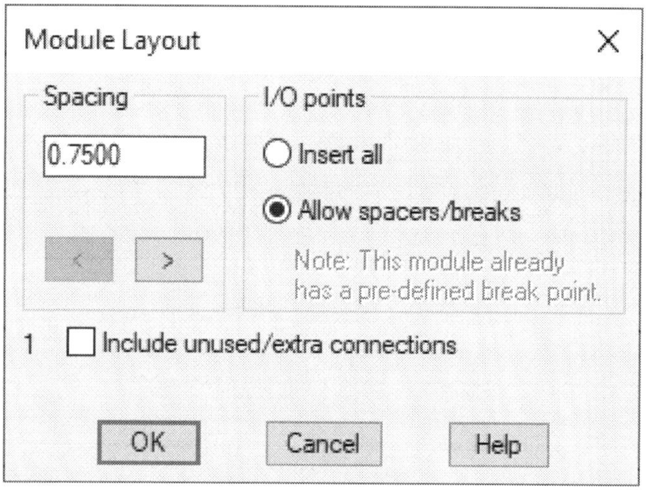

Figure 8–26

8. In the *I/O Point* dialog box that opens, set the following:
   * *RACK*: **1**
   * *SLOT:* **2**
9. Click **OK**.

10. In the *I/O Address* dialog box, in the *Quick picks* drop-down list, select **I:012** as shown in Figure 8–27. Click **OK**.

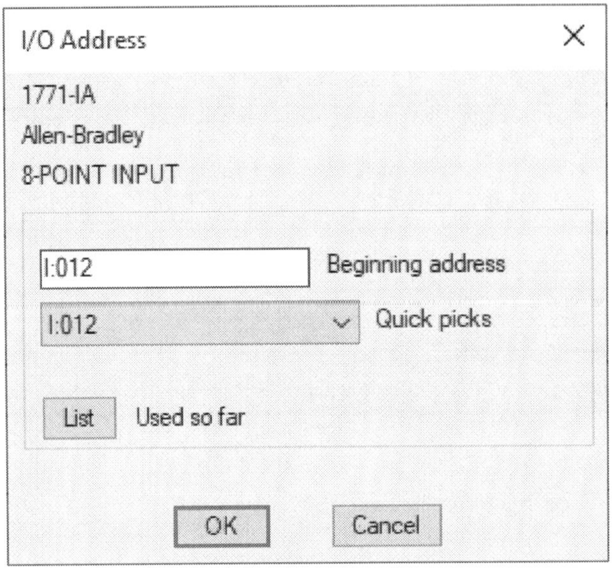

Figure 8–27

11. The *Custom Breaks/Spacing* dialog box opens as shown in Figure 8–28. Click **Insert Next I/O Point**.

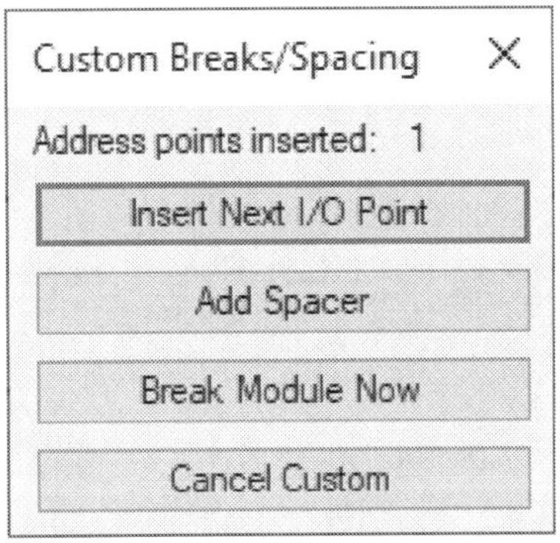

Figure 8–28

12. Click **Insert Next I/O Point** again.
13. Click **Add Spacer** to insert a spacer at line 323. A red **X** displays on line 323 to indicate that a spacer was inserted.
14. Click **Insert Next I/O Point** two more times to add I/O points on lines 324 and 325.
15. Click **Break Module Now** to break the module. The remainder of the PLC is attached to the cursor.

16. Click a point near the right end of the wire on line 326. Line 326 is at the top of the second ladder.
17. In the *Module Layout* dialog box, select **Insert all** and click **OK**.
18. In the *I/O Addressing* dialog box, click **Decimal**.

Task 4: Insert components.

1. Insert a normally open push button near the left side of the wire on line 326 ((Icon Menu)> (Push Buttons)> (Push Button NO)).
2. In the *Insert / Edit Component* dialog box, verify that the component tag is PB326. Click **OK**.
3. Insert another normally open push button, and place it on line 327, below the PB326. The *Insert / Edit Component* dialog box opens.
4. In the *Component Tag* area, click **Use PLC Address**. The component tag is changed to **PBI:018** and **fixed** is automatically selected, as shown in Figure 8–29. Click **OK**.

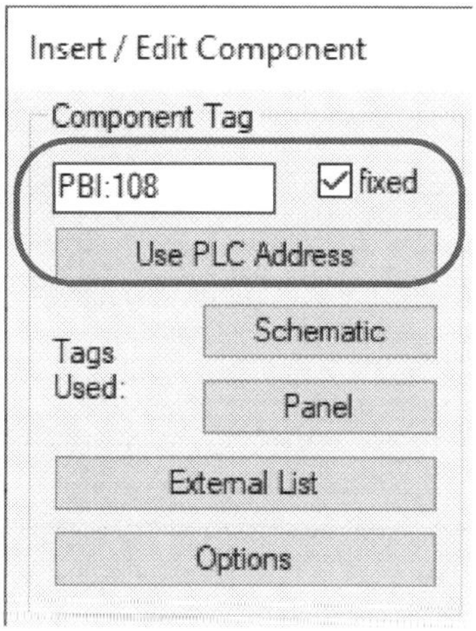

Figure 8–29

5. Trim the wire on line 323, which does not have an I/O point because a spacer was added.
6. Save and close **PLC Drawing.dwg**.

End of practice

Practice 8b
Insert a Full Units PLC Module

Practice Objective

- Insert a PLC module as a single component symbol.

In this practice, you will insert a ladder into an existing drawing. You will then insert a PLC module using the **Insert PLC (Full Units)** command. The final schematic displays as shown in Figure 8–30.

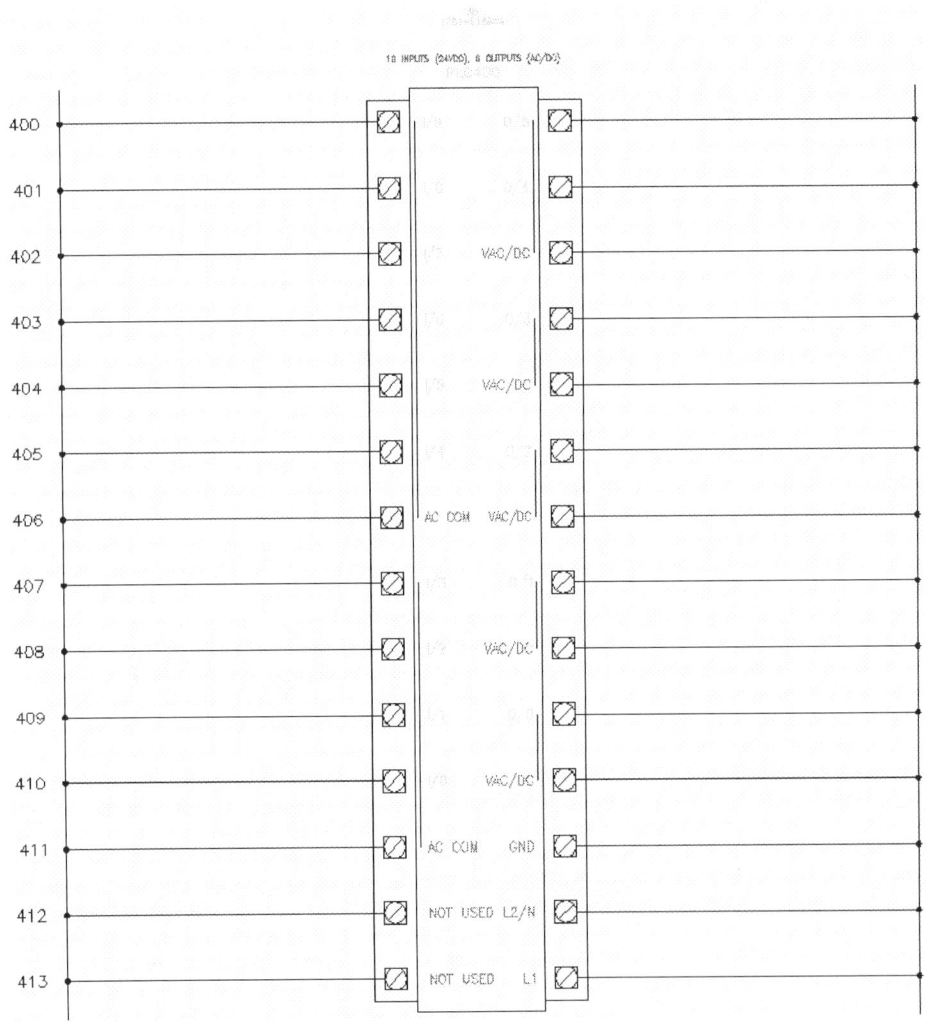

Figure 8–30

1. If the **Module 08** project is not active, open and activate it now.
2. In the **Module 08** project, open **PLC Drawing_02.dwg**.
3. Insert a ladder with **26** *Rungs* and set the *1st Reference* number to **400**, as shown in Figure 8–31. Leave the other settings as default. Click **OK** and pick **2,21** as the insertion point.

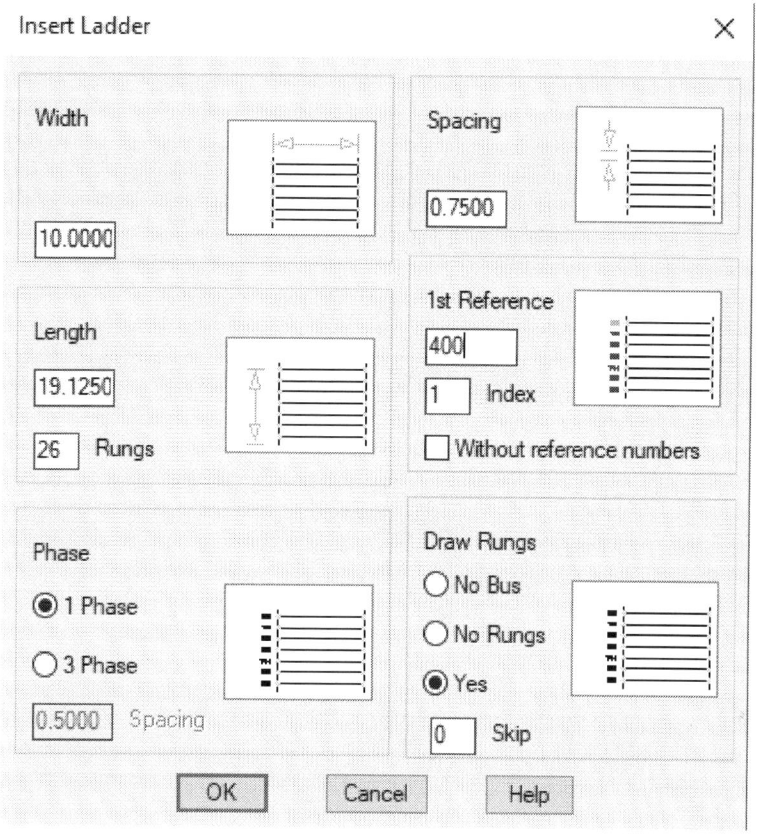

Figure 8–31

4. Zoom to the top portion of the ladder.

5. In the *Schematic* tab>*Insert Components* panel, click (Insert PLC (Full Units)).

6. The *Insert Component* dialog box opens. Click (AB 1761 MicroLogix (3/4" spacing)), as shown in Figure 8–32.

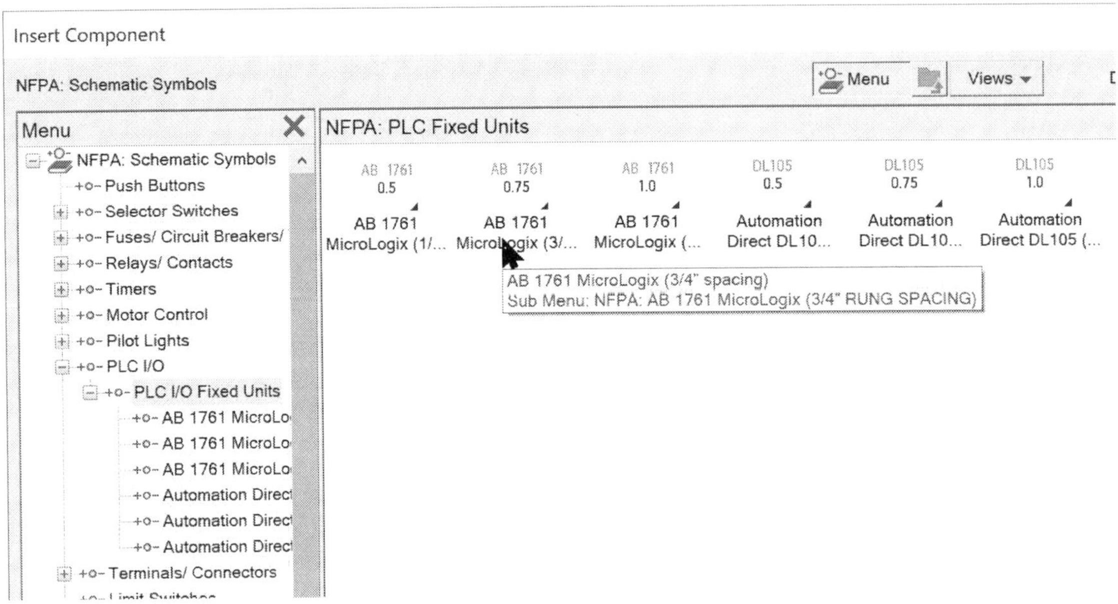

Figure 8–32

7. The **AB 1761 MicroLogix (3/4" RUNG SPACING)** submenu opens. Click (L16-AWA 10in/6out AC-DC/115AC-DC), which is the first entry, as shown in Figure 8–33.

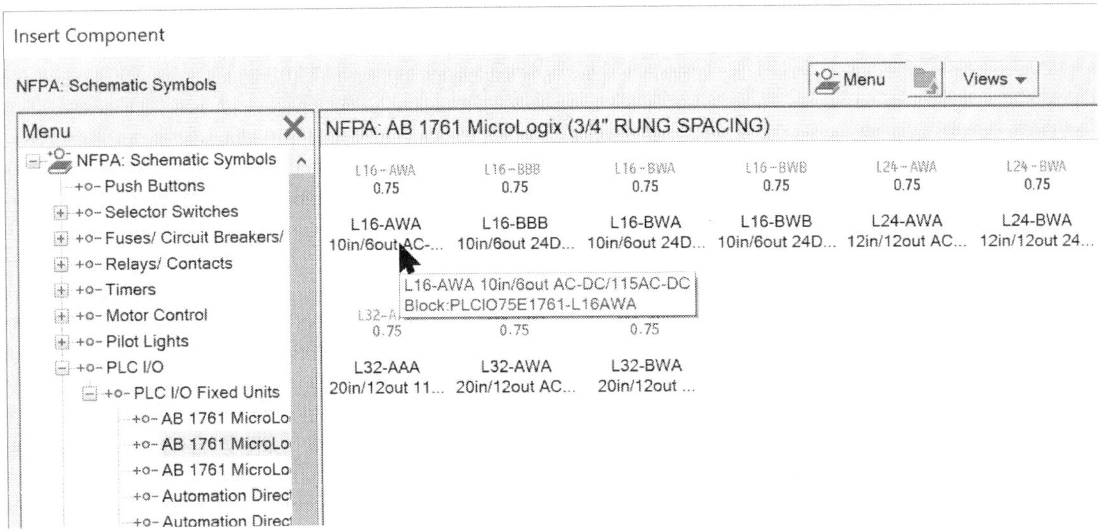

Figure 8–33

8. Pick a point near the middle of the wire on line 400.
9. The *Edit PLC Module* dialog box opens. Click **OK**. The full PLC module is inserted as a single component.
   - You might be required to map the symbol.
10. Save and close **PLC Drawing_02.dwg**.

End of practice

8.5 Spreadsheet to PLC I/O Utility

The **PLC I/O Utility** command is used to quickly generate multiple drawings containing PLC modules and their accompanying components. This command is most useful when you use similar drawings in multiple designs. When it is run, the AutoCAD Electrical software reads data from an Excel spreadsheet (as shown in Figure 8–34) and uses the information to generate drawings.

	A	B	C	D	E	F	G	
1	CODE	R	G	S	ADDR	RTP	DESC1	DESC2
2	1771-IAD	1	2	0	I:002/00	TB20	BANK #1 FIBER	WASTE
3					I:002/01		BANK #1 FIBER	WASTE
4					I:002/02		BANK #2 FIBER	WASTE
5					I:002/03		BANK #2 FIBER	WASTE
6					I:002/04		TUB OUTLET TEMPERATURE	NOT LC
7					I:002/05		TUB INLET TO HEATER FLOW	NOT LC
8					I:002/06		SPARE	
9					I:002/07		COMBUSTION BLOWER	RUNNI
10					I:002/10		INSTRUMENT AIR PRESSURE	NOT LC
11					SPACER			
12					I:002/11		AIR DAMPER	AT HIG
13					I:002/12		AIR DAMPER	AT LOV
14					I:002/13		PURGE AIR FLOW	NOT LC
15					I:002/14		COMBUSTION AIR PRESSURE	NOT LC
16					I:002/15		SPARE	

Figure 8–34

PLC I/O Utility

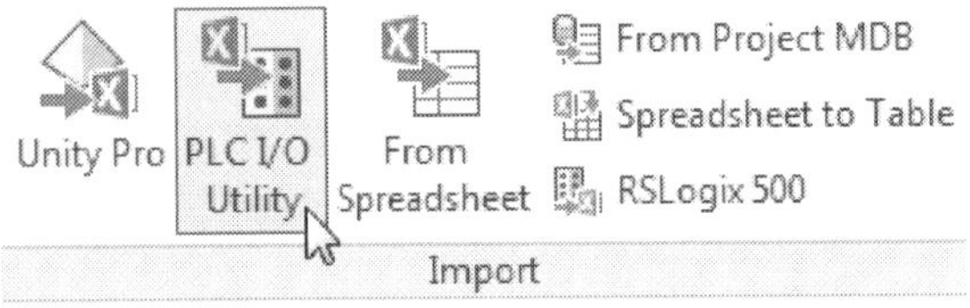

Ribbon: *Import/Export Data* tab>*Import* panel

Command Prompt: aess2plc

How To: Use the Spreadsheet to PLC I/O Utility Command

1. Start the **Spreadsheet to PLC I/O Utility** command. The *Select PLC I/O Spreadsheet Output File* dialog box opens.
2. Select the spreadsheet to use. Click **Open**. The *Spreadsheet to PLC I/O Utility* dialog box opens.
3. Click **Setup** to open the *Spreadsheet to PLC I/O Utility Setup* dialog box.

4. Click **Spreadsheet/Table Columns**. The *Spreadsheet to PLC I/O Drawing Generator* dialog box opens as shown in Figure 8–35. Verify that the data in the spreadsheet is mapped correctly and make any required changes. Click **OK**.

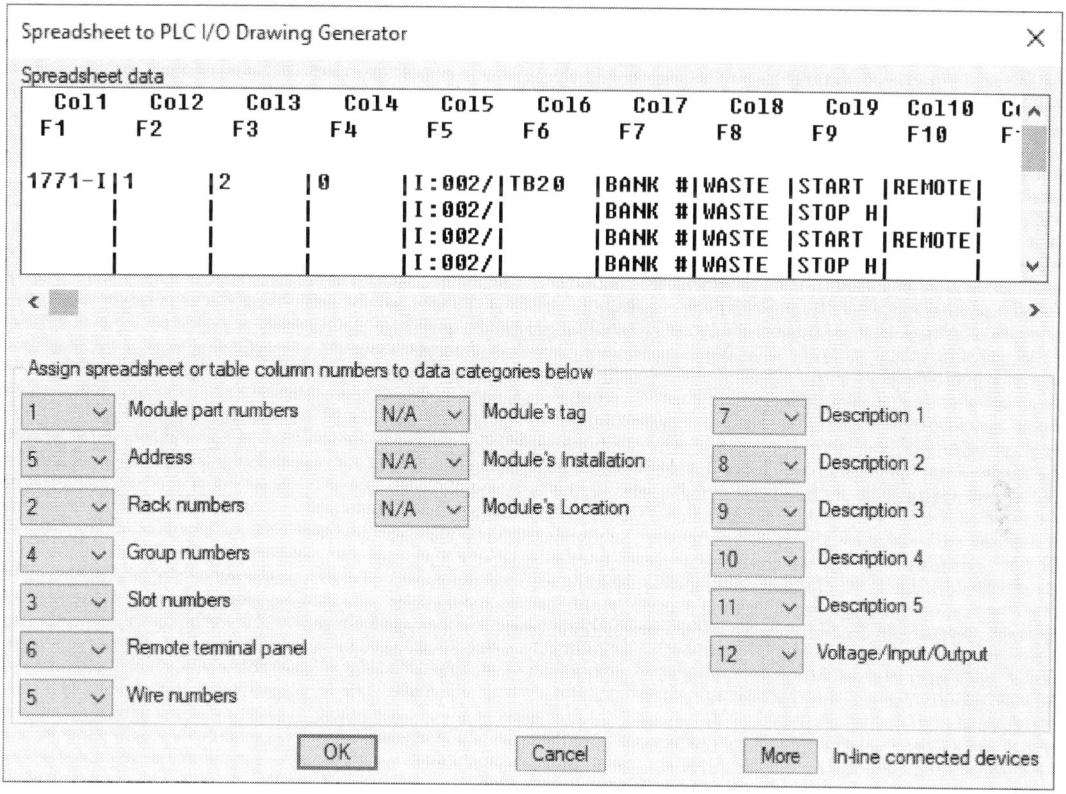

Figure 8–35

5. In the *Spreadsheet to PLC I/O Utility Setup* dialog box, configure any other required settings. Click **OK** to return to the *Spreadsheet to PLC I/O Utility* dialog box.
6. Set the reference number and other options. Click **Start**.
7. If the **Pause between drawings** option is selected, the *Spreadsheet to PLC I/O Utility* dialog box opens before each drawing is created. Change any settings and click **Start** to continue.

- The AutoCAD Electrical software installs with an example spreadsheet to be used with this command. It is called **demoplc.xls** and is located in *C:\Users\<user>\AppData\Roaming\Autodesk\AutoCAD Electrical <version>\<release>\<language>\Support\User* for Windows 10.
- The **Spreadsheet to PLC I/O Utility** command is driven by an Excel spreadsheet. Each column in the spreadsheet contains information (block name and its attributes) for the symbols to use. See the AutoCAD Electrical Help for a detailed description of the spreadsheet.

The *Spreadsheet to PLC I/O Utility* dialog box (shown in Figure 8–36) is used to configure the settings that can be saved to a .WDI file for later use.

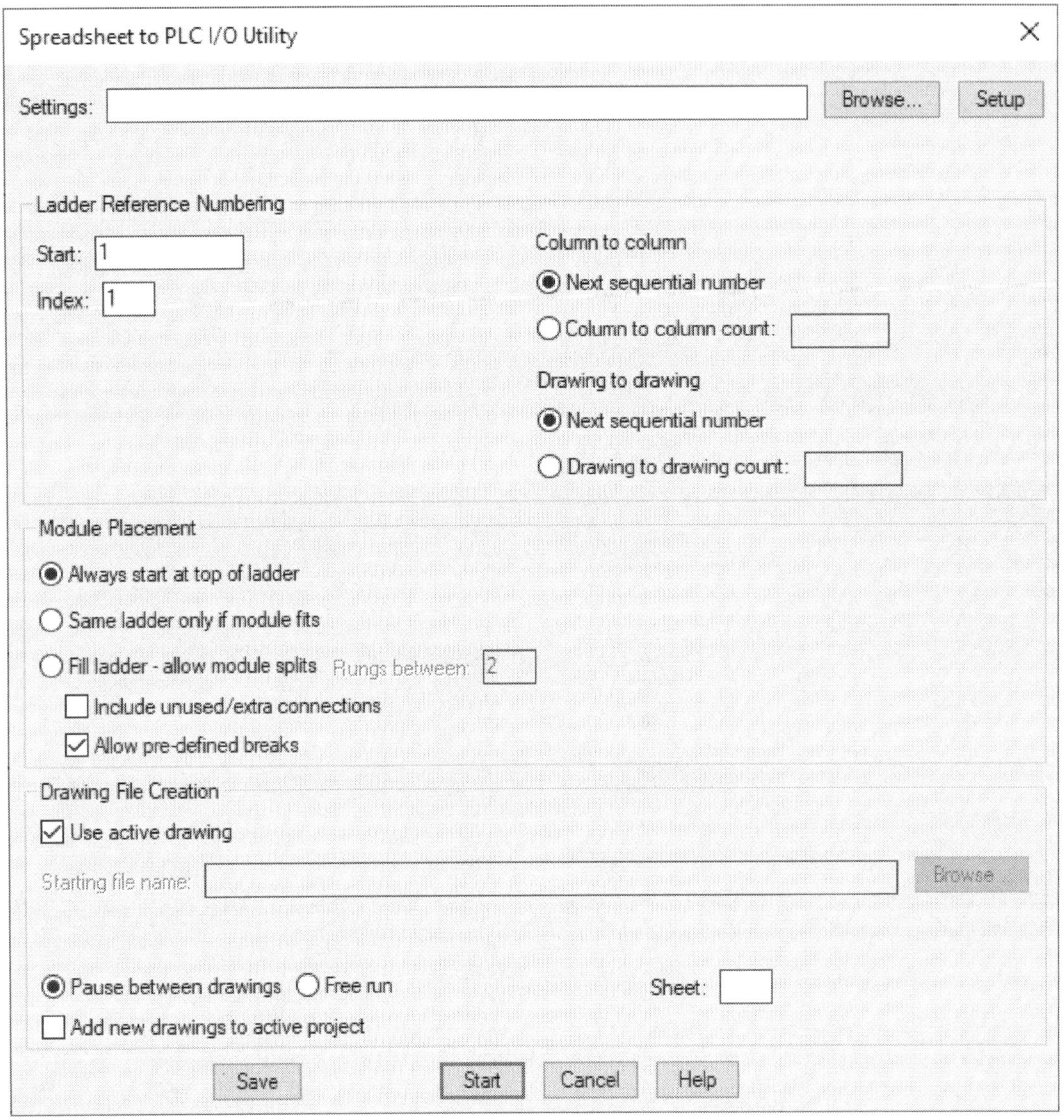

Figure 8–36

Browse	Opens the *Read Settings From* dialog box, where you can select a .WDI file to use.
Setup	Opens the *Spreadsheet to PLC I/O Utility Setup* dialog box, where you can configure settings for the size and position of ladders, PLC modules, and components.

Ladder Reference Numbering	Settings for ladder reference numbers, including the starting number, increment between reference numbers, and value to skip between columns and drawings.
Module Placement	Settings to control how modules are placed on ladders.
Drawing File Creation	Settings to control the starting drawing, pause, or free run, starting sheet number, and whether or not drawings are added to the active project.
Save	Saves the settings to a .WDI file to use later.
Start	Starts the creation of the drawings.

The *Spreadsheet to PLC I/O Utility Setup* dialog box (shown in Figure 8–37) contains various settings.

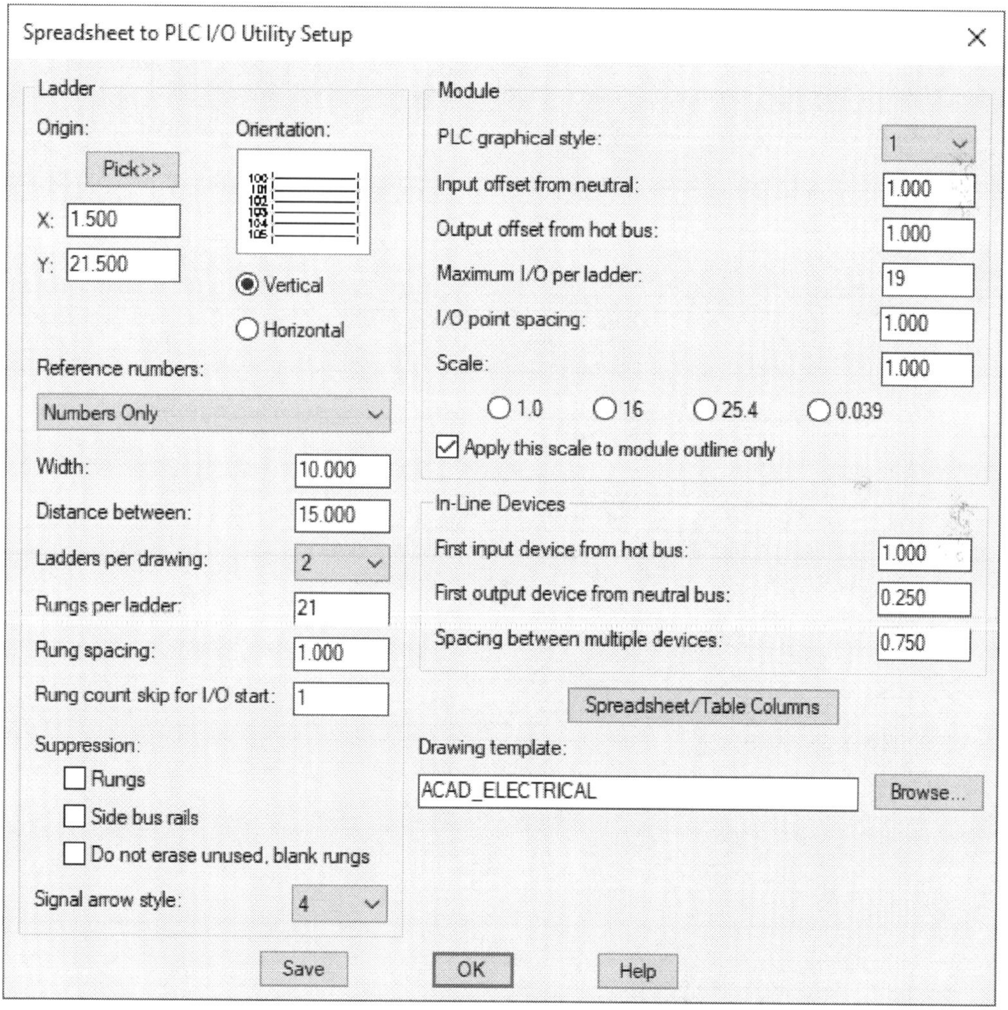

Figure 8–37

Ladder	Settings to control the position, size, and spacing of ladders and their rungs.
Module	Settings to control the appearance, spacing, and scale of PLC modules.
In-Line Devices	Settings to control the spacing of components.
Spreadsheet/ Table Columns	Opens the *Spreadsheet to PLC I/O Drawing Generator* dialog box. It controls the mapping of the data in the spreadsheet to the information required by the software.
Drawing template	Specifies the drawing template to use for drawings created by the utility. Click **Browse** to select a template.
Save	Saves the spreadsheet information to a .WDI file for later use.

- It is recommended that you start with a drawing name with a number at the end (e.g., **PLC_01.dwg**). Depending on the information in the spreadsheet, the AutoCAD Electrical software can create multiple drawings. Each new drawing uses the same name as the previous drawing. The number at the end increments (e.g., **PLC_02.dwg** would be the second drawing).

Practice 8c
Spreadsheet to PLC I/O Utility

Practice Objectives

- Generate several schematic drawings using an external spreadsheet file.
- Modify a spreadsheet and generate additional schematic drawings.

In this practice, you will use the **Spreadsheet to PLC I/O Utility** command to create several schematic drawings, as shown in Figure 8–38. You will then modify the spreadsheet to use different symbols and attributes. Finally, you will create drawings based on the new spreadsheet.

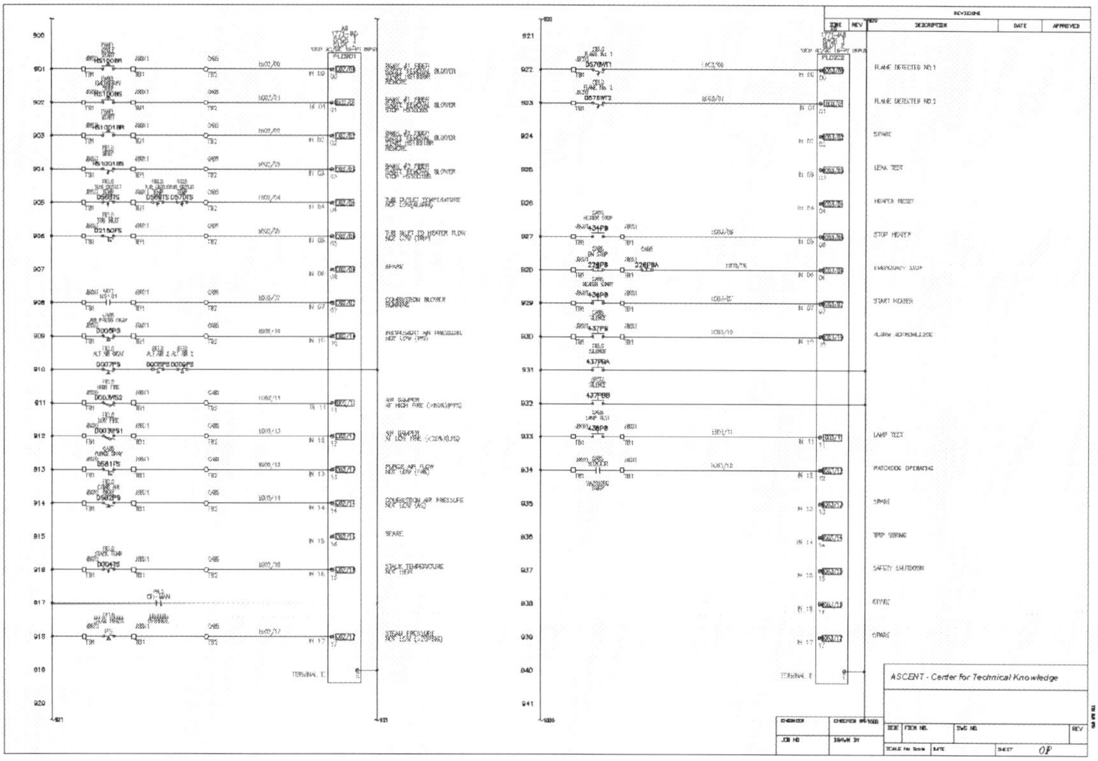

Figure 8–38

Task 1: Create drawings from a spreadsheet.

1. If the **Module 08** project is not active, open and activate it.
2. If no drawings are open, open any one drawing in the **Module 08** project. You must have a drawing open to access the AutoCAD Electrical commands.

3. In the *Import/Export Data* tab>*Import* panel, click  (PLC I/O Utility). The *Select PLC I/O Spreadsheet Output File* dialog box opens.
4. Browse to the *Module 08* folder in your practice files folder, as shown in Figure 8–39. Select **demoplc.xls**. Click **Open**.

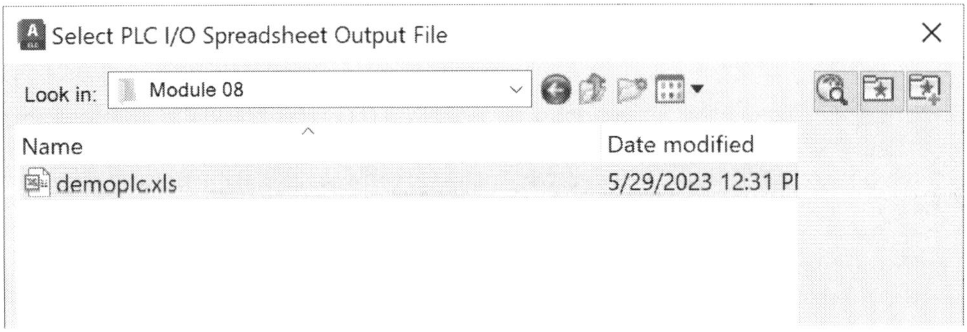

Figure 8–39

5. The *Spreadsheet to PLC I/O Utility* dialog box opens. Next to the *Settings* field, click **Setup** to open the *Spreadsheet to PLC I/O Utility Setup* dialog box.
6. In the *Drawing template* area, click **Browse**. In the *Select Prototype/Template (.dwg or.dwt)* dialog box, select and open **Electrical_template.dwt** from your practice files folder. It displays in the *Drawing template* field, as shown in Figure 8–40.

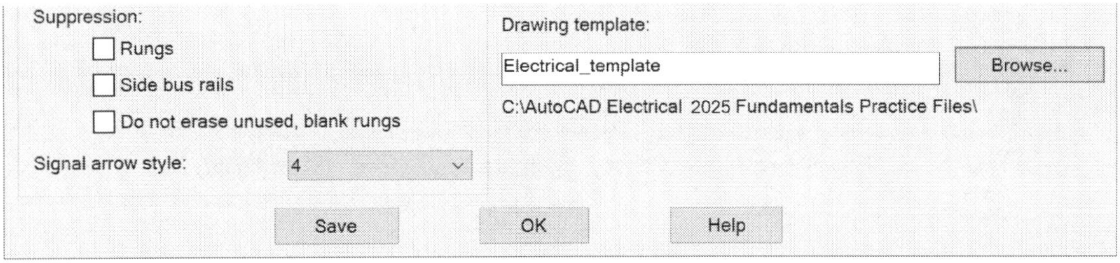

Figure 8–40

7. Click **OK** to close the *Spreadsheet to PLC I/O Utility Setup* dialog box.
8. You are returned to the *Spreadsheet to PLC I/O Utility* dialog box. In the *Ladder Reference Numbering* area, in the *Start* field, type **600**. Select the **Drawing to drawing count** option and leave the default as **100** in the field, as shown in Figure 8–41.

9. In the *Drawing File Creation* area, clear the **Use active drawing** option. Next to the *Starting file name* field, click **Browse**. In the *Starting File Name* dialog box, navigate to the *Module 08* folder in your practice files folder. In the *File name* field, type **PLC_01**, and click **Save**. Select **Free run** and the **Add new drawings to active project** options, as shown in Figure 8–41.

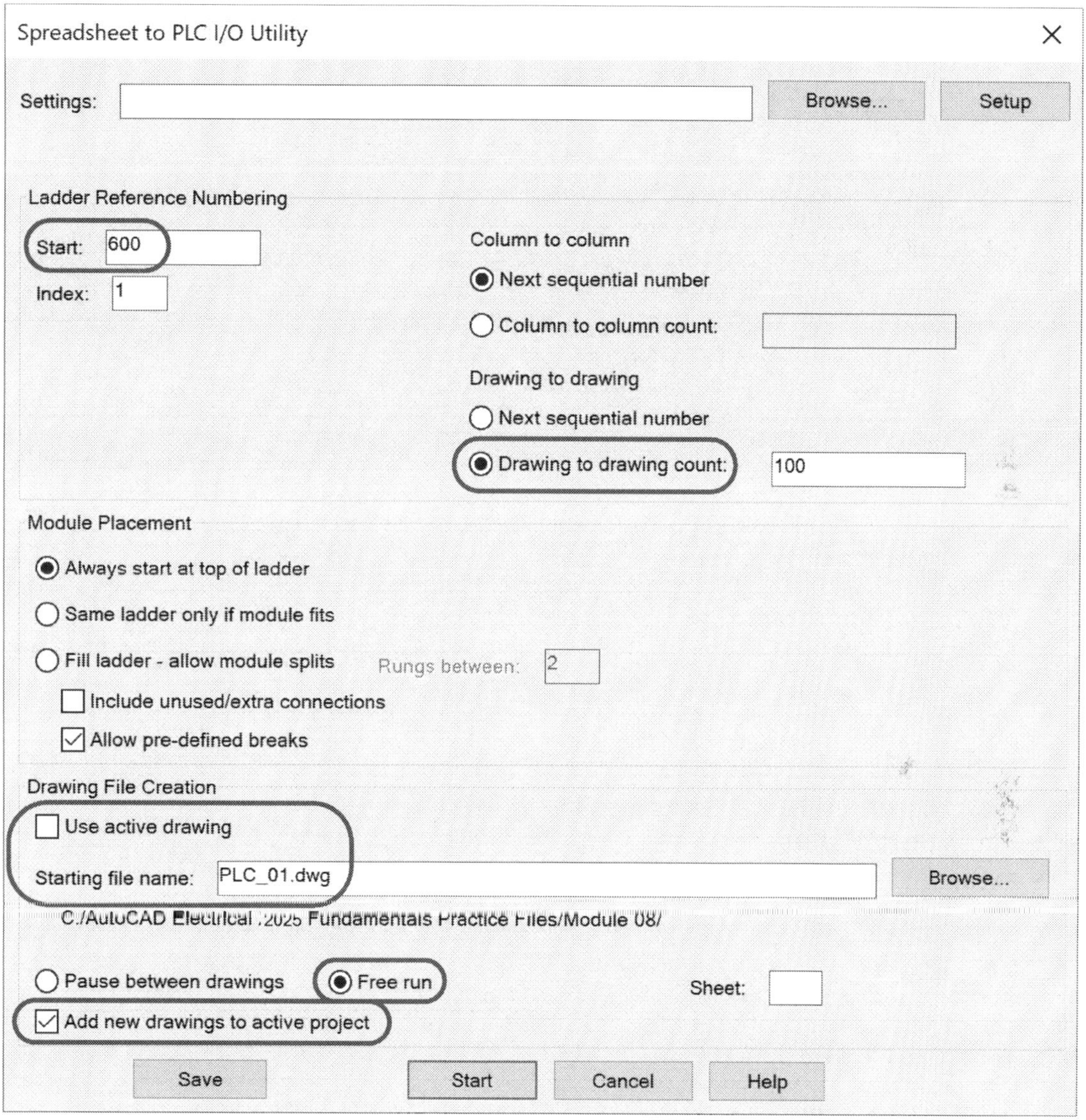

Figure 8–41

10. Click **Start** to begin creating drawings.

- The process of drawing creation might take a few minutes depending on computer speed and other programs running.

11. The software automatically creates three drawings (**plc_01.dwg**, **plc_02.dwg**, and **plc_03.dwg**) based on the data in the spreadsheet. The newly created drawings are automatically added to the *Project Manager* with **plc_03.dwg** open, as shown in Figure 8–42.

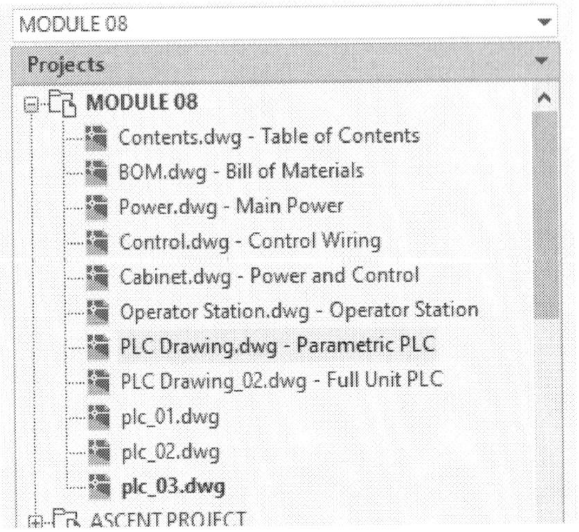

Figure 8–42

12. In the *Project Manager*, in the *Module 08* folder, open **plc_01.dwg**.
13. Zoom to lines 600 to 605.
14. Note the first symbols on the left side of the lines 601, 602, and 603, as shown in Figure 8–43. They are normally open push buttons and their descriptions are **CYCLE START**, **STOP**, and **START** respectively. Their location codes are set to **FIELD**.

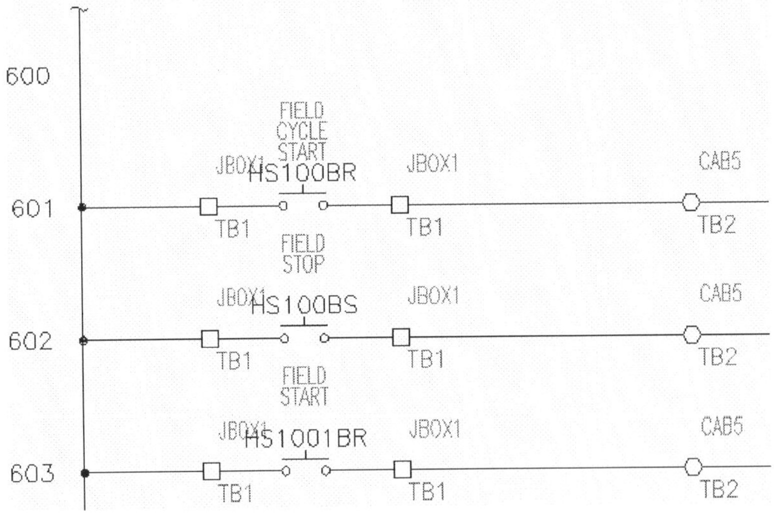

Figure 8–43

Task 2: Modify a spreadsheet.

1. Using Windows Explorer, navigate to the *Module 08* folder in your practice files folder and open **demoplc.xls** in Microsoft Excel.
2. Scroll to columns *Q* to *T*. The data in columns *Q* to *T* and rows *2* to *4* (as shown in Figure 8–44) corresponds to the push buttons you just viewed in drawing **PLC_01.dwg**.

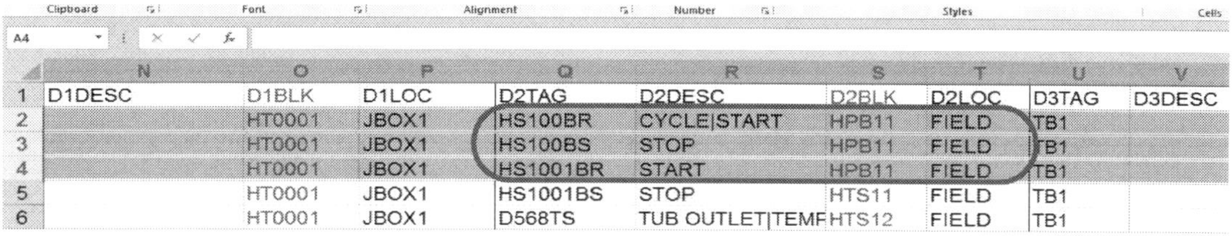

Figure 8–44

3. Change the text in cell *R3* from *STOP* to **EMERGENCY|STOP**.
4. Change the text in cells *S2*, *S3*, and *S4* from *HPB11* to **HPB11M**. This text is the block name for a normally open mushroom head push button.
5. Change the text in cells *T2*, *T3*, and *T4* from *FIELD* to **PANEL**. This text is the location code for the symbols.
6. The spreadsheet (columns *Q* through *T* and rows *2* through *4*) now display as shown in Figure 8–45. Save the spreadsheet as **demoplc_02.xls** in the *Module 08* folder in your practice files folder. Close Microsoft Excel.

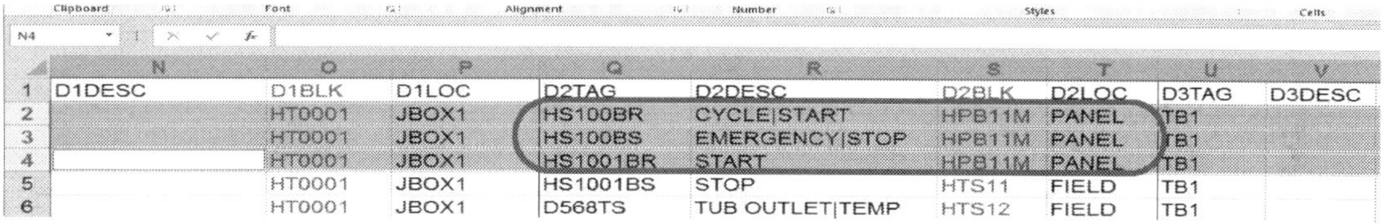

Figure 8–45

Task 3: Create drawings from a new spreadsheet.

1. In the AutoCAD Electrical software, in the *Import/Export Data* tab>*Import* panel, click  (PLC I/O Utility).
2. The *Select PLC I/O Spreadsheet Output File* dialog box opens. Browse to the *Module 08* folder in your practice files folder. Select **demoplc_02.xls** and click **Open**. The *Spreadsheet to PLC I/O Utility* dialog box opens.
3. Click **Setup** to open the *Spreadsheet to PLC I/O Utility Setup* dialog box.

4. For the *Drawing template*, click **Browse.** Select and open **Electrical_template.dwt** in your practice files folder.
5. Click **OK** in the *Spreadsheet to PLC I/O Utility Setup* dialog box.
6. In the *Spreadsheet to PLC I/O Utility* dialog box, in the *Ladder Reference Numbering* area, in the *Start* field, type **900**. Select the **Drawing to drawing count** option and leave the default **100** in the field.
7. In the *Drawing File Creation* area, verify that **Use active drawing** is cleared. In the *Starting file name* field, type **PLC2_01**. Select **Free run** and **Add new drawings to active project**, as shown in Figure 8–46.

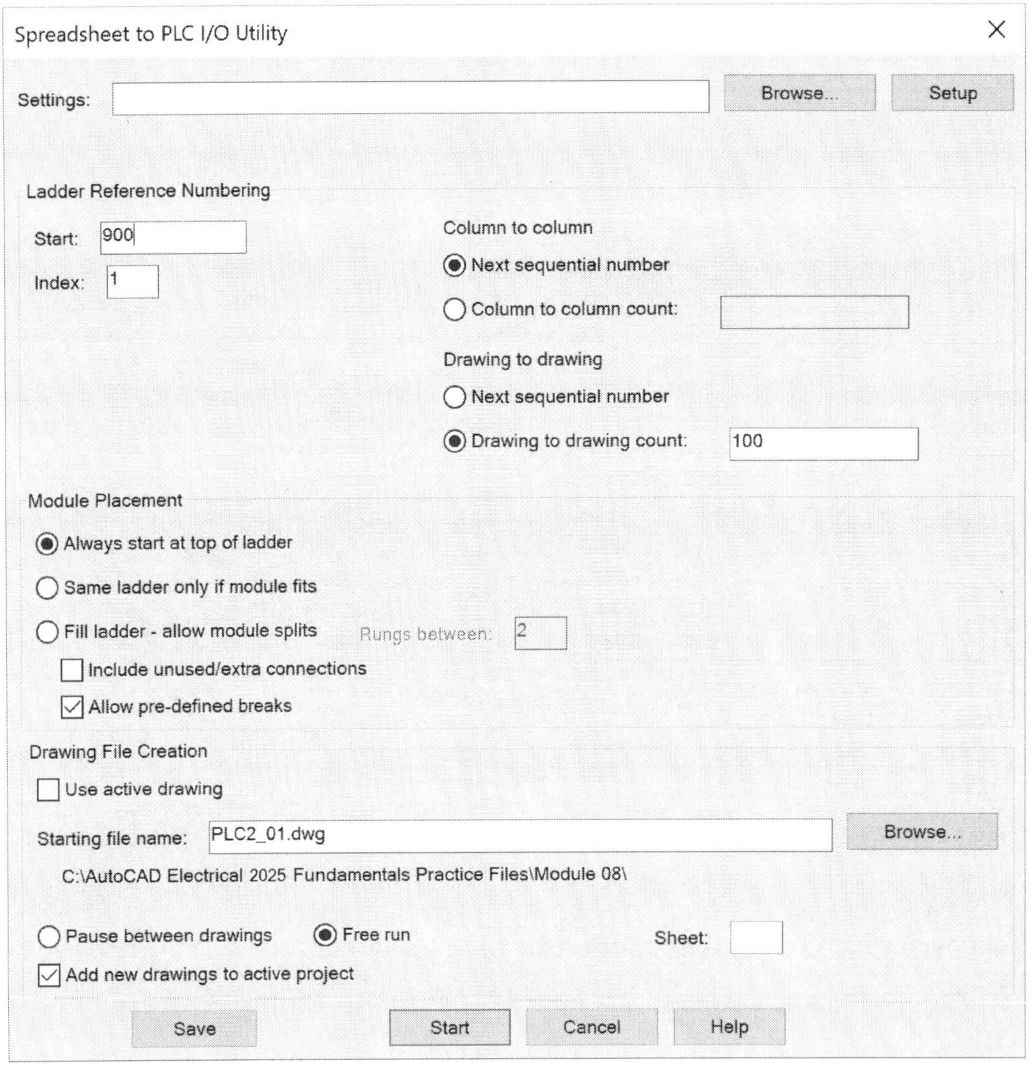

Figure 8–46

8. Click **Start** to begin creating drawings. The AutoCAD Electrical software creates three drawings (**plc2_01.dwg**, **plc2_02.dwg**, and **plc2_03.dwg**) based on the data in the spreadsheet. They are also displayed in the *Project Manager*.
9. In the *Module 08* project, open **plc2_01.dwg**.
10. Zoom to lines 900 through 905.
11. Note the first symbols on the left side of the lines 901, 902, and 903 as shown in Figure 8–47. They are normally open mushroom head push buttons and their descriptions are **CYCLE START**, **EMERGENCY STOP**, and **START** respectively. Their location codes are all set to **PANEL**.

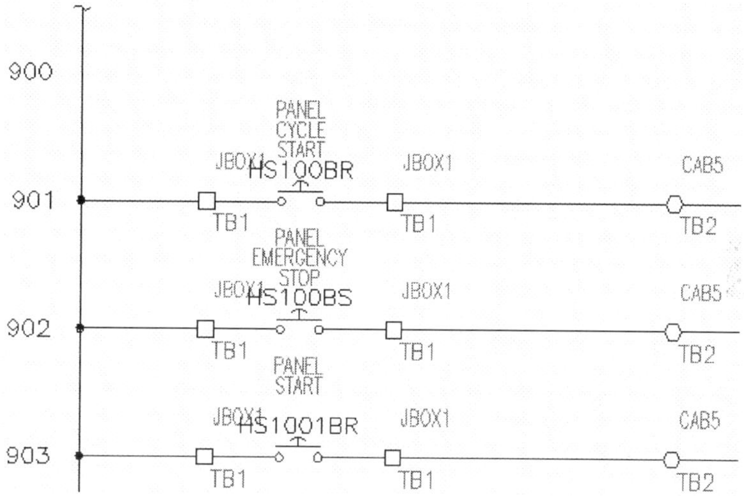

Figure 8–47

12. Save and close all of the drawings.

End of practice

Chapter Review Questions

1. What is the difference between the **Insert PLC (Parametric)** and the **Insert PLC (Full Units)** commands?
   a. **Insert PLC (Full Units)** does not adjust spacing between PLC I/O points.
   b. **Insert PLC (Full Units)** does not include PLC I/O point descriptions.
   c. **Insert PLC (Full Units)** does not break wires that intersect connection points.
   d. There is no difference between them.

2. How can you change the descriptions for the I/O points after a PLC is inserted?
   a. Use the **Edit Description** command to change I/O point descriptions.
   b. Use the **Insert PLC (Parametric)** command to change I/O point descriptions.
   c. Use the **Edit Component** command to display the *Edit PLC Module* dialog box.
   d. You cannot change the descriptions for the I/O points after a PLC is inserted.

3. You insert a PLC and then decide you need to insert components in parallel on a particular rung. What command would you use to adjust the spacing between the PLC I/O points to accommodate the components?
   a. Split PLC Module
   b. Move Component
   c. Stretch PLC Module
   d. Scoot

4. When using the **Insert PLC (Parametric)** command, how do you control the appearance of the I/O points?
   a. Set the style in the *Module Layout* dialog box.
   b. Set the style in the *Graphics Style* area in the *PLC Parametric* dialog box.
   c. Manually after it is placed using the **Edit PLC Module** command.
   d. You cannot control the appearance of the I/O points.

5. What command do you use to insert individual PLC I/O points?
   a. Use the **Insert Individual PLC I/O Points** command.
   b. Use the **Insert PLC (Full Units)** command.
   c. You cannot insert individual PLC I/O points.
   d. Use the **Insert Component** command and select **PLC I/O**.

Command Summary

Button	Command	Location
	**Drawing Properties**	• **Ribbon:** *Schematic* tab>*Other Tools* panel
	**Insert PLC (Full Units)**	• **Ribbon:** *Schematic* tab>*Insert Components* panel
	**Insert PLC (Parametric)**	• **Ribbon:** *Schematic* tab>*Insert Components* panel
	**PLC I/O Utility**	• **Ribbon:** *Import/Export Data* tab>*Import* panel

Chapter 9

Point-to-Point Wiring Drawings

Learn how to insert parametric connectors, components, wires, and splices to easily create usable and effective point-to-point schematic drawings. Additionally, knowledge on how to bend wires enables you to re-route existing wires that can sometimes get in the way of inserting new components and wires.

Learning Objectives

- Insert a parametric connector to an individual drawing or across multiple drawings.
- Modify the geometry and pin placement of an existing connector.
- Insert a splice symbol to an existing wire.
- Insert multiple wires that are automatically attached to component connection points.
- Re-route an existing wire network.

9.1 Insert Connectors

Point-to-point schematic drawings are created using many of the same commands as ladder style drawings. You insert components and wires and combine different styles. For example, adding connectors to PLC drawings. Many point-to-point drawings use the X-Y Grid or the X-Zone Referencing instead of Line Referencing.

Connectors

A connector is a parametric component and can be inserted using the **Insert Connector** command. The connector symbol (as shown in Figure 9–1) consists of a plug (the object with round corners), a receptacle (the object with square corners), pin numbers, and other attributes. The pin numbers can be displayed on either the plug side, the receptacle side, or on both sides. The component tag displays above the connector.

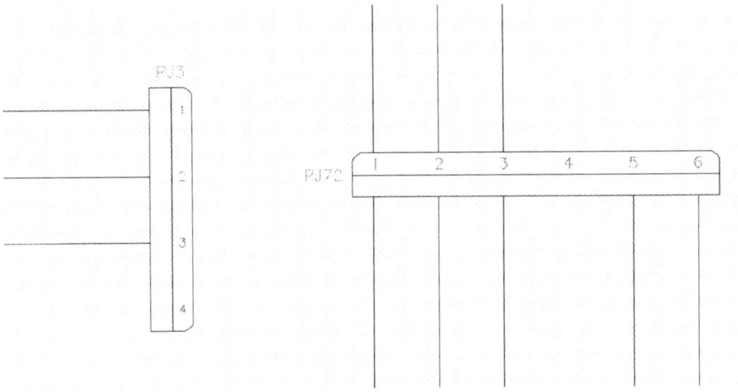

Figure 9–1

Insert Connector

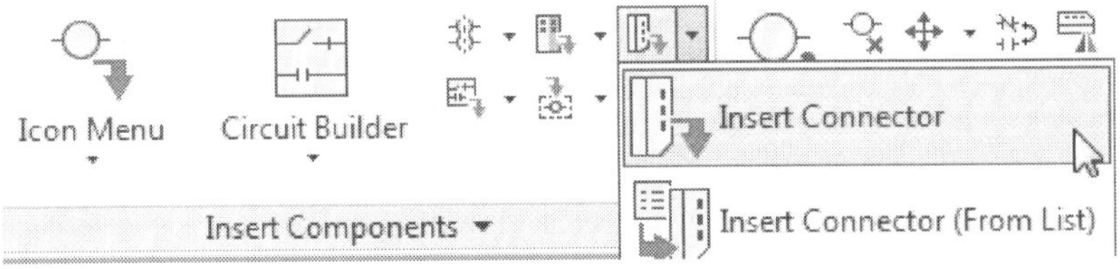

Ribbon: *Schematic* tab>*Insert Components* panel

Command Prompt: aeconnector

How To: Insert a Connector

1. Start the **Insert Connector** command. The *Insert Connector* dialog box opens.
2. Configure the orientation, pins, and geometry of the symbol.
   - Use **Details>>** to expand or collapse the dialog box.
3. Click **Insert**.
4. Pick the insertion point of the connector.
5. If the **Allow Spacers/Breaks** option was selected, you can insert pins, spacers, or breaks using the *Custom Pin Spaces/Breaks* dialog box.

The *Insert Connector* dialog box (shown in Figure 9–2), controls the spacing, number of pins, orientation, and other properties of a connector. It displays a simplified preview of the connector.

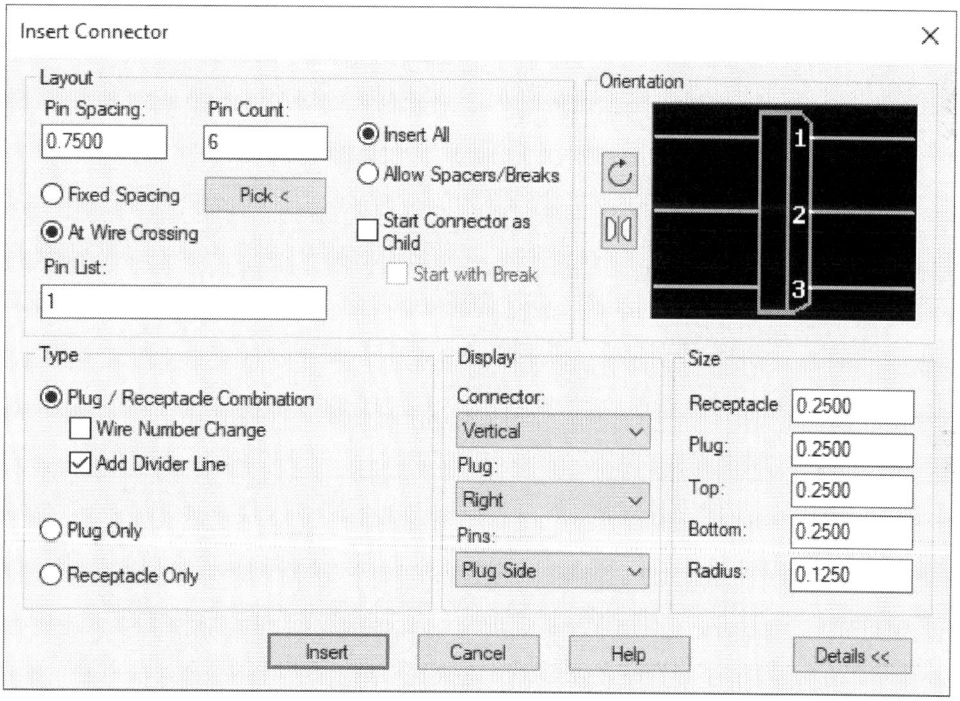

Figure 9–2

Pin Spacing	Sets the distance between the pins.
Fixed Spacing	Maintains the same distance between the pins.
At Wire Crossing	Adjusts the distance between the pins to intersect existing wires.

Pick<	Pick two points in the graphics window to determine the number of pins. If the line crosses wires, the number of pins is set to the number of wires intersected. If the line is drawn in blank space, its length is divided by the pin spacing to determine the number of pins.
Pin List	Format for the pin list. Either a single character or comma-delimited list. Can be any combination of numbers or letters.
Insert All	Insert all pins without interruption.
Allow Spacers/Breaks	Add spacers or breaks for each pin.
Start Connector as Child	Inserts the connector as a child component.
Start with Break	If selected, the connector is inserted with a break or jagged line at the top.
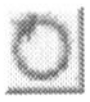	Rotates the connector between horizontal and vertical.
	Flips or mirrors the connector.
Type	Controls the portion of the connector symbol to be inserted.
Display	Controls the orientation of the symbol.
Size	Controls the size of the different parts of the symbol.

- The last settings used in the *Insert Component* dialog box become the default settings, which are used when inserting a new parametric component.
- When you insert a connector as a child component, use the **Edit Component** command to link the child to its parent.

9.2 Edit Connectors

Once a connector has been inserted, its attributes can be edited using the **Edit Component** command. This command functions as it would for other schematic components, except for the **List** option in the *Pins* area, which displays a list of the pins for that connector and enables you to modify the pin numbers or add descriptions to them. The **Edit Component** command is also used to link child connectors to their parent.

You can modify the geometry and pin placement of an existing connector using the various edit connector commands.

Edit Connectors

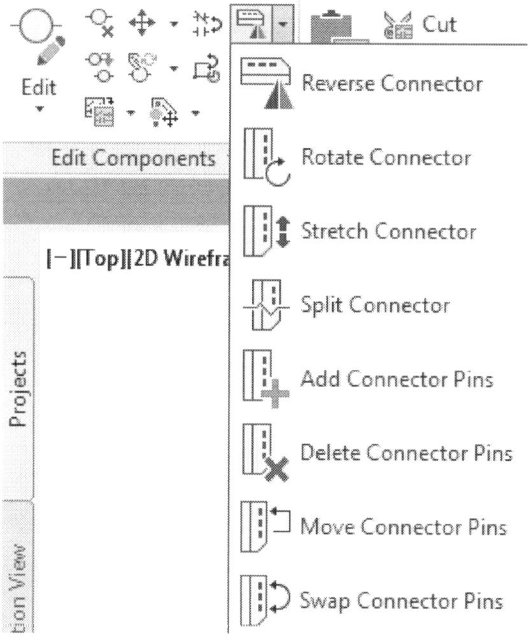

Ribbon: *Schematic* tab>*Edit Components* panel

 (Reverse Connector)	Select the connector to flip and press <Enter> or <Esc> to end the command.
 (Rotate Connector)	Select the connector to rotate and press <Enter> or <Esc> to end the command.
 (Stretch Connector)	Select the end of the connector to stretch and pick to define the new length of the connector.

(Split Connector)	Select the connector to split. Pick the location to split the connector. In the *Split Block* dialog box, configure the options for break type and repositioning. Click **OK**. Pick the location for the child connector.
(Add Connector Pins)	Select the connector to modify. Enter the Pin number. Pick the point(s) for the new pin(s). Press <Enter> or <Esc> to end the command.
(Delete Connector Pins)	Select the pin to delete and press <Enter> or <Esc> to end the command.
(Move Connector Pins)	Select the pin to move. Pick the new location for the pin. Press <Enter> or <Esc> to end the command.
(Swap Connector Pins)	Select the pin to swap. Select the pin to swap with the selected pin. Press <Enter> or <Esc> to end the command.

- If you need to add pins to a connector, but there is not enough room for the pins, use the **Stretch Connector** command to enlarge the connector, and the **Add Connector Pins** command to add the pins.
- The **Split Connector** command automatically creates a parent/child relationship between the existing connector and the split portion.

9.3 Insert Splices

If a design requires an additional lead or wire, you can add a splice symbol to an existing wire. You can then add the second wire branch to the splice, as shown in Figure 9–3. The **Insert Splice** command is used to add the splice to the wire.

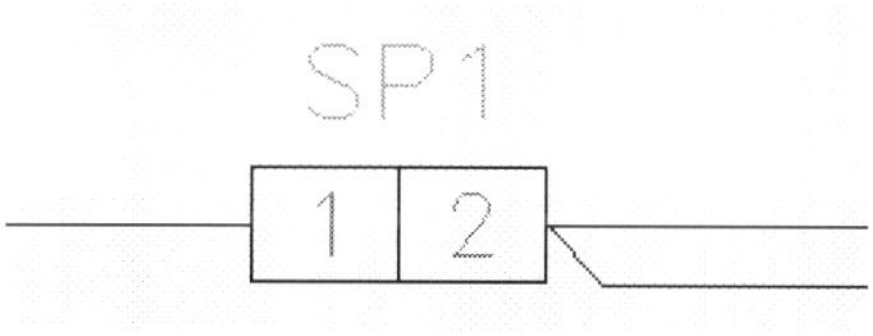

Figure 9–3

Insert Splice

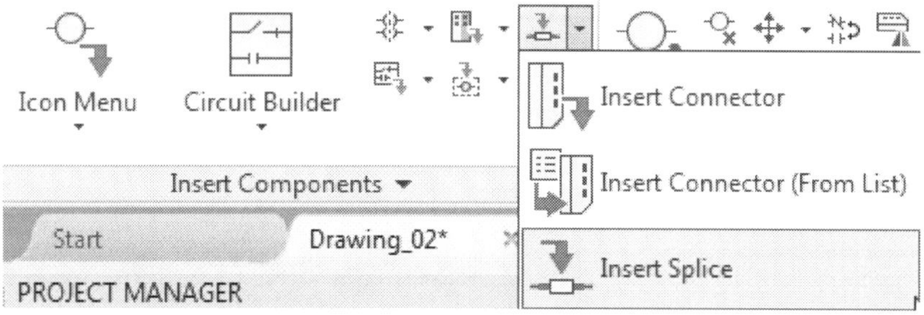

Ribbon: *Schematic* tab>*Insert Components* panel

Command Prompt: aesplice

How To: Insert a Splice

1. Start the **Insert Splice** command. The *Insert Component* dialog box opens with the Splice Symbols displayed.
2. Click 1|2 (Splice) to insert a splice.
3. Pick the insertion point for the splice. The *Insert / Edit Component* dialog box opens.
4. Define the properties.
5. Click **OK**.

- Use the **Edit Component** command to modify the attributes of the splice.
- To add the second wire, use the **Insert Wire** command and pick near the connection point of the existing wire. The second wire is automatically added with a 45° angle.

Practice 9a
Insert and Modify Connectors

Practice Objectives

- Insert connectors and then modify the connector's geometry.
- Insert a splice symbol on an existing wire.

In this practice, you will insert two connectors: one on existing wires and another in a blank area. You will then insert a splice on an existing wire. Finally, you will modify the connectors. The final circuit displays as shown in Figure 9–4.

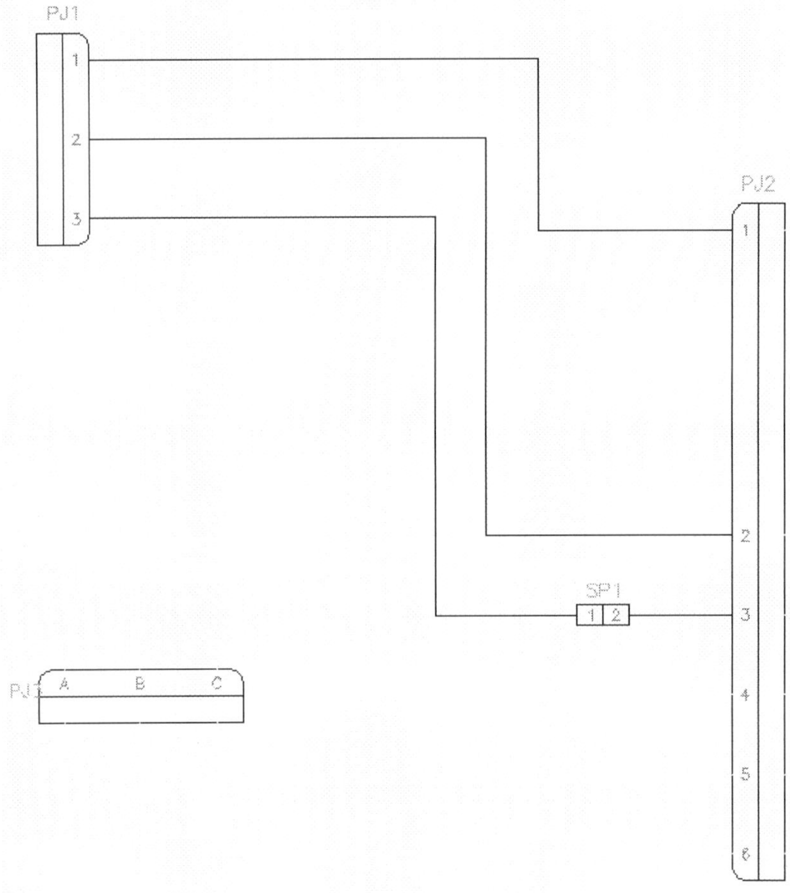

Figure 9–4

Task 1: Insert a connector on existing wires.

1. In your practice files folder, in the *Module 09* folder, open the **Module 09** project file.
2. In the **Module 09** project, open **Point_to_point_01.dwg**.
3. Zoom to the three wires and the pin in the drawing.
4. In the *Schematic* tab>*Insert Components* panel, click (Insert Connector).
5. The *Insert Connector* dialog box opens. Click **Details** (if required) to open the expanded view of the dialog box. Set the following options, as shown in Figure 9–5:
   - In the *Layout* area, set *Pin Count* to **6** and select **At Wire Crossing**.
   - In the *Type* area, select **Plug/Receptacle Combination** and **Add Divider Line**.
   - In the *Display* area, set *Connector* to **Vertical**, *Plug* to **Right**, and *Pins* to **Plug Side**. You can also use and to set the orientation display.

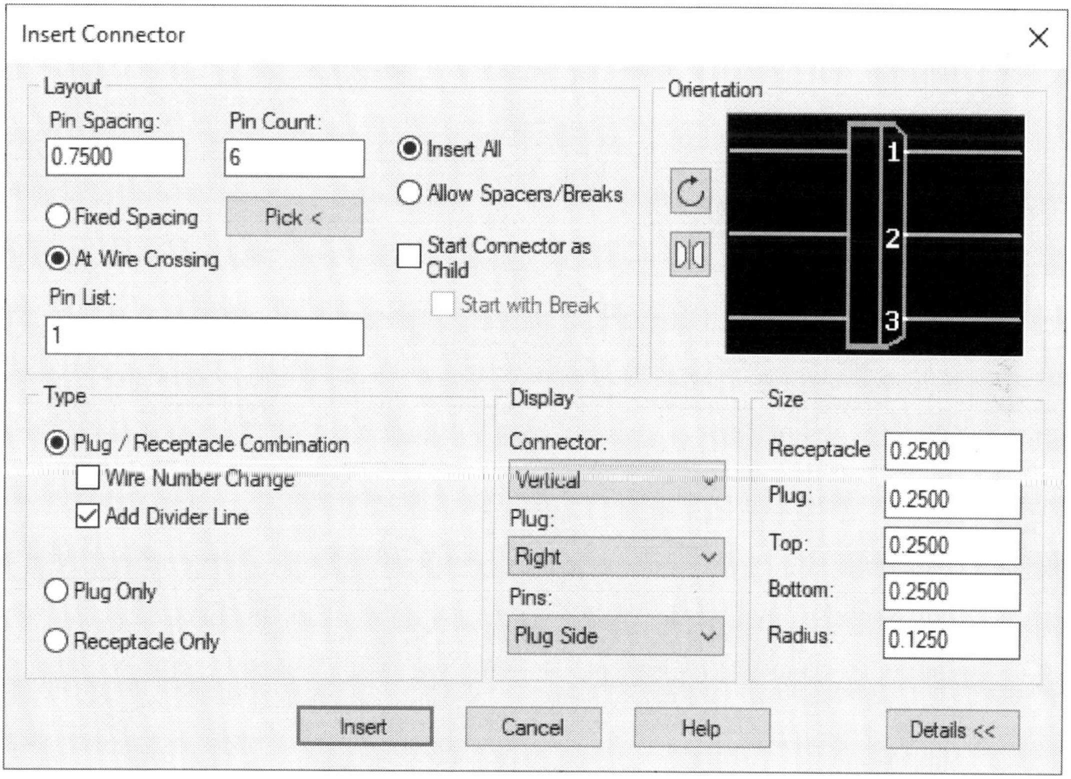

Figure 9–5

6. Click **Insert**.

7. Hover and pick near the end of the top right horizontal wire, as shown in Figure 9–6. Click **OK** in the *Insert / Edit Component* dialog box. The connector is inserted along the right side of the wires.

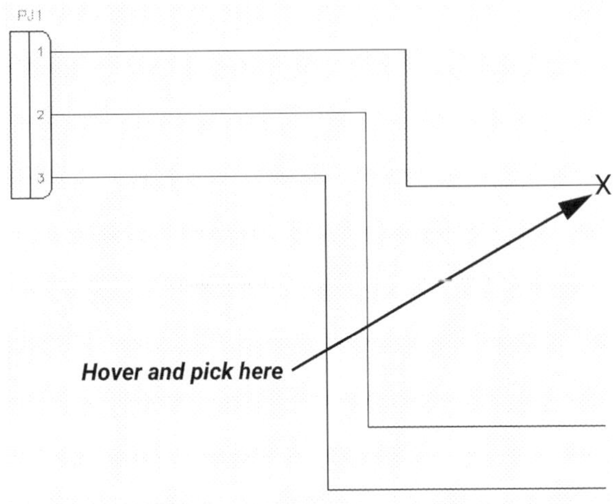

Figure 9–6

Task 2: Insert a connector in a blank area.

1. Click (Insert Connector).
2. The *Insert Connector* dialog box opens with the previous settings. Set the following options, as shown in Figure 9–7:
   - *Pin Count:* **3**
   - Select **Fixed Spacing**
   - *Pin List:* **A**

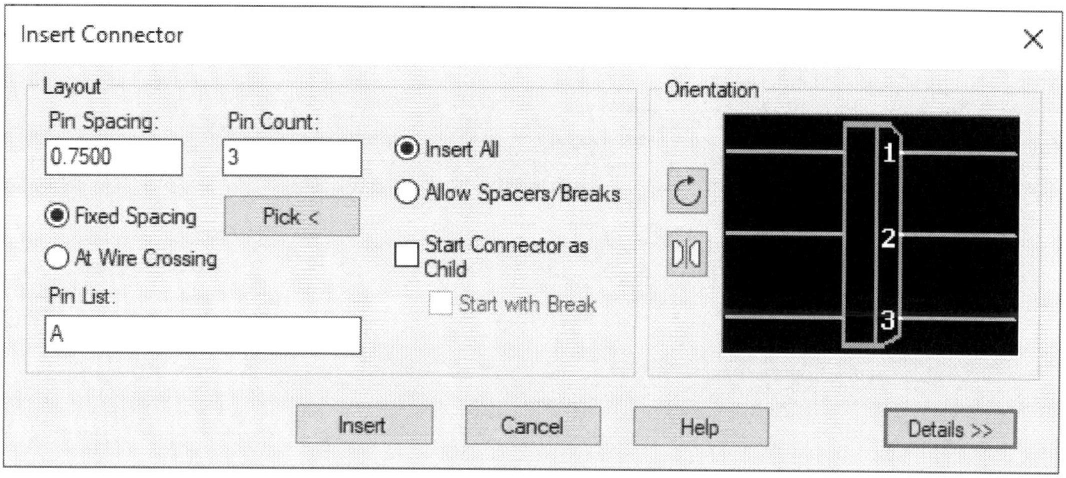

Figure 9–7

3. Click **Insert**.
4. Pick at **8,12** for the insertion point, as shown in Figure 9–8. Click **OK** in the *Insert / Edit Component* dialog box.

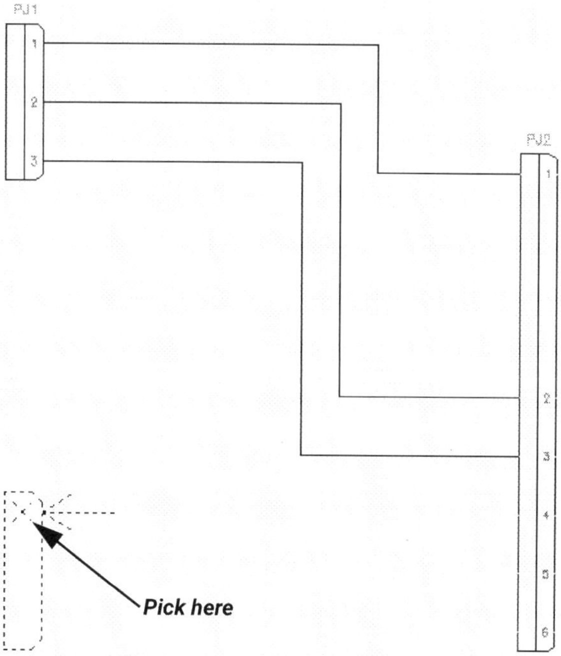

Figure 9–8

Task 3: Insert a splice.

1. In the *Schematic* tab>*Insert Components* panel, click (Insert Splice).
2. The *Insert Component* dialog box opens with the NFPA Splice Symbols. Click (Splice) to insert a splice.
3. Pick near the middle of the lower horizontal portion of the third wire, as shown in Figure 9–9.

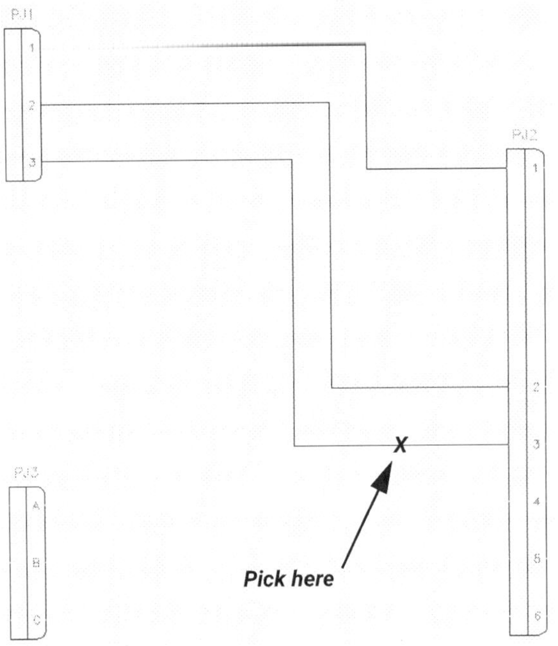

Figure 9–9

4. Click **OK** in the *Insert / Edit Component* dialog box. Note that a splice is inserted at the selected point.

Task 4: Edit connectors.

1. In the *Schematic* tab>*Edit Components* panel, click (Reverse Connector).
2. Select **PJ2**, the **6 pin** connector. The connector is reversed.
3. Press <Enter> to end the command.
4. In the *Schematic* tab>*Edit Components* panel, click (Rotate Connector).

5. Select **PJ3**, the **3 pin** connector that you inserted previously. It is rotated.
6. Press <Enter> to end the command.
7. Save and close **Point_to_point_01.dwg**.

End of practice

9.4 Insert Multiple Wires

Wires function the same way in point-to-point drawings as they do in schematic drawings. To insert individual wires, use (Wire) and pick the start and end points for the wire, or connection points on existing components. The wires are inserted at 90 degree angles and break across components at connection points.

You can insert multiple wires onto a connector using (Multiple Bus), as shown in Figure 9–10.

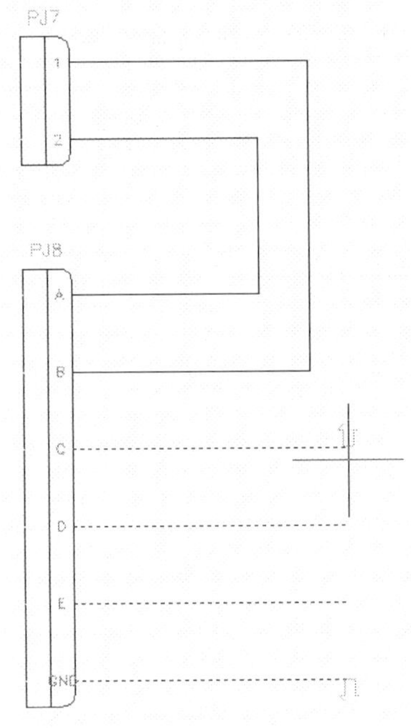

Figure 9–10

Multiple Bus

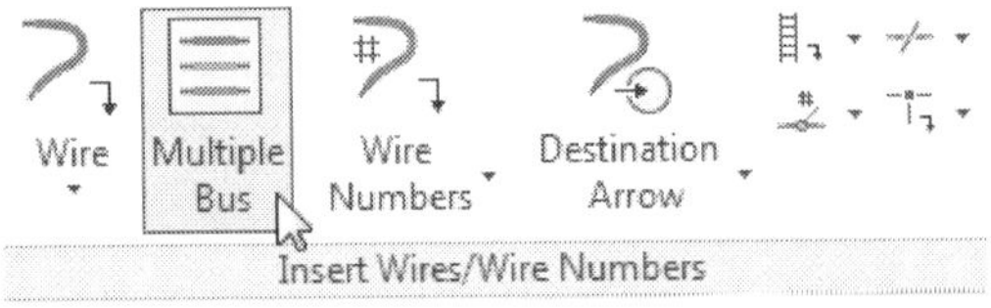

Ribbon: *Schematic* tab>*Insert Wires/Wire Numbers* panel

Command Prompt: aemultibus

How To: Insert a Multiple Wire Bus

1. Start the **Multiple Bus** command. The *Multiple Wire Bus* dialog box opens.
2. Specify the spacing in the *Horizontal* and *Vertical* areas.
3. Select **Component (Multiple Wires),** as shown in Figure 9–11.
   - **Component (Multiple Wires)** enables you to use a window to select the pins to which to connect, and inserts wires at each connection point in one command.

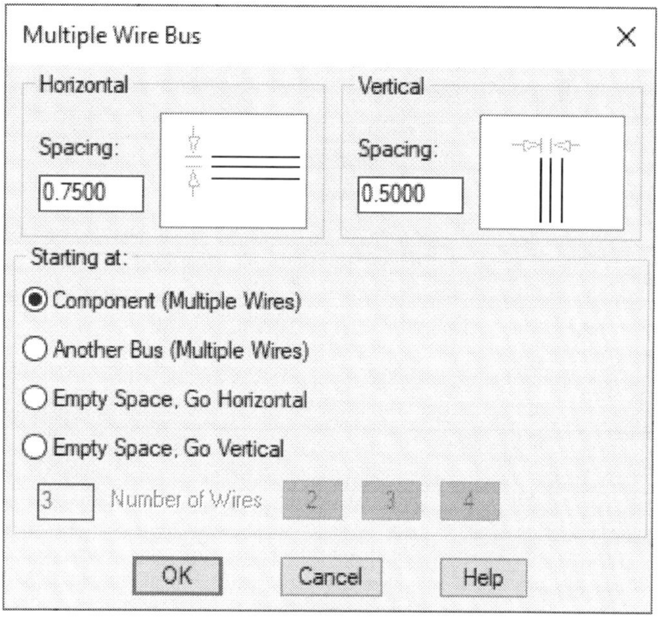

Figure 9–11

4. Click **OK**.
5. Pick the first corner of the selection window.
6. Pick the second corner of the selection window.
7. Continue selecting connection points. Press <Enter> to continue.
8. Pick the end point on the wires or the crossing window, depending on the method of insertion.

- At the Command Prompt, type **T** to switch the wire type before selecting the end point of the wires.
- At the Command Prompt, type **C** before selecting the end point of the wires to continue them.

9.5 Bend Wires

If you need to insert components or wires and there are existing wires in the way, the **Bend Wire** command can be used to re-route the existing wires. This command adds a 90 degree bend between two wires at selected points, as shown in Figure 9–12.

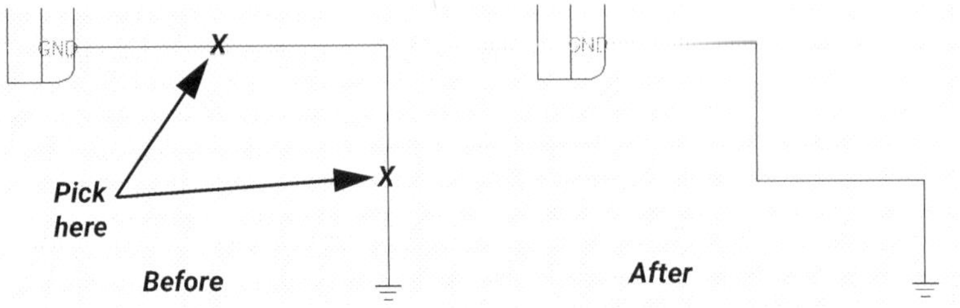

Figure 9–12

Bend Wire

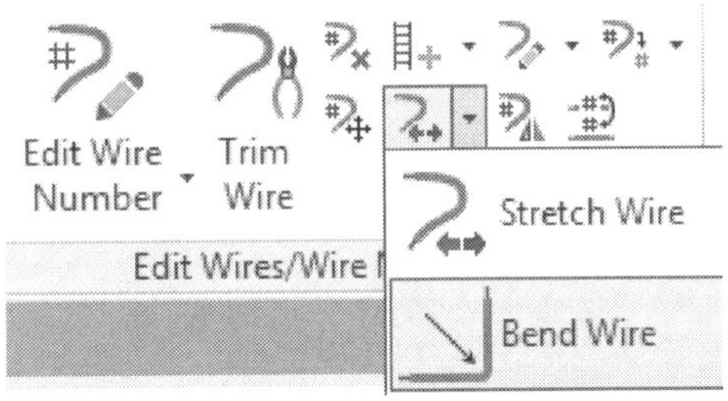

Ribbon: *Schematic* tab>*Edit Wires/Wire Numbers* panel

Command Prompt: aebendwire

How To: Bend a Wire

1. Start the **Bend Wire** command.
2. Pick the first wire at the point where you want the bend on that wire to be located.
3. Pick the second wire at the point where you want the bend on that wire to be located.
4. Continue picking wires. Press <Enter> or <Esc> to end the command.

- The two wire segments must be on the same network and they must share one end point.

Practice 9b
Wiring Tools

Practice Objectives

- Insert wires on existing connectors.
- Insert a splice component and add a bend to a wire network.

In this practice, you will insert multiple wires attached to a component's connectors. You will then insert a splice symbol on an existing wire and add an additional wire to the splice. Finally, you will bend a wire using the **Bend Wire** command. The final circuit displays as shown in Figure 9–13.

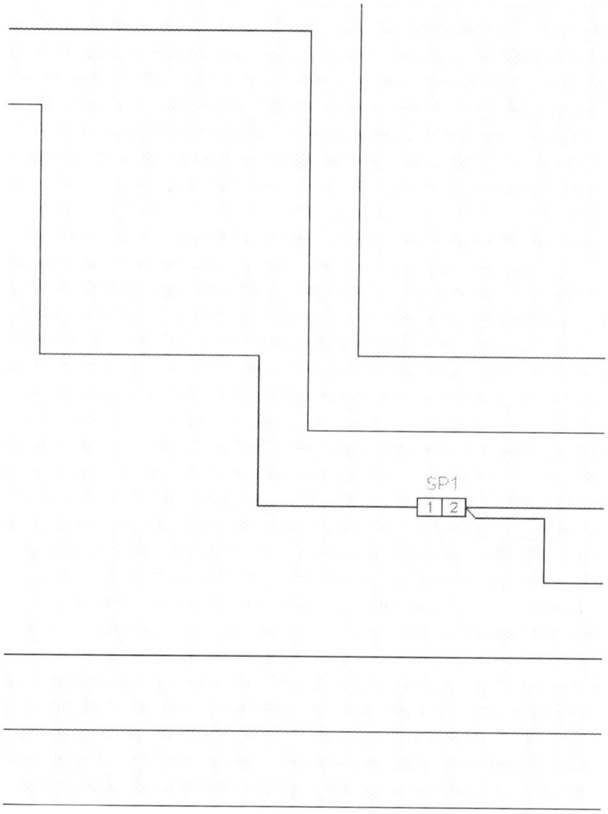

Figure 9–13

Task 1: Insert wires.

1. If the **Module 09** project is not active, open and activate it now.

2. In the **Module 09** project, open **Point_to_point_02.dwg**.
3. Zoom into the three pin connector, PJ4.
4. In the *Schematic* tab>*Insert Wires/Wire Numbers* panel, click  (Multiple Bus).
5. The *Multiple Wire Bus* dialog box opens. In the *Horizontal* area, set the *Spacing* as **0.7500**. In the *Starting at* area, select the **Component (Multiple Wires)** option, as shown in Figure 9–14. Click **OK**.

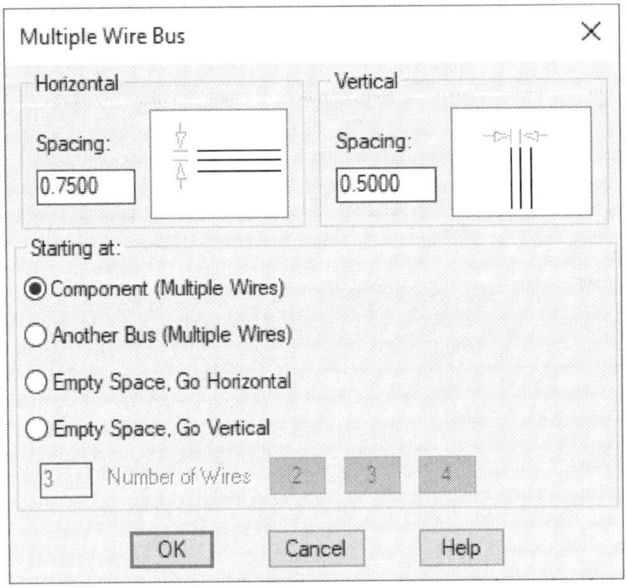

Figure 9–14

6. Window around the three pins on connector **PJ4**, as shown on the left in Figure 9–15. Note that the three red diamond symbols are displayed at the pins' locations, as shown on the right in Figure 9–15. Press <Enter>. Move the cursor and note the three preview lines indicating that wires are starting from the **PJ4** connector.

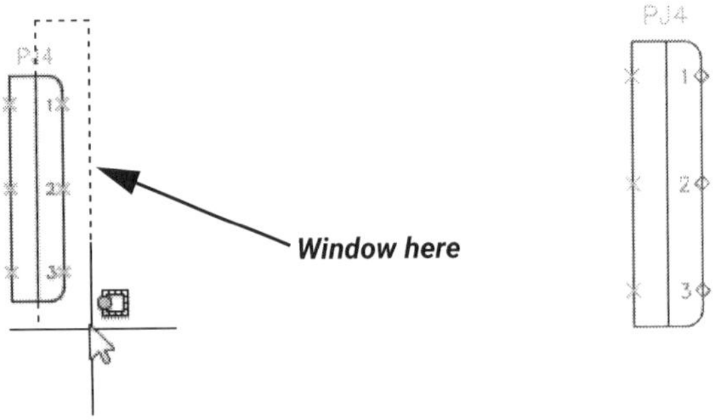

Figure 9–15

7. Move the cursor to the position shown in Figure 9–16. Type **C** and press <Enter>.

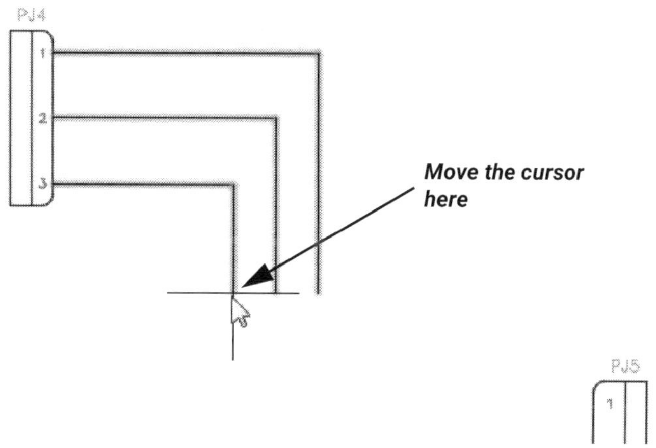

Figure 9–16

8. Select **pin 3** on connector **PJ5** to connect the wires, as shown in Figure 9–17.

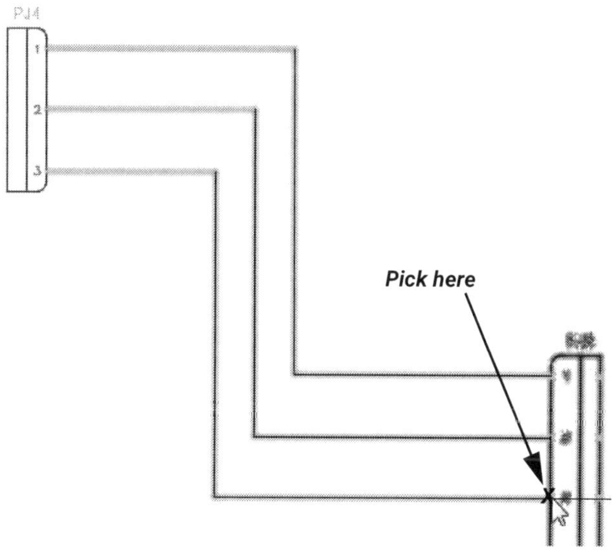

Figure 9–17

9. Click 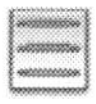 (Multiple Bus).
10. In the *Multiple Wire Bus* dialog box, verify that **Component (Multiple Wires)** is selected. Click **OK**.
11. Window around pins **A - C** on connector **PJ6**. Press <Enter>.

12. Select **pin 5** on connector **PJ5** to connect the wires, as shown in Figure 9–18.

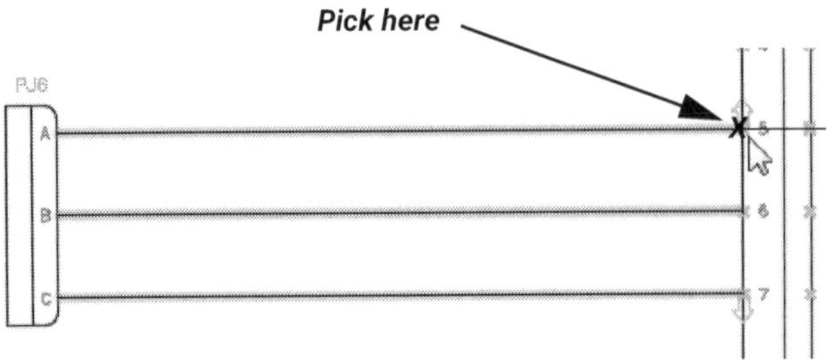

Figure 9–18

Task 2: Insert a splice.

1. In the *Schematic* tab>*Insert Components* panel, click 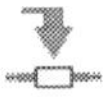 (Insert Splice).
2. In the *Insert Component* dialog box, click  (Splice).
3. Pick near the middle of the bottom wire connected to **pin 3** on **PJ5**, as shown in Figure 9–19.

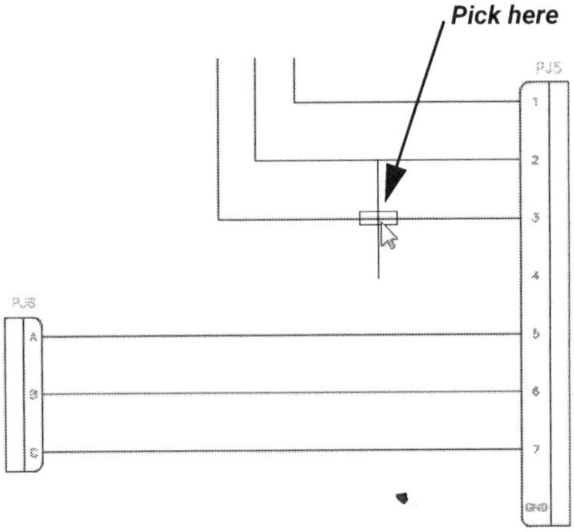

Figure 9–19

4. In the *Insert / Edit Component* dialog box, click **OK**.
5. Click  (Wire).

6. Pick the right endpoint of the splice symbol, as shown Figure 9–20.

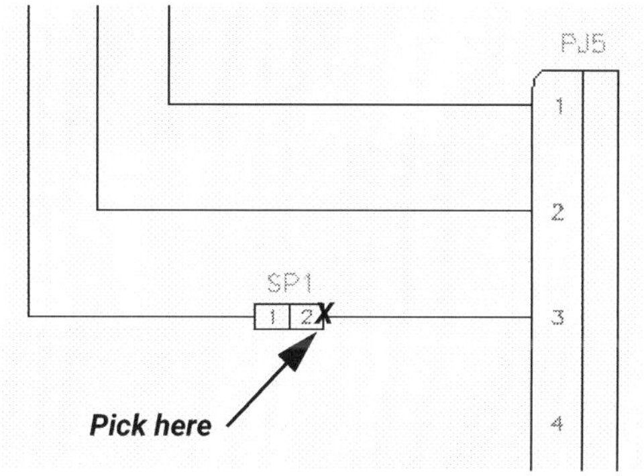

Figure 9–20

7. Select **pin 4** on **PJ5**, as shown in Figure 9–21.

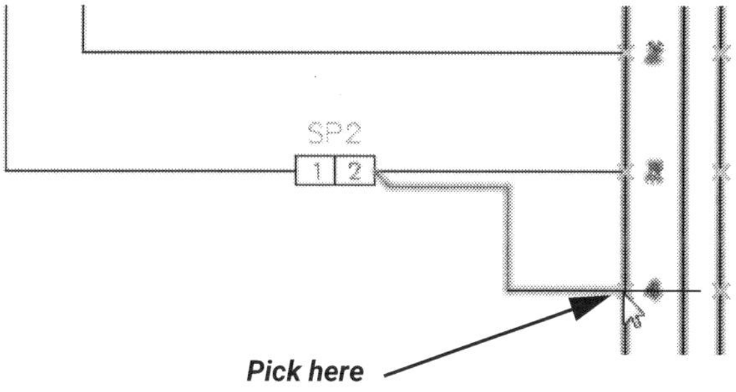

Figure 9–21

8. Press <Enter> to end the command.

Task 3: Bend a wire.

1. In the *Schematic* tab>*Edit Wires/Wire Numbers* panel, click  (Bend Wire).

2. Pick a point near the left end of the wire connected to **pin 3** on **PJ4**, as shown in Figure 9–22.

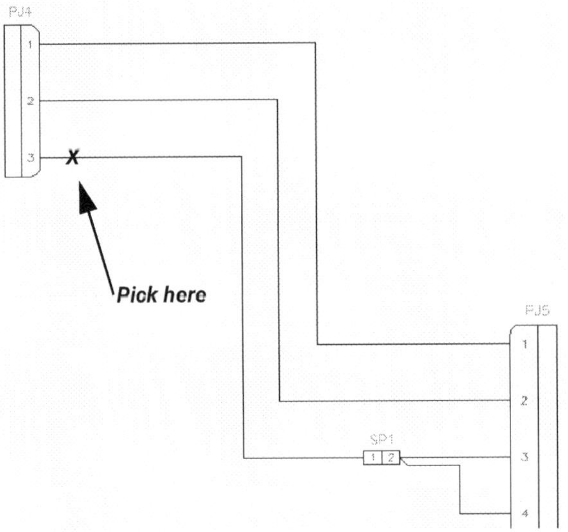

Figure 9–22

3. Pick a point on the vertical portion of the same wire, as shown in Figure 9–23. Note that the wire now travels vertically downward from the first selected point and then runs horizontally through the second selected point to create an additional bend in the wire, as shown previously in Figure 9–13.

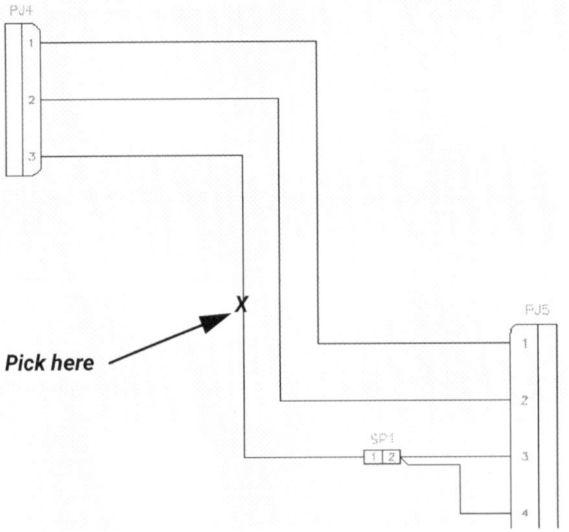

Figure 9–23

4. Press <Enter> to end the command.
5. Save and close **Point_to_point_02.dwg**.

End of practice

Chapter Review Questions

1. In the *Insert Connector* dialog box, which format can be used for the Pin List?
    a. A link to the spreadsheet only.
    b. Only a single character for an incrementing list.
    c. Only a comm-delimited list of pin numbers.
    d. A single character for an incrementing list or a comma-delimited list of pin numbers.

2. Which command is used to link a child connector to its parent?
    a. Link Component
    b. Edit Component
    c. Insert Connector
    d. Reverse Connector

3. If you need to insert pins on a connector, but there is not enough room for the new pins, how can you expand the connector?
    a. Use **Stretch Connector** then **Add Connector Pins**.
    b. Use **Stretch Connector** then **Insert Connector**.
    c. Use **Add Connector Pins** then the **Expand** option.
    d. The only way is to delete it entirely and reinsert the connector of the correct size.

4. When you insert a second wire on a splice, how is it visually different from the first wire?
    a. It has a curved wire added automatically.
    b. It has a dashed line to represent the second wire.
    c. It has a 45-degree angled wire added automatically.
    d. It is not visually different.

5. What two commands are used to insert wires into a point-to-point drawing?
   a. Insert Wire and Multiple Bus
   b. Multiple Bus and Insert Multiple Wires
   c. Multiple Bus and Insert Component
   d. Insert Wire and Insert Multiple Wires

6. When using the **Multiple Bus** command, how does the AutoCAD Electrical software determine the number of wires to insert?
   a. By the number of insertion points selected by the window selection polygon.
   b. At the Command Prompt, type **T** and enter the number of wires before selecting the end point of wires.
   c. By the number of unconnected insertion points in the entire drawing.
   d. By the length of the components selected.

7. When using the **Bend Wires** command, how does the AutoCAD Electrical software determine where to place the bend?
   a. By the midpoint of the wires selected.
   b. By the user-selected points of the wires.
   c. By the amount indicated in the project file.
   d. By the nearest components.

Command Summary

Button	Command	Location
	**Bend Wire**	• **Ribbon:** *Schematic* tab>*Edit Wires/Wire Numbers* panel
	**Insert Connector**	• **Ribbon:** *Schematic* tab>*Insert Components* panel
	**Insert Splice**	• **Ribbon:** *Schematic* tab>*Insert Components* panel
	**Multiple Wire Bus**	• **Ribbon:** *Schematic* tab>*Insert Wires/Wire Numbers* panel
	**Reverse Connector**	• **Ribbon:** *Schematic* tab>*Edit Components* panel
	**Rotate Connector**	• **Ribbon:** *Schematic* tab>*Edit Components* panel

Chapter

10

Symbol Creation

This chapter provides knowledge on how to create schematic symbols and panel footprints, use the *Icon Menu Wizard* and databases, as well as add objects to the Icon Menu, information to the Catalog database, or blocks to the Footprint Lookup database in order to facilitate adding PLC modules to the PLC database and pinning information to the Pin List database.

Learning Objectives

- Create AutoCAD® Electrical symbols.
- Identify symbols by their naming conventions and modify the library search paths.
- Insert a submenu trigger and a symbol icon.
- Recognize the use of databases in the AutoCAD Electrical software.
- Recognize the use and location of the project's scratch database.
- Recognize the use of and the directory search order for the catalog database and footprint lookup database.
- Add and modify an entry in the catalog database and footprint lookup database.
- Add a new module to the PLC database.

10.1 Schematic Symbols

The schematic symbols used by the AutoCAD Electrical software are AutoCAD blocks with attributes. The attributes have several functions, including displaying data, storing data, and controlling wire connection points. Although you can create AutoCAD Electrical symbols using traditional AutoCAD commands, the **Symbol Builder** command works in the AutoCAD Block Editor environment and it enables you to insert the attributes that define the AutoCAD Electrical intelligence.

Symbol Builder

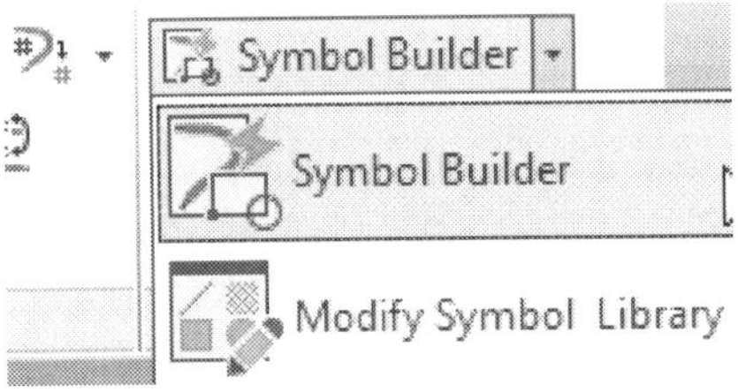

Ribbon: *Schematic* tab>*Other Tools* panel or *Panel* tab>*Other Tools* panel

Command Prompt: aesymbuilder

How To: Create an AutoCAD Electrical Symbol

1. Draw the symbol using AutoCAD commands.
2. Start the **Symbol Builder** command. The *Select Symbol / Objects* dialog box opens.
3. Fill out the dialog box by selecting a block or objects for the symbol, selecting its insertion point, and then selecting a **Symbol** and **Type**.
4. Click **OK** to continue. The geometry is loaded in the *AutoCAD Block Editor* environment with the *Symbol Builder Attribute Editor* palette and *Symbol Builder* tab open in the ribbon.
5. Insert the required and optional attributes such as the Wire Connection and the Link Line attributes.
6. Click (Done) or (Close Block Editor) to open the *Close Block Editor: Save Symbol* dialog box.
7. Fill out the dialog box and click **OK** to save the symbol.

The *Select Symbol / Objects* dialog box (shown in Figure 10–1) is used to specify the objects to use and specify the location for attribute templates.

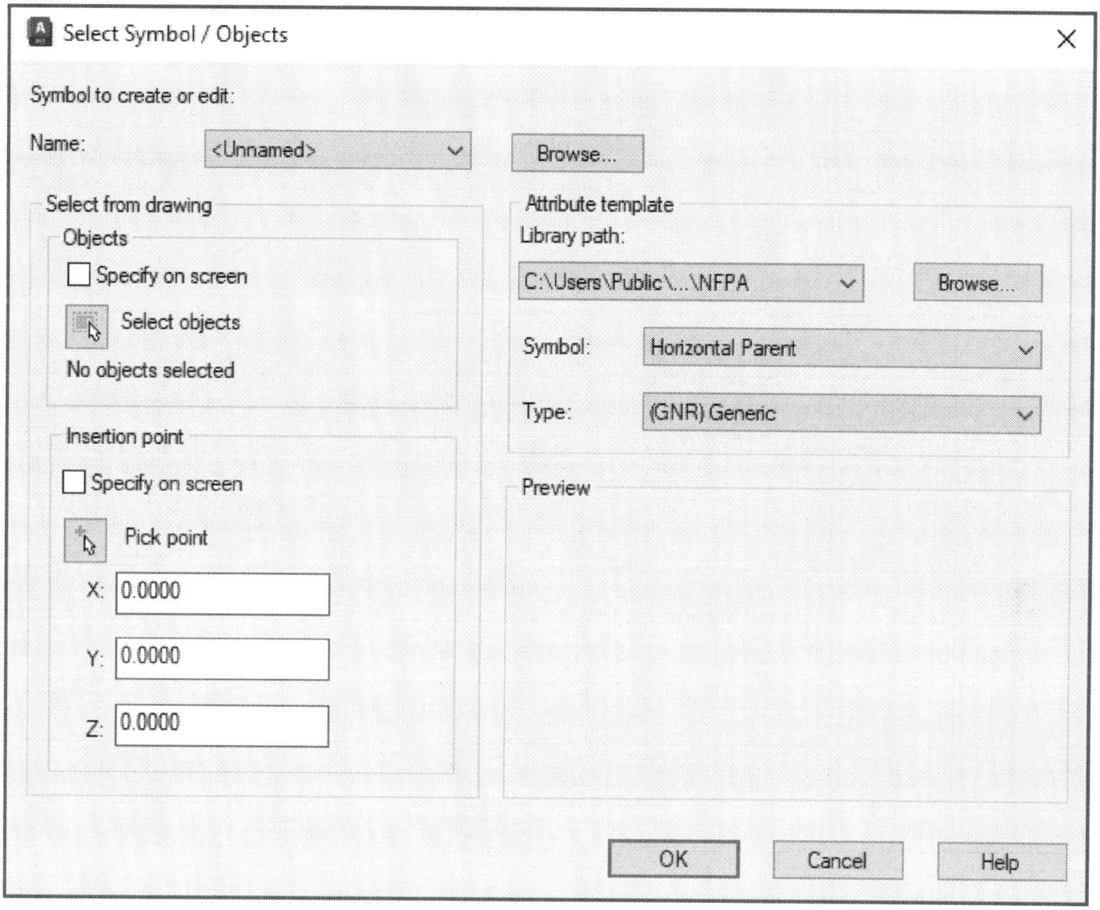

Figure 10–1

Name	Select from the list of existing blocks in the current drawing or click **Browse** to select a file.
Select from drawing	Select the objects and insertion point for the symbol if a block is not selected in the *Name* field. • **Objects:** Select any existing geometry, text, or attributes to include in the symbol. Click  (Select objects) to select objects immediately or select the **Specify on screen** option to select objects after the dialog box closes. • **Insertion point:** Specify the coordinates for the 0,0,0 point of the symbol. Click  (Pick point) to select a point immediately or select the **Specify on screen** option to select a point after the dialog box closes. Alternatively, you can type the coordinates in the *X,Y,Z* fields.

Attribute template	Specify the library path, symbol category, and symbol type. • **Library path:** Select a path in the drop-down list or click **Browse** to browse to a folder. The *Symbol* and *Type* fields are populated based on the attribute templates located in the selected directory. • **Symbol:** Select the category for the symbol. The category controls whether you are creating a schematic or panel symbol, the horizontal or vertical orientation, and the parent or child symbol. • **Type:** This field is populated based on the available attribute template files and the category selected in the *Symbol* field. The *Type* controls the family code for the symbol (push button, relay, terminal, etc).
Preview	Displays a preview of the symbol from the selected block or objects.

How To: Insert an Attribute

1. From the list in the *Symbol Builder Attribute Editor* palette, select the attribute to insert.
2. Click (Insert Attribute).
3. Pick the location for the attribute.
4. Repeat Steps 1 to 3 for each attribute that you want to insert.

- Use **Snap** to accurately position the attributes on the geometry.

How To: Insert Wire Connection Attributes

1. In the *Symbol Builder Attribute Editor* palette, in the Direction/Style drop-down list, select the wire connection type.
2. Click (Insert Wire Connection).
3. Pick the location for the wire connection.
4. Select one of the options to insert another wire connection or press <Enter> to end the command.

- Use **OSNAP** to accurately position the wire connection attributes on the geometry.

After you finish filling out the *Select Symbol / Objects* dialog box, the objects are opened in the AutoCAD Block Editor with the addition of the Symbol Builder Attribute Editor palette (as shown in Figure 10–2) and *Symbol Builder* tab in the ribbon (as shown in Figure 10–3).

- Geometry, attributes, and other objects can be added to the symbol using standard AutoCAD tools.
- The AutoCAD Electrical *intelligence* is added using the *Symbol Builder Attribute Editor* palette. Use the commands in the palette to insert attributes for the symbol information, wire connection positions, and link line locations.

- Attribute templates control the attributes expected for a symbol type and their default location. An attribute template is a DWG file that contains the attributes for that symbol type.
- Attribute template names start with AT_. The next two characters dictate the symbol category (HP = horizontal parent, HC = horizontal child, etc.). The last two characters dictate the type of symbol (PB = push button, FU = fuse, etc). For example, an attribute template name might be **AT_HP_PB.dwg** for a horizontal parent push button symbol.
- Several attribute templates are included in the libraries that are supplied with the software.
- Panel symbols do not require attributes. Any required data that does not have an associated attribute inserted is attached using xdata when the symbol is used. Xdata is invisible data attached to an AutoCAD block. The limitation of xdata is that it cannot be displayed on the symbol. You should insert attributes for any data that you want to display on the symbol.

The commands in the *Symbol Builder Attribute Editor* palette (as shown in Figure 10–2) can be used to insert attributes for the symbol information, wire connection positions, and link line locations.

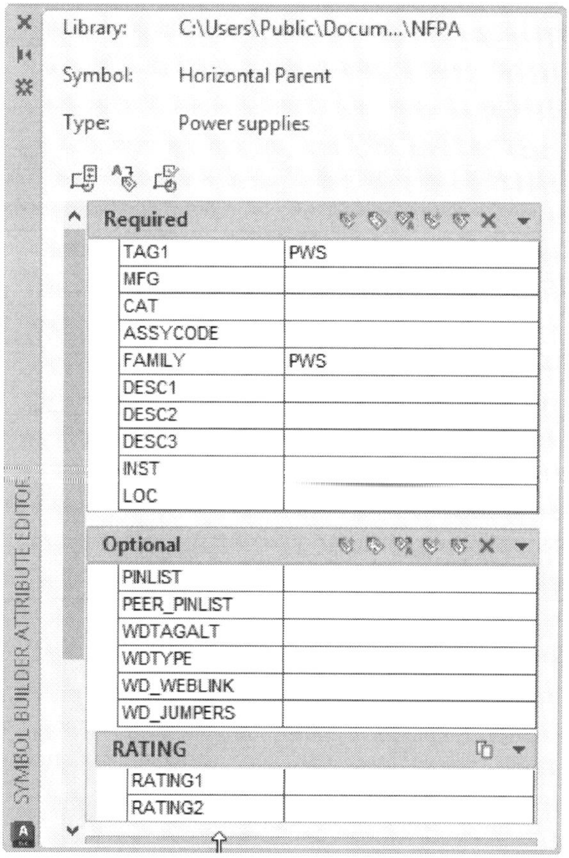

Figure 10–2

Different attributes are listed for different types of symbols.

	Symbol Configuration: Opens the *Symbol Configuration* dialog box in which you can change the library path, symbol category, symbol type, and insertion point.
	Convert Text to Attribute: Opens the *Convert Text to Attribute* dialog box, which enables you to map existing text to attributes for the symbol.
	Symbol Audit: Opens the *Symbol Audit* dialog box, which lists any issues with the attributes or symbol name.
Required	Lists attributes that are required or expected for Electrical Symbols. Use the commands or the shortcut menu to insert and modify the attributes. • **(Insert Attribute):** Inserts the selected attribute. • **(Properties):** Opens the *Insert / Edit Attributes* dialog box to modify the properties of the selected attribute. • **(Convert Text):** Converts existing text to the selected attribute. • **(Add Attribute):** Adds an attribute to the list of required attributes. • **(Remove Attribute):** Removes the selected attribute from the list. • **(Delete Attribute):** Deletes the selected attribute from the symbol.
Optional	Lists optional attributes from the attribute template. The commands that are available for **Required** attributes are also available for **Optional** attributes.
Wire Connection	Inserts wire connections based on a style and direction. Select the **Direction/ Style** in the drop-down list and then click (Insert Wire Connection) to insert the attributes. Select **Others...** in the drop-down list to open the *Insert Wire Connections* dialog box for more configuration options.
Pins	Automatically inserts pin attributes with the wire connection attributes. Use this area to manage the wire connection and pin attributes. • **(Properties):** Opens the *Insert / Edit Attributes* dialog box to modify the properties of the selected attribute. • **(Convert Text):** Converts existing text to the selected attribute. • **(Move Wire Connection):** Moves the selected wire connection attribute and its pin attribute. • **(Add Optional Attribute):** Adds an attribute to the list of required attributes. • **(Delete Wire Connection):** Deletes the selected attribute from the symbol.
Link Lines	Inserts link line attributes based on direction. Select the direction and then click (Insert Link Lines) to insert the attributes.

Inserted Link Lines	Lists information about the link line attributes that have been inserted. • **(Delete Link Lines):** Deletes the selected attribute from the symbol.

- Changes to the attribute list or the properties of attributes happen in the current session of the Symbol Builder and do not affect the attribute templates.
- displays next to attributes that have been inserted into the symbol.
- Use <Ctrl> or <Shift> to select multiple attributes before invoking a command.

In the ribbon, the *Symbol Builder* tab (shown in Figure 10–3) becomes available along with the AutoCAD *Block Editor* tab. Use these commands and the *Symbol Builder Attribute Editor* palette to complete the symbol.

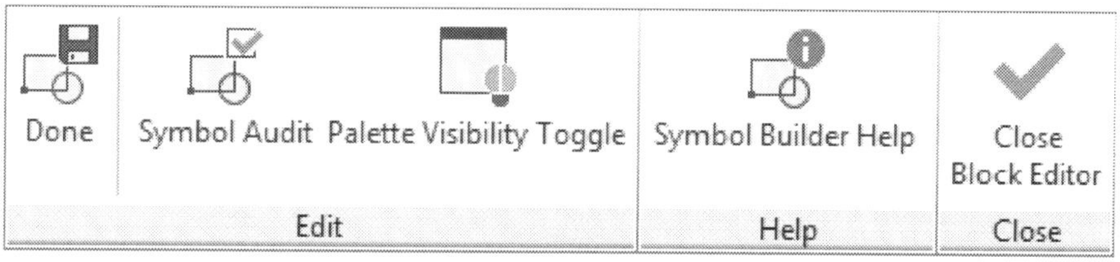

Figure 10–3

	Done: Opens the *Close Block Editor: Save Symbol* dialog box, which is used to configure the symbol name and location, base point, and image.
	Symbol Audit: Opens the *Symbol Audit* dialog box, which lists any issues with the attributes or symbol name.
	Palette Visibility Toggle: Controls the display of the *Symbol Builder Attribute Editor* palette.
	Symbol Builder Help: Displays help information for the Symbol Builder.
	Close Block Editor: Closes the *Block Editor* and returns to the active drawing.

- Clicking (Close Block Editor) to exit the AutoCAD Block Editor environment opens the *Close Block Editor: Save Symbol* dialog box.

The *Close Block Editor: Save Symbol* dialog box is shown in Figure 10–4.

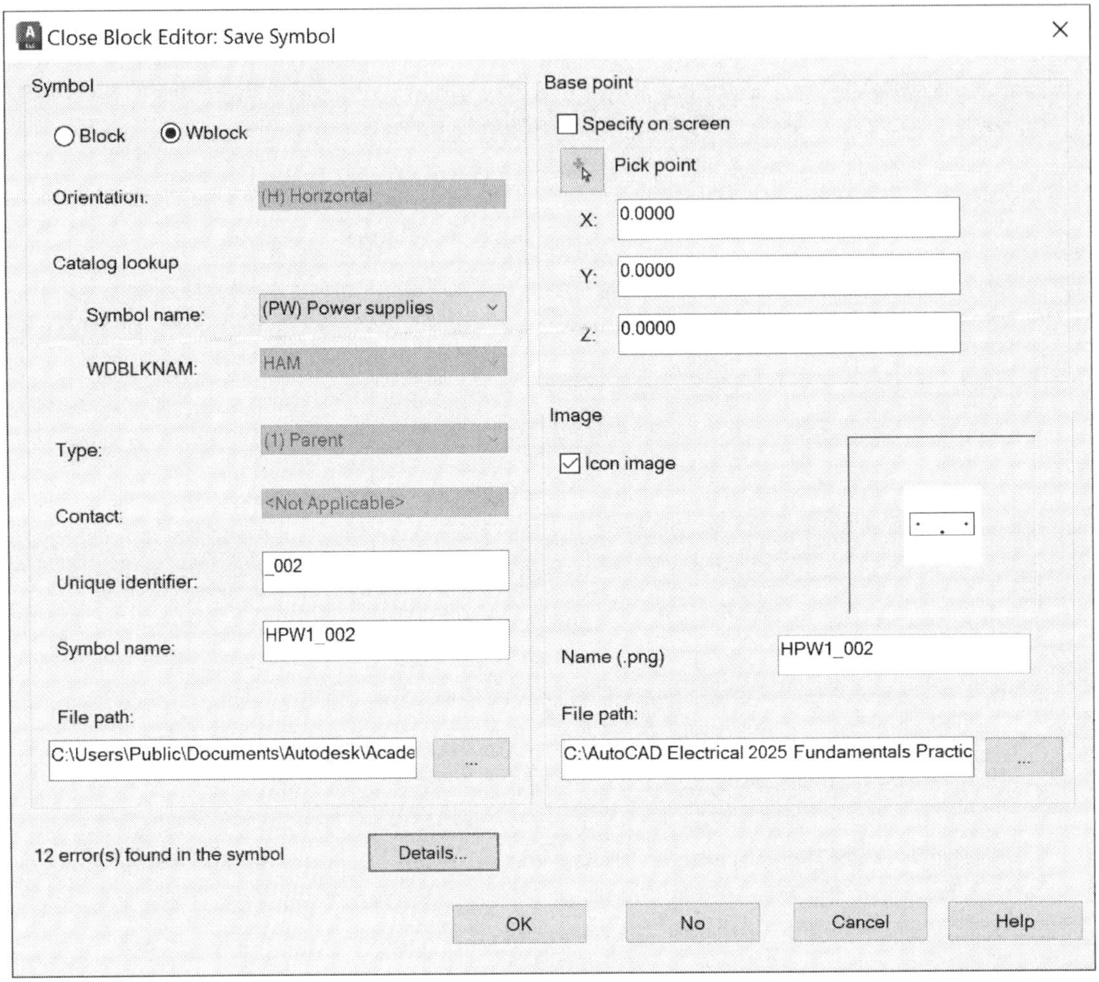

Figure 10–4

Symbol	Select **Block** to save the symbol in the current drawing or **Wblock** to save the block to the AutoCAD Electrical symbol library. The other fields are used to build the name in the *Symbol name* field (some fields are grayed out depending on the symbol type).
Base point	Specify the coordinates for the base point of the symbol. Click  (Pick Point) to select a point immediately or select the **Specify on screen** option to select a point after the dialog box closes. Alternatively, you can also enter the coordinates in the *X,Y,Z* fields.
Image	Select the **Icon image** option to create an image file (.PNG) to use if the symbol is added to the Icon Menu.

- The characters before the _ character in the symbol name must not be changed. The characters after the _ character can be changed. They are used to ensure that a unique filename is created for the DWG file.
- Once a symbol is created using the **Symbol Builder** command, you can access it through **Browse** in the Icon Menu. You can also use the **Icon Menu Wizard** to customize the Icon Menu to include your symbols.
- When converting AutoCAD blocks into AutoCAD Electrical intelligent symbols using the **Symbol Builder** command, first explode the block so that you can select the attributes in the Symbol Builder.
- If you accidentally exit the **Symbol Builder** command, start it again and select the block and attributes. The command resumes where you stopped.It is a good idea to save all custom symbols to a single location, but keep them separate from the standard AutoCAD Electrical symbols making it easier to share your symbols and to upgrade to later releases of the software.

10.2 Naming Convention

The AutoCAD Electrical software follows a specific naming convention for symbols and applies to both the block name and DWG filename for the block in the library.

- Depending on the symbol type, the first four or five characters in the name are used by the automated commands of the software. Some AutoCAD Electrical commands use these characters to determine the component type (push button, limit switch, etc.), orientation (horizontal or vertical), parent/child status, and whether it is normally open or normally closed.
- The naming convention is not mandatory, but is recommended so that you can take advantage of all of the AutoCAD Electrical commands.
- See the AutoCAD Electrical Help System under *symbols, naming convention* for information on the naming convention for all symbol types. Panel footprint symbols do not follow a specific naming convention.

1st Character	Either **H** for a horizontal symbol or **V** for a vertical symbol. Refers to the orientation of the wire on which the symbol is placed.
2nd and 3rd Characters	Family code for the symbol. For example, PB for push button, LS for limit switch, and CR for relays and contacts. • If the 3rd character is 0, the wire number does not change as it goes through the symbol.
4th Character	Either **2** for child symbols or **1** for everything else.
5th Character	For contact symbols only. Either **1** for normally open or **2** for normally closed.

Examples of symbols and their names:

HPB11	Horizontal push button, normally open.
HPB21	Horizontal push button, child contact, normally open.
HCR1	Horizontal relay coil.
VCR1	Vertical relay coil.
HCR21	Horizontal contact, normally open.
HCR22	Horizontal contact, normally closed.

- All characters after the fifth character are not used by the software and can be of any type as long as they are valid for a Windows filename. They are typically used to make DWG names unique. For example, in the naming convention for a normal push button and a mushroomhead push button, the first five characters for both symbols would be HPB11. Therefore, the mushroomhead push button is named HPB11M to be unique from the push button symbol name (HPB11).

Library files are stored in external folders until the symbol is used. When a symbol is used in a drawing, its block definition is copied into that drawing. When a symbol is inserted, the software searches for it in a series of locations in a specific order.

The search order is as follows:

1. Search the current drawing file for the block definition.
2. Check the specific directory if the full path name is provided.
3. Check the user subdirectory. (The user subdirectory is defined by the **WD_USER** parameter in the **wd.env** file).
4. Search the directory in which the active project file is located.
5. Search the directories listed in the *Project Settings* in the *Project Properties* dialog box.
6. Search the electrical support files.
7. Check the current directory.
8. Search the path specified by the **WD_LIB** parameter in the **wd.env** file.

- The **wd.env** file is a text file that contains settings for default directories that the software uses.
- This file can be edited using any text editor.
- The file is located in the following location in Windows 10: *C:\Users\<username>\Documents\Acade <version>\AeData*.

A project file can be configured to search multiple library directories. This configuration is controlled in **Project Properties** in the *Project Settings* tab and is useful if you use a custom library for special symbols and the default AutoCAD Electrical library for everything else. The libraries are searched in the order in which they are listed in the *Project Properties* dialog box, as shown in Figure 10–5.

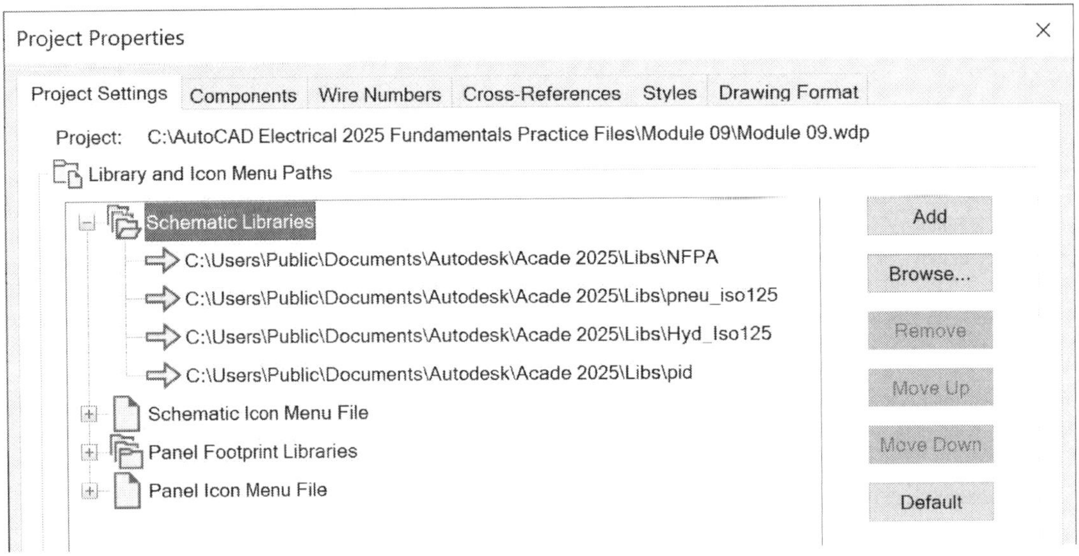

Figure 10–5

Add	Adds a new path to the end of the list.
Browse	Opens the Windows *Browse for Folder* dialog box. Select the folder to use for the path.
Remove	Removes the selected path from the list.
Move Up/Move Down	Moves the selected path up or down one position in the list.
Default	Restores the default paths from the **wd.env** file.

How To: Change the Library Search Paths

1. Activate the project file to be able to change its settings.
2. Right-click on the project file and select **Properties**. The *Project Properties* dialog box opens.
3. In the *Project Settings* tab, click **+** next to Schematic Libraries to expand the node.
4. Use the buttons on the right side of the dialog box to configure the library search paths.
5. Click **OK** to save the changes and exit the dialog box.

Practice 10a
Create a Custom Symbol

Practice Objectives

- Create and save an electrical symbol.
- Insert a custom symbol into a schematic drawing.

In this practice, you will use the **Symbol Builder** to create a custom symbol. You will first insert attributes to carry the AutoCAD Electrical intelligence and then save the symbol. You will then insert the symbol into an existing drawing, as shown in Figure 10–6.

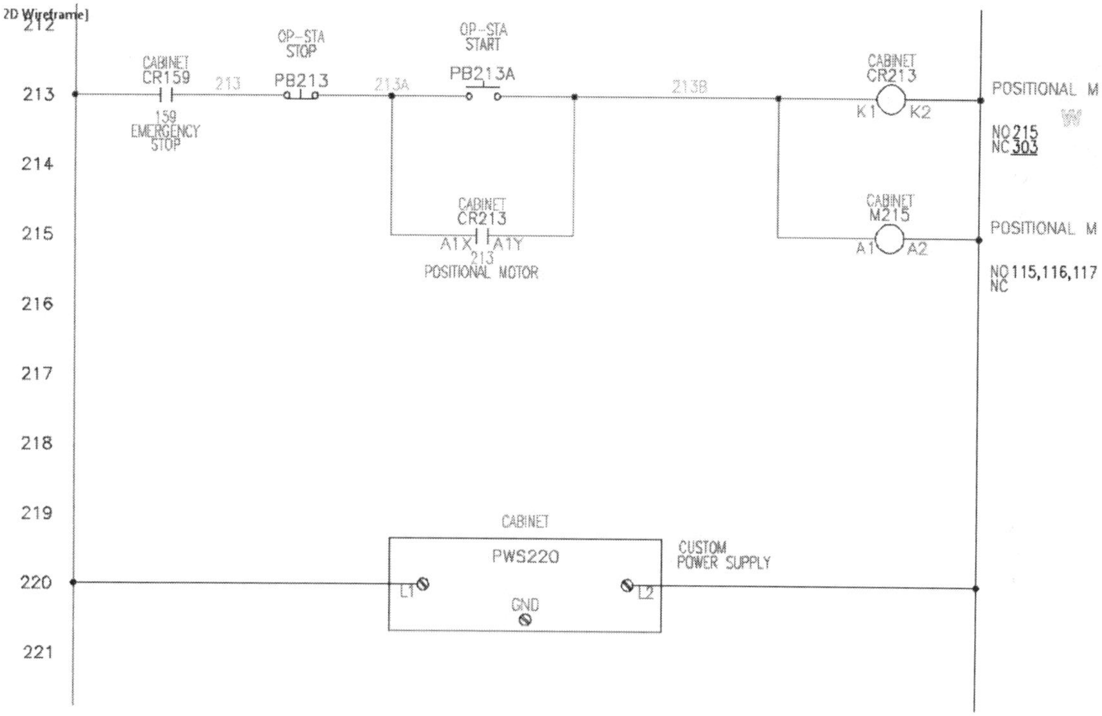

Figure 10–6

Task 1: Start the Symbol Builder command.

1. In your practice files folder, in the *Module 10* folder, open the **Module 10** project file.

2. Using the AutoCAD **Open** command (in the Quick Access Toolbar or use **Open files** in the *Start* tab), open **Custom_symbol_PS.dwg** from your *Module 10* practice files folder. The drawing opens as shown in Figure 10–7.
   - The drawing is not a part of the Module 10 project, but is a separate file provided in the *Module 10* folder in your practice files folder. You need to use the standard AutoCAD **Open** command to open it.
   - If the dialog box does not display, set the FILEDIA system variable to **1**.

Figure 10–7

3. In the *Schematic* tab>*Other Tools* panel, click (Symbol Builder). The *Select Symbol / Objects* dialog box opens.

4. In the *Objects* area, click (Select objects) and using window selection, select all of the geometry in the drawing. Press <Enter>.

5. In the *Insertion point* area, click (Pick point) and select a point in the center of the rectangle (use OSNAP).

6. In the *Attribute template* area, use **Browse** to set the *Library path* to the *NFPA* library by selecting **NFPA** in the *Autodesk\Acade 2025\Libs* directory, as shown in Figure 10–8.
7. Set the following, as shown in Figure 10–8:
   - *Symbol*: **Horizontal Parent**
   - *Type*: **(PW) Power supplies**

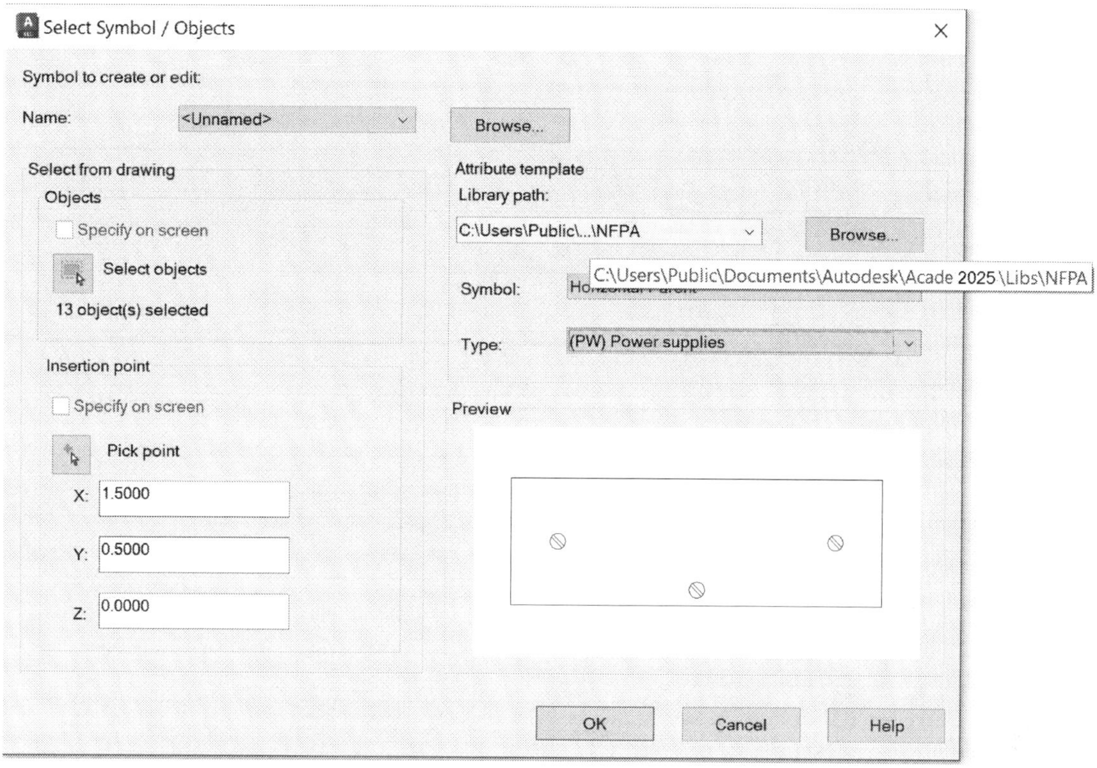

Figure 10–8

8. Click **OK** to load the geometry into the AutoCAD Block Editor environment. The *Symbol Builder Attribute Editor* palette opens. Note that the ribbon displays the *Symbol Builder* and *Block Editor* tabs.

Task 2: Insert standard attributes.

1. In the *Symbol Builder Attribute Editor* palette, in the *Required* area, note that *TAG1* is set as **PWS**, by the NFPA standard. This will insert the Power supply symbol in the drawing and is assigned [%f], a replaceable parameter. Set the *FAMILY* attribute to **PW**, as shown in Figure 10–9.

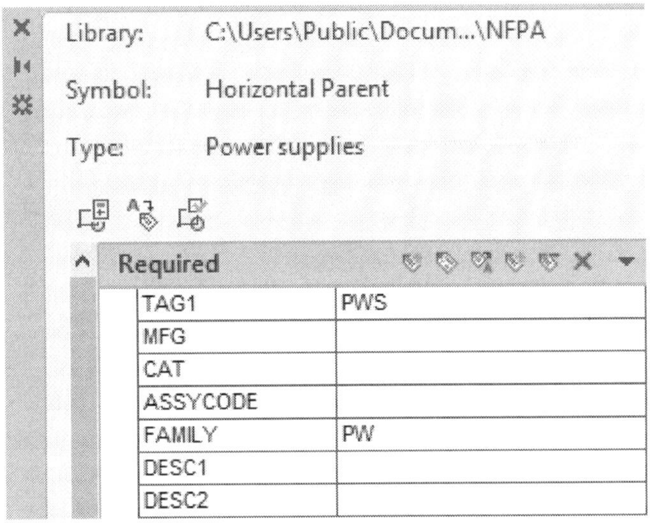

Figure 10–9

2. In the *Symbol Builder Attribute Editor* palette, in the *Required* area, click and hold **TAG1** attribute and drag it onto the drawing. Click to place it above the center of the rectangle below the top edge, as shown in Figure 10–10.

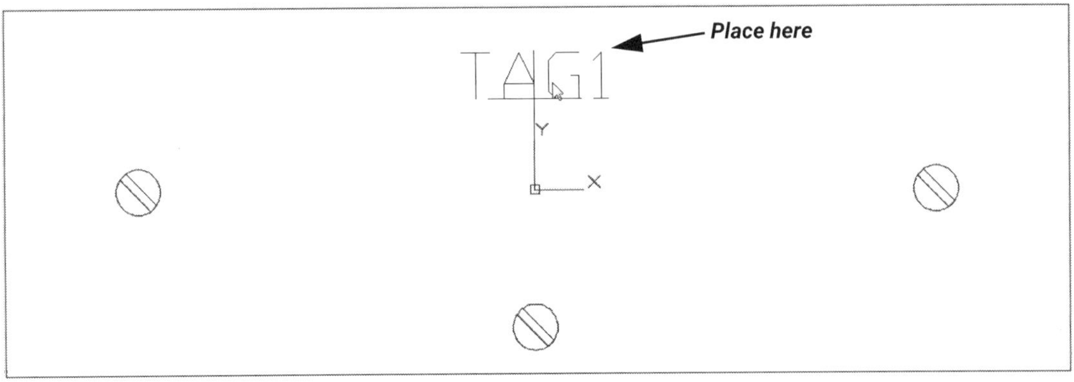

Figure 10–10

- Note that in the *Symbol Builder Attribute Editor* palette, ✔ displays next to **TAG1** (as shown in Figure 10–11), indicating that it has been inserted in the drawing.

3. In the *Symbol Builder Attribute Editor* palette, select **MFG**. Hold <Ctrl> and select **CAT**, **ASSYCODE**, and **FAMILY**, as shown in Figure 10–11.

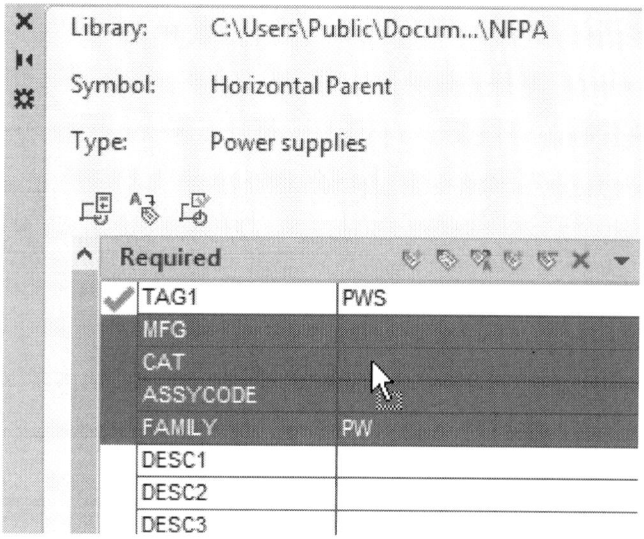

Figure 10–11

4. Drag and place them in the drawing near the right side of center point of the rectangle, as shown in Figure 10–12.

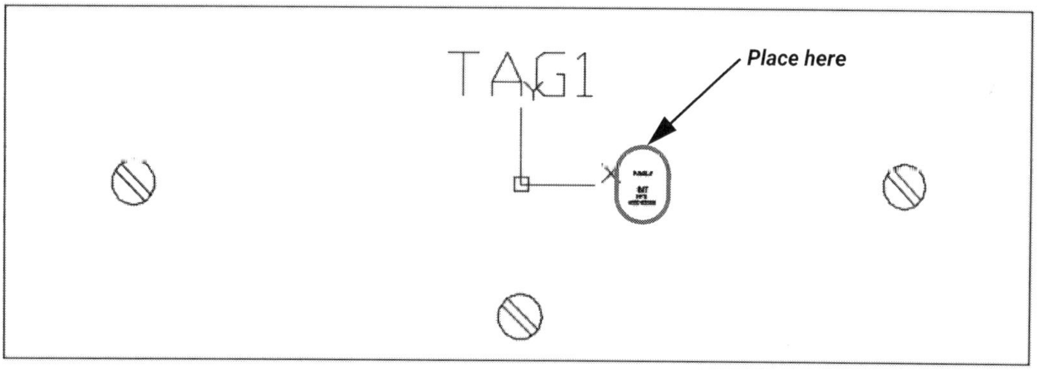

Figure 10–12

5. In the *Symbol Builder Attribute Editor* palette, using <Ctrl>, select **DESC1**, **DESC2**, and **DESC3**. Right-click and select **Properties**, as shown in Figure 10–13. *The Insert / Edit Attributes* dialog box opens. Set *Justify* to **Left**, as shown in Figure 10–14. Click **OK**.

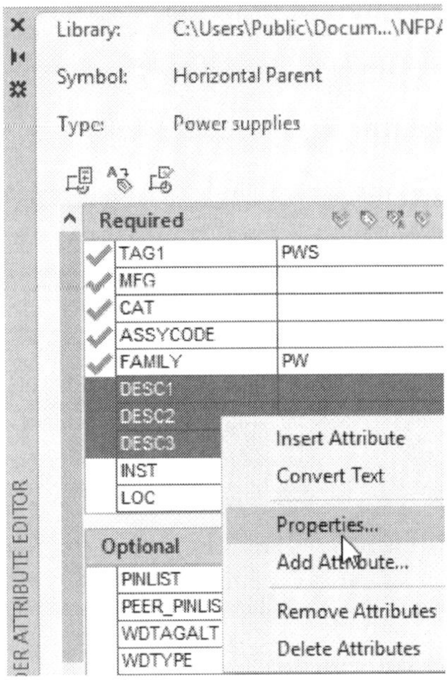

Figure 10–13

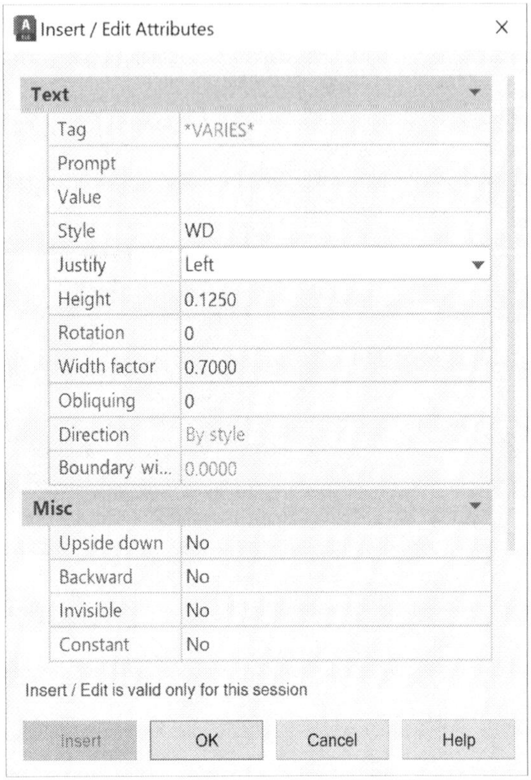

Figure 10–14

6. Drag the three selected **DESC** from the *Symbol Builder Attribute Editor* and place them on the drawing outside the right edge of the rectangle, as shown in Figure 10–15.

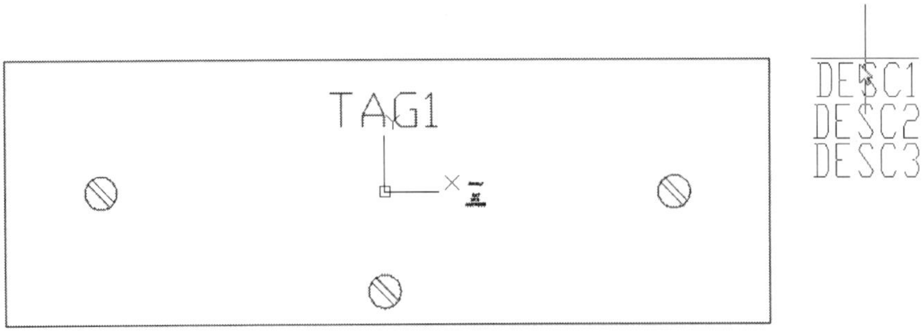

Figure 10–15

7. In the *Symbol Builder Attribute Editor* palette, in the *Required* area, drag and place **LOC** on the drawing on top of the rectangle, as shown in Figure 10–16.
8. In the *Symbol Builder Attribute Editor* palette in the *RATING* area, drag and place **RATING1** near the bottom right corner inside the rectangle, as shown in Figure 10–16.

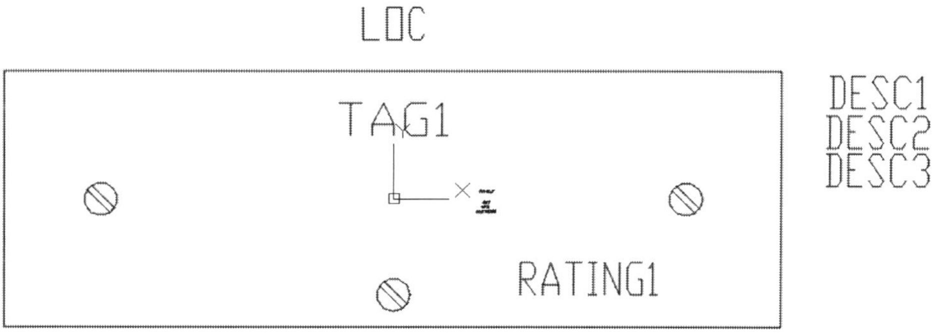

Figure 10–16

Task 3: Insert wire connection attributes.

1. In the *Symbol Builder Attribute Editor* palette, scroll down to the *Wire Connection* area and verify that *Direction/Style* is set to **Left/None**, as shown in Figure 10–17.

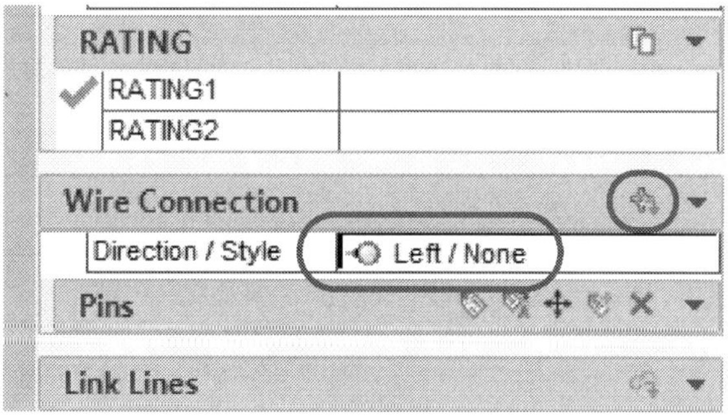

Figure 10–17

2. Near the right side of the *Wire Connection* title bar, click  (Insert Wire Connection), as shown in Figure 10–17.
3. Move the cursor over the drawing, and note that TERM01 is attached to the cursor. Pick the left quadrant of the left connection circle, as shown in Figure 10–18.
   - To locate the point precisely, use the **Quadrant** Object Snap. You might need to toggle the **Snap** off.

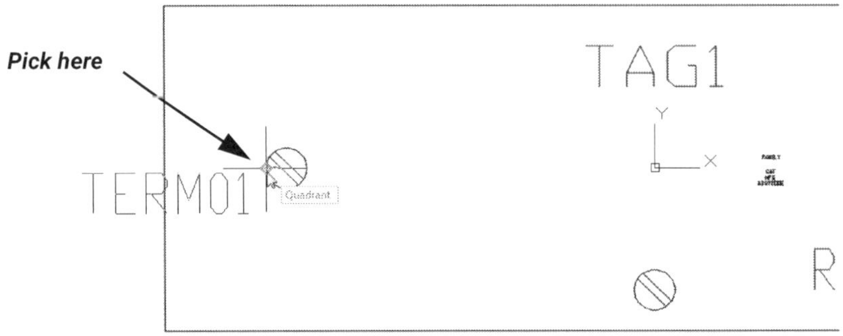

Figure 10–18

4. Note that TERM02 displays with the cursor. In the *Symbol Builder Attribute Editor* palette, in the *Wire Connection* area, change the *Direction / Style* is set to **Right/None** and click  (Insert Wire Connection) again.
5. Pick the right quadrant of the right connection circle, as shown in Figure 10–19.

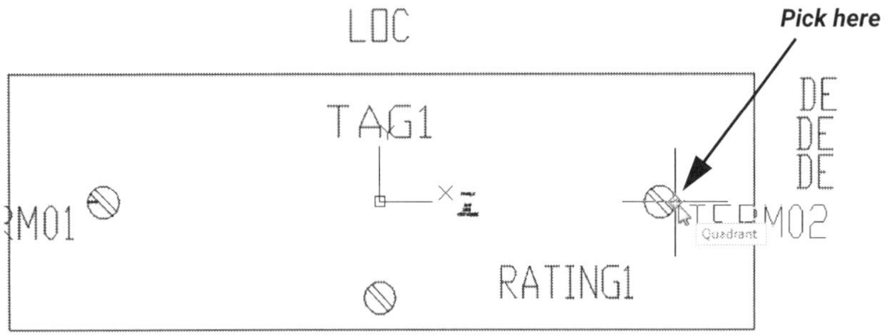

Figure 10–19

6. With TERM03 displayed at the cursor, pick the bottom quadrant of the bottom pin circle. Press <Enter> to exit the command.

7. Using the AutoCAD **Move** command, move **TERM03** and position it above the bottom middle pin, as shown in Figure 10–20.

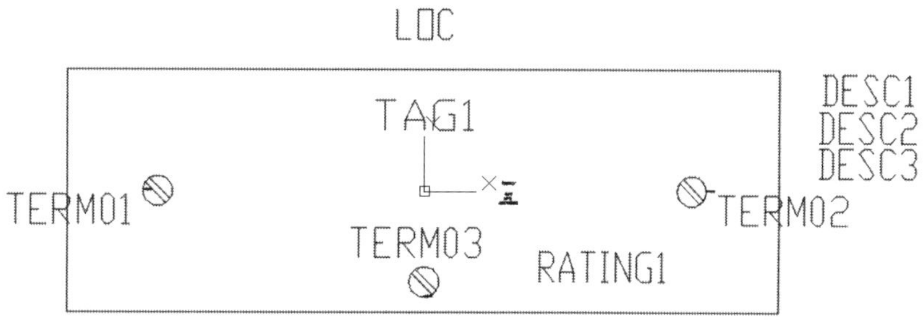

Figure 10–20

8. In the *Symbol Builder Attribute Editor* palette, in the *Pins* area, set the following, as shown in Figure 10–21:

- *TERM01*: **L1**
- *TERM02*: **L2**
- *TERM03*: **GND**

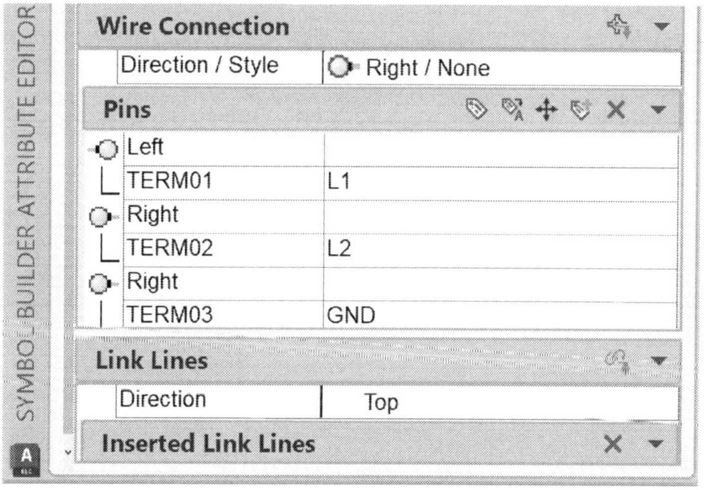

Figure 10–21

Task 4: Save the symbol.

1. In the ribbon, in the *Symbol Builder* contextual tab>*Edit* panel, click (Done). The *Close Block Editor: Save Symbol* dialog box opens.
2. In the *Symbol* area, verify that **Wblock** is selected. In *Unique identifier* field, type **_POWERSUPPLY**. Select the *Symbol name* field and note that **_POWERSUPPLY** is appended to **HPW1** as shown in Figure 10–22.

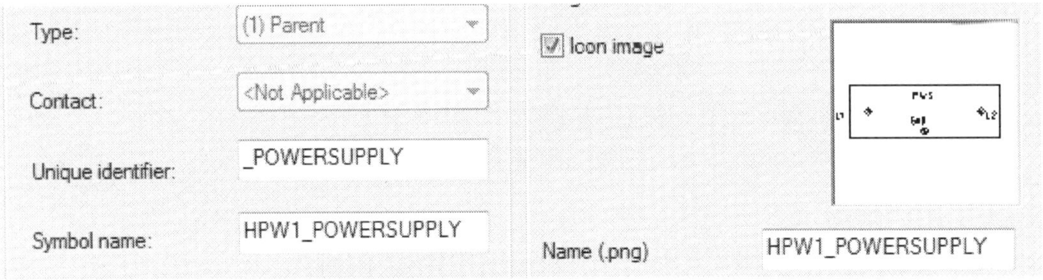

Figure 10–22

3. Click **OK** to save the symbol.
4. In the *Close Block Editor* warning dialog box, click **No**. If *Close Block Editor* is opened, click **No** again to close it.
5. Close **Custom_symbol_PS.dwg**. Do **NOT** save the changes. This symbol has been provided for you and is available in your practice files folder.

Task 5: Insert a new symbol.

1. In the **Module 10** project, open **Control.dwg**.
2. Zoom to the location of wire number 220.

3. In the *Schematic* tab>*Edit Wires/Wire Numbers* panel, click (Add Rung). Add a rung at 220, as shown in Figure 10–23.

Figure 10–23

4. In the *Schematic* tab>*Insert Components* panel, click (Icon Menu (Insert Component)). The *Insert Component* dialog box opens.
5. In the *Insert Component* dialog box, click **Browse**. Navigate to your practice files folder and in *Module10* folder, and open **HPW1_POWERSUPPLY.dwg**.
6. Note that the drawing is attached to the cursor. Pick the midpoint of rung 220 (as shown in Figure 10–24) to place the component.

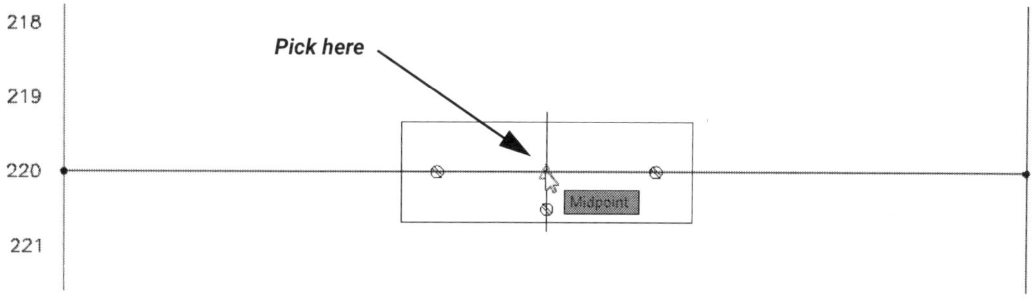

Figure 10–24

7. In the *Insert / Edit Component* dialog box that opens, set the following, as shown in Figure 10–25:
   - *Line 1*: **CUSTOM**
   - *Line 2*: **POWER SUPPLY**
   - *Location code:* **CABINET** (use **Project** and select **CABINET**)

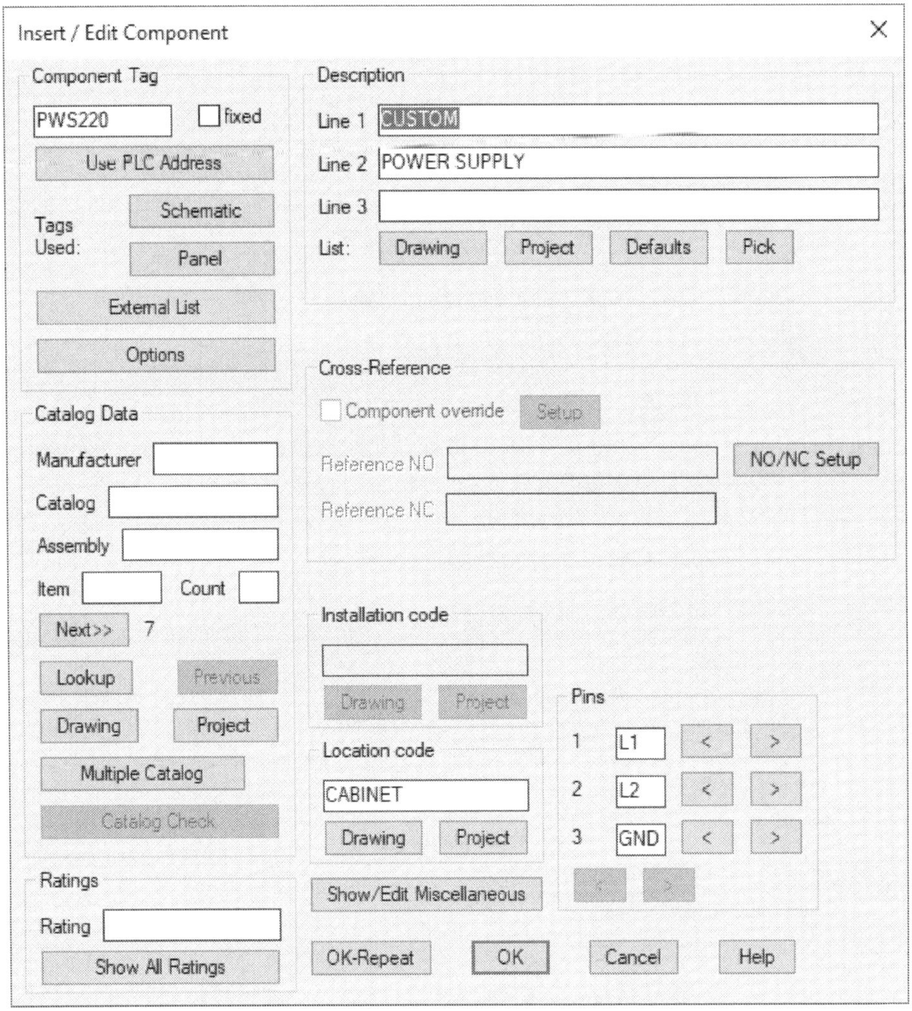

Figure 10–25

8. Click **OK**. The Power supply is placed on rung 220.
9. Close **Control.dwg** and do **NOT** save the drawing file.

End of practice

10.3 Icon Menu Wizard

The *Icon Menu Wizard* is used to add menus and symbols to the Icon Menus. The AutoCAD Electrical software uses text files to control the menus. The default menu files are:

- **ace_nfpa_menu.dat** for schematic symbols.
- **ace_panel_menu_nfpa.dat** for panel symbols.

Note: The DAT files can also be edited using any text editor.

When working with the *Icon Menu Wizard*, the Icon Menu you are editing opens. It looks exactly as it would if you were using the **Insert Component** or **Insert Footprint** commands. To modify existing icons or add new icons, use the shortcut menus in the *Icon Menu Wizard* dialog box.

Icon Menu Wizard

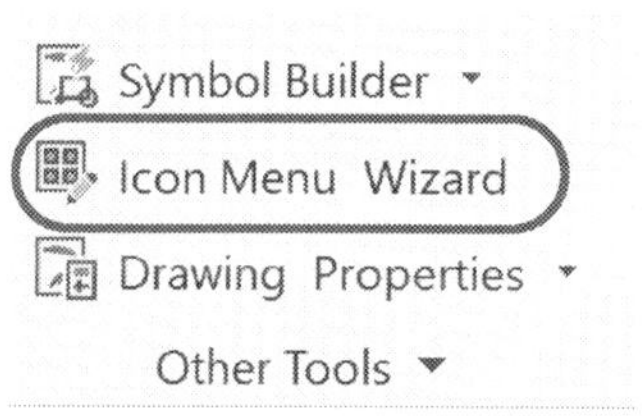

Ribbon: *Schematic* tab>*Other Tools* panel or *Panel* tab>*Other Tools* panel

Command Prompt: aemenuwiz

How To: Insert a Submenu Trigger

1. Start the **Icon Menu Wizard** command. The *Select Menu File* dialog box opens.
2. Select the menu file to edit. The *Icon Menu Wizard* opens.
3. Navigate to the menu in which you want to add a new submenu.
4. Right-click in a blank area and select **New submenu**. The *Create New Submenu* dialog box opens.
5. Fill in the *Name*, *Image file*, and *Menu title* fields and click **OK**. The *Icon Menu Wizard* opens.
6. Click **OK** to save the Icon Menu.

How To: Insert a Symbol Icon

1. Start the **Icon Menu Wizard** command. The *Select Menu file* dialog box opens.
2. Select the menu file to edit. The *Icon Menu Wizard* opens.
3. Navigate to the menu in which you want to add a new icon.
4. Right-click in a blank area and select **Add icon>Component**. The *Add Icon - Component* dialog box opens.
5. Fill in the *Name*, *Image file*, and *Block name* fields and click **OK**. The *Icon Menu Wizard* opens.
6. Click **OK** to save the Icon Menu.

- A submenu trigger is an icon that displays a submenu when clicked.
- To edit an existing submenu, double-click it in the *Icon Menu Wizard*.
- To create a new submenu, right-click in a blank area in the *Icon Menu Wizard* and select **New submenu**.
- When creating a new submenu trigger, the *Create New Submenu* dialog box opens, as shown in Figure 10–26.

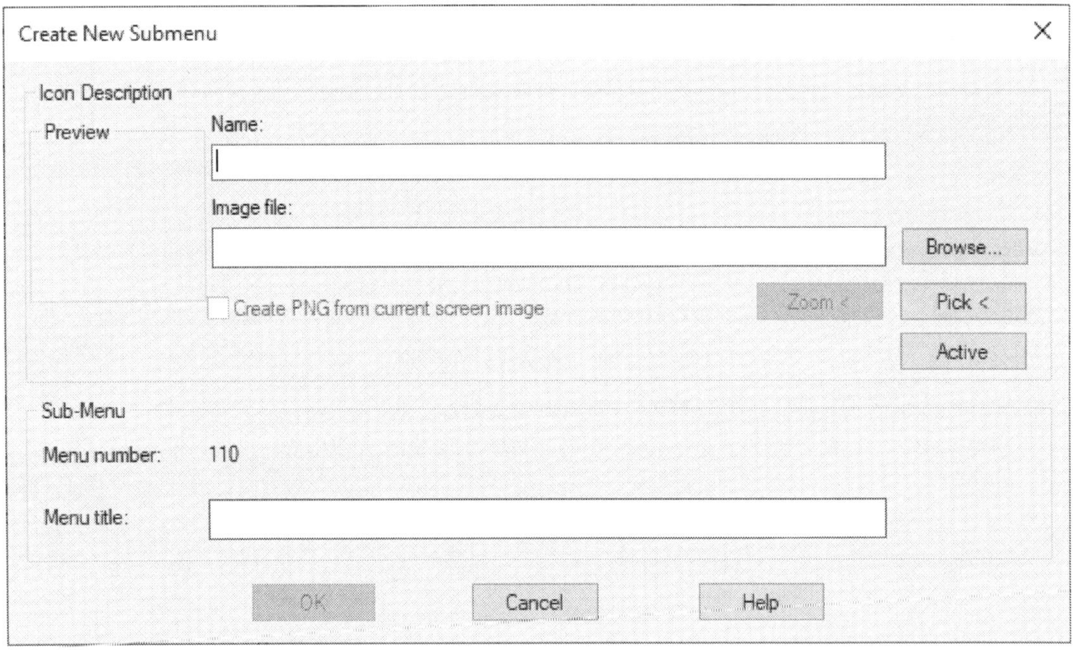

Figure 10–26

Name	Name that displays for the icon in the menu that is being edited.
Image file	Name of the image file to use for the icon. You can use an AutoCAD slide file (SLD) or a PNG file.
Preview	Preview of the image file used for the icon.
Browse	Browse for an existing PNG or slide file.
Pick <	Assigns an image name that matches a selected block in the drawing.
Active	Assigns an image name that matches the current drawing name.
Zoom<	Temporarily hides the dialog box, enabling you to zoom or pan in the drawing window to capture.
Create PNG from current screen image	If selected, a PNG file is created from the current screen image. The PNG file is used as the icon for the new menu.
Location	Displays the path for the image file.
Menu number	Displays the menu number of the menu that is created.
Menu title	The title that displays in the new menu. This can be different from the menu name.

- An AutoCAD slide file is a file containing a raster image of the objects in the drawing window. Slide files have an SLD file extension. They can be created using the AutoCAD **Mslide** command.
- A PNG file is a bitmapped image file. PNG files can be created using the **Pngout** command in the AutoCAD software or the *Icon Menu Wizard*. Most graphics editors can also create PNG files.
- The AutoCAD Electrical software uses a menu number to identify each menu. Menu numbers 1-99 are reserved for the software. Menu numbers 100 and higher are used for user-defined menus.

- You can also create icons that trigger the insertion of components. To create a new component icon, right-click in a blank area in the *Icon Menu Wizard* and select **Add icon> Component**. The *Add Icon – Component* dialog box opens, as shown in Figure 10–27.

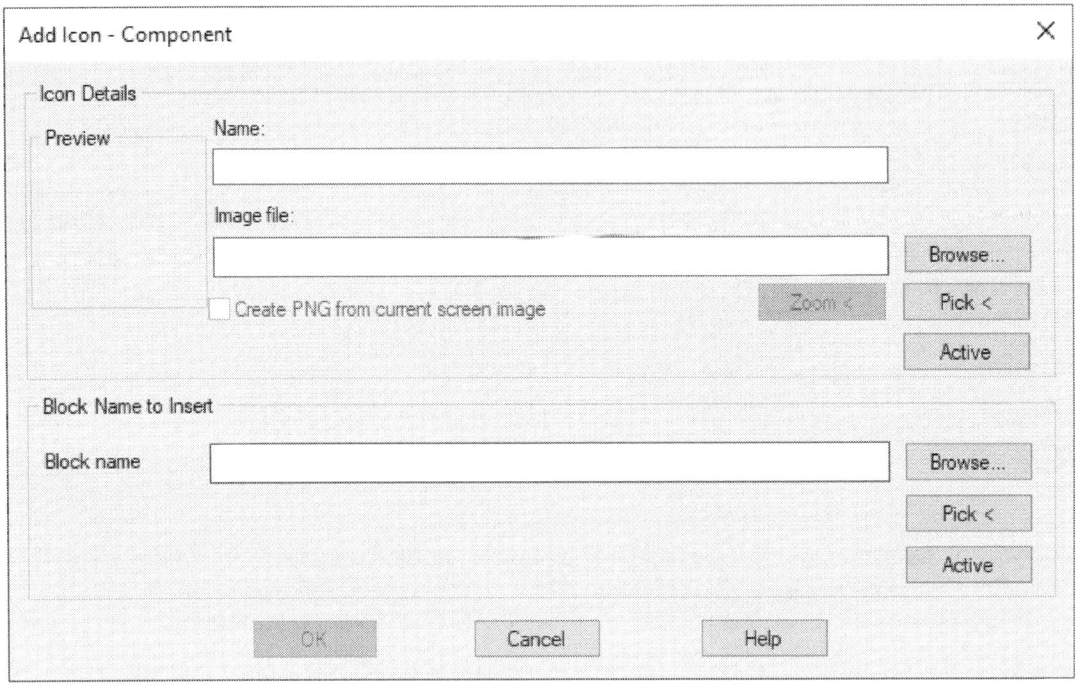

Figure 10–27

The *Icon Details* area of the dialog box has options similar to the *Icon Description* area of the *Create New Submenu* dialog box. The *Add Icon* dialog box has an additional *Block Name to Insert* area with the following options:

Block name	The name of the block that is inserted when the icon is clicked.
Browse	Browse for an existing DWG file to use.
Pick <	Pick a block in the current drawing to assign. A version of the block must exist external to the active drawing.
Active	Assigns the contents of the active drawing as the block.

- It is recommended that you backup the default Icon Menu before making any edits.
- You can modify existing icons in the *Icon Menu Wizard* by right-clicking on the icon and selecting **Properties**.
- For information on the other options in the *Icon Menu Wizard*, see **Icon Menu Wizard** in the AutoCAD Electrical Help.

Practice 10b
Customize the Icon Menu

Practice Objectives

- Create a submenu trigger and a symbol icon.
- Insert a component using the newly added submenu trigger and icon symbols.

In this practice, you will add a submenu trigger to the schematic icon menu using the *Icon Menu Wizard*. You will then add a button to insert a custom component. Finally, you will open an existing drawing and use the new buttons to insert a symbol as shown in Figure 10–28.

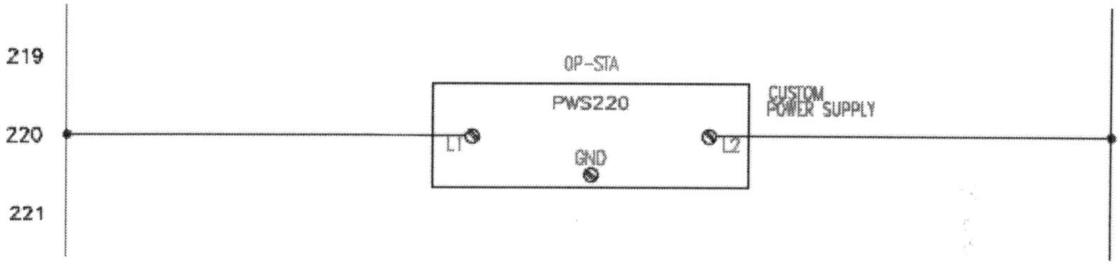

Figure 10–28

Task 1: Create a submenu trigger.

1. If the **Module 10** project is not active, open and activate it now.
2. In the **Module 10** project, open **Control.dwg**.
3. In the *Schematic* tab>*Other Tools* panel, click  (Icon Menu Wizard).

4. The *Select Menu file* dialog box opens. Verify that it references **ACE_NFPA_MENU.DAT**, as shown in Figure 10–29. Click **Browse** to open the *Select ".dat" icon menu file* dialog box. Note that the .DAT file is located in the *Module 10* folder of your practice files folder. In the dialog box, click **Cancel**. In the *Select Menu file* dialog box, click **OK**. The *Icon Menu Wizard* dialog box opens.

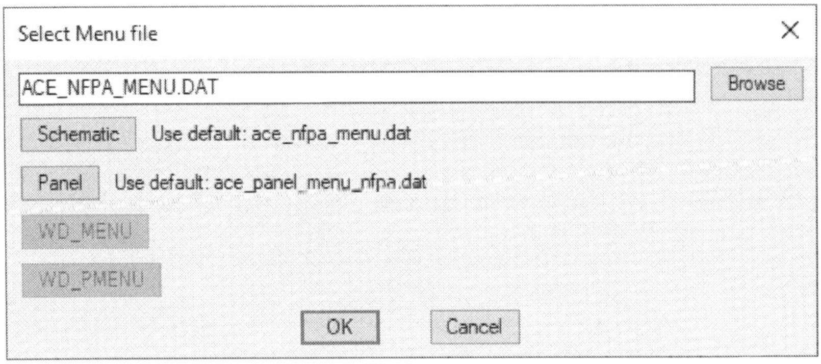

Figure 10–29

5. Right-click in a blank area and select **New submenu**, as shown in Figure 10–30. The *Create New Submenu* dialog box opens.

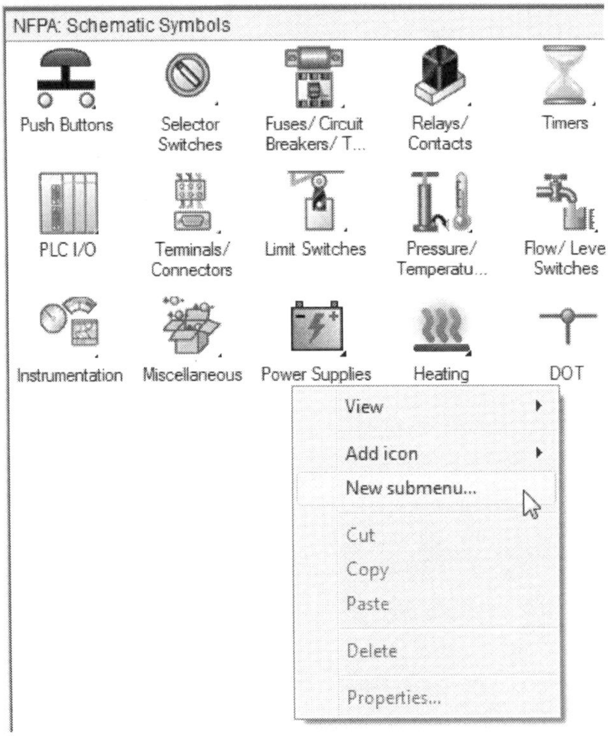

Figure 10–30

6. In the *Name* field, type **My Menu**. For the *Image file,* click **Browse**. Navigate to the *Module 10* folder in your practice files folder and select and open **My Menu.png**. Note that the preview of the selected image displays in the *Create New Submenu* dialog box, as shown in Figure 10–31. Click **OK**.

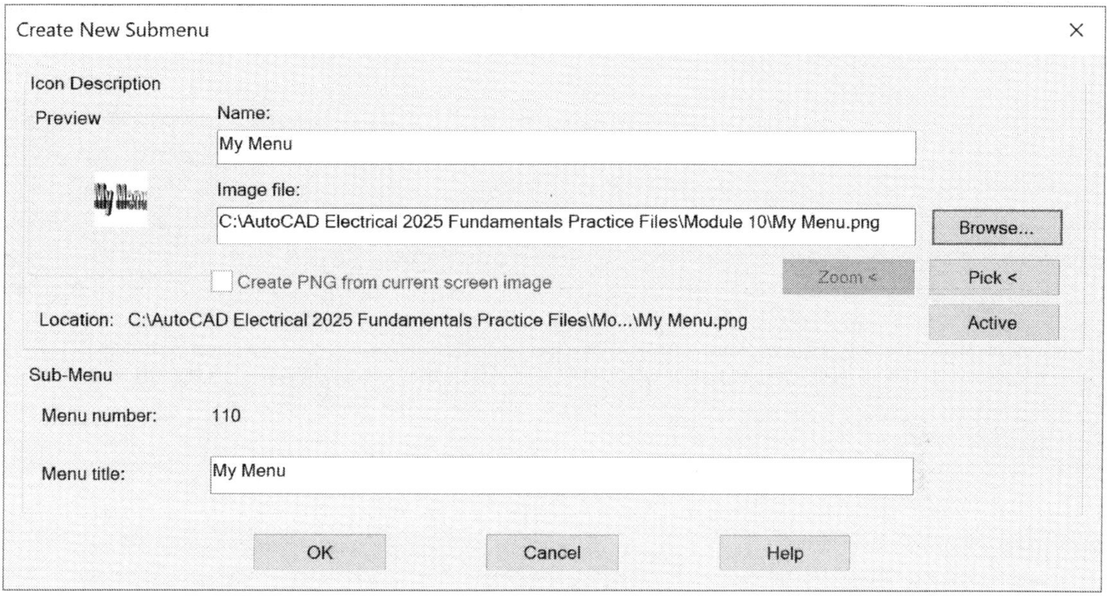

Figure 10–31

7. The new icon displays in the *Icon Menu Wizard* dialog box, as shown in Figure 10–32. Remain in this dialog box for the next task.

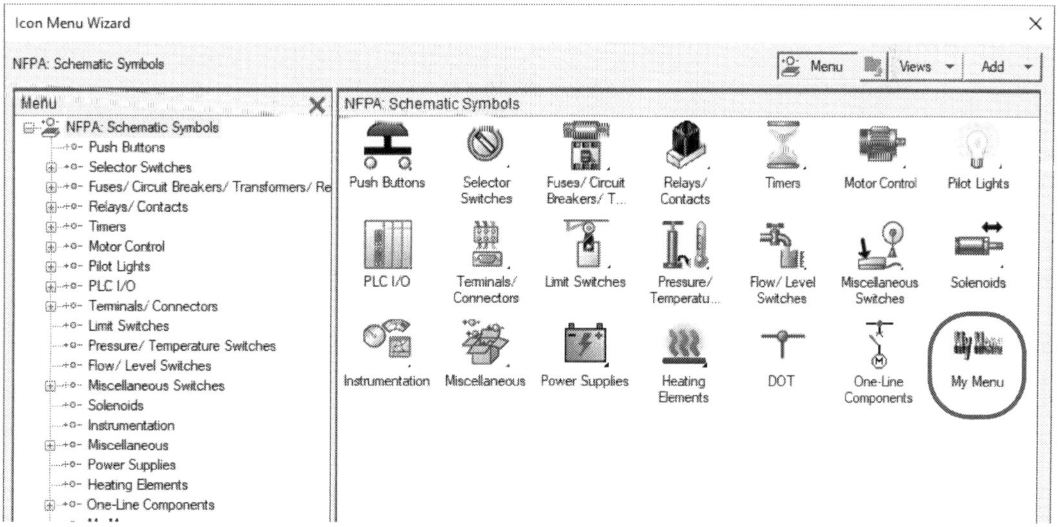

Figure 10–32

Task 2: Create an Insert Component button.

1. In the *Icon Menu Wizard*, double-click on  (My Menu). A blank menu opens.
2. Right-click and select **Add icon>Component** as shown in Figure 10–33. The *Add Icon – Component* dialog box opens.

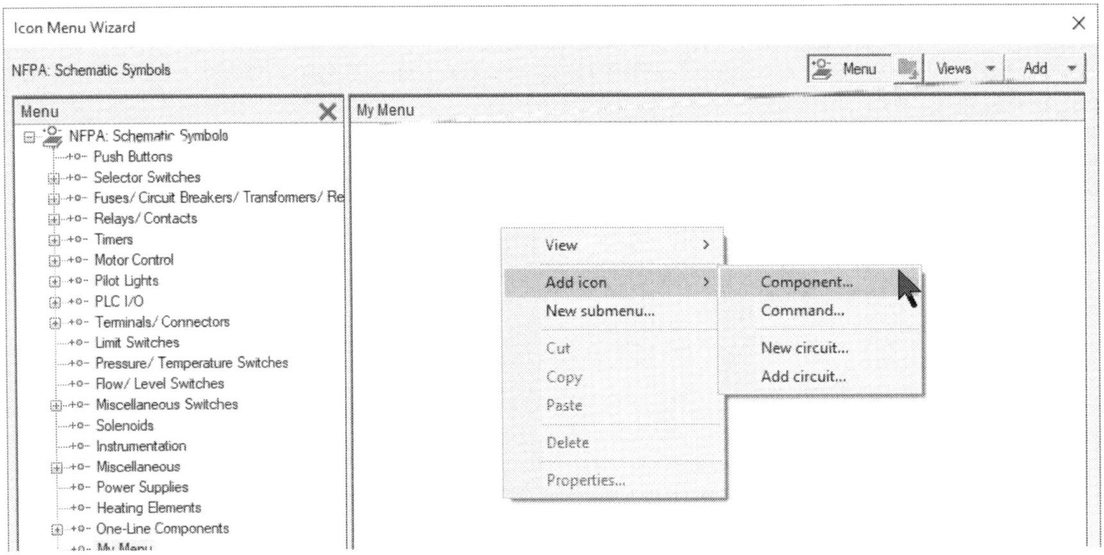

Figure 10–33

3. In the *Name* field, type **My Power Supply**. Next to the *Image file* field, click **Browse**. In the *Module 10* folder in your practice files folder, select **HPW1_POWERSUPPLY_ Done.png** and click **Open**. The image displays in the *Preview* area in the *Add Icon - Component* dialog box.
4. Next to the *Block name* field, click **Browse**. In the *Module 10* folder in your practice files folder, select **HPW1_POWERSUPPLY_Done.dwg** and click **Open**. Click **OK** in the *Add Icon - Component* dialog box.

5. You are returned to the *Icon Menu Wizard* with the new icon as shown in Figure 10–34. Click **OK**.

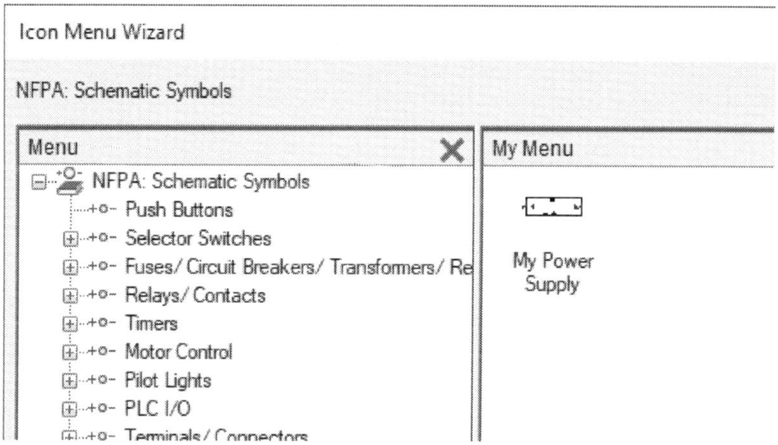

Figure 10–34

Task 3: Use the new buttons.

1. Zoom to line 220 in **Control.dwg**. Add a rung on line 220 and press <Enter> to exit the command.
2. In the *Project Manager*, select the Module 10 project. Right-click and select **Properties** to open the *Project Properties* dialog box.
3. In the *Project Settings* tab, expand **Schematic Libraries**, as shown in Figure 10–35.

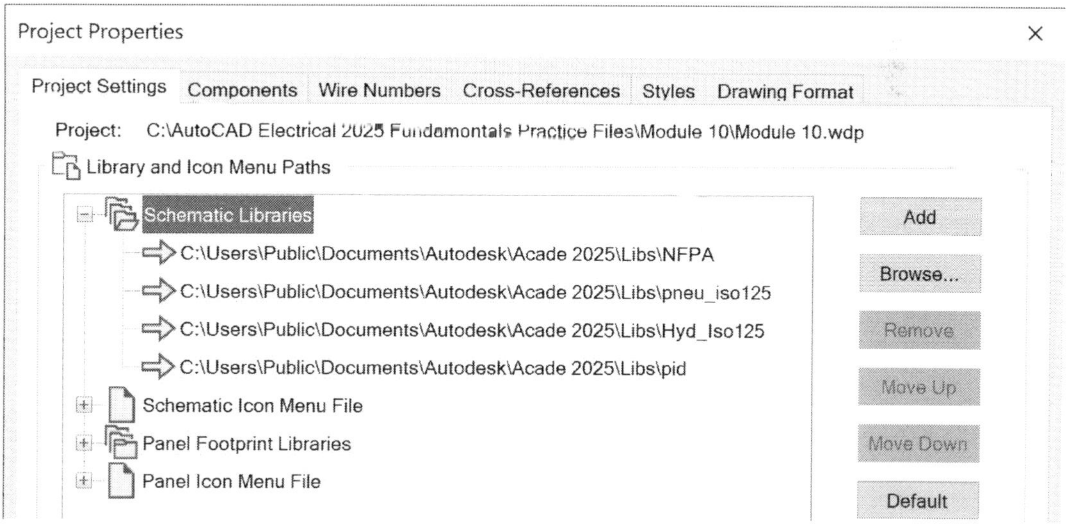

Figure 10–35

4. Click **Add** and note that an empty edit box is created with the cursor placed in it. Click **Browse** and select the *Module 10* folder in your practice files folder. Click **OK**. Note that the path is added to the bottom of the *Schematic Libraries* list.
5. With the Module 10 path selected, click **Move Up** until this path is at the top of the list, as shown in Figure 10–36. This enables the Module 10 project to look in the *Module 10* practice files folder for custom schematic symbols. Click **OK**.

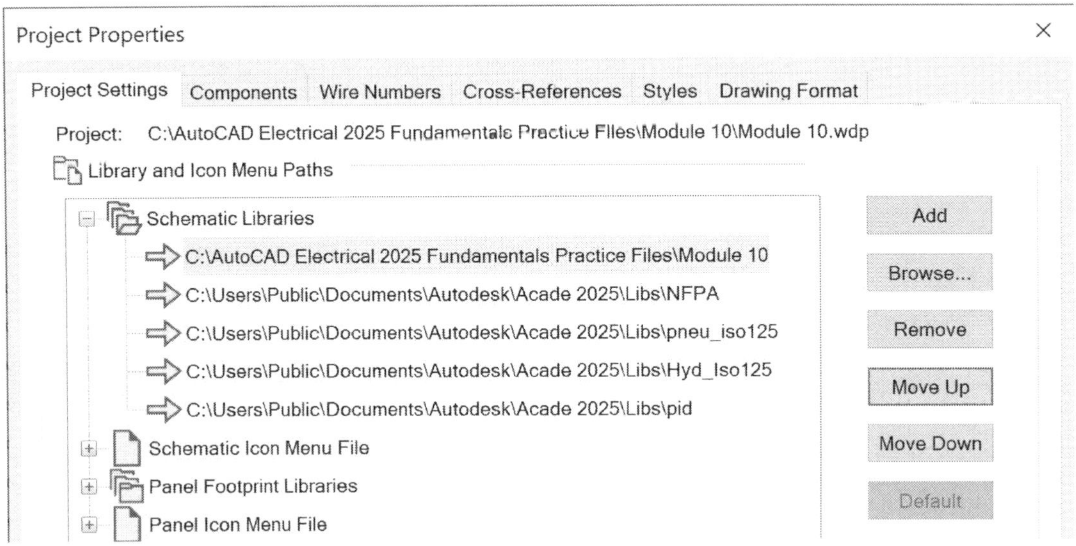

Figure 10–36

6. Click  (Icon Menu (Insert Component)).
7. The *Insert Component* dialog box opens. Click  (My Menu).
8. The **My Menu** submenu opens. Click  (My Power Supply).
9. Pick a point near the middle of rung 220 as shown in Figure 10–37.

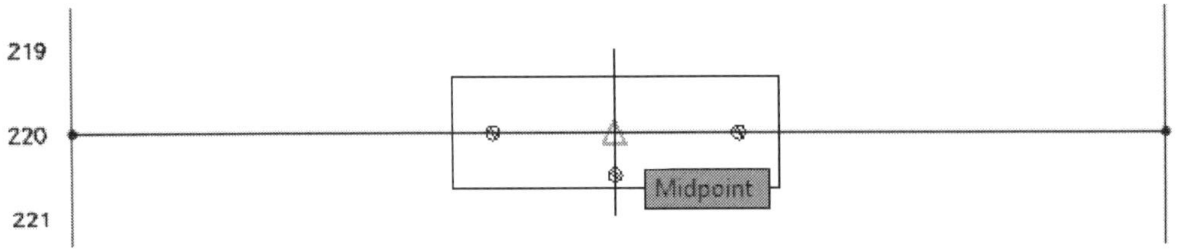

Figure 10–37

10. The *Insert / Edit Component* dialog box opens. Set the following options:
    - *Line 1*: **CUSTOM**
    - *Line 2*: **POWER SUPPLY**
    - *Location code*: **OP-STA** (Use **Project** and select **OP-STA**.)
11. Click **OK**. The custom power supply is inserted.
12. Save and close **Control.dwg**.

End of practice

10.4 AutoCAD Electrical Databases

- The AutoCAD Electrical software uses Access databases for many functions, which typically involves searching the database for information. For example, in the Catalog Lookup database, when you click **Lookup** in the *Insert / Edit Component* dialog box, the software queries a database to build the list of available bill of materials information for that component type.
- Similar to the search for library blocks, the software searches for these databases in a specific order. The path(s) searched depend on the database that is being searched for.
- The AutoCAD Electrical software contains tools for editing the databases. Alternatively, you can edit them using Microsoft Access or any other database editing tool.

10.5 Project Database

The Project database is a scratch database created for each project file. Information about catalog data, component relationships, and other component data is stored in this database. It is used to speed-up some project-wide commands. The AutoCAD Electrical software automatically maintains this database. Therefore, you should not have to modify it. If the database is missing or corrupt, it is automatically re-created.

- The database is named **<project name>.mdb** where <project name> is the name of the project's .WDP file.
- In Windows 10, the databases are stored in the following folder: *C:\Users\<user>\AppData\Roaming\Autodesk\AutoCAD Electrical <version>\ <release>\<language>\Support\User*

10.6 Catalog Database

The Catalog database contains all of the bill of materials information for the AutoCAD Electrical software. This database is queried when catalog data is assigned to a symbol or when various reports are run.

The Catalog database contains several tables. Each table contains data for a specific type of symbol (push buttons, lights, etc.). This configuration is the reason you are only presented with catalog numbers for a specific component type when you click **Lookup** in the *Insert / Edit Component* dialog box. Each table contains the available catalog numbers and associated bill of material information.

- For a project specific database, the database is named **<project name>_cat.mdb** where <project name> is the name of the project's .WDP file. The default database is named **default_cat.mdb**.
- The software searches several paths for the database, using the first one it finds. It first searches for the project specific database (**<project name>_cat.mdb**) in the project directory. If that file does not exist, it searches for **default_cat.mdb** in several directories.

The directories are searched in the following order:

1. The **<project name>_cat.mdb** file in the directory that contains the project's .WDP file.
2. The **default_cat.mdb** file in the directory that contains the project's .WDP file.
3. The user subdirectory.
    - Windows 10: *C:\Users\<user>\AppData\Roaming\Autodesk\AutoCAD Electrical <version>\<release>\<language>\Support\User*
4. The catalog lookup subdirectory.
    - Windows 10: *C:\Users\<user>\My Documents\Acade <version>\AeData\<language>\Catalogs*
5. The AutoCAD Electrical support directory.
    - Windows 10: *C:\Users\<user>\AppData\Roaming\Autodesk\AutoCAD Electrical <version>\<release>\<language>\Support\AeData*
6. The AutoCAD Electrical support directory.
    - Windows 10: *C:\Users\<user>\AppData\Roaming\Autodesk\AutoCAD Electrical <version>\<release>\<language>\Support*
7. The AutoCAD Electrical support directory.
    - Windows 10: *C:\Program Files\Autodesk\Acade <version>\Support*
8. The AutoCAD Electrical support directory.
    - Windows 10: *C:\Program Files\Autodesk\Acade <version>*
9. All directories defined in the AutoCAD **Options>Files>Support File Search Path**.

Catalog Browser

You can modify the existing data or add new records using the *Catalog Browser* in the Edit mode. An easy way of adding new records is to copy a complete row that has similar columns with similar content and then modify the individual cells to suit your requirements.

- You can open the Catalog Browser as a palette using (Catalog Browser) in the *Schematic* tab>*Insert Components* panel.
- To edit or add a record, open the database in the Edit mode in the *Catalog Browser*.
- You can also open the *Catalog Browser* (in the form of a dialog box) by using **Edit Component** to open the *Insert / Edit Component* dialog box and then clicking **Lookup** to open the *Catalog Browser* dialog box. The *Catalog Browser* displays in **Lookup mode** (as shown in Figure 10–38) in which you can search for the database records in the catalog by entering a search string and clicking .

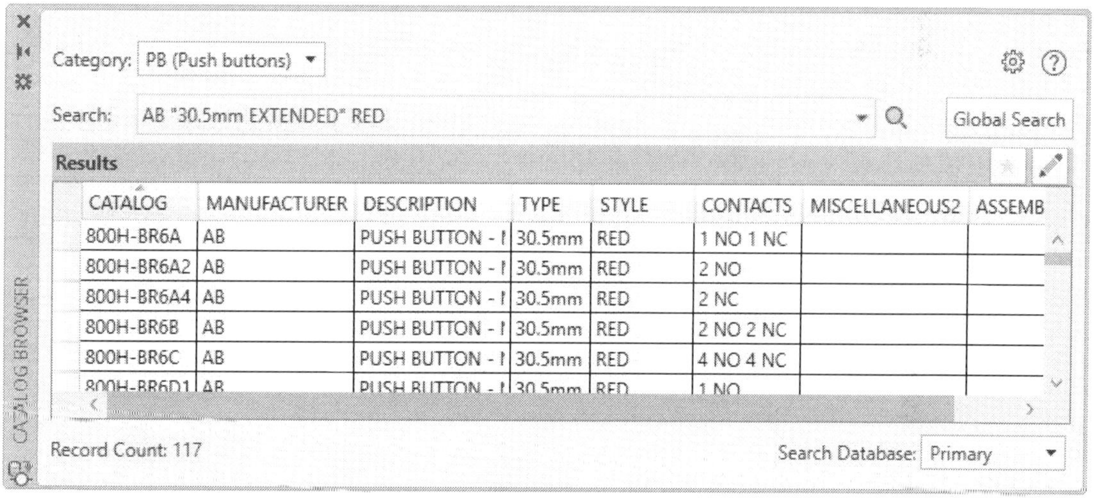

Figure 10–38

- When the *Catalog Browser* is opened as a palette, other commands can be used. When the *Catalog Browser* is opened as a dialog box, you need to close the *Catalog Browserr* before you can work with other commands.

- Use to display the records in **Edit mode** (as shown in Figure 10–39) in which you can add a record or edit the selected record. Once you are in Edit mode, you can click:
    - to accept the edits to the catalog database, or
    - to cancel the edits.

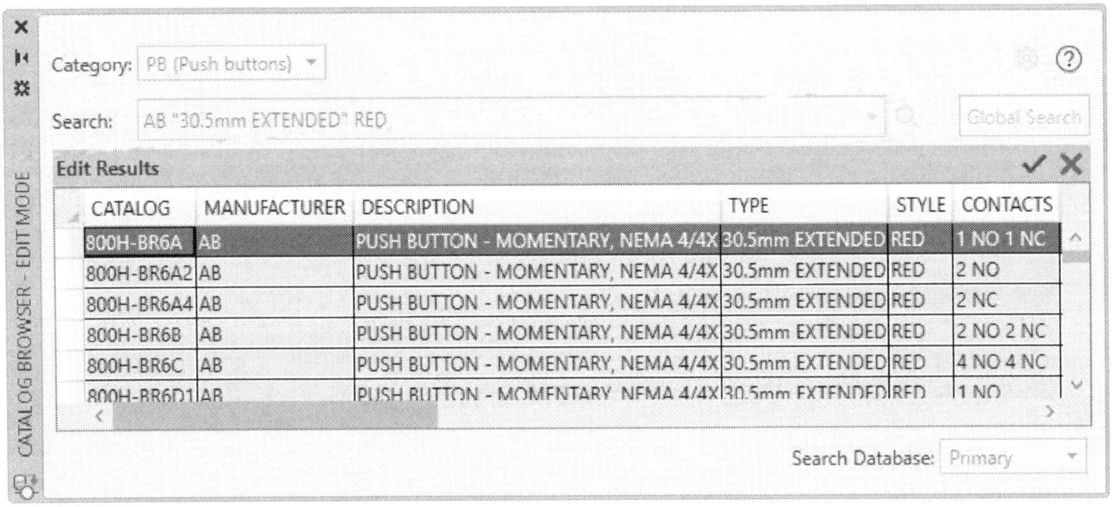

Figure 10–39

- In Lookup mode, right-click on the column heading to display the shortcut menu, which lists the columns that display in the *Catalog Browser*, as shown in Figure 10–40. Select **More** in the shortcut menu to display the Columns to display dialog box (shown in Figure 10–41) in which you can select additional columns for display. Using the shortcut menu to control the display of the columns is only available in Look-up mode. When the *Catalog Browser* is in Edit mode, all of the columns display for editing.

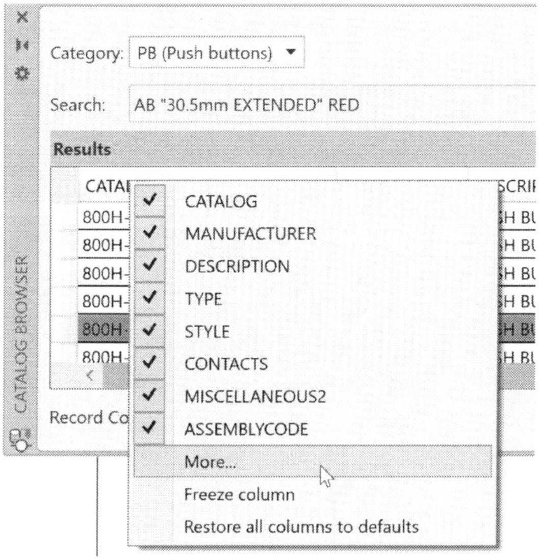

Figure 10–40

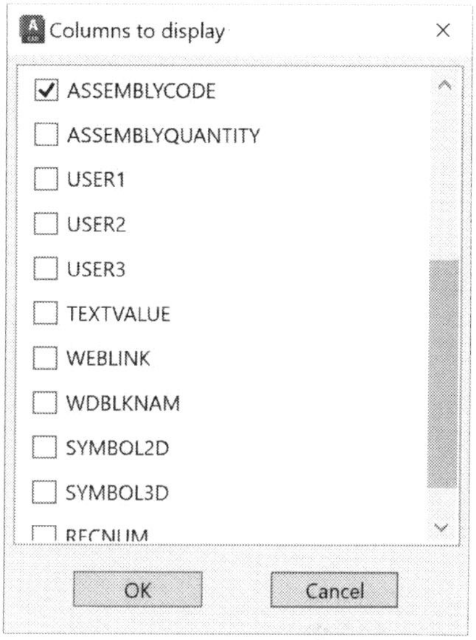

Figure 10–41

Some of the columns that are available are as follows:

CATALOG	Enter the catalog number for the item.
MANUFACTURER	Enter the manufacturer of the item.
DESCRIPTION	Enter the description of the item.
TYPE	Enter the type of item.
STYLE	The title of this field varies depending on the component type. Enter the style, coil, voltage, color, etc., of the item.
CONTACTS	The title of this field varies depending on the component. Enter either the contacts or a miscellaneous field.
MISCELLANEOUS2	Enter miscellaneous text for the item.
ASSEMBLYCODE	Flags the item as having subassembly items. The code is used to link the main assembly to the subassembly items.
USER1 – USER3	Fields available for user properties.
ASSEMBLYLIST	Flags the item as a subassembly item. The code is used to link the main assembly to the subassembly items.
TEXTVALUE	Populates attributes in the symbol. Format is <att name>=<value> (e.g., RATING=30A).
WEBLINK	Specifies a web URL or .PDF file to associate with the symbol.
WDBLKNAM	Specifies the schematic block name to use for the item.

- In Edit mode, right-clicking in a cell displays a context menu, as shown in Figure 10–42. You can copy and paste the content from one cell to another. Using the **Copy Row** and **Paste Row** options, you can copy and paste complete rows.

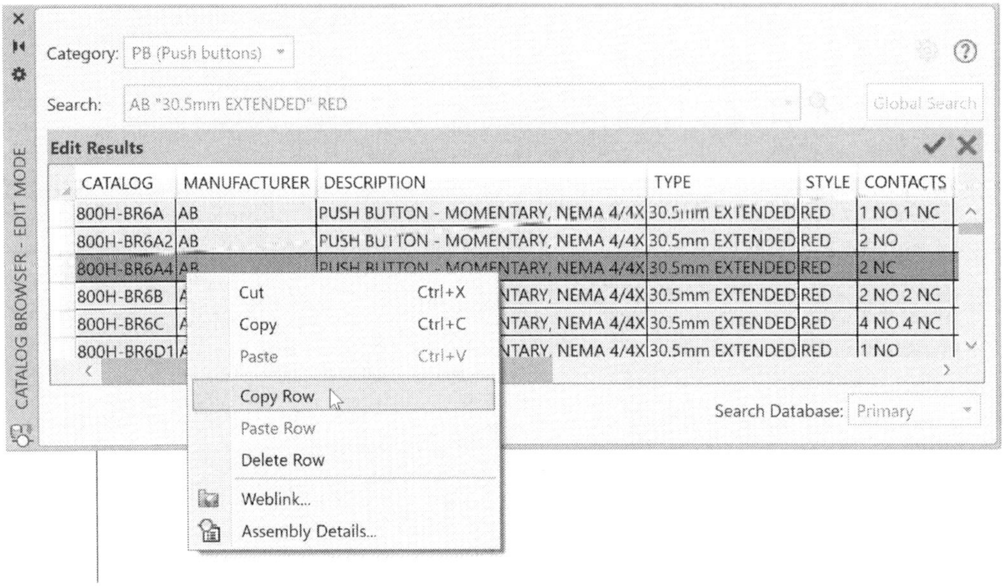

Figure 10–42

- Click once in a cell to overwrite the contents.
- Double-click in a cell to add text to the existing content in the cell.
- Some cell content requires special formatting. In that case when you double-click in that cell, [...] displays in the cell. Clicking [...] opens an associated dialog box in which you can modify the content.
- *WDBLKNAM* is used to sort the records based on the symbol block name. For example, a green pilot light's block name is HLT1G. If *WDBLKNAM* is populated for the records in the LT table, only records with LT1G display (the block name minus its first character).

How To: Add an Entry to the Catalog Database

1. Open the *Catalog Browser* using (Catalog Browser), which opens the palette or by clicking **Lookup** in the *Insert / Edit Component* dialog box (editing a component), which opens the dialog box.
2. In Lookup mode, search the catalog for a similar database record.
3. Click to change the *Catalog Browser* to Edit mode from Lookup mode.

4. Copy and paste the complete row or scroll down to the bottom where an empty row is provided to be populated.
5. Type or edit the column contents of the newly added record.
6. Click ✓ to accept the changes.

Subassemblies

Subassemblies are useful if a component requires multiple items, such as a push button with contact blocks. In the main component record, assign an assembly code. It can be any combination of characters including spaces and is used to link the main assembly item to its subassembly items. Create a second record for the subassembly item and assign the same value to the *ASSEMBLYLIST* field. When you assign the main assembly item to a symbol, the subassembly items are also included in its bill of materials information. Use **CatalogCheck** to verify this.

How To: Add a Subassembly to the Catalog Database

1. Open the *Catalog Browser* using (Catalog Browser), which opens the palette or by clicking **Lookup** in the *Insert / Edit Component* dialog box (editing a component), which opens the dialog box.
2. In the Lookup mode, search the catalog for a similar database record.
3. Click to change the *Catalog Browser* to Edit mode from Lookup mode.
4. Copy and paste the complete row or scroll down to the bottom where an empty row is provided to be populated.
5. Type or edit the column contents of the newly added record.
6. Enter a code in the *ASSEMBLYCODE* field. (This value defines it as the main assembly.)
7. Click ✓ to accept the changes and switch back to Lookup mode.
8. In the *Catalog Browser*, select the main assembly database record (for which you assigned a value for the *ASSEMBLYCODE* field).
9. Click to change the *Catalog Browser* to Edit mode from Lookup mode.
10. Copy and paste the complete main row.
11. Change the column contents of the newly added record. Leave the *ASSEMBLYCODE* field empty.
12. In the *ASSEMBLYLIST* field, select the code. It must be the same code as the *ASSEMBLYCODE* that was entered in Step 6.
13. Enter a value in the *ASSEMBLYQUANTITY* field if more than one of these items is required.
14. Repeat Steps 10 to 12 to add any other sub-assemblies items.

15. Click ✓ to accept the changes.
16. Click **OK** to exit the *Catalog Browser*. The *Insert / Edit Component* dialog box opens.
17. Click **OK** to end the command.

Pin List Numbers

The *Catalog Browser* also includes columns for pin numbers. For each catalog number, a Coil Pin and a Pin List can be entered. The Coil Pins indicate the default pin numbers for the coil or parent symbol. The Pin List indicates the number of available contacts (if applicable) and their default pin numbers. The Pin List information is used when inserting the child symbol and determines how the AutoCAD Electrical software verifies the maximum number of contacts during real time error checking.

The format for the pin list is contact type followed by pin numbers. The items are separated by commas and each set of pins is separated by a semicolon. Valid contact type codes are:

0	Convertible contact.
1	Normally open contact.
2	Normally closed contact.
3	Form-C contact (NO/NC pair).
4	Multiple-pole terminal strips or undefined type.
5	Multiple-pin or stacked contacts.

Terminal Symbol Properties

The *Catalog Browser* includes additional columns for properties of Terminal Symbols. For each terminal symbol catalog number, information pertaining to the number of levels and wires is included in specific columns. These terminal properties are used when inserting and associating terminals between parent and child terminal symbols.

Terminal Symbol properties include the following:

LEVELS	Number of levels for multiple-level terminals.
LEVELDESCRIPTION	Descriptions for each level, separated by commas.
TPINL	Pin label definition for the left side of the terminal.
TPINR	Pin label definition for the right side of the terminal.
WIRESPERCONNECTION	Number of wires for each level of the terminal, separated by commas.

10.7 Footprint Lookup Database

The Footprint Lookup database is used to determine which block to insert as the footprint for a particular catalog number. The Footprint Lookup database contains a separate table for each manufacturer. The name of each table is based on the **MFG CODE** attribute. Each table is basically a list of catalog numbers and the block to use for each of them.

When a footprint is inserted into a panel drawing, the AutoCAD Electrical software opens the table for its manufacturer and searches for the catalog number. If an exact match is not found, the last character on the right is dropped and the search is performed again. This procedure is continued until a match is found or all characters are dropped.

The software searches for the Footprint Lookup database in a similar manner to searching for the Catalog database.

- For a project specific database, the database is named **<project name>_footprint_lookup.mdb** where <project name> is the name of the project's .WDP file. The default database is named **footprint_lookup.mdb**.
- The software searches several paths for the database, using the first one it finds. It first searches for the project specific database (**<project name>_footprint_lookup.mdb**) in the project directory. If that file does not exist, it searches for **footprint_lookup.mdb** in several directories.

The directories are searched in the following order:

1. The **<project name>_footprint_lookup.mdb** file in the directory that contains the project's .WDP file.
2. The **footprint_lookup.mdb** file in the directory that contains the project's .WDP file.
3. The user subdirectory.
    - Windows 10: *C:\Users\<user>\AppData\Roaming\Autodesk\AutoCAD Electrical <version>\<release>\<language>\Support\User*
4. The catalog lookup subdirectory.
    - Windows 10: *C:\Users\<user>\My Documents\Acade <version>\AeData\<language>\Catalogs*
5. The Panel Footprint Library directory.
    - Windows 10: *C:\Users\Public\Documents\Autodesk\ Acade <version>\Libs*
6. The AutoCAD Electrical support directory.
    - Windows 10: *C:\Users\<user>\AppData\Roaming\Autodesk\AutoCAD Electrical <version>\<release>\<language>\Support\AeData*
7. The AutoCAD Electrical support directory.
    - Windows 10: *C:\Users\<user>\AppData\Roaming\Autodesk\AutoCAD Electrical <version>\<release>\<language>\Support*

8. The AutoCAD Electrical support directory.
    - Windows 10: *C:\Program Files\Autodesk\Acade <version>\Support*
9. The AutoCAD Electrical support directory.
    - Windows 10: *C:\Program Files\Autodesk\Acade <version>*
10. All directories defined in the AutoCAD **Options>Files>Support File Search Path**.

Footprint Database Editor

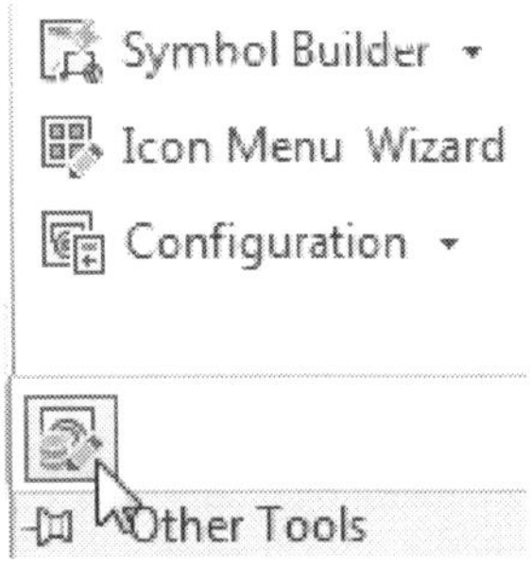

Ribbon: *Panel* tab>expanded *Other Tools* panel

Command Prompt: aefootprintdb

How To: Add to the Footprint Lookup database

1. Start the **Footprint Database File Editor** command. The *Panel Footprint Lookup Database File Editor* opens.
2. Click **Edit Existing Table.** The *Table Edit* dialog box opens.
3. Select the table to edit and click **OK**. The *Footprint lookup* dialog box opens.
4. Click **Add New**. The *Add footprint record* dialog box opens.
5. Fill in the fields, as required.
6. Click **OK**. The *Footprint lookup* dialog box opens.
7. Repeat Steps 4 to 6 to add another record or click **OK/Save/Exit** to save the changes and exit the command.

You can modify the table to add your own records or to modify existing records. This can be done using Microsoft Access, another database editor, or the AutoCAD Electrical Footprint File Database Editor.

- When using the *Footprint File Database Editor*, you first select whether to edit an existing table or to create a new one.
  - If editing an existing table, you are presented with a list of available tables from which to select.
  - If creating a new table, you are prompted for the table name. The table name should match the manufacturer code in the Catalog database.
  - After you have selected the table, the *Footprint lookup* dialog box opens, as shown in Figure 10–43.

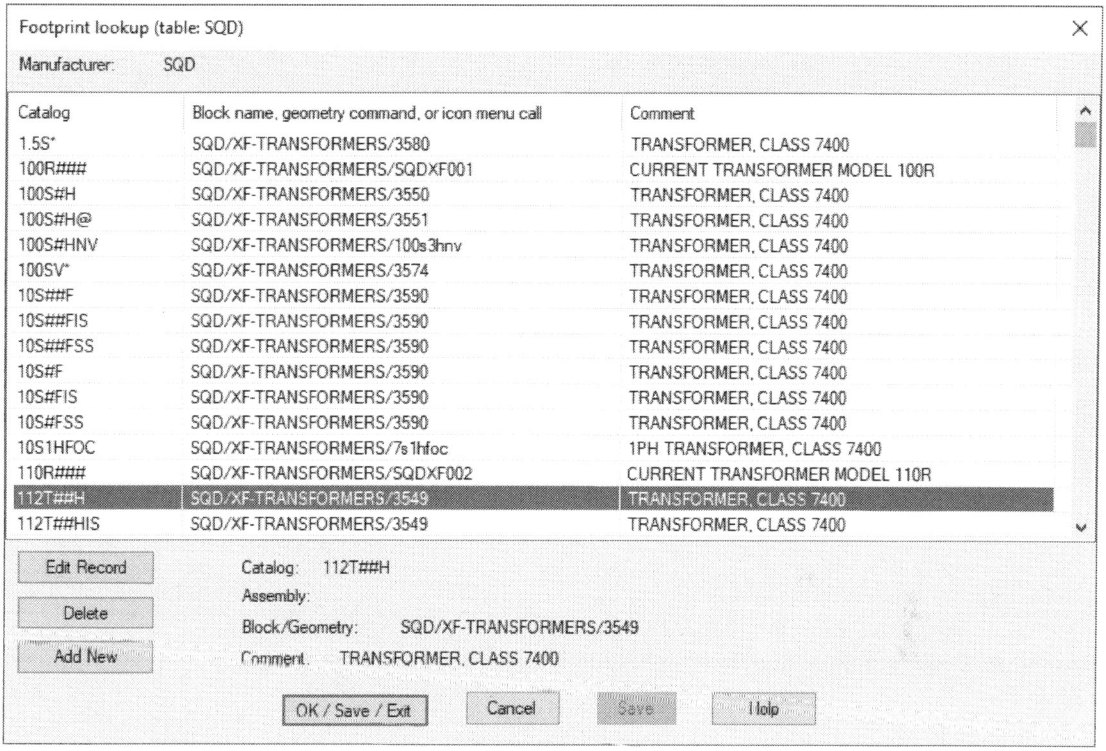

Figure 10–43

Edit Record	Displays the *Edit footprint record* dialog box for the selected record.
Delete	Deletes the selected record.
Add New	Displays the *Add footprint record* dialog box to add a new record.
OK/Save/Exit	Saves the changes to the table and exits the command.
Save	Saves the changes to the table and maintains the command.

After editing or adding a new record, Edit footprint record or Add footprint record displays in the title bar, as shown in Figure 10–44.

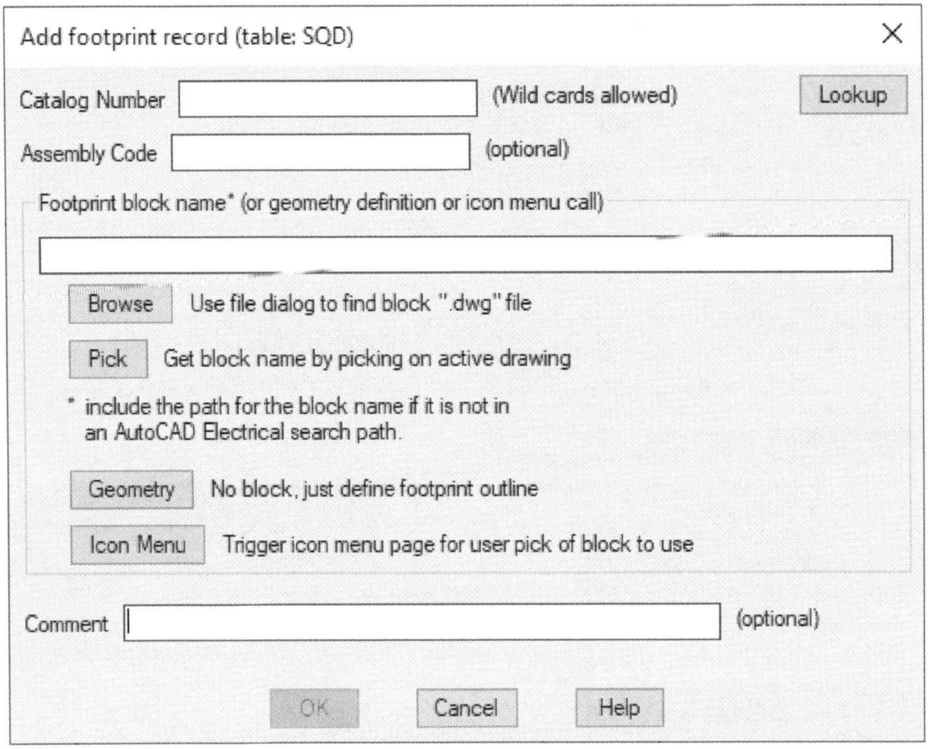

Figure 10–44

Catalog Number	Specifies the catalog number for the footprint.
Assembly Code	Specifies the assembly code for the footprint.
View	Opens a dialog box that lists catalog numbers in the catalog database.
Footprint block name	Blocks the name or geometry information for the footprint.
Browse	Browses for a Wblocked drawing file to use as the footprint.
Pick	Picks a block in the current drawing to use as the footprint.
Geometry	Uses simplified geometry for the footprint rather than an AutoCAD block.
Icon Menu	Specifies an Icon Menu page to display rather than inserting a block.
Comment	Enables you to enter an optional comment for the record. This is not used in any other AutoCAD Electrical commands.

- *Catalog Number* and *Footprint block name* are required fields.
- Wild card characters are used to help you link several catalog numbers to one AutoCAD block. For example, you might want to link all Allen Bradley items starting with 80 to one footprint. To do so, you would type **80*** for the catalog number.
- Valid wild card characters are:

*	Matches any character.
?	Matches a single character (alphabetic or numeric).
#	Matches a single numeric character.
@	Matches a single alphabetic character.

When entering a block name you must use the name of the DWG file and the path to the file if it is not an AutoCAD Electrical search path. If providing geometry instead of a block name, the *Define Footprint Shape* dialog box opens, as shown in Figure 10–45.

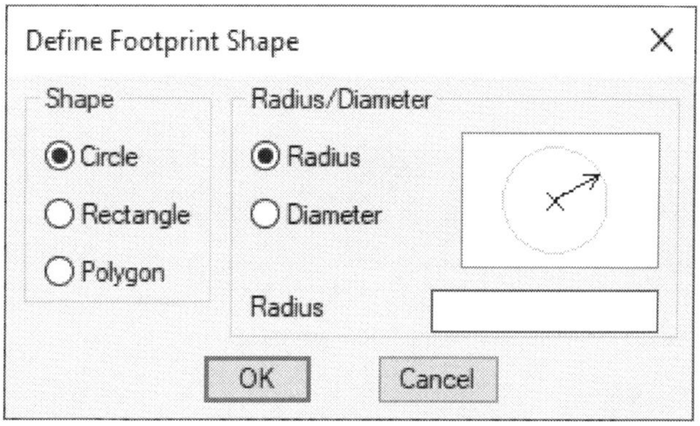

Figure 10–45

On the left side of the dialog box, select the shape you want to use. On the right side of the dialog box, enter the information to draw the shape. When you click **OK**, the information required to draw the shape in the block name field displays.

10.8 PLC Database

The PLC database is referenced by the **Insert PLC (Parametric)** command. The database contains the manufacturer and module type information and the geometric information for a module. This includes the blocks to use for the PLC, the number of inputs, and the margins for the rectangle drawn around the PLC block.

- The database is named **ace_plc.mdb**.
- It is located in *C:\Users\<user>\Documents\Acade <version>\AeData\<language>\Plc* for Windows 10.

PLC Database File Editor

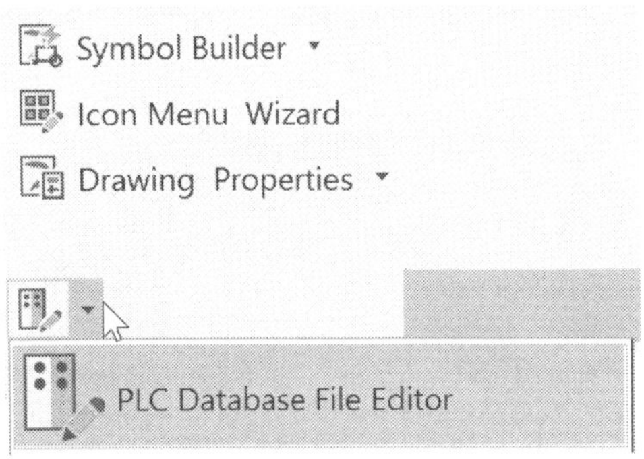

Ribbon: *Schematic* tab>expanded *Other Tools* panel

Command Prompt: aeplcdb

How To: Add a New Module to the PLC Database

1. Start the **PLC Database File Editor** command. The *PLC Database File Editor* dialog box opens.
2. Click **New Module**. The *New Module* dialog box opens.
3. Fill in the *Manufacturer*, *Series Type*, *Series*, *Code*, and *Terminals* fields. Fill in any of the optional fields, as required.
4. Click **Module Box Dimensions**. The *Module Box Dimensions* dialog box opens.
5. Specify the module box dimensions. Click **OK** to return to the *New Module* dialog box.
6. Click **Module Prompts** to open the *Prompts at Module Insert Time* dialog box where you can specify any prompts for the module. Click **OK** to return to the *New Module* dialog box.
7. Click **OK** to return to the *PLC Database File Editor*.

8. Specify the *Terminal Type*, *Show*, *Optional Re-prompt*, *Break After*, and *Spacing Factor* for each terminal.
9. Click **Save Module**.
10. Click **Done** to end the command.

The *PLC Database File Editor* dialog box is shown in Figure 10–46.

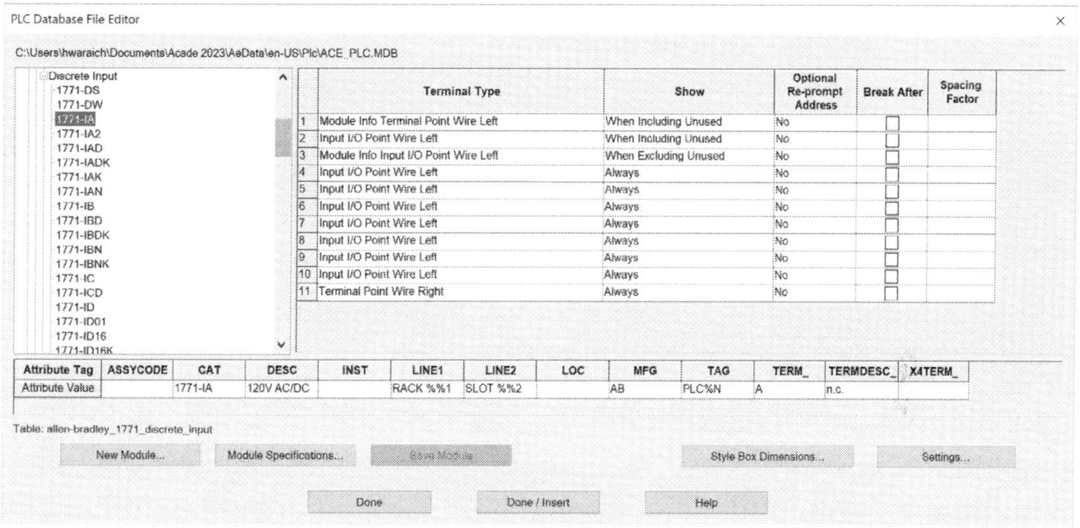

Figure 10–46

The tree on the left side is used to browse the existing modules. Click **+** next to an entry to expand its branch. The area on the right side of the tree lists the I/O points for the selected module. The area below the tree lists the available attributes for a selected terminal and their default values.

Terminal Type	Specifies the type of terminal. Select from the list of available types. Controls which block is used for that I/O point.
Show	Determines when a terminal is shown. Use to configure the unused/extra terminals. Options are **Always**, **When Excluding Unused**, or **When Including Unused**.
Optional Re-prompt	Prompts you for a new address. Options are **No**, **Input**, or **Output**.
Break After	Forces the module to break after that point enabling you to continue it in a different area of the drawing.
Spacing Factor	Overrides the current rung spacing for that point by the specified factor.

- To edit the terminal, select in the drop-down list or right-click and select **Edit Terminal**.

The *New Module* and *Module Specifications* dialog boxes contain the same information. However, some of the fields in the *Module Specifications* dialog box are grayed out. This differences are that the *Module Specifications* dialog box is used to edit existing modules and some data cannot be changed. The *New Module* dialog box is used to add new modules to the database, as shown in Figure 10–47.

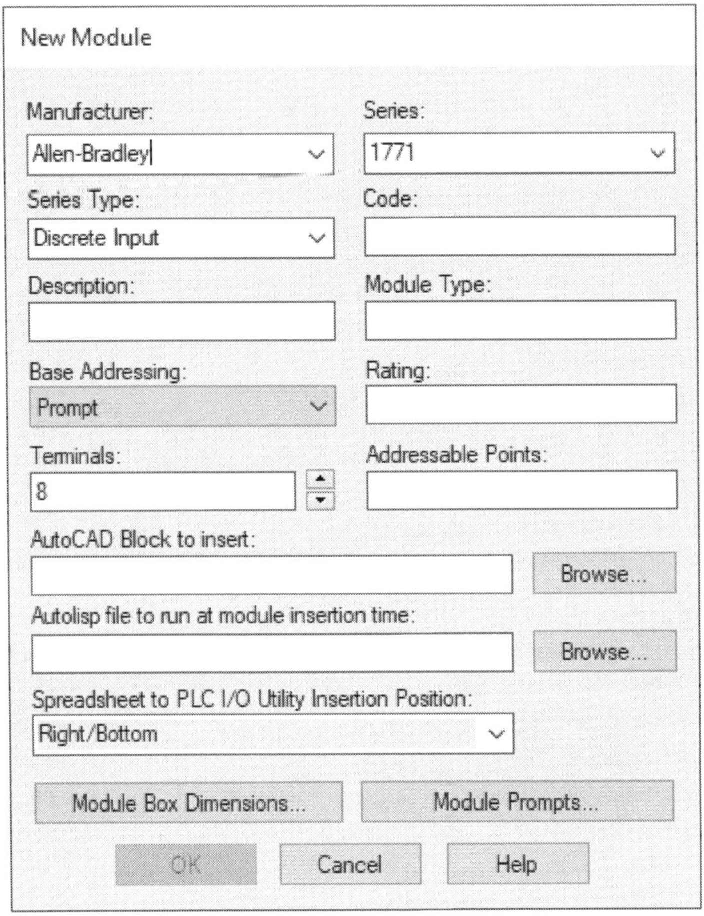

Figure 10–47

Manufacturer	Specify the manufacturer of the PLC module. Enter the value or select in the drop-down list of existing manufacturers in the database.
Series	Specify the series number for the PLC module. Enter the value or select from the drop-down list of existing manufacturers in the database.
Series Type	Specify the series type of PLC module. Enter the value or select in the drop-down list of existing manufacturers in the database.
Code	Specify the code or catalog number for the PLC module.

Description	Enter a description of the PLC module.
Module Type	Specify the type of PLC module.
Base Addressing	Select from **Prompt**, **Octal**, **Decimal**, or **Hexadecimal**. **Prompt** opens a dialog box at the time of insertion enabling you to select the addressing type.
Rating	Specify the power rating value for the PLC module.
Terminals	Specify the total number of terminals for the PLC module.
Addressable Points	Specify the number of addressable points on the PLC module.
AutoCAD Block to Insert	Specify an AutoCAD block to insert after the last I/O point of the module. Typically used for DIP switches or notes about the PLC module.
Autolisp file to run at module insertion time	Specify an Autolisp program to run after the module is inserted.
Browse	Browse for the AutoCAD block or Autolisp program.
Spreadsheet to PLC I/O Utility Insertion Position	Set as either **Center**, **Left/Top**, or **Right/Bottom**.
Module Box Dimensions	Opens the *Module Box Dimensions* dialog box to configure the dimensions of the module box.
Module Prompts	Opens the *Prompts at Module Insertion Time* dialog box. Used to define up to nine prompts to be used at the time of insertion. Typically used for **Rack number** and **Slot number**.

The *Style Box Dimension* and *Module Box Dimensions* dialog boxes contain the same information. However, the *Style Box Dimension* dialog box contains an additional *Graphics Style* area, as shown in Figure 10–48. Both of these dialog boxes are used to define the size and line properties of the box that is drawn around the PLC module at the time of insertion.

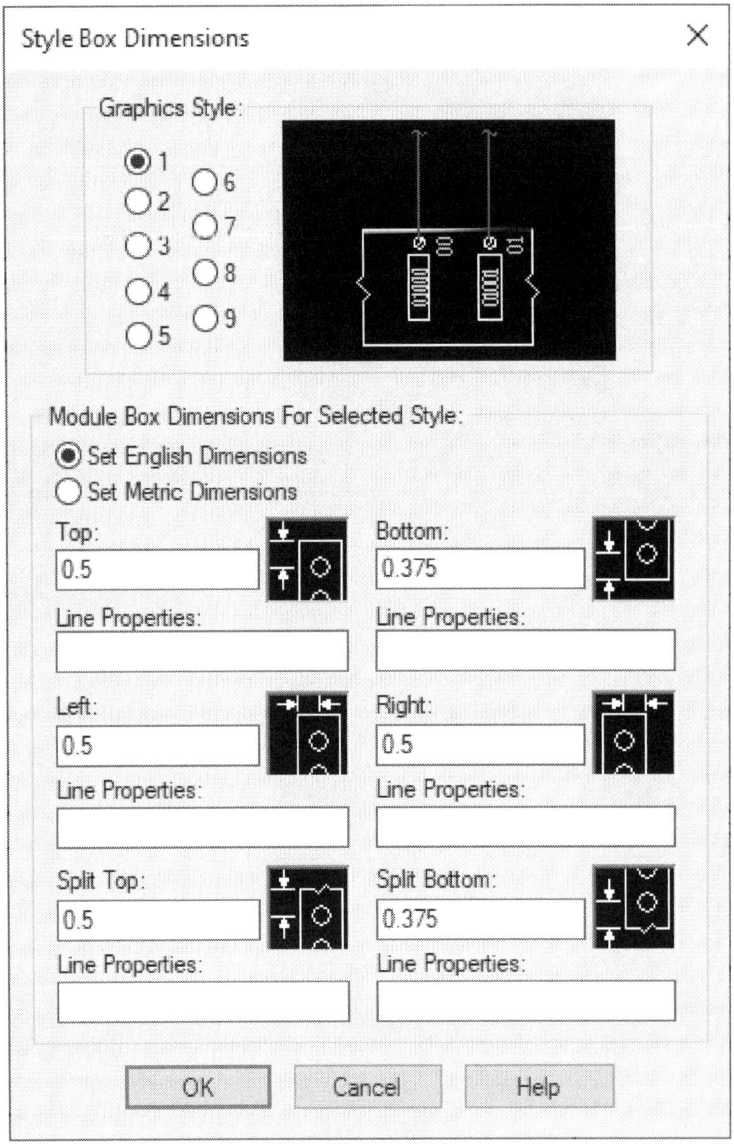

Figure 10–48

The *Prompts at Module Insertion Time* dialog box is used to define up to nine prompts for the PLC module, as shown in Figure 10–49. These are used at the time of insertion and are populated in attributes in the symbol.

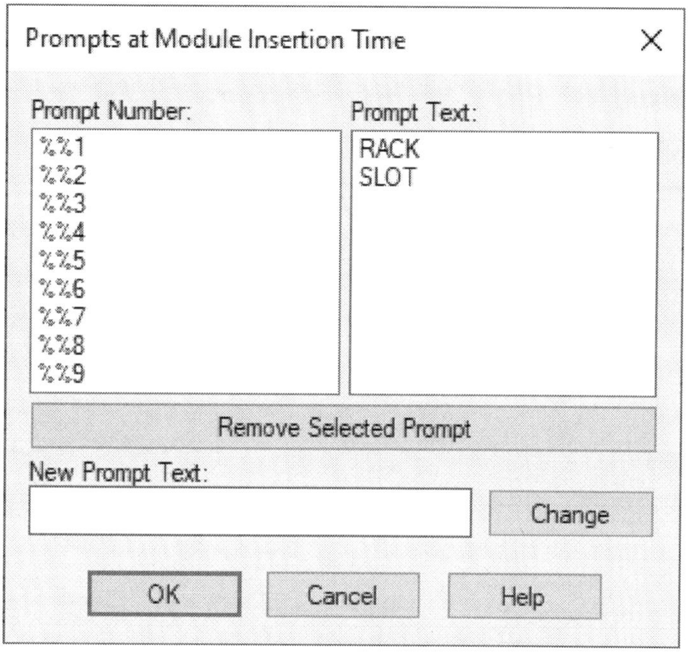

Figure 10–49

Practice 10c
Catalog Database

Practice Objective

- Add a new record and a subassembly record to the catalog database.

In this practice, you will add new records to the catalog database. First you will add a record for a single component and then you will add records to build a subassembly, as shown in Figure 10–50.

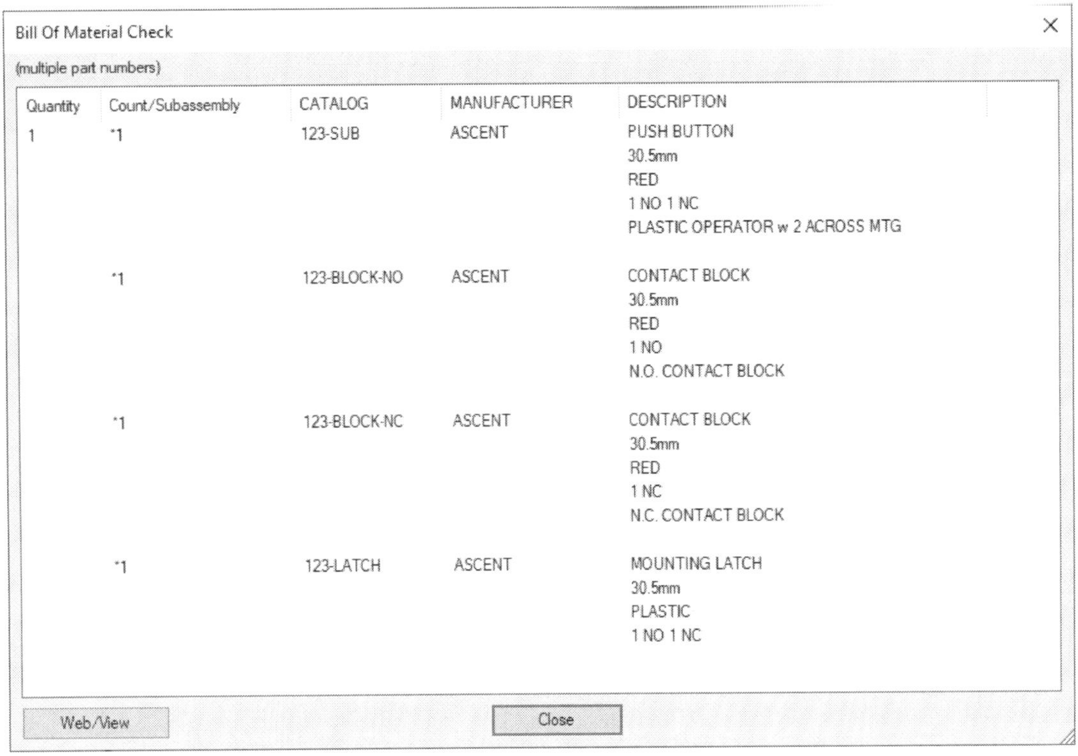

Figure 10–50

Task 1: Add a single record.

1. If the **Module 10** project is not active, open and activate it now.
2. In the **Module 10** project, open **Control.dwg**.
3. Zoom to lines 200 to 209.
4. Edit the component **PB201A**.

5. The *Insert / Edit Component* dialog box opens. Note the Description as **START** in *Line 1* and **FORWARD** in *Line 2*. In the *Catalog Data* area, click **Lookup**.

6. The Catalog Browser opens with **800H-BR6D1** record selected. Click  (Edit catalog database) to display the records in Edit mode, as shown in Figure 10–51.

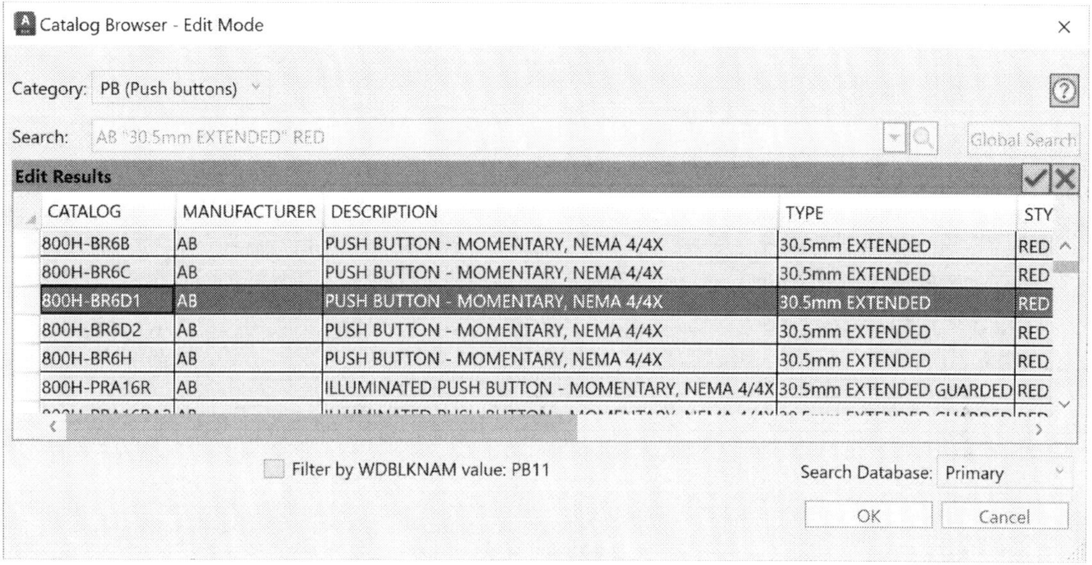

Figure 10–51

7. Right-click on the selected row (**800H-BR6D1**) and select **Copy Row**.
8. Right-click again and select **Paste Row**. It automatically pastes the copy of the record at the bottom of the list.

9. Scroll to the left and note that you are already placed in the *CATALOG* column cell of the copied row, which is indicated by a bold black border around the cell (you do not need to click once the first time). If you are not placed in the required column cell, click inside the cell. Type **123-A** to overwrite the original content, as shown in Figure 10–52.

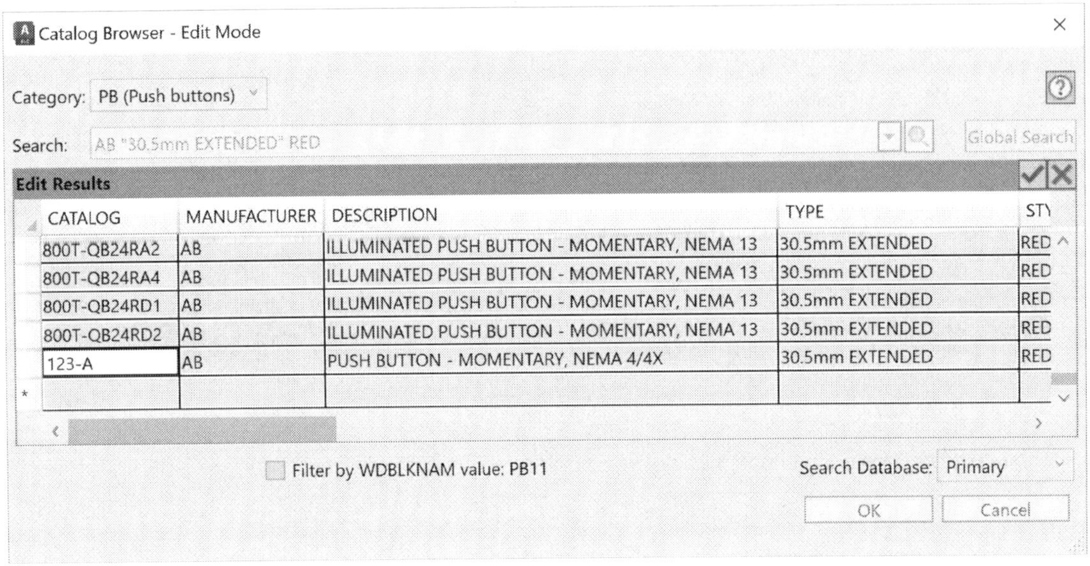

Figure 10–52

10. In the *DESCRIPTION* field, double-click and modify the content to **PUSH BUTTON – ALTERNATE ACTION OPERATORS**.

11. Modify the content in the *TYPE* field to **30.5mm**.

 Note: *Use the horizontal scroll bar along the bottom to display other columns in the dialog box.*

12. In the *TEXTVALUE* field, click once and type **DESC1=PUSH; DESC2=BUTTON**, as shown in Figure 10–53.

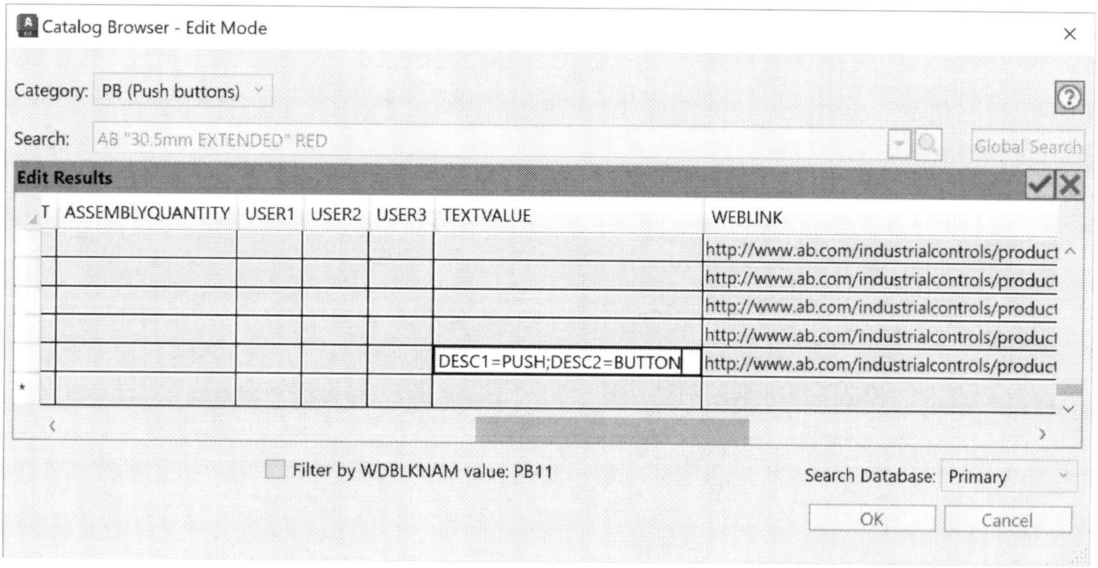

Figure 10–53

13. Click (Accept changes) to accept the changes. Note that you are returned to the Lookup mode of the Catalog Browser.
14. In the *Search* field, change the string to **AB "30.5mm" RED**, and click . Locate the newly added record (**123-A**) and select it, as shown in Figure 10–54. (You might need to select the *CATALOG* column heading to sort this column in ascending order and display this record on the top of the list).

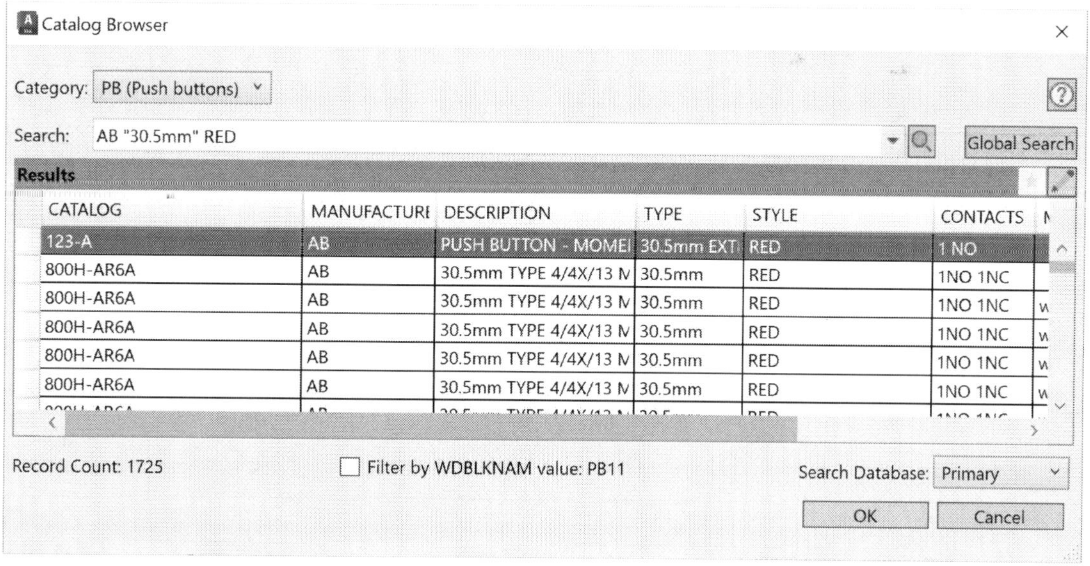

Figure 10–54

15. Click **OK**. You are returned to the *Insert / Edit Component* dialog box. Note that the following are set, as shown in Figure 10–55:

- *Line 1*: **PUSH**
- *Line 2:* **BUTTON**
- *Catalog:* **123-A**

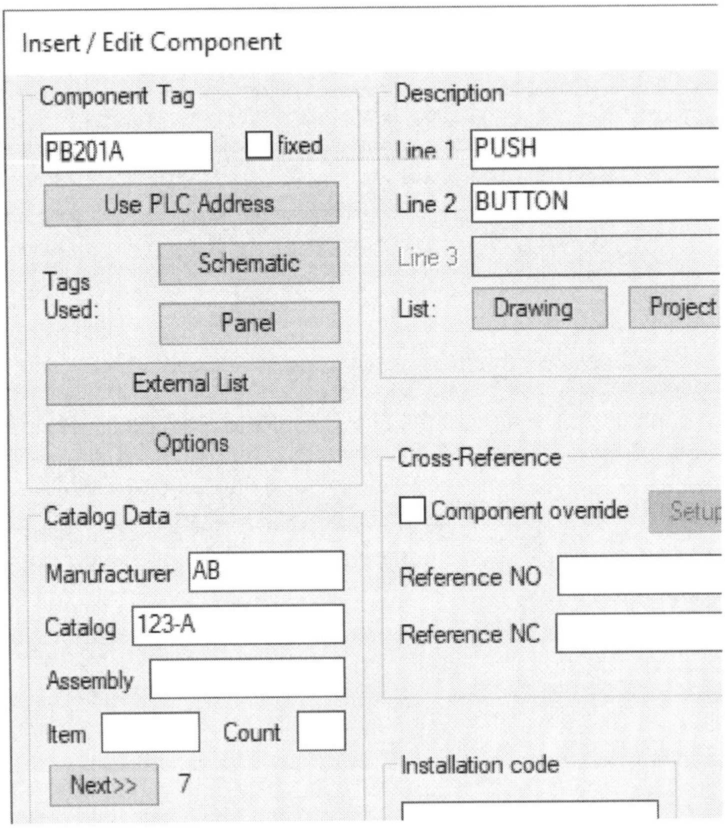

Figure 10–55

16. Click **Catalog Check**. The *Bill of Material Check* dialog box opens. The BOM information for the selected catalog number displays as shown in Figure 10–56. Click **Close**.

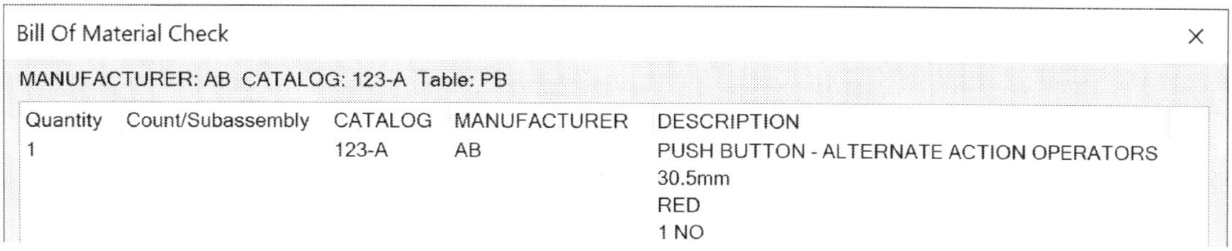

Figure 10–56

17. In the *Insert / Edit Component* dialog box, click **OK**.
18. In the *Footprint Symbol Missing* dialog box, select **Update the catalog on the footprint but leave the footprint symbol as is.**
19. In the *Update other drawings* dialog box, click **OK**. Click **OK** to **QSAVE**.
20. Note in the drawing, for PB201A, **PUSH BUTTON** displays as the description.

Task 2: Add a main subassembly record.

1. Edit **PB207** on line 207.
2. In the *Insert / Edit Component* dialog box opens, click **Lookup**.
3. The Catalog Browser opens with the record selected. Click (Edit catalog database) to display the records in Edit mode.
4. Right-click on the selected row and select **Copy Row**.
5. Right-click and select **Paste Row** to automatically paste the copy of the record at the bottom of the list.

6. Edit the copied record with the following content, as shown in Figure 10–57:
   - *CATALOG:* **123-SUB**
   - *MANUFACTURER:* **ASCENT**
   - *DESCRIPTION:* **PUSH BUTTON**
   - *TYPE*: **30.5mm**
   - *STYLE:* **RED**
   - *CONTACTS:* **1 NO 1 NC**
   - *MISCALLANEOUS2:* **PLASTIC OPERATOR w 2 ACROSS MTG**
   - *ASSEMBLYCODE:* **123-SUB_2_BLOCKS** (This defines it as a main assembly.)
   - *WDBLKNAM:* **PB11,PB12**

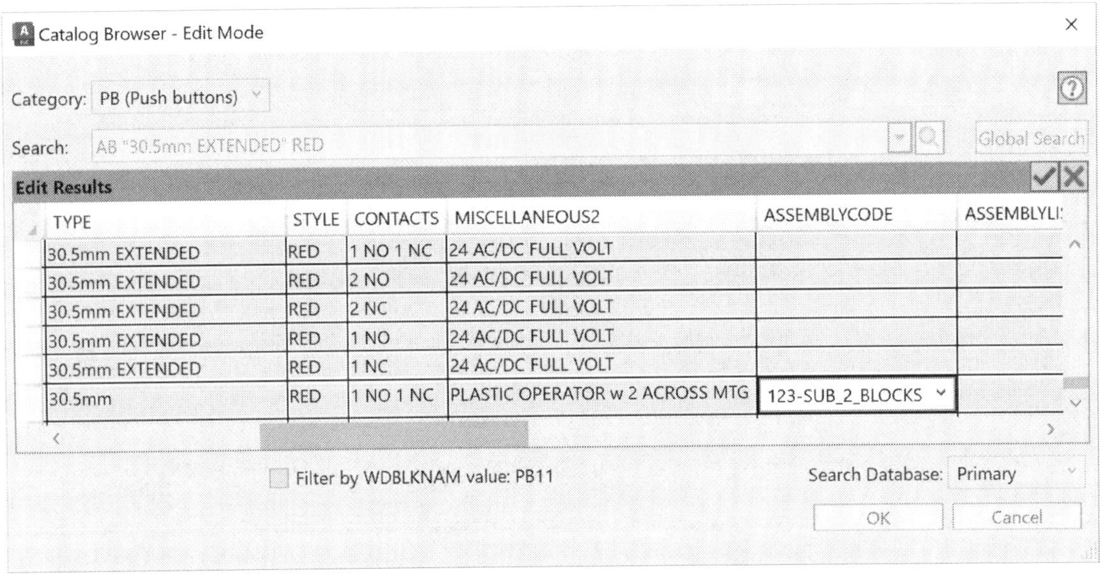

Figure 10–57

7. Click ✓ to accept the changes. Note that you are in Lookup mode in the Catalog Browser.

8. In the *Search* field, type **ASCENT** and click the search icon. Only the newly created record is available. Select it (**123-SUB**) and click **OK**. You are returned to the updated *Insert / Edit Component* dialog box. Do not close the dialog box.

Task 3: Add records for the subassembly components.

1. In the *Insert / Edit Component* dialog box, click **Lookup** to open the Catalog Browser again.
2. Note that **123-SUB** record is selected. In the *Search* field, type **ASCENT** for searching, and click (Search).
3. Change the Catalog Browser to Edit mode by clicking (Edit catalog database).
4. Copy and paste the entire **123-SUB** row.
5. Edit the copied record with the following content. (You will select the **ASSEMBLYCODE** value in the ASSEMBLYLIST content to make it a subassembly of the main assembly):
   - *CATALOG:* **123-BLOCK-NO**
   - *MANUFACTURER:* **ASCENT**
   - *DESCRIPTION:* **CONTACT BLOCK**
   - *TYPE:* **30.5mm**
   - *STYLE:* **RED**
   - *CONTACTS:* **1 NO**
   - *MISCALLANEOUS2:* **N.O. CONTACT BLOCK**
   - *ASSEMBLYCODE:* Blank (delete everything).
   - *ASSEMBLYLIST:* Click ▾ and select **123-SUB_2_BLOCKS**, as shown in Figure 10–58. (This defines it as the subassembly of the main 123-Sub assembly.)
   - *WDBLKNAM:* **PB11,PB12,PB11M,PB12M**

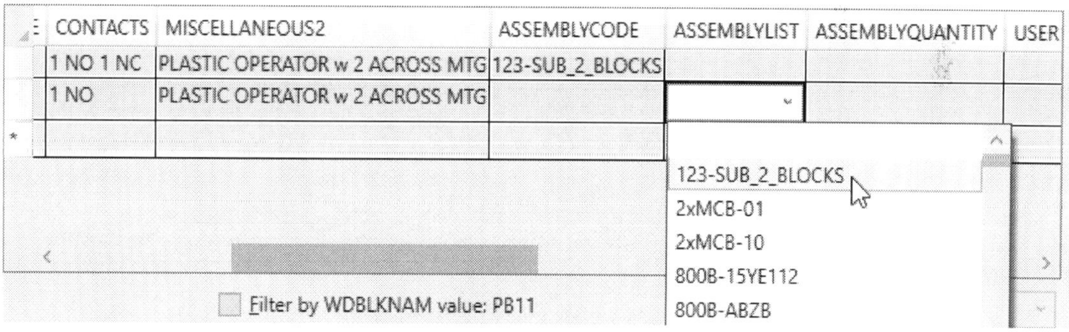

Figure 10–58

6. Click to accept all of the changes. Note that you are in Lookup mode in the Catalog Browser and as the last search was **ASCENT**, only one main assembly displays.

   Note: *The subassemblies do not display in Lookup mode in the Catalog Browser.*

7. Change the Catalog Browser to Edit mode by clicking (Edit catalog database).
8. Repeat to create another subassembly. Copy and paste the entire **123-BLOCK-NO** row.
9. Edit the copied record with the following content, as shown in Figure 10–59:
    - *CATALOG:* **123-BLOCK-NC**
    - *MANUFACTURER:* **ASCENT**
    - *DESCRIPTION:* **CONTACT BLOCK**
    - *TYPE:* **30.5mm**
    - *STYLE:* **RED**
    - *CONTACTS:* **1 NC**
    - *MISCALLANEOUS2:* **N.C. CONTACT BLOCK**
    - *ASSEMBLYCODE:* Blank (delete everything, if required).
    - *ASSEMBLYLIST:* Click ▾ and select **123-SUB_2_BLOCKS**
      (Delete the **123-SUB_2_BLOCKS** and select it from the list again even if it displays from copying the row. It sometimes conflicts while saving the records.)
    - *WDBLKNAM:* **PB11,PB12,PB11M,PB12M**

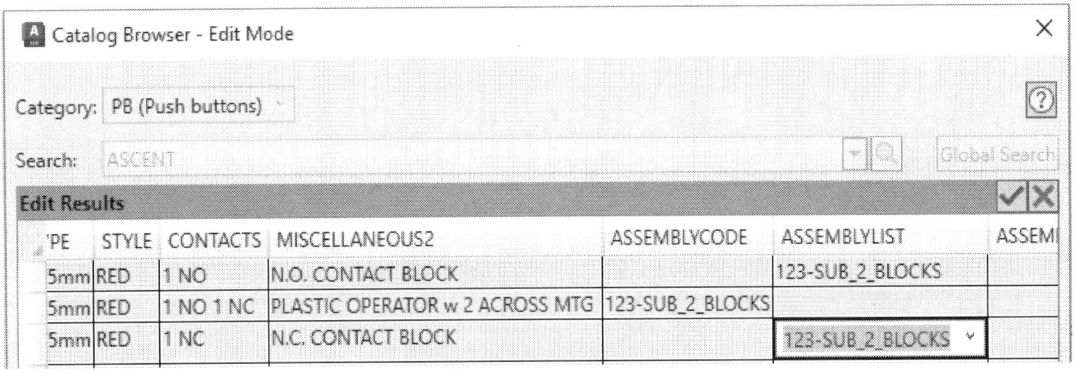

Figure 10–59

10. Still in the Edit mode, repeat to create another subassembly. Copy and paste the entire **123-BLOCK-NC** row.

11. Edit the copied record with the following content, as shown in Figure 10–60:
    - *CATALOG:* **123-LATCH**
    - *MANUFACTURER:* **ASCENT**
    - *DESCRIPTION:* **MOUNTING LATCH**
    - *TYPE:* **30.5mm**
    - *STYLE:* **PLASTIC**
    - *CONTACTS:* **1 NO 1 NC**
    - *MISCALLANEOUS2:* Blank (delete everything).
    - *ASSEMBLYCODE:* Blank (delete everything, if required).
    - *ASSEMBLYLIST:* Click ▾ and select **123-SUB_2_BLOCKS**.
    - *WDBLKNAM:* **PB11,PB12,PB11M,PB12M**

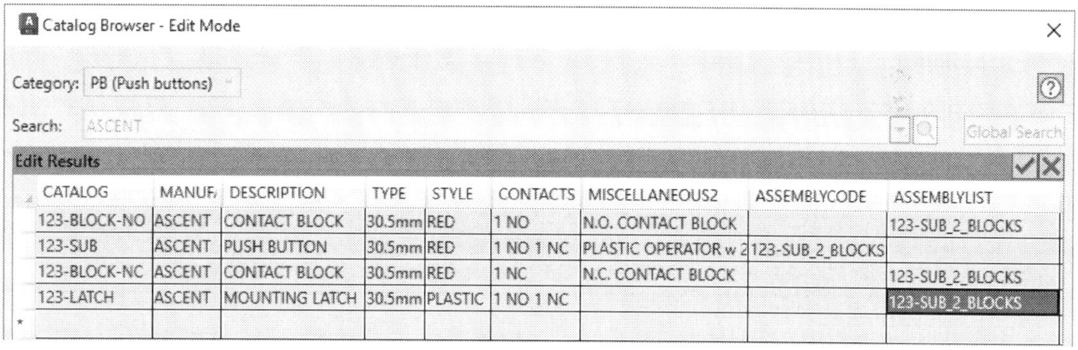

Figure 10–60

12. Click ✔ to accept all of the changes. Note that you are in Lookup mode in the Catalog Browser. As the last search was **ASCENT**, only one main assembly displays.
13. Select the main assembly and click **OK**. You are returned to the *Insert / Edit Component* dialog box.

14. In the *Insert / Edit Component* dialog box, click **Catalog Check**. The *Bill of Material Check* dialog box opens. Note the subassembly information, as shown in Figure 10–61. Click **Close**.

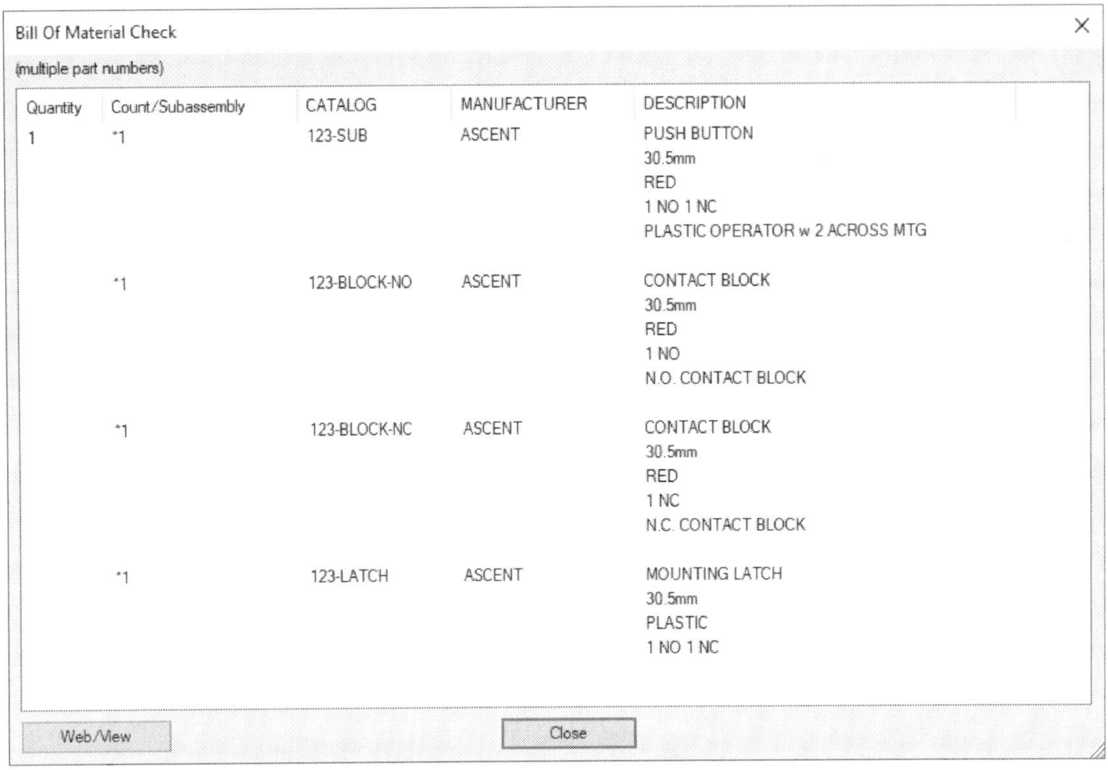

Figure 10–61

15. In the *Insert / Edit Component* dialog box, click **OK**.
16. If the *Footprint Symbol Missing* dialog box, select **Update the catalog on the footprint but leave the footprint symbol as is.**
17. Update and save the drawing.
18. Close **Control.dwg**.

End of practice

Practice 10d
Pin List Database

Practice Objective

- Add a pin list record to a catalog entry in the Pin List database.

In this practice, you will insert components with a catalog number that is not in the Pin List database. Next, you will erase the components and edit the Pin List database to add a record for the catalog number. Finally, you will insert the same components, noting that they have now been assigned pin numbers, as shown in Figure 10–62.

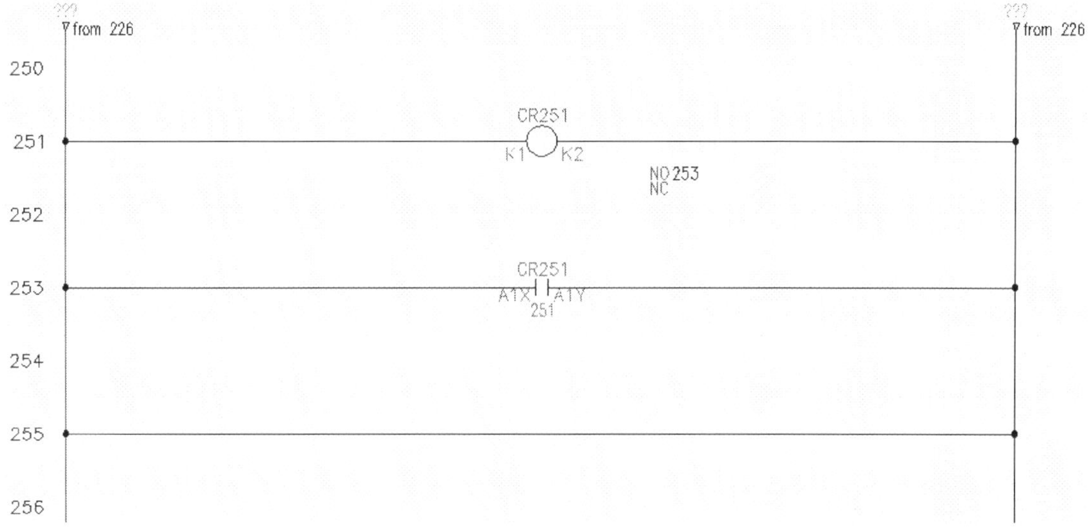

Figure 10–62

Task 1: Insert components.

1. If the **Module 10** project is not active, open and activate it now.
2. In the **Module 10** project, open **Control.dwg**.
3. Zoom into the area of 250 to 256.
4. Click (Add Rung).

5. Add rungs to lines 251, 253, and 255 as shown in Figure 10–63. Press <Enter> to end the command.

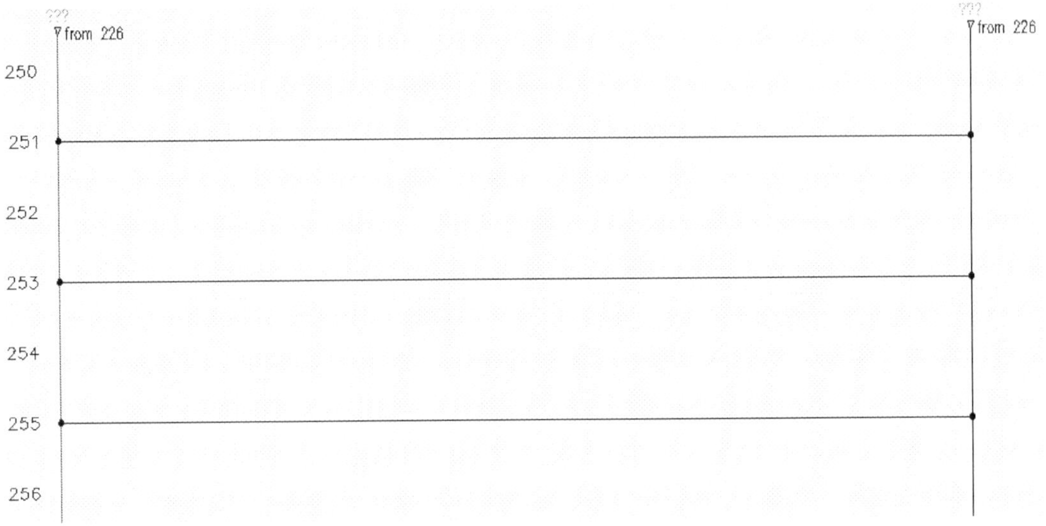

Figure 10–63

6. Click (Icon Menu).

7. Click (Relays/Contacts) and then click (Relay Coil) to insert a relay coil.

8. Insert the coil anywhere (near the middle) on line 251.

9. The *Insert / Edit Component* dialog box opens. Click **Lookup**.

10. The *Catalog Browser* dialog box opens. Search for **OMRON**, select **P2CM-S** and click **OK**.

11. The *Catalog Data* area in the *Insert / Edit Component* dialog box is updated, but in the *Pins* area the fields are blank, as shown in Figure 10–64. Click **OK**.

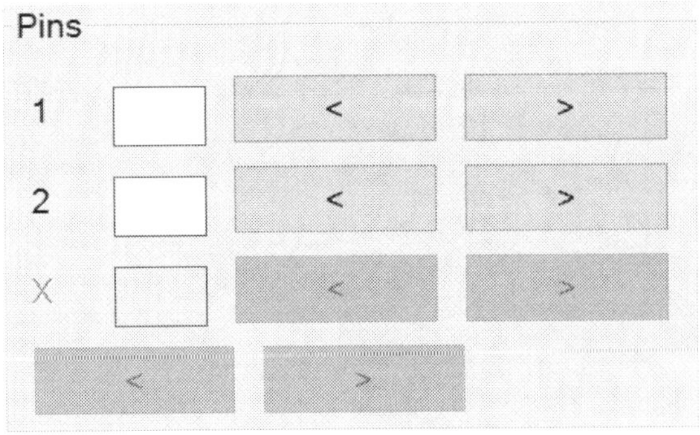

Figure 10–64

12. Click (Icon Menu).

13. Click (Relays/Contacts) and then click (Relay NO Contact) to insert a normally open contact.

14. Insert the contact anywhere on line 253.

15. The *Insert / Edit Child Component* dialog box opens. Click **Parent/Sibling** and select **CR251**. The *Insert / Edit Child Component* dialog box opens again with the fields in the *Pins* area still blank. Click **OK**.

16. Click (Delete Component) and delete the two symbols that you just inserted. In the *Search for/Surf to Children?* dialog box, click **No**.

Task 2: Edit the Pin List database.

1. In the *Schematic* tab>*Insert Components* panel, click (Catalog Browser) to open the *Catalog Browser* palette.

2. Search for **OMRON** and select **P2CM-S**.

3. Change the *Catalog Browser* to Edit mode (as shown in Figure 10–65) by clicking (Edit catalog database).

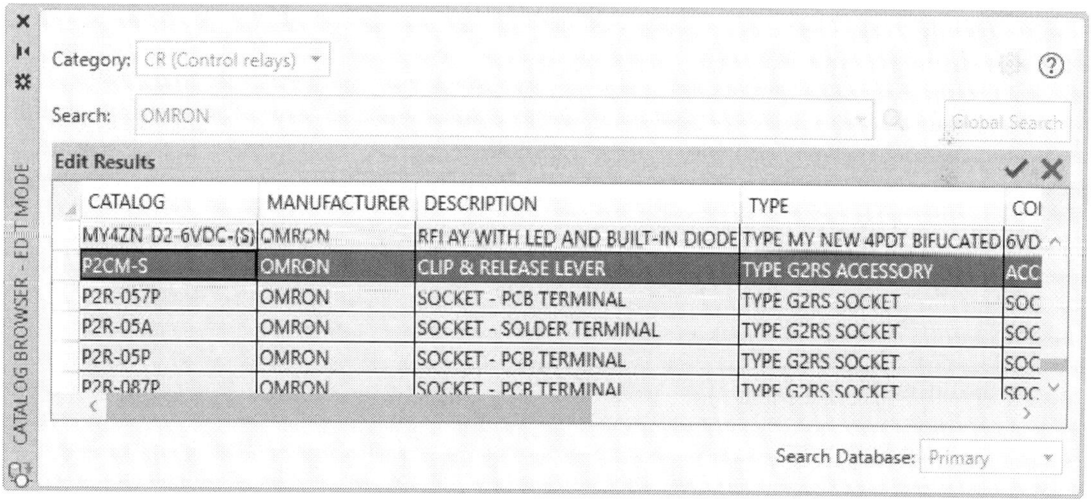

Figure 10–65

4. Scroll right until the *COILPINS* and *PINLIST* columns display in the *Catalog Browser* Note that they are empty for the selected component (**P2CM-S**).

5. In the *COILPINS* column, type **K1,K2** and in the *PINLIST* column, type **0,A1X,A1Y;0,A4X,A4Y**, as shown in Figure 10–66.

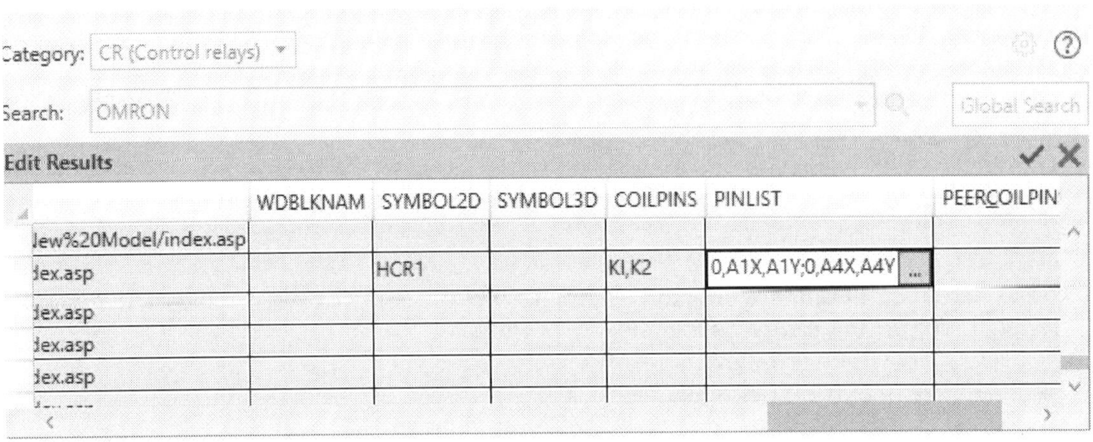

Figure 10–66

6. Click ✓ to accept all of the changes. Note that you are in Lookup mode in the *Catalog Browser*. Close the *Catalog Browser*.

Task 3: Insert components.

1. Click (Icon Menu).
2. In the *Insert Component* dialog box, in the *Recently Used* area, click (Relay Coil) to insert a relay coil.
3. Insert the coil anywhere on line 251 (near the middle).
4. The *Insert / Edit Component* dialog box opens. Click **Lookup**.
5. The *Catalog Browser* dialog box opens. Search for **OMRON** and select **P2CM-S**. Click **OK**.

6. The *Insert / Edit Component* dialog box updates. Note that in the *Pins* area, the fields are updated, as shown in Figure 10–67. Click **OK**.

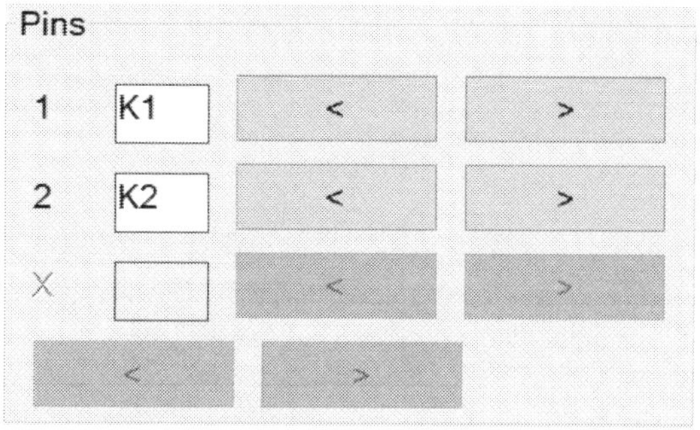

Figure 10–67

7. Click (Icon Menu).

8. In the *Recently Used* list, click (Relay NO Contact) and insert the contact anywhere on line 253.

9. The *Insert / Edit Child Component* dialog box opens. Note that the *Pins* area is empty. Click **Parent/Sibling** and select **CR251**. The dialog box updates. Note that in the *Pins* area, the fields are updated, as shown in Figure 10–68. Click **OK**. Note that the pin numbers display with the components in the drawing.

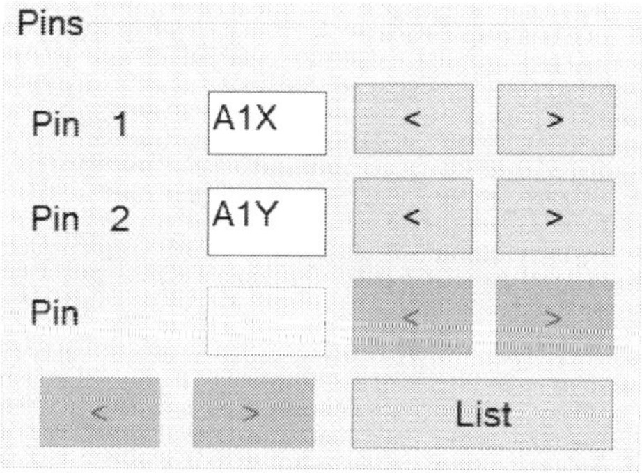

Figure 10–68

10. Save and close **Control.dwg**.

End of practice

Practice 10e
Footprint Database

Practice Objective

- Add records to the Footprint Lookup database.

In this practice, you will add a new component to the BOM database. You will also create a new footprint and add the footprint block link to the Footprint database. Finally, you will insert the power supply footprints over a DIN rail, as shown in Figure 10–69.

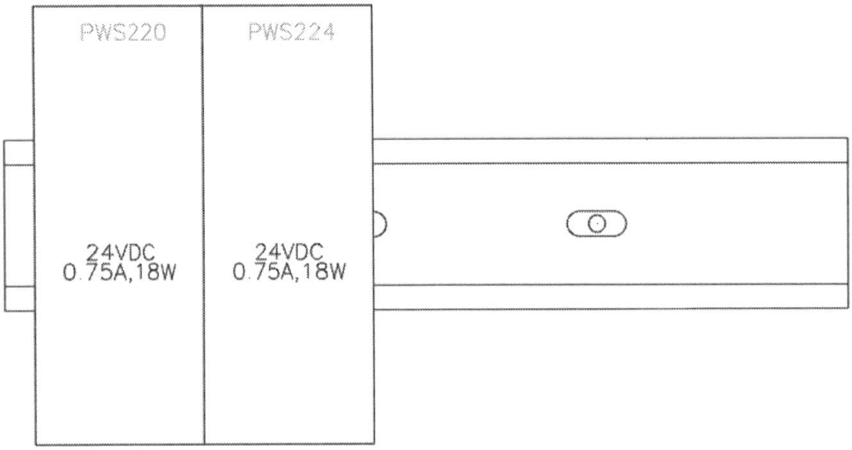

Figure 10–69

Task 1: Add a new record to the BOM database.

1. If the **Module 10** project is not active, open and activate it now.
2. In the **Module 10** project, open **Control.dwg**.
3. Zoom to rung 220 and note the custom power supply.
4. Edit the power supply component.
5. In the *Insert/Edit Component* dialog box, in the *Catalog Data* area, click **Lookup**.
6. In the *Catalog Browser*, verify that the category is set to **PW (Power supplies)**.
7. Change the *Catalog Browser* to Edit mode by clicking  (Edit catalog database).

8. Scroll down to the bottom of the list and locate the last empty row. Enter the following information, as shown in Figure 10–70:
   - *CATALOG:* **2868635**
   - *MANUFACTURER:* **PHOENIX CONTACT**
   - *DESCRIPTION:* **SINGLE PHASE DIN RAIL POWER SUPPLY**
   - *RATING:* **0.75A,24VDC**
   - *TYPE:* **SINGLE-PHASE**
   - *MISCALLANEOUS1:* **INPUT VOLTAGE: 110VAC TO 240VAC**
   - *MISCALLANEOUS2:* **OUTPUT POWER 18W**
   - *TEXTVALUE:* **RATING1=24VDC;RATING2=0.75A,18W**

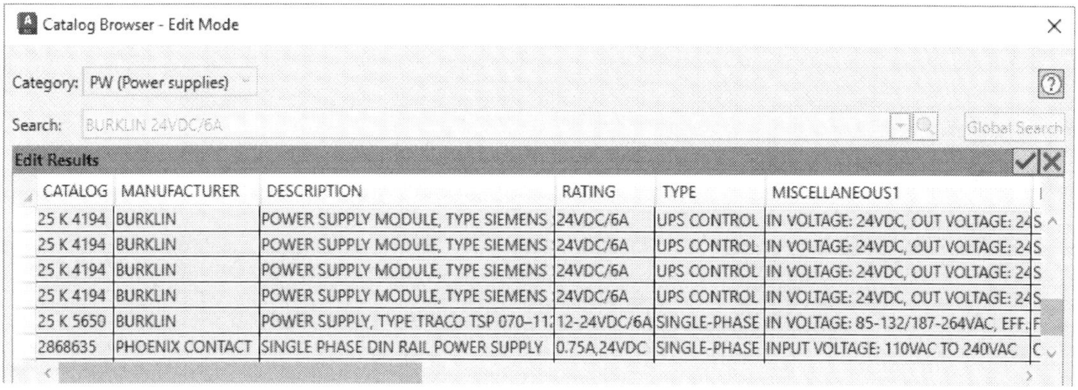

Figure 10–70

9. Click ✓ to accept all of the changes.
10. Search for **PHOENIX** and select the newly created entry. Click **OK** in the *Catalog Browser*.
11. The *No Pinlist Defined for Catalog Selection* dialog box opens. Select **Assign the catalog data, leave the existing pinlist values,** as shown in Figure 10–71.

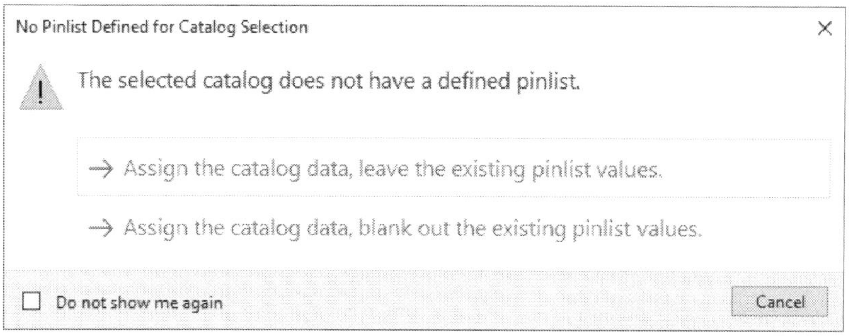

Figure 10–71

12. In the *Insert/Edit Component* dialog box, click **Catalog Check** to display the *Bill Of Material Check* dialog box, as shown in Figure 10–72.

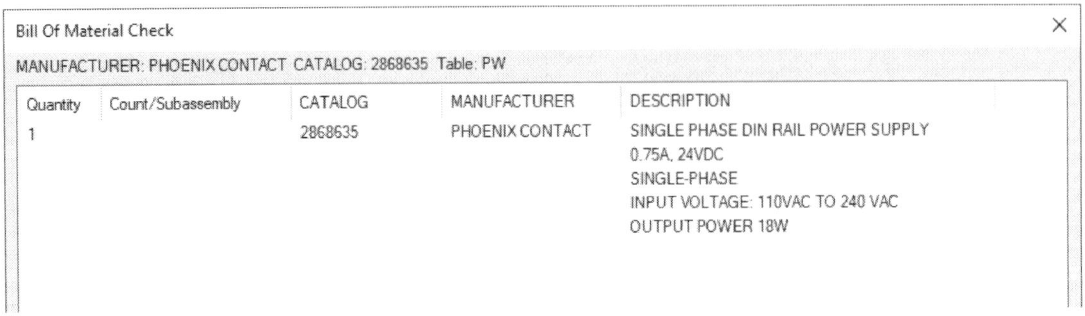

Figure 10–72

13. Click **Close**. In the *Insert/Edit Component* dialog box, click **OK**. Select **Map symbol to the catalog number**.
14. In the drawing, insert a rung at line 224.
15. Use **Copy Component** to copy the power supply from rung 220 to rung 224. Click **OK** in the *Insert/Edit Component* dialog box. The two power supplies are displayed, as shown in Figure 10–73.

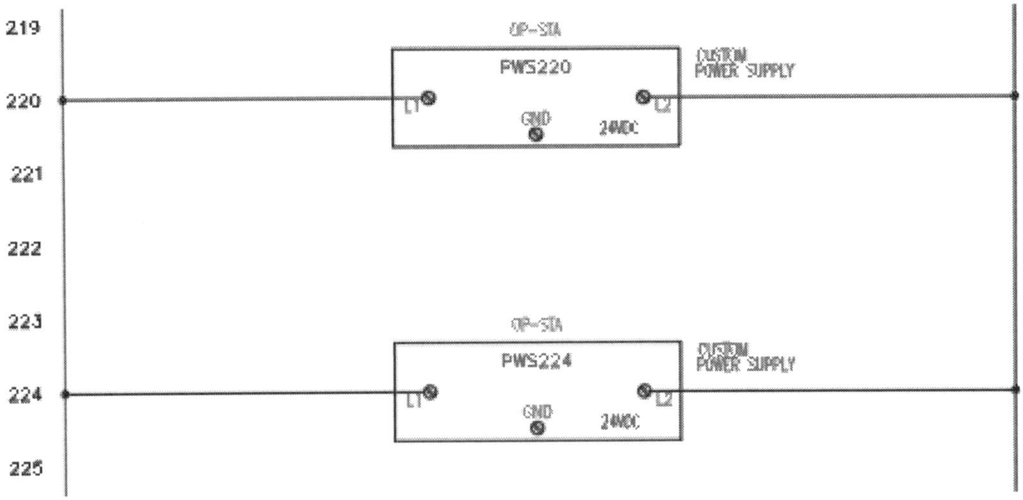

Figure 10–73

16. Save and close **Control.dwg**.

Task 2: Create the footprint symbol.

1. In the **Module 10** project, open **Operator Station.dwg**.
2. Pan to the empty space along the right side to create the footprint symbol.
3. Make layer **0** the current layer.
4. Start the AutoCAD **Rectangle** command. For the first corner of the rectangle, click at coordinate point **80,14**. Right-click and select **Dimensions**. For the *length* of the rectangle, enter **1.417**. For the *width*, enter **3.54**. Click in the upper right quadrant to create the rectangle, as shown in Figure 10–74.
    - The power supply dimensions specified in the catalog are **Width: 36mm or 1.417**" and **Height: 90mm or 3.54**".

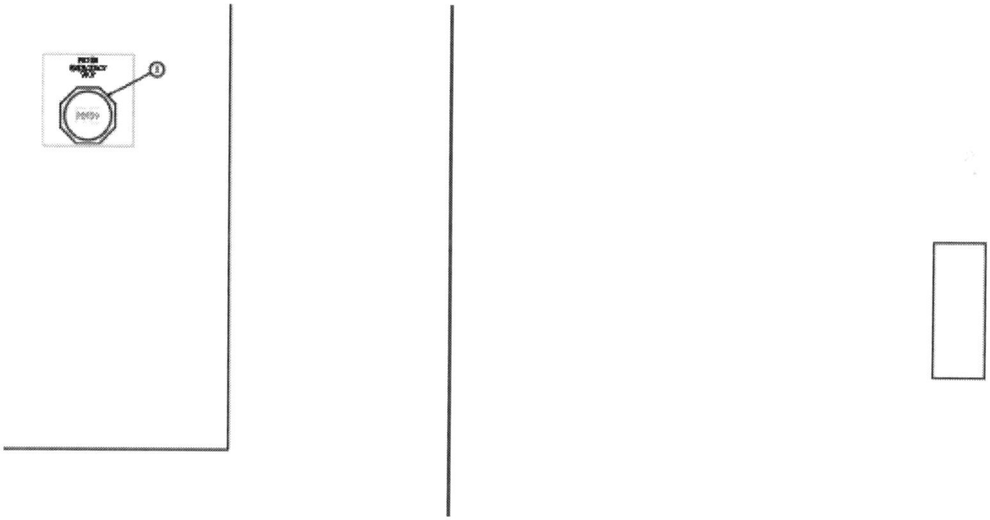

Figure 10–74

5. In the *Panel* tab>*Other Tools* panel, click  (Symbol Builder). The *Select Symbol / Objects* dialog box opens.
6. In the *Objects* area, click  (Select objects) and select the new rectangle in the drawing. Press <Enter>.
7. In the *Insertion point* area, click  (Pick point) and using the **Midpoint** OSNAP, select the midpoint of the left vertical edge of the rectangle.

8. In the *Attribute template* area, for *Symbol*, select **Panel Footprint**. The dialog box displays as shown in Figure 10–75.

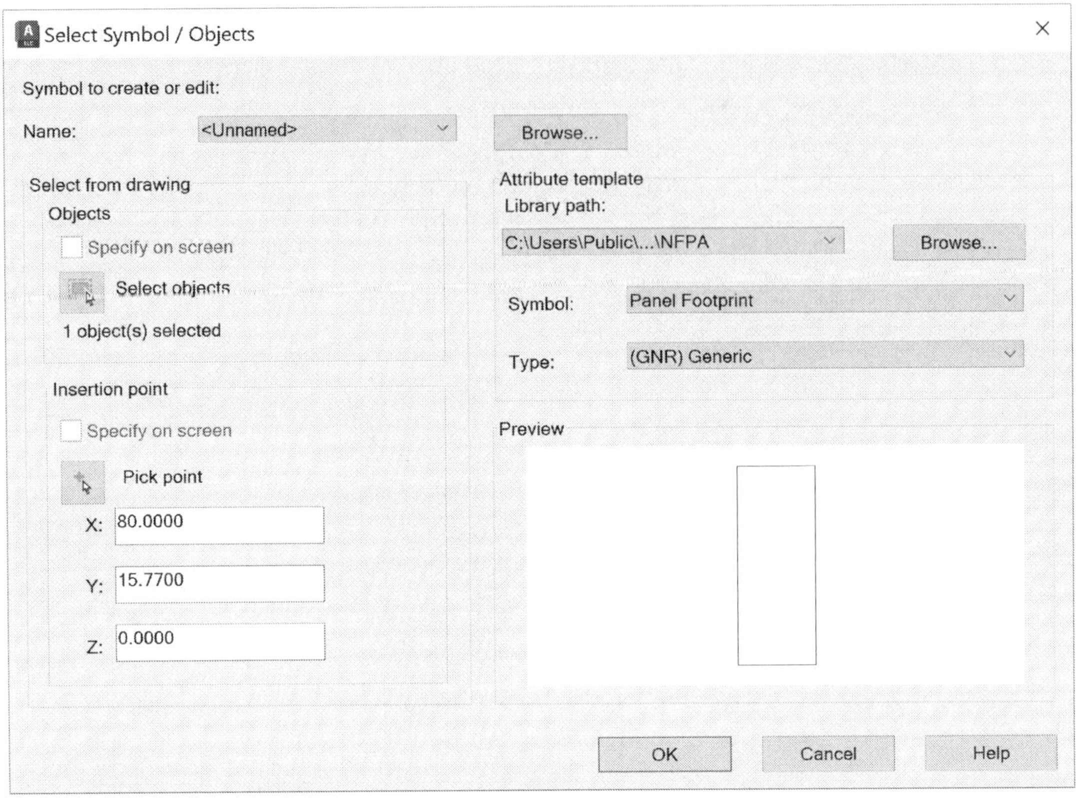

Figure 10–75

9. Click **OK** to load the geometry into the AutoCAD Block Editor environment. The *Symbol Builder Attribute Editor* palette opens. Note that the ribbon displays the *Symbol Builder* and *Block Editor* contextual tabs.
10. Select the **Endpoint** object snaps and toggle on **Object Snaps**, if required.
11. In the *Home* tab>expanded *Draw* panel, click  (Wipeout).
12. Select the four corners of the rectangle to create the wipeout.
13. In the *Symbol Builder Attribute Editor* palette, in the *Required* area, drag the **P_TAG1** attribute below the top horizontal edge of the rectangle and then click to place it, as shown in Figure 10–76.

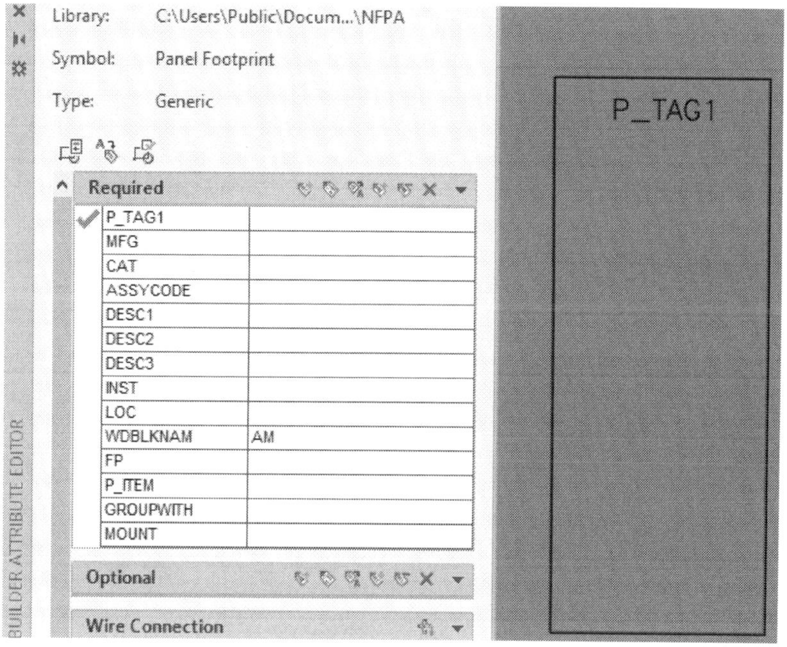

Figure 10–76

14. In the ribbon, in the *Block Editor* tab, click  (Close Block Editor).
15. In the *Close Block Editor: Save Symbol* dialog box, in the *Symbol* area, for *File path* click 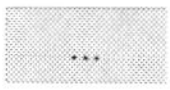.
16. In the *Browse For Folder* dialog box, navigate to *C:\Users\Public\Public Documents\Autodesk\Acade 2025\Libs\panel\PHOENIX CONTACT*.
17. Right-click on **PHOENIX CONTACT** and select **New>Folder**. Create a folder with the name **PW-POWER SOURCES**, as shown in Figure 10–77.

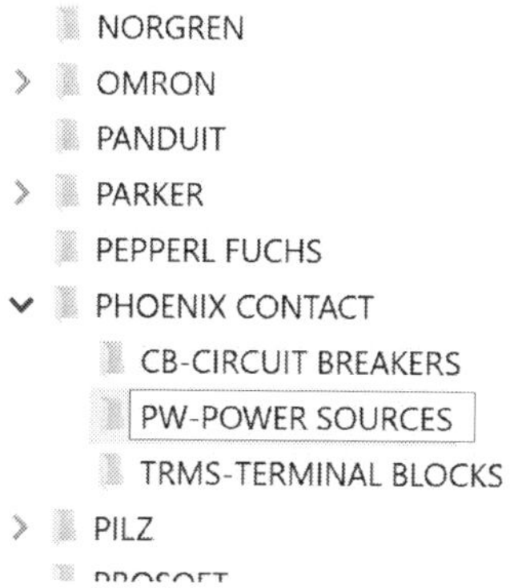

Figure 10–77

18. Select the folder and click **OK**. This sets the path for saving the symbol, as shown in Figure 10–78.
19. For *Symbol name*, enter **FP_2868635**. Clear the **Icon image** option. The *Close Block Editor: Save Symbol* dialog box should display as shown in Figure 10–78.

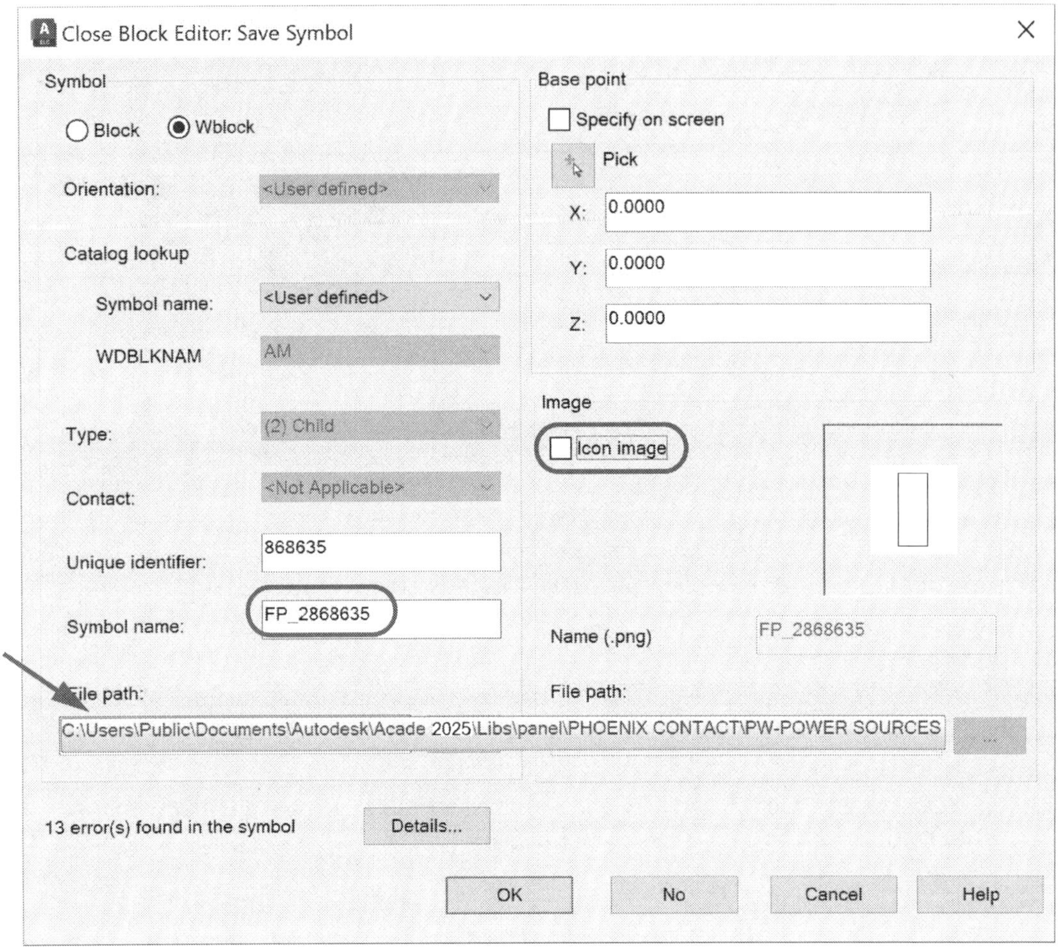

Figure 10–78

20. Click **OK**. Click **No** in the *Close Block Editor* dialog box.
21. Using the AutoCAD **Erase** command, delete the rectangle.

Task 3: Add record to the Footprint Lookup database.

1. In the *Panel* tab>expanded *Other Tools* panel, click (Footprint Database Editor).
2. In the *Panel Footprint Lookup Database Editor*, click **Edit Existing Table**, as shown in Figure 10–79.

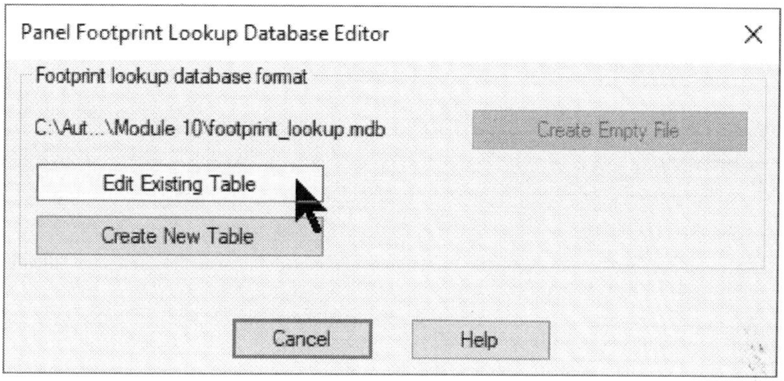

Figure 10–79

3. In the *Table Edit* dialog box, select **PHOENIX CONTACT** (as shown in Figure 10–80) and click **OK**.

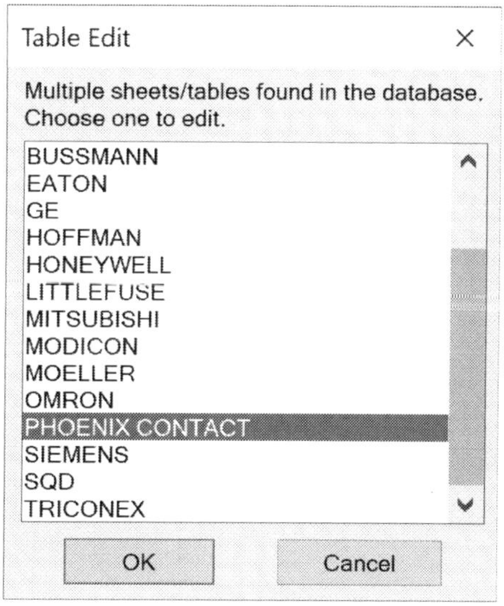

Figure 10–80

4. In the *Footprint lookup (table PHOENIX CONTACT)* dialog box that opens, click **Add New**.

5. In the *Add footprint record (table PHOENIX CONTACT)* dialog box, for *Catalog Number*, enter **2868635**.
6. Click **Browse**. In the *Select Footprint Block* dialog box, navigate to *C:\Users\Public\Public Documents\Autodesk\Acade 2025\libs\panel\PHOENIX CONTACT\PW-POWER SOURCES* and open **FP_2868635.dwg and click Open**.
7. The complete path is displayed in the *Add footprint record* dialog box. Delete the path from C: until PHOENIX CONTACT, as shown in Figure 10–81.

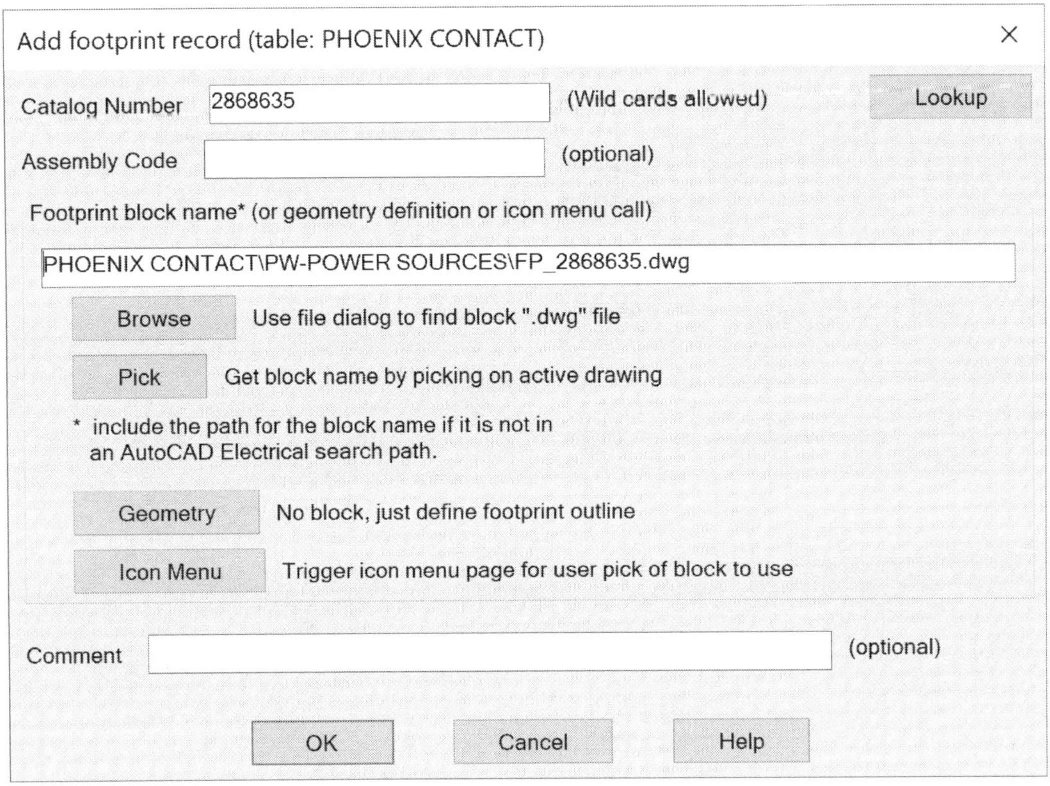

Figure 10–81

8. In the *Add footprint record* dialog box, click **OK**.
9. In the *Footprint lookup table* dialog box, click **OK/Save/Exit**.

Task 4: Insert a DIN rail.

1. Verify that **Operator Station.dwg** is open.
2. In the *Panel* tab>*Insert Component Footprints* panel, click  (Insert Footprint [Icon Menu]).

3. In the *Insert Footprint* dialog box, click  (DIN Rail).
4. The *Din Rail* dialog box opens. Note that the *Rail Type* is set as default **AB, 199-DR1**. Set the following, as shown in Figure 10–82:
   - *Length:* **7**
   - *X*: **40**
   - *Y*: **16**

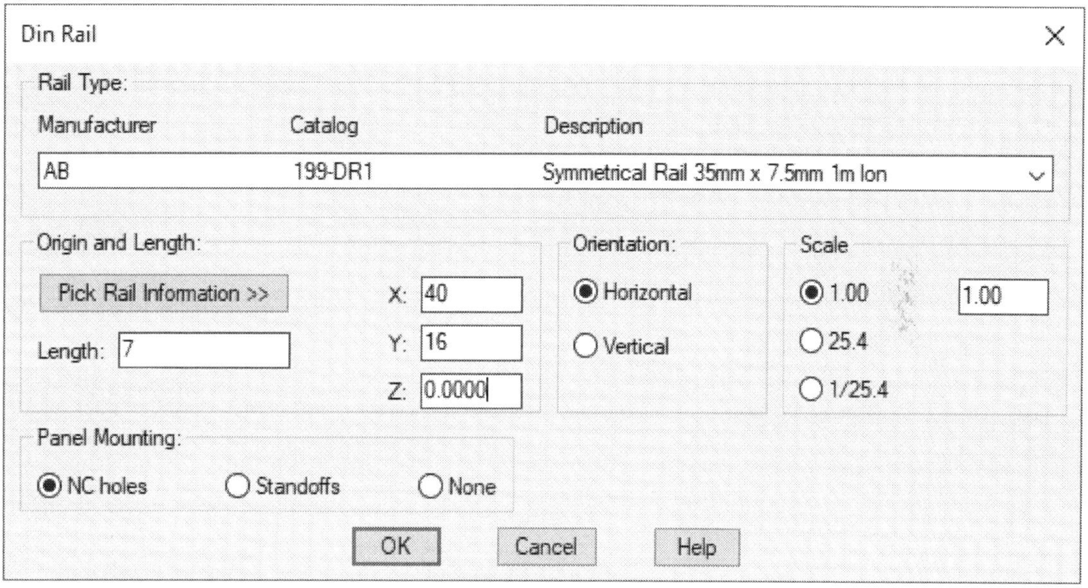

Figure 10–82

5. Click **OK**.
6. The *Panel Layout – Component Insert/Edit* dialog box opens. In the *Location* column, click **Project**, select **OP-STA**, and click **OK**. It is displayed as Location, as shown in Figure 10–83.

Figure 10–83

7. Click **OK**. Note that a DIN rail is inserted in the drawing, as shown in Figure 10–84.

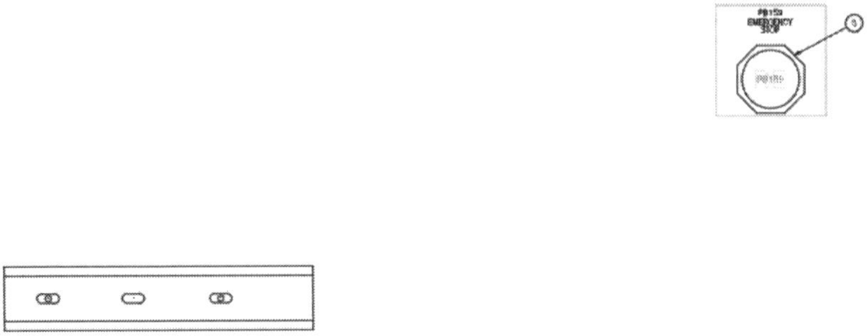

Figure 10–84

Task 5: Insert power supplies footprints.

1. In the *Panel* tab>*Insert Component Footprints* panel, click (Schematic List).
2. In the *Schematic Components List* dialog box, click **OK** to accept the default values.
3. In the *Select Drawings to Process* dialog box, click **Do All**. All of the drawings are moved to the bottom panel. Click **OK**.
4. In the *Schematic Components* dialog box that opens, click **Mark Existing**. A checkmark is placed in front of the components that are already placed in the Panel layout. Click **Hide Existing** to hide those components.
5. Click **Sort List**. In the *Sort* dialog box, in the *Primary sort* drop-down list, select **LOC**. In the *Secondary sort* drop-down list, select **MFG**, as shown in Figure 10–85.

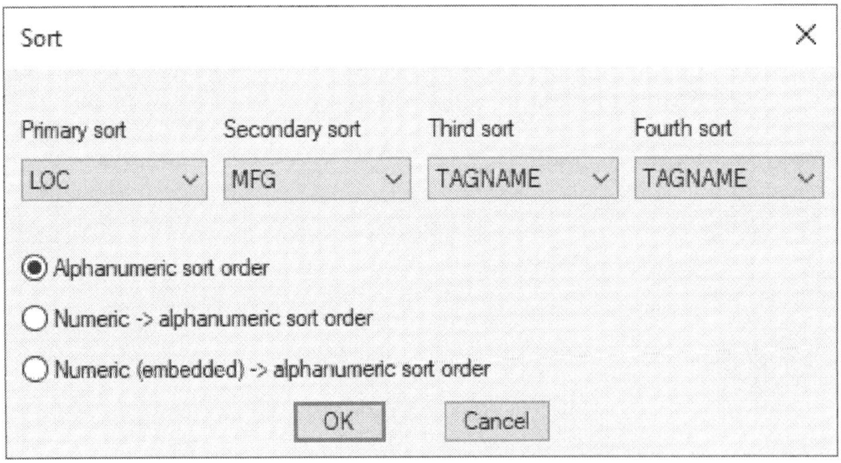

Figure 10–85

6. Click **OK**.
7. In the *Schematic Components* dialog box, for Rotate (blank="ask"), enter **0** (as shown in Figure 10–86) to set the rotation angle to 0.
8. Near the bottom of the list, select **PWS220** (as shown in Figure 10–86). Click **Insert**.

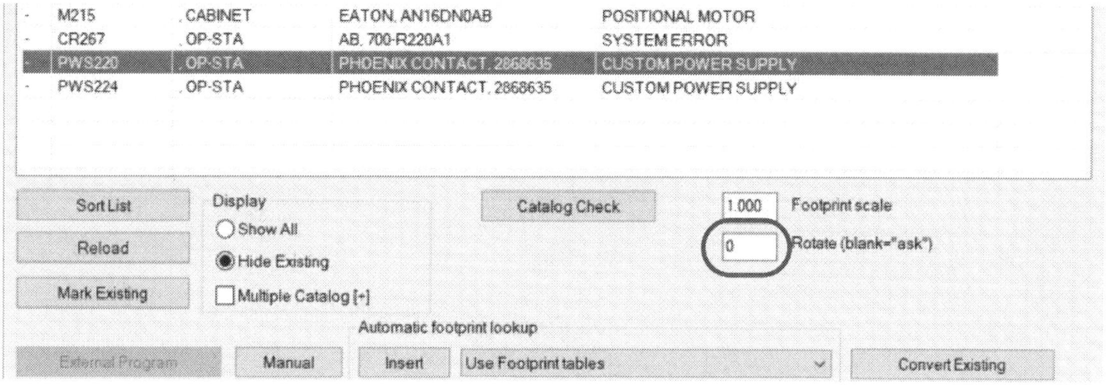

Figure 10–86

9. The component is attached to the cursor. Insert it 0.25 to the right of the left wall of the DIN rail, as shown in Figure 10–87.

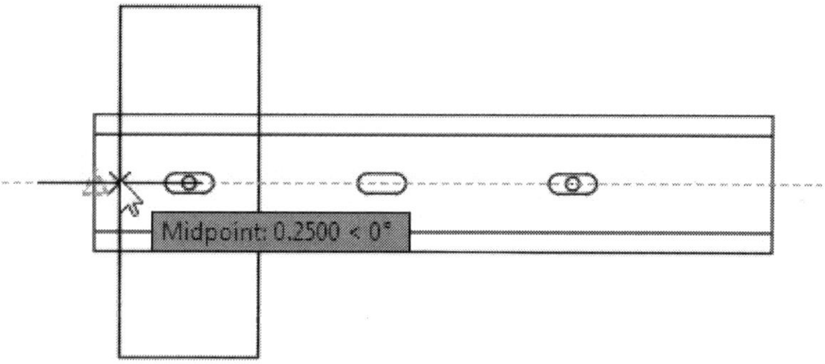

Figure 10–87

10. In the *Panel Layout* dialog box, click **OK**.
11. In the *Schematic Components* dialog box, select **PWS224**. Click **Insert**.

12. Insert the component flush to the right wall of PWS220, as shown in Figure 10–88.

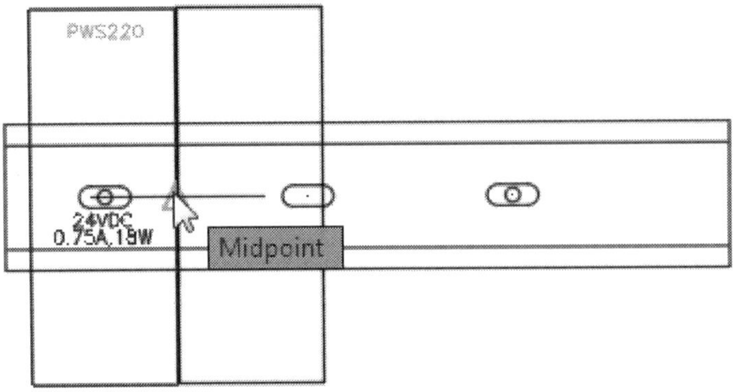

Figure 10–88

13. In the *Panel Layout* dialog box, click **OK**.
14. In the *Schematic Components* dialog box, click **Close**.
15. If the DIN rail overlays the power supplies, in the *Home* tab>extended *Modify* panel, use the AutoCAD  (Send to Back) command to send the DIN rail behind the power supplies.
16. Save and close all the open drawings.

End of practice

Chapter Review Questions

1. When you save a symbol with the **Wblock** option selected in the *Close Block Editor: Save Symbol* dialog box, where is the information saved?

    a. In the AutoCAD Electrical symbol library.

    b. In the project file.

    c. In the current/active drawing.

    d. In a text file.

2. Using the AutoCAD Electrical software naming convention, what does a block named **HPB11** represent?

    a. A horizontal parent normally open mushroom head.

    b. A horizontal parent normally open push button.

    c. A horizontal parent normally closed push button.

    d. A vertical parent normally closed push button.

3. How do you specify the library directories to search for the symbol blocks?

    a. In the Project Properties>*Project Settings* tab, set the Schematic Libraries directories.

    b. In the Schematic Properties>*Drawing Settings* tab, set the Schematic Libraries directories.

    c. In the Project Properties>*Drawing Settings* tab, set the Schematic Libraries directories.

    d. In the *Project Manager* toolbar, click **Library Directory**.

4. When using the *Icon Menu Wizard*, how do you create a new submenu?

    a. Click **Show Submenu**.

    b. Click **Submenu** in the ribbon.

    c. Right-click in empty space and select **New submenu**.

    d. Double-click on the icon.

5. When creating a new icon, how is the picture for the icon created?
   a. From an AutoCAD drawing file.
   b. From an AutoCAD slidefile or PNG file.
   c. From an AutoCAD block.
   d. From a PNG file or WDT file.

6. What is the function of the Project scratch database?
   a. It holds all deleted component data for later use.
   b. It holds all deleted component data for report purposes.
   c. It holds component data for back-up purposes.
   d. It holds component data for faster access during project-wide commands.

7. Which command is used to access the Catalog database so that information can be added to it?
   a. The **Edit Component** command and click **Lookup**.
   b. The **Catalog Database File Editor** command.
   c. The **Component Database File Editor** command.
   d. The **Edit Component** command and click **Edit Database**.

8. The Footprint Lookup database contains a separate table for each manufacturer.
   a. True
   b. False

Command Summary

Button	Command	Location
	**Catalog Browser**	• **Ribbon:** *Schematic* tab>*Insert Components* panel>*Icon Menu* drop-down list
	**Footprint Database File Editor**	• **Ribbon:** *Panel* tab>*Other Tools* panel flyout
	**Icon Menu Wizard**	• **Ribbon:** *Schematic* tab>*Other Tools* panel or *Panel* tab>*Other Tools* panel
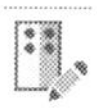	**PLC Database File Editor**	• **Ribbon**: *Schematic* tab>*Other Tools* panel flyout
	**Symbol Builder**	• **Ribbon:** *Schematic* tab>*Other Tools* panel or *Panel* tab>*Other Tools* panel

Chapter 11

Titleblocks

Typically, a drawing includes a titleblock that contains all the important information about the drawing. Learning to update the information in the titleblock enables you to keep it up to date and relevant to the current status of the drawing.

Learning Objectives

- Update attribute values in a titleblock.
- Create a new titleblock mapping file.

11.1 Update Titleblocks

The AutoCAD® Electrical software can update the values of attributes in your titleblock with properties from the drawing or project. You can update an individual active drawing or all of the drawings in a project. Properties include drawing name, sheet number, and project descriptions.

Title Block Update

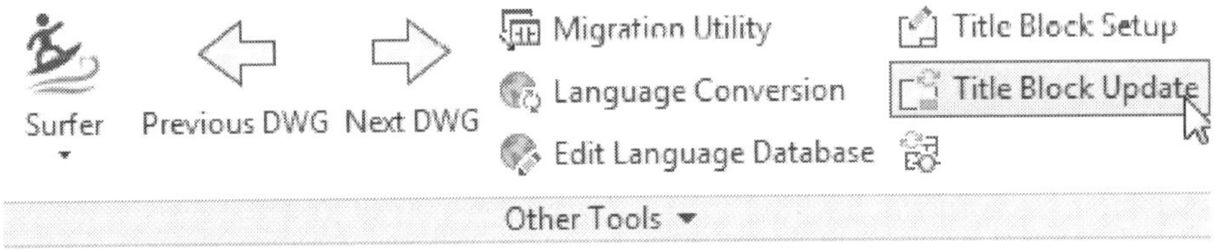

Ribbon: *Project* tab>*Other Tools* panel

Command Prompt: aeupdatetitleblock

How To: Update Titleblocks in a Project

1. Start the **Title Block Update** command. The *Update Title Block* dialog box opens.
2. Select the parameters that you want to update.
3. Click **OK Project-wide** to update specific drawings from the entire project. (You can also click **OK Active Drawing Only** to only update the titleblock of the active drawing.) The *Select Drawings to Process* dialog box opens.
4. Select the drawings you want to update and click **OK**.
5. If the *Qsave* dialog box opens, click **OK**.

You can control the parameters that you want to update in the *Update Title Block* dialog box, as shown in Figure 11–1.

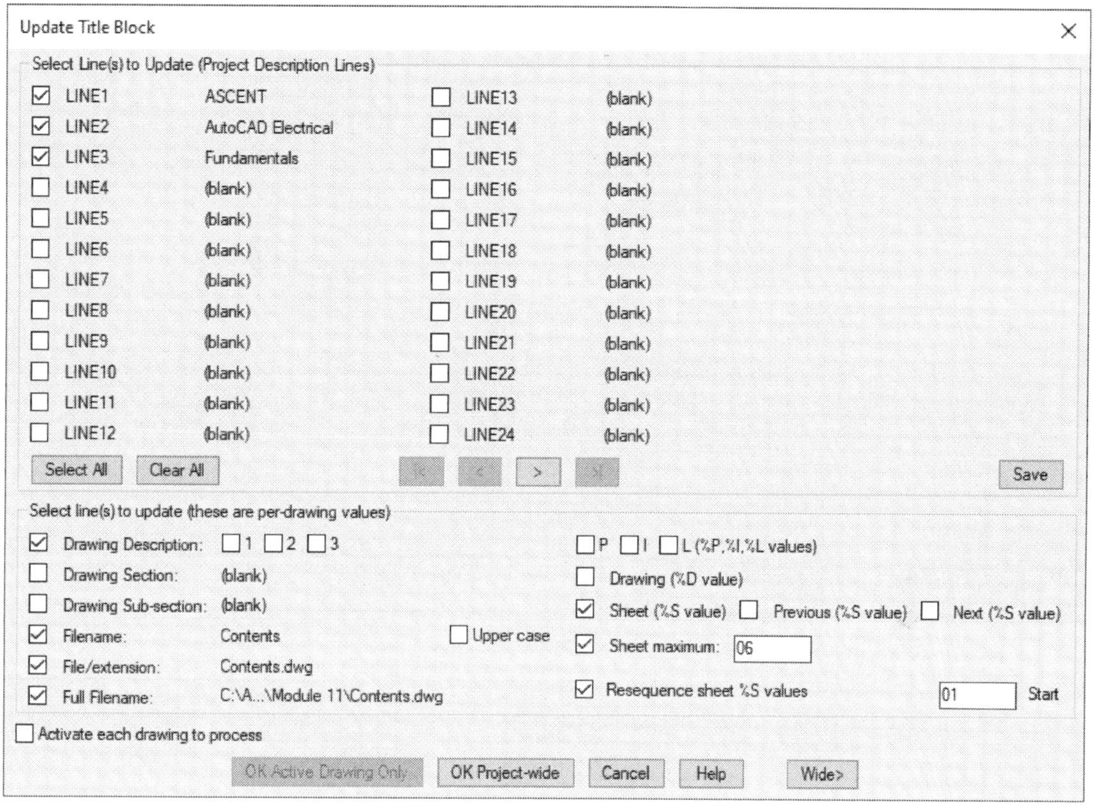

Figure 11–1

Select Line(s) to Update (Project Description Lines)	Parameters that are the Project Description lines assigned by you when the project file is created.
Select All/Clear All	Selects or clears all Project Description lines.
</>	Navigates to the previous or next page of Project Descriptions.
Select line(s) to update (these are per-drawing values)	These parameters are assigned to each drawing.

- You can update the **Sheet** parameter, which is assigned to each drawing and is its sheet number in the project, by selecting **Resequence – sheet %S values** option and entering a starting value.
- Alternatively, you can update titleblocks using the **Project-Wide Update/Retag** command. Select **Title Block Update** and click **Setup** to open the *Update Title Block* dialog box, and then configure the parameters to update in the titleblock. If a parameter is selected, its corresponding attribute in the titleblock is updated.

- Some of the Project Description lines might have a value different from the default **Line #**. This differentiation is controlled through a text file called **<project name>_wdtitle.wdl** or **default_wdtitle.wdl**. The file is searched for values similar to the catalog database and can be configured for a specific project or for the AutoCAD Electrical software in general.
- The example dataset installed in *C:\Users\<user>\Documents\Acade <version>\Proj\Demo* in Windows 10, has a titleblock configured for the automatic update.

Practice 11a
Update Titleblocks

Practice Objective

- Modify project description and drawing properties and update the titleblocks.

In this practice, you will first populate the project descriptions and the drawing properties for two drawings. You will then run the **Title Block Update** command to update the sheet property and the titleblock as shown in Figure 11–2.

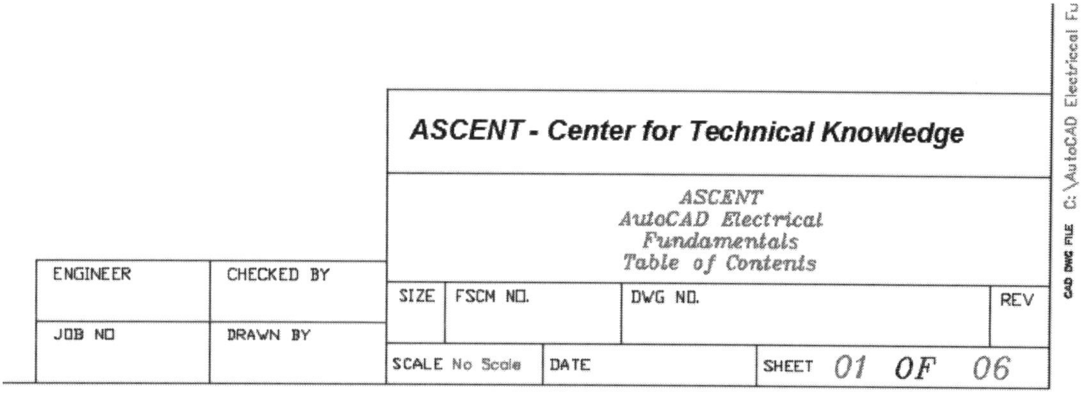

Figure 11–2

Task 1: Populate properties.

1. In your practice files folder, in the *Module 11* folder, open the **Module 11** project file.
2. In the **Module 11** project, open **Contents.dwg**.

3. Right-click on **MODULE 11** and select **Descriptions...**, as shown in Figure 11–3.

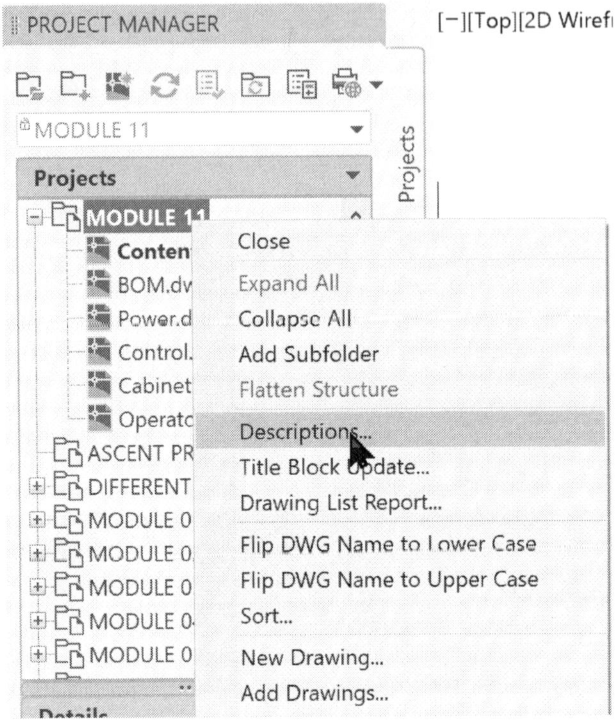

Figure 11–3

4. In the *Project Description* dialog box that opens, set the following, as shown in Figure 11–4:
   - *Line1*: **ASCENT**
   - *Line2*: **AutoCAD Electrical**
   - *Line3*: **Fundamentals**

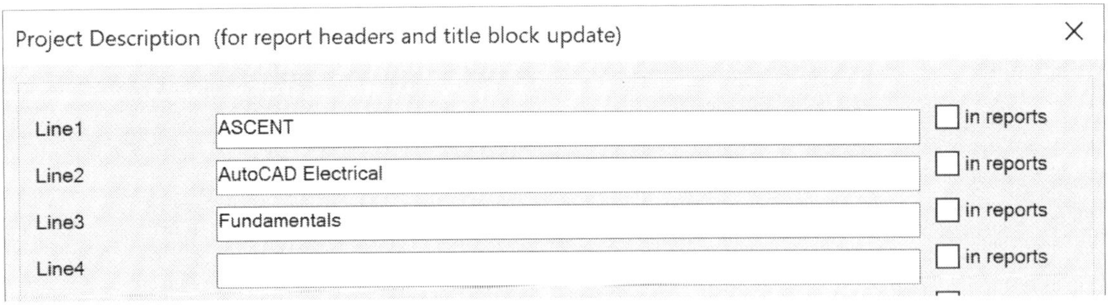

Figure 11–4

5. Click **OK**.

6. In the *Project Manager* palette, right-click on **Contents.dwg** and select **Properties>Drawing Properties,** as shown in Figure 11–5.

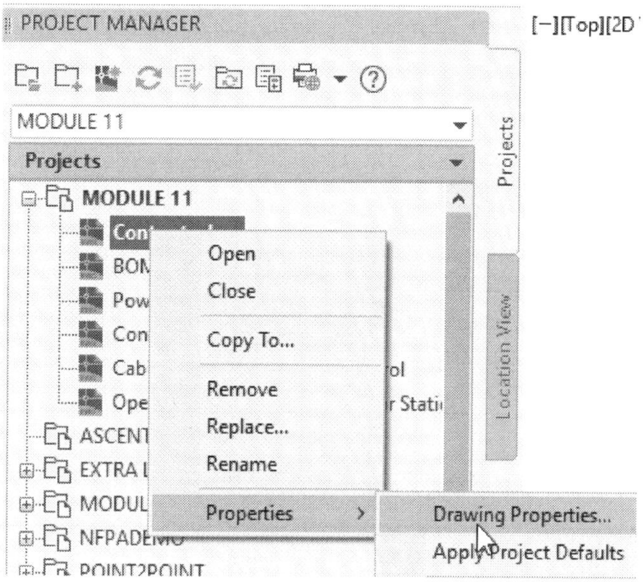

Figure 11–5

7. The *Drawing Properties* dialog box opens. For *Description 1*, type **Table of Contents**, as shown in Figure 11–6. Note that, in the *Sheet Values* area, the *Sheet* field is blank (this will automatically update later). Click **OK**.

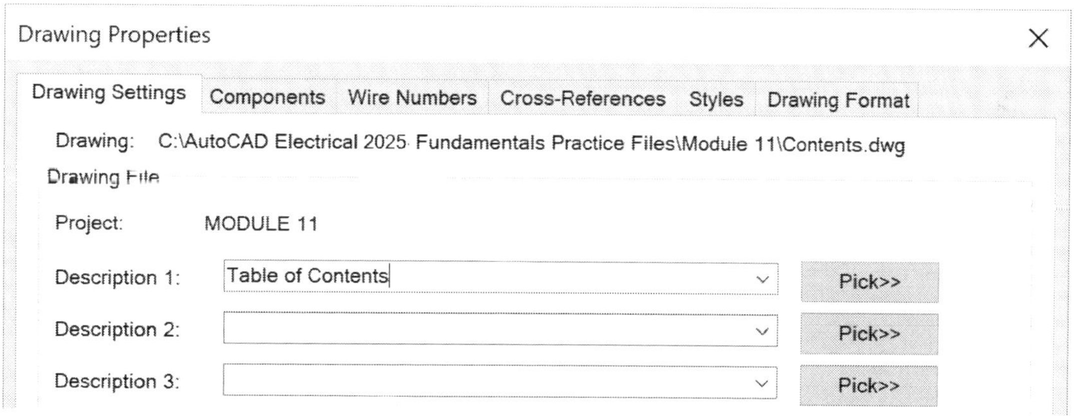

Figure 11–6

8. In the *Project Manager*, note that the **Table of Contents** description is added to **Contents.dwg**.

9. In the *Project Manager*, right-click on **Power.dwg** and select **Properties>Drawing Properties**.

10. In the *Drawing Properties* dialog box, set the following:
    - *Description 1:* **Main Power**
    - *Description 2:* **Schematic**
11. Note that, in the *Sheet Values* area, the *Sheet* field is blank (this will automatically update later). Click **OK**.

Task 2: Update titleblocks.

1. In the *Project* tab>*Other Tools* panel, click (Title Block Update).
2. The *Update Title Block* dialog box opens. Select the various checkboxes, as shown in Figure 11–7, and additionally set the following:
    - *Sheet maximum*: **06**
    - *Start*: **01**

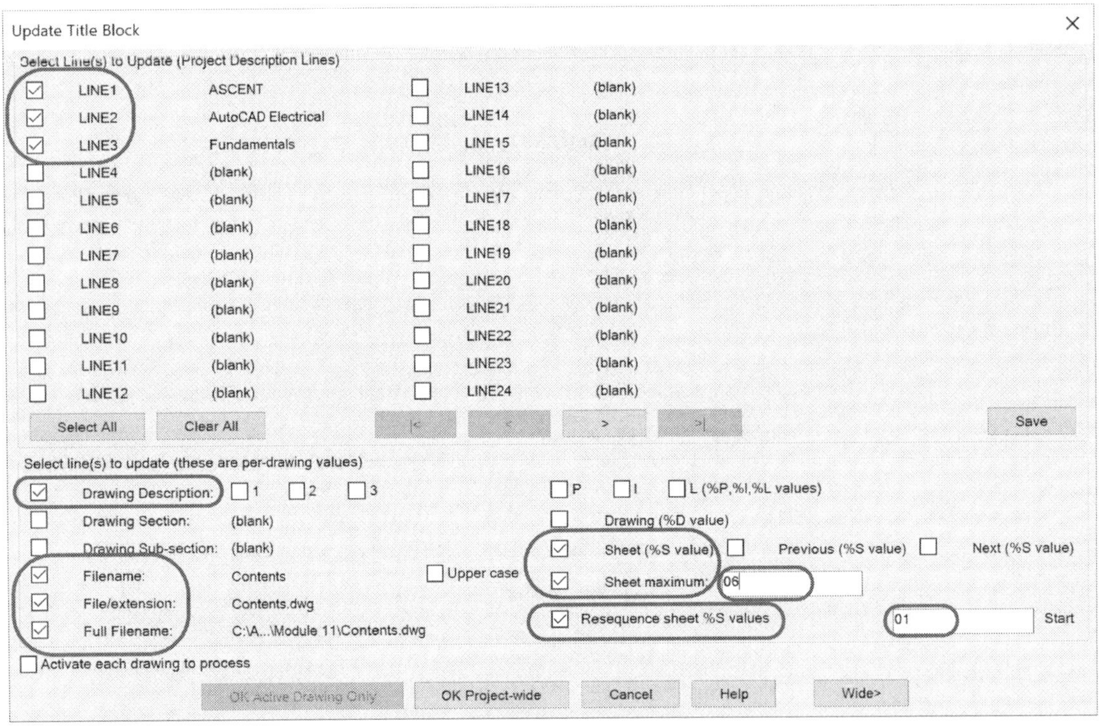

Figure 11–7

3. Click **OK Project-wide**.
4. The *Select Drawings to Process* dialog box opens. Click **Do All** and **OK**. If prompted, save the drawing.

5. The AutoCAD Electrical software processes each drawing. When the command is complete, zoom in to the lower right corner of the titleblock. The attributes are now filled in as shown for **Contents.dwg** in Figure 11–8.

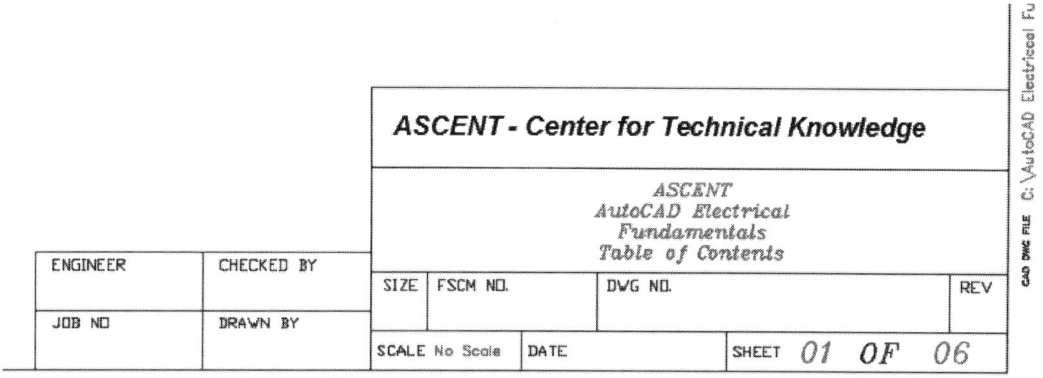

Figure 11–8

6. Right-click on **Contents.dwg** and select **Properties>Drawing Properties**.
7. In the *Drawing Properties* dialog box, note that the *Sheet* field is now populated, as shown in Figure 11–9. Click **OK**.

Figure 11–9

8. Zoom extents.
9. Save and close the drawing.

End of practice

11.2 Titleblock Setup

You can configure any AutoCAD block to work with the *Title Block Update* feature in the **Project-Wide Resequence/Retag** command. You can also have the **Title Block Update** command update multiple blocks in a drawing. This type of update is controlled through an attribute named **WD_TB** in a block or a text file with a .WDT file extension.

When the command is run, the AutoCAD Electrical software searches for the configuration information in a specific order.

1. The **WD_TB** attribute in any block in the drawing.
2. The **<project name>.wdt** file in the directory that contains the .WDP file of the active project.
3. The **default.wdt** file in the directory that contains the .WDP file of the active project.
4. The **default.wdt** file in the default AutoCAD Electrical support folder.

- The software uses the first method it finds. If using the **WD_TB** attribute, any block with the **WD_TB** attribute is updated. The attribute can be created using the AutoCAD **Insert Attribute** command or the AutoCAD Electrical **Title Block Setup** command. The format for the value of the **WD_TB** attribute is <attribute name>=<parameter name>. If the attribute name contains special characters (#, @, ?, etc.) they must be preceded by an `. Each attribute set is separated by a ;. For example, a **WD_TB** attribute is: **SH`#=SHEET ; SHTS=SHEETMAX ; DWGNO=DWGNAM**.
- The .WDT file is a text file and can be edited using any text editor, as shown in Figure 11–10, or using the **Title Block Setup** command. The first line of the file dictates the block to update. Its format is **BLOCK = <block name>**. You can configure multiple blocks by separating the block names with a comma or by creating multiple **BLOCK = entries**. The attribute mappings follow the block name. Their format is <attribute name> = <parameter name> with the same special character restrictions as the **WD_TB** attribute.

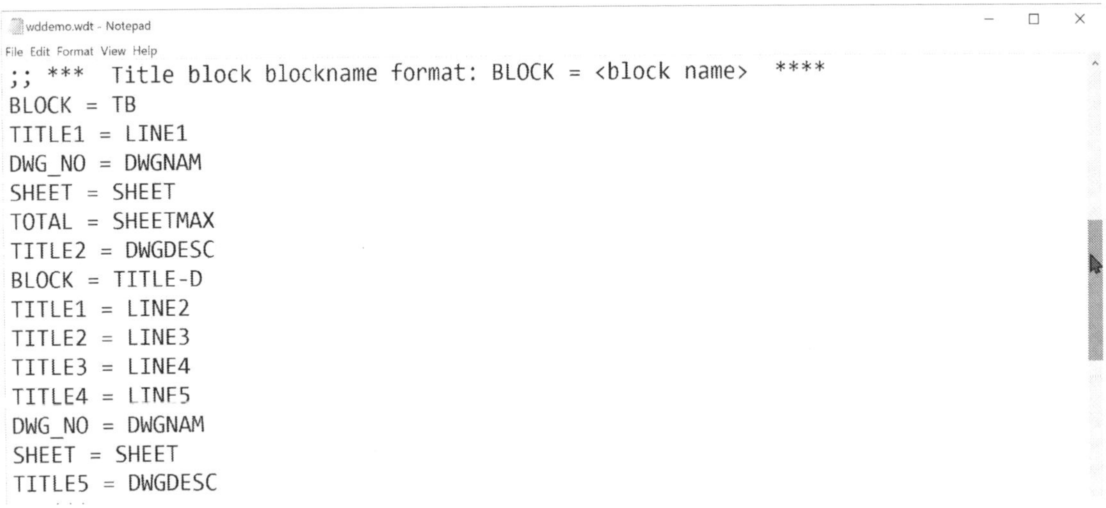

Figure 11–10

The easiest method of creating the titleblock mapping is to use the **Title Block Setup** command. This method enables you to pick blocks and attributes in the drawing window or from a list, eliminating any typos or the need to remember parameter names and formats.

Title Block Setup

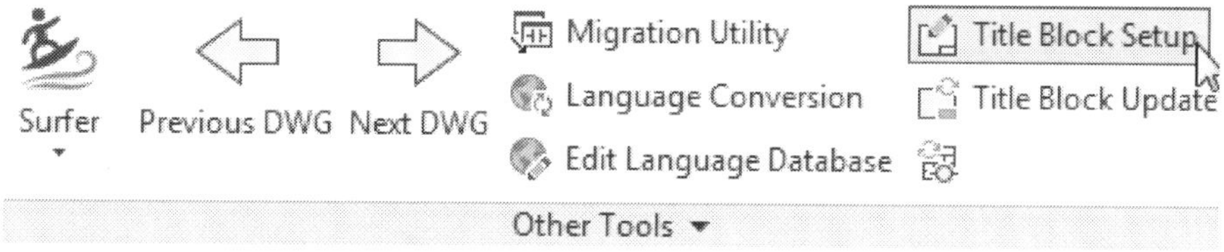

Ribbon: *Project* tab>*Other Tools* panel

Command Prompt: aesetuptitleblock

How To: Create a New Titleblock Mapping File

1. Open a drawing file that contains the titleblock.
2. Start the **Title Block Setup** command. The *Setup Title Block Update* dialog box opens.
3. Select the method of storing the attribute mapping information. The *Enter Block Name* dialog box opens.
4. Enter the block name to map. The *Title Block Setup* dialog box opens.
5. Map the attributes to the AutoCAD Electrical parameters using **Pick** or the drop-down list.
6. Click **OK** to save the mapping information.

In the *Setup Title Block Update* dialog box, select the required method of storing the data, as shown in Figure 11–11.

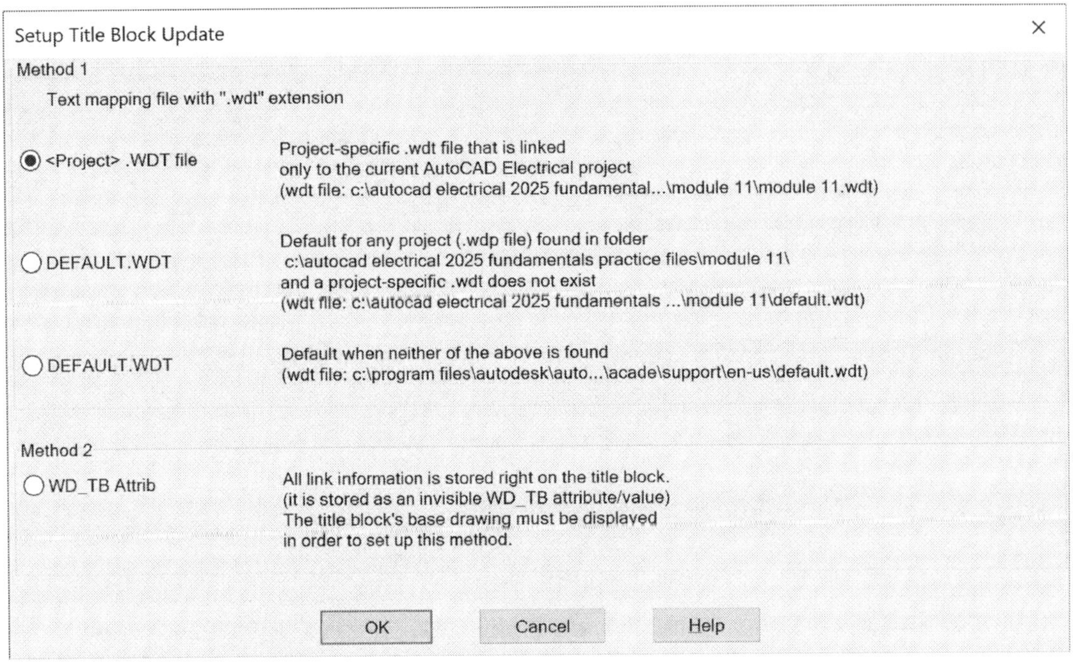

Figure 11–11

Method 1

- Uses a .WDT file to store the mapping information. The different options for Method 1 control where the .WDT file is stored.
- If the .WDT file does not exist, the *Enter Block Name* dialog box opens, as shown in Figure 11–12. You can enter the block name and use the Pick Block and Active Drawing to select the block.

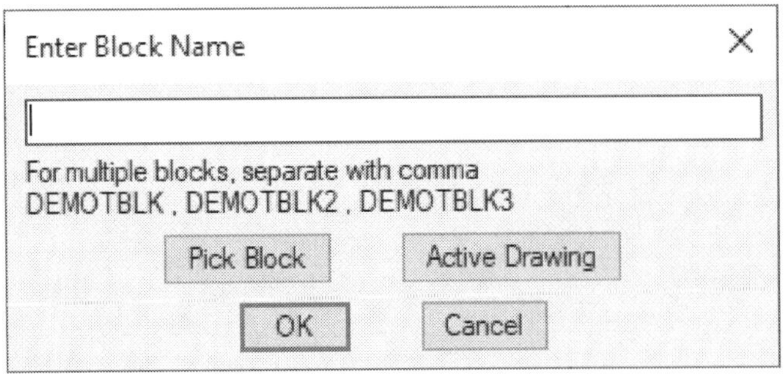

Figure 11–12

- If a .WDT file already exists, the *.WDT File Exists* dialog box opens as shown in Figure 11–13. From here, you can view, edit, or overwrite the existing .WDT file.

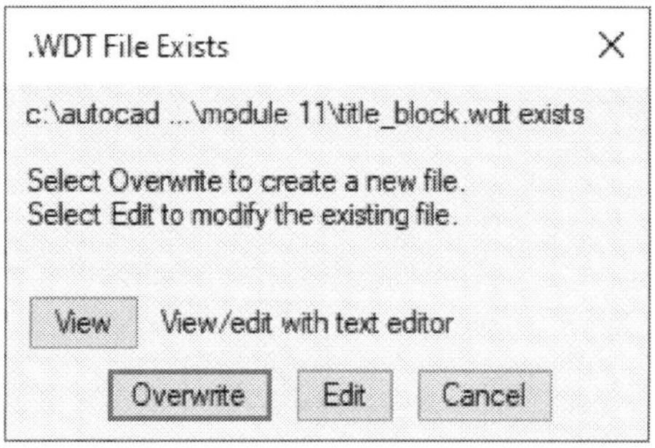

Figure 11–13

Method 2

- Uses the WD_TB attribute to store the mapping information.
- The base drawing for the titleblock must be open to insert the attribute.

When the Method selection is completed, the *Title Block Setup* dialog box displays. The *Project Values* in the dialog box are shown in Figure 11–14. You can map the existing attributes in the block to the AutoCAD Electrical parameters. The field next to the drop-down list describes the AutoCAD Electrical parameter.

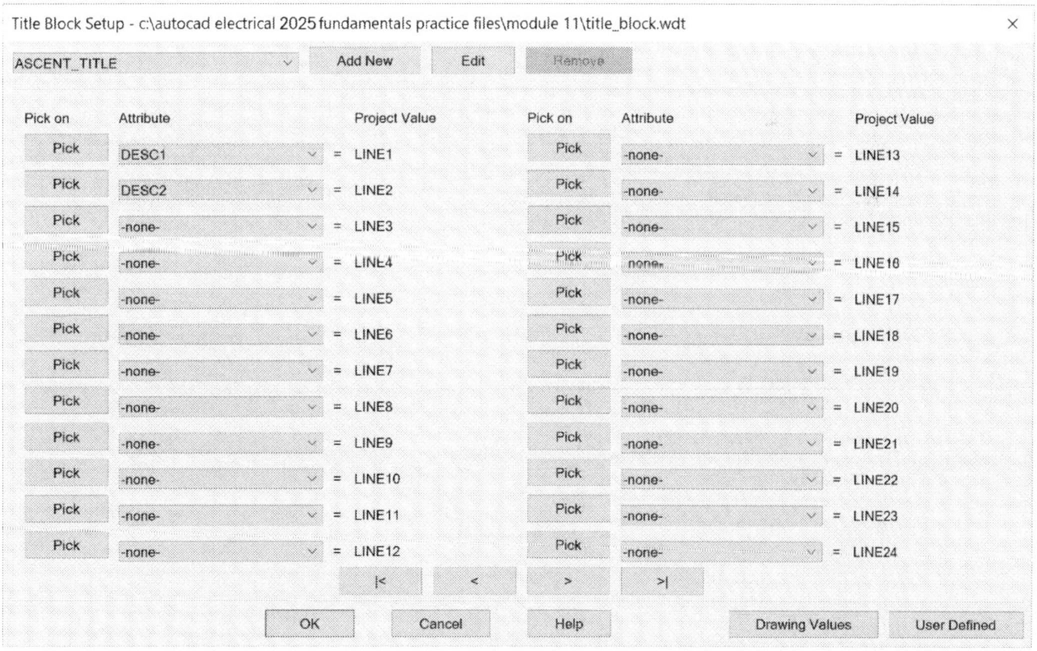

Figure 11–14

The *Drawing Values* in the *Title Block Setup* dialog box are shown in Figure 11–15.

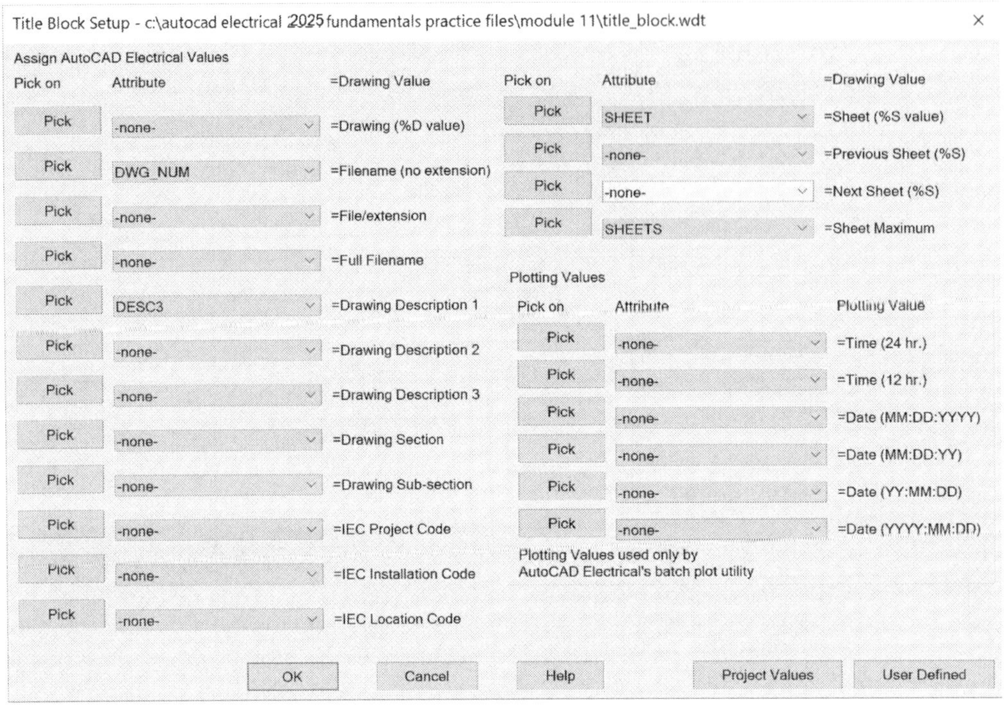

Figure 11–15

Add New	Add a new block to the .WDT file.
Edit	Returns to the *Enter Block Name* dialog box.
Remove	Removes the selected block from the .WDT file.
Pick	Pick the attribute in the drawing window.
	Select the attribute from a list in the selected block.
</>	Navigates to the previous/next page of Project Parameters.
Drawing Values/Project Values	Toggles between Drawing Parameters and Project Parameters display.
User Defined	Map text constants or Autolisp programs to the attributes.

- The filename and path of the .WDT file being edited display in the title bar in the *Title Block Update* dialog box.
- The advantage of using the **WD_TB** attribute is that there is no additional file to keep track of when using the **Update** command. The disadvantage is that it is more difficult to edit the attribute mapping.

Practice 11b
Titleblock Setup

Practice Objective

- Map attributes in the titleblock and update it.

In this practice, you will create a new drawing and see that the titleblock is mapped using the **WD_TB** attribute. You will then open an existing drawing and run the **Title Block Update** command on a titleblock that has not been mapped to the AutoCAD Electrical properties. Next, you will use the **Title Block Setup** command to map attributes in the titleblock to AutoCAD Electrical properties using a .WDT file. Finally, you will run the **Title Block Update** command again to update the titleblock. The final titleblock will display as shown in Figure 11–16.

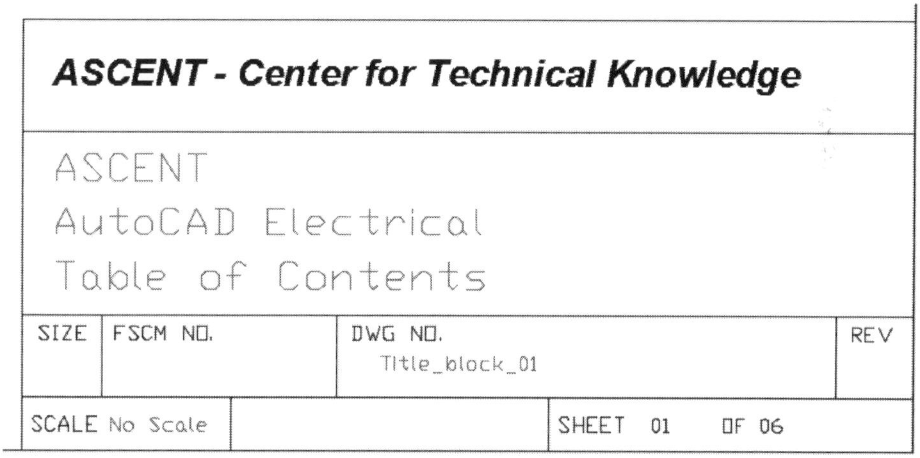

Figure 11–16

Task 1: Explode the titleblock.

1. In your practice files folder, in the *Module 11* folder, open the **Title_block.wdp** project file.
2. Create a new drawing using the AutoCAD **New** command (in the Quick Access Toolbar). Use **Electrical_template.dwt**, in your practice files folder, as the template.
3. Zoom to the lower right corner of the titleblock.

4. At the Command Prompt, type **EXPLODE** and press <Enter>. Select the titleblock and press <Enter>. The titleblock is exploded. The **WD_TB** attribute at the bottom of the titleblock, as shown in Figure 11–17, controls its attribute mapping.

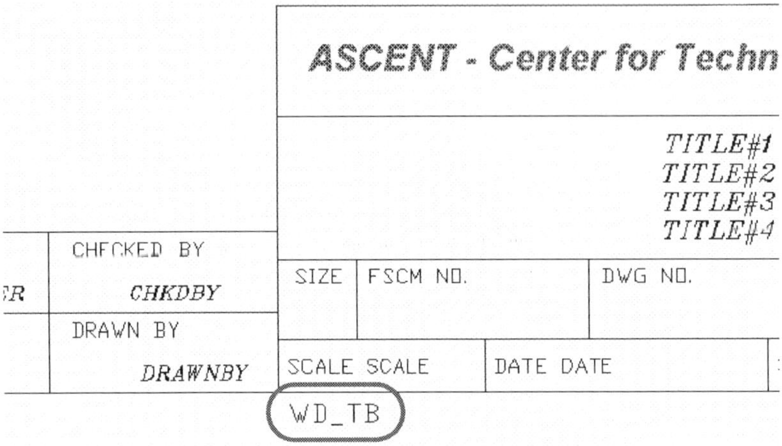

Figure 11–17

5. Double-click on the **WD_TB** attribute. (You might need to toggle off **Snap** to do this). The *Edit Attribute Definition* dialog box opens, as shown in Figure 11–18. Note the value of the attribute. This value controls the mapping of the AutoCAD Electrical properties to attributes in the block.

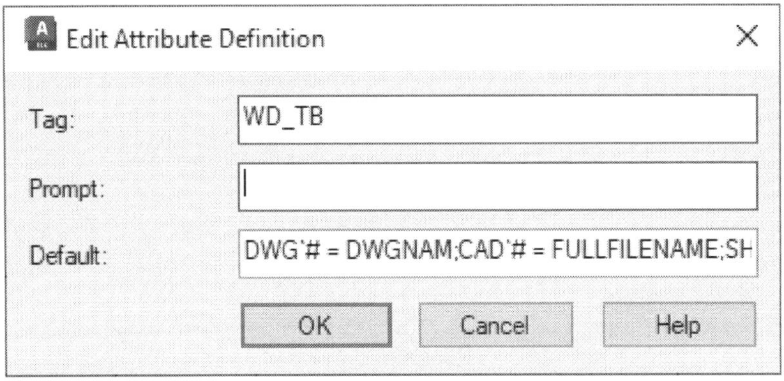

Figure 11–18

6. Click **Cancel**.
7. Close the drawing without saving changes.

Task 2: Attempt to update titleblocks.

1. In the **TITLE_BLOCK** project, open **Title_block_01.dwg**.
2. In the *Project Manager*, right-click on **TITLE_BLOCK** and select **Title Block Update**, as shown in Figure 11–19.

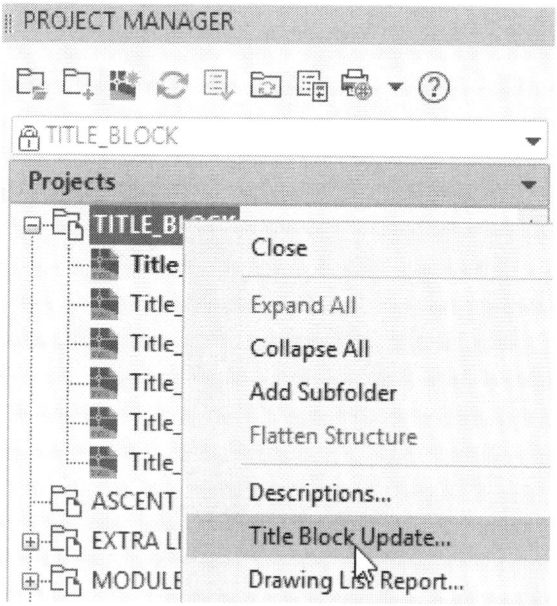

Figure 11–19

3. The *Update Title Block* dialog box opens. Select the various checkboxes, as shown in Figure 11–20, and additionally set the following:
    - *Sheet maximum*: **06**
    - *Resequence sheet %S values*: **01**

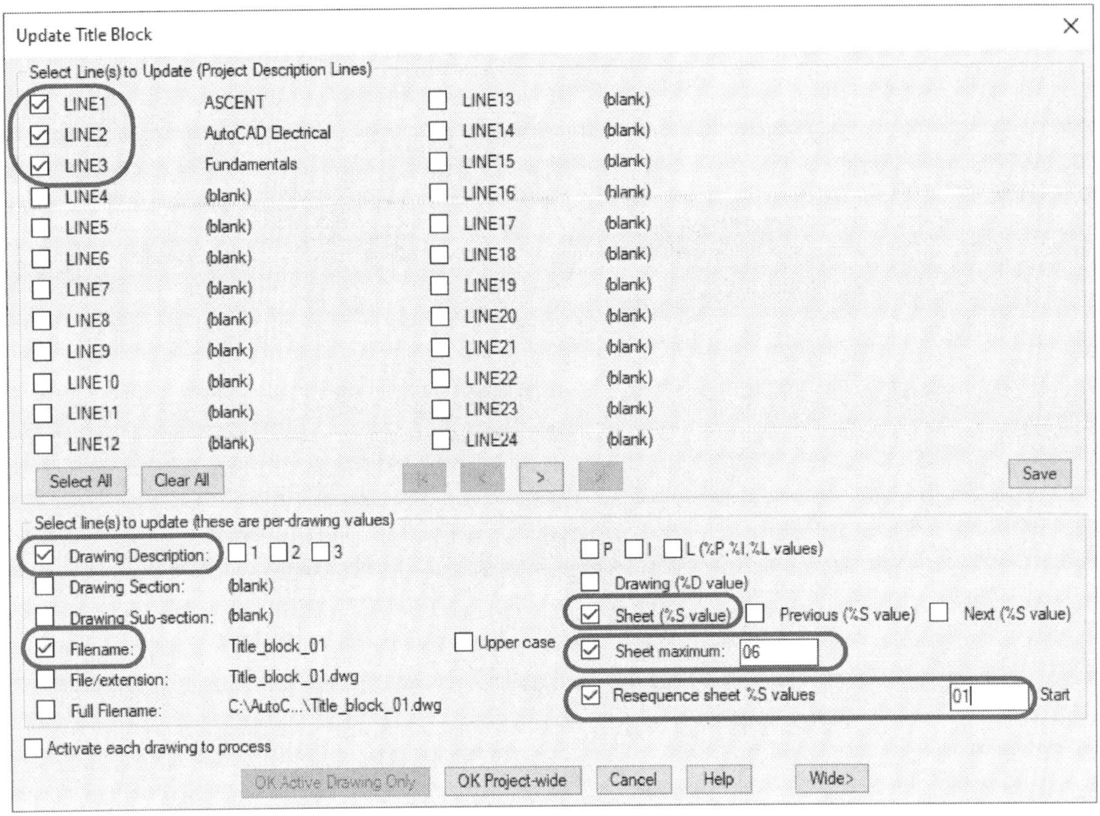

Figure 11–20

4. Click **OK Project-wide**.
5. The *Select Drawings to Process* dialog box opens. Click **Do All** and **OK**.
6. Note that the titleblock is not updated. You need to map the attributes to the AutoCAD Electrical properties.

Task 3: Map attributes to AutoCAD Electrical properties.

1. In the *Project* tab>*Other Tools* panel, click (Title Block Setup).
2. The *Setup Title Block Update* dialog box opens with **<Project> .WDT file** in the *Method 1* area selected. Click **OK**.
3. The *Enter Block Name* dialog box opens. Click **Pick Block** and select the titleblock in the drawing window. Press <Enter>.
4. The *Enter Block Name* dialog box updates with the block name **ASCENT_TITLE**, as shown in Figure 11–21. Click **OK**.

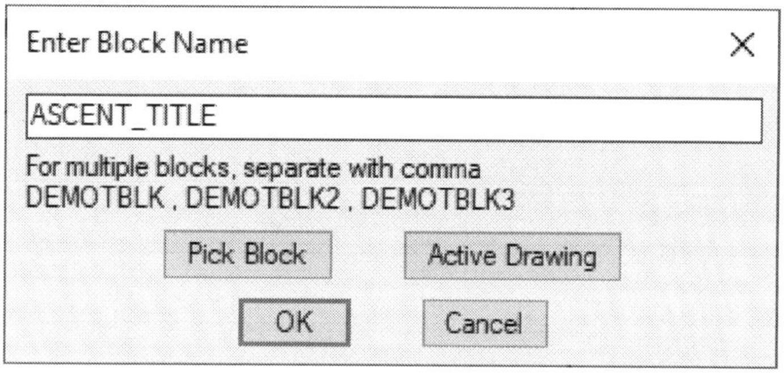

Figure 11–21

5. The *Title Block Setup* dialog box opens. In *Line 1*, using the down arrow, select **DESC1** from the drop-down list. Similarly, in *Line 2,* select **DESC2**, as shown in Figure 11–22.

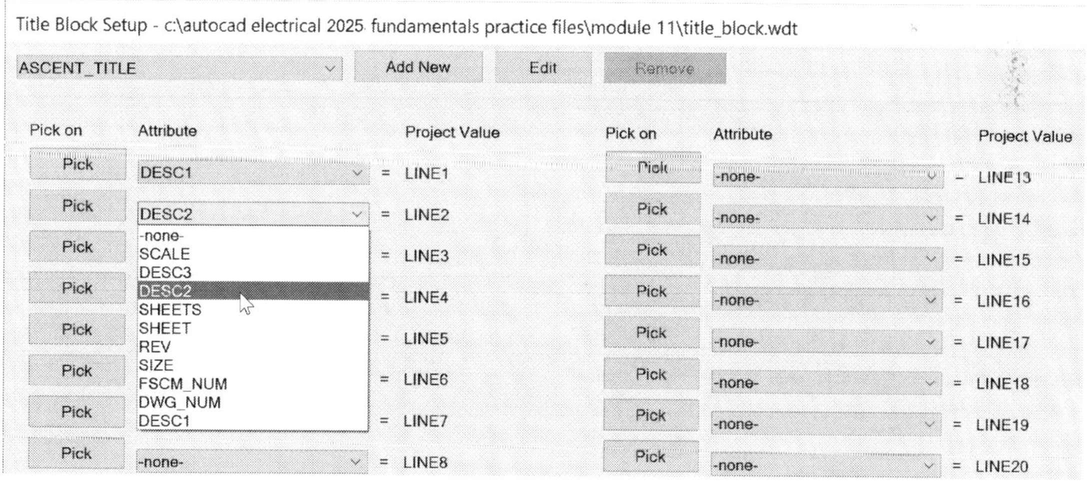

Figure 11–22

6. Near the bottom right of the dialog box, click **Drawing Values** to display the drawing values in the dialog box.
7. For *Filename (no extension)*, select **DWG_NUM**; for *Sheet (%S value)*, select **SHEET**; for *Sheet Maximum*, select **SHEETS**; and for *Drawing Description 1*, select **DESC3** (as shown in Figure 11–23). Click **OK**.

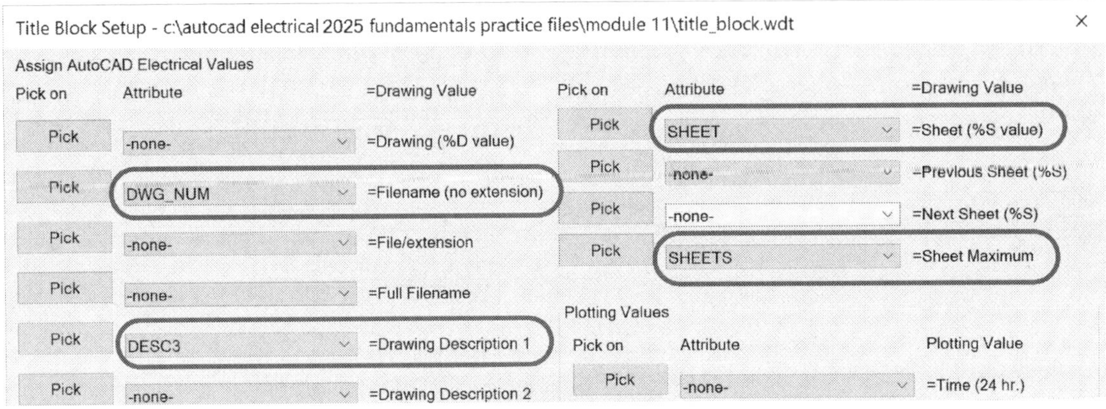

Figure 11–23

Task 4: Update titleblocks.

1. In the *Project Manager*, right-click on **TITLE_BLOCK** and select **Title Block Update**.

2. The *Update Title Block* dialog box opens. Select the checkboxes and set the following, as shown in Figure 11–24:
   - *Sheet maximum*: **06**
   - *Resequence sheet %S values*: **01**

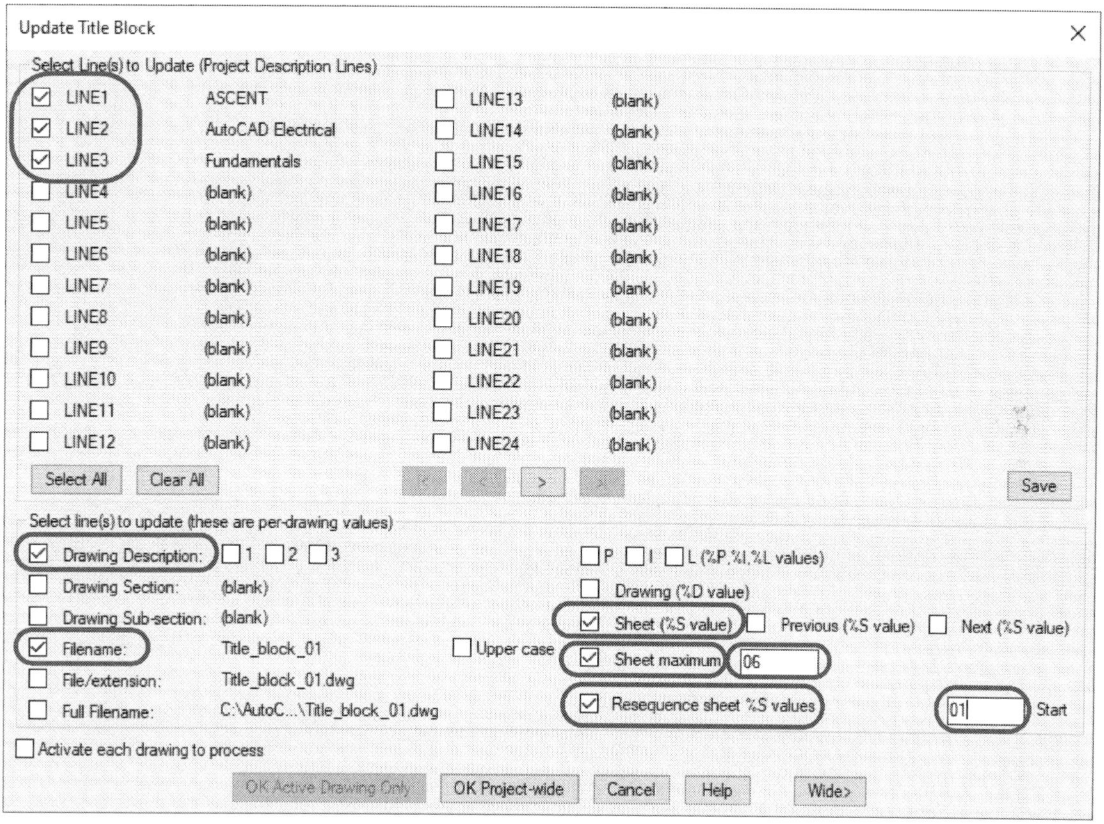

Figure 11–24

3. Click **OK Project-wide**.
4. The *Select Drawings to Process* dialog box opens. Click **Do All** and **OK**.

5. Zoom in on the titleblock. It is now populated, as shown in Figure 11–25.

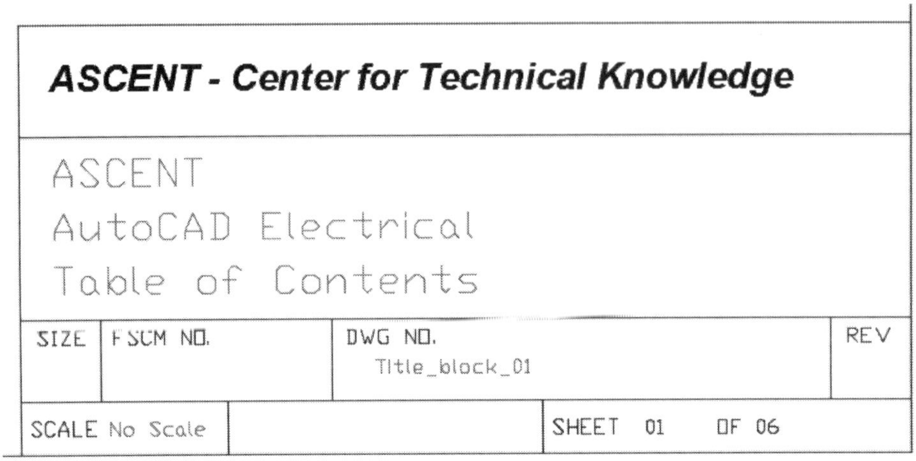

Figure 11–25

6. Zoom extents.
7. Save and close **Title_block_01.dwg**.

End of practice

Chapter Review Questions

1. How do you access the **Title Block Update** command?
   a. In the ribbon, using the **Title Block Update** command or using the **Title Block Update** option in the **Project-Wide Update/Retag** command.
   b. In the ribbon, using the **Title Block Update** command or through the Project Settings.
   c. Using the Project Settings or using the **Title Block Update** option in the **Project-Wide Update/Retag** command.
   d. Using the **Project-Wide Utilities** command or in the ribbon, using the **Title Block Update** command.

2. What does a .WDT file control?
   a. Project Settings for the entire project.
   b. Line titles for the Project descriptions.
   c. Attribute mapping for the **Title Block Update** command.
   d. Library and icon menu paths for the project.

3. What does a .WDL file control?
   a. Project Settings for the entire project.
   b. Line titles for the Project descriptions.
   c. Attribute mapping for the **Title Block Update** command.
   d. Library and icon menu paths for the project.

4. If you run the **Title Block Setup** command and a .WDT file already exists, which option creates a new file to replace the existing file?
   a. View
   b. Overwrite
   c. Edit
   d. Cancel

5. When mapping attributes in the *Title Block Setup* dialog box, what does 

display?
    a. AutoCAD Electrical parameters.
    b. A list of drawing property values.
    c. A list of project file property values.
    d. A pick list of attributes on the block.

Command Summary

Button	Command	Location
	**Title Block Setup**	• **Ribbon:** *Project* tab>*Other Tools* panel
	**Title Block Update**	• **Ribbon:** *Project* tab>*Other Tools* panel

Chapter 12

Reporting Tools

When working on a project, it is important to generate several reports, such as the schematic component list, bill of material list, panel nameplate report, etc. Knowledge on how to run multiple reports simultaneously reduces the time required to configure and run reports. Also, knowledge on how to create an error report is helpful in detecting and correcting errors at the designing stage.

Learning Objectives

- Create schematic and panel reports for project components.
- Save a report on various external file formats.
- Configure a table of a project report and place it into a drawing.
- Configure and save the report format settings to a file and then create multiple reports using the report files.
- Scan all of the drawings in the active project for issues.

12.1 Create Reports

The AutoCAD® Electrical software contains reporting commands used to extract data from drawings. The commands use a combination of attributes in the drawings and other databases to generate the reports.

The commands also provide different report options because schematic drawings and panel drawings contain different data.

- **Schematic Reports:** This command only pulls data from schematic drawings (drawings containing the **WD_M** block).
- **Panel Reports:** This command only pulls data from panel drawings (drawings with the **WD_PNLM** block).

Schematic Reports

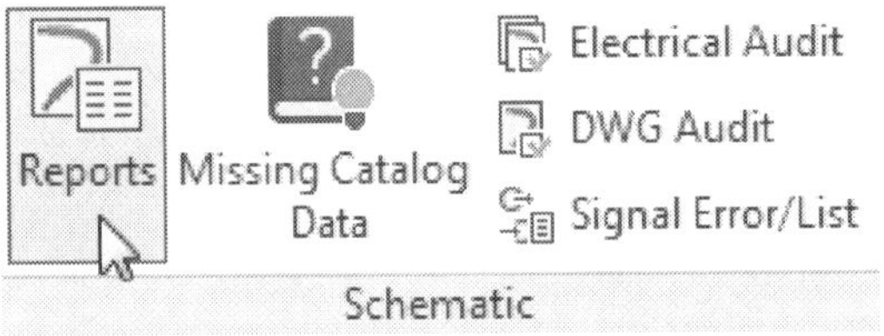

Ribbon: *Reports* tab>*Schematic* panel

Command Prompt: aeschematicreport

Panel Reports

Ribbon: *Reports* tab>*Panel* panel

Command Prompt: aepanelreport

How To: Create a Report

1. Start the **Schematic Reports** or **Panel Reports** command. The *Schematic Reports* or *Panel Reports* dialog box opens, as shown in Figure 12–1.

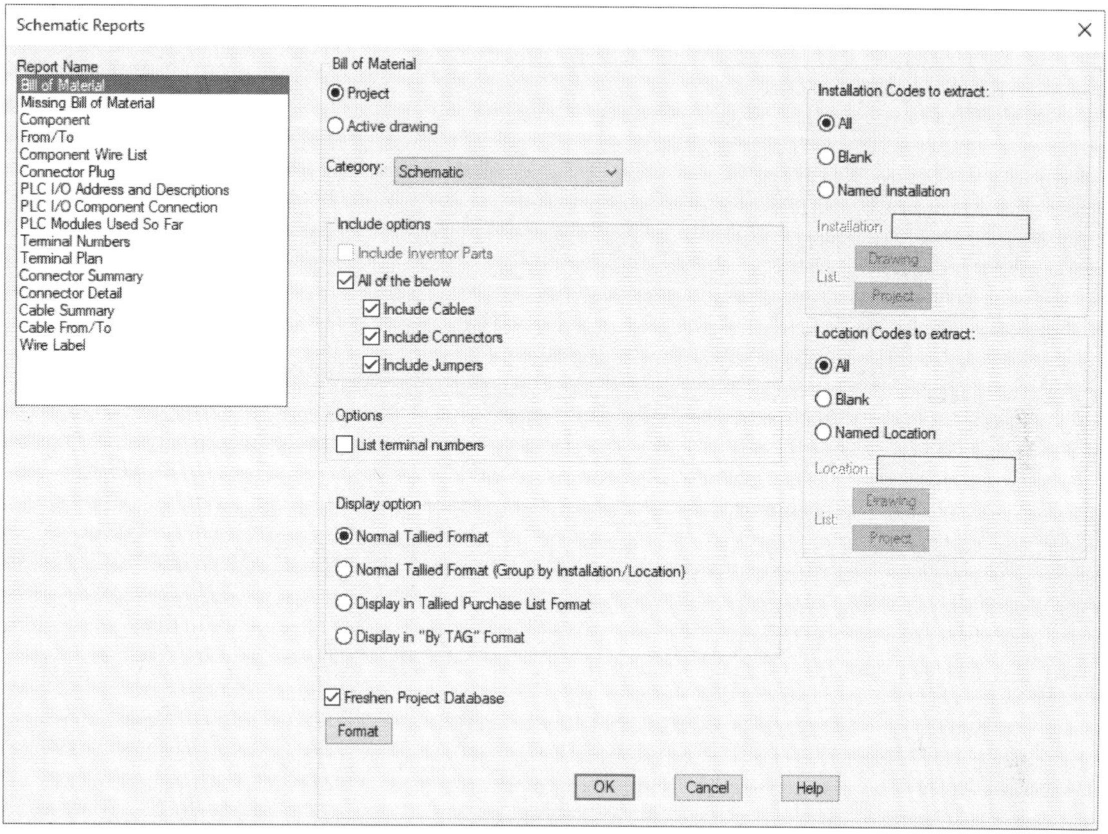

Figure 12–1

Report Name	Lists the available report types.
Bill of Material	Contains options for the selected report. The column changes depending on the selected report.
Installation Codes to extract	Select the **Installation** code on which to run the report.
Location Codes to extract	Select the **Location** code on which to run the report.
Include Options (Bill of Material)	Enables you to include the selected items in the Bill of Material. The **Include Inventor Parts** option creates a bill of materials that displays the parts as Electrical only, Inventor only, and parts in both.

2. In the *Report Name* area, select the report you want to run. Configure the options for the report and select the **Installation** or **Location** code for which to run the report. Click **OK**. The *Select Drawings to Process* dialog box opens.
3. Select the drawings to process for the report and click **OK**. The *Report Generator* dialog box opens.
4. Configure the report and then click **Put on Drawing**, **Save to File**, or **Print**.
5. Configure the options for the selected report method (drawing, file, or print) and click **OK**.
6. Click **Close** to close the *Report Generator* dialog box.

Report Generator

The *Report Generator* dialog box displays the preview of the report, as shown in Figure 12–2.

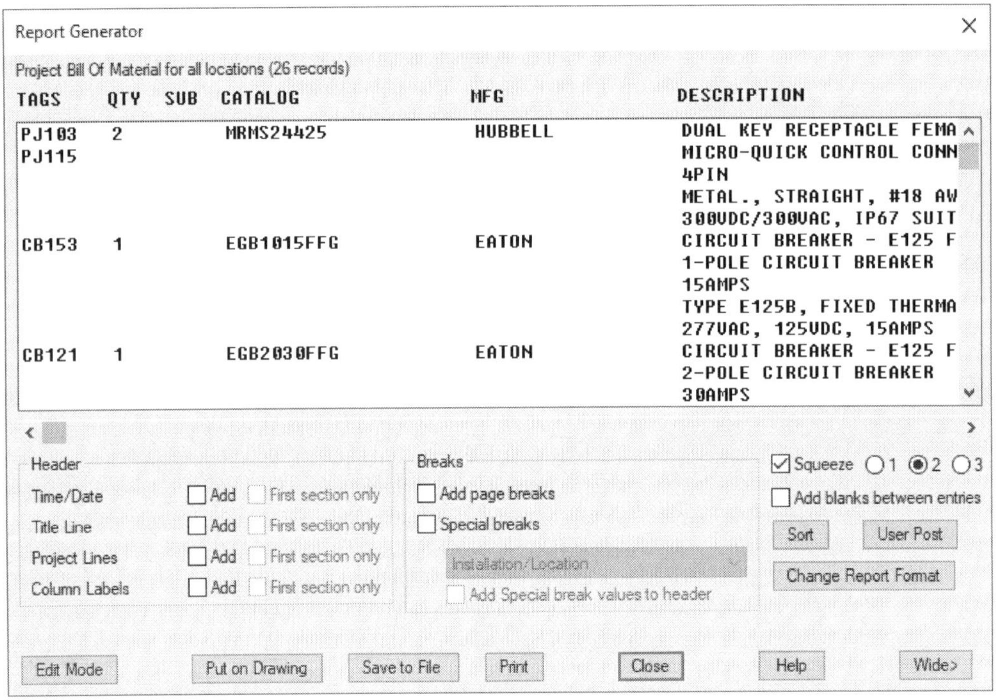

Figure 12–2

Report Preview	White area in the dialog box. Previews the report data.
Header	Adds information to the report header. **Add** includes its information in the header. **First Section only** limits the information to only displaying in the first area.
Breaks	Adds breaks to the report. These can be page breaks or breaks on **Installation/Location** codes or manufacturers.

Squeeze	Reduces the width of the report. For *maximum reduction*, select **1** and for *minimum reduction*, select **3**.
Add blanks between entries	Adds a blank line between report entries.
Sort	Changes the sorting of the report. You can sort using up to four fields.
User Post	Runs an Autolisp routine against the report and returns the results to the Report Generator.
Change Report Format	Configure the column order and data in each column.
Edit Mode	Edit the contents of the report. You can modify existing rows, add from the catalog, delete rows, and reorder data. This does not affect the data in the drawing files.
Put on Drawing	Opens the *Table Generation Setup* dialog box. Use it to configure the report table and to add it to the current drawing.
Save to File	Opens the *Save Report to File* dialog box. Use it to select the type of file to create and to save the data to a file.
Print	Opens the *Print* dialog box to print the report from the Report Generator.

Hint: Drawing List Report

The **Drawing List Report** command creates a report listing all of the drawings that are included in the project. It is similar to the **Schematic Reports** and **Panel Reports** commands in functionality and is only accessible in *Project Manager*. Right-click on the project name and select **Drawing List Report**, as shown in Figure 12–3.

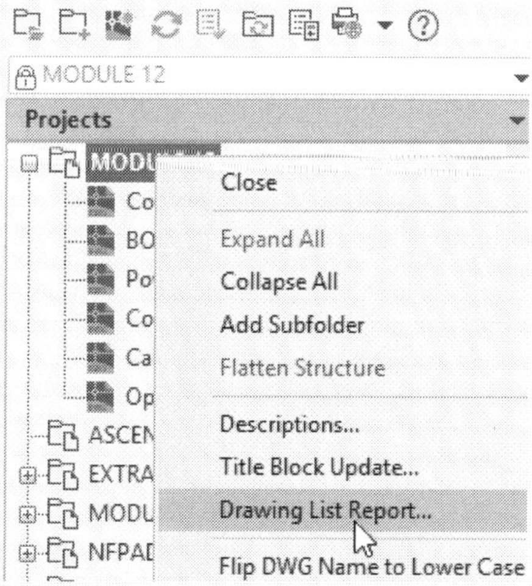

Figure 12–3

Save to File

In the *Save Report to File* dialog box (shown in Figure 12–4), you can select the file format to create (ASCII text file, Excel spreadsheet, Access database, XML file, and comma delimited text file) and click **OK**. The *Select file for report* dialog box opens and you can save the file.

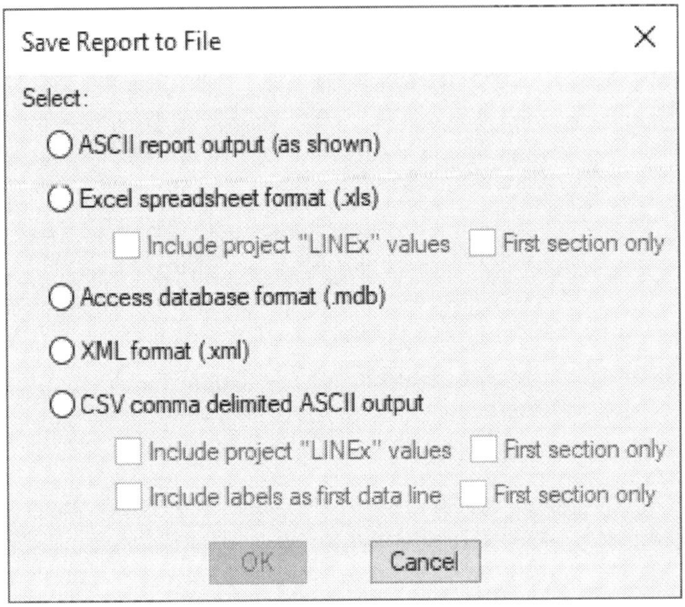

Figure 12–4

Put on Drawing

The *Table Generation Setup* dialog box (shown in Figure 12–5) configures the table to be inserted into the drawing.

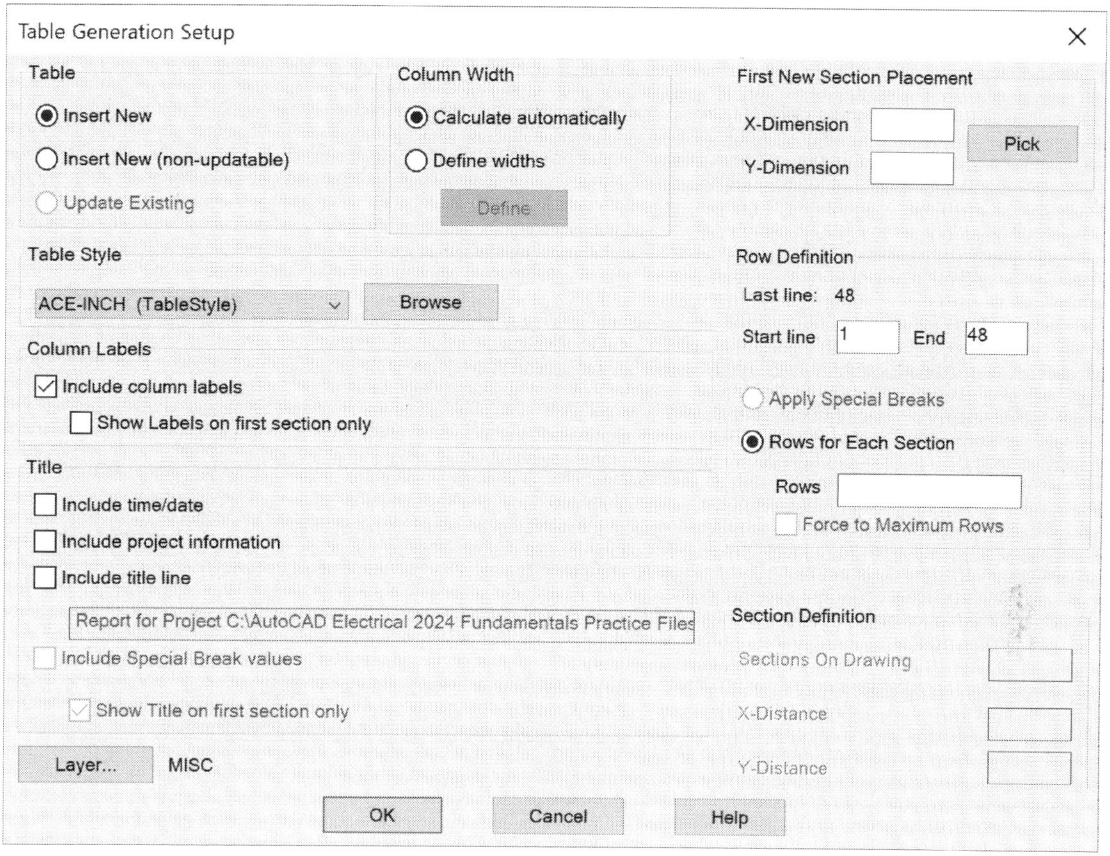

Figure 12–5

Table	Selects an option to insert a new table, new non-updatable table, or update an existing table.
Column Width	Selects an option to calculate automatically or define widths of individual columns.
First New Section Placement	Specifies the coordinates for the insertion point of the table. You can enter values or pick points on the screen. If left blank, you can pick the point after clicking **OK**.
Table Style	Select a Table Style in the drop-down list that contains the table styles that are included with the software. The style controls the text properties, borders, etc. You can use Browse to include a table style from another drawing and then select it in the list.
Column Labels	Controls whether to display column labels and the color of the labels.
Row Definition	Controls the table rows, number of rows per section, and whether to build the table from the bottom up.

Title	Controls the information included in the title.
Section Definition	When there are multiple sections for a report, specifies the number of sections per drawing and the x and y spacing between the sections.
Layer	Controls the layer on which the table is created.

Practice 12a
Create Reports

Practice Objectives

- Save a project report to an external file.
- Place and update a project report.

In this practice, you will create a schematic component report and save it to an Excel spreadsheet. You will then create a panel nameplate report and put it on a drawing. Finally, you will update a panel bill of material report. The updated panel bill of material displays in Figure 12–6.

ITEM	TAGS	QTY	SUB	CATALOG	MFG	DESCRIPTION
1	LT151 LT169 LT262 LT263 LT264	5		800T-P16H	AB	GREEN PILOT LIGHT – STANDARD, NEMA 4/13 30.5mm 120VAC XFMR GLASS LENS
2	PB167 PB207 PB213A	3		800H-BR6D1	AB	PUSH BUTTON – MOMENTARY, NEMA 4/4X 30.5mm EXTENDED RED 1 NO
3	LT161	1		800T-P16J	AB	RED PILOT LIGHT – STANDARD, NEMA 4/13 30.5mm 120VAC XFMR GLASS LENS
4	PB201 PB213	2		800H-BR6D2	AB	PUSH BUTTON – MOMENTARY, NEMA 4/4X 30.5mm EXTENDED RED 1 NC
5	PB159	1		800T-D6D2	AB	PUSH BUTTON – MUSHROOM, NEMA 4/13 30.5mm RED 1 NC
6	LT151 LT161 LT169 LT262 LT263 LT264 PB159 PB167 PB201 PB201A PB207 PB213 PB213A	13		800H-W100A	AB	Name Plate 800H Automotive Gray Blank
7	CB101	1		EGB3100FFG	EATON	CIRCUIT BREAKER – E125 FRAME 3-POLE CIRCUIT BREAKER 100AMPS TYPE E125B, FIXED THERMAL & MAGNETIC TRIP 480VAC, 250VDC, 100AMPS

Figure 12–6

Task 1: Save a report to an external file.

1. In your practice files folder, in the *Module 12* folder, open the **Module 12** project file.
2. Open any drawing in the Module 12 project.

3. Using the AutoCAD Electrical (New Drawing) command, set the following for the new drawing, as shown in Figure 12–7:
   - *Name*: **Reports**
   - *Location:* Verify that the *Module 12* folder in your practice files folder is set.
   - *Description 1*: **Project Reports**

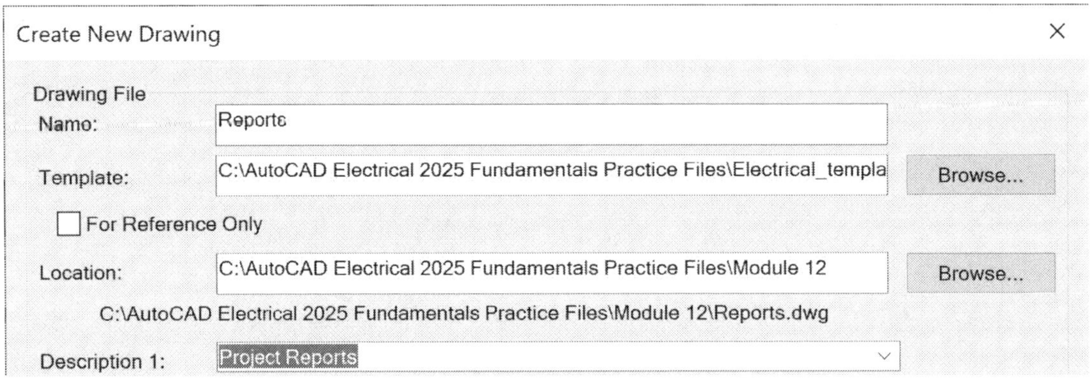

Figure 12–7

4. Click **OK**. In the *Apply Project Defaults to the Drawing Settings* dialog box, click **Yes**. Note that the new drawing (**Reports.dwg**) is created and opened.

5. In the *Reports* tab>*Schematic* panel, click (Reports, Schematic).

6. The *Schematic Reports* dialog box opens. In the *Report Name* list, select **From/To**. In the right-hand pane of the *Schematic Reports* dialog box, the *From/To* options are displayed (as shown in Figure 12–8).

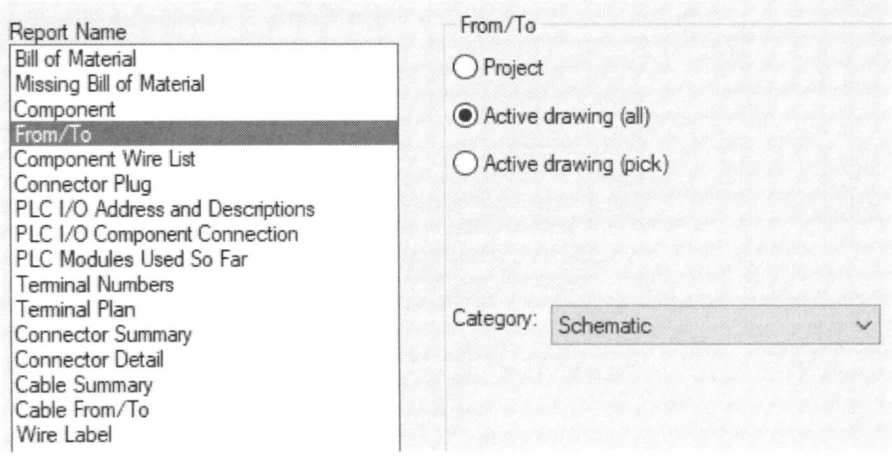

Figure 12–8

7. In the *Report Name* list, select **Component**. The dialog box displays the options for the Component report. Leave the default settings and click **OK**.
8. The *Select Drawings to Process* dialog box opens. Click **Do All** and **OK**. Click **OK** to QSAVE.
9. The *Report Generator* dialog box opens and should display the alphabetically sorted *TAGNAME* list, as shown in Figure 12–9.
   - If *TAGNAME* column is not displayed, click **Change Report Format**, add **TAGNAME** to the *Fields to report* list, and click **OK**.
   - If the *TAGNAME* list is displayed but not sorted alphabetically, click **Sort**. In the *Primary sort* field, in the drop-down list, select **TAGNAME** and click **OK**.

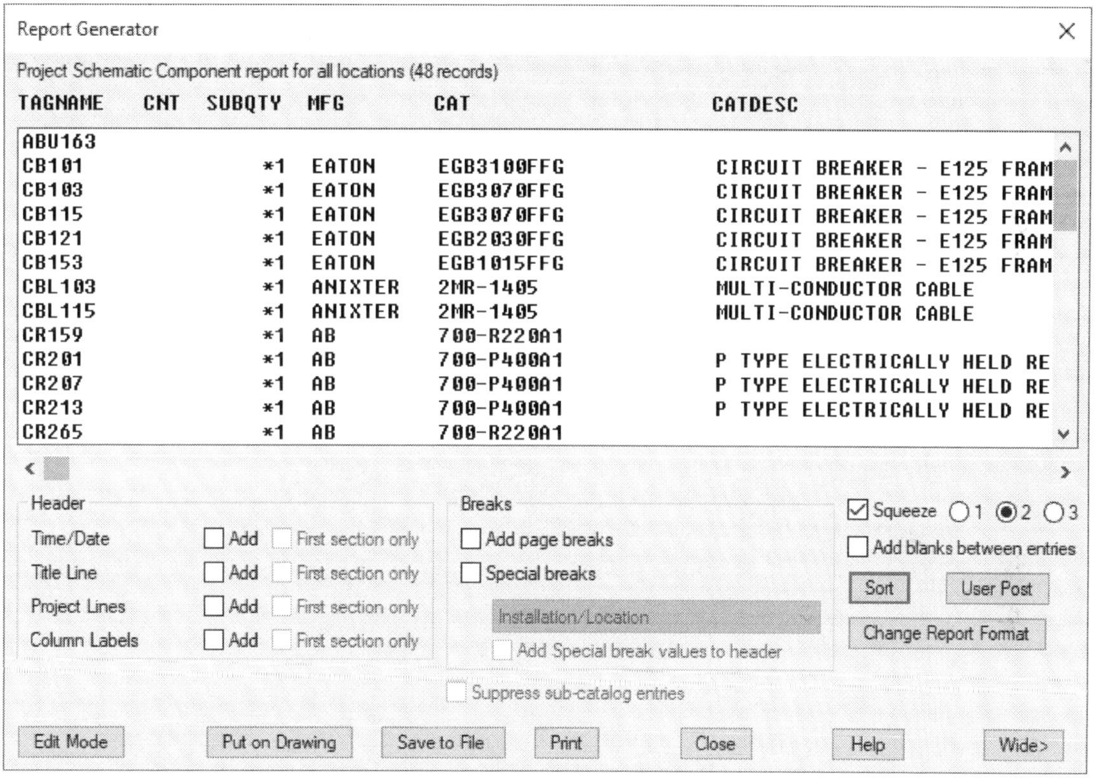

Figure 12–9

10. Click **Save to File**.

11. The *Save Report to File* dialog box opens. Select **Excel spreadsheet format (.xls)** (as shown in Figure 12–10) and click **OK**.

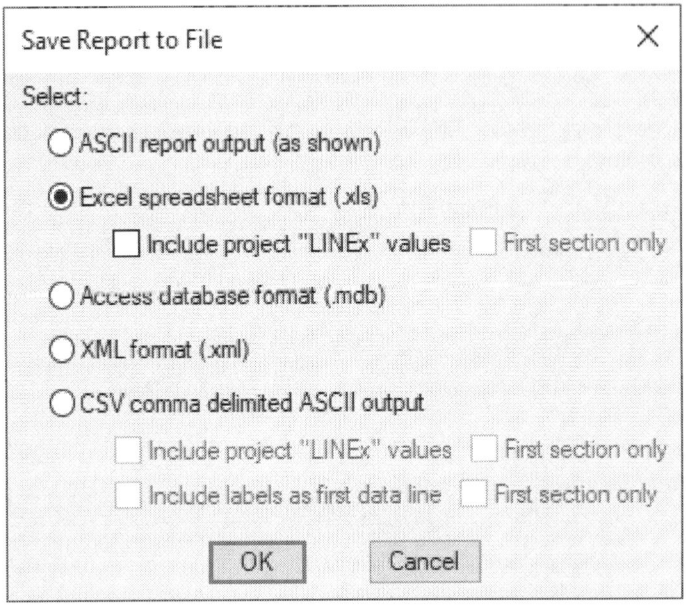

Figure 12–10

12. The *Select file for report* dialog box opens. Browse to the *Module 12* folder in your practice files folder. Leave the default name (**COMP.XLS**) and click **Save**.
13. The *Optional Script File* dialog box opens. Click **Close - No Script**.
14. You are returned to the *Report Generator* dialog box. Click **Close**.
15. Using Windows Explorer, navigate to your practice files folder and, in the *Module 12* folder, open the file **COMP.XLS** in Microsoft Excel.
16. Note the data in cells A1 (TAGNAME) and A2 (ABU163) and close the file.
17. Return to the AutoCAD Electrical software.

Task 2: Put a report on a drawing.

1. In the *Reports* tab>*Panel* panel, click  (Reports, Panel) for the panel.
2. The *Panel Reports* dialog box opens. In the *Report Name* list, select **Nameplate** and in the *Panel Nameplate* area, select **Project** as shown in Figure 12–11. Click **OK**.

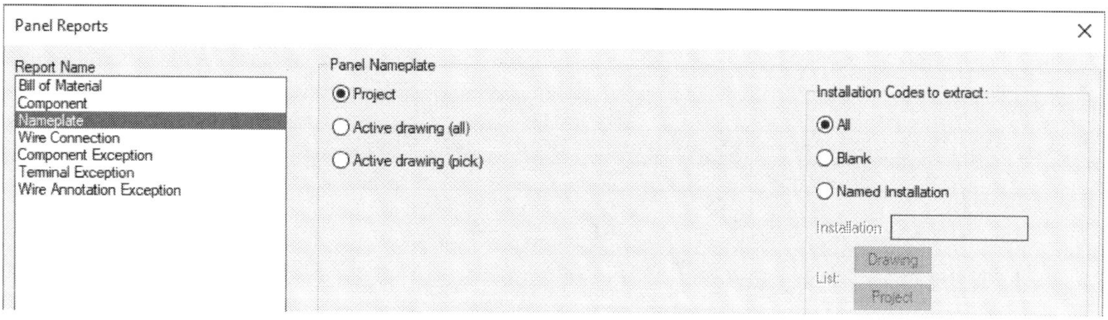

Figure 12–11

3. The *Select Drawings to Process* dialog box opens. Click **Do All** and **OK**.
4. The *Report Generator* dialog box opens as shown in Figure 12–12. Click **Put on Drawing**.

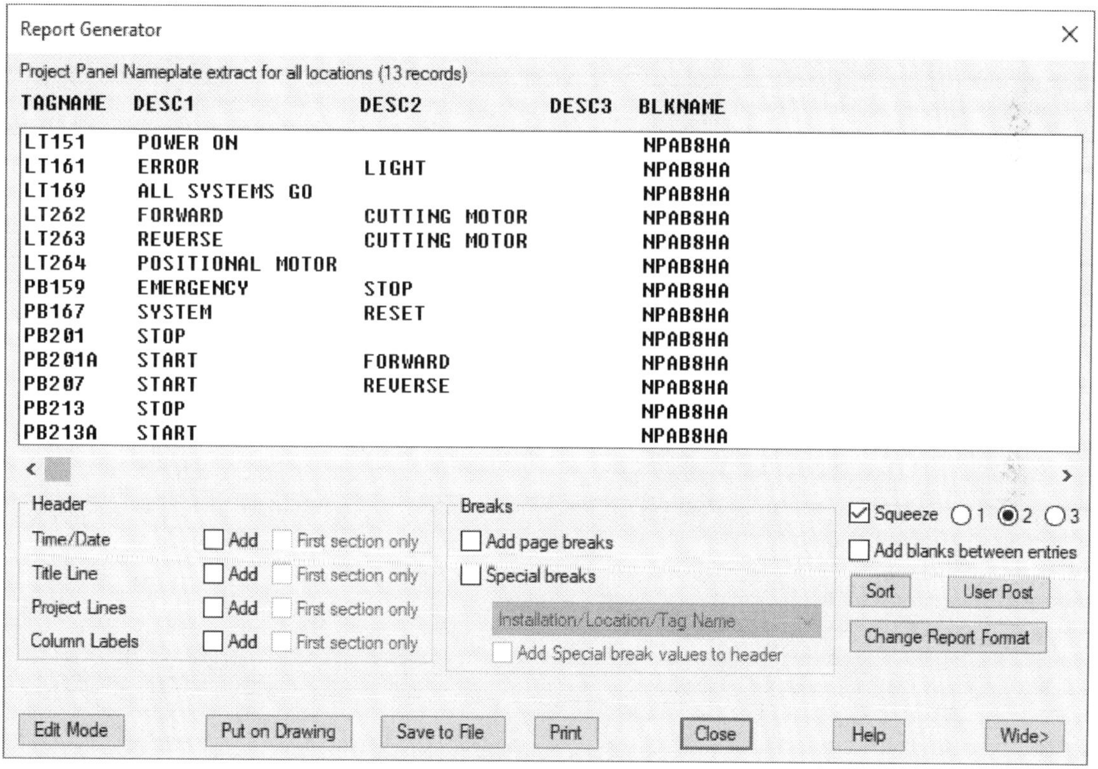

Figure 12–12

5. The *Table Generation Setup* dialog box opens. In the *Table Style* area, select **Standard (Table Style)**, as shown in Figure 12–13. Click **OK**.

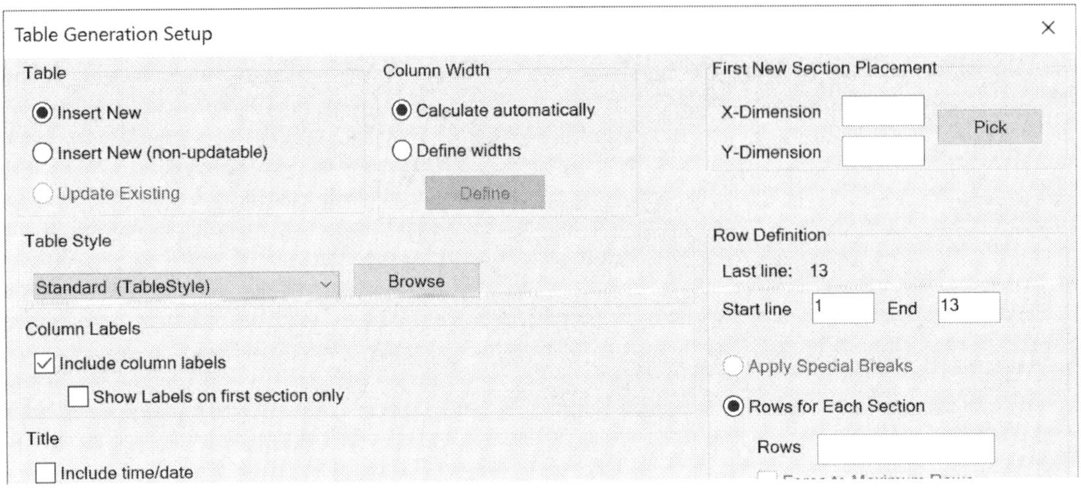

Figure 12–13

6. Pick **2,20** as the insertion point.
7. You are returned to the *Report Generator* dialog box. Click **Close**.
8. Zoom into the report, as shown in Figure 12–14.

TAGNAME	DESC1	DESC2	DESC3	BLKNAME
LT151	POWER ON			NPAB8HA
LT161	ERROR	LIGHT		NPAB8HA
LT169	ALL SYSTEMS GO			NPAB8HA
LT262	FORWARD	CUTTING MOTOR		NPAB8HA
LT263	REVERSE	CUTTING MOTOR		NPAB8HA
LT264	POSITIONAL MOTOR			NPAB8HA
PB159	EMERGENCY	STOP		NPAB8HA
PB167	SYSTEM	RESET		NPAB8HA
PB201	STOP			NPAB8HA
PB201A	START	FORWARD		NPAB8HA
PB207	START	REVERSE		NPAB8HA
PB213	STOP			NPAB8HA
PB213A	START			NPAB8HA

Figure 12–14

9. Zoom extents.
10. Save and close **Reports.dwg**.

Task 3: Update an existing report.

1. In the **Module 12** project, open **Operator Station.dwg**.

2. Zoom into the top portion of the report. Note that the row for **Item 6** is missing, as shown in Figure 12–15.

ITEM	TAGS	QTY	SUB	CATALOG	MFG	DESCRIPTION
1	LT151 LT159 LT262 LT263 LT264	5		800T-P16H	AB	GREEN PILOT LIGHT - STANDARD, NEMA 4/13 30.5mm 120VAC XFMR GLASS LENS
2	PB167 PB201A PB207 PB213A	4		800H-BR6D1	AB	PUSH BUTTON - MOMENTARY, NEMA 4/4X 30.5mm EXTENDED RED 1 NO
3	LT161	1		800T-P16J	AB	RED PILOT LIGHT - STANDARD, NEMA 4/13 30.5mm 120VAC XFMR GLASS LENS
4	PB201 PB213	2		800H-BR6D2	AB	PUSH BUTTON - MOMENTARY, NEMA 4/4X 30.5mm EXTENDED RED 1 NC
5	PB159	1		800T-D6D2	AB	PUSH BUTTON - MUSHROOM, NEMA 4/13 30.5mm RED 1 NC
7	CB101	1		EGB3100FFG	EATON	CIRCUIT BREAKER - E125 FRAME 3-POLE CIRCUIT BREAKER 100AMPS TYPE E125B, FIXED THERMAL & MAGNETIC TRIP 480VAC, 250VDC, 100AMPS
8	CB103 CB115	2		EGB3070FFG	EATON	CIRCUIT BREAKER - E125 FRAME 3-POLE CIRCUIT BREAKER 70AMPS TYPE E125B, FIXED THERMAL & MAGNETIC TRIP 480VAC, 250VDC, 70AMPS

Figure 12–15

3. In the *Reports* tab>*Panel* panel, click (Reports) for the panel.
4. The *Panel Reports* dialog box opens. In the *Report Name* list, select **Bill of Material**, as shown in Figure 12–16. Click **OK**.

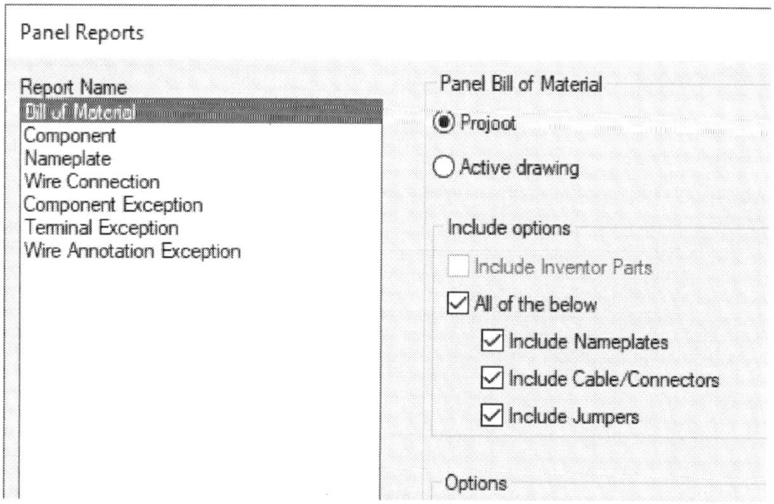

Figure 12–16

5. The *Select Drawings to Process* dialog box opens. Click **Do All** and **OK**.
6. The *Report Generator* dialog box opens, as shown in Figure 12–17. Click **Put on Drawing**.

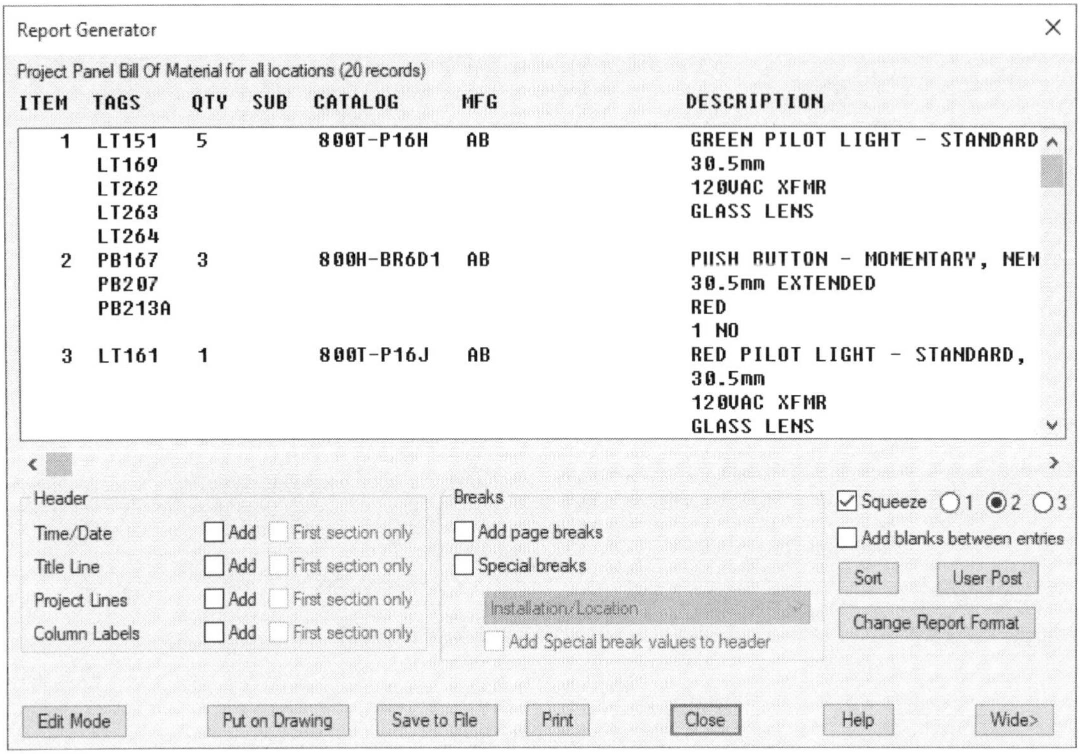

Figure 12–17

7. The *Table Generation Setup* dialog box opens. In the *Table* area, note that **Insert New** is grayed out and **Update Existing** is selected, as shown in Figure 12–18. This indicates that an existing BOM report is already inserted into a drawing in the project. Click **OK**.

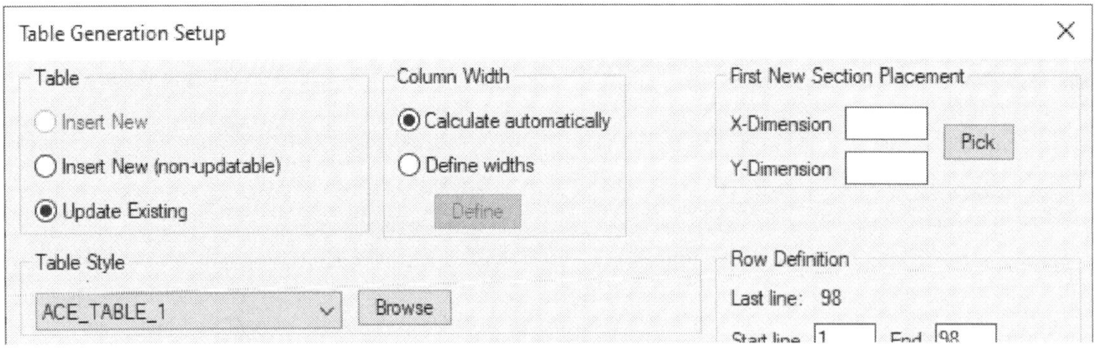

Figure 12–18

8. You are returned to the *Report Generator*. Click **Close**. The table is updated and the row for *Item* 6 has been inserted, as shown in Figure 12–19.

ITEM	TAGS	QTY	SUB	CATALOG	MFG	DESCRIPTION
1	LT151 LT169 LT262 LT263 LT264	5		800T-P16H	AB	GREEN PILOT LIGHT - STANDARD, NEMA 4/13 30.5mm 120VAC XFMR GLASS LENS
2	PB167 PB207 PB213A	3		800H-BR6D1	AB	PUSH BUTTON - MOMENTARY, NEMA 4/4X 30.5mm EXTENDED RED 1 NO
3	LT161	1		800T-P16J	AB	RED PILOT LIGHT - STANDARD, NEMA 4/13 30.5mm 120VAC XFMR GLASS LENS
4	PB201 PB213	2		800H-BR6D2	AB	PUSH BUTTON - MOMENTARY, NEMA 4/4X 30.5mm EXTENDED RED 1 NC
5	PB159	1		800T-D6D2	AB	PUSH BUTTON - MUSHROOM, NEMA 4/13 30.5mm RED 1 NC
6	LT151 LT161 LT169 LT262 LT263 LT264 PB159 PB167 PB201 PB201A PB207 PB213 PB213A	13		800H-W100A	AB	Name Plate 800H Automotive Gray Blank
7	CB101	1		EGB3100FFG	EATON	CIRCUIT BREAKER - E125 FRAME 3-POLE CIRCUIT BREAKER 100AMPS TYPE E125B, FIXED THERMAL & MAGNETIC TRIP 480VAC. 250VDC. 100AMPS

Figure 12–19

9. Zoom extents.
10. Save and close **Operator Station.dwg**.

End of practice

12.2 Configure Report Templates

When working on a project, you might need to run several different reports or to run the same report several times throughout the design cycle. Using the **Report Format Setup** command, you can save report settings to a file to use later. The settings for a report are saved to a text file with a .SET extension. The report format files can then be used when running reports with the **Schematic Reports**, **Panel Reports**, or **Automatic Report Selection** commands.

Report Format Setup

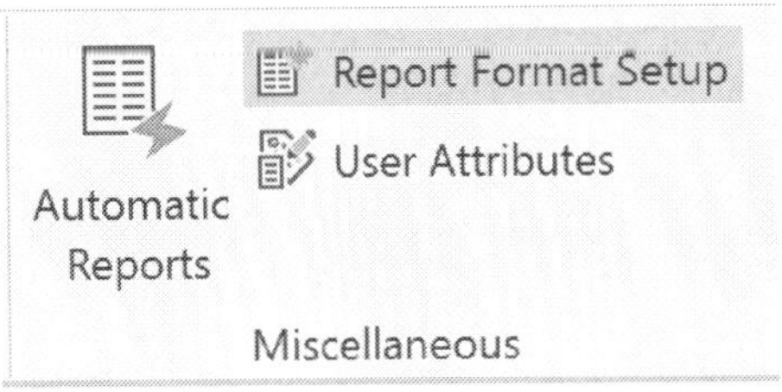

Ribbon: *Reports* tab>*Miscellaneous* panel

Command Prompt: aeformatfile

How To: Create a Report Format File

1. Start the **Report Format Setup** command. The *Report Format File Setup* dialog box opens.
2. In the *Report Name* list, select the type of report or click **Open Format File** to open an existing report format file.
3. Configure the settings and select the **Installation** and/or **Location** codes as you would when running a report.
4. Configure the output for the report (put it on a drawing or save it to an external file and set the fields to include). A format file can be configured to put the report on a drawing and save it to a file.
5. Save the report format file.

The *Report Format File Setup* dialog box (shown in Figure 12–20) is used to open/save format files and to configure the report output.

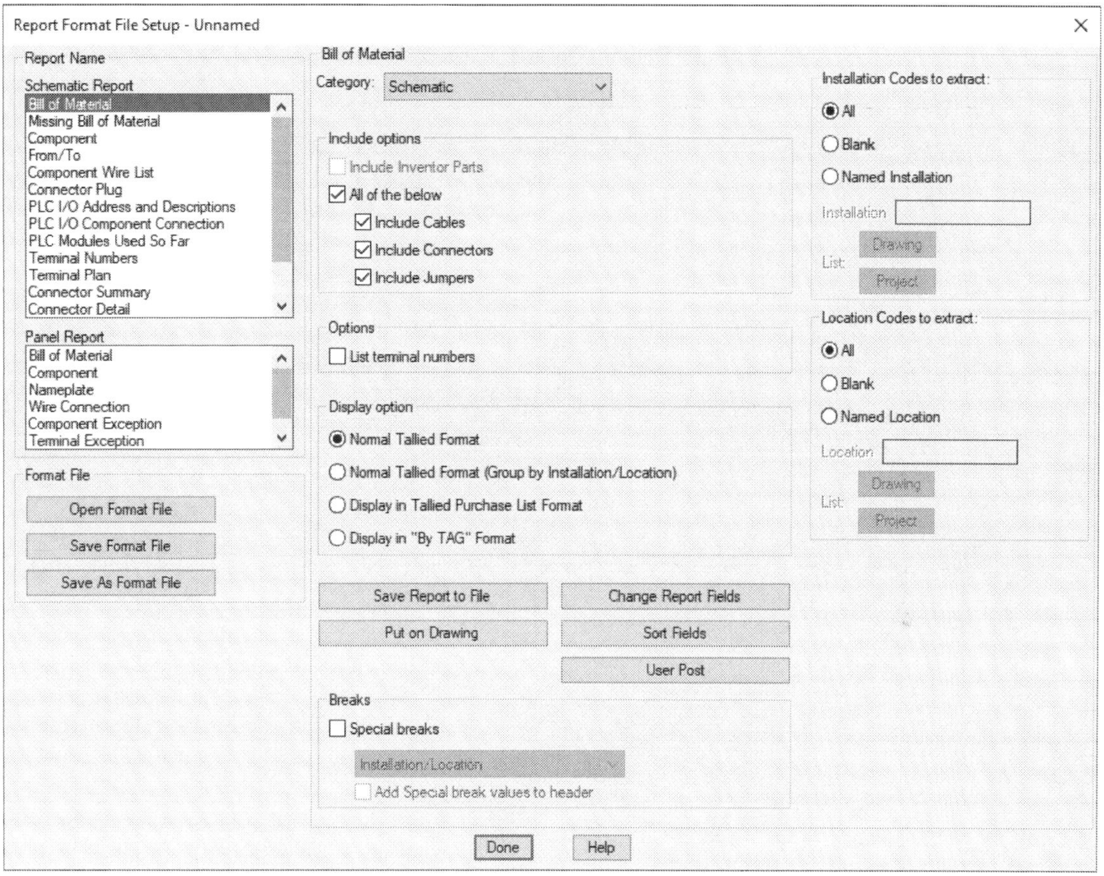

Figure 12–20

Report Name	Lists the available report types.
Bill of Material	Contains options for the selected report. This column changes depending on the selected report.
Installation Codes to extract	Select the **Installation** code on which to run the report.
Location Codes to extract	Select the **Location** code on which to run the report.
Save Report to File	Flags the format file to save to a file and opens the *Save Report to File* dialog box. Select the type of file to save to in the dialog box.
Put on Drawing	Flags the format file to put the report on a drawing and opens the *Table Generation Setup* dialog box enabling you to configure the table.
Change Report Fields	Opens the *<report name> Data Fields to Report* dialog box. Configure the columns for the report.
Sort Fields	Opens the *Sort Fields* dialog box. Configure the sort order for the report in the dialog box.

User Post	Opens the *Reports Data Post-processing Options* dialog box. Select the options that are applied to the data when generating the report.
Open Format File	Opens an existing format file to make changes to the file.
Save Format File	Save the settings to the current format file.
Save As Format File	Save the settings to a new format file.

12.3 Running Automatic Reports

The **Automatic Reports** command uses report format files to run multiple reports in one command. The command enables you to select existing format files and run them simultaneously, drastically reducing the time required to configure and run reports.

Automatic Reports

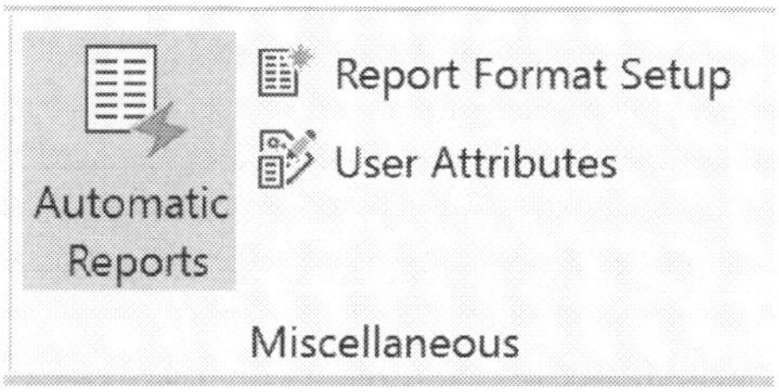

Ribbon: *Reports* tab>*Miscellaneous* panel

Command Prompt: aeautoreport

How To: Run Multiple Reports Using Automatic Reports

1. Start the **Automatic Reports** command. The *Automatic Report Selection* dialog box opens.
2. In the *Report Name* list, select the report type.
3. In the *Format File Name* list, select the file to add.
4. Click **Add>>** to add the report.
5. Repeat to add all required reports.
6. In the *Drawing Information for Table Output* area, specify the information.
7. Click **OK** to run the reports.

The *Automatic Report Selection* dialog box (shown in Figure 12–21) has various options from to select from.

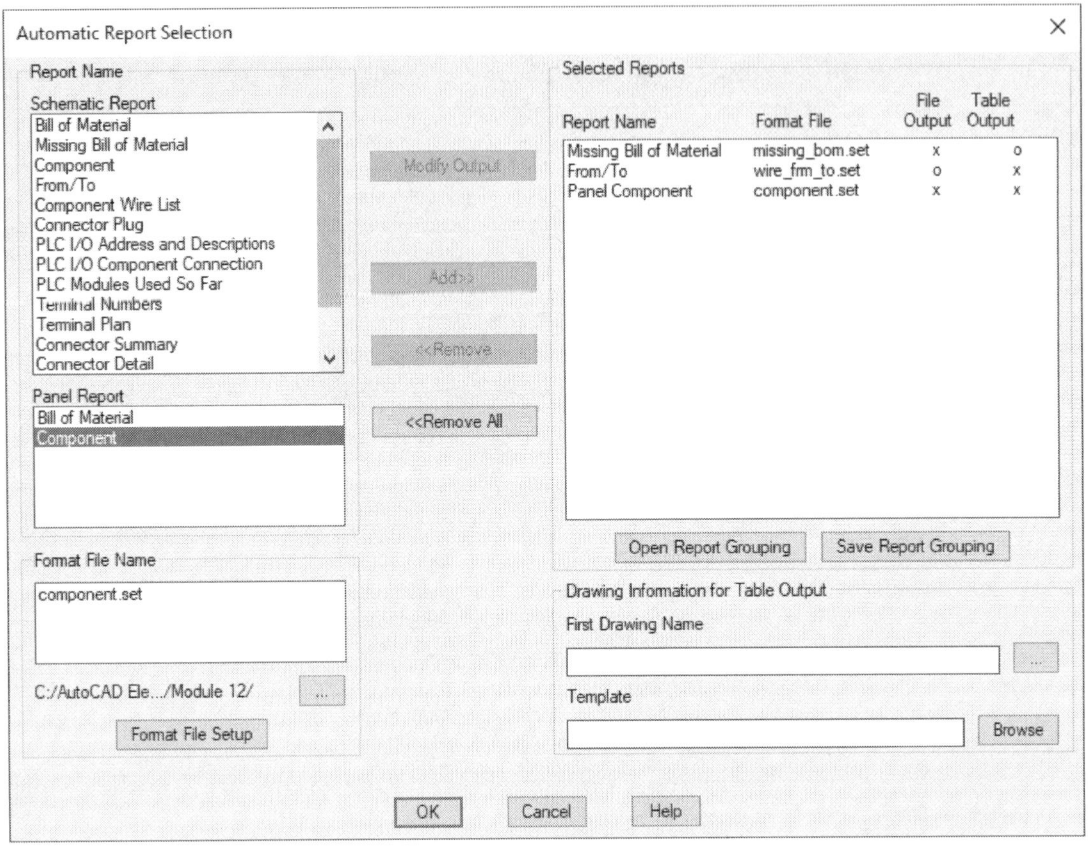

Figure 12–21

- It creates a report grouping file with an .RGF extension that can be used later to run the same group of reports on this project or any other project

Report Name	Lists the available report types.
Format File Name	Lists the available format file for the selected report type. Change the directory for the format files by clicking .... Click **Format File Setup** to open the *Report Format File Setup* dialog box in which to change the format file.
Modify Output	Opens the *Report Output Options* dialog box. Change the output options in the dialog box.
Add>>	Adds the selected format file to the *Selected Reports* list.
<<Remove	Removes the selected format file from the *Selected Reports* list.

<<Remove All	Removes all format files from the *Selected Reports* list.
Selected Reports	Lists the format files to be run when you click **OK**.
Open Report Grouping	Opens the *Enter name for Automatic Report Group file* dialog box. Select a report group file (.RGF) here.
Save Report Grouping	Opens the *Enter name for Automatic Report Group file* dialog box. Specify a name for the report group file.
Drawing Information for Table Output	Specify the name, directory, and template for the drawing files to be created for the reports. It is recommended that you end the name with a number suffix such that it is incremented for any subsequent drawing files that are created.

Practice 12b
Automatic Reports

Practice Objective

- Create report format files and run the reports.

In this practice, you will create three report format files: one to save to an Excel spreadsheet, one to put the report on a drawing, and one to do both. You will then use the **Automatic Reports** command to group the format files and run the reports. Finally, you will open the four files to verify that the reports are complete. One of the reports will display as shown in Figure 12–22.

ITEM	TAGNAME	CNT	UNITS	SUBQTY	MFG	CAT	CATDESC
1	LT151			*1	AB	800T–P16H	GREEN PILOT LIGH
1	LT169			*1	AB	800T–P16H	GREEN PILOT LIGH
1	LT262			*1	AB	800T–P16H	GREEN PILOT LIGH
1	LT263			*1	AB	800T–P16H	GREEN PILOT LIGH
1	LT264			*1	AB	800T–P16H	GREEN PILOT LIGH
2	PB167			*1	AB	800H–BR6D1	PUSH BUTTON – N
2	PB207			*1	AB	800H–BR6D1	PUSH BUTTON – N
2	PB213A			*1	AB	800H–BR6D1	PUSH BUTTON – N
3	LT161			*1	AB	800T–P16J	RED PILOT LIGHT -
4	PB201			*1	AB	800H–BR6D2	PUSH BUTTON – N
4	PB213			*1	AB	800H–BR6D2	PUSH BUTTON – N
5	PB159			*1	AB	800T–D6D2	PUSH BUTTON – N
6	LT151			*1	AB	800H–W100A	Name Plate
6	LT161			*1	AB	800H–W100A	Name Plate
6	LT169			*1	AB	800H–W100A	Name Plate
6	[illegible]			*1	[illegible]	[illegible]	[illegible]

Figure 12–22

Task 1: Create a report format file that saves to a spreadsheet.

1. If the **Module 12** project is not active, open and activate it now.
2. In the **Module 12** project, open **Contents.dwg**.
3. In the *Reports* tab>*Miscellaneous* panel, click  (Report Format Setup).
4. The *Report Format File Setup – Unnamed* dialog box opens. In the *Schematic Report* list, select **Missing Bill of Material**. Click **Save Report to File**.
5. The *Save Report to File* dialog box opens. In the *Excel Spreadsheet* area, select **Excel spreadsheet format (.xls)**.
6. For *File Name*, click **Browse**. Browse to the *Module 12* folder in your practice files folder. In the *File name* field, type **missing_bom.xls** and click **Save**.
7. You are returned to the *Save Report to File* dialog box, with the new filename and path listed in the *File Name* field, as shown in Figure 12–23. Click **OK**.

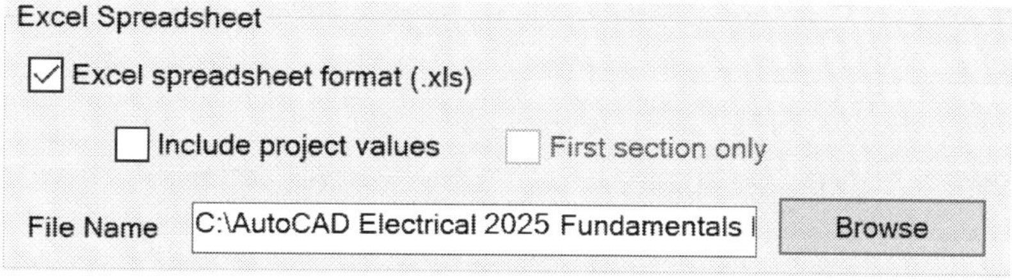

Figure 12–23

8. You are returned to the *Report Format File Setup* dialog box. In the *Format File* area, click **Save As Format File**.
9. In the *Select Missing Bill of Material *.set format file* dialog box, navigate to the *Module 12* folder in your practice files folder. In the *File name* field, type **missing_bom.set** and click **Save**.

Task 2: Create a report format file that saves to a drawing.

1. You are returned to the *Report Format File Setup* dialog box. In the *Schematic Report* list, select **From/To** and click **Put on Drawing**.
2. In the *Table Generation Setup* dialog box, set the following, as shown in Figure 12–24:
   - *X-Dimension*: **2**
   - *Y-Dimension*: **20**
   - *Table Style* drop-down list: **Standard (TableStyle)**

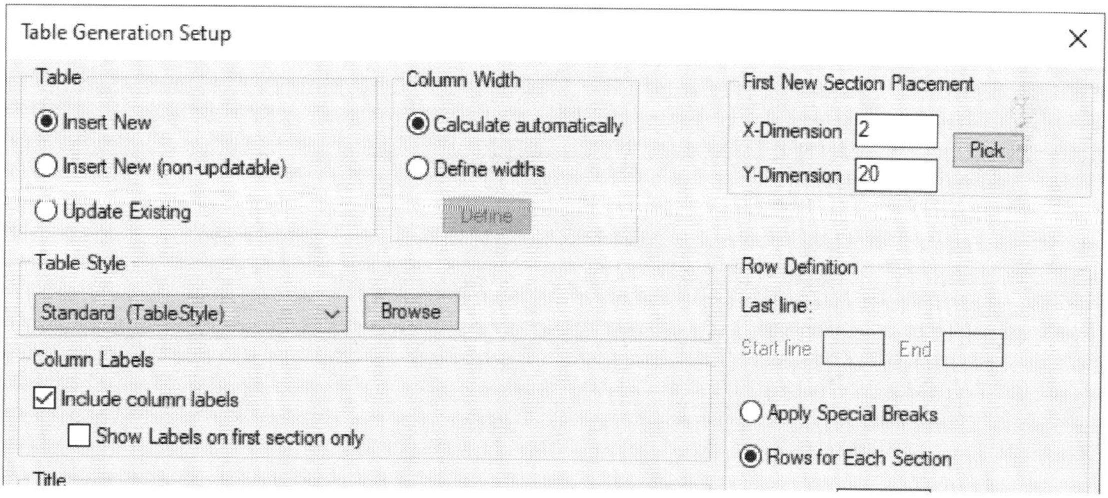

Figure 12–24

3. Click **OK**.
4. You are returned to the *Report Format File Setup* dialog box. Click **Save As Format File**.

5. The *Select From/To*.set format file* dialog box opens. Navigate to the *Module 12* folder in your practice files folder. In the *File name* field, type **wire_frm_to** and click **Save**. The file is saved as a .SET file.

Task 3: Create a report format file that saves to a spreadsheet and a drawing.

1. You are returned to the *Report Format File Setup* dialog box. In the *Panel Report* list (lower list), select **Component,** as shown in Figure 12–25. Click **Save Report to File**.

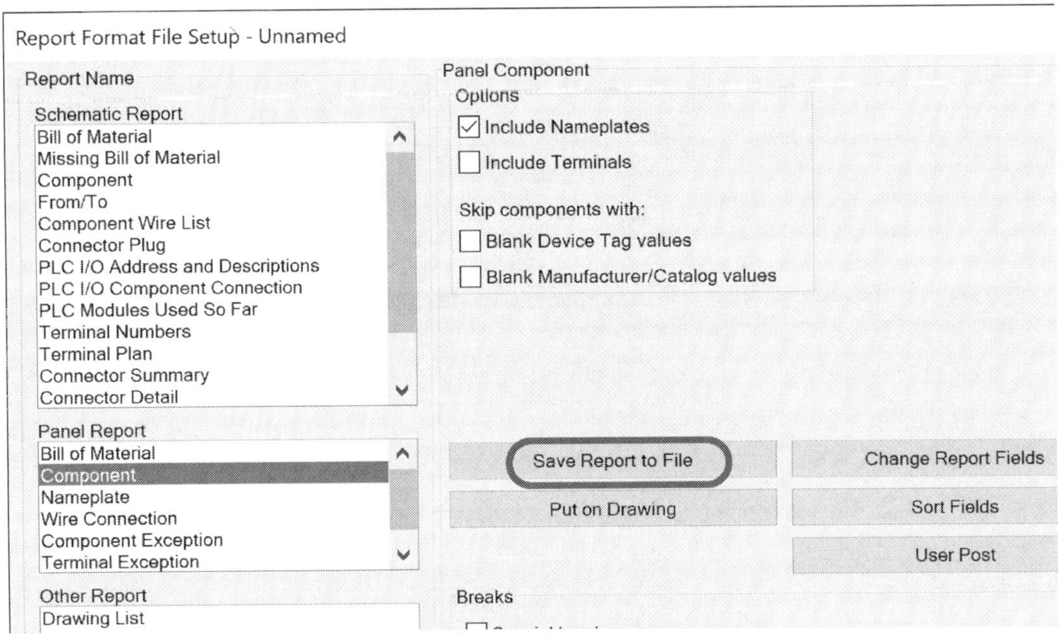

Figure 12–25

2. In the *Save Report to File* dialog box, select **Excel spreadsheet format (.xls)**.
3. For *File Name*, click **Browse**. Browse to the *Module 12* folder in your practice files folder. In the *File name* field, type **component** and click **Save**. The file is saved as an .XLS file.
4. You are returned to the *Save Report to File* dialog box. Click **OK**.
5. You are returned to the *Report Format File Setup* dialog box. Click **Put on Drawing**.
6. In the *Table Generation Setup* dialog box that opens, set the following:
   - *X-Dimension*: **2**
   - *Y-Dimension*: **20**
   - Table Style drop-down list: **Standard (TableStyle)**
7. Click **OK**.
8. You are returned to the *Report Format File Setup* dialog box. Click **Save As Format File**.

9. The *Select Panel Component *.set format file* dialog box opens. Browse to the *Module 12* folder in your practice files folder. In the *File name* field, type **component** and click **Save**.
10. You are returned to the *Report Format File Setup* dialog box. Click **Done**.

Task 4: Group the report format files and run the reports.

1. In the *Reports* tab>*Miscellaneous* panel, click  (Automatic Reports).
2. The *Automatic Report Selection* dialog box opens. In the *Format File Name* area, click **...** (Browse), as shown in Figure 12–26.

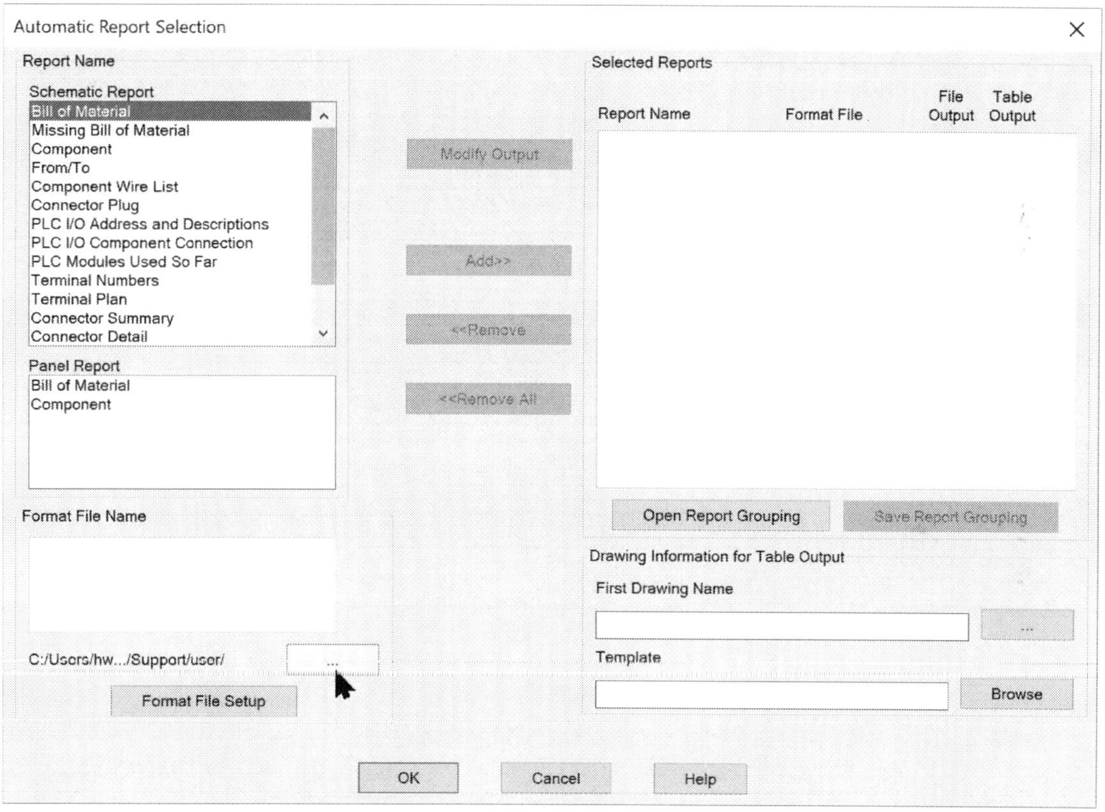

Figure 12–26

3. The *Browse for Folder* dialog box opens. Navigate to the practice files folder, select the *Module 12* folder, and click **OK**.

4. You are returned to the *Automatic Report Selection* dialog box, with the folder name and path displayed below the *Format File Name* area. In the *Schematic Report* area, select **Missing Bill of Material** and in the *Format File Name* area, select **missing_bom.set** (as shown in Figure 12–27). Click **Add>>**. The report is listed in the *Selected Reports* area. Note that an **X** displays under the *File Output* column and a **0** displays under the *Table Output* column (as shown in Figure 12–27) indicating that the file only displays as a file output.

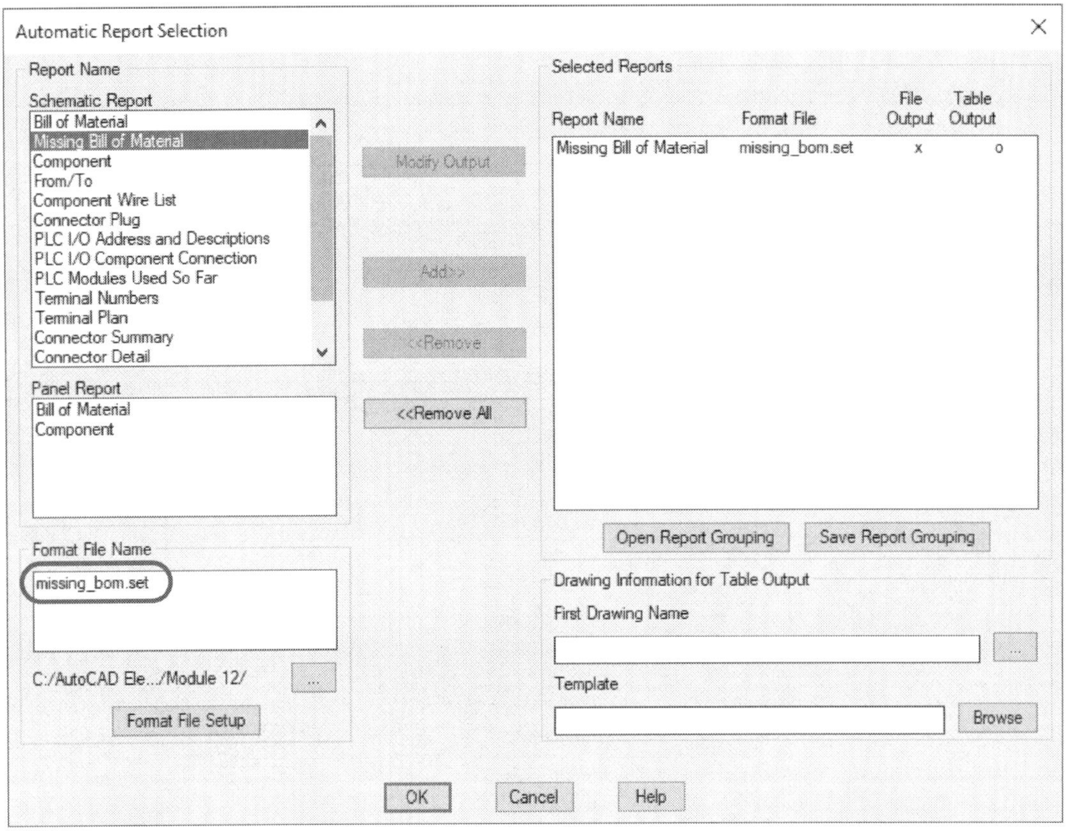

Figure 12–27

5. In the *Schematic Report* list, select **From/To**. In the F*ormat File Name* area, select **wire_frm_to.set**. Click **Add>>**. This report only displays table output (**X** for *Table Output*), as shown in Figure 12–28.

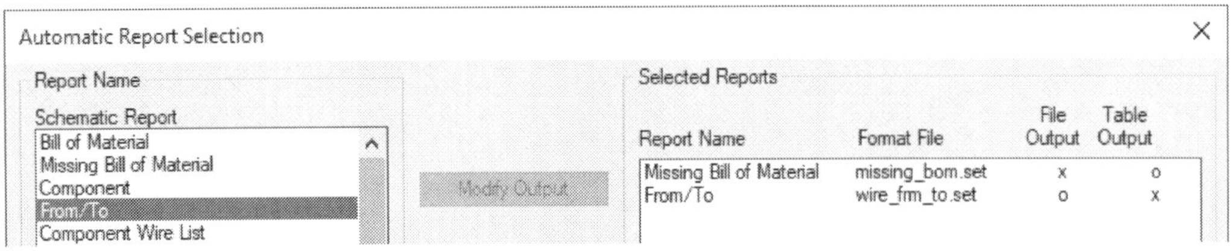

Figure 12–28

6. In the *Panel Report* list, select **Component**. In the Format File Name list, select **component.set**. Click **Add>>**. This report displays both the file and table output (**X** for both *File Output* and *Table Output*), as shown in Figure 12–29.

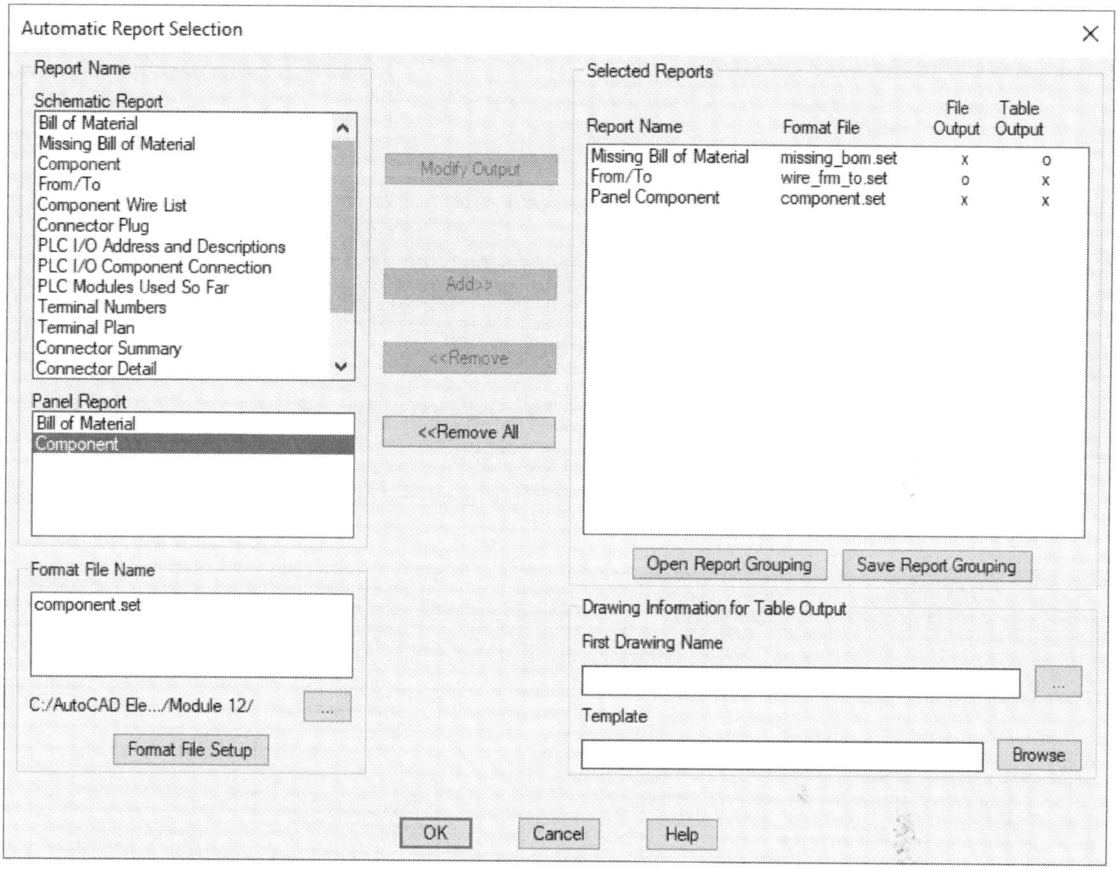

Figure 12–29

7. Click **Save Report Grouping**.

8. The *Enter name for Automatic Report Group* file dialog box opens. Browse to the *Module 12* folder in your practice files folder. In the *File name* field, type **fundamentals** (it will be saved as an .RGF file) and click **Save**.

9. You are returned to the *Automatic Report Selection* dialog box. Next to the *First Drawing Name* field, click **...**.

10. The *Enter Name for First Drawing* dialog box opens. Browse to the *Module 12* folder in your practice files folder, if required. In the *File name* field, type **Report_01** (it will be saved as a .DWG file) and click **Save**.

11. Next to the *Template* field, click **Browse**. In the *Select Template* dialog box, browse to your practice files folder, select **Electrical_template.dwt** and click **Open**.

12. You are returned to the *Automatic Report Selection* dialog box with the selected folders and paths displayed, as shown in Figure 12–30. Click **OK**.

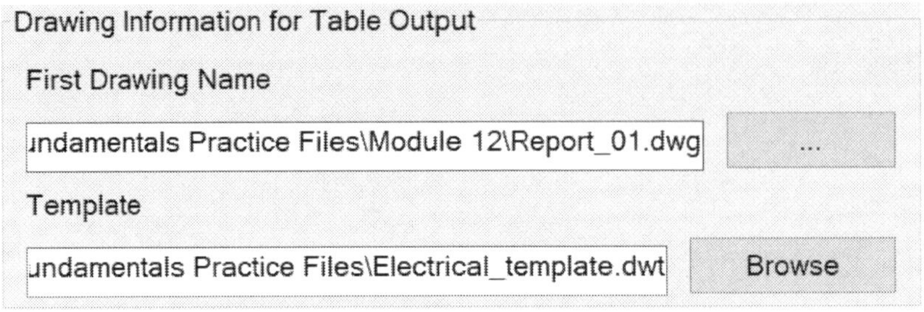

Figure 12–30

Task 5: Verify that reports were created.

1. When the **Automatic Reports** command is complete, **REPORT_01.DWG** is added to the project. Open the file.
2. Delete the titleblock. Zoom in to the top portion of the report, as shown in Figure 12–31. Save and close **REPORT_01.dwg**.

WIRENO	LOC1	CMP1	PIN1	LOC2	CMP2	PIN2	WLAY1
		MOT116		FLOOR	PJ115	3	BLK_14AWG
		MOT116		FLOOR	PJ115	4	BLK_14AWG
		MOT104		FLOOR	PJ103	3	BLK_14AWG
		MOT104		FLOOR	PJ103	4	BLK_14AWG
	CABINET	TB	6	FLOOR	PJ115	3	BLU_14AWG
	CABINET	M215	T3	CABINET	TB	6	BLK_14AWG
	CABINET	TB	5	FLOOR	PJ115	2	RED_14AWG
	CABINET	M215	T2	CABINET	TB	5	BLK_14AWG
	CABINET	TB	4	FLOOR	PJ115	1	BLK_14AWG
	CABINET	M215	T1	CABINET	TB	4	BLK_14AWG
	CABINET	TB	3	FLOOR	PJ103	3	BLU_14AWG
	CABINET	M203	T3	CABINET	TB	3	BLK_14AWG
	CABINET	TB	3	CABINET	M209	T3	BLK_14AWG
	CABINET	TB	2	FLOOR	PJ103	2	RED_14AWG
	CABINET	M203	T2	CABINET	TB	2	BLK_14AWG
	CABINET	TB	2	CABINET	M209	T2	BLK_14AWG
	CABINET	TB	1	FLOOR	PJ103	1	BLK_14AWG

Figure 12–31

3. In the practice files folder, in the *Module 12* folder, open **component.xls** in Microsoft Excel, as shown in Figure 12–32. Close **component.xls.**

	A	B	C	D	E	F	G	H	I	J
1	ITEM	TAGNAME	CNT	UNITS	SUBQTY	MFG	CAT	CATDESC	QUERY1	
2	1	LT151			*1	AB	800T-P16H	GREEN PIL	30.5mm	
3	1	LT169			*1	AB	800T-P16H	GREEN PIL	30.5mm	
4	1	LT262			*1	AB	800T-P16H	GREEN PIL	30.5mm	
5	1	LT263			*1	AB	800T-P16H	GREEN PIL	30.5mm	
6	1	LT264			*1	AB	800T-P16H	GREEN PIL	30.5mm	
7	10	CB153			*1	EATON	EGB1015FI	CIRCUIT BI	1-POLE CIRCUIT BREAKER	
8	11	PS155								
9	12	XF123			*1	SQD	500SV1B	1PH TRAN	DRY TRANSFORMER	
10	13	PLC251			*1	AB	1771-IA	1771 PLC-	1771	
11	14	PLC261			*1	AB	1771-OA	1771 PLC-	1771	
12	15	CR201			*1	AB	700-P400A	P TYPE ELE	TYPE P	
13	15	CR207			*1	AB	700-P400A	P TYPE ELE	TYPE P	
14	15	CR213			*1	AB	700-P400A	P TYPE ELE	TYPE P	
15	16	CR159			*1	AB	700-R220A1			
16	16	CR265			*1	AB	700-R220A1			

Figure 12–32

4. Return to the AutoCAD Electrical software.
5. Save and close the open drawings.

End of practice

12.4 Electrical Audit

The **Electrical Audit** command is an error-checking command. It scans all drawings in the active project for problems and lists them in relevant tabs.

Electrical Audit

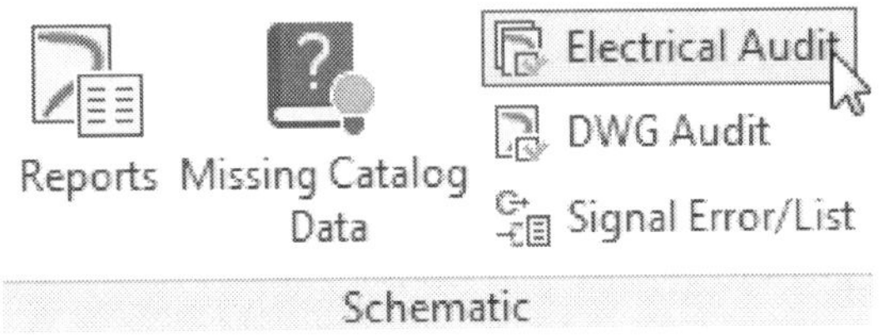

Ribbon: *Reports* tab>*Schematic* panel

Command Prompt: aeaudit

How To: Run the Electrical Audit

1. Start the **Electrical Audit** command.
    - The progress bar displays while the drawings are being processed. When the process is complete, the number of errors is listed in the text field.
2. Click **Details** to expand the dialog box.
3. Select the tab you want to investigate.
4. Select the error you want to correct. Click **Go To** that opens the drawing that contains the error and zooms in to the symbol.
5. Use the standard AutoCAD Electrical commands to fix the error (do not close the *Electrical Audit* dialog box).
    - With the *Electrical Audit* dialog box open, you can run other commands.
6. Repeat Steps 3 to 5 to correct other errors.
7. Click **Close** to close the *Electrical Audit* dialog box.

The *Electrical Audit* dialog box (shown in Figure 12–33) contains multiple tabs that organize the list of errors by error type. Any tab displaying a red circle with a white x indicates errors.

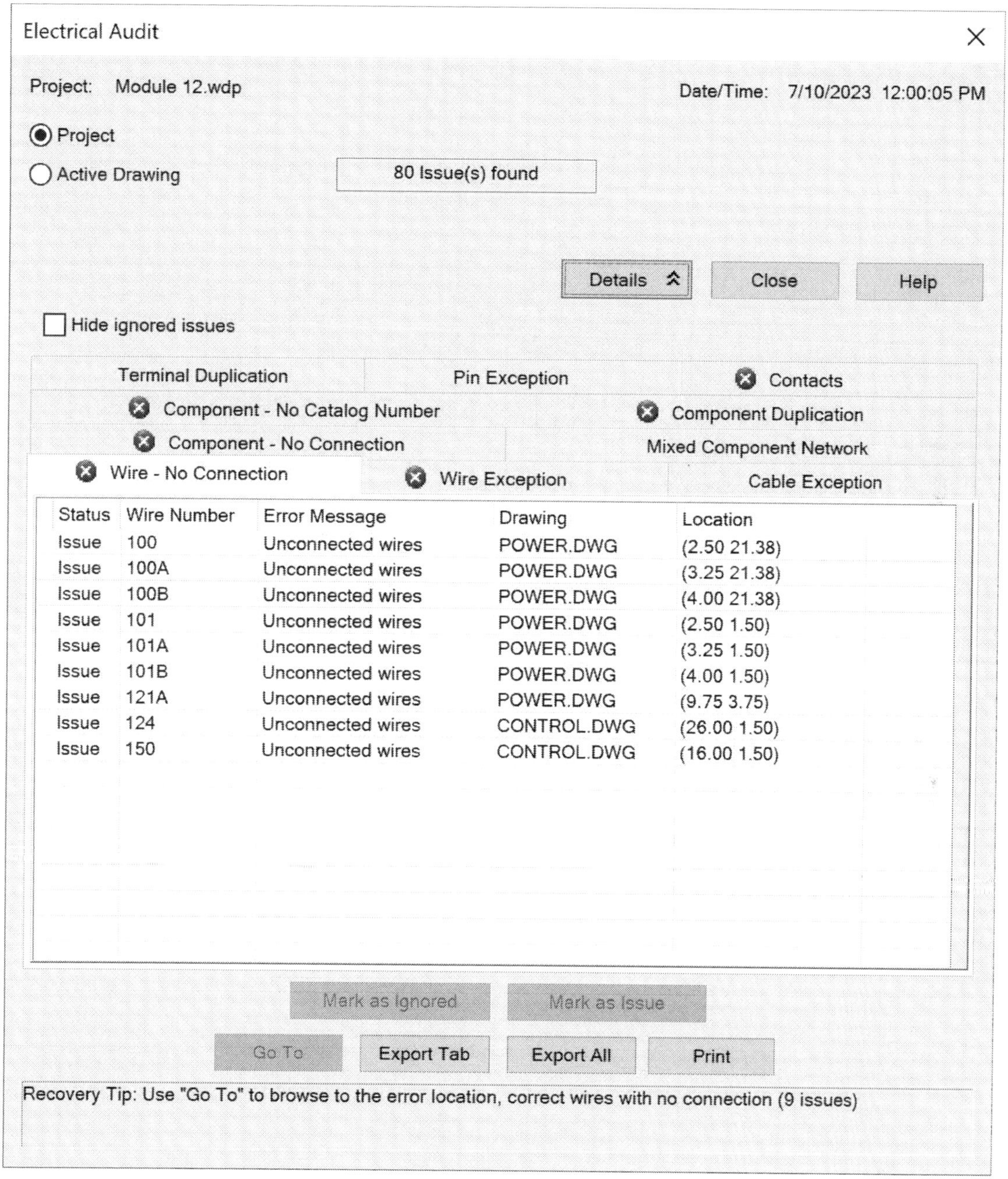

Figure 12–33

Details	Expands or collapses the tabbed section in the dialog box.
Hide ignored issues	Enables you to hide issues that you do not want to fix. Only issues that are **Marked as Ignored** are hidden.
Terminal Duplication	Duplicate schematic terminal numbers.
Pin Exception	Duplicate pin number assignments.
Contacts	Orphaned child schematic components (child components without a parent).
Component – No Catalog Number	Components without assigned catalog data.
Component Duplication	Duplicate schematic or panel components.
Component – No Connection	Components without a connected wire.
Mixed Component Network	Displays Components in the wire network with varying WDTYPE variables.
Wire – No Connection	Wires without a connection.
Wire Exception	Missing or duplicate wire numbers.
Cable Exception	Duplicate cable and wire id.
Mark as Ignored	The issues that are not required to be fixed are marked with the **Ignored** label in the *Status* column. These can be then hidden using the **Hide ignored issues** option.
Mark as Issue	Changes the label of the Ignored errors to **Issue** in the *Status* column.
Go To	Opens the drawing containing the selected error and zooms to the appropriate wire or component and is highlighted. After an error has been viewed, an **X** is placed next to the record in the *Electrical Audit* dialog box.
Export Tab/Export All	Saves the information (audit report) of the active tab/all tabs to a text file.
Print	Prints the information in all tabs.

Practice 12c
Electrical Audit

Practice Objective

- Scan, correct, and verify errors in the active project.

In this practice, you will run the **Electrical Audit** command on a project. The audit returns errors in the project, as shown in Figure 12–34. You will fix two of these errors and then re-run **Electrical Audit** to verify that they have been resolved.

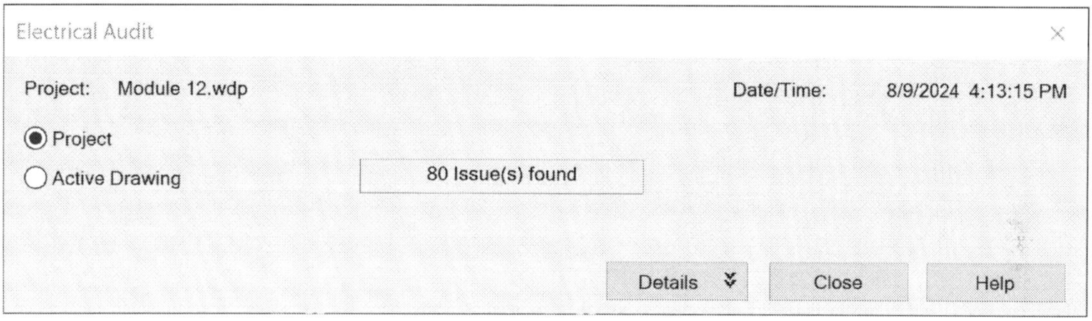

Figure 12–34

Task 1: Run the Electrical Audit command.

1. If the **Module 12** project is not active, open and activate it now.
2. In the **Module 12** project, open **Contents.dwg**.
3. In the *Reports* tab>*Schematic* panel, click (Electrical Audit).
4. The *Electrical Audit* dialog box opens. There are 80 possible errors in this project.

Task 2: Fix one error.

1. In the *Electrical Audit* dialog box, click **Details** to expand the tabbed section, as shown in Figure 12–35. Note that there are 80 issues found in the project.
2. In the expanded *Electrical Audit* dialog box, select the *Component – No Catalog Number* tab.
3. Select all of the issues except for PB201A. You will fix issue PB201A later in this practice.
4. Click **Mark as Ignored**. Note that **Ignored** displays in the *Status* column for the selected components. Only PB201A displays **Issue** in the *Status* column, as shown in Figure 12–35. Also note that the number of issues found has changed to 74, as six issues are now ignored.

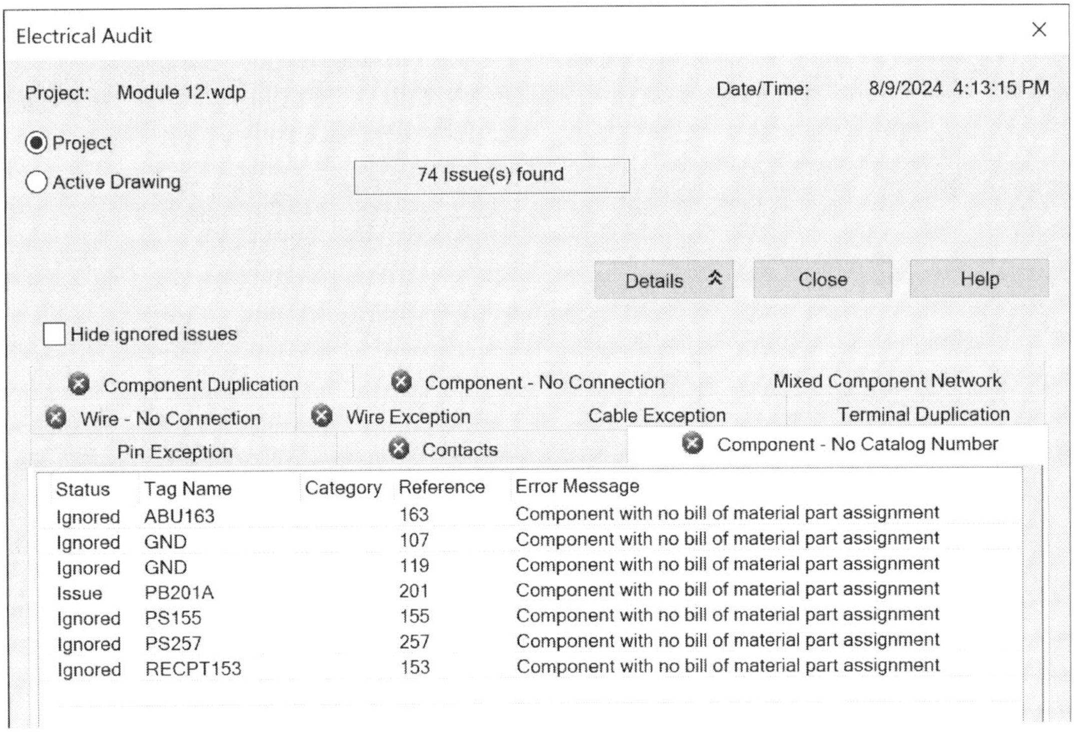

Figure 12–35

5. Select **Hide ignored issues**. Only PB201A displays in the list.
6. Select **PB201A** and click **Go To**.
7. **Control.dwg** is opened and zoomed to highlighted component PB201A. If the *Electrical Audit* dialog box is blocking the component, move it to the side.
8. In the drawing, right-click on PB201A and select **Edit Component**.
9. The *Insert / Edit Component* dialog box opens. In the *Catalog Data* area, click **Lookup**.

10. The Catalog Browser opens with **AB** manufacturer and **Push Button** category searched. Select **800H-BR6D1** and click **OK**.
11. The *Insert / Edit Component* dialog box is populated. Click **OK**.
12. In the *Update other drawings?* dialog box, click **OK**. Click **OK** to **QSAVE**.

Task 3: Fix another error.

1. In the expanded *Electrical Audit* dialog box, select the *Contacts* tab. Select the only record listed (CR 209), as shown in Figure 12–36, and click **Go To**.

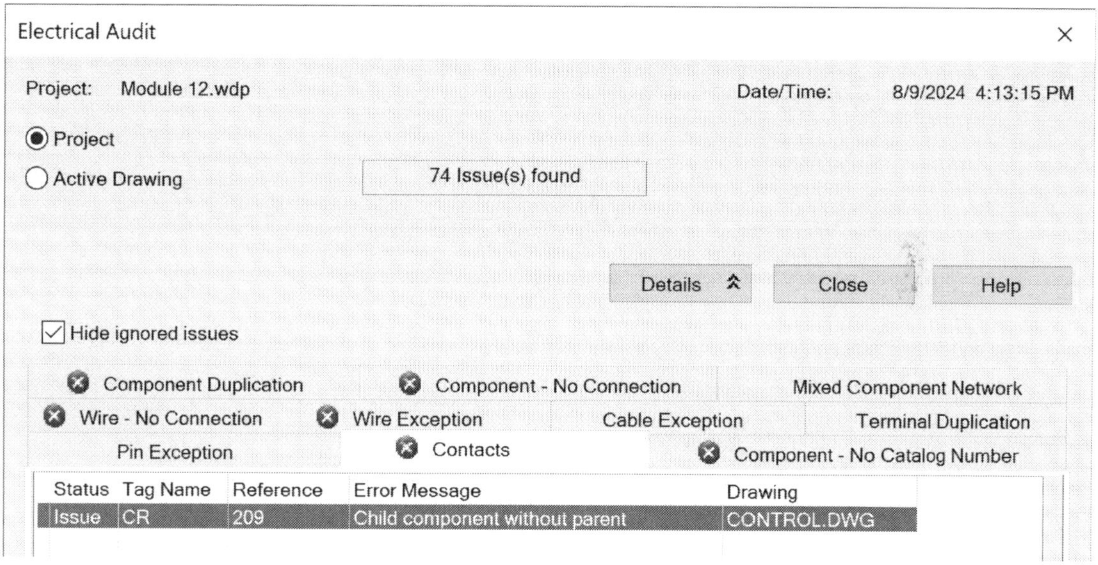

Figure 12–36

2. The drawing window is zoomed to a normally open contact that has a tag of **CR** and is highlighted. This contact has not been linked to a parent.
3. Right-click on the contact and select **Edit Component**.
4. The *Insert / Edit Child Component* dialog box opens. In the *Component Tag* area, click **Drawing**.
5. In the *Active Drawing list for FAMILY="CR"* dialog box, select **CR207** and click **OK**.
6. You are returned to the updated *Insert / Edit Child Component* dialog box. Click **OK**. Note that in the drawing all of the linked labels display for the contact.
   - You might be required to map the symbol to the catalog number.
7. Click **Close** in the *Electrical Audit* dialog box.

Task 4: Run the Electrical Audit command to verify errors have been fixed.

1. Click (Electrical Audit).
2. The *Electrical Audit* dialog box opens. There are now 72 errors in this project, as shown in Figure 12–37. The six errors are ignored and two errors were corrected in the previous tasks.

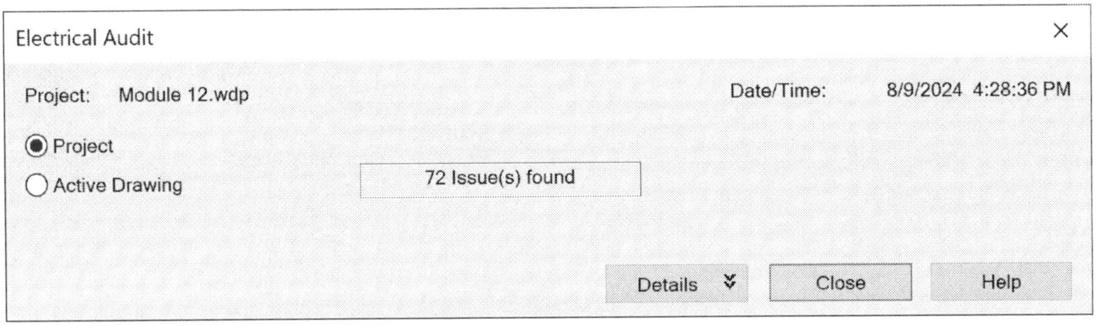

Figure 12–37

3. Click **Close** in the *Electrical Audit* dialog box.
4. Zoom extents.
5. Save and close **Control.dwg**.

End of practice

Chapter Review Questions

1. What is the difference between the **Panel Reports** and **Schematic Reports** commands?
   a. **Schematic Reports** only create spreadsheet reports; **Panel Reports** can only place reports on drawings.
   b. **Schematic Reports** only report on data in a single drawing; **Panel Reports** report on data on all drawings in the project.
   c. There is no difference between **Schematic Reports** and **Panel Reports**.
   d. **Schematic Reports** only report on data in schematic drawings; **Panel Reports** only report on data in panel drawings, with the ability to include schematic components.

2. What is the function of the *Report Generator* dialog box?
   a. It collects the data for a report.
   b. It previews the report and enables data format and placement.
   c. It determines what data to report on.
   d. It determines which drawing to generate the report from.

3. When configuring a report format file, how do you control the output for the report?
   a. Click **Save Report to File** or **Put on Drawing**.
   b. Click **Save As Format File** or **Save Format File**.
   c. Click **Put on Drawing** or **Save Format File**.
   d. Click **Save Report to File** or **Change Report Fields**.

4. How do you determine which tabs in the *Electrical Audit* dialog box contain errors?
   a. Only tabs that contain errors display.
   b. The tabs that contain errors display in bold.
   c. The tabs that contain errors display a red circle with a white x.
   d. Toggle the **Show Errors** option to display only the tabs that contain errors.

5. If you want to resolve or investigate an error, how can you find the appropriate drawing and symbol?
   a. Select the error in the dialog box and click **Find**.
   b. Select the error in the dialog box and click **Go To**.
   c. Right-click the error in the dialog box and click **Find**.
   d. Select the error in the dialog box and click **Save As**.

6. What does **Export All** do?
   a. It saves all the drawings with errors to a new Error project.
   b. It saves all errors listed in the *Electrical Audit* dialog box to a spreadsheet file.
   c. It saves all errors listed in the *Electrical Audit* dialog box so that they are not re-audited when the command is launched again.
   d. It saves all errors listed in the *Electrical Audit* dialog box to a text file.

Command Summary

Button	Command	Location
	**Automatic Reports**	• **Ribbon:** *Reports* tab>*Miscellaneous* panel
NA	**Drawing List Report**	• **Project Manager**
	**Electrical Audit**	• **Ribbon:** *Reports* tab>*Schematic* panel
	**Panel Reports**	• **Ribbon:** *Reports* tab>*Panel* panel
	**Report Format File Setup**	• **Ribbon:** *Reports* tab>*Miscellaneous* panel
	**Schematic Reports**	• **Ribbon:** *Reports* tab>*Schematic* panel

Chapter 13

Settings and Templates

Project properties are settings that are used for the entire project, whereas drawing properties are settings that control individual drawings in a project. Panel drawings have some additional settings that are required to be set at an individual drawing level. Learning to save the settings in a template file is also useful when creating new drawings.

Learning Objectives

- Modify the settings and formatting for an individual drawing or an entire project.
- Compare and match a drawing's properties to the project's properties.
- Modify the configurations and default values for panel drawings.
- Create AutoCAD® Electrical specific template files.
- Set up the AutoCAD Electrical software for multiple users.

13.1 Project Properties

The **Project Properties** command controls the default settings and formatting for the entire project. When a drawing is added to the project, you have the option of applying the project settings to the drawing settings. The Project Properties are also used as the default properties when a new drawing is created for a project.

Project Properties

Shortcut Menu: *(on project name in Project Manager)* **Properties**

How To: Change the Project Properties

1. Start the **Project Properties** command. The *Project Properties* dialog box opens.
2. Select the tab for the properties you want to update.
3. Configure the required properties.
4. Click **OK**.

- The values in Project Properties are saved in the project file.
- Denotes a setting that applies to the project file.
- Denotes a setting that is a drawing default.

In the *Project Properties* dialog box, the *Project Settings* tab (shown in Figure 13–1) controls the library and catalog file path information.

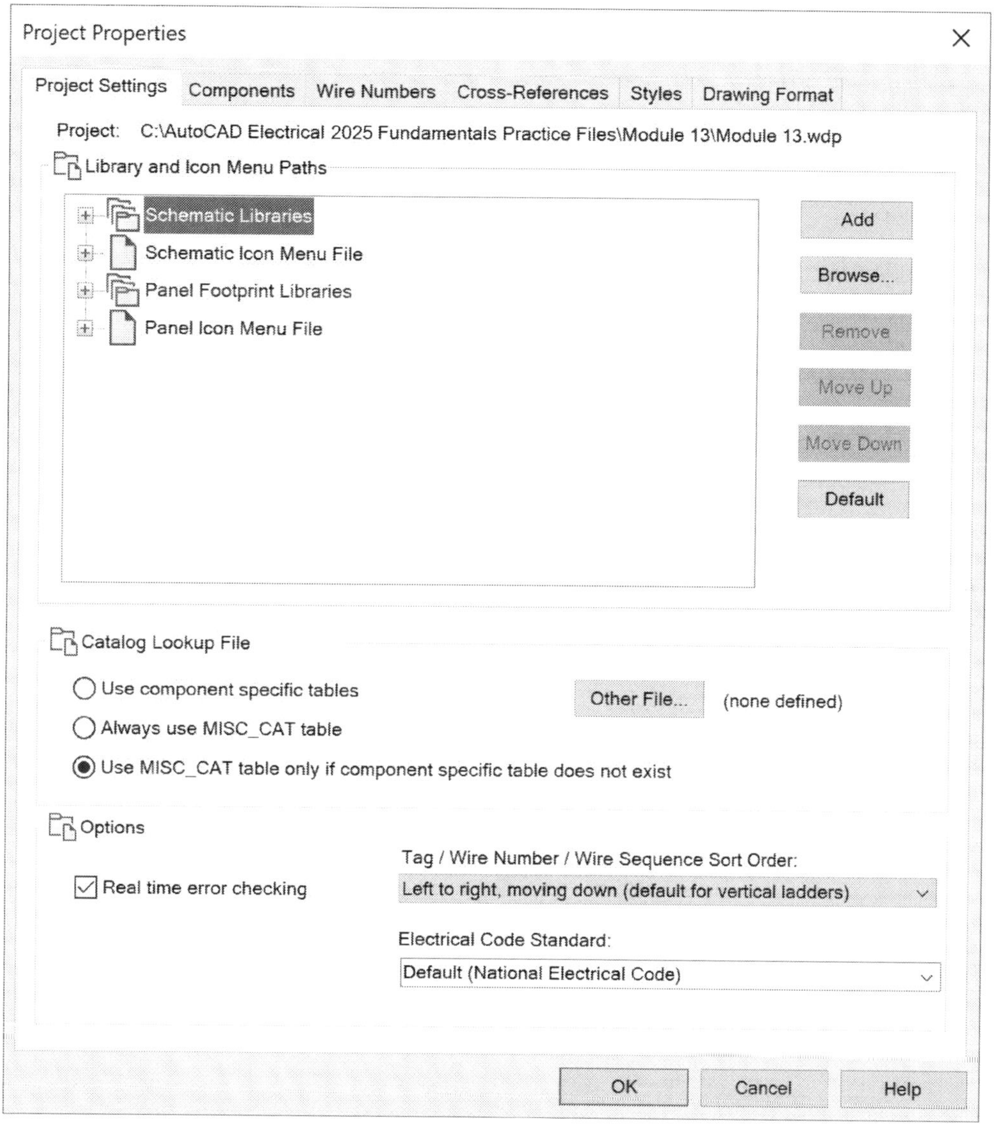

Figure 13–1

Library and Icon Menu Paths	Controls the paths that are searched for block files and which menu files are used. These are the last paths to be searched for library symbols.
Catalog Lookup File	Controls the preferences for searching the bill of material catalog database.
Options	Controls real time error checking and the sort order for tagging and wire numbering. Also sets the Electrical Code Standard to be used in the project.

In the *Project Properties* dialog box, the *Components* tab (shown in Figure 13–2) controls component tagging options.

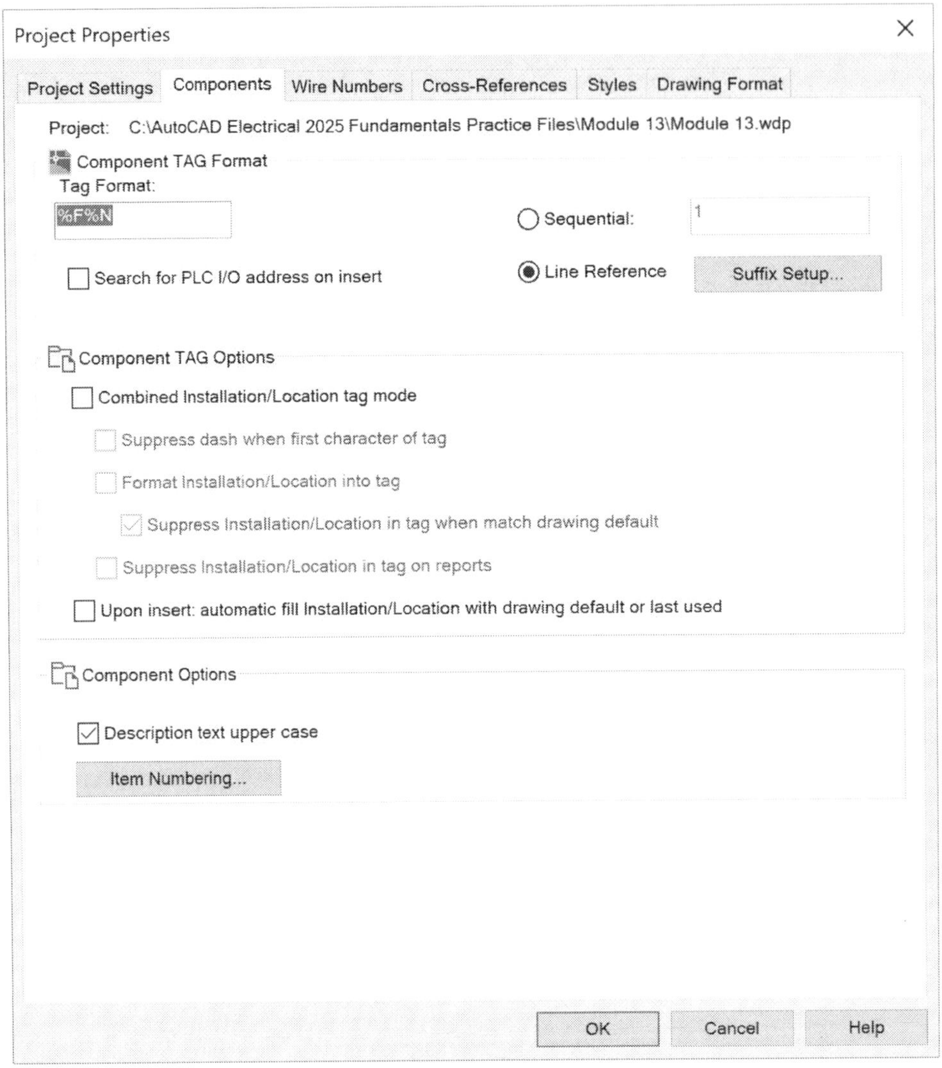

Figure 13–2

Component TAG Format	Controls the component tag. Select from sequential tagging or referenced based tagging.
Component TAG Options	Controls the **Installation/Location** code options with component tags, and the automatic code fill option.
Component Options	Forces the description text to be in upper case letters and controls the **Item Numbering** behavior.

In the *Project Properties* dialog box, the *Wire Numbers* tab (shown in Figure 13–3) controls wire options, such as number format and wire type.

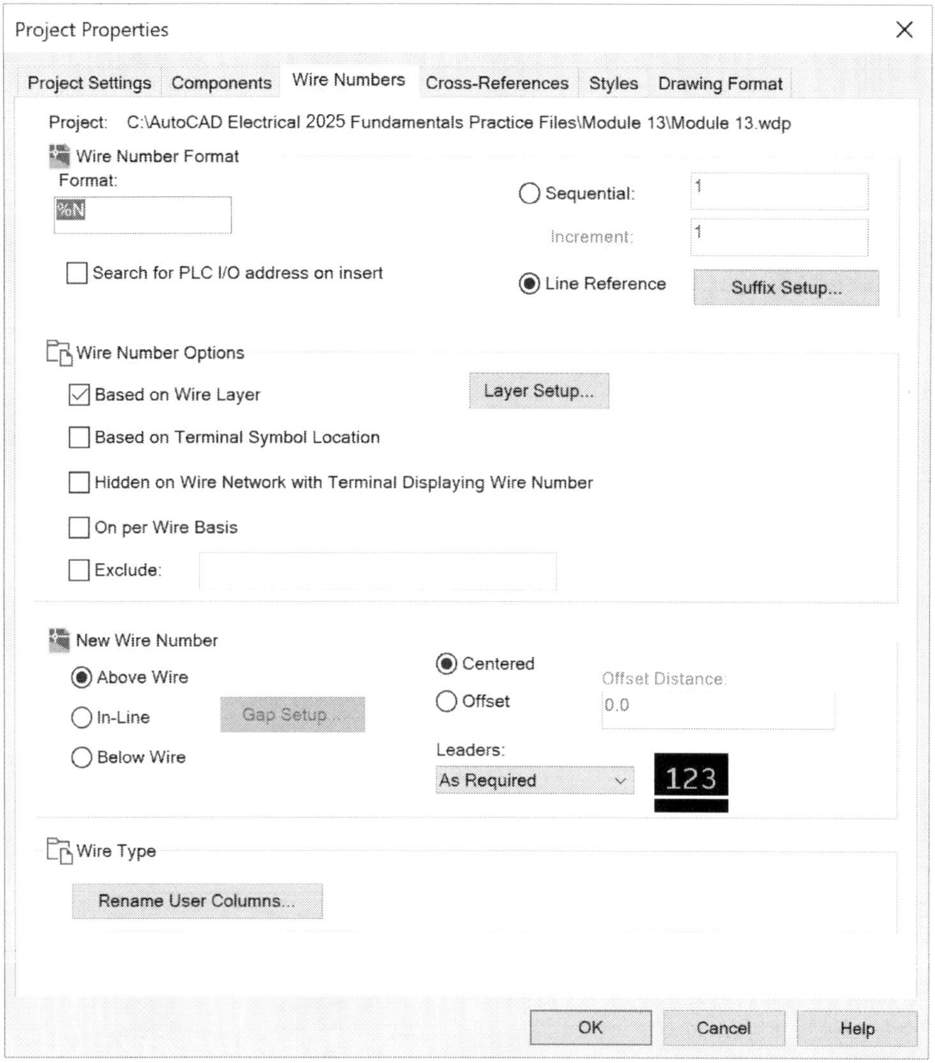

Figure 13–3

Wire Number Format	Controls the formatting of the wire number. Select from sequential tagging or referenced based tagging.
Wire Number Options	Controls various options for the wire number source information.
New Wire Number	Controls the location of the wire numbers relative to the wire.
Wire Type	Controls the names of the *User1* through *User20* fields.

In the *Project Properties* dialog box, the *Cross-References* tab (shown in Figure 13–4) controls the cross-reference format and options for the same drawing or between drawings, including Parent/Child cross-referencing.

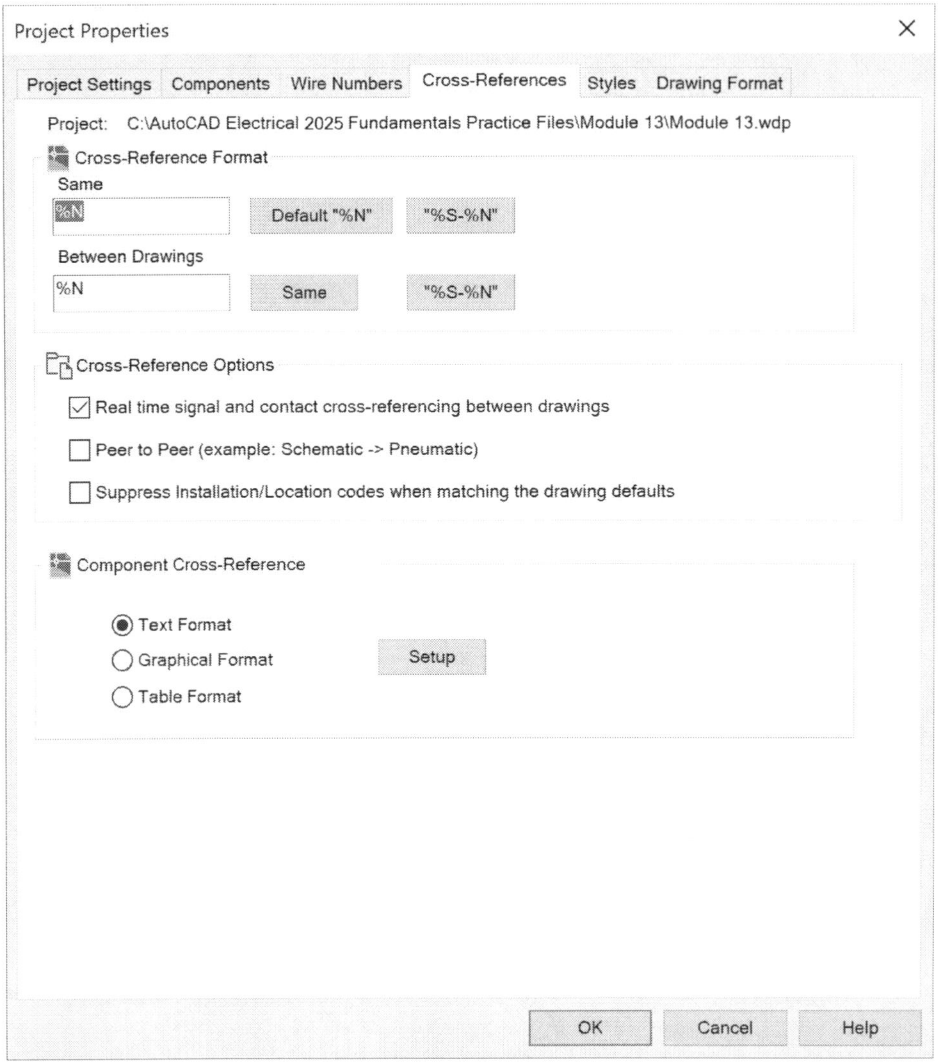

Figure 13–4

Cross-Reference Format	Controls the format for cross-referencing in the same drawing and between drawings.
Cross-Reference Options	Controls the cross-referencing options.
Component Cross-Reference	Controls the format used to display the cross-referencing information.

In the *Project Properties* dialog box, the *Styles* tab (shown in Figure 13–5) controls the default styles for Source/Destination arrows, PLCs, Wiring, and Fan-In/Out Markers.

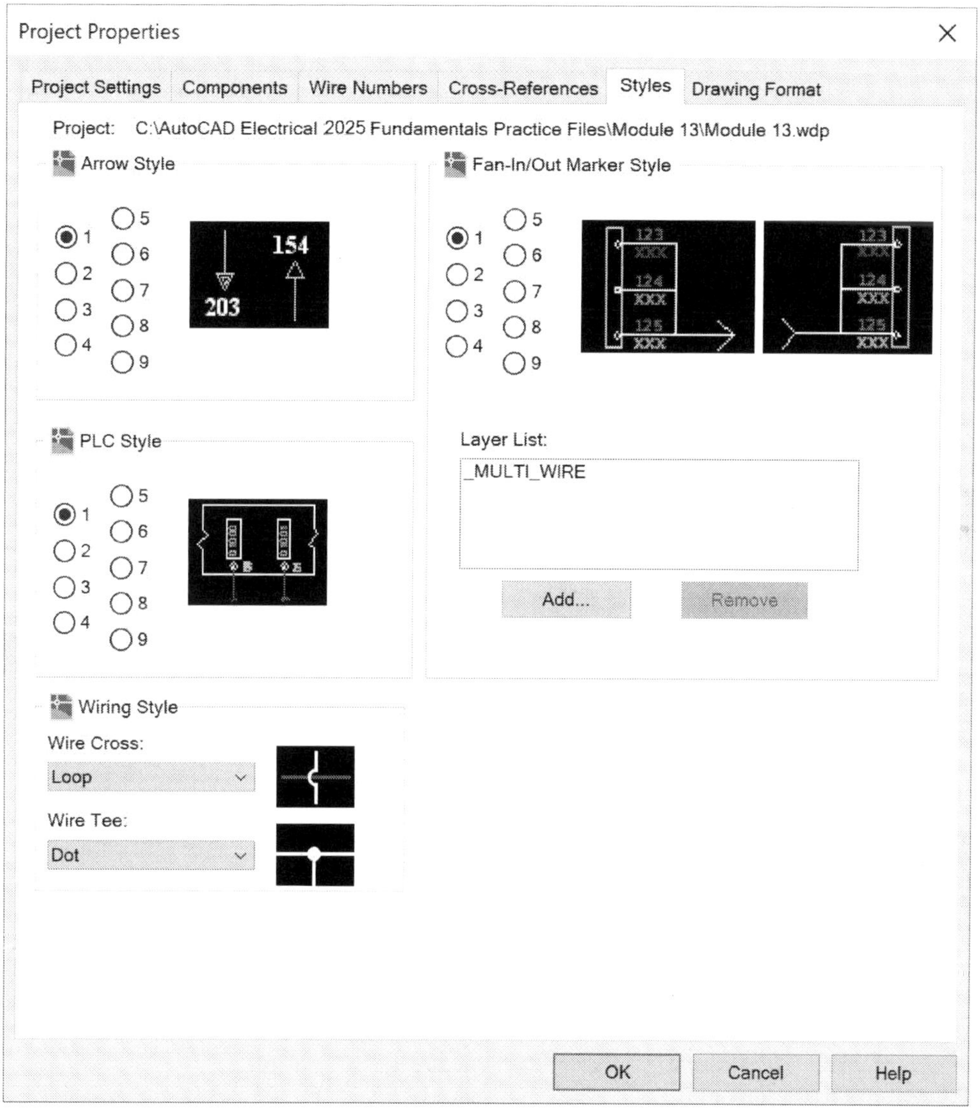

Figure 13–5

Arrow Style	Controls the default style for the Source and Destination arrows.
Fan-In/Out Marker Style	Controls the default style for the Fan In/Out marker symbols.
PLC Style	Controls the default symbol for PLC modules.
Wiring Style	Controls the symbol used for wires that intersect.

In the *Project Properties* dialog box, the *Drawing Format* tab (shown in Figure 13–6) controls the default formats for drawings, including Ladders, Referencing, and Layers.

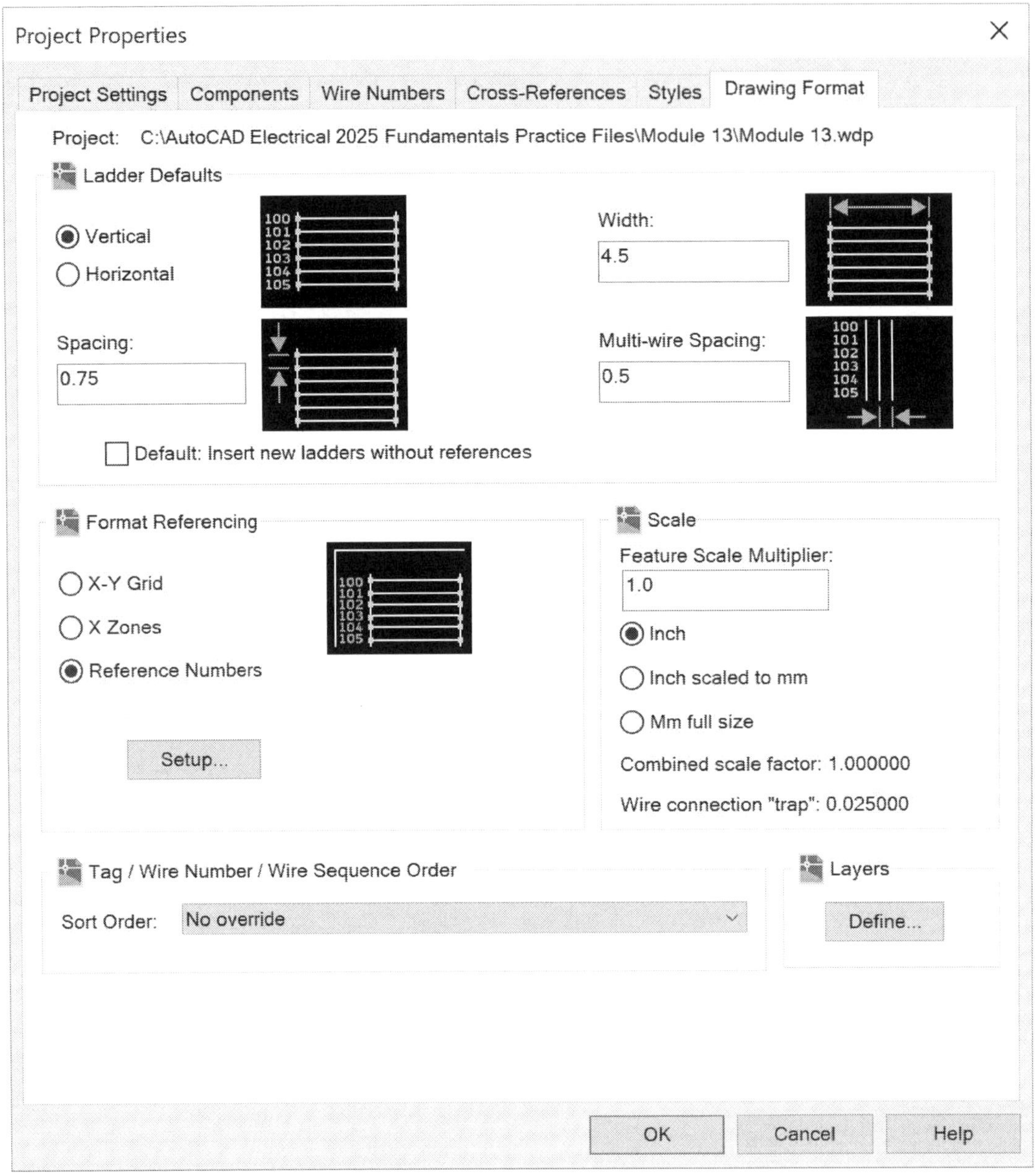

Figure 13–6

Ladder Defaults	Controls the default spacing and orientation for ladders.
Format Referencing	Controls the default format for reference numbers on ladders.
Scale	Controls the scale for inserting components and wire numbers.
Tag/Wire Number/Wire Sequence Order	Controls the way component tags and wire numbers are calculated.
Layers	Controls the layers for AutoCAD Electrical information.

The AutoCAD Electrical software uses replaceable parameters when defining the format for component tags, wire numbers, and other data. Replaceable parameters are codes that represent AutoCAD Electrical data. For example, %S represents the sheet number and %F represents the family code.

> ***Note:*** *For detailed information on all of the options, see the AutoCAD Electrical Help system.*

13.2 Drawing Properties

Drawing properties are similar to project properties. They are settings that control the format for data fields and the default settings for commands. Each drawing has its own settings. They override the settings in the Project Properties.

Drawing Properties

Ribbon: *Schematic* tab>*Other Tools* panel

Command Prompt: aeproperties

Shortcut Menu: *(on drawing name in Project Manager)* **Properties>Drawing Properties**

How To: Change the Drawing Properties

1. Start the **Drawing Properties** command. The *Drawing Properties* dialog box opens.
2. Select the tab that contains the properties that you want to update.
3. Configure the required properties.
4. Click **OK**.

- The values of the drawing properties are stored in the **WD_M** block in the drawing file.

In the *Drawing Properties* dialog box, the *Drawing Settings* tab (shown in Figure 13–7) controls drawing descriptions and default values for codes and sheet information.

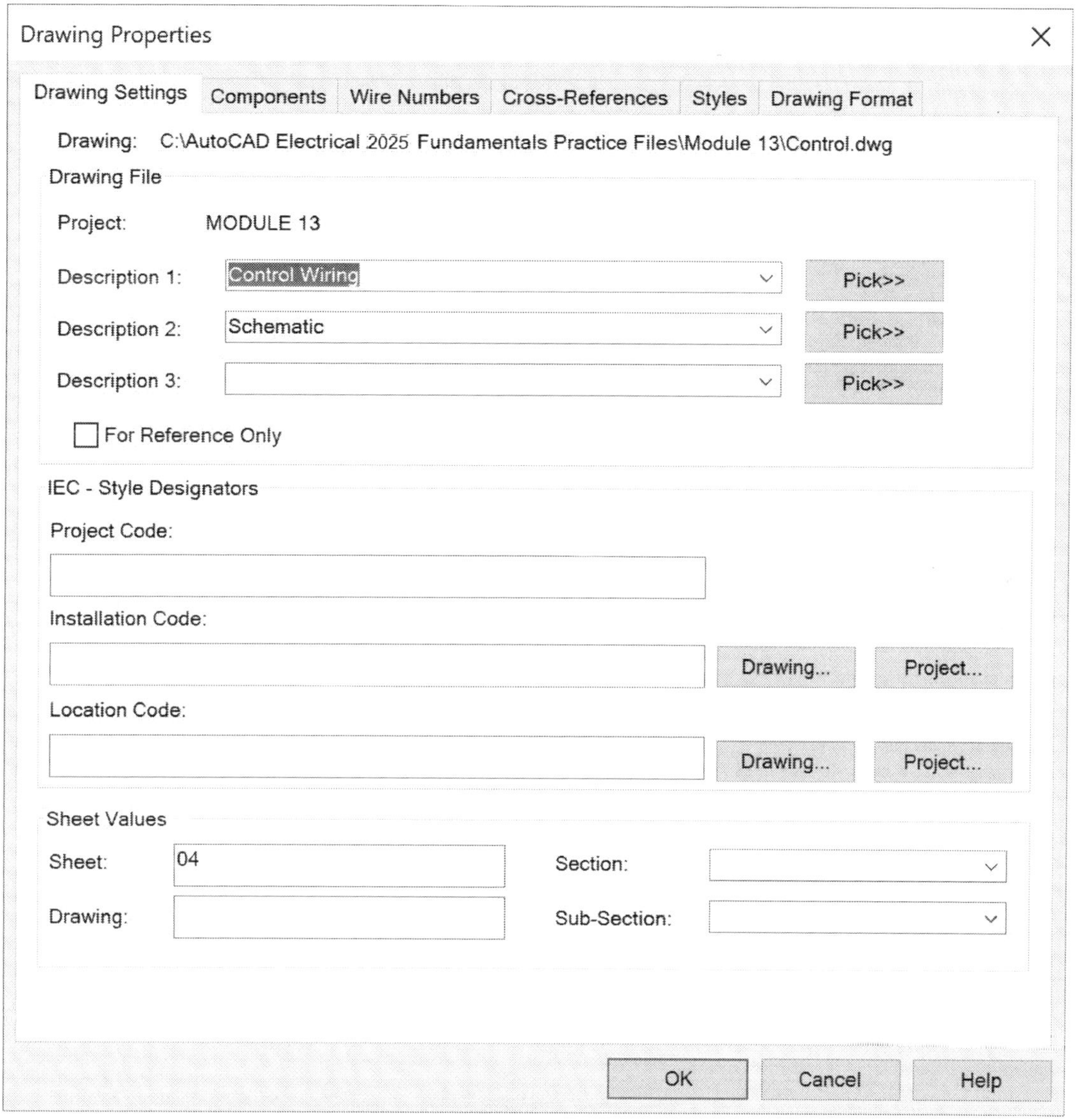

Figure 13–7

Drawing File	Controls descriptions for the drawing file and controls the reference status.
IEC - Style Designators	Controls the default values for Project Code (%P), Installation Code (%I), and Location Code (%L).
Sheet Values	Controls the values for drawing sheet properties.

In the *Drawing Properties* dialog box, the *Components* tab (shown in Figure 13–8) controls component tagging options for this drawing only.

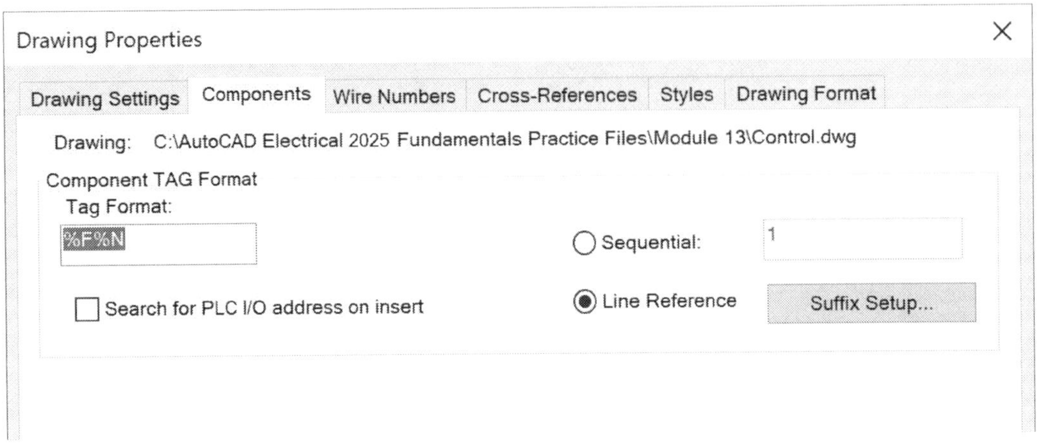

Figure 13–8

Component TAG Format	Controls the component tag. Select from sequential tagging or referenced based tagging.

In the *Drawing Properties* dialog box, the *Wire Numbers* tab (shown in Figure 13–9) controls wire number formatting and number placement for this drawing only.

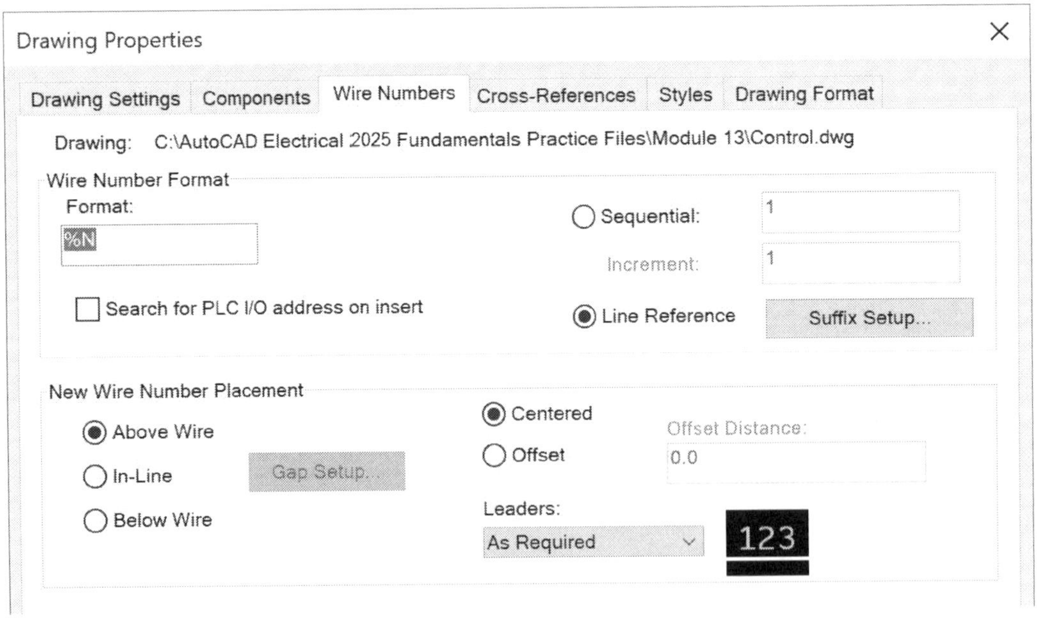

Figure 13–9

Wire Number Format	Controls the formatting of the wire number. Select from sequential tagging or referenced based tagging.
New Wire Number Placement	Controls the location of the wire numbers relative to the wire.

In the *Drawing Properties* dialog box, the *Cross-References* tab (shown in Figure 13–10) controls cross-reference formatting in the same drawing and between drawings.

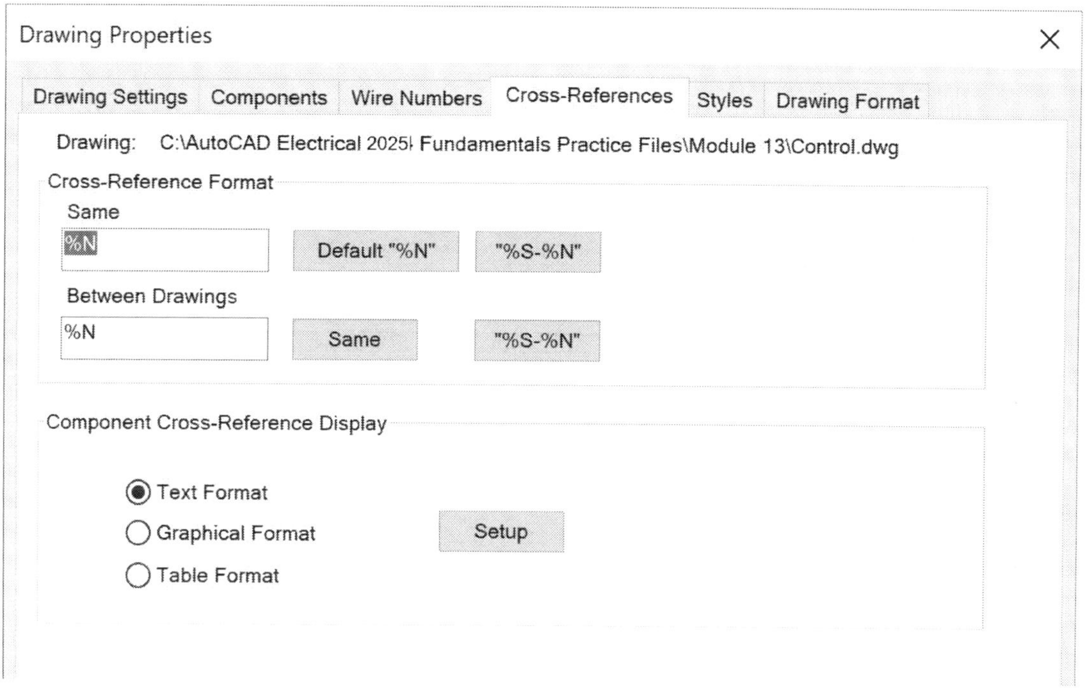

Figure 13–10

Cross-Reference Format	Controls the format for cross-referencing in the same drawing and between drawings.
Component Cross-Reference Display	Controls the format used to display the cross-referencing information.

In the *Drawing Properties* dialog box, the *Styles* tab (shown in Figure 13–11) controls the default styles for Source/Destination arrows, PLCs, Wiring, and Fan-In/Out Markers for this drawing only.

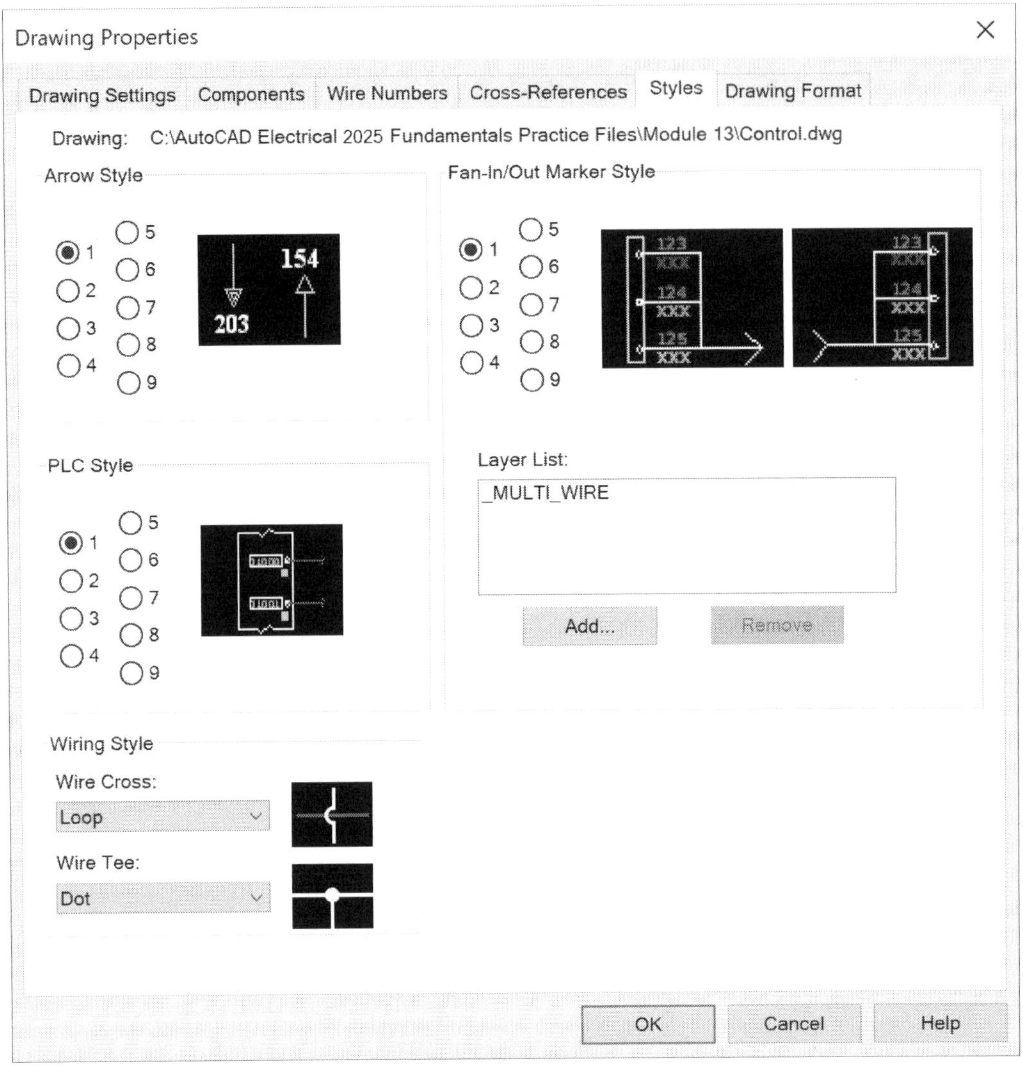

Figure 13–11

Arrow Style	Controls the default style for the Source and Destination arrows.
Fan-In/Out Marker Style	Controls the default style for the Fan In/Out marker symbols.
PLC Style	Controls the default symbol for PLC modules.
Wiring Style	Controls the symbol used for wires that intersect.

In the *Drawing Properties* dialog box, the *Drawing Format* tab (shown in Figure 13–12) controls the default formats for Ladders, Referencing, and Layers, for this drawing only.

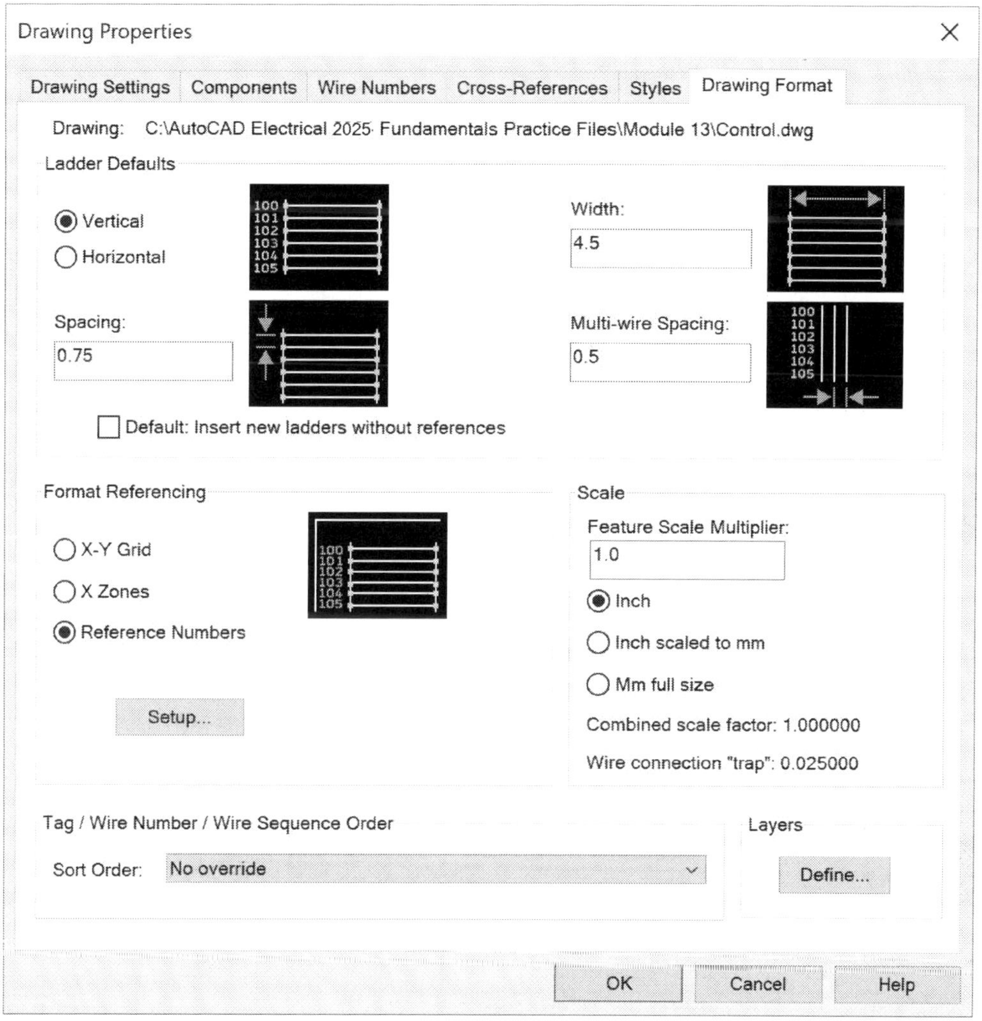

Figure 13–12

Ladder Defaults	Controls the default spacing and orientation for ladders.
Format Referencing	Controls the default format for reference numbers on ladders.
Scale	Controls the scale for inserting components and wire numbers.
Tag/Wire Number/Wire Sequence Order	Controls the way component tags and wire numbers are calculated.
Layers	Controls the layers for AutoCAD Electrical information.

Compare Settings

This **Settings Compare** command compares the values stored in Drawing Properties to the values in Project Properties.

Settings Compare

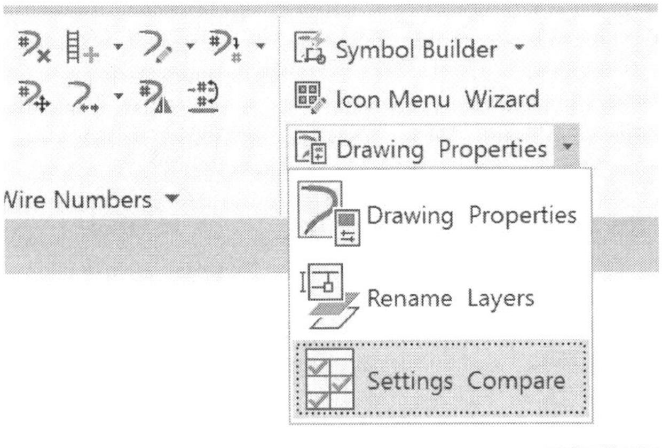

Ribbon: *Schematic* tab>*Other Tools* panel

Command Prompt: aesheetcompare

Shortcut Menu: *(on drawing name in Project Manager)* **Properties>Settings Compare**

Starting this command opens the *Compare Drawing and Projects Settings* dialog box, as shown in Figure 13–13. You can then update the drawing to match the project or the project to match the drawing.

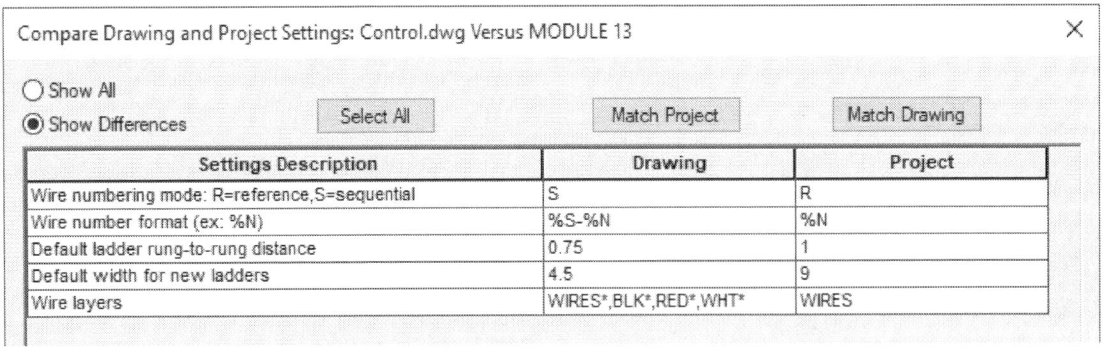

Compare Drawing and Project Settings: Control.dwg Versus MODULE 13

Show All
Show Differences
Select All
Match Project
Match Drawing

Settings Description	Drawing	Project
Wire numbering mode: R=reference,S=sequential	S	R
Wire number format (ex: %N)	%S-%N	%N
Default ladder rung-to-rung distance	0.75	1
Default width for new ladders	4.5	9
Wire layers	WIRES*,BLK*,RED*,WHT*	WIRES

Figure 13–13

13.3 Panel Drawing Configuration

Panel drawings have a set of properties controlled by the **Panel Configuration** command in addition to those in Drawing Properties. These settings control the default values for commands and the formatting for symbols.

Panel Configuration

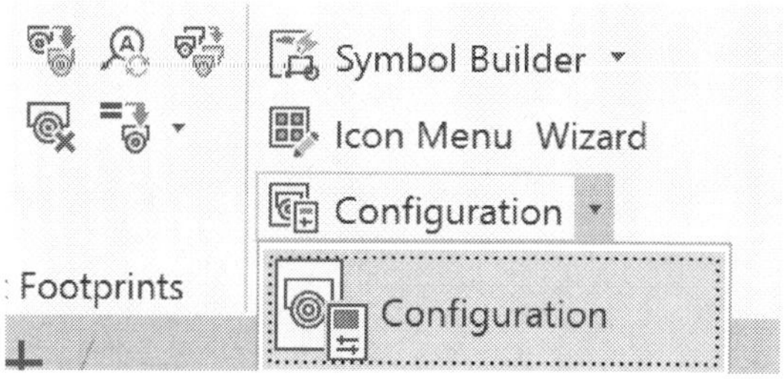

Ribbon: *Panel* tab>*Other Tools* panel

Command Prompt: aepanelconfig

How To: Change the Panel Drawing Properties

1. Start the **Panel Configuration** command. The *Panel Drawing Configuration and Defaults* dialog box opens.
2. Configure the properties in the dialog box, as required.
3. Click **OK**.

- The values for the Panel Configuration are stored in the **WD_PNLM** block in the drawing.

The *Panel Drawing Configuration and Defaults* dialog box (shown in Figure 13–14) controls panel drawing properties, for the current drawing only.

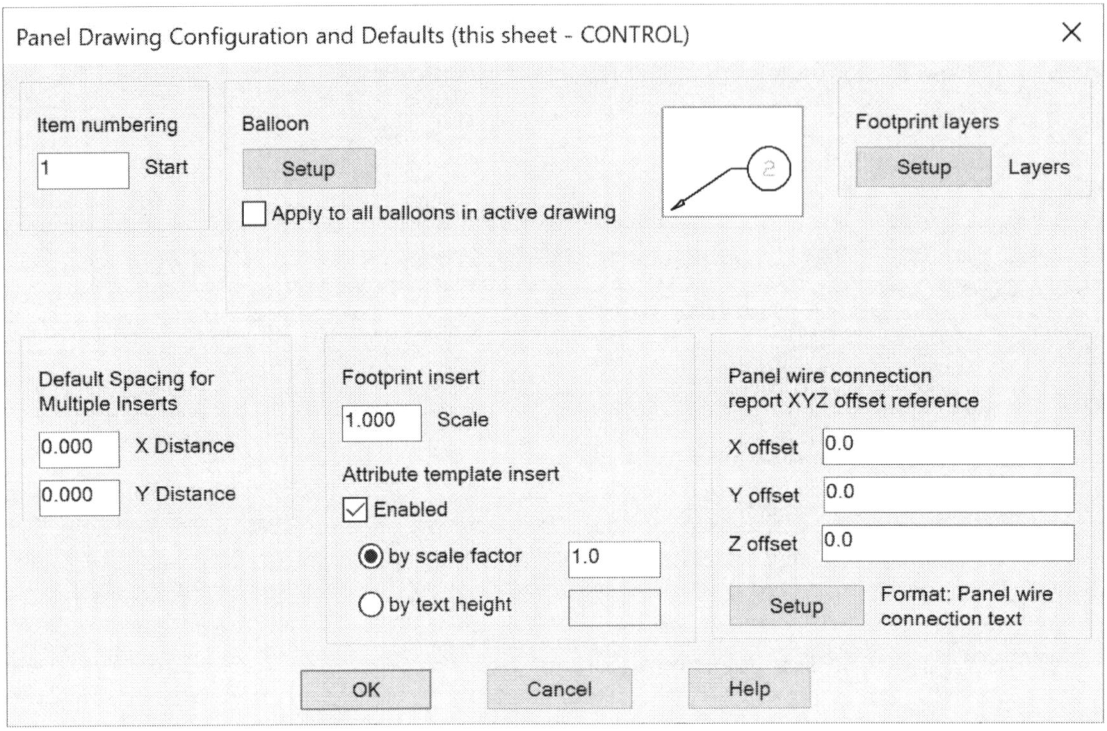

Figure 13–14

Item numbering	Controls the first item number used.
Balloon	Controls the default balloon shape and size.
Footprint layers	Controls the layers for AutoCAD Electrical information.
Default Spacing for Multiple Inserts	Controls the default spacing between footprints when using the **Multiple Insert** option.
Footprint insert	Controls the default scales for inserting a footprint.
Panel wire connection report XYZ offset reference	Controls the default offset and format for the text added when the wire connection information displays.

Practice 13a
Drawing and Project Properties

Practice Objectives

- Modify property settings for a single drawing and for the entire project.
- Compare the project and drawing settings.

In this practice, you will change the drawing properties for wire numbers in a drawing, as shown in Figure 13–15, and then update the wire numbers to see the changes. You will then change the project properties and do a compare to the drawing properties. Finally, you will create a new drawing using the updated project properties.

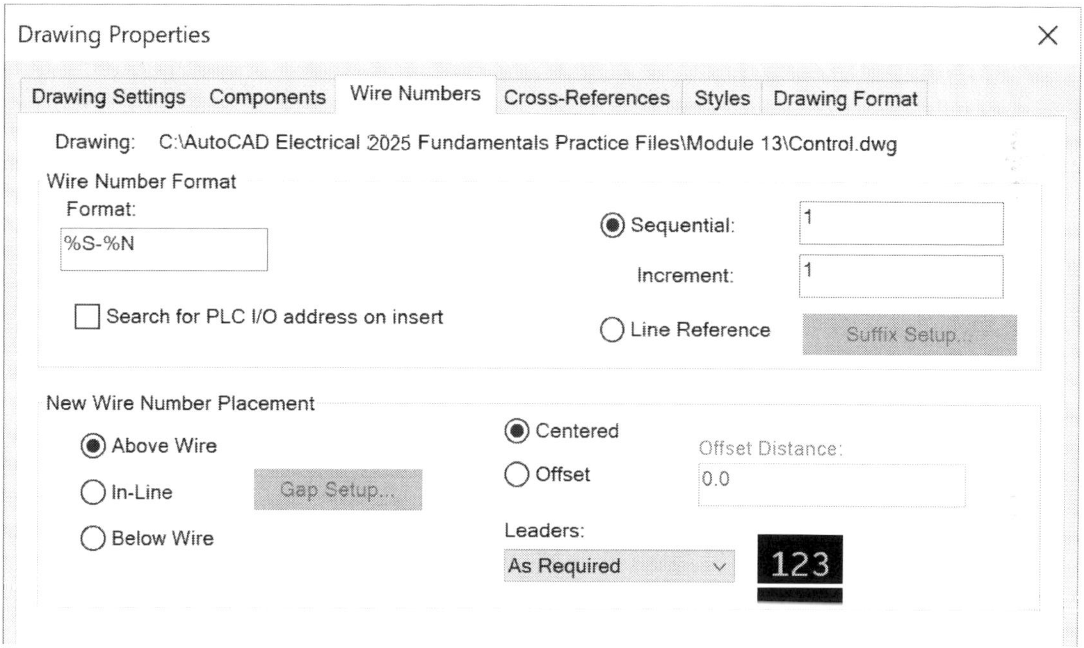

Figure 13–15

Task 1: Change drawing properties.

1. In your practice files folder, in the *Module 13* folder, open the **Module 13** project file.
2. In the *Module 13* project, open **Control.dwg**.
3. Zoom into lines 200 to 207. Note that the wire numbers are line reference based, such as 201, 201A, 201B, etc.
4. In the *Schematic* tab>*Other Tools* panel, click  (Drawing Properties).

5. The *Drawing Properties* dialog box opens. Select the *Wire Numbers* tab. In the *Wire Number Format* area, change the *Format* field to **%S-%N** and select **Sequential**, as shown in Figure 13–16. Click **OK**.

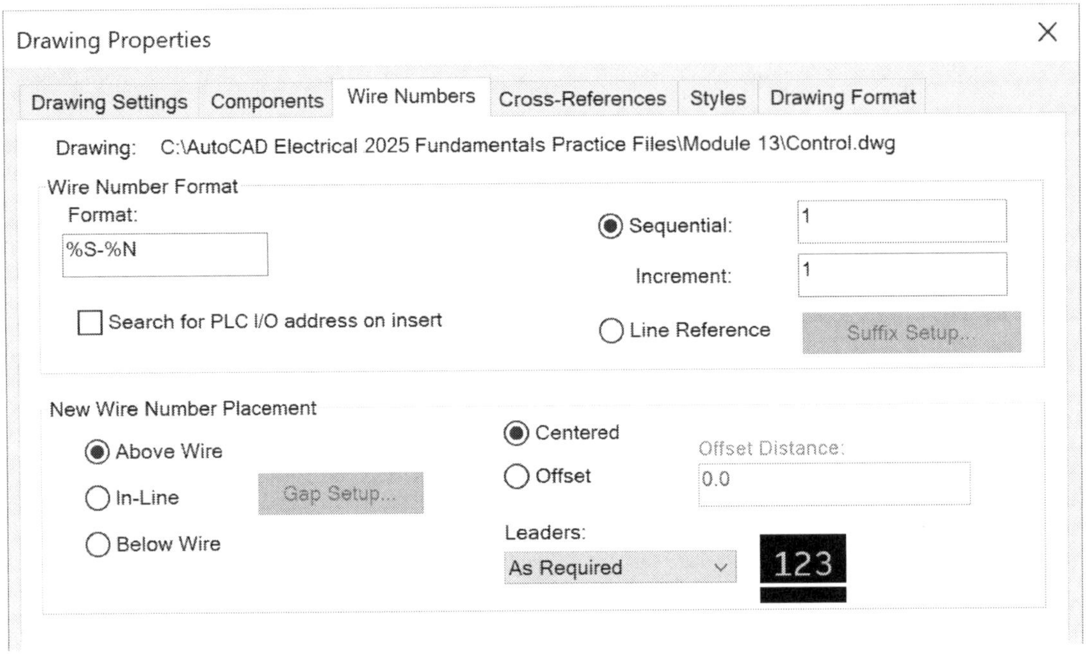

Figure 13–16

6. Click (Wire Numbers). The *Sheet 04 - Wire Tagging* dialog box opens.
7. Click **Drawing-wide**. The wire numbers update to match the new format, such as 04-1, 04-2, etc., as shown in Figure 13–17.

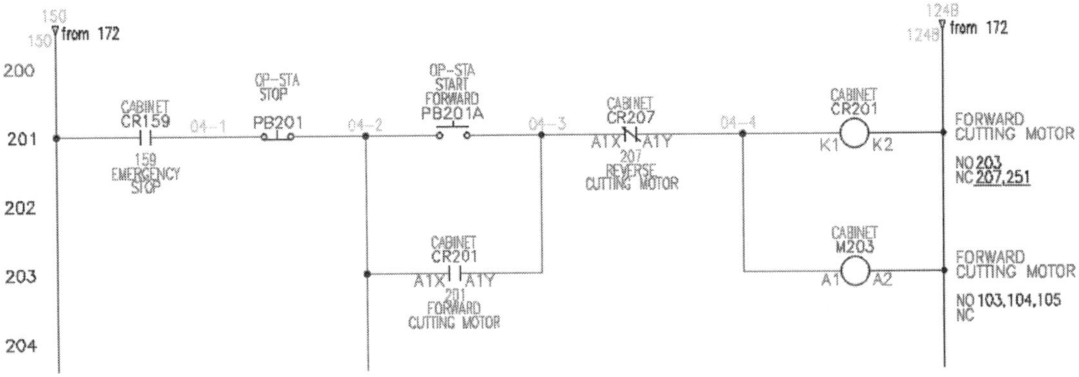

Figure 13–17

Task 2: Change project properties.

1. In the *Project Manager*, right-click on the **Module 13** project and select **Properties**.
2. In the *Project Properties* dialog box that opens, select the *Drawing Format* tab and set the following, as shown in Figure 13–18:
    - *Spacing*: **1**
    - *Width*: **9**

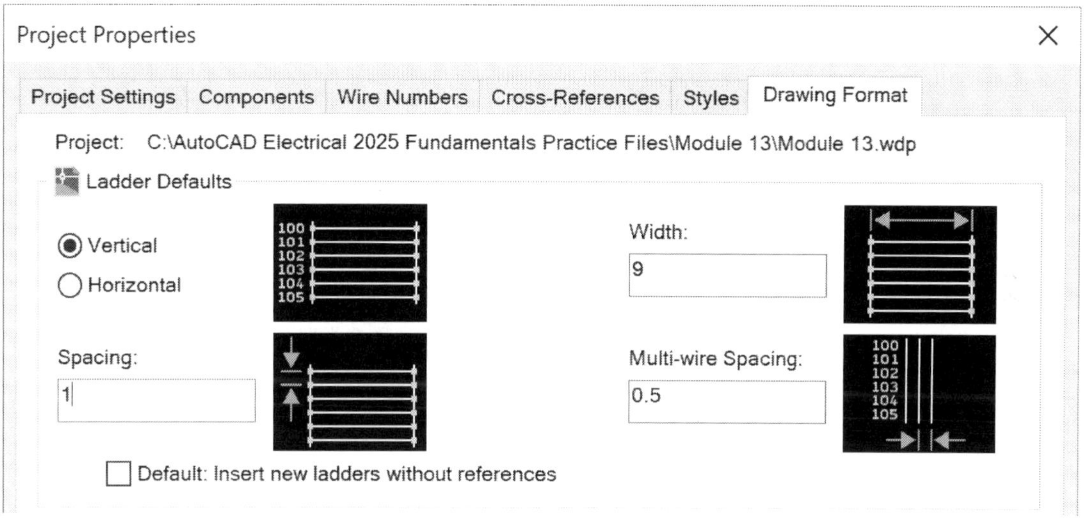

Figure 13–18

3. Click **OK**.

Task 3: Compare project and drawing properties.

1. In the *Schematic* tab>*Other Tools* panel> (Drawing Properties) flyout, click (Settings Compare).

2. The *Compare Drawing and Project Settings: Control.dwg Versus MODULE 13* dialog box opens. Note that the values in the *Drawing* and *Project* columns are different for all of the settings. Hold <Ctrl> and select the **Wire numbering mode**, **Wire number format**, and **Wire layers**, as shown in Figure 13–19. (The rows get selected.) Click **Match Drawing**. Note that the values in *Project* column for the three selected settings are updated to match the drawing values.

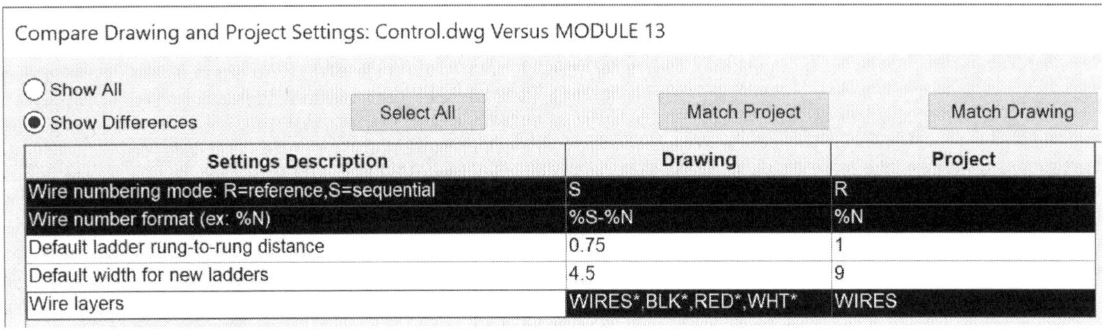

Figure 13–19

3. Select the **Default ladder rung-to-rung distance** and **Default width for new ladders**, as shown in Figure 13–20. Click **Match Project**. The values in the *Drawing* column for the two selected settings are updated to match the project values. All of the **Control.dwg** drawing and **Module 13** project properties are now the same. Click **OK**.

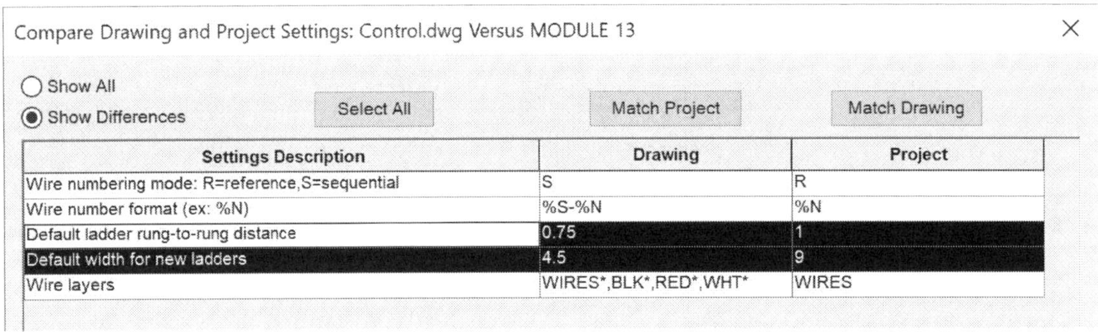

Figure 13–20

Task 4: Create a new drawing.

1. Using the AutoCAD Electrical (New Drawing) command, create a new drawing with the name **Settings**, as shown in Figure 13–21. Verify that the **Electrical_template** is used from your practice files folder and the *Location* path points to the *Module 13* folder, as shown in Figure 13–21. Click **OK-Properties**. In the *Apply Project Default to Drawing Settings* dialog box, click **Yes**.

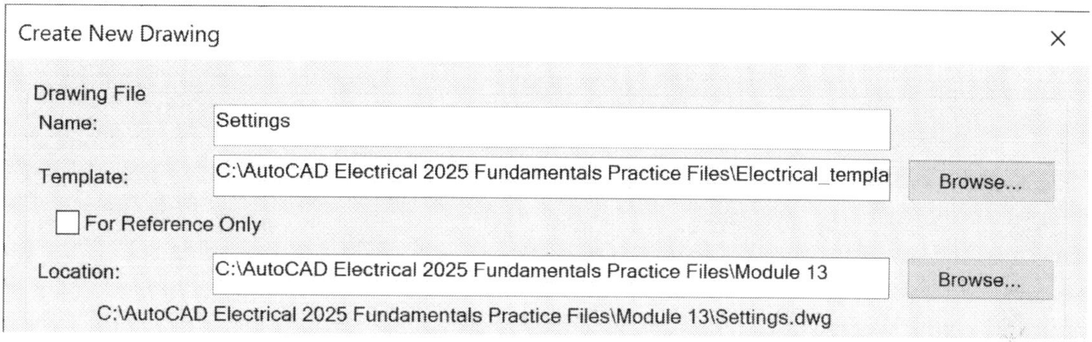

Figure 13–21

2. The *Drawing Properties* dialog box opens. Click the *Drawing Format* tab, as shown in Figure 13–22. The settings match those configured in the Project Properties. Click **OK**.

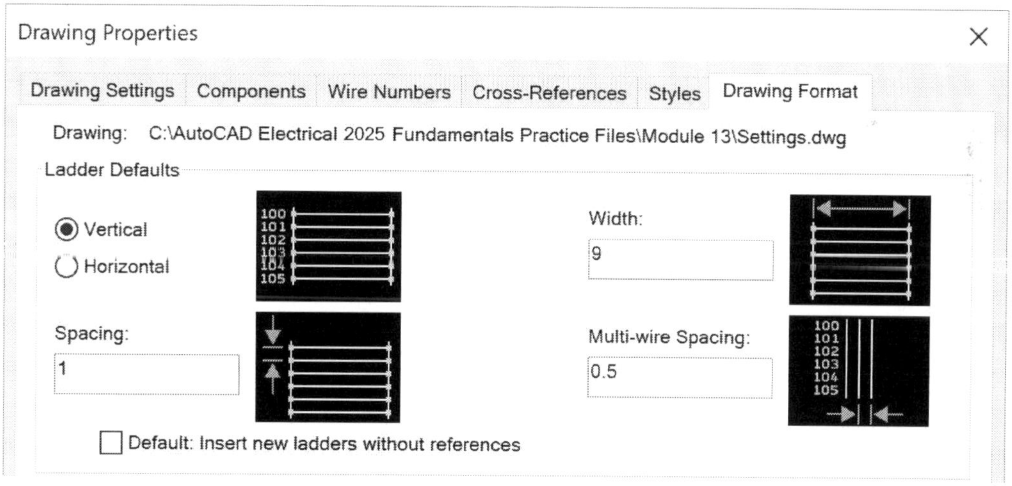

Figure 13–22

3. Save and close **Settings.dwg**.

End of practice

13.4 Template Files

When creating a new file, you are required to select a template file, as shown in Figure 13–23. Template files in the AutoCAD Electrical software function as they do in the base AutoCAD® software. They contain default geometry, blocks, titleblocks, layer information, etc.

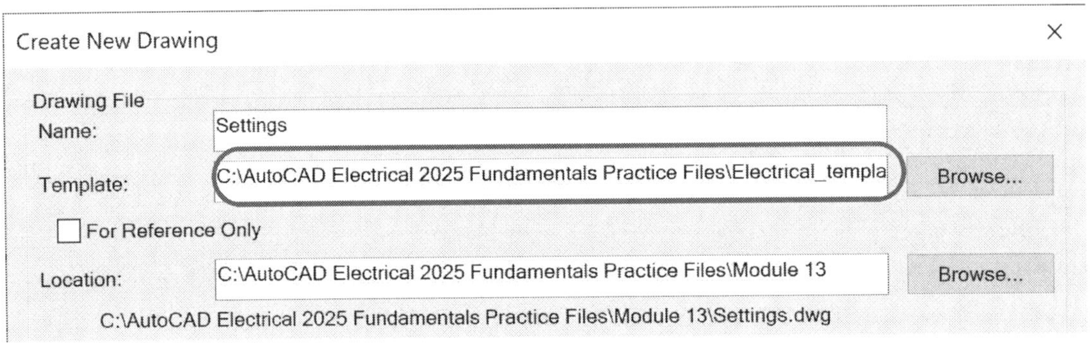

Figure 13–23

How To: Create a Template File

1. Open an existing DWG file or create a new DWG file.
2. Create and configure the required layers.
3. If this is a panel template, configure the panel settings.
4. If this is a schematic template, insert any default ladders.
5. Insert any other default geometry (titleblock, key, etc.).
6. In the Application Menu, select **Save As>Drawing Template**. The *Save Drawing As* dialog box opens.
7. Browse to the folder in which you want to save the template.

8. In the *File name* field, type the template name as shown in Figure 13–24.

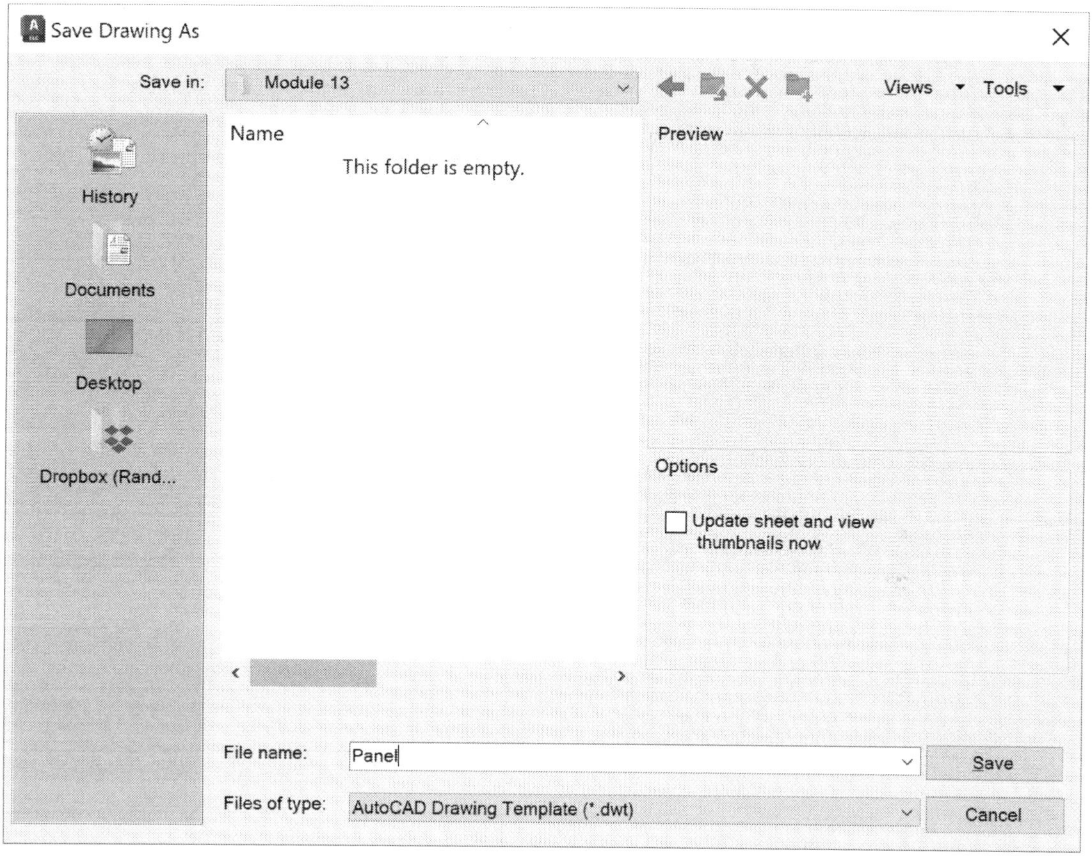

Figure 13–24

9. Click **Save**.

10. The *Template Options* dialog box opens, as shown in Figure 13–25. Enter a description for the template and specify the type of units in the *Measurement* drop-down list. Click **OK**.

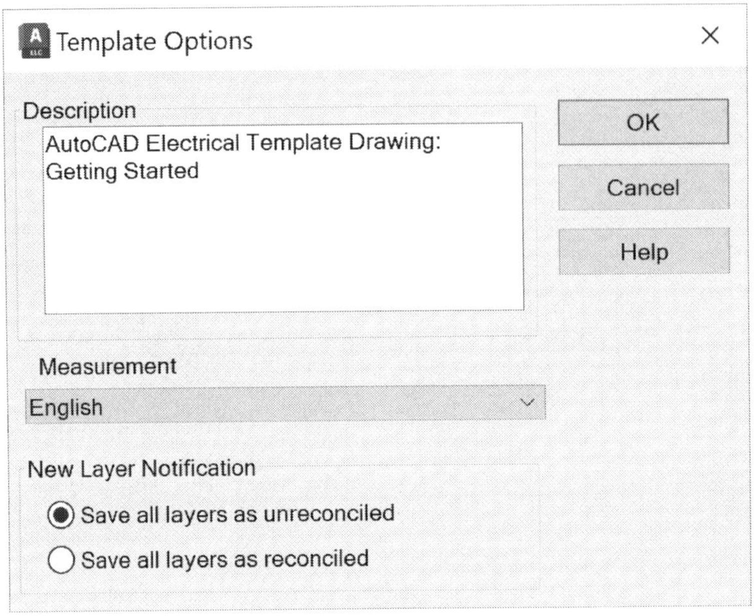

Figure 13–25

- When creating templates, it is recommended that you add and configure layers with the required colors and linetypes.
- Template files have a .DWT file extension.

- You can specify the default template location in the *Options* dialog box, in the *Files* tab, as shown in Figure 13–26. Expand **Template Settings>Drawing Template File Location** and change the path.

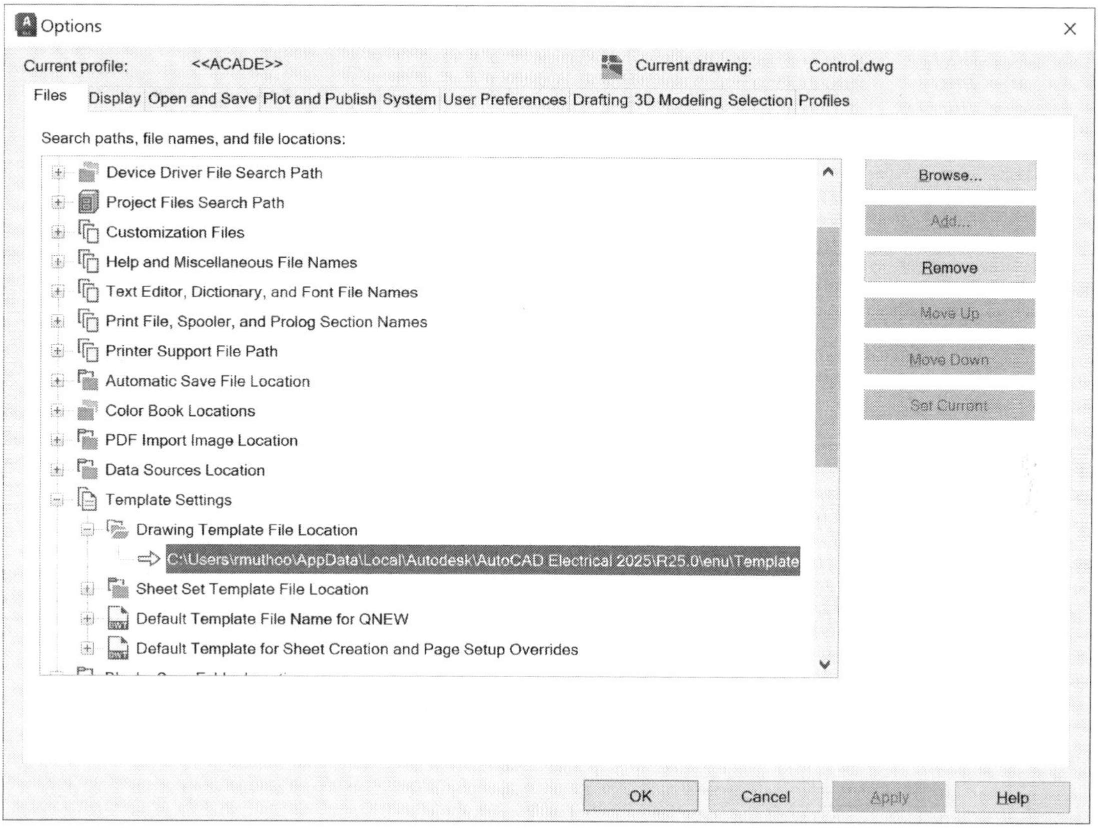

Figure 13–26

Practice 13b
Template File

Practice Objective

- Create and save an AutoCAD Electrical specific template file.

In this practice, you will create a new drawing, configure the panel settings, and insert an enclosure. You will then save the drawing as a template file. Finally, you will use the new template to create a new drawing, as shown in Figure 13–27.

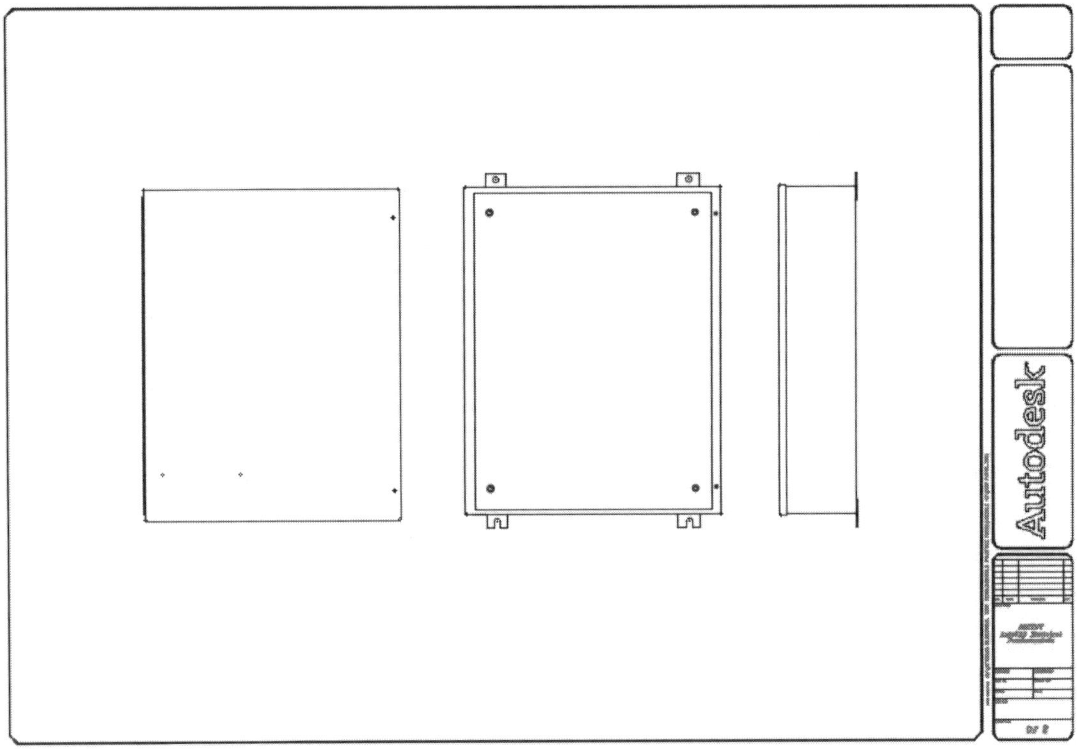

Figure 13–27

Task 1: Create a new drawing, configure settings, and insert an enclosure.

1. If the **Module 13** project is not active, open and activate it now.

2. Create a new drawing using AutoCAD 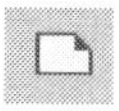 (New) command in the Quick Access Toolbar. For the template, use **ACAD_ELECTRICAL.dwt**, which is provided with the software, as shown in Figure 13–28.

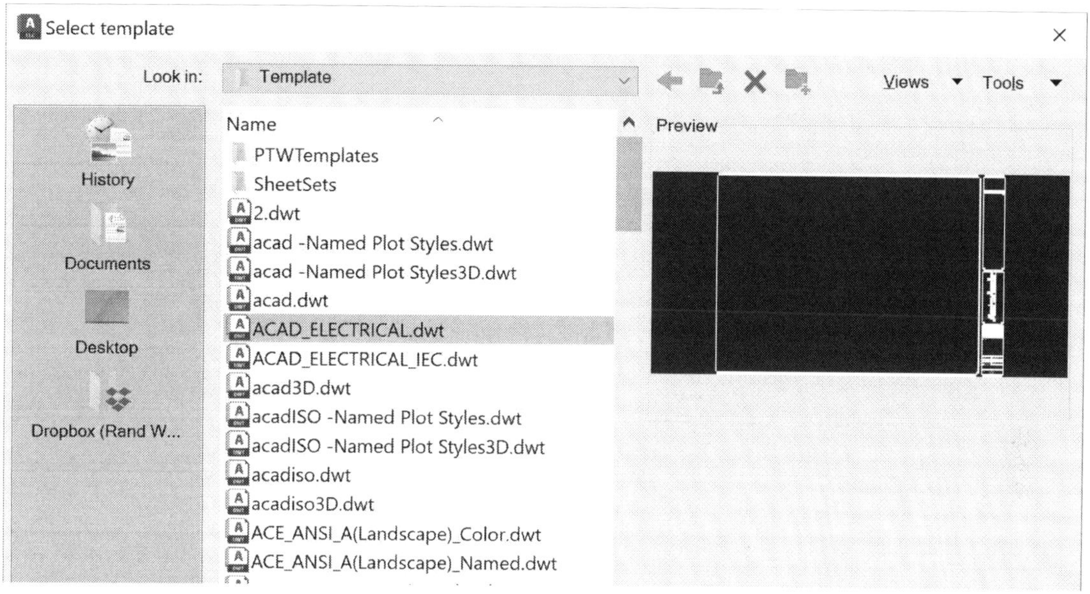

Figure 13–28

3. In the *Panel* tab>*Other Tools* panel, click  (Panel Configuration).
4. The *Alert* dialog box opens, as shown in Figure 13–29. This template file is a new file, so the **WD_PNLM** block must be inserted. Click **OK**.

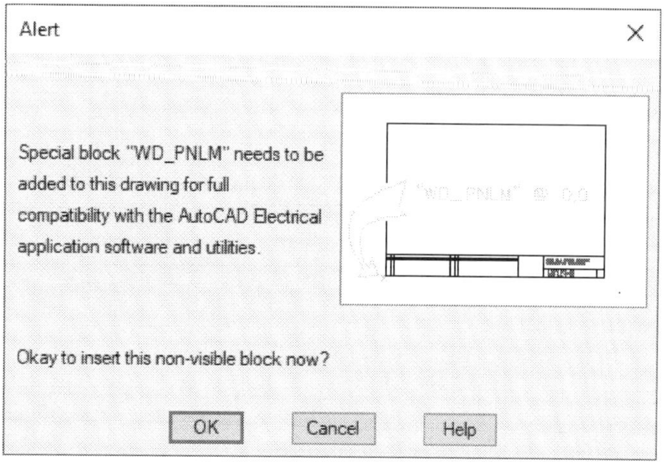

Figure 13–29

5. The *Panel Drawing Configuration and Defaults* dialog box opens. In the *Balloon* area, click **Setup**.
6. The *Panel balloon setup* dialog box opens. In the *Balloon* area, select **Ellipse** as the balloon type (as shown in Figure 13–30) and click **OK**.

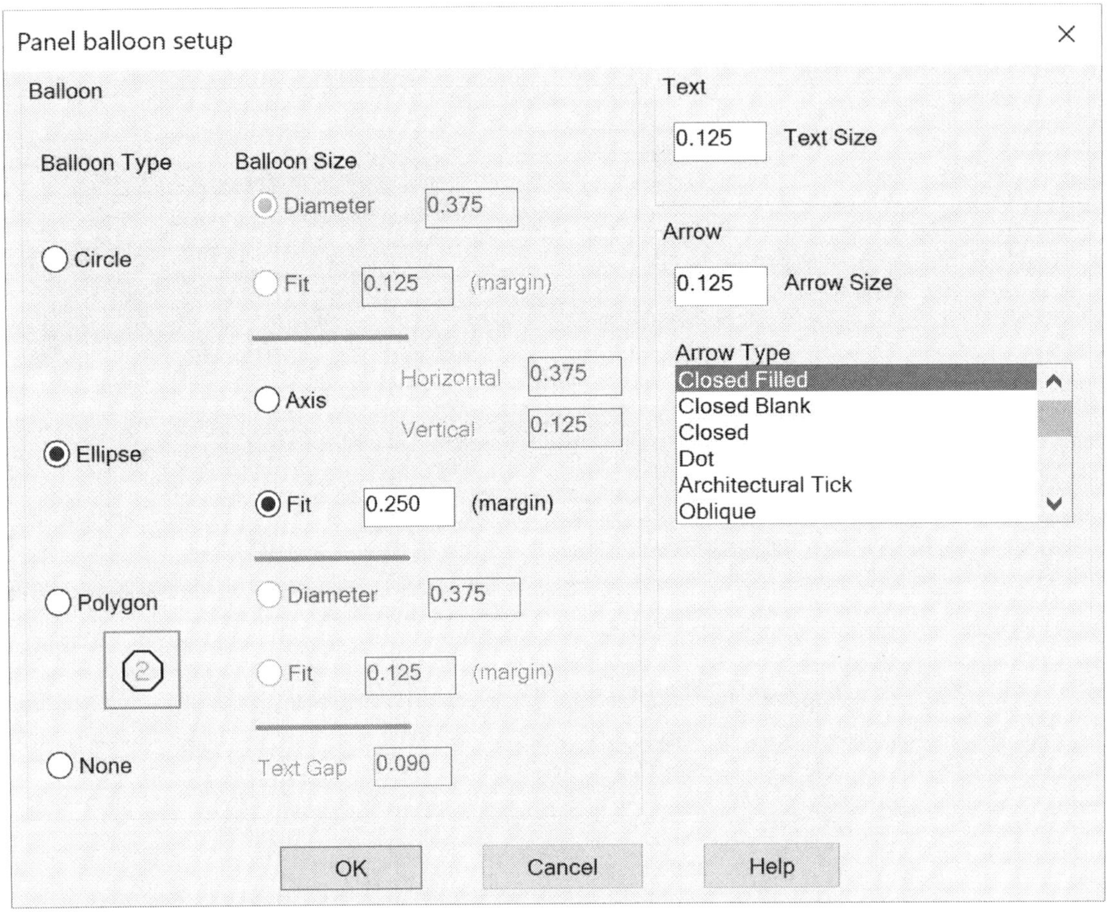

Figure 13–30

7. You are returned to the *Panel Drawing Configuration and Defaults* dialog box. Click **OK**.
8. Scale the titleblock by a factor of **3**.
9. Zoom to the extents of the drawing.

10. Click  (Insert Footprint (Icon Menu)) and insert an enclosure. In the *Footprint* dialog box, in **Choice A**, set the following (use **Catalog lookup** to select the required footprint), as shown in Figure 13–31:

- *Manufacturer*: **HOFFMAN**
- *Catalog*: **A30C24ALP**

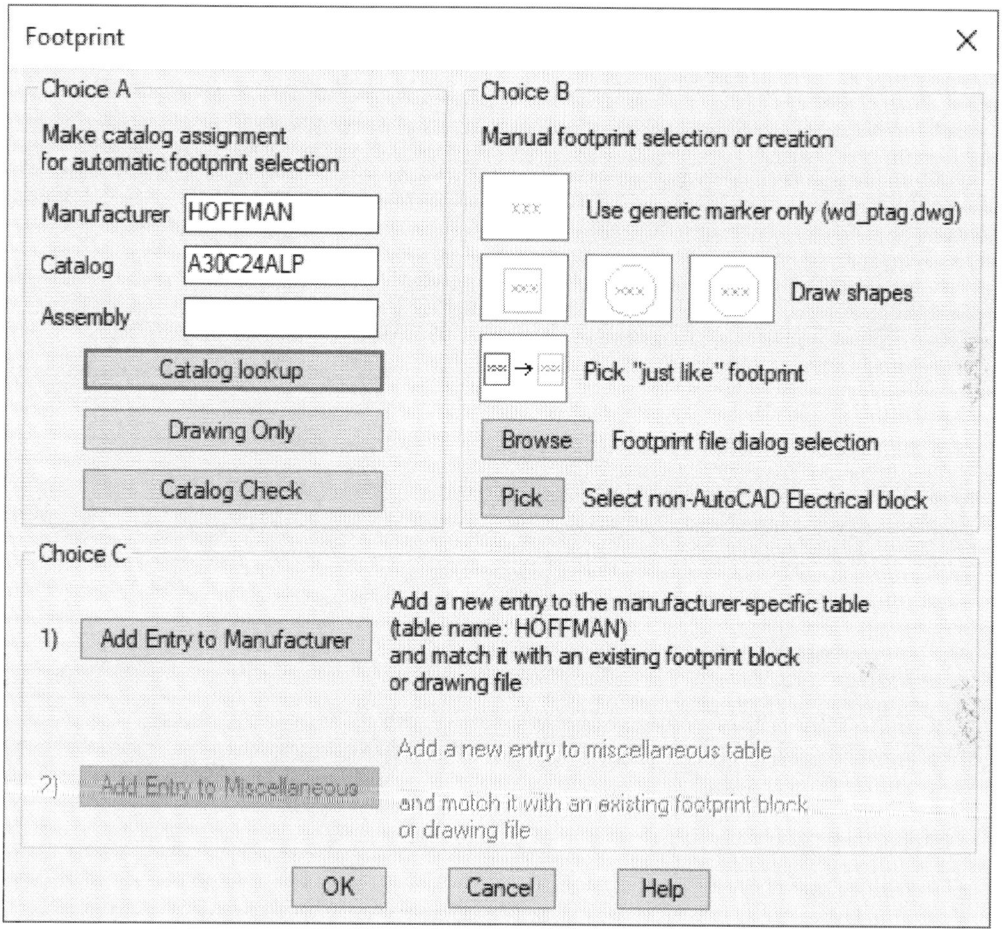

Figure 13–31

11. Click **OK**.

12. Place the enclosure blocks so that they are approximately at the center of the titleblock, as shown in Figure 13–32 (the drawing grid has been toggled off). In the *Panel Layout - Component Insert/Edit* dialog box, click **OK**.

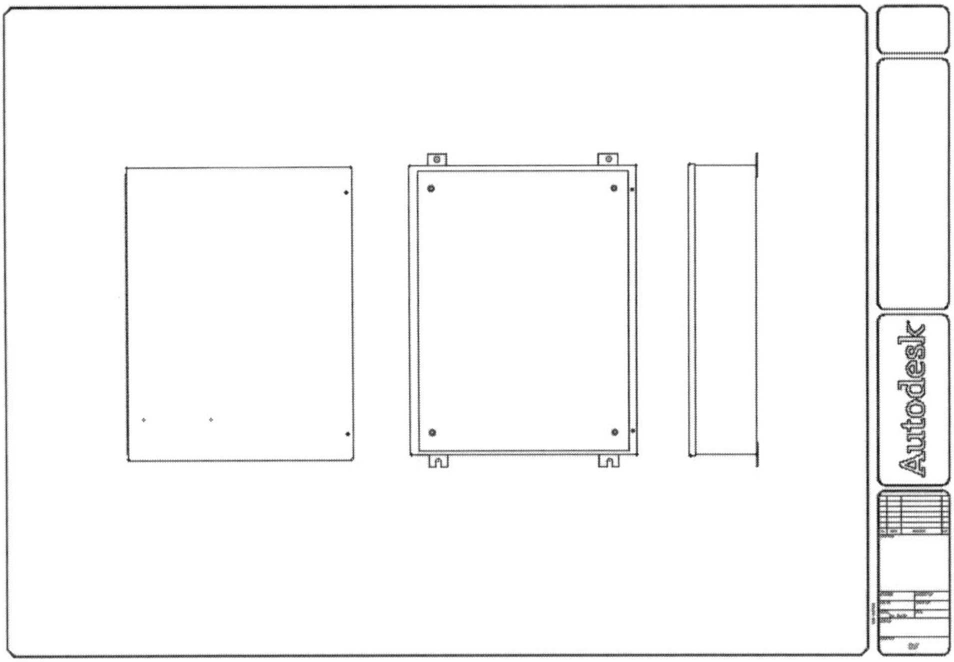

Figure 13–32

Task 2: Save as template file.

1. In the Application Menu, select **Save As>Drawing Template**.
2. The *Save Drawing As* dialog box opens. Browse to the *Module 13* folder in your practice files folder and in the *File name* field, type **Panel**, as shown in Figure 13–33. Click **Save**.

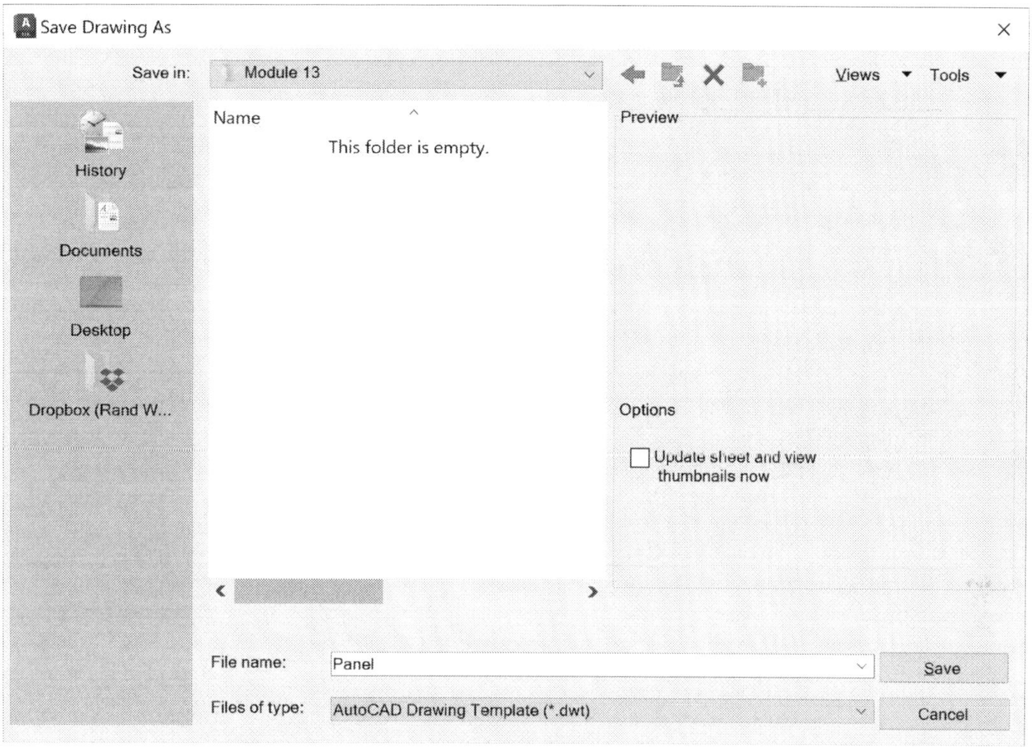

Figure 13–33

3. The *Template Options* dialog box opens. In the *Description* field, type **Panel template for AutoCAD Electrical**, as shown in Figure 13–34. Click **OK**.

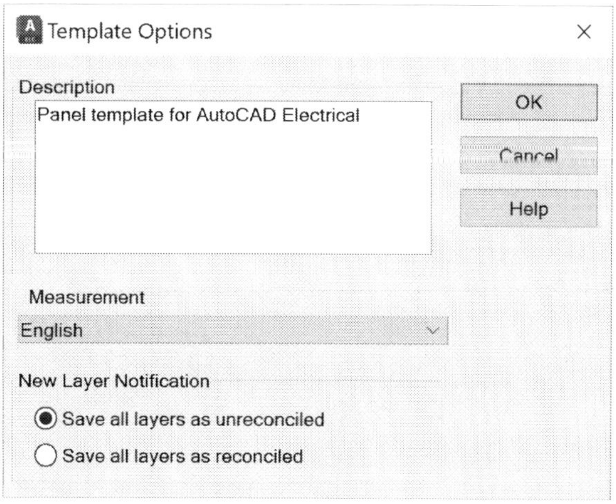

Figure 13–34

4. Close **Panel.dwt**.

Task 3: Create a new drawing using the new template.

1. In the **Module 13** project, open **Operator Station.dwg**.
2. In the *Project Manager*, click  (New Drawing) to create a new drawing.
3. In the *Create New Drawing* dialog box, set *Name* as **New Panel** and for *Template*, use **Browse** and navigate to the *Module 13* folder in your practice files folder. Select **Panel.dwt** and verify that the path is displayed as shown in Figure 13–35. Click **OK**.
   - This is the template that you created in Task 2.

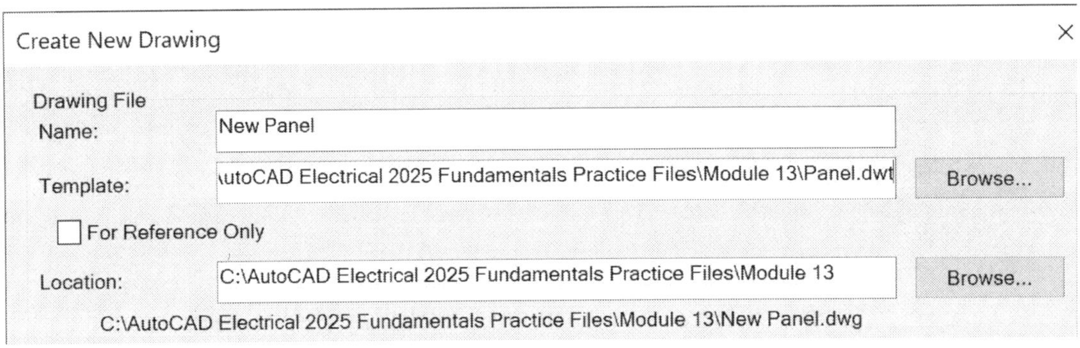

Figure 13–35

4. In the *Apply Project Defaults to Drawing Settings* dialog box, click **Yes**.
   - The **New Panel** drawing is created and opened. It has the title block and the enclosures already inserted, as shown in Figure 13–36.

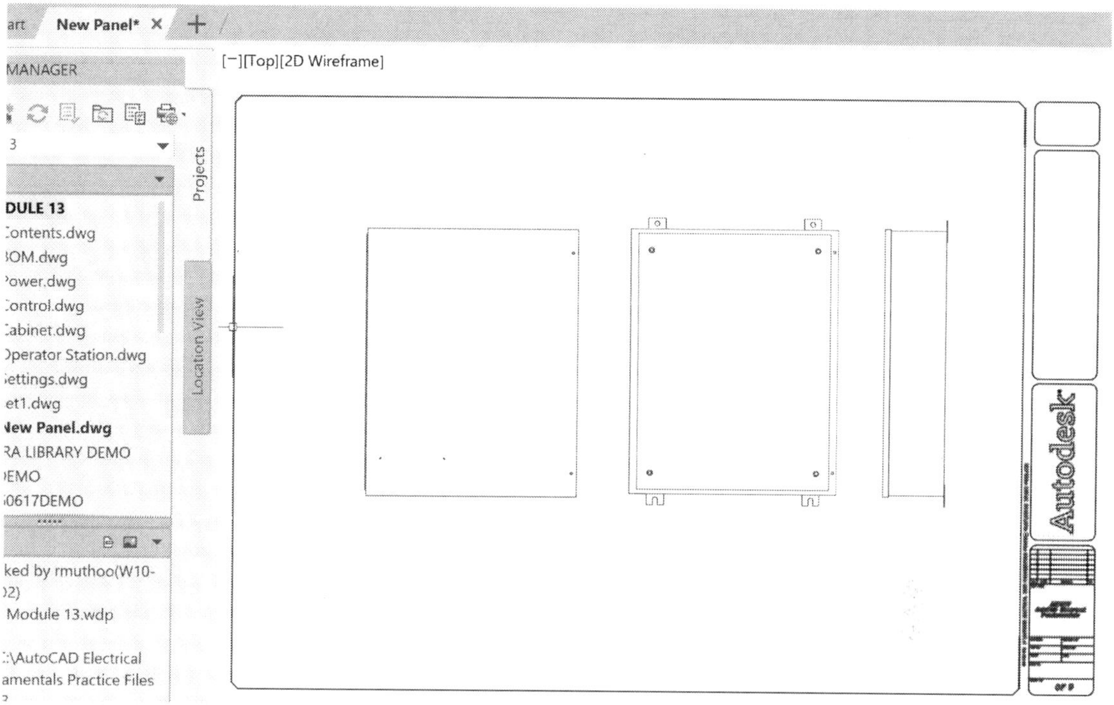

Figure 13–36

5. In the *Panel* tab>*Other Tools* panel, click (Panel Configuration).
   - The *Panel Drawing Configuration and Defaults* dialog box opens. The *Balloon shape* is set to **Ellipse** and the *Alert* dialog box prompting you to insert **WD_PNLM** did not open. This is because you had saved those settings while creating the template file.
6. In the *Panel Drawing Configuration and Defaults* dialog box, click **OK**.
7. Save and close **New Panel.dwg**.

End of practice

13.5 Sharing Symbol Libraries and Databases

If multiple users are using the AutoCAD Electrical software, you can setup the software to share the library symbols and databases to ensure that everyone has the same information.

- Copy the data to a shared location on the network using Windows Explorer or another tool for everyone to access.
- It is recommended that you also backup the data and then remove it from the local drive. This removal ensures that you are not using the local data.

You then need to change the support paths in the AutoCAD Electrical software to point to the new path. This adjustment might include changing the Icon Menu path for the **Schematic** and **Panel** menus, updating the AutoCAD support paths, or changing the **wd.env** file.

- The **wd.env** file is a text file that lists the default support paths for the AutoCAD Electrical software. It can be edited with any text editor and contains comments describing the function of the different information.
- See *About Setting Up AutoCAD Electrical for Multiple Users* in the AutoCAD Electrical Help system for a detailed list of the files to move and how to update the required AutoCAD Electrical support paths.

You can also use the **Network Install Wizard (NIW)** to set up the shared libraries and databases. This setup can be done even if you have standalone licenses, but must be done before you install the AutoCAD Electrical software on the workstations. Otherwise, you must share the data using the method described above.

How To: Set Up AutoCAD Electrical Software to Share Library Files and Databases

1. Back up your data.
2. Copy the required files to the shared location using Windows Explorer.
3. Update the required support paths in the AutoCAD Electrical software.
4. Remove the data from the local drive.

Chapter Review Questions

1. If the Drawing Properties have different values than the Project Properties, which settings are used?
   a. Drawing Properties
   b. Project Properties

2. Which command enables you to compare the values in Drawing Properties to the defaults in Project Properties?
   a. Edit Settings
   b. Edit Properties
   c. Settings Compare
   d. Properties Compare

3. What does %F represent in the *Drawing Properties* or *Project Properties* dialog boxes?
   a. Sheet Number
   b. Family Code
   c. File Code
   d. Reference Number

4. You can change the default location of the template files.
   a. True
   b. False

5. What is the function of the **wd.env** file?
   a. A text file that lists support paths for the AutoCAD Electrical software.
   b. A text file that lists the drawings for a project.
   c. A text file that lists the settings for a project.
   d. A text file that lists the shared library files and databases for the AutoCAD Electrical software

Command Summary

Button	Command	Location
	**Drawing Properties**	• **Ribbon:** *Schematic* tab>*Other Tools* panel
	**Panel Configuration**	• **Ribbon:** *Panel* tab>*Other Tools* panel
NA	**Project Properties**	• **Project Manager:** (*shortcut menu*)
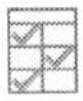	**Settings Compare**	• **Ribbon:** *Schematic* tab>*Other Tools* panel

Chapter 14

Drawing Update Tools

Working on multiple drawings in a project saves time and increases the efficiency of designing in the software. Knowledge of project-based commands, such as the Project-Wide Update/Retag, Project-Wide Utilities, Plot Project, Copy Project, and Swap/Update Block, enables you to perform a variety of actions on multiple drawings. Learning to export data from drawings to a spreadsheet and then updating drawings from that spreadsheet also makes it easier to design and create electrical drawings.

Learning Objectives

- Update selected drawings in a project.
- Reset data in project drawings.
- Plot all of the drawings or a select group of drawings in a single command.
- Export data from the drawings to a file.
- Modify component and wire data in drawings from an external file.
- Copy a project file to a new directory and project name.
- Replace a component symbol block with a different block.
- Mark a drawing and then verify whether it was modified since it was last marked.

14.1 Project-Wide Update/Retag

The **Project-Wide Update/Retag** command updates selected drawings in a project. This command is useful for updating many settings in multiple drawings at once. For example, you can re-sequence ladders, retag components, renumber wires, or change the drawing settings.

Project-Wide Update/Retag

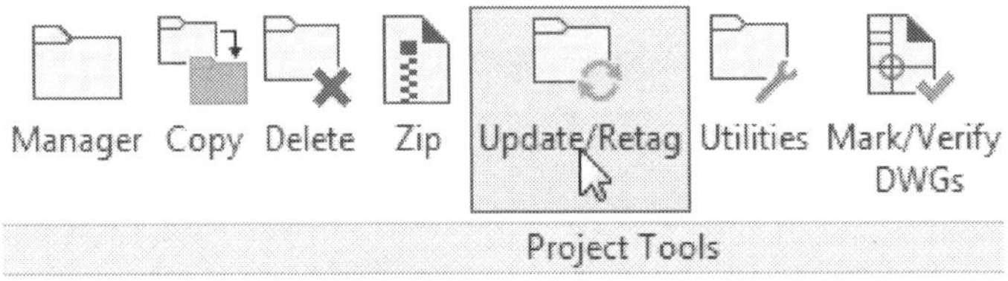

Ribbon: *Project* tab>*Project Tools* panel

Command Prompt: aeprojupdate

How To: Use the Project-Wide Update/Retag Command

1. Start the Project-Wide **Update/Retag** command. The *Project-Wide Update or Retag* dialog box opens.
2. Select the options for the information you want to update.
3. If required, use **Setup** to configure the options for the selected options.
4. Click **OK**. The *Select Drawings to Process* dialog box opens.
5. Select the drawings to process. Click **OK**.

- Verify that all appropriate options have been selected when updating the information. If you update the ladder reference numbers, you must also select the options to update component tags and wire numbers. Otherwise, they are not updated and do not match the ladder reference numbers.

The *Project-Wide Update or Retag* dialog box, shown in Figure 14–1, contains the options for the type of objects to update.

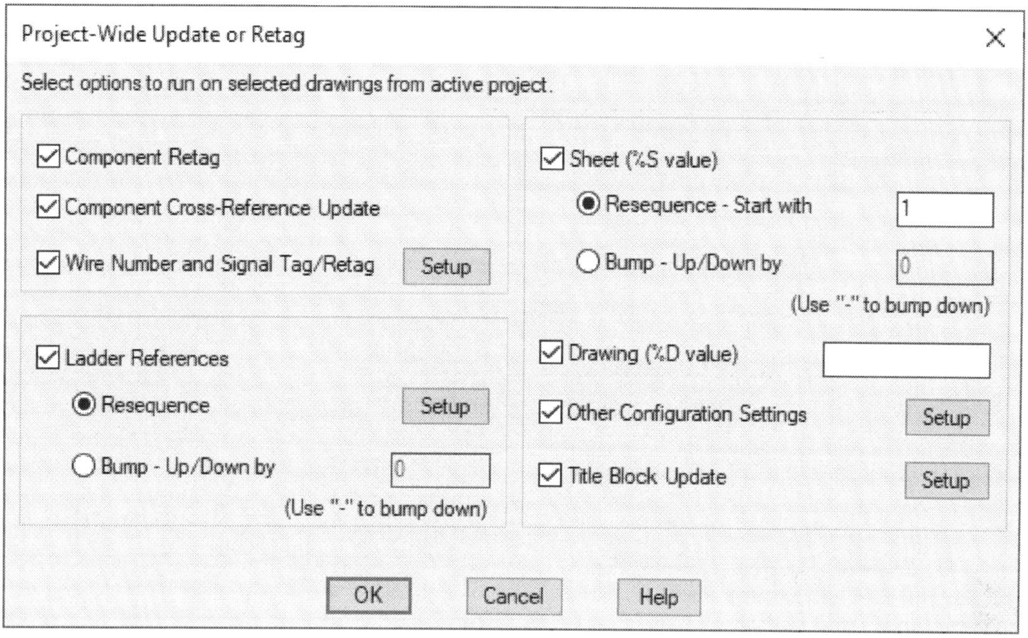

Figure 14–1

Component Retag	Retags all components that are not marked as fixed.
Component Cross-Reference Update	Updates cross-referencing on components.
Wire Number and Signal Tag/ Retag	Updates all wire numbers that are not marked as fixed and updates the signal symbols. Click **Setup** to configure the new tagging.
Ladder Reference	Renumbers the ladders. Click **Setup** to input the first reference number and value to skip between drawings.
Sheet (%S value)	Updates the sheet number parameter. Select to re-sequence or add a value to each sheet number.
Drawing (%D value)	Updates the drawing parameter with the specified value.
Other Configuration Settings	Updates drawing settings relating to formatting for wire numbers, component tags, and cross-referencing. Click **Setup** to select which settings to update and to input new formatting.
Title Block Update	Updates the attributes in the titleblock that are mapped to AutoCAD® Electrical parameters. Click **Setup** to select which parameters to update.

The *Wire Tagging (Project-wide)* dialog box (shown in Figure 14–2) opens when you use **Setup** for **Wire Number and Signal Tag/Retag**.

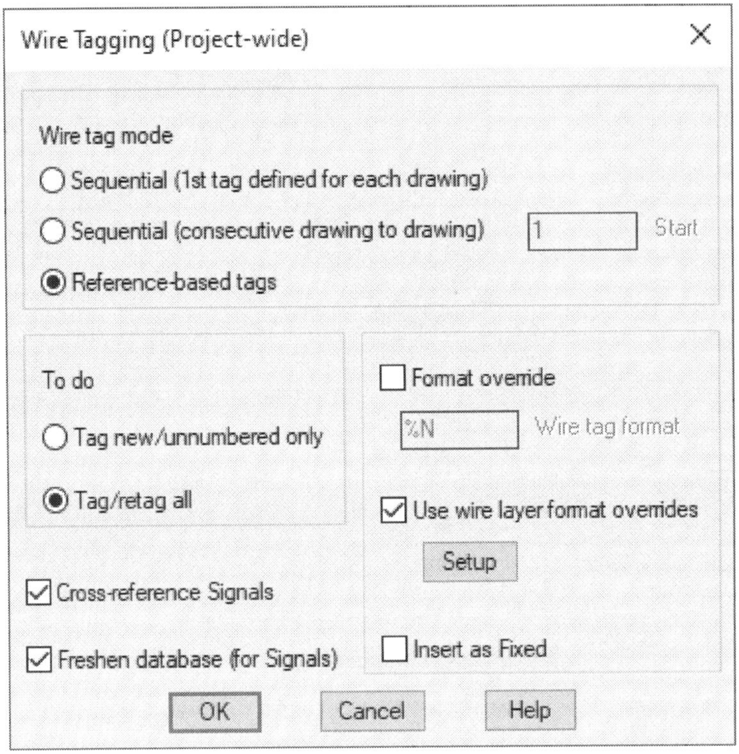

Figure 14–2

Wire tag mode	Configures the method to use for wire numbers.
To do	Controls which wires to number.
Cross-reference Signals	Updates the cross-reference information on signal symbols (source and destination arrows).
Freshen database (for Signals)	Updates the database with source and destination signal information.
Format override	Overrides the default wire number format.
Use wire layer format overrides	Setup overrides for the default wire layer.
Insert as Fixed	Inserts wire numbers as fixed (they do not update automatically).

The *Renumber Ladders* dialog box (shown in Figure 14–3) opens when you use **Setup** for **Ladder References**.

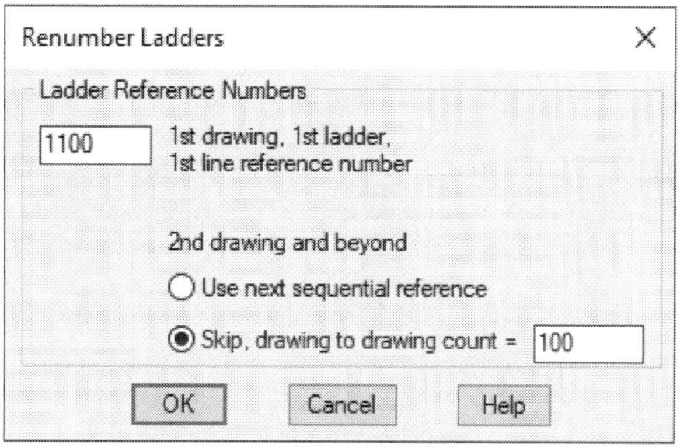

Figure 14–3

1st line reference number	Specifies the reference number for the first line of the ladder in the first drawing.
2nd drawing and beyond	Specifies what to do for the first reference number in each successive drawing.

The *Change Each Drawing's Settings – Project-wide* dialog box (shown in Figure 14–4) opens when you use **Setup** for **Other Configuration Settings**.

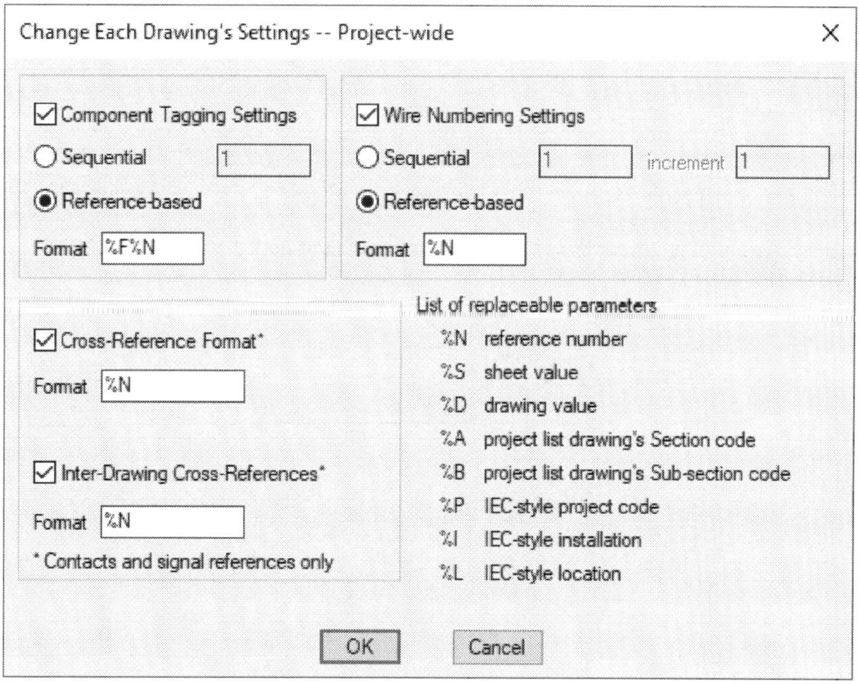

Figure 14–4

Component Tagging Settings	Configures new settings for component tags.
Cross-Reference Format	Configures the format for cross-reference information.
Inter-Drawing Cross-References	Configures the information for inter-drawing cross-reference information.
Wire Numbering Settings	Configures new settings for the wire numbers.

The *Update Title Block* dialog box (shown in Figure 14–5) opens when you use **Setup** for **Title Block Update**.

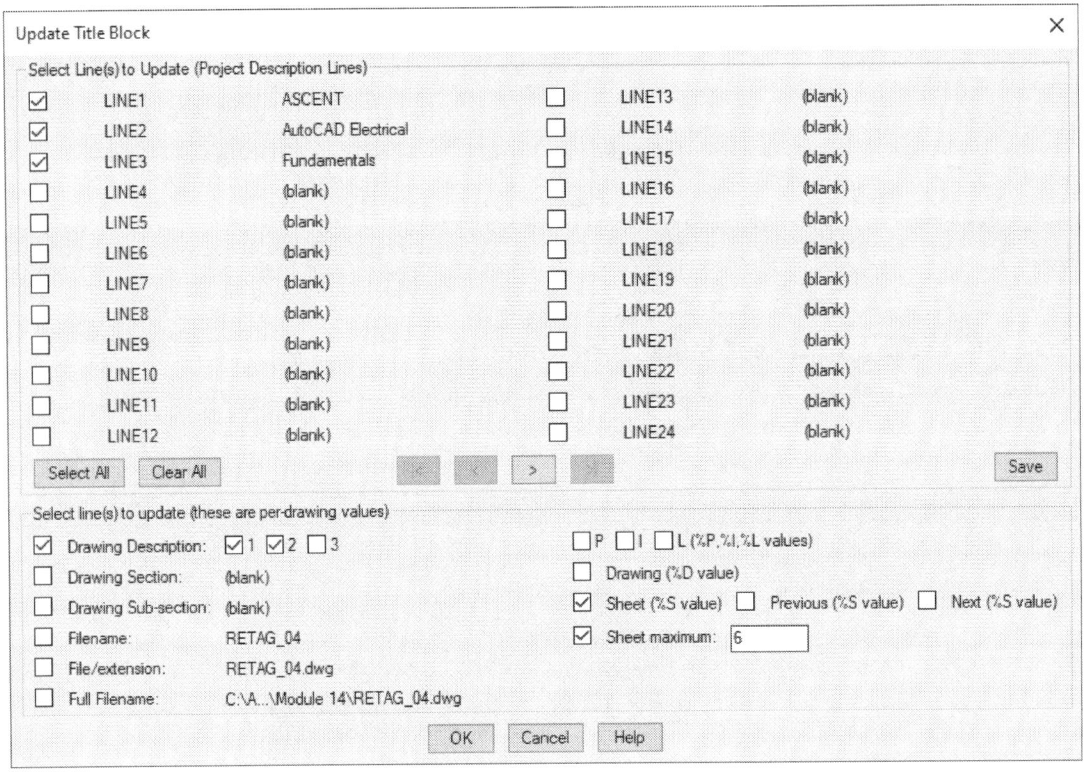

Figure 14–5

Select Line(s) to Update (Project Description Lines)	Selects which descriptions to update in the titleblock. These items are the descriptions from the project file.
Select line(s) to update (these are per-drawing values)	Selects which properties to update in the titleblock. These items are the properties for each drawing.

14.2 Project-Wide Utilities

The **Project-Wide Utilities** command is used to reset or remove data in AutoCAD Electrical project drawings. This removal includes wire numbers, signal wires, component tags, and other data.

Project-Wide Utilities

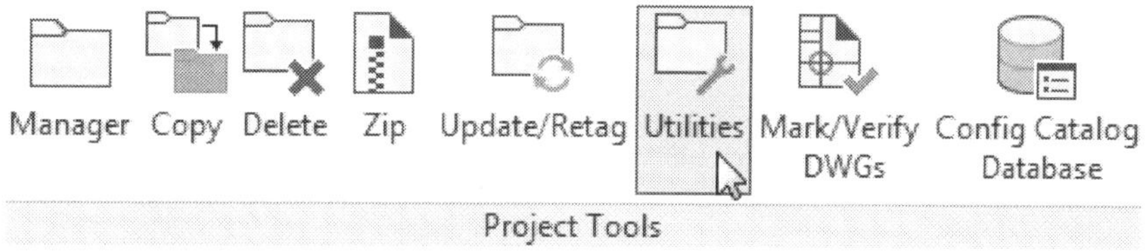

Ribbon: *Project* tab>*Project Tools* panel

Command Prompt: aeutilities

How To: Use the Project-Wide Utilities Command

1. Start the **Project-Wide Utilities** command. The *Project-Wide Utilities* dialog box opens.
2. Select the options for the information you want to update.
3. If required, use **Setup** to configure the options for the selected information.
4. Click **OK**. The *Select Drawings to Process* dialog box opens.
5. Select the drawings to process. Click **OK**.

The *Project-Wide Utilities* dialog box (shown in Figure 14–6) contains various options for configuring the reset or removal of data.

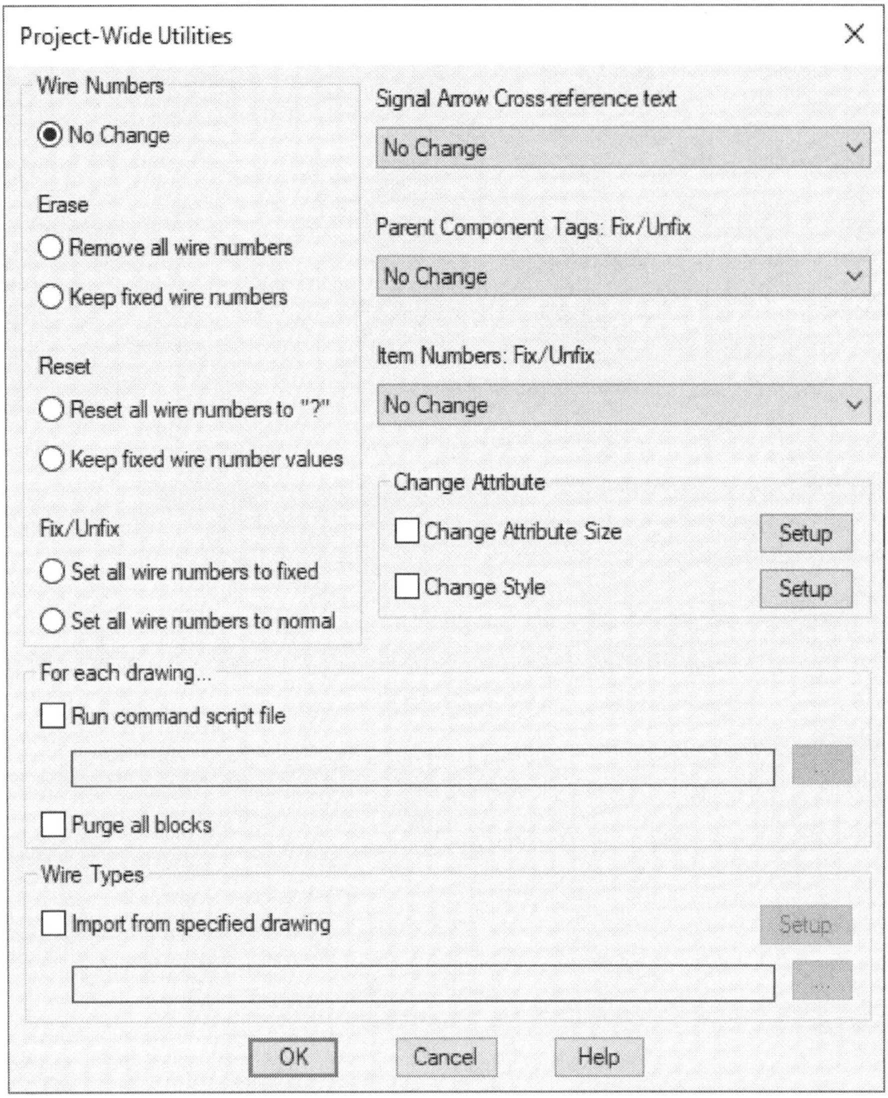

Figure 14–6

Wire Numbers	Select a single option for all wire numbers: • **No Change:** Leaves all wire numbers as they are. • **Erase:** Erases all wire numbers from selected drawings. Select to erase all or leave only numbers marked as fixed. • **Reset:** Clears all wire number values, but leaves the attributes in the drawing. Select to set all wire number attributes to ? or leave any numbers marked as fixed. • **Fix/Unfix:** Resets the *fixed* attribute of all wire numbers. Select to set all wire numbers to either fixed or normal.
Signal Arrow Cross-reference text	Removes all cross-reference text from signal arrows.
Parent Component Tags	Resets the *fixed* attribute for parent symbols. Select to set all Parent Component Tags to either fixed or normal.
Item Numbers	Resets the *fixed* attribute for panel components. Select it to set all Item Numbers to be either fixed or normal.
Change Attribute	Changes the attribute size and/or style in each drawing. Setup's specify which specific attributes to update and which styles to use.
For each drawing...	Select to run a user-defined script on each drawing or to purge all unused blocks from each drawing.
Wire Types	Imports wire types from another drawing. Select options if wire types already exist (overwrite or update color and linetype).

Practice 14a
Project-Wide Update/Retag and Utilities

Practice Objectives

- Update/retag all of the component and wire data.
- Reset all of the component tags to their normal state.

In this practice, you will use the **Project-Wide Update/Retag** command to change the ladder reference numbers on all drawings in a project. You will then edit a component to set its tag to **fixed**. Next, you will use the **Project-Wide Update/Retag** command to update all component tags and wire numbers. Finally, you will use the **Project-Wide Utilities** command to set all component tags to **normal** and then update all component tags. The final circuit will display as shown in Figure 14–7.

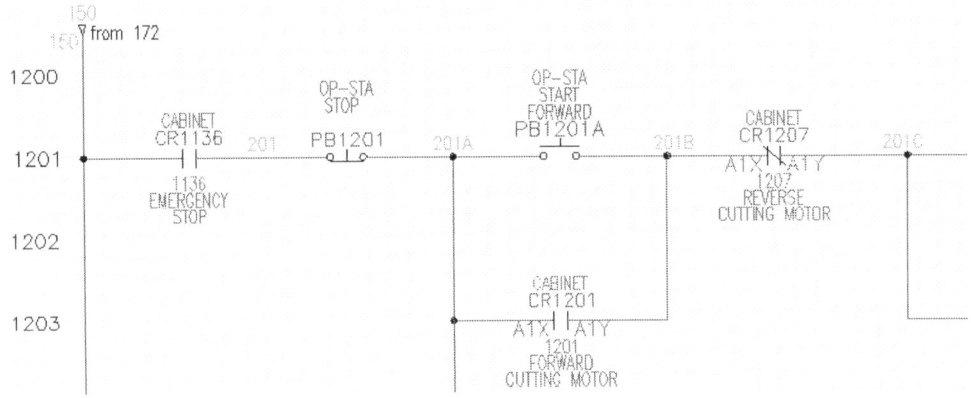

Figure 14–7

Task 1: Update ladder reference numbers.

1. In your practice files folder, in the *Module 14* folder, open the **RETAG.wdp** project file.
2. In the **RETAG** project, open **RETAG_03.dwg**. Note that all ladder reference numbers, component tags, and wire numbers are based on three digits starting at 100.
3. Click (Next Drawing) to open the next drawing in the project list (**RETAG_04.dwg**). Note that the reference numbers, component tags, and wire numbers start at 200 and are based on three digit numbers.
4. In the *Project* tab>*Project Tools* panel, click (Update/Retag).
5. The *Project-Wide Update or Retag* dialog box opens. Select **Ladder References**. Next to **Resequence**, click **Setup**.

6. The *Renumber Ladders* dialog box opens. Set *1st drawing, 1st ladder* to **1100**. Select **Skip, drawing to drawing count =** and in the field, type **100**, as shown in Figure 14–8. Click **OK**.

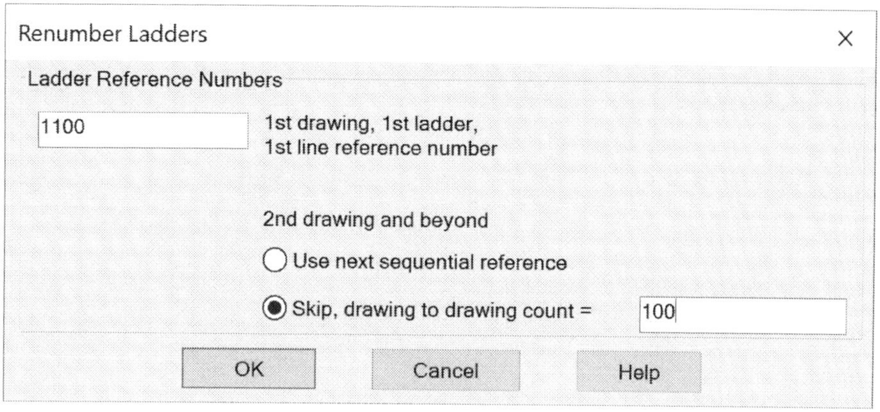

Figure 14–8

7. You are returned to the *Project-Wide Update or Retag* dialog box. Verify that only **Ladder References** and **Resequence** are still selected and that all of the other checkboxes are cleared. Click **OK**.

8. The *Select Drawings to Process* dialog box opens. Select **RETAG_03.dwg** through **RETAG_06.dwg** and click **Process**. Note that the four selected drawings are moved to the lower portion of the dialog box, as shown in Figure 14–9. Click **OK**.

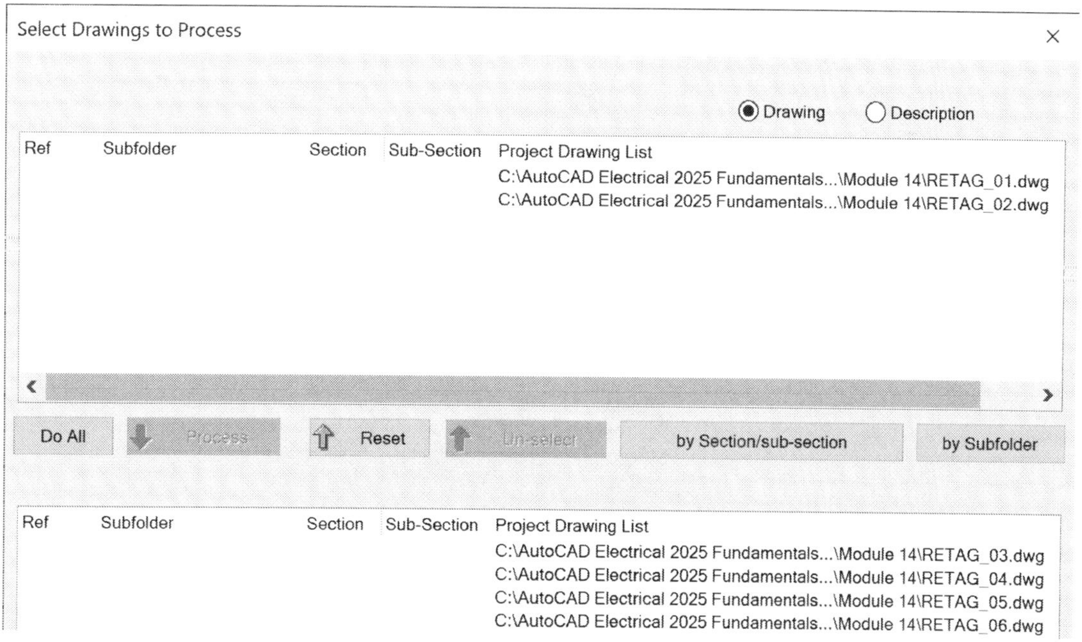

Figure 14–9

9. When the command is complete, all ladder reference numbers have been updated (starting from 1200), but the component tags and wire numbers have not, as shown in Figure 14–10. They are omitted because you did not select these options in the *Project-Wide Update or Retag* dialog box.

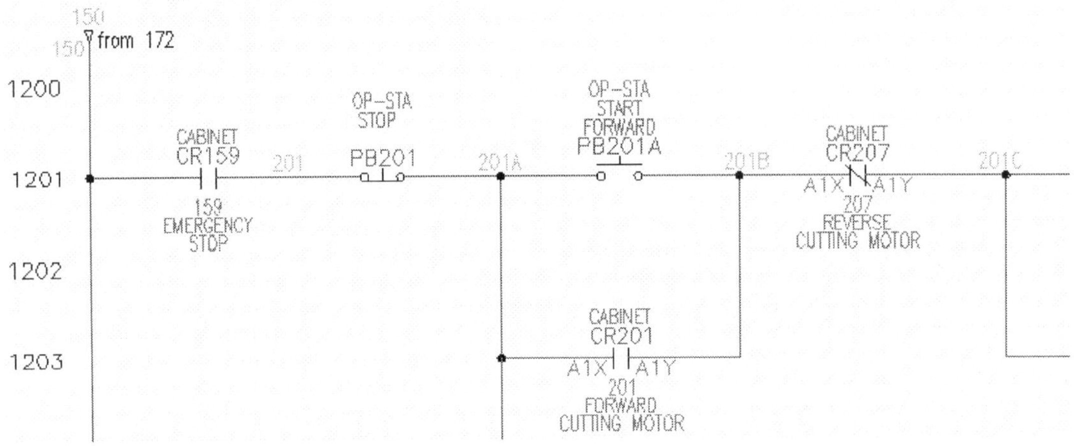

Figure 14–10

Task 2: Retag components and update wire numbers.

1. Edit PB201. Change the *Component Tag* to **PB201-STOP**. Select the **fixed** option (as shown in Figure 14–11), and click **OK**.

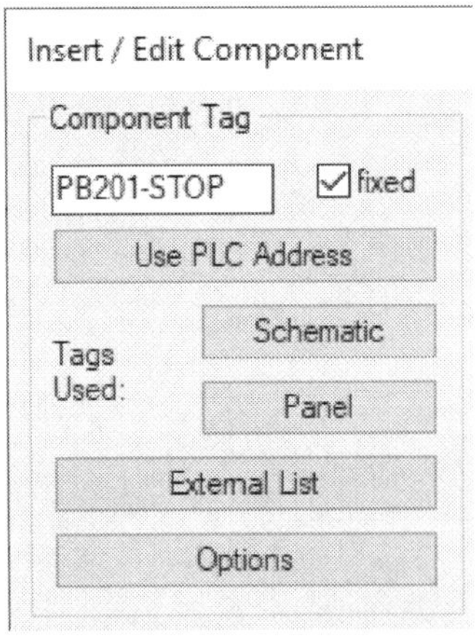

Figure 14–11

2. Update and save the drawings. Note that *PB201* has been updated to **PB201-STOP**.

3. In the *Project* tab>*Project Tools* panel, click  (Update/Retag).

4. The *Project-Wide Update or Retag* dialog box opens. Select the **Component Retag**, **Component Cross-Reference Update**, and **Wire Number and Signal Tag/Retag** options. Clear the **Ladder References** option as shown in Figure 14–12, and click **OK**.

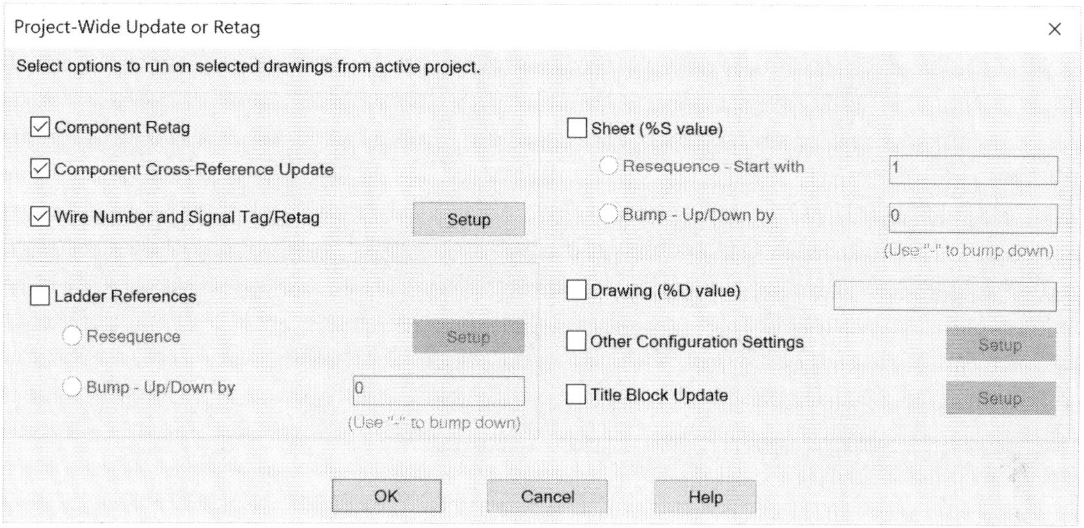

Figure 14–12

5. The *Select Drawing to Process* dialog box opens. Click **Do All** and click **OK**.
6. When the command has completed, note that all the components and wire numbers are updated, as shown in Figure 14–13. However, **PB201-STOP** is not updated because you marked this component tag as **fixed**.
   - You can update ladder reference numbers, component tags, and wire numbers in one command. For demonstration purposes, the process is separated in this practice.

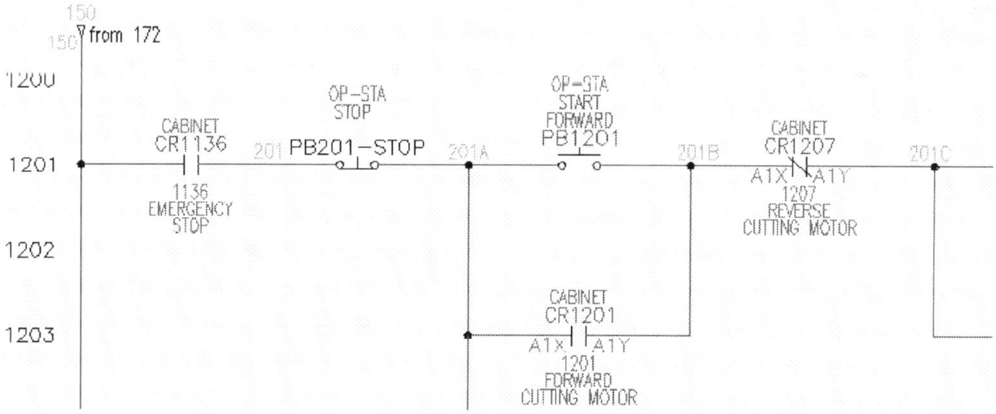

Figure 14–13

Task 3: Set component tags to normal.

1. In the *Project* tab>*Project Tools* panel, click (Project-Wide Utilities).
2. The *Project-Wide Utilities* dialog box opens. For the *Parent Component Tags: Fix/Unfix* field, select **Set all to normal** (as shown in Figure 14–14) and click **OK**.

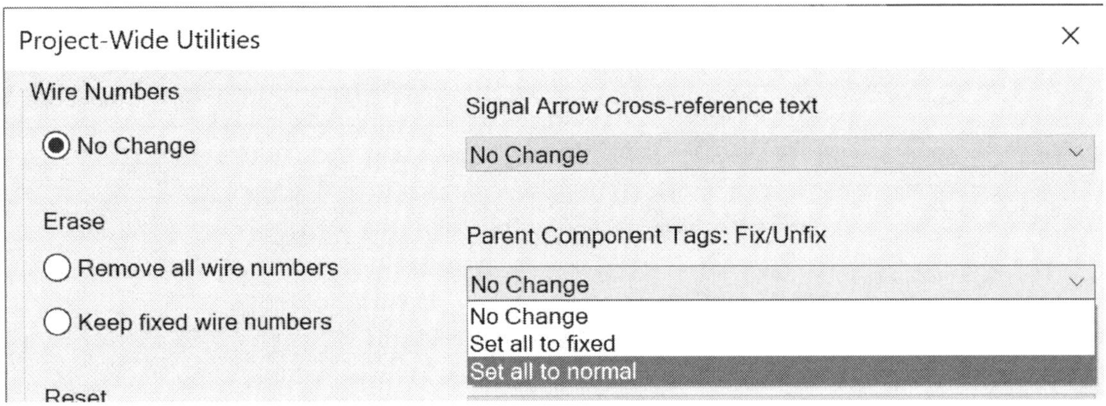

Figure 14–14

3. The *Batch Process Drawings* dialog box opens with the default **Project** and **All** selected. Click **OK**.
4. The *Select Drawings to Process* dialog box opens. Click **Do All** and click **OK**. Click **OK** to **QSAVE**.

Task 4: Retag components.

1. In the *Project* tab>*Project Tools* panel, click (Update/Retag).
2. The *Project-Wide Update or Retag* dialog box opens. Verify that **Component Retag** is selected and clear all of the other options, as shown in Figure 14–15. Click **OK**.

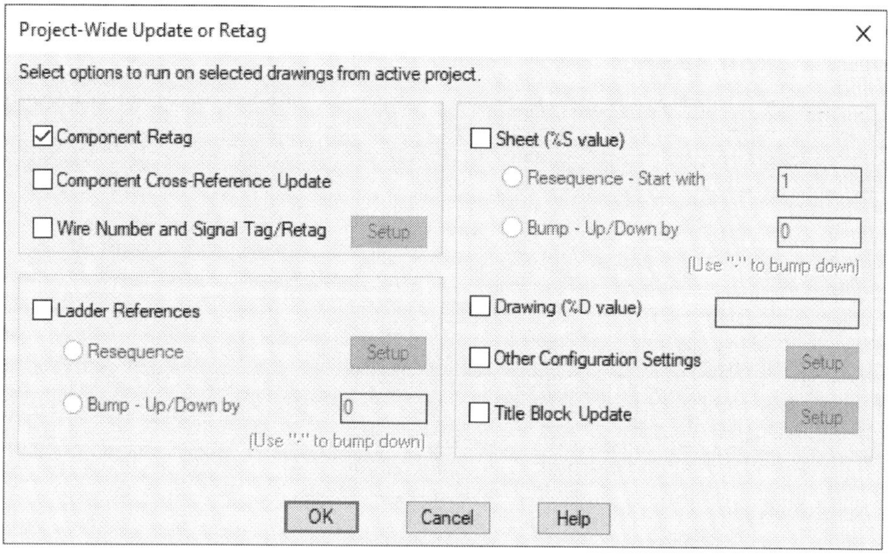

Figure 14–15

3. The *Select Drawing to Process* dialog box opens. Select **RETAG_04.dwg**. Click **Process** to move only the **RETAG_04.dwg** to the lower area. Click **OK**.
4. Zoom in to line 1201 and note that *PB201-STOP* has changed to **PB1201**, as shown in Figure 14–16. This is because you selected **Set all to normal** and then retagged the drawing.

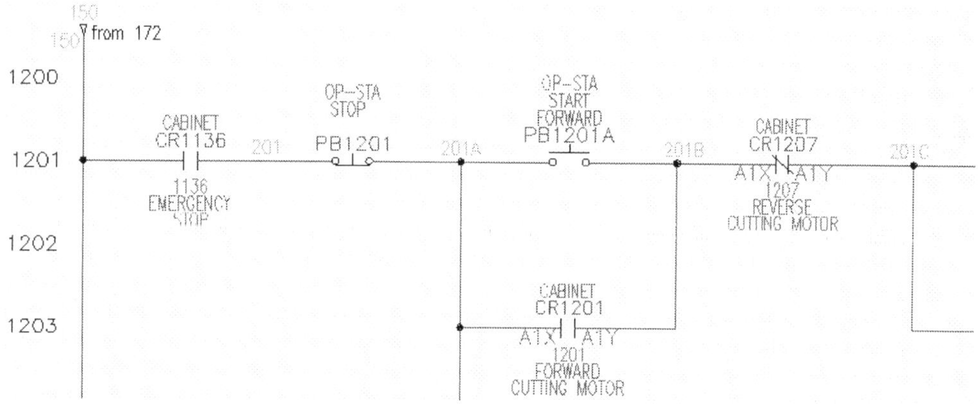

Figure 14–16

5. Zoom extents.
6. Save and close all of the drawings.

End of practice

14.3 Plot Project

The **Plot Project** command is a batch plotting routine that works with the active project file. Using this command, you can plot all drawings or a select group of drawings from the active project file. The **Plot Project** command is only accessible through the *Project Manager* palette. If you have to plot individual files, you can also use the AutoCAD® **Plot** command.

Plot Project

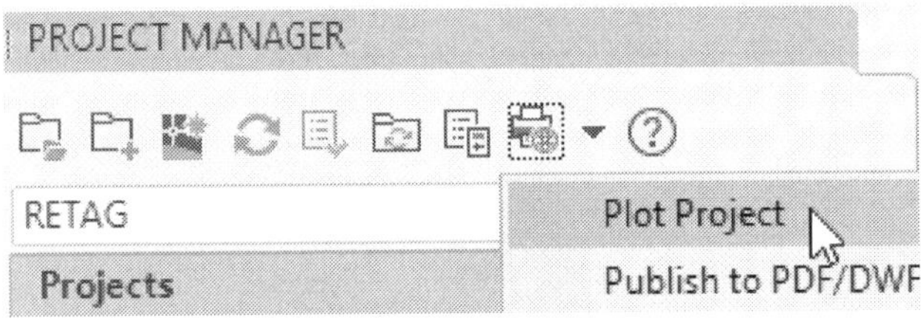

Project Manager: *Toolbar>Publish/Plot* drop-down list

Shortcut menu: *(on project name in Project Manager)* **Publish>Plot Project**

How To: Batch Plot a Project's Drawings

1. Start the **Plot Project** command. The *Select Drawings to Process* dialog box opens.
2. Select the drawings that you want to plot, move them to the lower portion by using **Do All** or **Process**, and then click **OK**.
3. The *Batch Plotting Options and Order* dialog box opens. Configure the plot options in the dialog box.
4. Click **OK** to plot the drawings in the order in which they are listed in the dialog box, or click **OK-Reverse** to plot the drawings in the reverse order.

The *Batch Plotting Options and Order* dialog box (shown in Figure 14–17) contains options to configure the batch plotting process.

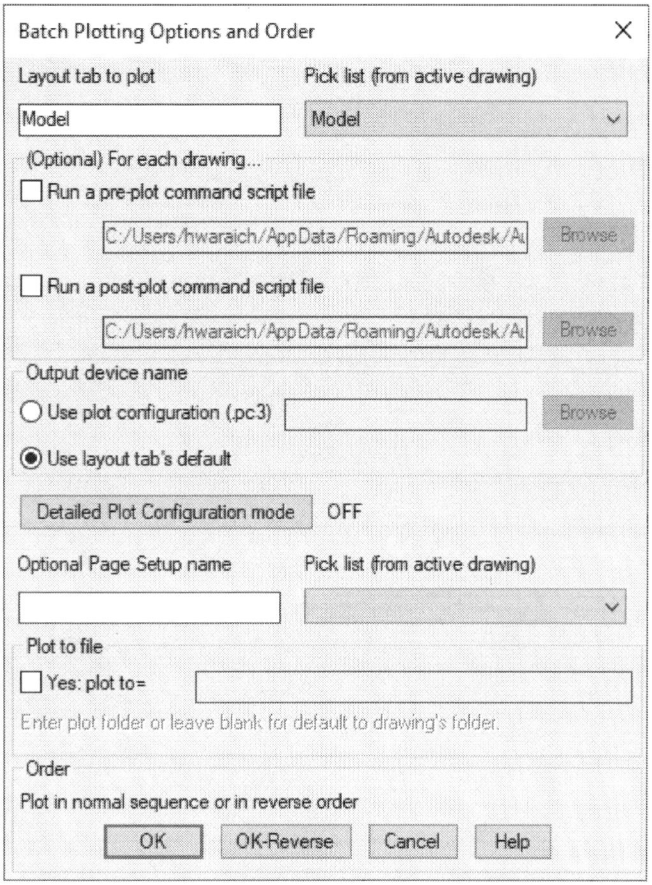

Figure 14–17

Layout tab to plot	Enter the name of the layout you want to plot.
Pick list (from active drawing)	Select the layout to plot from a list of layout tabs in the active drawing.
(Optional) For each drawing	Select to run a script file before plotting, after plotting, or both. Select the script file using Browse.
Output device name	Specify the output device by selecting an existing PC3 file or select to use the device specified in the layout tab.
Detailed Plot Configuration mode	Opens the *Detailed Plot Configuration Option* dialog box. Use this mode to configure plot options instead of using a Page Setup.
Optional Page Setup name	Enter the name of the Page Setup to use for the plots.

Pick list (from active drawing)	Select the Page Setup from a list of setups in the active drawing.
Plot to file	Send the plot to a PLT file instead of a plot device.
OK/OK-Reverse	Plots drawings in the order/reverse order in which they are listed in the project file.

The *Detailed Plot Configuration Option* dialog box displays as shown in Figure 14–18.

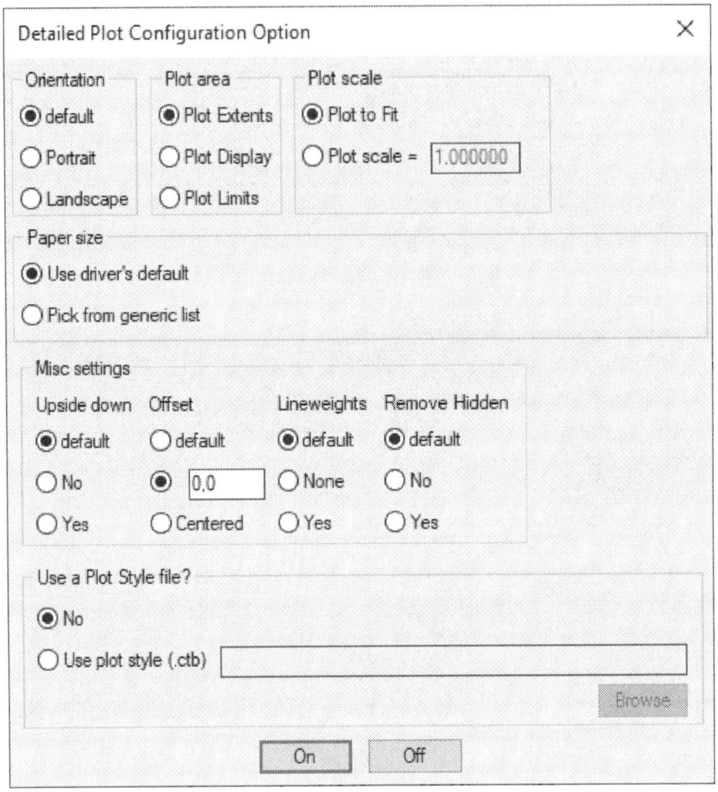

Figure 14–18

Orientation	Select from default, portrait, or landscape. Default uses the orientation specified in the page setup.
Plot area	Specifies the area to plot.
Plot scale	Specifies a plot scale.
Paper size	Specifies the Paper size for the plots.
Misc settings	Miscellaneous settings for the plots, including orientation, offsets, lineweights, and **Remove Hidden**.
Use a Plot Style file?	Selects a color-based plot style.

On	The **Plot Project** command uses the Detailed Plot Configuration settings.
Off	The **Plot Project** command uses the Page Setup settings.

Hint: Publish to PDF/DWF/DWFx

You can also publish your drawing as a .PDF file with bookmarks and hyperlinks added. This command enables you to output your project drawings from the active project file. The **Publish to PDF/DWF/DWFx** command can be accessed in the *Project Manager* toolbar> *Publish/Plot* drop-down list, as shown in Figure 14–19.

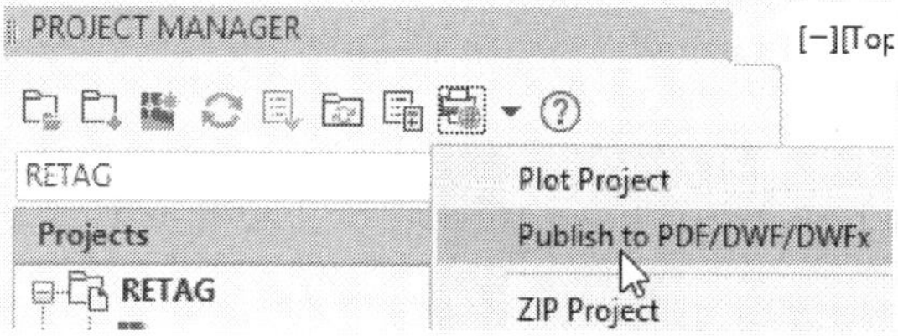

Figure 14–19

Select the drawings that you want to output from a list in the active project file. Then configure the options in the *Publish Setup* dialog box, as shown in Figure 14–20. Using this command, you can add hyperlinks that are similar to the Surfer feature. Using cross-referencing you can display a parent component to a child component. Alternatively, by selecting the child tag in the .PDF file, you can display its parent. In the .PDF file created, you can also search for text and display the related component, wire number, or report table.

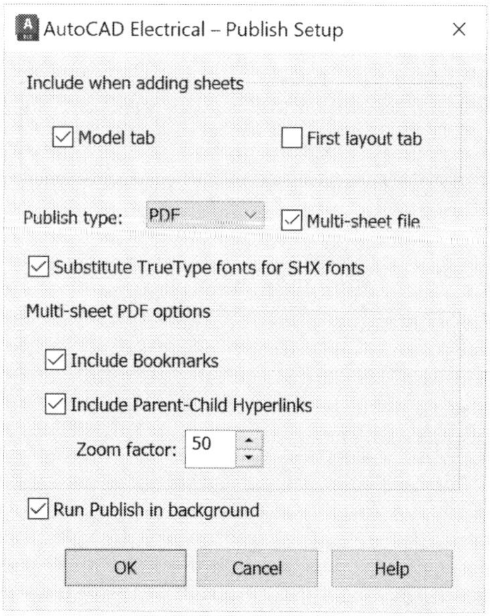

Figure 14–20

Practice 14b
Plot Project

Practice Objective

- Set up a batch plot of all of the drawings in a project.

In this practice, you will start the **Plot Project** command and observe the options at each step in the process. Since you might not be connected to a plotter in the classroom, you will cancel the command at the last step, rather than plot the drawings.

1. If the **RETAG** project is not active, open it from the *Module 14* folder and activate it now.
2. In the **RETAG** project, open **RETAG_01.dwg**.
3. In the *Project Manager* toolbar, in the *Publish/Plot* drop-down list, select **Plot Project** (as shown in Figure 14–21). You can also right-click on the **RETAG** project and select **Publish> Plot Project.**

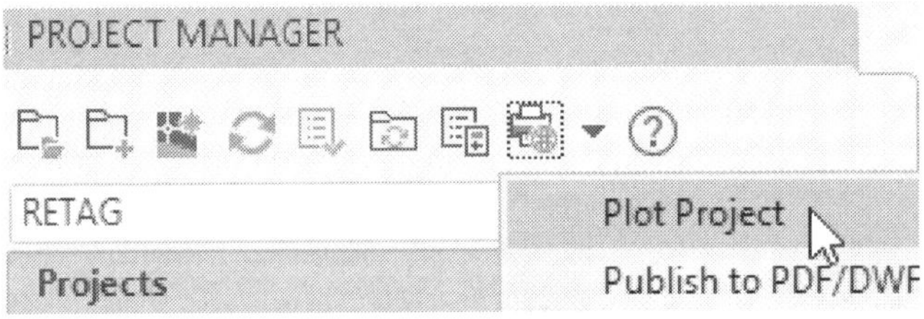

Figure 14–21

4. The *Select Drawings to Process* dialog box opens. Click **Do All** and click **OK**.
5. The *Batch Plotting Options and Order* dialog box opens. Click **Detailed Plot Configuration mode**.
6. In the *Detailed Plot Configuration Option* dialog box, note the available options. Click **Off**.

7. You are returned to the *Batch Plotting Options and Order* dialog box, as shown in Figure 14–22. You might not be connected to a plotter in the classroom. Click **Cancel**.

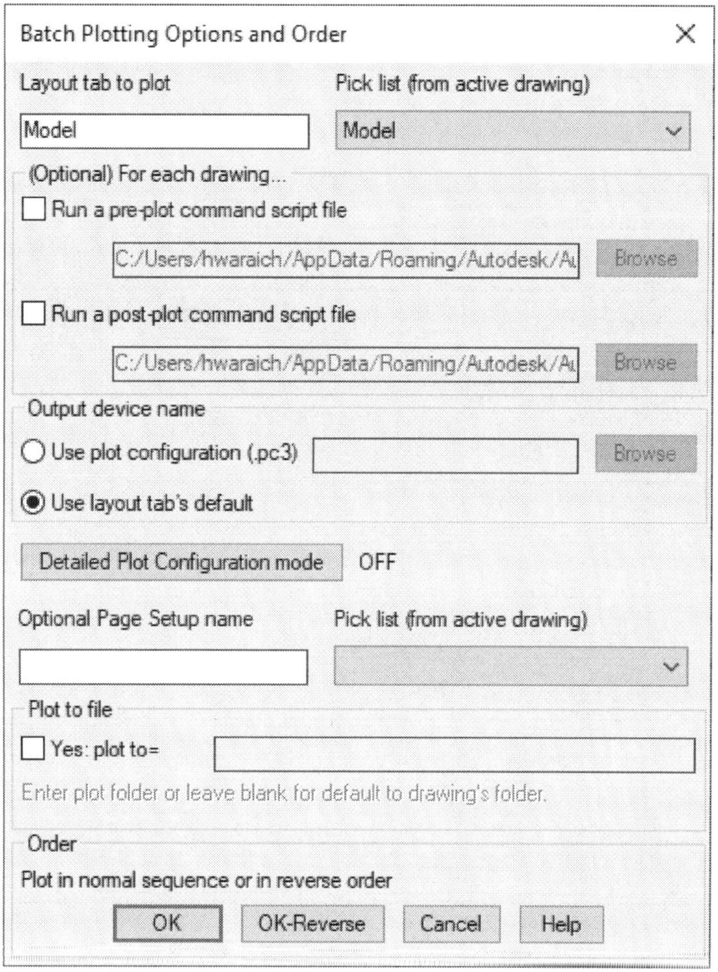

Figure 14–22

8. Close **RETAG_01.dwg**.

End of practice

14.4 Export to Spreadsheet

The **Export to Spreadsheet** command takes the data in the AutoCAD Electrical drawings of the active project and exports it to a file (typically Excel or Access). This command can be used for reporting purposes, importing into a different database or software, or modifying the data for use with the **Update from Spreadsheet** command.

Export to Spreadsheet

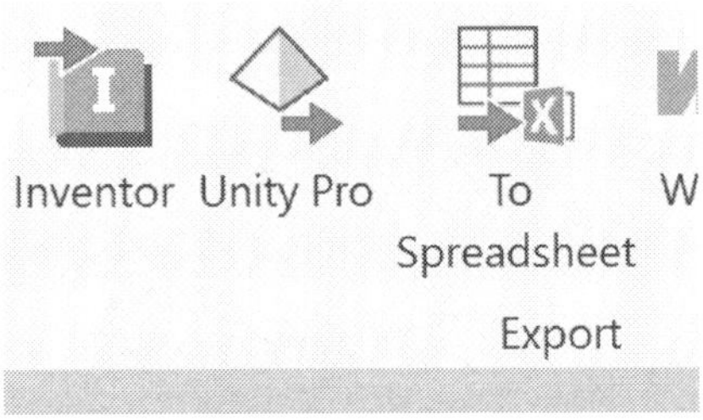

Ribbon: *Import/Export Data* tab>*Export* panel

Command Prompt:aeexport2ss

How To: Export Data to a Spreadsheet

1. Start the **Export to Spreadsheet** command. The *Export to Spreadsheet* dialog box opens.
2. Select the report to run and click **OK**.
3. The *<report name> Data Export* dialog box opens. Configure the options and click **OK**.
4. The *Select Drawings to Process* dialog box opens. Select the drawings to process and click **OK**.
5. The *Select file name for Project-wide output* dialog box opens. Browse to the required directory and enter a name for the new file. Click **Save**.

- If you make changes to the drawings, you must run the **Export to Spreadsheet** command again to update the report.
- The report created is a static file.

The *Export to Spreadsheet* dialog box (shown in Figure 14–23) contains the options for the type of data to export.

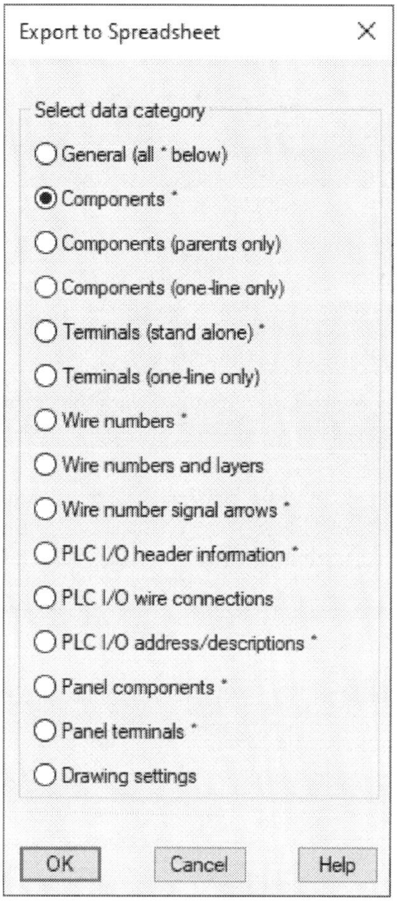

Figure 14–23

General (all * below)	Creates a report containing all reports marked with an * in the dialog box. Each report is put on a separate tab or table depending on the output type.
Components	Component related data including component tag, manufacturer and catalog number, and other attribute values.
Components (parents only)	Only exports data for parent components.
Components (one-line only)	Only exports data for one-line components.
Terminals (stand alone)	Reports on terminals in schematic drawings. Includes attribute values and wire numbers.
Terminals (one-line only)	Reports on terminals in schematic drawings that are one-line only.
Wire numbers	Report containing all wire numbers.
Wire numbers and layers	Report containing all wire numbers and their associated wire layer.

Wire number signal arrows	Report containing all signal codes in the schematic drawing. Includes signal codes, wire number, and source or destination status.
PLC I/O header information	Report containing the header attribute values for each PLC I/O module.
PLC I/O wire connections	Report containing wire numbers for each I/O point for all PLC modules in the project.
PLC I/O address/descriptions	Report containing address description attribute values for each PLC I/O point in the project.
Panel components	Report containing attribute values for components in the panel drawings of the project.
Panel terminals	Report containing attribute information for terminals in the panel drawing of the project.

The dialog box varies slightly depending on the report selected in the *Export to Spreadsheet* dialog box. The **Output format** options might be limited depending on the report type, but contain some variation of what is shown in Figure 14–24. Not all reports have the **Location Codes to extract** option.

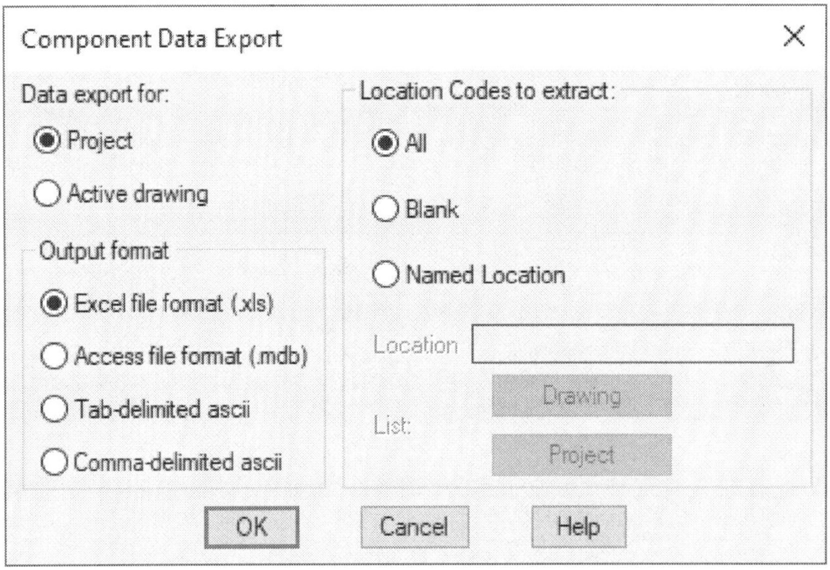

Figure 14–24

Data export for	Exports data for the project or active drawing. If **Project** is selected, the *Select Drawings to Process* dialog box opens when you click **OK**.
Output format	Select the format for the output. The list varies depending on the selected report.
Location Codes to extract	Select the **Location** code to process. This option is not available for all reports.

All reports contain an *(HDL)* and *(FILENAME)* column among other reference type data. These columns have headings in parenthesis. DO NOT modify the data in these columns. The AutoCAD Electrical software uses this data to link the information in the spreadsheet to the geometry in the drawing when updating from a spreadsheet.

14.5 Update from Spreadsheet

The **Update from Spreadsheet** command modifies the drawings in the active project according to the information in a selected spreadsheet or database.

Update from Spreadsheet

Ribbon: *Import/Export Data* tab>*Import* panel

Command Prompt: aeimportss

How To: Update Drawings from a Spreadsheet

1. Start the **Update from Spreadsheet** command. The *Update Drawings from Spreadsheet File* dialog box opens.
2. Select the source file and click **Open**.
3. The *Update Drawing per Spreadsheet Data* dialog box opens. Configure the options and click **OK**.
4. The *Select Drawings to Process* dialog box opens. Select the drawings to update and click **OK**.

- The command only updates existing symbols in the drawings. It cannot add or remove symbols.

The **Update from Spreadsheet** command can be used with a *template* project file and drawing set to start a new project. Copy the project, drawings, and exported spreadsheet to a new location. Change the values in the spreadsheet to meet the new design criteria. Finally, use the **Update from Spreadsheet** command to process the drawings and create a new design.

The *Update Drawings per Spreadsheet Data* dialog box (shown in Figure 14–25) contains various options for configuring the update drawing process.

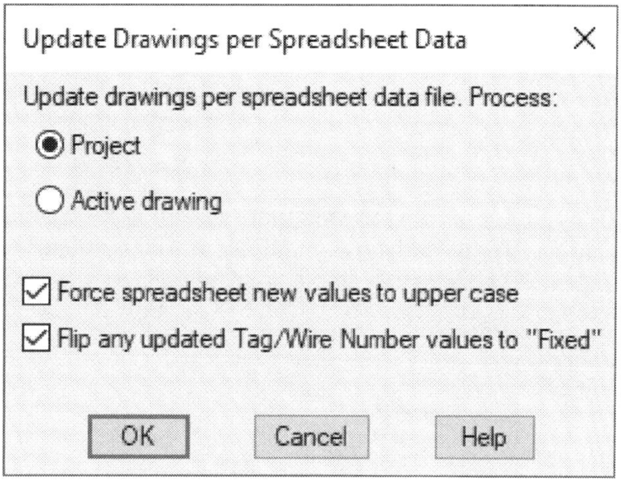

Figure 14–25

Update drawings per spreadsheet data file. Process:	Select whether to process the active project or active drawing.
Force spreadsheet new values to upper case	Any attributes updated by the command are forced to be upper case.
Flip any updated Tag/Wire Number values to "Fixed"	Any component tags or wire numbers that are updated are set to **Fixed** so that they are not accidentally updated later.

Practice 14c
Export to and Update from a Spreadsheet

Practice Objective

- Export component data to an external file, modify the data, and import the modified data back into the drawing.

In this practice, you will export data to a spreadsheet from all drawings in a project. You will then edit some of the data in the spreadsheet. Finally, you will update the active drawing using the spreadsheet. The updated drawing will display as shown in Figure 14–26.

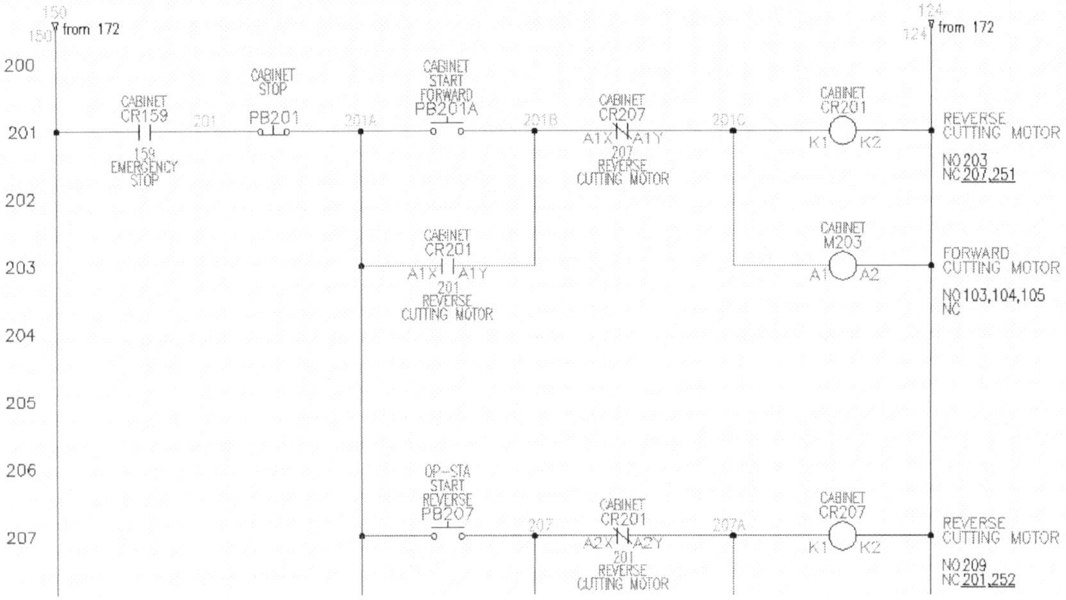

Figure 14–26

Task 1: Export to spreadsheet.

1. In your practice files folder, in the *Module 14* folder, open the **UPDATE.wdp** project file.
2. In the **Update** project, open **UPDATE_04.dwg**.
3. Zoom to Lines 200 to 203. Note on line 201, some of the components have descriptions and location codes such as **FORWARD** and **OP-STA**, as shown in Figure 14–27.

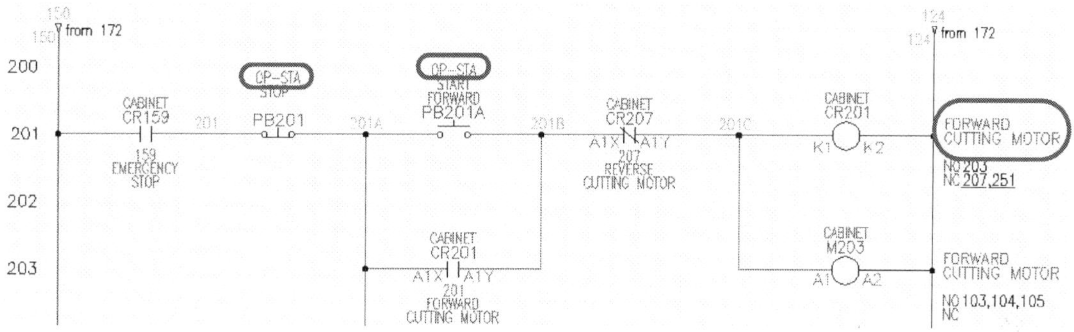

Figure 14–27

4. In the *Import/Export Data* tab>*Export* panel, click (To Spreadsheet).
5. The *Export to Spreadsheet* dialog box opens. Select **General (all * below)**, as shown in Figure 14–28, and click **OK**.

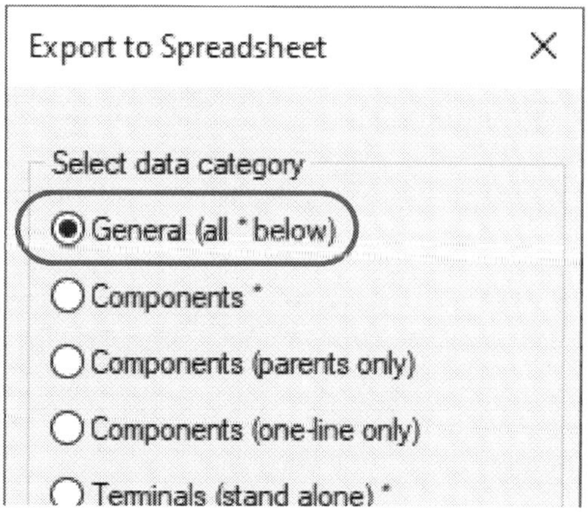

Figure 14–28

6. The *General Data Export* dialog box opens, as shown in Figure 14–29. With the default options selected, click **OK**.

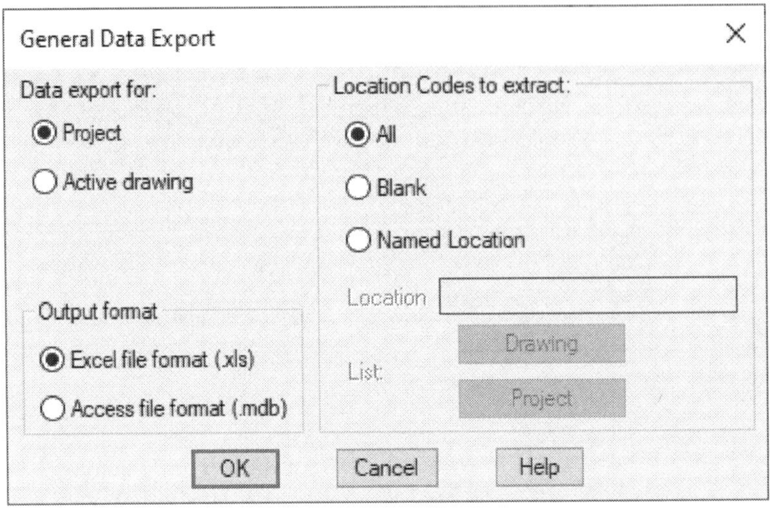

Figure 14–29

7. The *Select Drawings to Process* dialog box opens. Click **Do All** and click **OK**.
8. The *Select file name for Project-wide XLS output* dialog box opens. Browse to the *Module 14* folder in your practice files folder. Leave the filename as **UPDATE**, verify that *Save as type* is ***.xls** (as shown in Figure 14–30), and click **Save**.

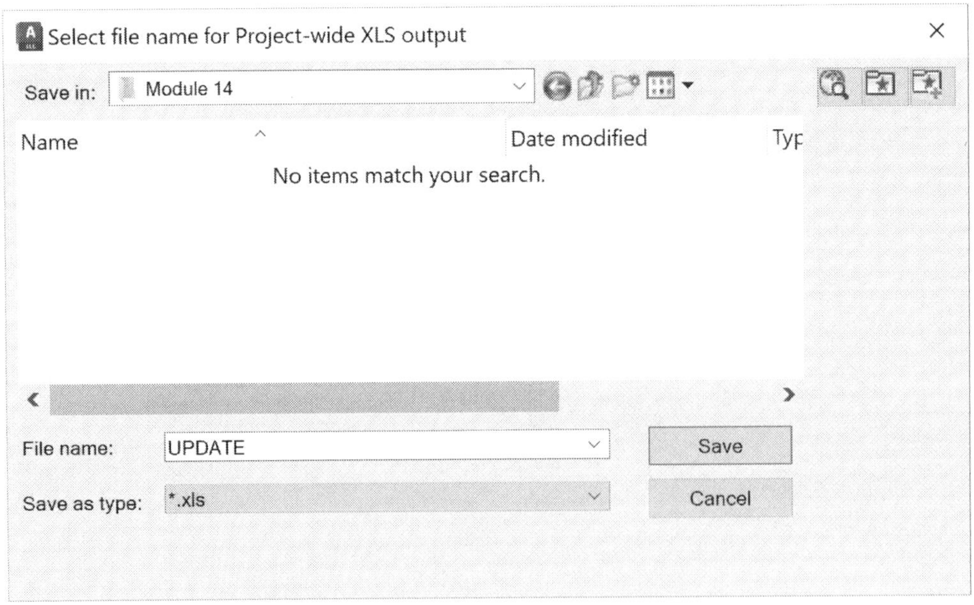

Figure 14–30

Task 2: Modify the spreadsheet.

1. Using Microsoft Excel, open the newly created **UPDATE.XLS** spreadsheet located in the *Module 14* folder in your practice files folder.
2. Note the different tabs near the bottom in the spreadsheet, such as *COMP*, *TERM*, *PLCMOD*, etc. Each tab is a different report from the *Export to Spreadsheet* dialog box category list. Select the *COMP* tab. Scroll to the extreme left to display cell **A1**.and select it, as shown in Figure 14–31.

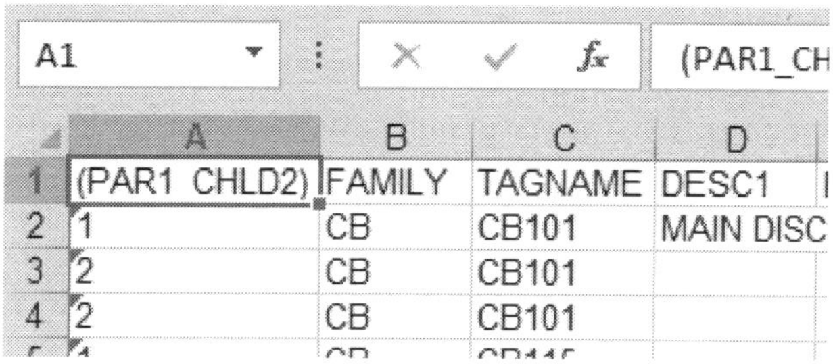

Figure 14–31

3. In the Excel ribbon, in the *Data* tab>*Sort & Filter* panel, begin the **Sort** command, as shown in Figure 14–32.

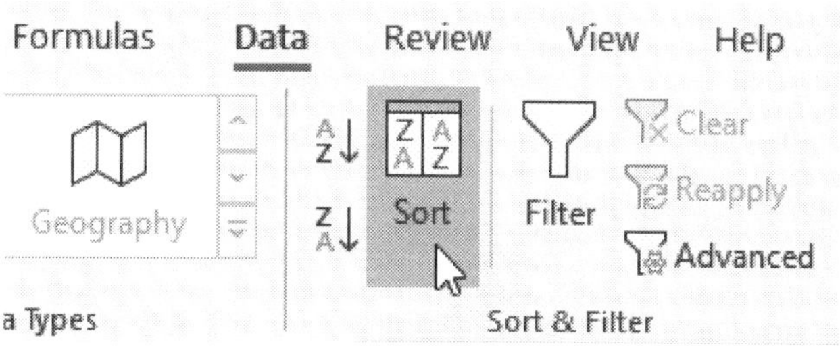

Figure 14–32

4. The *Sort* dialog box opens. In the *Sort by* drop-down list, select **TAGNAME**, as shown in Figure 14–33. Click **OK**.

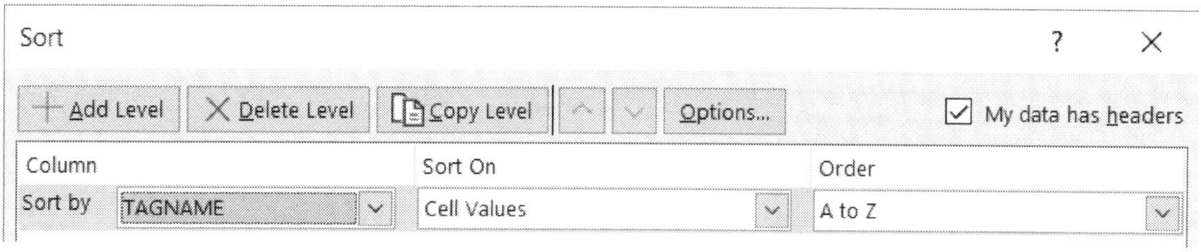

Figure 14–33

5. Scroll down to CR201 (row numbers 27-30). The data in *column D* for CR201 is **FORWARD**. Change it to **REVERSE** for each row for CR201, as shown in Figure 14–34. There is a row for each symbol in the drawings labeled CR201. These rows include the parent (relay) and children (contacts). That is why there are multiple entries for CR201.

	A	B	C	D	E	F	G	H	I
25	2	CR	CR159	EMERGENCY	STOP		201		
26	2	CR	CR159	EMERGENCY	STOP		254		
27	2	CR	CR201	REVERSE	CUTTING MOTOR		203		
28	2	CR	CR201	REVERSE	CUTTING MOTOR		251		
29	2	CR	CR201	REVERSE	CUTTING MOTOR		207		
30	1	CR	CR201	REVERSE	CUTTING MOTOR		201	AB	700-P400A1
31	2	CR	CR207	REVERSE	CUTTING MOTOR		209		
32	2	CR	CR207	REVERSE	CUTTING MOTOR		252		
33	2	CR	CR207	REVERSE	CUTTING MOTOR		201		

Figure 14–34

6. Scroll down to PB201 and PB201A (row numbers 76 and 77). The data in *column Q* for both is **OP-STA**. Change it to **CABINET** for both rows, as shown in Figure 14–35.

	A	B	C	D	E	F	G	H	I	J	K	L	M	N	O	P	Q	R
71	1	M	M215	POSITIONAL MOTOR			215	EATON	AN16DN0AB		3	0	0	0			CABINET	
72	1	MTR	MOT104	CUTTING	MOTOR		104	AB	1329RS-ZA00218VNC									
73	1	MTR	MOT116	POSITIONAL	MOTOR		116	AB	1329RS-ZA00318VNC-DH									
74	1	PB	PB159	EMERGENCY	STOP		159	AB	800T-D6D2						NC		OP-STA	
75	1	PB	PB167	SYSTEM	RESET		167	AB	800H-BR6D1						NO		OP-STA	
76	1	PB	PB201	STOP			201	AB	800H-BR6D2						NC		CABINET	
77	1	PB	PB201A	START	FORWARD		201	AB	800H-BR6D1						NO		CABINET	
78	1	PB	PB207	START	REVERSE		207	AB	800H-BR6D1						NO		OP-STA	
79	1	PB	PB213	STOP			213	AB	800H-BR6D2						NC		OP-STA	
80	1	PB	PB213A	START			213	AB	800H-BR6D1						NO		OP-STA	
81	1	PJ	PJ103				103	HUBBELL	MRMS24425					3			FLOOR	

Figure 14–35

7. Save and close **UPDATE.XLS**.
8. Return to the AutoCAD Electrical software.

Task 3: Update drawings from a spreadsheet.

1. In the *Import/Export Data* tab>*Import* panel, click (From Spreadsheet).
2. The *Update Drawing from Spreadsheet File* dialog box opens. In the *Module 14* folder in your practice files folder, select **UPDATE.XLS** and click **Open**.
3. The *Update Drawings per Spreadsheet Data* dialog box opens. Select **Active drawing**, as shown in Figure 14–36, and click **OK**.

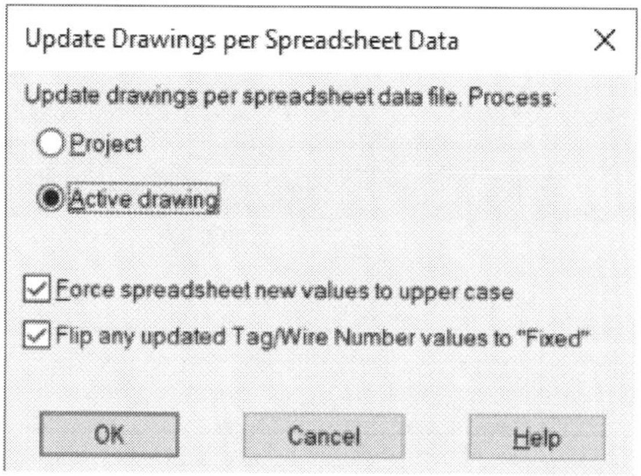

Figure 14–36

4. Zoom to lines 200 to 207 as shown in Figure 14–37. The location codes for PB201 and PB201A have changed to **CABINET** and the description for CR201 on lines 201, 203, and 207 has changed to **REVERSE**.

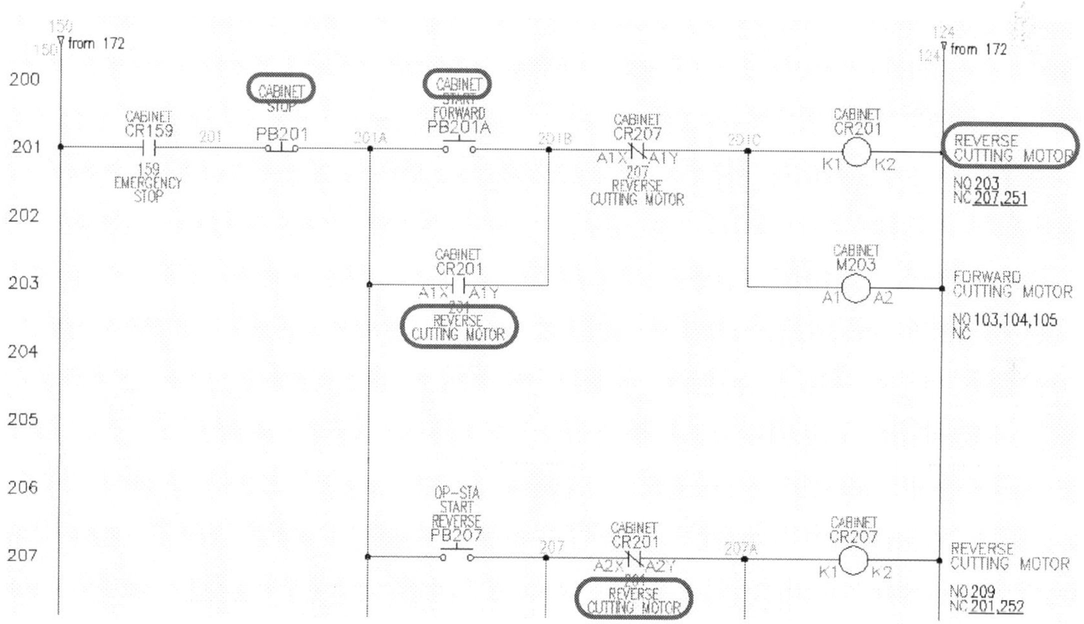

Figure 14–37

5. Zoom extents.
6. Save and close **Update_04.dwg**.

End of practice

14.6 Copy Project

The **Copy Project** command copies a project file, its associated drawings, and support files to a user-specified directory and project name. The advantage of using this command over simply copying in Windows Explorer is that the new project file is updated to reflect the new drawing names and a search for support files is performed.

Copy Project

Ribbon: *Project* tab>*Project Tools* panel

Command Prompt: aecopyproject

How To: Copy a Project

1. Start the **Copy Project** command. The *Copy Project: Select Existing Project to Copy* dialog box opens, as shown in Figure 14–38.

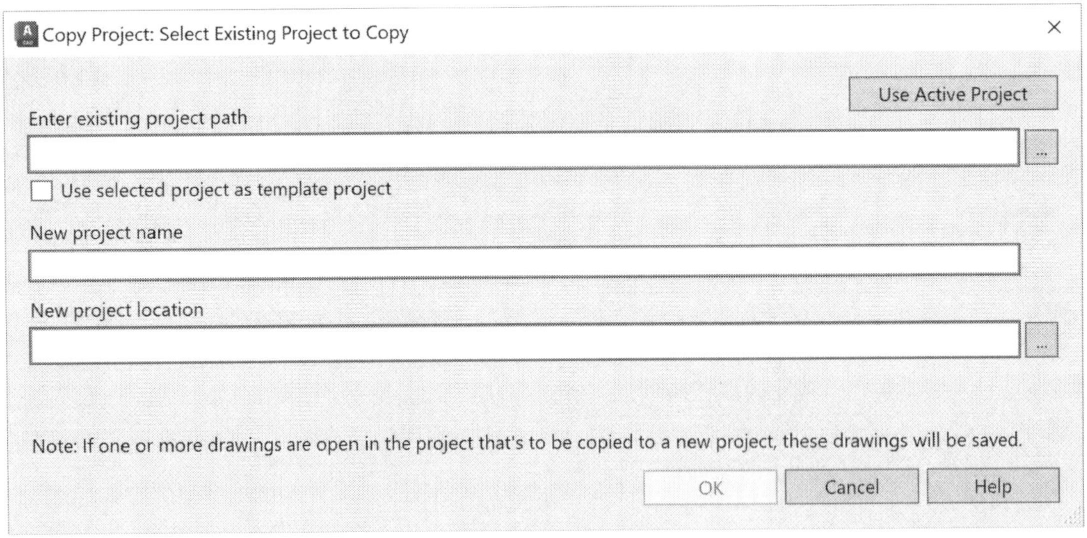

Figure 14–38

2. Enter the name of the project file to copy including the path. You can either select **Use Active Project** or click  to select the project. You can clear the **Use selected project as template project** option to customize the selections for the new project.
3. In the *New project name* field, you can enter the name for the new project, as shown in Figure 14–39. Use  to browse to the folder for the new project location. Click **OK**.

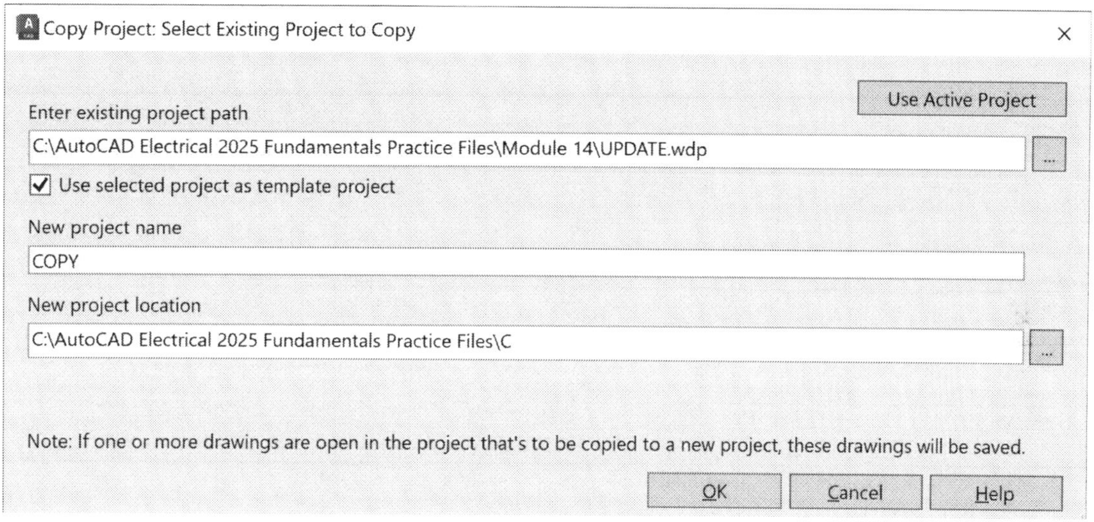

Figure 14–39

4. The *Select Drawings to Process* dialog box opens. Select the drawings to process and click **OK**.

5. The *Copy Project: Enter Base Path for Project Drawings* dialog box opens, as shown in Figure 14–40. Select the project-specific support files to copy. If a support file does not exist, it is grayed out in the dialog box. Click **OK**.

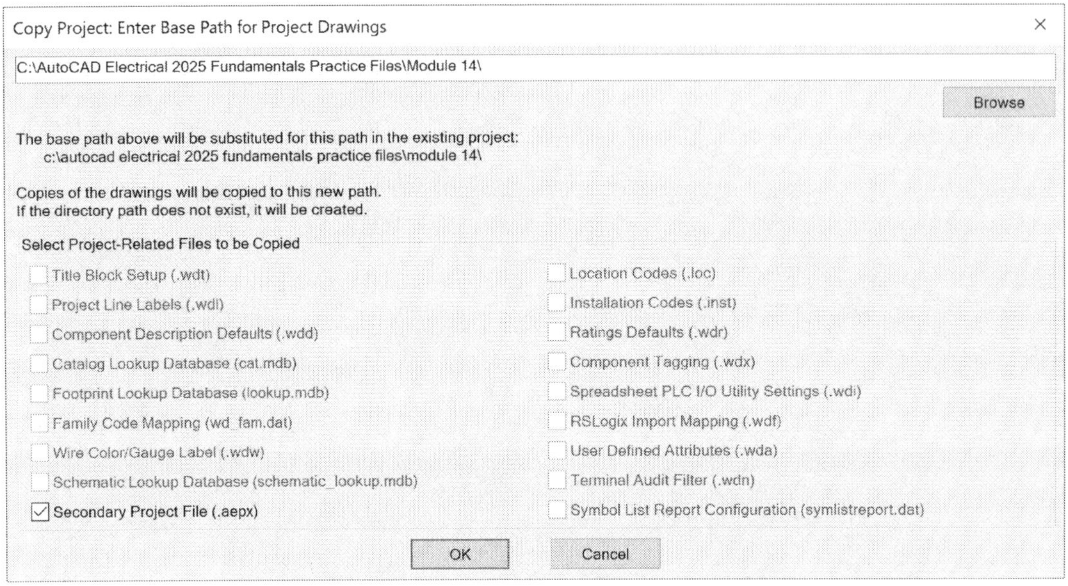

Figure 14–40

6. The *Copy Project: Adjust new drawing file names* dialog box opens, as shown in Figure 14–41. Use **Edit** to enter a new filename or use **Find/Replace** to search and replace the text in the filenames. Click **OK**.

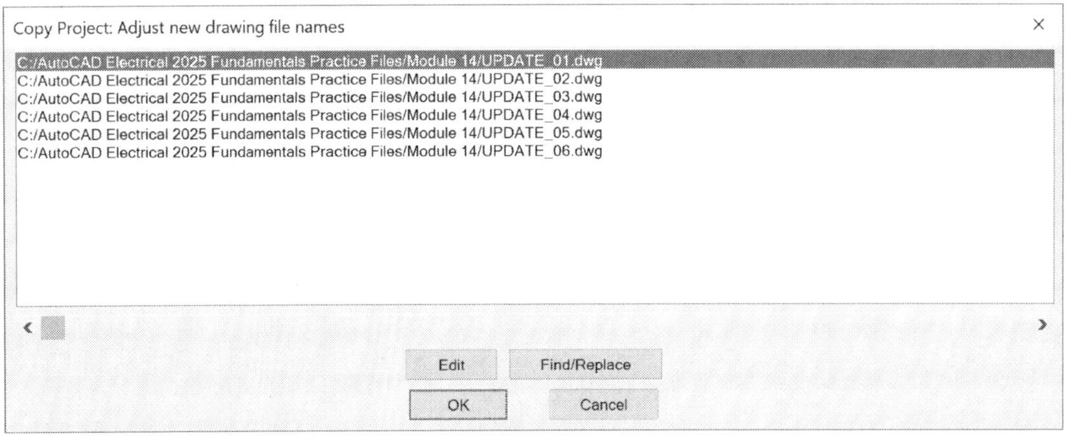

Figure 14–41

- The **Copy Project** command is useful when you are creating a new design that is similar to something you had previously created.
- You must have a drawing file open to run this command.
- You cannot have one of the drawings open that belongs to the project file that is being copied.

Practice 14d
Copy Project

Practice Objective

- Copy a project file.

In this practice, you will copy the active project along with its associated drawings and support files to a new directory. A new project will be created and activated, as shown in Figure 14–42.

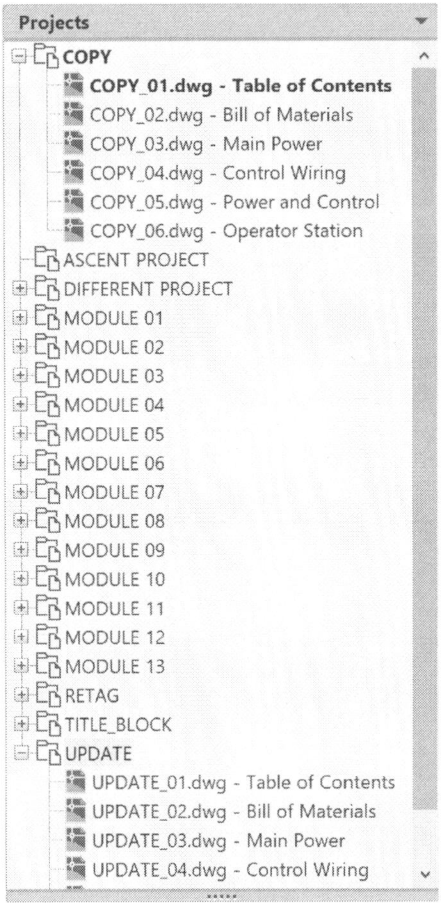

Figure 14–42

1. If the **UPDATE.wdp** project is not active, open it from the *Module 14* folder and activate it now.
2. Create a new drawing using the AutoCAD **New** command (in the Quick Access Toolbar). Use **Acad_Electrical.dwt** (provided with the software) for the template.

- A new drawing with the name **Drawing#** is created and opened. This step is required because you must have a drawing open to use the **Copy Project** command and the drawing cannot be part of the project you are copying.

3. In the *Project* tab>*Project Tools* panel, click (Copy).
4. The *Copy Project: Select Existing Project to Copy* dialog box opens. Click **Use Active Project**. The path and .WDP file is acquired from your active project. Clear **Use selected project as template project**, if required, as shown in Figure 14–43.

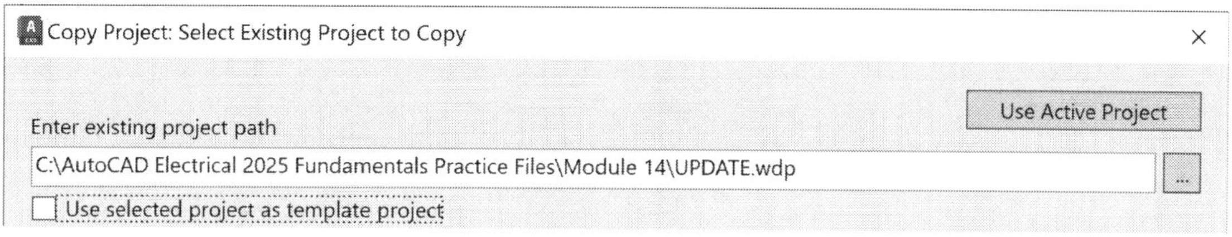

Figure 14–43

5. In the *New project name* field, type **COPY**. For *New project location*, click and select **Module 14** from your practice files folder.
6. The fields in *Copy Project: Select Existing Project to Copy* dialog box should display as shown in Figure 14–44. Click **OK**.

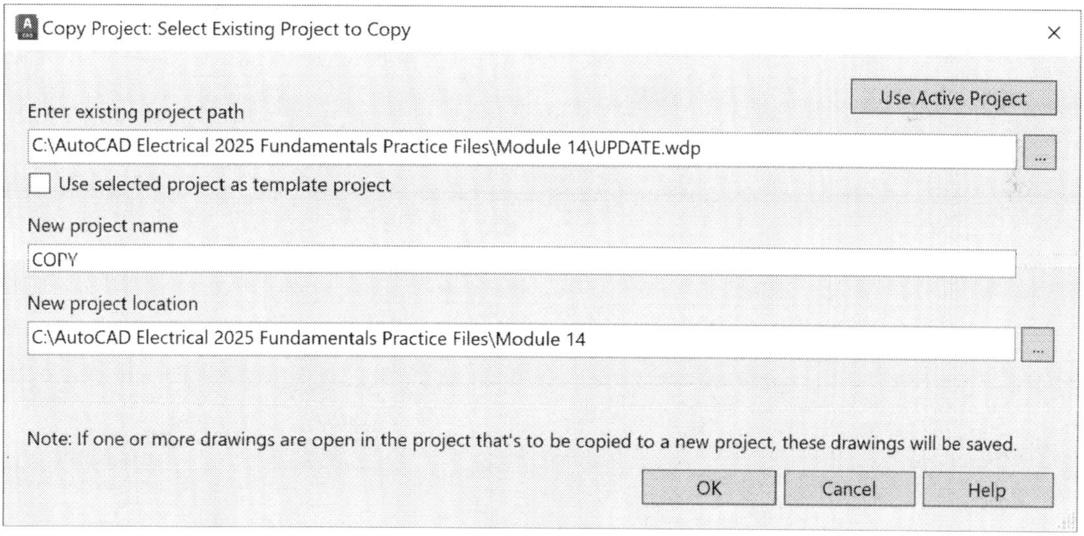

Figure 14–44

7. The *Select Drawings to Process* dialog box opens. Click **Do All** and click **OK**.

8. The *Copy Project: Enter Base Path for Project Drawings* dialog box opens. All boxes are grayed out because none of the support files exist for this project. Click **OK**.
9. The *Copy Project: Adjust new drawing file names* dialog box opens displaying all the files in the project, as shown in Figure 14–45. Click **Find/Replace**.

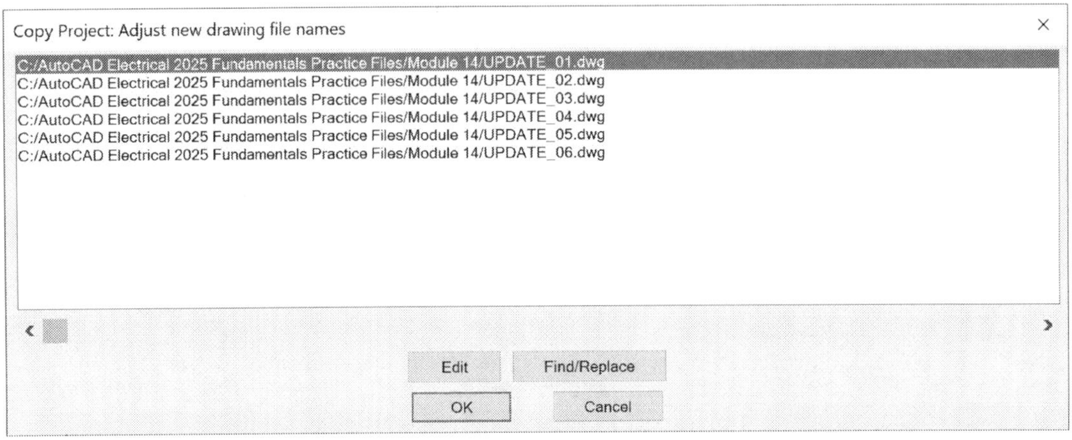

Figure 14–45

10. In the *Find/Replace* dialog box that opens, set the following, as shown in Figure 14–46:
    - *Find*: **UPDATE**
    - *Replace*: **COPY**

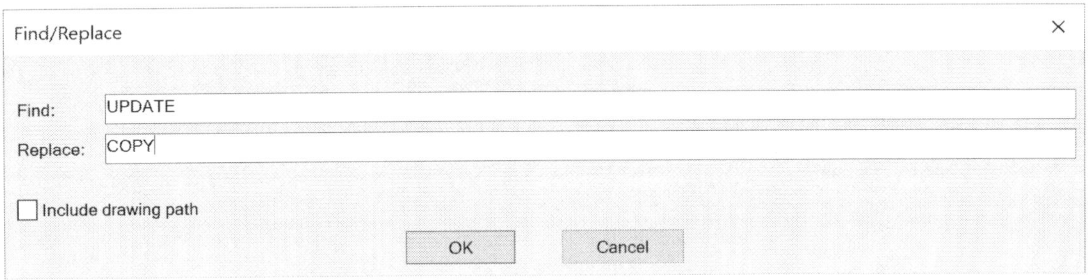

Figure 14–46

11. Click **OK**.
12. You are returned to the *Copy Project: Adjust new drawing file names* dialog box. The new drawing filenames have changed to display COPY, as shown in Figure 14–47. Click **OK**.

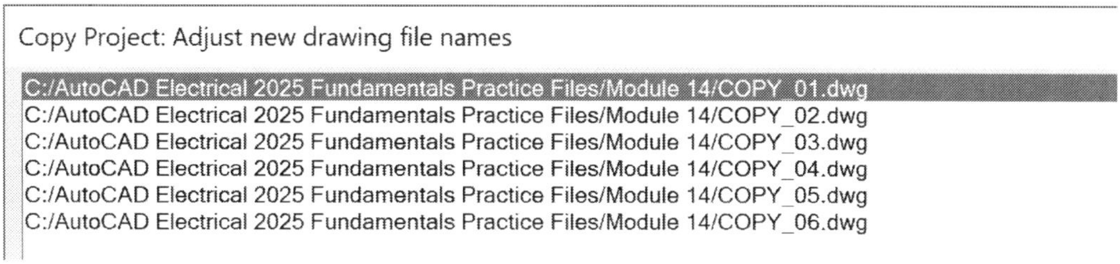

Figure 14–47

13. The **COPY** project and associated drawing files are created. The **COPY** project is activated and **COPY_01.dwg** is opened, as shown in Figure 14–48.

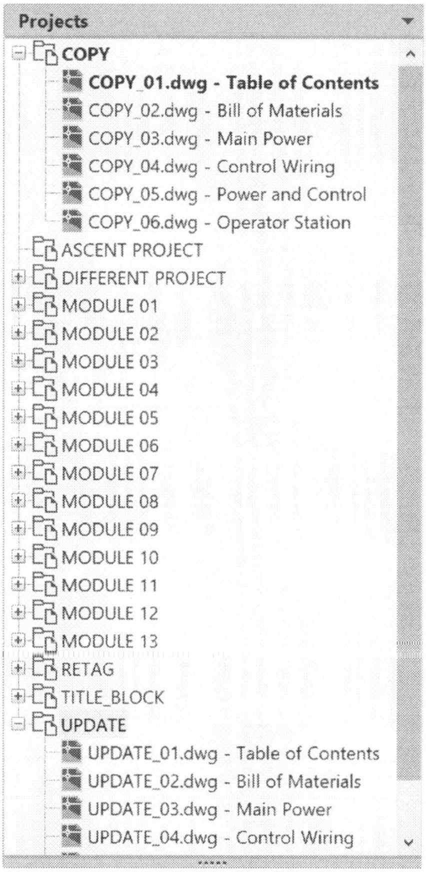

Figure 14–48

14. Close all of the drawings. Do not save the open drawings.

End of practice

14.7 Swap/Update Block

The **Swap/Update Block** command replaces one block instance with another block. It can be used to swap a single block, many of the same blocks, or update drawings after a library has been changed. The command maintains attribute values and wire connections for the new block as long as it contains the attributes.

- **Option A** of the command swaps a block instance for a block of a different name (for example, swap a push button for a mushroom head push button). This option is used if your design changes and you want to change components.
- **Option B** of the command swaps a block instance with a block of the same name. This option is used if you modify your library blocks or if you decide to switch to a different library.

Swap/Update Block

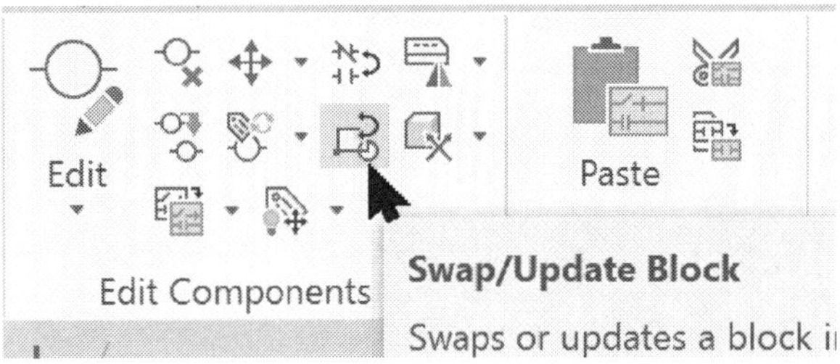

Ribbon: *Schematic* tab>*Edit Components* panel

Command Prompt: aeswapblock

How To: Swap/Update a Block with Option A

1. Start the **Swap/Update Block** command. The *Swap Block/Update Block/Library Swap* dialog box opens.
2. Under Option A, select the replacement method (one at a time, drawing wide, or project wide).
3. Select the method to select the new block.
4. Configure the other options and select the attribute mapping method. Click **OK**.
5. Select the new block using the method selected in step 3.
6. Select the block instance to replace in the drawing window.
7. If performing a project wide swap, the *Select Drawings to Process* dialog box opens. Select the drawings to process and click **OK**.

How To: Swap/Update a Block with Option B – Update a Block

1. Start the **Swap/Update Block** command. The *Swap Block/Update Block/Library Swap* dialog box opens.
2. Under Option B, select **Update a Block** and click **OK**.
3. Pick the block instance to replace in the drawing window.
4. The *Update Block – New block's path\filename* dialog box opens. Specify the path and filename for the new block definition.
5. Configure the scale and attribute options.
6. Click **Project** to swap the block project wide or **Active Drawing** to swap the block in the active drawing.
7. If replacing project wide, the *Select Drawings to Process* dialog box opens. Select the drawings to process and click **OK**.

How To: Swap/Update a Block with Option B – Library Swap

1. Start the **Swap/Update Block** command. The *Swap Block/Update Block/Library Swap* dialog box opens.
2. Under Option B, select **Library Swap** and click **OK**.
3. The *Library Swap – All Drawing* dialog box opens. Specify the path for the new library.
4. Configure the **Scale** and **Attribute** options.
5. Click **Project** to swap the block project wide, **Active Drawing** to swap the block in the active drawing, or **Pick** to select the block instances in the drawing.
6. If replacing project wide, the *Select Drawings to Process* dialog box opens. Select the drawings to process and click **OK**.

The *Swap Block / Update Block / Library Swap* dialog box (shown in Figure 14–49) contains various selections in the different option areas.

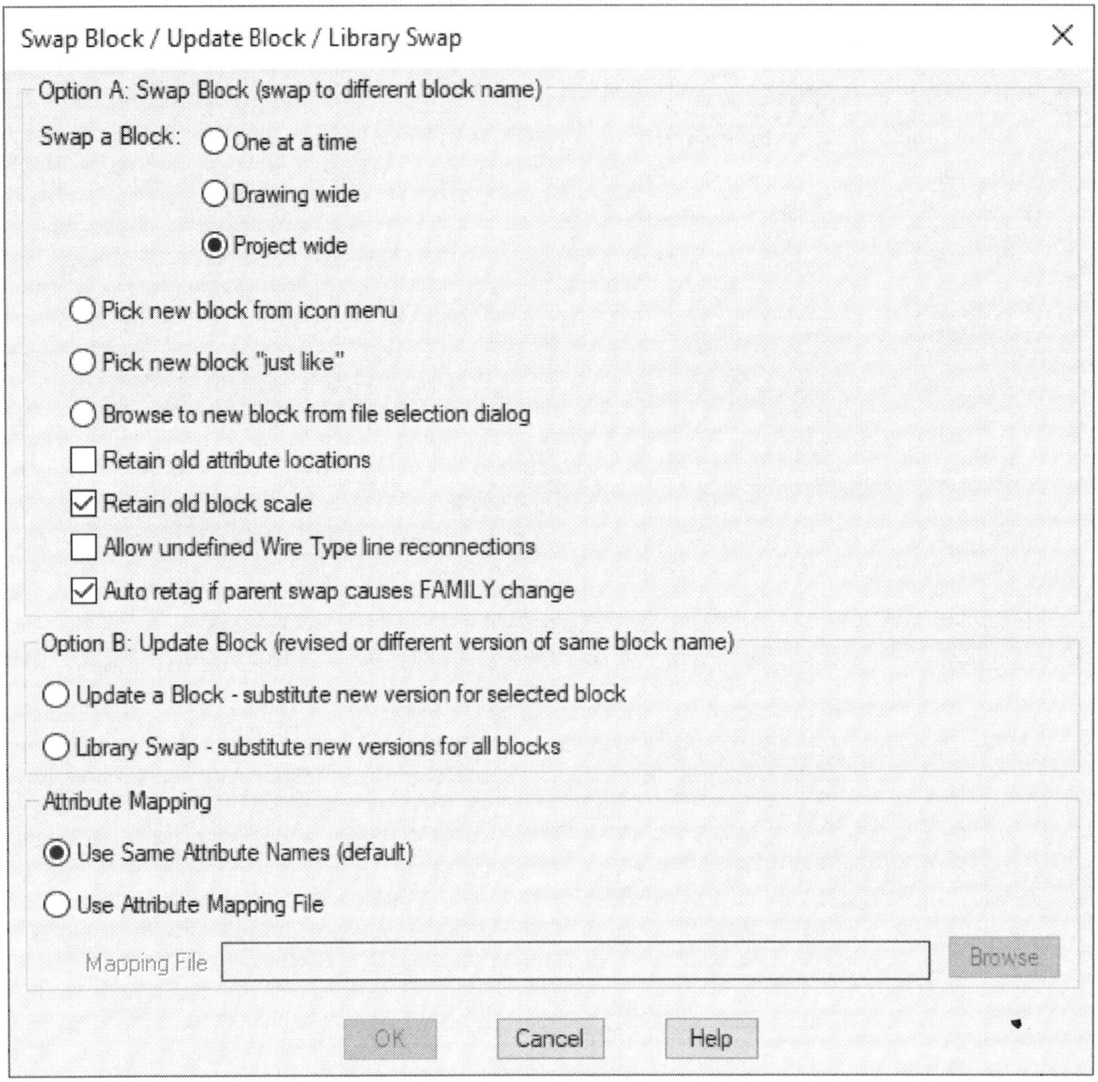

Figure 14–49

Option A:

One at a time	Swaps only the selected block instance.
Drawing wide	Swaps all instances of a selected block in the active drawing.
Project wide	Swaps all instances of a selected block in selected drawings in the active project.
Pick new block from icon menu	Select the new block in the Icon Menu.
Pick new block "just like"	Select the block to replace in the active drawing window.
Browse to new block from file selection dialog	Select the block to replace from the hard drive using the *File selection* dialog box.
Retain old attribute locations	Maintains the attribute position of the old block when inserting the new block.
Retain old block scale	Maintains the scale of the original block when inserting the new block.
Allow undefined Wire Type line reconnections	Includes non-wire lines for connections when the block is exchanged.
Auto retag if parent swap causes FAMILY change	If the family code changes, the component tag is updated.

Option B:

Update a Block	Updates all instances of a selected block with the definition that is in the library.
Library Swap	Updates all blocks in the selected drawings with the definition that is in the library.

Attribute Mapping:

Use Same Attribute Names	Maintains the attribute data for any attributes with names that match an attribute on the old block.
Use Attribute Mapping File	Uses a mapping file to map attribute names on the old block to attribute names on the new block.
Mapping File	Browse to select the mapping file. Supported file formats are XLS, CSV, and TXT.

The *Update Block – New block's path\filename* dialog box (shown in Figure 14–50) opens when **Update a Block** is selected under Option B.

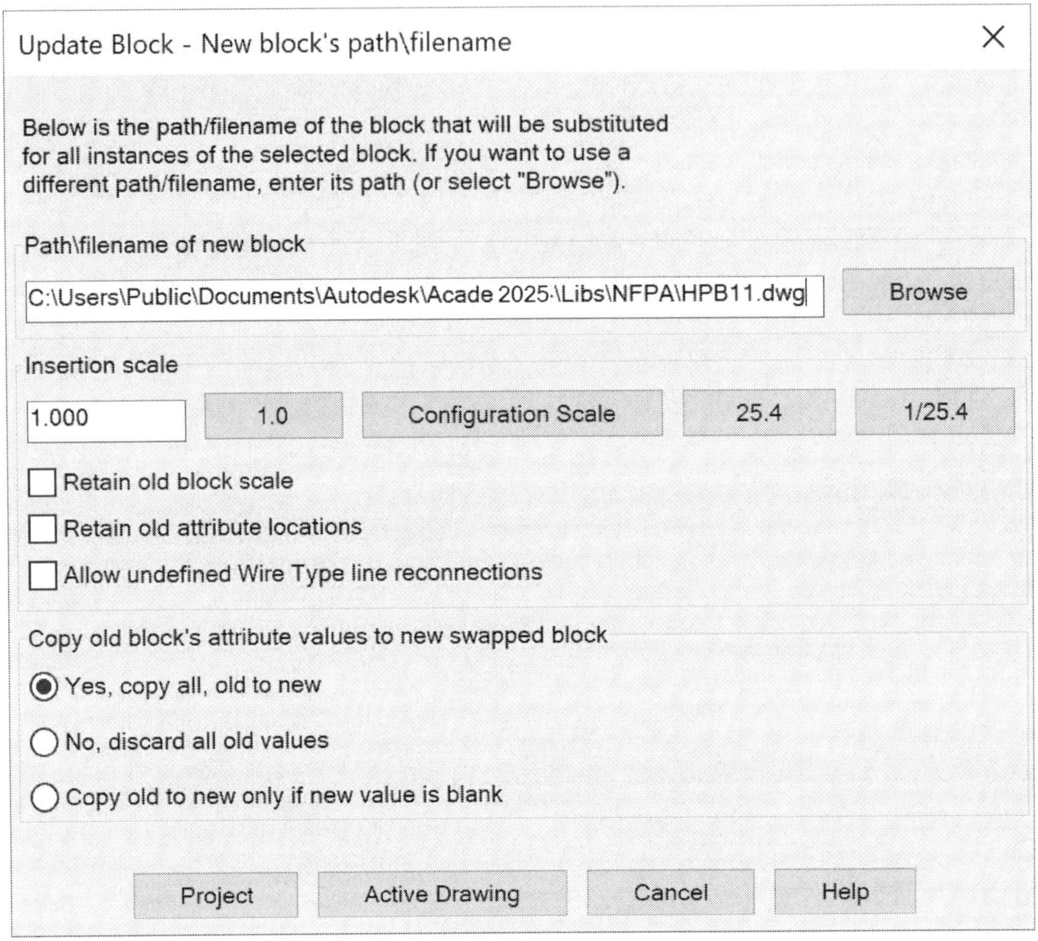

Figure 14–50

Path\filename of new block	Specify the path and filename for the new block. Click **Browse** and select the file in the *Select a substitute* dialog box.
Insertion scale	Specify the scale to use to insert the new block.
Copy old block's attribute values to new swapped block	Select how to handle the attribute values on the existing block.
Project	Click to swap blocks for the entire project. Use the *Select Drawing to Process* dialog box to select the drawings to update.
Active Drawing	Swap blocks in the active drawing only.

The *Library Swap – All Drawing* dialog box (shown in Figure 14–51) opens when **Library Swap** is selected under Option B. All the options work in the same way as in the *Update Block – New block's path\filename* dialog box. The *Library Swap – All Drawing* dialog box has the additional option to **Pick**, which enables you to select the blocks to be replace in the active drawing window.

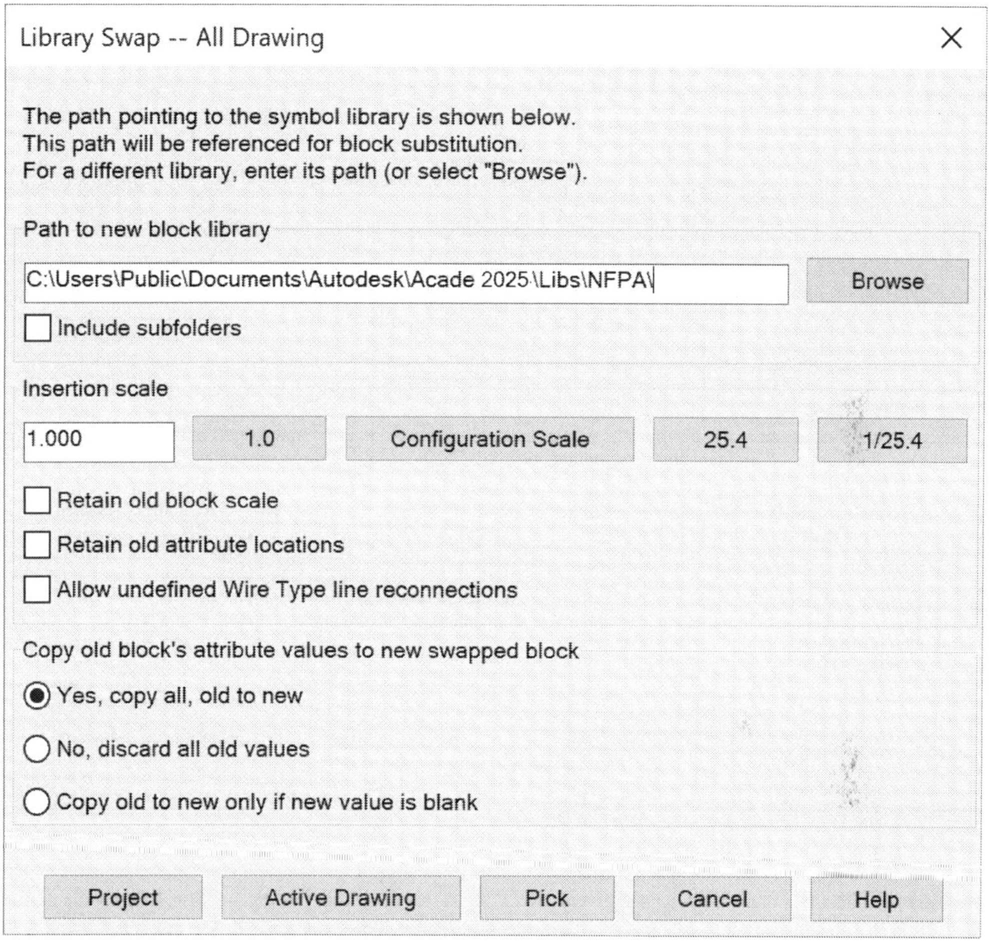

Figure 14–51

- The **Swap/Update Block** command can be used to swap blocks that are not AutoCAD Electrical symbols. For example, use the command to change the title blocks in the drawings of an entire project.

Practice 14e
Swap/Update Block Option A

Practice Objective

- Replace a component block with a different one.

In this practice, you will use **Swap Block** with Option A to exchange green lights for red lights, as shown in Figure 14–52. You then update the catalog data for one component and use **Copy Catalog Assignment** to update the other components.

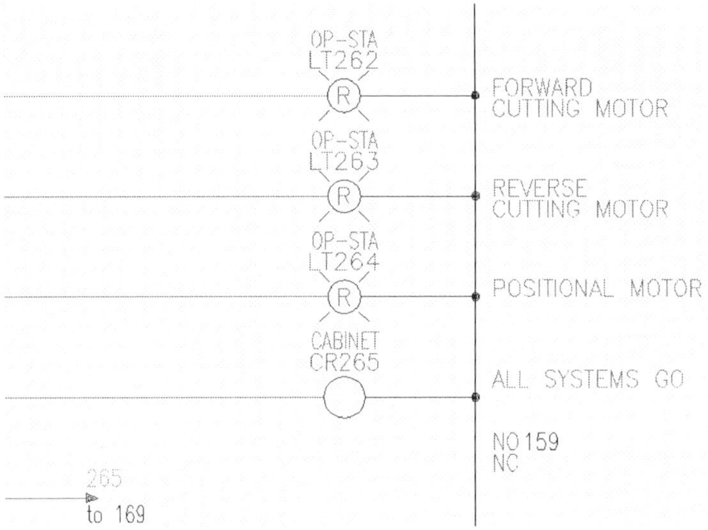

Figure 14–52

1. In your practice files folder, in the *Module 14* folder, open the **VERIFY.wdp** project file.
2. In the **Verify** project, open **VERIFY_04.dwg**.
3. Zoom to lines 260 to 268 (as shown in Figure 14–53) and note the three lights on lines 262, 263, and 264. They display **G** inside the circle indicating that these are green lights.

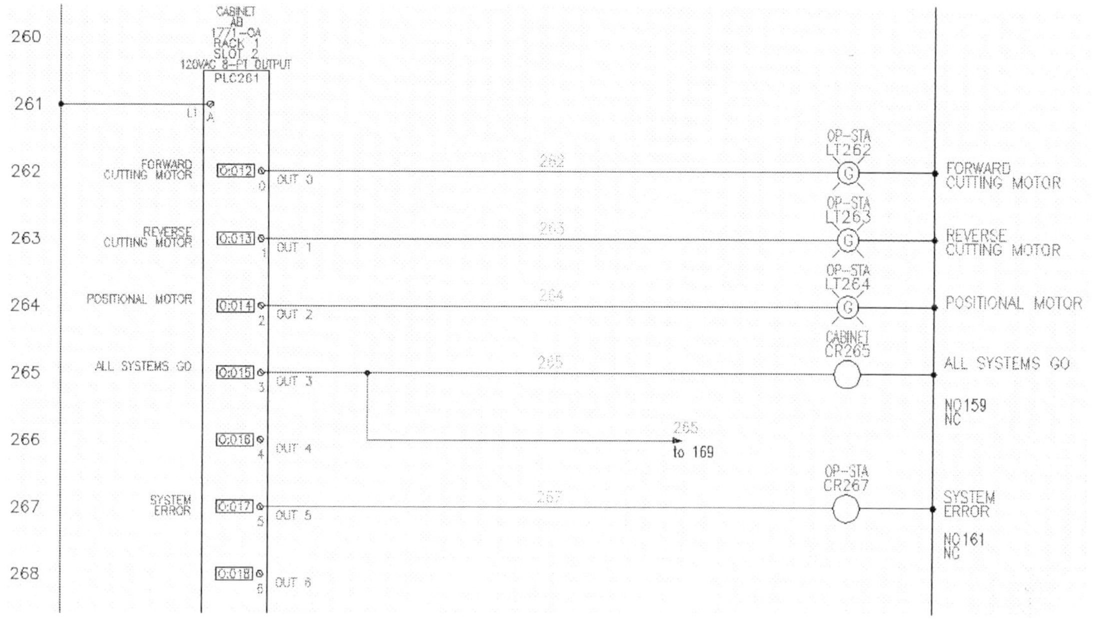

Figure 14–53

4. In the *Schematic* tab>*Edit Components* panel, click (Swap/Update Block).
5. The *Swap Block/Update Block/Library Swap* dialog box opens. In Option A, for **Swap a Block:**, select **Drawing wide**. Select **Pick new block from icon menu**, as shown in Figure 14–54. Click **OK**.

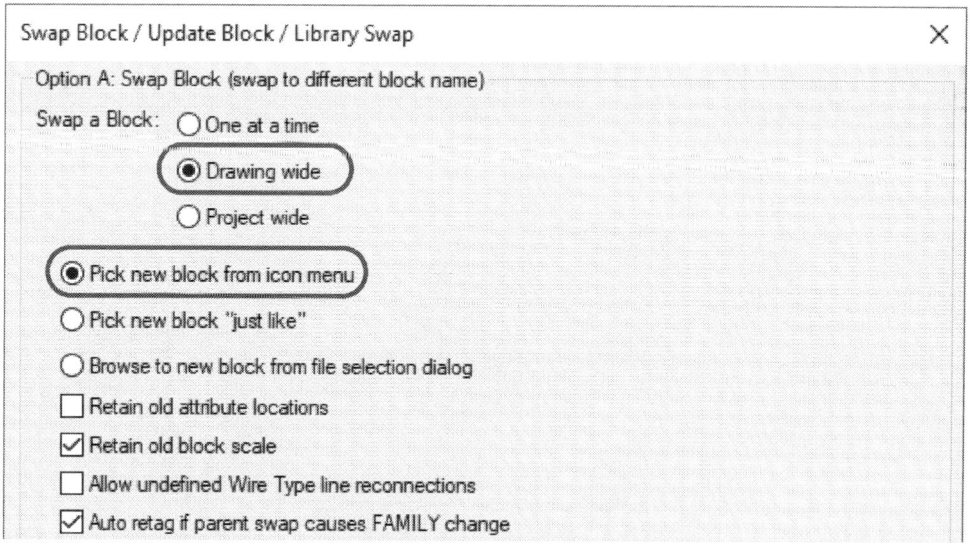

Figure 14–54

6. The *Insert Component* dialog box opens. Click (Pilot Lights) and (Red Standard) to insert a Red Standard light.
7. Pick LT262 as the component type to swap out. Note that the three green lights on lines 262, 263, and 264 have changed to red lights (symbol with an R in the center), as shown in Figure 14–55.

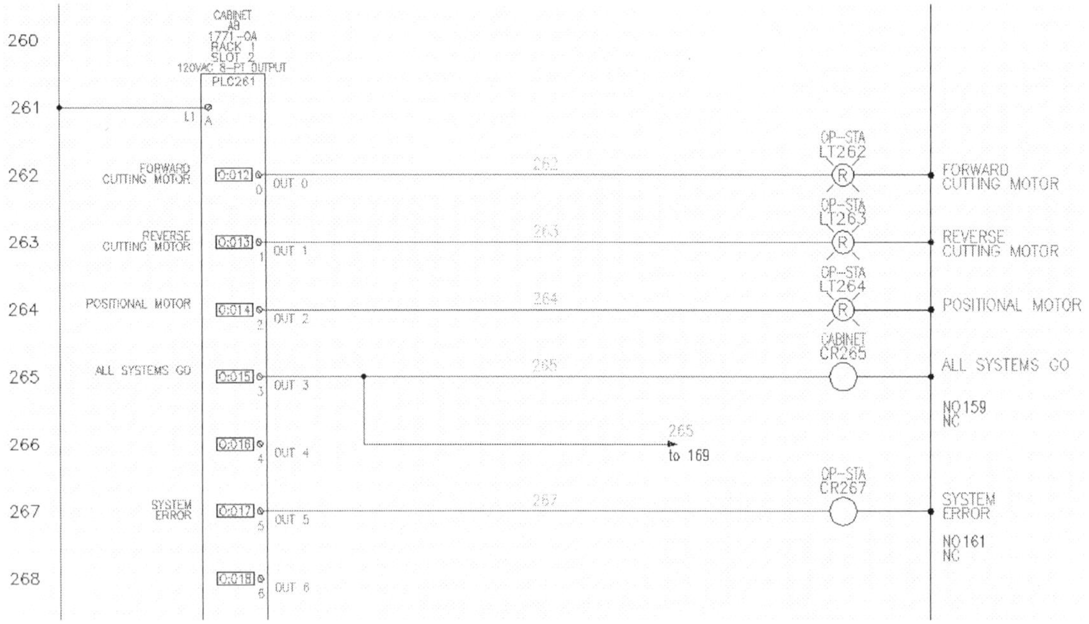

Figure 14–55

8. Edit the component LT262.
9. The *Insert / Edit Component* dialog box opens. In the *Catalog Data* area, Click **Lookup**.

10. The *Catalog Browser* opens. Note that 800T-P16H is already selected in the list. (If it is not listed, clear the **Filter by WDBLKNAM value** option.) Select **800T-P16J**, as shown in Figure 14–56, and click **OK**.

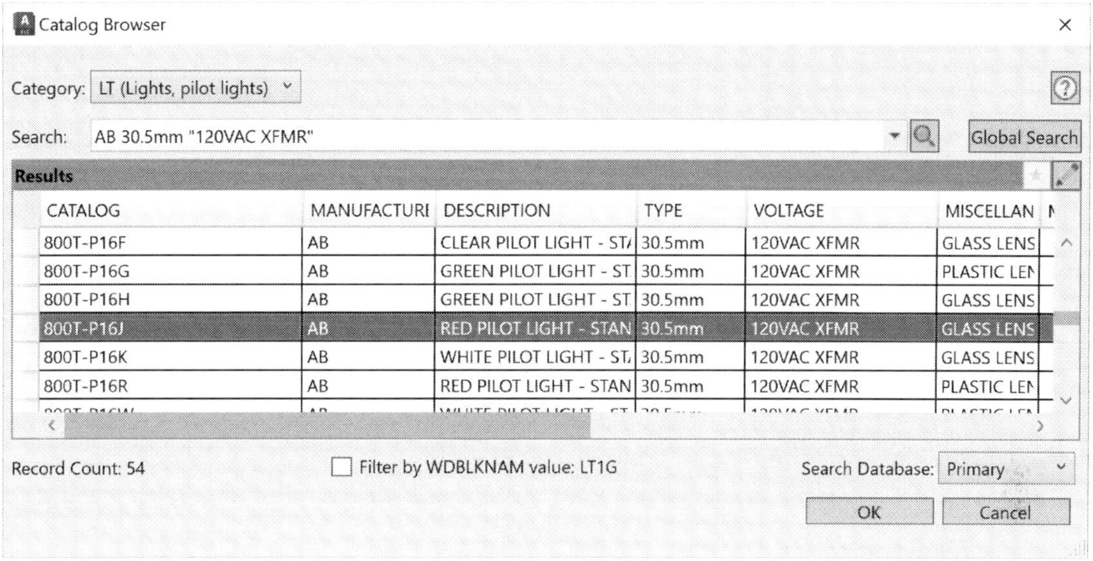

Figure 14–56

11. You are returned to the *Insert / Edit Component* dialog box, with the updated catalog data, as shown in Figure 14–57. Click **OK**.

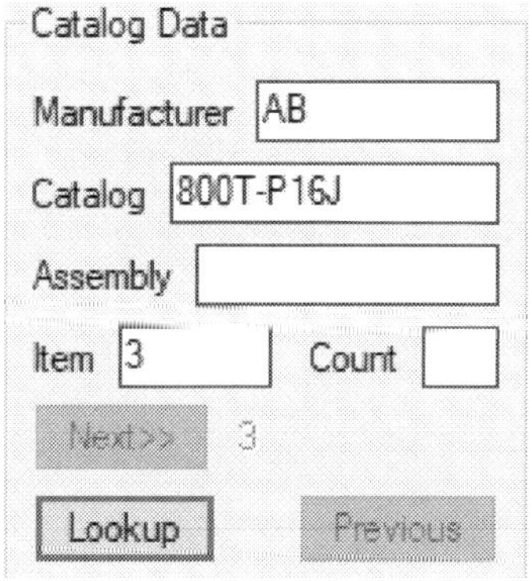

Figure 14–57

12. In the *Update other drawings?* dialog box, click **Task**.

13. In the *Schematic* tab>*Edit Components* panel, in the *Edit* flyout, click  (Copy Catalog Assignment).

14. Select LT262 as the master component.

15. The *Copy Catalog Assignment* dialog box opens, as shown in Figure 14–58. Click **OK**.

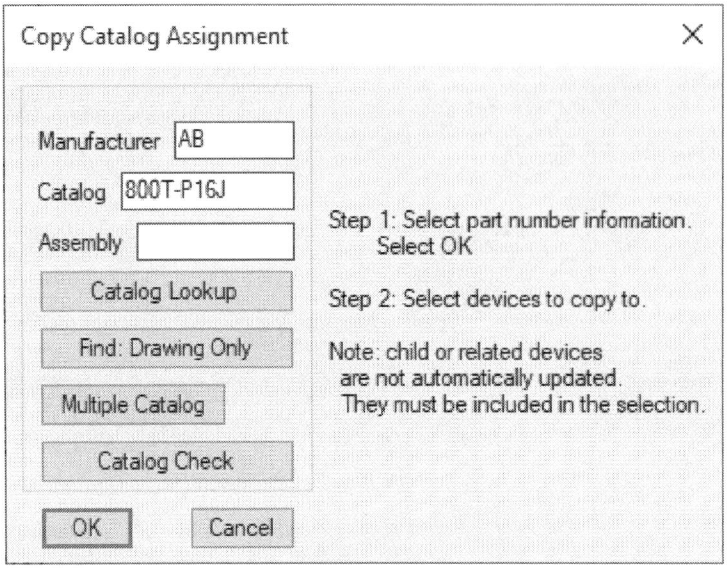

Figure 14–58

16. Select LT263 and LT264 as the *Target* components, and press <Enter>.

17. A green diamond displays on LT263 in the drawing and the *Caution: Existing Data on Target* dialog box opens, as shown in Figure 14–59. Click **Overwrite**.

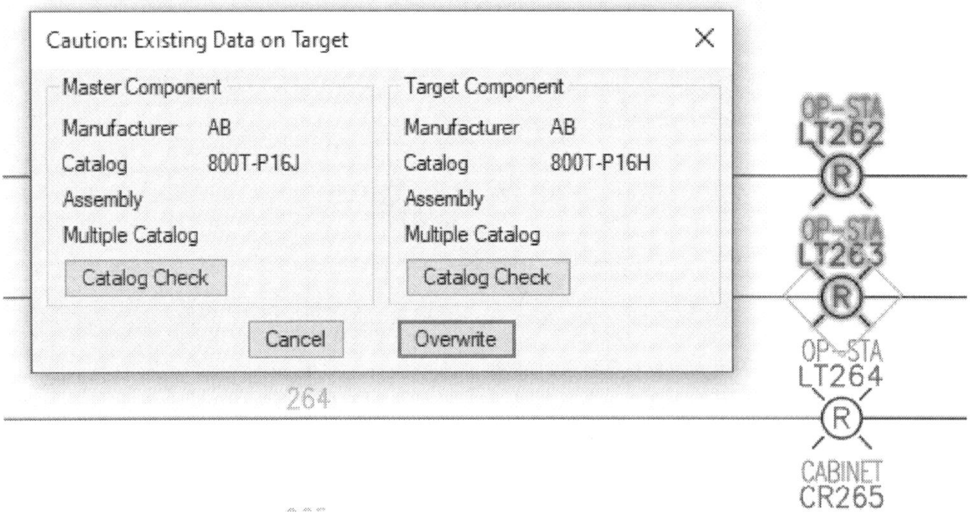

Figure 14–59

18. The *Caution: Existing Data on Target* dialog box opens again (for LT264). Click **Overwrite**.

19. In the *Update other drawings?* dialog box, click **Task**.

20. In the *Project Manager*, click (Project Task List).

21. The *Task List* dialog box opens, similar to that shown in Figure 14–60. Click **Select All** and click **OK**. Click **OK** to QSAVE. The other drawings are updated with the new catalog data.

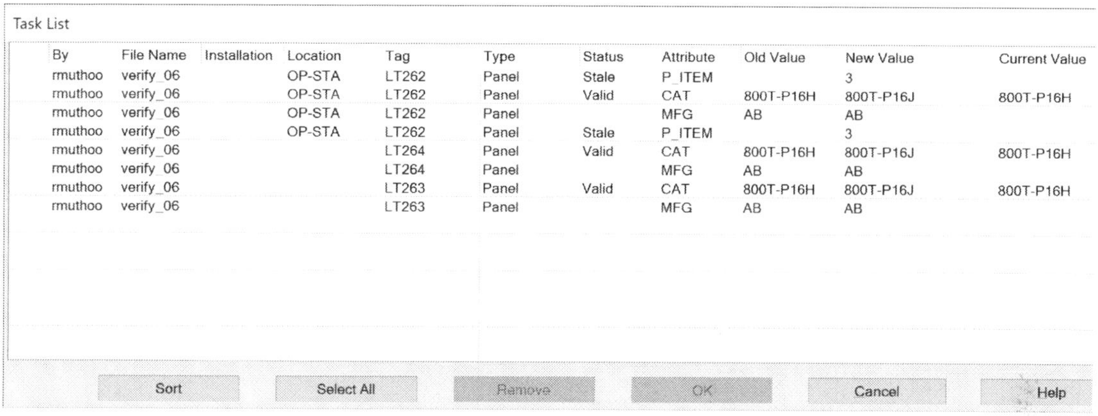

Figure 14–60

22. Zoom extents.

23. Save and close **VERIFY_04.dwg**.

End of practice

Practice 14f
Swap/Update Block Option B

Practice Objective

- Substitute all of the component symbol blocks in a drawing with a new library of blocks.

In this practice, you will use the **Swap/Update Block** command to update all symbols in the active drawing. The symbols will be changed to a library that contains blocks with smaller text, as shown in Figure 14–61.

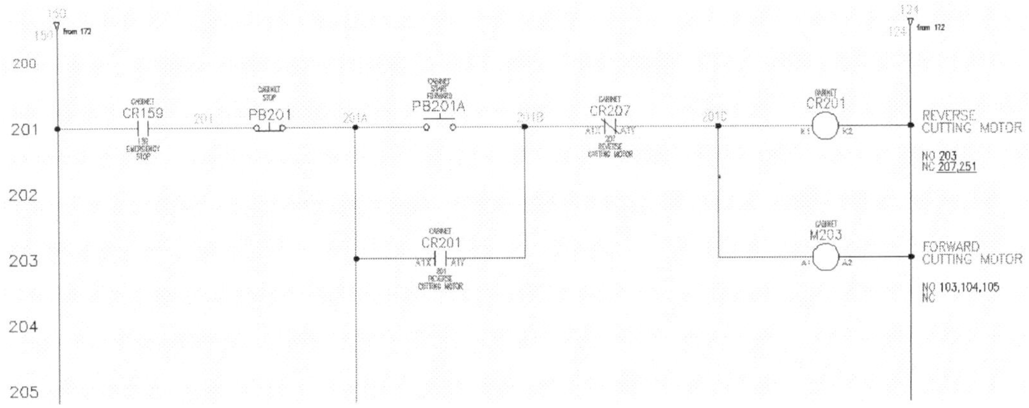

Figure 14–61

1. If the **VERIFY** project is not active, open it from the *Module 14* folder and activate it now.
2. In the **VERIFY** project, open **VERIFY_04.dwg**, if it is not already open.
3. Zoom to lines 200 to 205, as shown in Figure 14–62. Note the size of the text for the Location codes and descriptions on the symbols.

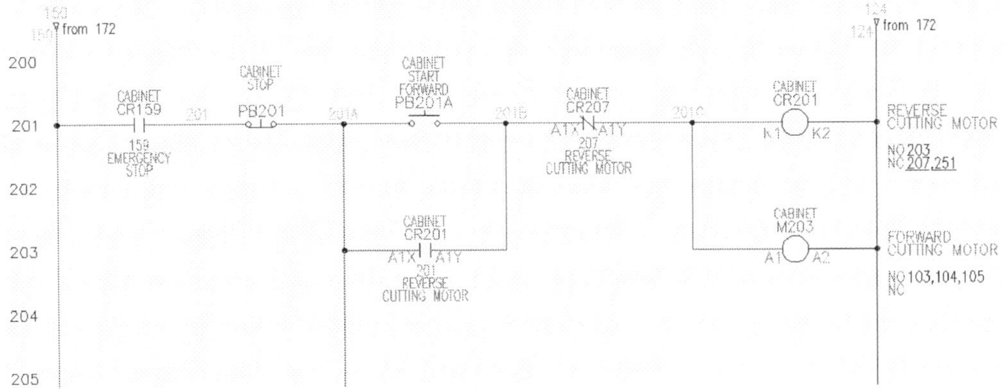

Figure 14–62

4. In the *Schematic* tab>*Edit Components* panel, click (Swap/Update Block).
5. The *Swap Block/Update Block/Library Swap* dialog box opens. In the *Option B* area, select **Library Swap - substitute new versions for all blocks**, as shown in Figure 14–63. Click **OK**.

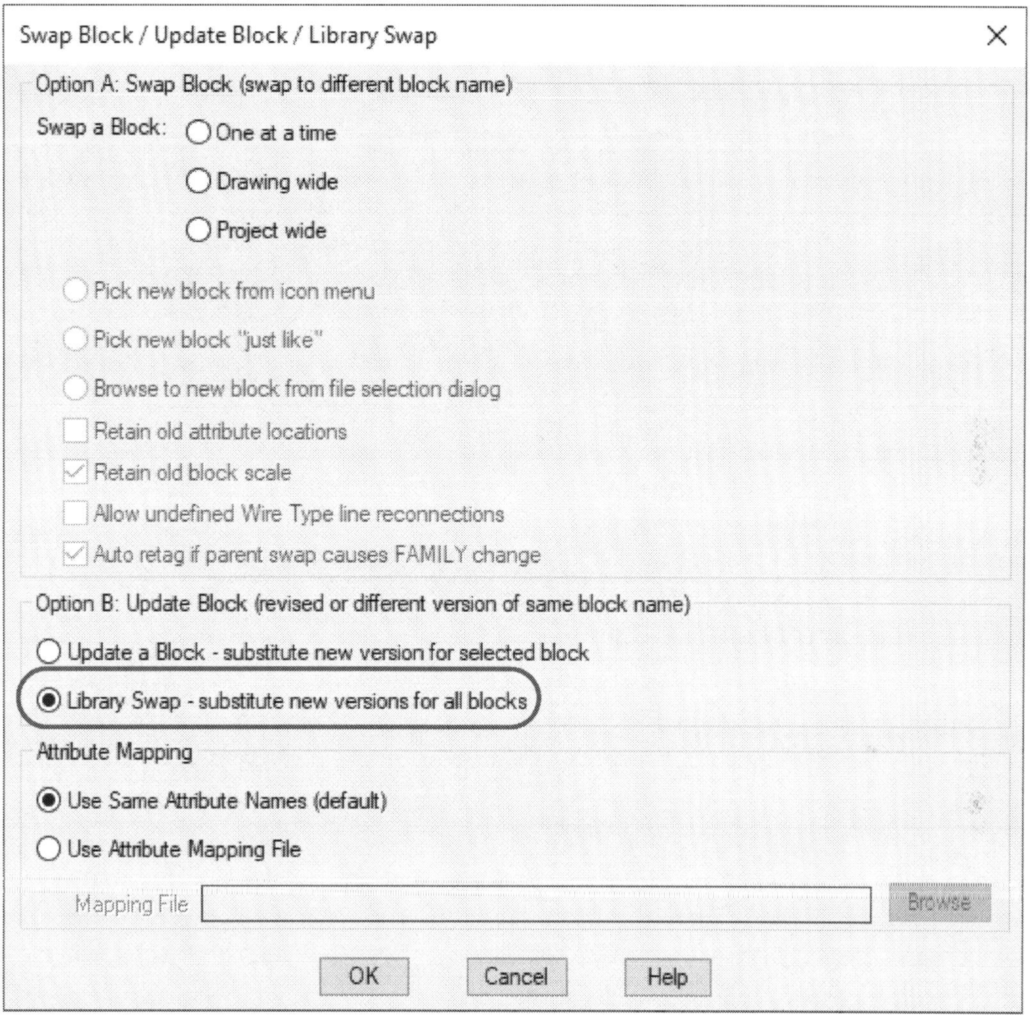

Figure 14–63

6. The *Library Swap – All Drawing* dialog box opens. In the *Path to new block library* area, click **Browse**.

7. The *Browse For Folder* dialog box opens. In the *Acade 2025/Libs* folder, select **jic1**, as shown in Figure 14–64. Click **OK**.

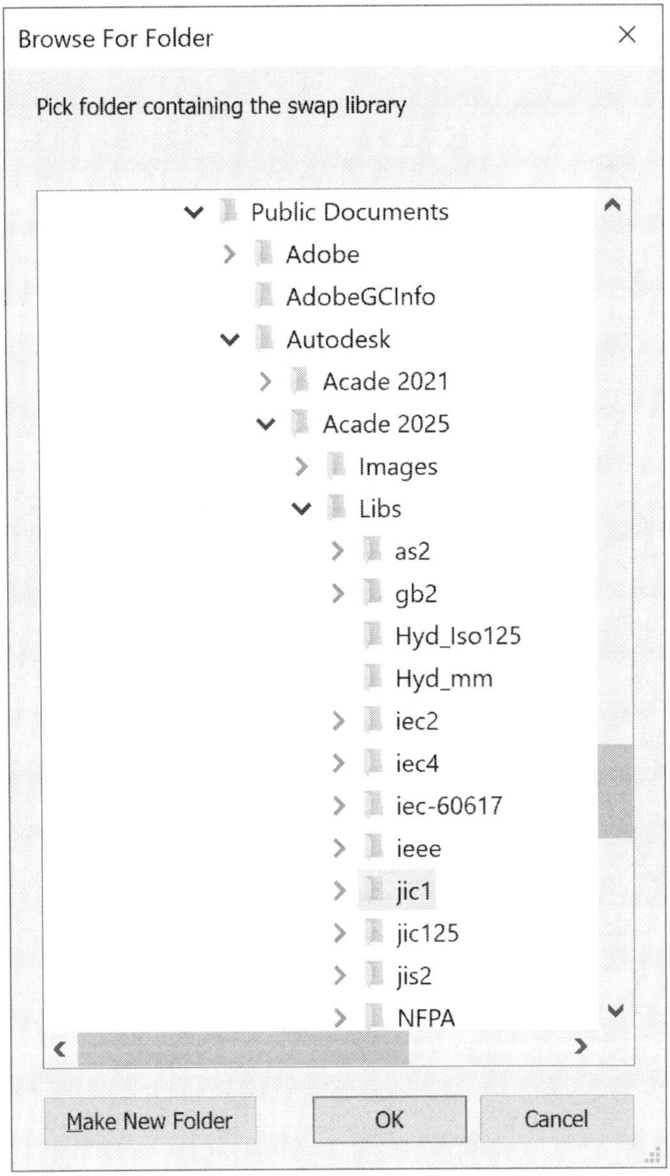

Figure 14–64

8. You are returned to the *Library Swap – All Drawing* dialog box, which displays the new path, as shown in Figure 14–65. Click **Active Drawing**.

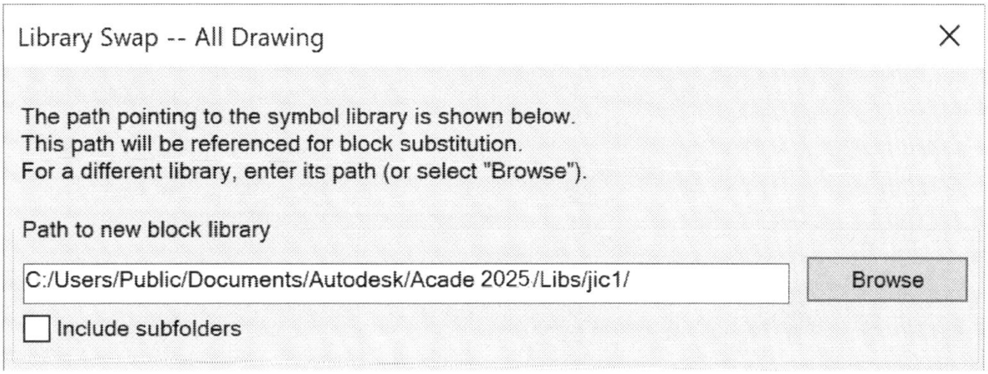

Figure 14–65

- Note the new size of the text in the drawing, as shown in Figure 14–66. The **jic1** library contains symbols with a 0.100" text size. The default **NFPA** library contains symbols with a 0.125" text size. The **Swap/Update Block** command replaces all of the current **NFPA** symbols in the active drawing with **jic1** symbols.

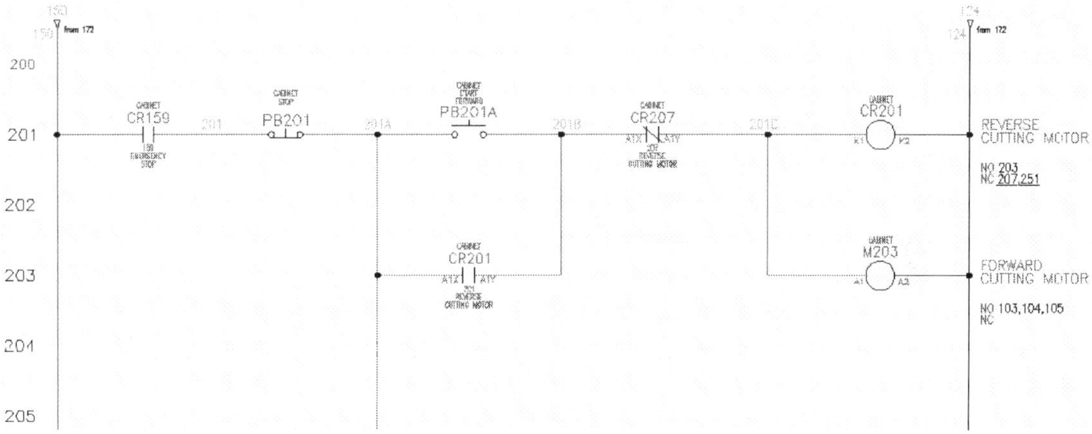

Figure 14–66

9. Zoom extents.

10. Save and close **VERIFY_04.dwg**.

End of practice

14.8 Mark/Verify Drawings

Mark Drawings

The **Mark** option in the **Mark/Verify DWGs** command takes a snapshot of the data in the drawing(s) and an invisible mark is added to each component and wire.

Mark/Verify DWGs

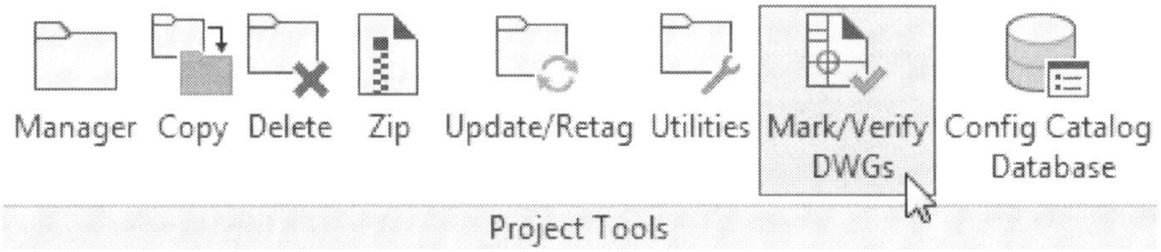

Ribbon: *Project* tab>*Project Tools* panel

Command Prompt: aemarkverify

How To: Mark Drawings

1. Start the **Mark/Verify DWGs** command. The *Mark and Verify* dialog box opens.
2. Select whether to mark the active drawing or all drawings in the project.
3. In the *What to do* area, select **Mark**. Click **OK**.
4. If Project was selected, the *Select Drawings to Process* dialog box opens. Select the drawings to mark and click **OK**.

The *Mark and Verify* dialog box (shown in Figure 14–67) contains the options for marking a drawing or project.

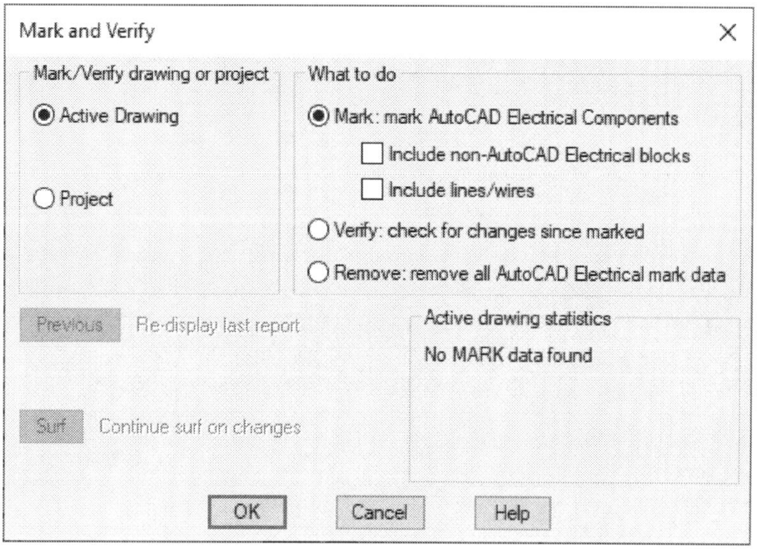

Figure 14–67

Mark/Verify drawing or project	Select **Active Drawing** to mark the active drawing or **Project** to mark all drawings in the active project.
What to do	Select **Mark:** to add an invisible mark to each component and wire.
Active drawing statistics	Displays the status of the active drawing including when the drawing was last marked, by whom, and the comments that were added.

Verify Drawings

The **Verify** option in the **Mark/Verify DWGs** command, compares the current state of the drawings to the last information marked.

How To: Verify a Drawing

1. Start the **Mark/Verify DWGs** command. The *Mark and Verify* dialog box opens.
2. Select whether to verify the active drawing or all drawings in the project.
3. In the *What to do* area, select **Verify** and then click **OK**.
4. If **Project** was selected, the *Select Drawings to Process* dialog box opens. Select the drawings to verify and click **OK**.
5. The *Report* dialog box opens. Click **Display: Report Format** to create a report of changes or **Surf** to open the *Surf* dialog box and examine the changes in the drawing window.

The *Mark and Verify* dialog box (shown in Figure 14–68) contains the options for verifying a drawing or project.

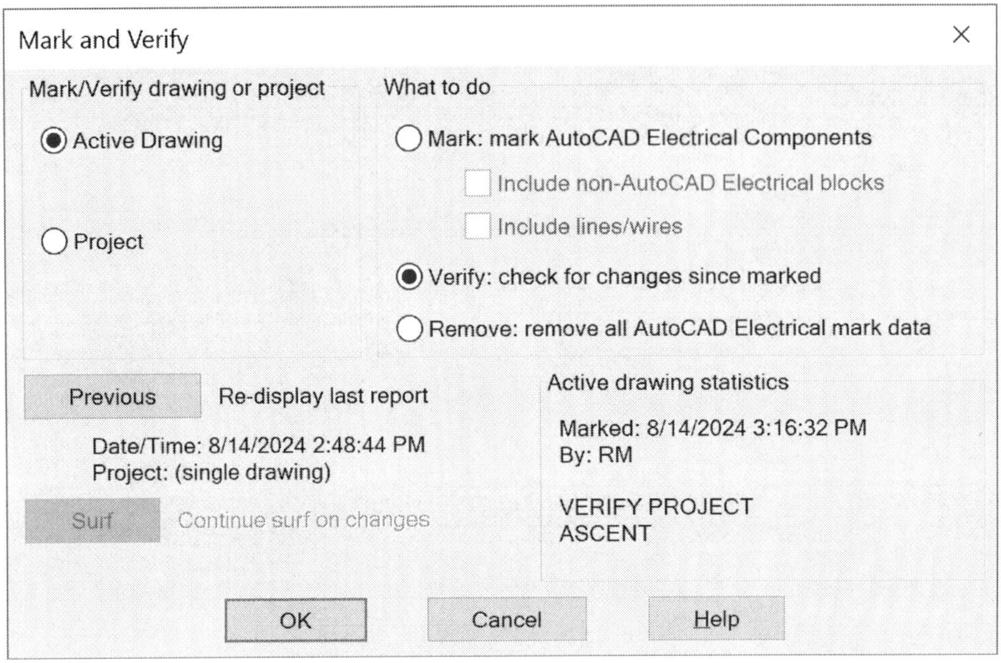

Figure 14–68

Mark/Verify drawing or project	Select **Active Drawing** to verify the active drawing or **Project** to verify all drawings in the active project. If **Project** is selected, the *Select Drawings to Process* dialog box opens.
What to do	Select **Verify:** to compare the drawing(s) to the last marked data.
Previous	Displays the last verify report that was run.
Surf	Surf through the changes that have been made since the data was last marked.
Active drawing statistics	Displays the status of the active drawing including when the drawing was last marked, by whom, and the comments that were added.

If changes have been made since the drawings were last marked, the *REPORT* dialog box opens, as shown in Figure 14–69. It lists the changes made and provides options to either examine the changes or create a report.

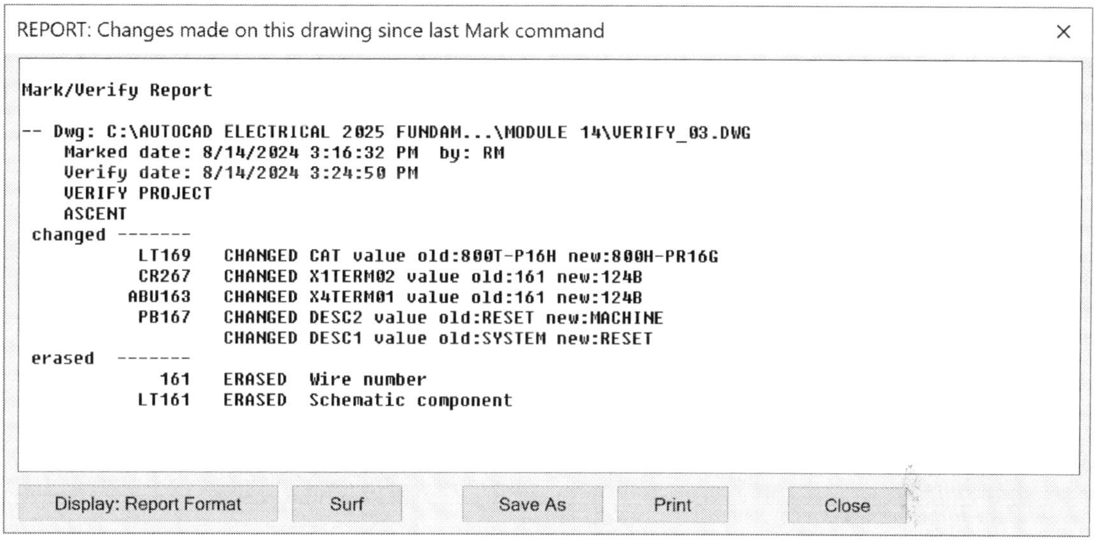

Figure 14–69

Display: Report Format	Displays the Mark/Verify Report in the *Report Generator*.
Surf	Opens the *Surf* dialog box with the changes listed. Used to examine changes in the drawing window.
Save As	Saves the list of changes to an external file.
Print	Sends the report directly to a printer.

Practice 14g
Mark and Verify a Drawing

Practice Objective

- Mark, modify, and verify a drawing.

In this practice, you will mark an existing drawing. You will then change some of the symbols in the drawing. Finally, you will verify the drawing and create a report, which displays a list of the changes, as shown in Figure 14–70.

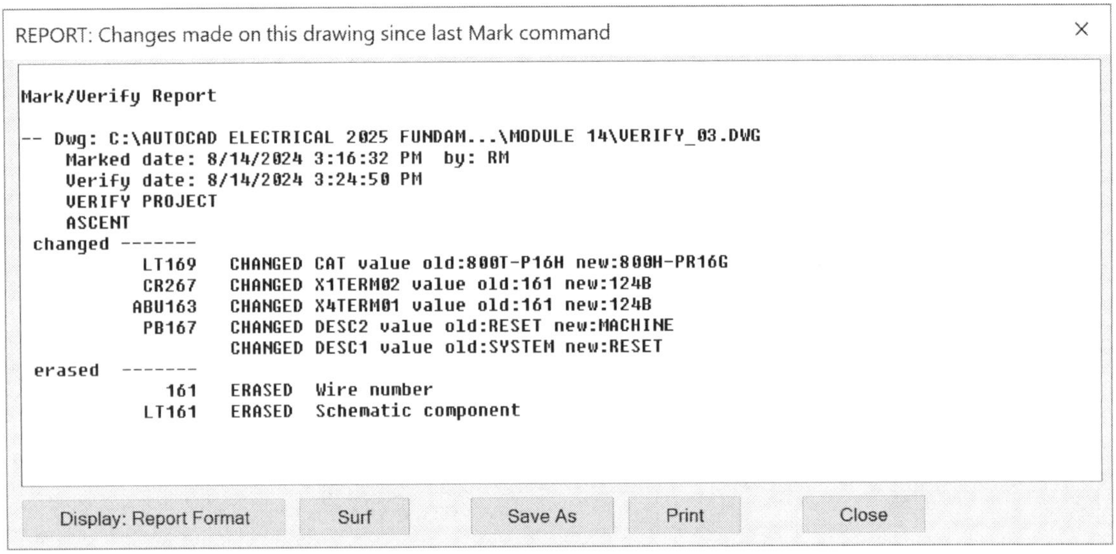

Figure 14–70

Task 1: Mark the drawing.

1. If the **VERIFY** project is not active, open it from the *Module 14* folder and activate it now.
2. In the **VERIFY** project, open **VERIFY_03.dwg**.
3. In the *Project* tab>*Project Tools* panel, click  (Mark/Verify DWGs).

4. The *Mark and Verify* dialog box opens. In the *What to do* area, select **Mark: mark AutoCAD Electrical Components**. In the *Mark/Verify drawing or project* area, verify that **Active Drawing** is selected, as shown in Figure 14–71. Click **OK**.

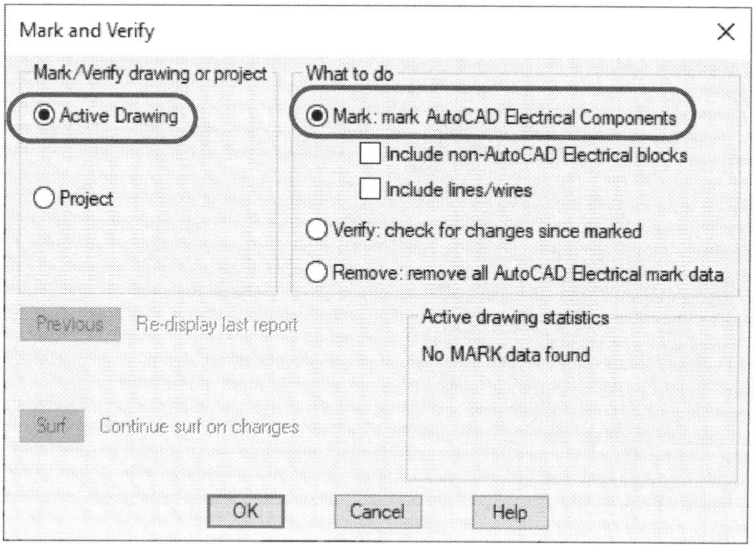

Figure 14–71

5. In the *Enter Your Initials* dialog box that opens, set the following, as shown in Figure 14–72:
   - *Initials*: your initials
   - *Comment 1*: **VERIFY PROJECT**
   - *Comment 2*: **ASCENT**

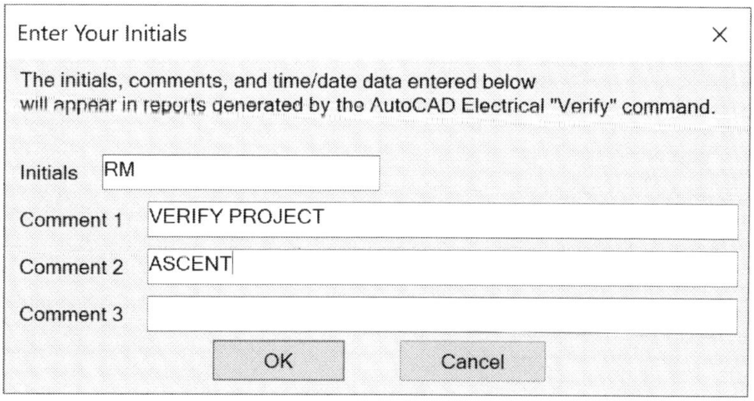

Figure 14–72

6. Click **OK**.

Task 2: Modify the drawing.

1. Zoom to lines 161 through 169.

2. Click  (Delete Component) and delete **LT161**. In the *Search for/Surf to Children?* dialog box, click **No**.

3. Edit **PB167**. Change *Line 1* to **RESET** and *Line 2* to **MACHINE**, as shown in Figure 14–73. Click **OK**.

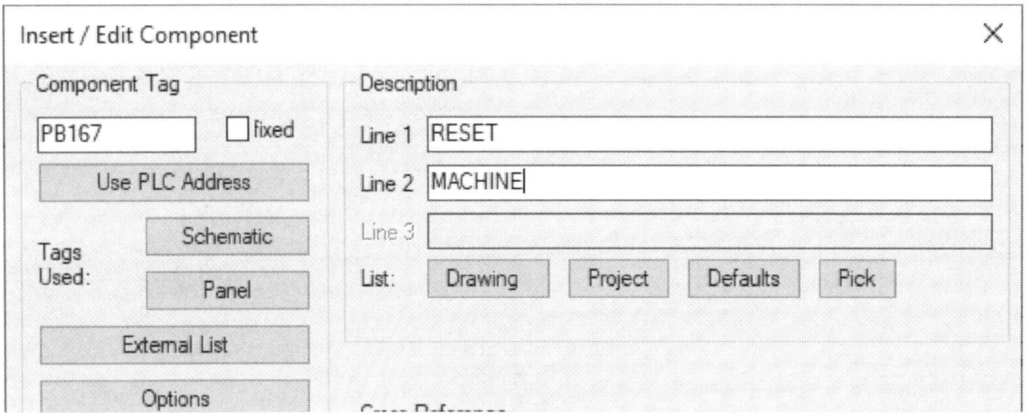

Figure 14–73

4. The *Update other drawings?* dialog box opens. Click **Task**.

5. Edit **LT169**. Change the *Catalog* information to **800H-PR16G**, as shown in Figure 14–74. Click **OK**.

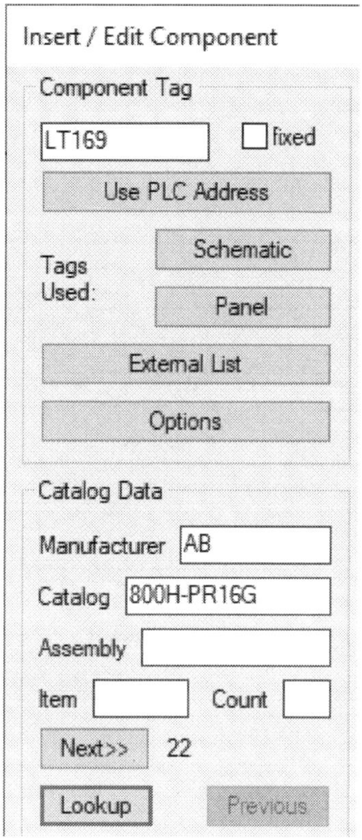

Figure 14–74

6. In the *Update other Drawings?* dialog box, click **Task**.

Task 3: Verify the drawings and save to a file.

1. In the *Project* tab>*Project Tools* panel, click  (Mark/Verify DWGs).

2. The *Mark and Verify* dialog box opens. Your comments display in the *Active drawing statistics* area. In the *What to do* area, verify that **Verify: check for changes since marked** is selected, as shown in Figure 14–75. Click **OK**.

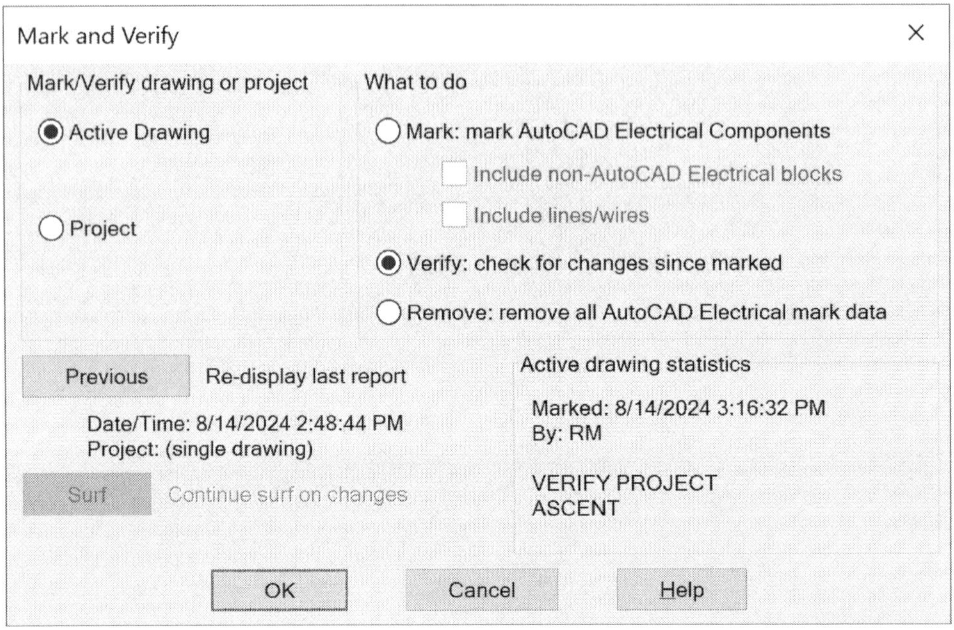

Figure 14–75

3. The *Report* dialog box opens, as shown in Figure 14–76. Click **Display: Report Format**.

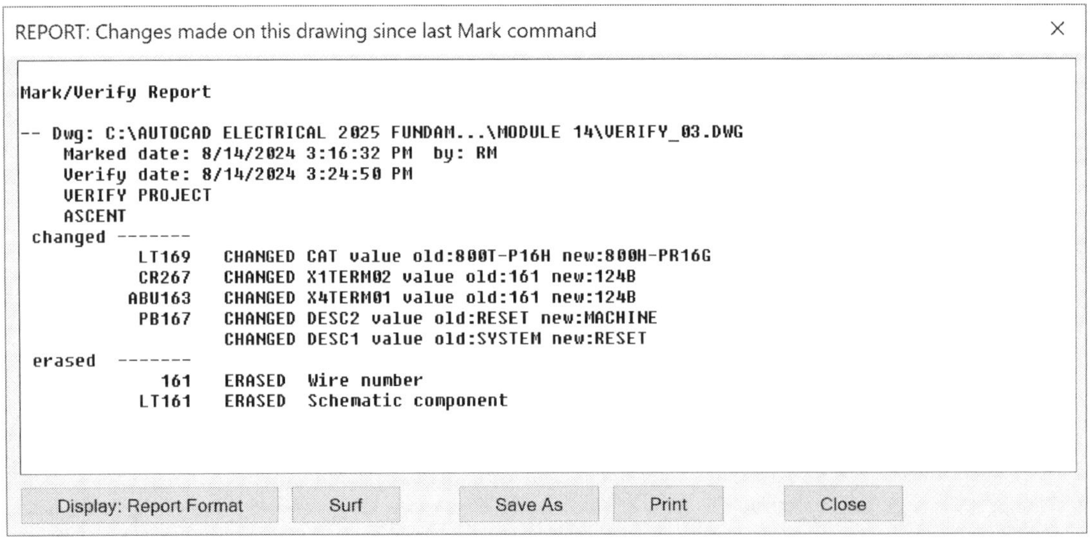

Figure 14–76

4. The *Report Generator* dialog box opens, as shown in Figure 14–77. Click **Save to File**.

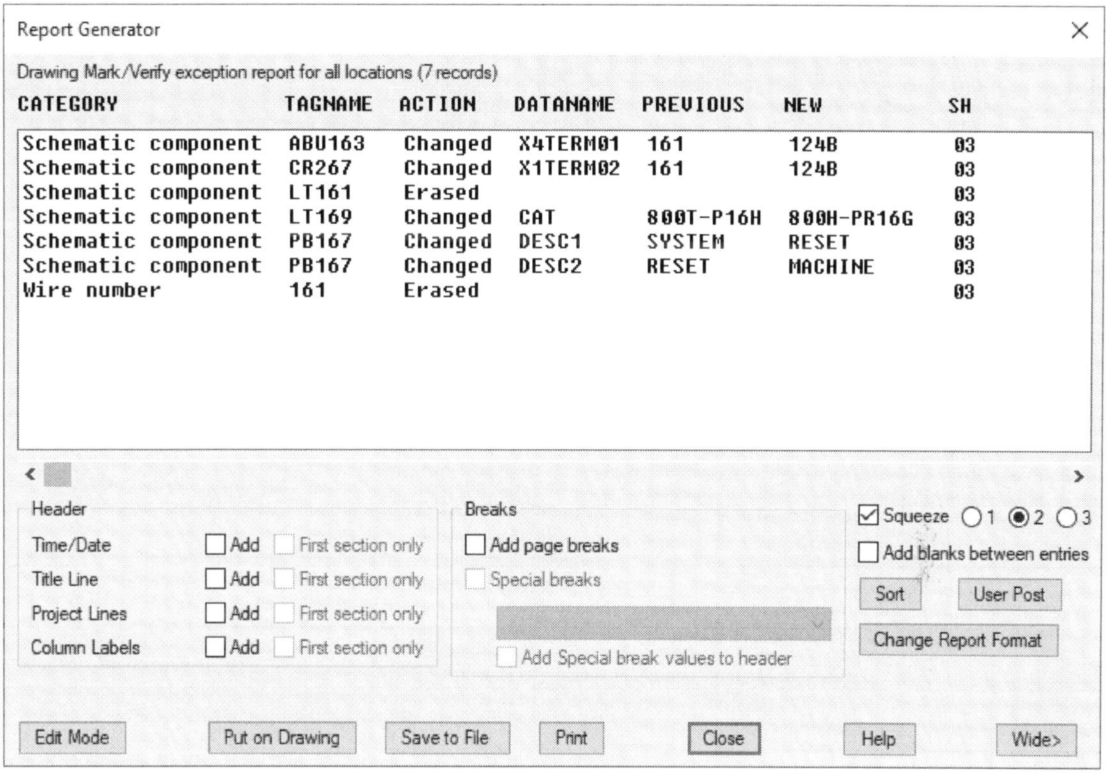

Figure 14–77

5. The *Save Report to File* dialog box opens. Select **Excel spreadsheet format** and click **OK**.
6. The *Select file for report* dialog box opens. Browse to the *Module 14* folder in your practice files folder. Leave the default filename as **VERIFY** and ensure that *Save as type* is ***.xls** and click **Save**.
7. The *Optional Script File* dialog box opens. Click **Close-No Script**.
8. You are returned to the *Report Generator*. Click **Close**.

Task 4: Verify drawings and surf to symbols.

1. In the *Project* tab>*Project Tools* panel, click  (Mark/Verify DWGs).
2. The *Mark and Verify* dialog box opens. In the *What to do* area, verify that **Verify: check for changes since marked** is selected. Click **OK**.
3. In the *Report* dialog box, click **Surf**.

4. The *Surf* dialog box opens. Select **PB167**, as shown in Figure 14–78, and click **Go To**. The drawing window is zoomed to **PB167** and an **x** is placed in the row for **PB167** in the *Surf* dialog box.

   - You might need to move the *Surf* dialog box so that the component is visible in the drawing window.

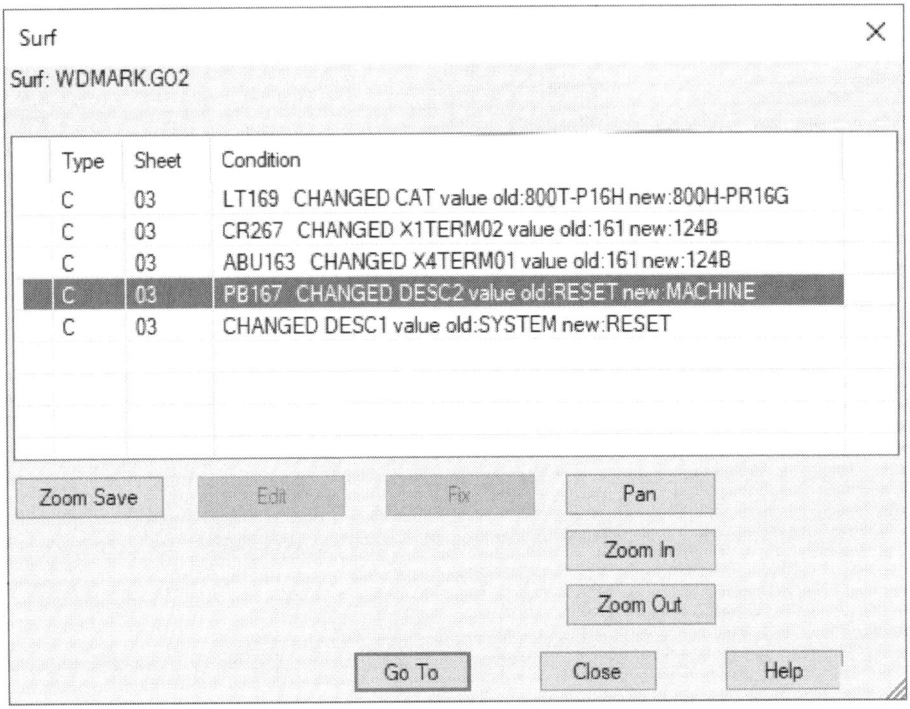

Figure 14–78

5. Select **LT169**, as shown in Figure 14–79, and click **Go To**. The drawing window is zoomed to **LT169** and an **x** is placed in its row.

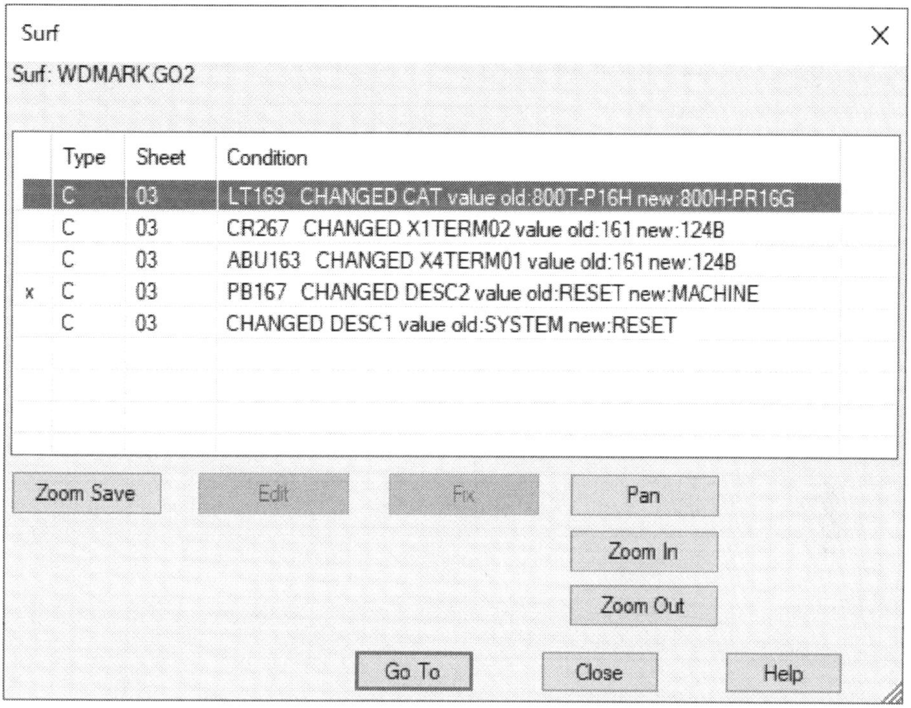

Figure 14–79

6. Click **Close**.
7. Zoom extents.
8. Save and close **VERIFY_03.dwg**.

End of practice

Chapter Review Questions

1. Which command do you use to erase all wire numbers from your project?
   a. **Update/Retag** and select **Remove all wires**.
   b. **Update/Retag** and select **Remove all wire numbers**.
   c. **Project-Wide Utilities** and select **Remove all wires**.
   d. **Project-Wide Utilities** and select **Remove all wire numbers**.

2. What is the advantage of the AutoCAD Electrical **Plot Project** command over the AutoCAD **Plot** command?
   a. **Plot Project** plots all drawings using the same titleblock.
   b. **Plot Project** plots multiple drawings in one command.
   c. **Plot Project** plots the project properties.
   d. There is no advantage to using the AutoCAD Electrical **Plot Project** command.

3. How can you configure the plotting settings in the **Plot Project** command instead of using the page setup?
   a. Click **Detailed Plot Configuration mode** and select **Project Plot Settings**.
   b. Toggle off each drawing's Plot Page Setup settings individually.
   c. Click **Detailed Plot Configuration mode**, configure the settings, and click **On**.
   d. You cannot configure the plotting settings in the **Plot Project** command.

4. The spreadsheet created using the **Export to Spreadsheet** command dynamically updates as the drawings change.
   a. True
   b. False

5. You can add new symbols to the drawings using the **Update from Spreadsheet** command.
   a. True
   b. False

6. Which of the following is not copied when using the **Copy Project** command?
   a. Associated drawings
   b. Support files
   c. Library files
   d. Project file

7. If you wanted to change all your green pilot lights in a drawing to red pilot lights, which option in the **Swap/Update Block** command would you use?
   a. Swap a Block - Drawing wide
   b. Swap a Block - Select a block
   c. Library Swap
   d. Update a block

8. How is data marked by the **Mark/Verify Drawings** command?
   a. The special **WD_M** or **WD_PNLM** block retains attributes of changes.
   b. The project file retains all marked data information.
   c. An invisible block is added to the drawing, retaining all changes.
   d. An invisible mark is added to each component and wire.

9. Which option do you use to see the changes, discovered by the **Mark/Verify DWGs** command, in the drawing window?
   a. Click **Report** in the *REPORT* dialog box.
   b. Click **Display: Report Format** in the *REPORT* dialog box.
   c. Click **Surf** in the *REPORT* dialog box.
   d. Click **Save As** in the *REPORT* dialog box.

Command Summary

Button	Command	Location
	**Copy Project**	• **Ribbon:** *Project* tab>*Project Tools* panel
	**Export to Spreadsheet**	• **Ribbon:** *Import/Export Data* tab>*Export* panel
	**Mark/Verify Drawings**	• **Ribbon**: *Project* tab>*Project Tools* panel
	**Plot Project**	• **Project Manager:** *Toolbar>Publish/Plot* drop-down list
	**Project-Wide Update/ Retag**	• **Ribbon:** *Project* tab>*Project Tools* panel
	**Project-Wide Utilities**	• **Ribbon:** *Project* tab>*Project Tools* panel
	**Publish to PDF/DWF/DWFx**	• **Project Manager:** *Toolbar>Publish/Plot* drop-down list
	**Swap/Update Block**	• **Ribbon:** *Schematic* tab>*Edit Components* panel
	**Update from Spreadsheet**	• **Ribbon:** *Import/Export Data* tab>*Import* panel

Appendix A

Skills Assessment

The following assessment has been provided to test your skills and understanding of the topics covered in this training guide. Select the best answer for each question.

1. Reference drawings are included in the project, but are not included in the tagging, cross-referencing, or reporting processes.
   a. True
   b. False

2. What is the best way to rename a drawing in a project?
   a. Change the drawing's filename in Windows Explorer.
   b. Open the drawing in the AutoCAD® Electrical software and use the **Save As** command.
   c. Right-click on the drawing name in the Project Manager and use the **Rename** option.
   d. You cannot rename a drawing in a project.

3. To force start a wire in the horizontal direction...
   a. Start the **Wire** command and type **X** at the Command Prompt.
   b. Start the **Wire** command, specify a start point, and type **H** at the Command Prompt.
   c. Start the **Wire** command, specify a start point, and right-click to select **Horizontal**.
   d. You cannot force start a wire in the horizontal direction.

4. When using the **Surfer** command, the *Surf* dialog box enables you to:
   a. Go to a component.
   b. Edit a component.
   c. Delete a component.
   d. All of the above.

5. Which command would you use to add a footprint to a panel drawing that is cross-referenced to an existing component symbol on a schematic drawing?
   a. Insert Footprint - Catalog List
   b. Insert Footprint - Panel List
   c. Insert Footprint - Schematic List
   d. Insert Footprint - Icon Menu

6. To insert a jumper chart of a terminal strip into a panel drawing, which option in the *Layer Preview* tab in the *Terminal Strip Editor* dialog box would you use?
   a. Graphical Terminal Strip
   b. Tabular Terminal Strip
   c. Jumper Chart
   d. None of the above.

7. You can create user-defined styles of PLCs.
   a. True
   b. False

8. Which of the following is true for connectors?
   a. You can insert spacers and breaks in connectors.
   b. You can continue a connector in a different drawing.
   c. Connectors can search for and attach to existing wires.
   d. All of the above.

9. Which of the following is an Optional attribute when creating a new symbol?
   a. MFG
   b. DESC3
   c. PINLIST
   d. INST

10. Which of the following file formats controls the Project Description lines?
    a. .WDL
    b. .WDT
    c. .WDP
    d. .ENV

11. How would you create a list of wires indicating what they are connecting?
    a. In the *Schematic Reports* dialog box, use the **Wire Label** option in the *Report Name* area.
    b. Right-click on a Project in the *Project Manager* and select **Drawing List Report**.
    c. In the *Schematic Reports* dialog box, use the **From/To** option in the *Report Name* area.
    d. Right-click on a wire in a drawing and select **Report**.

12. Which of the following can you control in the *Panel Drawing Configuration* dialog box?
    a. Tag Format
    b. Panel Balloons
    c. Terminal Strip Layouts
    d. Wiring Style

13. You cannot update a titleblock using the **Project-Wide Update/Retag** command.
    a. True
    b. False

Index

T

U

W

Made in United States
Orlando, FL
04 November 2026

90200805R00409